W9-AVG-876

PERSPECTIVES
in
Cultural
Anthropology

PERSPECTIVES

in

Cultural

Anthropology

Edited

by

Herbert Applebaum

State University of New York Press

To: Miles Richardson

Published by
State University of New York Press, Albany

© 1987 State University of New York

For information, address State University of New York
Press, State University Plaza, Albany, N.Y., 12246

Library of Congress Cataloging in Publication Data

Perspectives in cultural anthropology.

Bibliography: p.
Includes index.
1. Ethnology. 2. Anthropology. I. Applebaum,
Herbert A.
GN316.P4 1987 306 86-19168
ISBN 0-88706-438-8
ISBN 0-88706-439-6 (pbk.)

10 9 8 7 6 5 4 3 2 1

Contents

IX. Structuralism and Cognitive Anthropology

Introduction: Herbert Applebaum

X. Sociobiology

Introduction: Herbert Applebaum

XI. Symbolic and Humanistic Anthropology

Introduction: Herbert Applebaum

XII.   Concluding Remarks

Herbert Applebaum

Preface

Anthropology is a social science based on empirical data, most often compiled by observers who live among the people they are investigating. Being empirically based and interested in all aspects of every society and in every period, anthropology has the best chance of providing a unified theory about the social life of human beings. It has a chance to compile the most comprehensive record of the life of human beings in all the rich diversity recorded on the complex and colorful tapestry of world history. The anthropological mission was never more eloquently expressed than in this quote from Conrad Arensberg (1981:564):

As heirs of nature history, we, too, are observers. We too, are recorders, systematizers of the record, searchers for process, pattern, structure, emergence, evolution, and even law.

Process, pattern, structure, and even law is what this book is about. It will present the major theoretical orientations which historically and presently guide anthropological research and understanding. Studying different societies and compiling and comparing data requires that some central body of theory be used as an aid to the collection and ordering of the results of research. Hence, theory is the starting point for understanding. It is a good way for the student to start upon the anthropological mission. Anthropology is a way of looking at the world; thus, theory should be central to the concerns of anthropologists and their students.

Human beings are rational beings, in the sense that what makes them human is the need to search for meanings and understandings of the human, as well as the natural, world. This includes concrete behavior, along with the grand structures, contexts, institutions, and societies. Anthropology, as a discipline oriented toward compiling the entire human record, is well-suited for the enterprise of presenting the theoretical and practical endeavors of human life in all types of societies and cultures. This book presents some of the main, but certainly not all, of the theoretical perspectives of cultural anthropologists in the United States.

As the reader and student follow the line and arguments of the various theories presented in this book, they should realize that there is a process at work in the history of anthropological theory. Each body of

xi

theory inevitably leads to examination and critique. This healthy process then calls for adjustments and readjustments in theoretical thinking. This constant refining and fine-tuning all helps to improve the way we look at human society, enlarging our information and our methods.

Herbert Applebaum

I

Overview

Anthropology can be said to have been born with the first human search into the meanings of human life and the search for knowledge about the human and natural world. These beginnings trace back to remote times in human history. Knowledge obtained then was based on common sense, untrained observations, myths, folk tales, and mystical and poetic concepts of the world of man and the forces of nature. Knowledge was also based on authority and cultural habit that was passed from one generation to another, dressed in the form of received wisdom from dimly conceived ancestors thought to have been the progenitors of family, kinship, and community groups containing folk inhabiting various niches in the world's surface.

As a scientific discipline, anthropology developed on the basis of the rationalist revolution in thought and philosophy which followed the Renaissance period in western Europe. Anthropology rests on the modern development of scientific aims and methods which seeks through systematic observation and classification to discover theories capable of providing plausible and testable hypotheses about human phenomena. The refutations of the parochialism and distortions of nonscientific ideas laid the foundations for the development of the empirical sciences. Anthropology is an empirical science. It was born during the last quarter of the nineteenth century, when it became a recognized social science discipline. It later organized its own learned society, developed systems of training and education, and began to compile a body of knowledge and theory. The chapter which follows this introduction by Murphy, deals with the historical process in the development of anthropological theory and method.

Evolution as a theory attracted scientists and thinkers in the nineteenth century. The attraction of evolutionary theory is that it provides a

1

system of classification and hypothesizes a rational succession of forms of life and society which implies the notion of progress. People like to believe that the world is constantly getting better, especially if it is all happening inevitably and in spite of what human beings do to hold it back. Though it seems hard to accept today, during the nineteenth century and up until World War I, in Europe there was a generally optimistic view of world history, with mankind experiencing general improvement through the advances of science, technology, and culture. The fact that evolutionary theory was supported by the scientific investigations of people like Darwin, Bachofen, and Maine increased its stature as a theory. Thus, when anthropology emerged as a recognized discipline during the last half of the nineteenth century, it was no surprise that it was strongly influenced by the concepts of evolution.

One of the most influential of the early anthropologists guided by evolutionary theory was Edward Tylor (1865). Tylor postulated societal development as moving from primitive to advanced stages, the latter being equated with the United States and Europe. The early evolutionists in anthropology relied upon the reports of travellers, missionaries, reporters, and untrained observers for their data. Most of them were "armchair" anthropologists, meaning that they did not go into the field to live with the people they studied. They did their research in libraries and museums. The rigidity of their evolutionary schemes and the tenuousness of their data caused later anthropologists to criticize their methods and results.

One of those who reacted against nineteenth century evolutionary theory was Franz Boas, a German-born scientist, who became the dominant figure in American anthropology from 1920 until the Second World War. Boas stressed scientific data gathering and the use of the participant observation method in anthropology, i.e., researchers living among the people they are studying for extended periods so as to learn, first hand, about their ways and customs. Boas was also opposed to evolutionary schemes based on cultural traits taken out of the context of their living societies. He stressed the uniqueness and wholeness of every society and thought that isolating a trait, for purposes of study and classification, inevitably distorted it when removed from its cultural context. Boas has been described as a particularist because of his stress on the uniqueness of each culture and its historical particularity. At the turn of the century, Boas argued against large integrations of cultures and broad classifications, believing that not enough scientifically collected data was available for such grand theory. He continued to take this position most of his life, right up until his death in 1942.

Other reactions to nineteenth century evolutionary theories were the theory of functionalism, espoused by Bronislaw Malinowski (1944), and the theory of structuralism, developed by Alfred R. Radcliffe-Brown (1952). Radcliffe-Brown taught at the University of Chicago for six years, and Malinowski taught at Yale for three years. Both influenced and trained many American anthropologists. The structural-functional approach saw society as composed of a set of integrated institutions. Malinowski stressed the notion that these institutions functioned to satisfy culturally formed needs of individuals. Radcliffe-Brown placed his stress on the permanence of the structure, which gave shape and form to a society and endured regardless of which individuals entered or left the institutions which made up the structure. Structural-functionalism tends to focus on those aspects of a society which tend to further its maintenance and stability and does not address those elements leading to instability and change. During the period after World War II, when the world was changing so rapidly, particularly in the former colonial territories, anthropologists found structural-functionalism inadequate for furnishing guides for understanding the transformations taking place in societies and cultures throughout the world.

After World War II, there was an explosion of theories and new orientations in the field of anthropology. There was a rebirth of interest in the theory of evolution. Leslie White related evolution to energy systems (1959). Julian Steward thought that social evolution functioned through cultural ecology systems. There was a rise of various forms of cognitive anthropologies, including semiotics and symbolic anthropology. There was also, in the post–World War II period, a vigorous emergence of various forms of materialism, including Marxist anthropology, cultural materialism, economic anthropology, and the anthropology of work.

A new form of structuralism emerged in the 1950s and the 1960s, that of Claude Lévi-Strauss. He presented structural models which he proclaimed to contain universal human behavioral characteristics. Like Marxism, Lévi-Strauss's theory was overarching and was therefore bound to attract a wide range of people in various disciplines, from the humanities to the social sciences.

Robert Murphy (1976:19) sums up the state of theory in anthropology today:

There has been a burgeoning of schools of thought that are all with us today—structural-functionalism, structuralism, Marxism in several different varieties, personality and culture, cultural ecology, cognitive anthropologies, neo-evolutionisms, cultural materialism, and so forth—and none is dominant. Indeed, this may just be the future condition of anthropology: a pluralistic discipline that loosely shelters a plethora of interest and which lacks a center.

What follows in this volume is a guide for the student and reader as to the various forms of theory, as presented by the theorists, in their own words, with the editor's introductions meant to serve as guides to the meaning of the various theories and how they relate to one another.

The first chapter in Part I, by Murphy, will present some of the history and the theoretical issues in outline. These issues will be dealt with in detail throughout this book. Murphy provides the historical context for the debate which took place in the twentieth century in the United States. Theoretical issues, while they may appear to have a life of their own, are the property of human beings, who argue for and against them within the framework of their own positions and educational training. The influences which mold a particular anthropologist's thinking are specific and concrete, relating to place and educational institutions, to period and current dominating ideas, and to traditions and intellectual accomplishments of particular theoreticians. Murphy provides, in his chapter, this valuable background for understanding the milieu in which anthropological ideas were formulated and fought over during the development of important and relevant theories.

Robert F. Murphy

1. A Quarter Century of American Anthropology

The Executive Board of the American Anthropological Association paid me the honor in 1974 of inviting me to edit a selection of articles from the *American Anthropologist* for the period of 1946 to 1970, in celebration of the 75th anniversary of the journal. George Stocking of the University of Chicago was asked at the same time to edit an anthology of the years 1921 to 1945, both volumes to be published with a reissue of Dr. Frederica de Laguna's earlier collection of essays from the first years of the journal. Our mandate was to choose articles that reflect the highest qualitative standards of the *American Anthropologist* and the discipline it serves and, at the same time, represent trends and interests within anthropology at various phases of its history.

The constraint upon length dictated by the economics of publishing have made for an extraordinarily high degree of selectivity, and less than two percent of the articles published during the period were chosen. Every effort was made to include selections from the major anthropological persuasions, but this was not always possible, often owing to the fact that my criteria of excellence and representativeness were in conflict. In this enterprise, I have tried to maintain a stance of neutrality, sometimes in the face of my own predelictions, and I have avoided overrepresentation in the volume of my closest personal and theoretical affinities.

A measure of evenhandedness was also maintained through the simple expedient of not consulting with others regarding my choices in cultural anthropology, though I profited from the kind advice of Ralph Holloway in physical anthropology, Harvey Pitkin in linguistics, and Richard Keatinge in archaeology. This social anthropological exclusiveness is in keeping with the first principal of etic anthropology, which is: "Objectivity begins at home." The only exception to the rule has been an exchange of views and procedures with George Stocking, the editor of the 1921–45 volume. Our correspondence had less to do with the choices themselves, however, than with deciding upon matters of length, format, and criteria. I would like to take this opportunity to gratefully acknowledge his help and cooperation. Morton Fried was also kind enough to read this essay and to suggest certain changes, all of which were made.

The *American Anthropologist* was published as a quarterly journal from its inception through 1952; after that year, each annual volume was issued in six separate numbers. The 25-year period, then, encompasses 136 different issues of the journal. By my count, some 1,006 articles were published during this time, not including brief communications, letters to the editor, book reviews, and obituaries. This remarkable outpouring of anthropological erudition required that only articles be reviewed for inclusion, though there were some true gems published as brief communications. In all candor, I found it impossible to reread all 1,006 essays with care, and a first winnowing was done by scanning the contents of each issue and selecting those articles having the greatest intrinsic merit. These articles were then read and culled again for theoretical and substantive importance, and the final selection took into account the problem of representativeness of authors, disciplinary subfields, and theoretical perspectives. Finally, the limits posed by economy upon the length of the volumes forced both Stocking and me to adopt a rule of thumb excluding articles of over 30 pages.

The reader will immediately note that most of the selections fall within the general area of cultural-social anthropology. Of the 22 essays, there are two in archaeology, two in physical anthropology, and one in linguistics. This disparity is less a function of my interests than of the publishing patterns characteristic of the four fields of anthropology. Despite the fact that cultural anthropologists form a majority of the profession, there was no American journal exclusively devoted to that branch until the appearance of *Ethnology* in 1962. Like the *American Anthropologist*, the *Southwestern Journal of Anthropology* accepted articles from all four fields of anthropology, as did the major foreign journals. In contrast, each of the three smaller subfields had its own publications: *American Antiquity* for archaeology, physical anthropology's *American Journal of Physical Anthropology* and *Human Biology*, and the *International Journal of Linguistics* and *Language* for anthropological and other linguists. There were also smaller journals specializing in these fields both in this country and abroad. The editors of the *American Anthropologist*, however, always attempted to observe the catholicity of the discipline, and each volume usually contained a sample from around the profession. Of the 1,006 articles published from 1946 to 1970, 805 were in cultural anthropology, 86 in archaeology, 68 in physical anthropology, and 47 in linguistics. The selections in this volume are in the same rough proportion.

My review of articles in archaeology, physical anthropology and linguistics reveals a pattern that must be discussed, however contrary it may be to our goal of synthesis. This is, baldly, that the best writings in the three minor fields are usually sent to specialized journals and not to the *American Anthropologist*. The reasons for this are clear. One makes his way in the discipline, and in our institutions, as a specialist, and the archaeologist wishing to reach a broad audience of his peers will send an essay to *American Antiquity*, where it will receive maximum archaeological readership and discussion. Similarly, a linguist presenting what he considers to be a broadly significant paper will publish it in a journal that will be read by non-anthropological linguists, just as the physical anthropologist will choose the *American Journal of Physical Anthropology* or *Human Biology* as the vehicle to reach not only his subdisciplinary colleagues but also those in medicine, anatomy, zoology, and so forth, who regularly read those journals. The result of this is that only a limited number of essays having broad theoretical significance in a subfield, or in anthropology at large, reach the pages of the *American Anthropologist*. That I could find only one in this category in linguistics should not, then, be taken as a reflection upon that profession but as an indiciation that their best work is sent elsewhere.

A reading of the journal leads to another conclusion that contradicts anthropology's self-image. This is that, for all our vaunted "holism," there were very few articles in this entire quarter-century period that reached beyond their subfield, except, perhaps, by the readers' own processes of extrapolation. Certain of the essays chosen do have such a function, especially the two archaeological selections written by Julian Steward and by Philip Philips and Gordon Willey. Given the two problems posed by the inadequacy of publishing outlets in the field of cultural anthropology and the lack of synthesizing articles that span parochial frontiers, one can only applaud the Association's decision to found the *American Ethnologist* and to continue the *American Anthropologist* as a vehicle for broadly conceived essays.

In addition to quality, theoretical significance, and representativeness, I sought also to include essays by the leading anthropologists of the time, a consideration that was easier to observe for the early part of my period than for recent years. Most of the names listed in the table of contents are familiar to all anthropologists, but there are also certain significant omissions. No author was chosen twice, and Stocking and I agreed to minimize overlap in our selections; the only authors appearing in both volumes are Fred Eggan, Julian Steward, Carl Voegelin, and

Leslie White, all major figures in the history of our discipline and authors of essays which, for each period, could not be overlooked.

That some eminent anthropologists, both living and dead, were omitted from my list is a result, in some cases, of their not having published much in the *American Anthropologist* during the period in question. Certain others published only a limited amount in the journal, none of which contributions were appropriate for inclusion. Some of the selection problems may be illustrated by concrete examples. Claude Lévi-Strauss wrote one article for the *American Anthropologist* during the period which, under the title "Language and the Analysis of Social Laws" (Lévi-Strauss 1951), attempted to find an isomorphism between kinship structures and linguistic structures. The effort was doomed to failure, for it was based upon continent-wide generalizations regarding both languages and kinship systems, yielding results of the most impressionistic sort. Neither Lévi-Strauss nor his students ever attempted to follow up the hypothesis, and I saw no reason to revive it in these pages. And although Lévi Strauss's admirers are inclined to consider much more important his paper "Reciprocity and Hierarchy" (Lévi-Strauss 1944), it unfortunately appeared too early to be included in this volume. Radcliffe-Brown presented a somewhat different problem. He published a number of items during the early part of our period, but these were either brief communications or articles written in direct response to another article in the journal. It is obvious that one-half of an argument between two scholars cannot be published, and I did not find any of the debates of sufficient lasting interest to merit publication of both sides. Again, any sense of constraint that so noted an anthropologist as Radcliffe-Brown must be included at all costs was eased by the fact that Stocking has selected his 1935 article on California kinship systems (Radcliffe-Brown 1935). The supplementary functions of the two volumes for each other was reciprocal, for Stocking was able to find but one appropriate article by Julian Steward during the period 1921–45 and was gratified by my selection of "Cultural Causality and Law" (Steward 1948). Steward is an interesting example, for in all his long and remarkably productive career, he published very few articles in the *American Anthropologist*. Excluding letters, reviews, obituaries, and comments appended to papers written by others, he wrote only seven articles for the journal, most of which were short ethnographic or archaeological notes. The essay included in this volume was indeed the only one in which he attempted to draw broad conclusions or addressed a wide audience.

Steward's case was not unusual, for there is a tendency with growing professional prestige for most of a scholar's later publications to be by invitation, and edited volumes preempt a good deal of the production of mature anthropologists. This is to be deplored, in one sense, for the journal of our Association is subscribed to and read by almost the entire profession, whereas the books on special subjects are directed toward more limited audiences. One could accept this state of affairs more cheerfully if the edited volumes were of greater significance, but most are eminently forgettable, however much interest they may draw immediately after publication. With regard to age of the authors chosen for this volume, most are indeed elder statesmen in the profession, and a few are no longer with us. Lest it be thought that the volume reflects the gerontocratic bent of the discipline, however, it should be stressed that most of the writers were either young or in their middle years at the time of publication. That is, in turn, a function of the fact that most scholars—though not all—say what they are going to say by the age of 50, after which they usually become rather repetitive. Such a progression in the life cycle is in keeping with Murphy's Law of Academic Careers, which states that there are two stages to the scholar's life—during the first he is anxious as to whether he will be discovered; in the second he is worried about whether he will be found out.

An Anthropological Quarter-Century: 1946–70

The place of our selections within the discipline may best be seen against the background of anthropology during the 25 years from 1946 to 1970. The years of World War II were a fallow period in most scholarly disciplines, and anthropology was especially affected by the virtual discontinuation of overseas research, except for strategic and military purposes. The universities had been stripped of male students at both the graduate and undergraduate levels, and most younger professional anthropologists were either members of the military or assigned to government agencies directly connected with the war effort. It may be apposite for younger members of the American Anthropological Association to learn that there was no debate among anthropologists, nor were there significant reservations, about the role of the profession in the conduct of the war. Anthropologists served in the Office of Strategic Services, Naval Intelligence, the War Resources Board, and numerous other organizations, and their participation was considered to be appropriate and professionally beneficial. Such positive sanction was in marked and dramatic contrast to the bitter division that occurred within the Association during World War I and, to a far greater extent, the Vietnam War. World War II, of course, was strongly and unequivocally supported by the entire population, including intellectuals, as opposed to the Vietnam

War, but it is well to remember that the pattern of professional involvement was established during the former conflict.

The end of the war brought the anthropologists back to the campuses but with empty notebooks, and the *American Anthropologist* reflected this lack of a research backlog for the first few years of our period. The hiatus continued for two years or so after the war, for it took time to readapt foundations and public agencies to peacetime research and to regroup the personnel of the profession before sending them off again. Research began early in the Trust Territory of the Pacific under the sponsorship of the naval administrators of the region, but the full reestablishment of field investigations waited until about 1948.

The immediate post-war period continued the research interlude, but it was a time of intense educational activity, foreshadowing the enormous growth of the discipline for the next quarter century. Anthropology was among the smallest of the scholarly disciplines at the time, and the full fellow roster of the American Anthropological Association in 1947 was only 408, as compared to the 1976 figure of 2,526. The war contributed to the expansion of the discipline in many ways. First, several million young Americans had been exposed to overseas experience and had been scattered throughout the world, often in the remote outlying districts so favored by anthropologists. It was an unusual kind of experience, to be sure, but it broke the insularity of the American population and served as a forerunner to the extension of American influence throughout the world. Minimally, it awakened us to cultural diversity, and, maximally, it excited a desire to understand this array of cultures. Another effect of the war came about through a large package of veteran's benefits which included comprehensive educational subsidies. Public Law 346 provided full tuition, books and supplies, and a living stipend to all veterans of military service for a period of up to the time they spent in the military plus a year. For many, it subsidized a complete college education and all or part of graduate school. The veterans returned to the campuses in the millions, and they entered anthropology in unprecedented numbers. Even those who did not take advantage of the educational part of the "GI Bill of Rights" contributed by applying the housing benefits to the purchase of small houses, where they raised rather large families; the children from this "baby-boom" completed the process of inundating the universities in the 1960s, anthropology's greatest period of expansion.

The GI Bill of Rights changed the profile as well as the numbers of the anthropological profession. In common with the rest of the academic disciplines, anthropology had been largely a white, middle class domain. The expenses of schooling effectively screened out lower class and lower middle class students who, if they made it as far as post-graduate education, were better advised to seek the superior economic rewards of medicine and other professions. As for persons of minority background, there were no professionally established black anthropologists at all until after the war, and even so eminent a scholar as Edward Sapir experienced Ivy League anti-Semitism in the immediate pre-war period. Public Law 346 changed the recruitment situation completely, although discriminatory patterns of employment were to persist for a longer period. For the first time, the young, bright and indigent could not only afford to go to graduate school but, given the economic incentives, they could hardly afford not to. A small number of black students enrolled in our graduate departments of anthropology along with a much larger number of members of other minorities. That students of the lower class were now entering the scholarly disciplines did not have as much effect as might be anticipated, however, for their conditions of employment soon made them members of the same middle class that had previously rejected them.

Ironically, the same movement that brought large numbers of young men of diverse backgrounds into anthropology also saw a decline of female participation in the discipline relative to the feminist ferment of the 1920s. In keeping with the ethos of the time, women redirected their interests to family and children or, in a more negative sense, found themselves squeezed out of graduate schools and jobs by the returning veterans. It was not until the late 1960s that women would return with renewed vitality into academic life. This decline of female involvement is manifest in the authorship of *American Anthropologist* articles. I did a count of sex of all authors of articles during the 1946–70 period. The total number of authors was 1,219—a number greater than the total number of articles, due to co-authorships—of whom 1,060 were men and 158 women. For the entire period, then, 13% of the authors were female. The male-female ratio of authorship was further broken down by five-year periods, yielding the following percentages of women authors: 1966–70—12%; 1961–65—13%; 1956–60—10%; 1951–55—13%; 1946–50—22%. By themselves, these figures might be straws in the wind, but they follow the pattern already documented by careful studies of women in the academic professions.

Nourished by growing graduate and undergraduate enrollments, anthropology departments slowly increased in size and number during the early part of our period, but the expansion was miniscule compared to what happened in the 1960s. Looking back at my own personal experience in the profession, I was trained in the Columbia department in the late 1940s and early 1950s with a group of graduate students numbering close to 150 being taught by a faculty of ten; this made it one of the largest in the United States. When I went to the University of Illinois in 1953, there were only three anthropologists in a Department of Sociology and Anthropology which offered no advanced degrees in our subject. In 1955, I joined the University of California at Berkeley, where I became the ninth person in the department; by 1960 it had doubled in size. The change was of the same order nationwide.

The immediate post-war years from 1946 to 1950 saw a considerable change in the areal and theoretical interests of anthropology. The bulk of our research had previously been in the study of the American Indian, which served more than any other influence to produce the rather flat, descriptive tone of our writings. It was the reservation situation, the culling of memory culture unvitalized by extant patterns of activity, that led to Americanist nominalism, and not the anti-evolutionism of Boas. By the end of the 1930s, however, American anthropologists were becoming interested in culture change and "acculturation" studies, and they were already venturing into other areas. Melville Herskovits began his African studies during this decade, and Ruth Bunzel and Robert Redfield were working in Guatemala and Mexico as early as the 1920s. This is also the time that saw Margaret Mead undertake her pioneering researches in the Pacific, which serve as well as a landmark of the development of "culture and personality" studies in the 1930s.

The basis for change and diversification of interest was laid down during the pre-war years, but the post-war period brought it to fruition. American anthropologists, financed by an influx of new funds that were clearly responsive to the country's expanded overseas interests, broke out of their traditional insularity and embarked on research on a global scale. In the beginning their efforts were hesitant and often blocked by scholarly hegemonies. If one wanted to do African research, he had to work under the auspices of one of the British universities or through Northwestern, and Columbia's control of South American fieldwork dated back to the group sent there by Ruth Benedict in the late 1930s. By the mid-1950s, these barriers had broken down, departments were expanding, and the major universities sponsored research on almost every continent. The turn to foreign research, backed by the Social Science Research Council, the Ford Foundation and the National Institute of Mental Health, was so complete that by the late 1950s universities were experiencing difficulty in locating younger North Americanists.

The post-war group was not just studying in different places, for they were branching out into types of societies that were not within the traditional purview of anthropology. The study of peasants and complex societies began in the 1920s and 1930s with research among the Indian populations of highland Middle and South America. What had been a marginal interest during that period had now become a major preoccupation, and I would estimate that by the 1950s most anthropologists were no longer working with primitive peoples. Younger scholars such as Morton Fried and G. William Skinner, trained in the Chinese language and in general Sinology, undertook the study of Chinese communities, John Embree initiated his Japanese research, and such well known students of the American Indian as Morris Opler and David Mandelbaum redirected their energies to India. Julian Steward initiated a program of Latin American studies through the Smithsonian Institution's Institute of Social Anthropology during World War II, and in 1948 launched a Columbia University research program that attempted a comprehensive understanding of the island of Puerto Rico (Steward et al. 1956).

The spate of research in communities and districts of complex societies set anthropologists adrift on uncharted seas, and they were soon forced to sit back and conceptualize the units they were dealing with and try to place these units in larger structures. Steward's monograph *Area Research: Theory and Practice* (Steward 1950) presented a framework for the study of national, or horizontal, institutions, and local, or vertical, ones. The book also elaborated for the first time Steward's theory of levels of sociocultural integration, an idea that was seen to have wide evolutionary significance but which was devised as a means of studying acculturation. Robert Redfield had earlier drawn on Weberian theory to develop a polar typology of folk and urban society, with peasants occupying an intermediate position on the continuum (Redfield 1940). Three of the articles in this volume emerged directly from the community study method. Eric Wolf's "Types of Latin American Peasantry" (1955) was one of the first, and surely one of the more influential of papers essaying a typology of communities (cf. Wagley and Harris 1955). In this paper, Wolf juxtaposes a closed or corporate type of community to an open type and relates the differences to modes of land tenure. George Foster's "Peasant Society and the Image of Limited Good" (1965) was one among a number of attempts to find a consistent definition of the characteristics of peasant populations. Foster outlines one element of what he considers peasant world view and relates it to the economic processes inherent to peasant society. Conrad Arensberg's paper "The Community as Object and as Sample" (1961) tried to place the locality within the context of larger social systems and considers the always vexatious problems of community boundaries and representativeness. The major significance of Arensberg's article is a methodological one, for the change in scale of the research subject wrenched anthropology out of its age of

innocence and ended forever (or at least until the rise of cognitive studies) ethnographies written from the head of one old informant sitting in
the anthropologist's hotel room. Although quantification, sampling,
and so forth, are used even in the study of primitive villags today, the
more sophisticated techniques of our sociological colleagues first entered
the profession through the study of peasant communities. And as early
as 1950, Ralph Beals in his presidential address to the American Anthropological Association (Beals 1951) warned his colleagues in the budding
field of urban anthropology that they were reinventing survey research
and statistics without bothering to inquire into sociological methods
first.

American anthropology's expansion in scope and numbers had ramifications that extended deep into the realm of theory. By the end of
World War II, we had already come far from the period of Boas, Wissler,
and the other dominant figures of early 20th century anthropology.
There was a pervasive interest in culture change that had transformed
the research being done among the American Indians and was a dominant theme in the community study approach as well. The study of
social and cultural change is probably the most consistent thread binding
our twenty-five year period, a fact that owes less to theoretical consistency than to the simple premise that change and transformation were
inescapable parts of most research situations. Interest in the phenomenon was not so much a theoretical concern as the very ethnography
itself.

Studies of change were gaining greatly in sophistication, as compared
to the first formulations of "acculturation" studies (cf. Redfield, Linton,
and Herskovits 1936), and they were increasingly focused on specific
problem areas. One of the better examples of the new kind of study was
a comparative analysis entitled "Navaho and Zuni Veterans: A Study of
Contrasting Modes of Culture Change" by John Adair and Evon Vogt
(1949). This well known paper reported a radically different response of
the Navaho and Zuni to their returning war veterans: the Navaho regarded the demobilized soldiers as positive influences toward culture
change, while the Zuni looked upon their veterans as potential threats to
the tranquility of the community and the integrity of traditional values.
The authors related these differential attitudes to the histories of the two
societies, the physical layout of their communities and to the values of
each group. The latter emphasis was in keeping with the major orientation of the Harvard group, especially of those associated with the Department of Social Relations, to the key function of value orientations as
guarantors of cultural integration and as selective elements in culture
change.

The two other preoccupations of the discipline at the end of the war were a continuing interest in personality and culture studies and a newly reawakened fascination with theories of cultural evolution. I will turn to personality studies first, because the development of a psychological anthropology was aborted during our period, an unraveling that I consider one of the more unfortunate episodes in the history of anthropology. This field, begun by Freud and continued by psychoanalysts such as Kardiner and Fromm and such anthropologists as Mead, Benedict, Hallowell, and Henry, attempted to relate the symbolic aspects of culture to intra-psychic process through the study of the basic institutions of family and socialization. The psychological orientation of the field was Freudian, which can be explained by the dominance of this theoretical persuasion during the 1920s and 1930s and also by the manifest applicability of its theory of symbolism to cultural materials. Personality and culture studies went into sharp decline by the early 1950s, a function of diversification of psychoanalytic theory and the rise of neo- (and anti-) Freudian schools on the psychological side. Within anthropology, psychological anthropology experienced heavy criticism from both the cultural evolutionists and the structural-functionalists. The latter two groups, so frequently at odds with each other, managed to agree that culture and personality studies were a form of "reductionism" in that they sought to explain cultural facts by psychological ones, a stand that was usually sanctified by reference to a much overworked passage of Emile Durkheim's *Rules of Sociological Method* (1964:104). Reductionism, of course, really means explaining the particular and the variable by invocation of a general principle and by no means were all of the personality and culture specialists guilty of this sin. A much better example of reductionism would be Radcliffe-Brown's use of the principle of the unity of the sibling group to explain the terminological merging of father and father's brother in some kinship systems.

The attack upon personality and culture studies was highly successful, but it had some help from within the ranks of the psychologically oriented. One of the great weaknesses of the group was its espousal of the notion of "modal personality," an assumption of a degree of personality homogeneity in primitive societies that was mercilessly lampooned by C. W. M. Hart in a lovely essay entitled "The Sons of Turimpi" (Hart 1954). The apotheosis of modal personality, the idea of national character, probably did as much damage to psychological anthropology as did all the writings of Leslie White, its most trenchant opponent. Personality and culture studies did not end completely, and the interest has been continued by a growing band of anthropologists who are pronouncedly less optimistic and self-confident than their predecessors. Freud, however, did give us the only cross-culturally applicable theory of symbolism that is available in anthropology, and the approach remains useful and productive in the interpretation of mythology and the more symbolically stylized aspects of culture that we were wont to refer to as "projective." After all, what else are you going to say about the New Guinea group in which young male initiates practice fellatio on their mother's brothers?

It is in the firm belief that we will have to return to the depth psychologies if we are going to escape from an anthropology that has become sterile of lust and will that I have selected what I believe to be the best representative of the genre to appear in the *American Anthropologist:* "Earth-Diver: Creation of the Mythopoeic Male" by Alan Dundes (1962). This is a classically Freudian piece, both in conception and execution, in which Dundes relates the very widespread myth of the animal or bird who retrieves the earth from the primeval flood to the womb-envying urges of males and the fantasy of anal birth. One can easily see the structural dimensions of the myth as well, but structuralism deals with relationships between symbols rather than with the content of the symbols themselves, and it should be clear that the two approaches are complementary. In passing, it must be remarked that scholarship suffers from a propensity to say "If this, then *not* that," which leads to all or nothing theorization and ideological imperialism. As in the earth-diver myth, there is no reason why two approaches may not be thoroughly compatible with each other, representing merely two questions that one asks of the same material.

The revival of evolutionism in the early part of our period was largely the work of two men, Leslie White and Julian Steward. Leslie White was one of the more interesting figures in recent anthropology. Scrappy, pugnacious, unflinching in the defense of his ideas, he remained marginal to the mainstream of anthropology by choice. His closest ties were to his students, not his peers, and he had little to do with the anthropological establishment. Starting with a series of papers written during the early 1940s, he championed the discredited theories of Lewis Henry Morgan in a campaign that was dignified by its lack of political and professional wisdom. He argued for Morgan's ideas and for philosophical materialism at a time when Senator Joseph McCarthy, Congressman Richard Nixon and a host of other political troglodytes and opportunists were combing the campuses and the media for signs of subversion, and he took on an entire profession, most of which had not read Morgan but were sure he was wrong. White's evolutionism was not simply Morgan warmed over, but a systematic theory that related the progression of culture to technology and man's control over forms of energy. It suffered from being disembodied in time and space, an essential ahistoricism, but this was a function of its universal generality. Although White's most important paper on evolution, "Energy and the Evolution of Culture" (1943), falls outside the span of years covered by this volume, I have chosen to include his paper, "The Definition and Prohibition of Incest" (1948). The essay has an evolutionary theme insofar as White saw the incest taboo and marriage as an essential means for the establishment of larger social units through marital alliance. He goes beyond this idea, however, to present what he called a "culturalogical" interpretation of the taboo, which can be translated here as one that does not rely upon biological and psychological explanations. White always found satisfaction in finding old precedents for his ideas, and he attributed the genesis of the theory to St. Augustine's admonition that people must either marry out or die out. In a sense, White's views on incest are a continuation of his anti-Freudianism but, while writing this preface, I met a psychoanalyst who had done his undergraduate work at Michigan and told me that he was directly motivated into his calling by attending White's course on the mind of primitive man. It was White's fervor and dedication that had inspired my acquaintance, and not what he said about the mind. This is what attracted us all to the man.

White's theories had a certain following but, except for a common theme of materialism, they seldom influenced empirical research, including White's own fieldwork among the Rio Grande pueblos. The reasons for this lay in the very general and global nature of his notions on evolution and the difficulty of translating them into the analysis of ethnographic data. Julian Steward's evolutionism, however, was more a methodology than a schema of cultural development, and his influence was, therefore, more lasting. Multilinear evolutionism—a term coined by Robert Lowie to describe the *kulturkreiselehre* (1948:33-35)—was predicated on the naturalistic maxim that what has happened once in a universe governed by law can happen again—and given the same conditions probably will. The natural conditions for recurrence, and cultural regularity, lay in the domain of the cultural ecological equation in Steward's view. This, in turn, is the premise that the relationship between society and environment is a function of tools and techniques brought to bear upon resources through the process of work, which is a creative part of any social system. Following this logic, the regular appearance of any constellation of basic social characteristics indicates a similar causal process at work and suggests that common ecological features underlie all cases. Translated into working terms, the strategy of multilinear evolution is to look for similarities between cultures and, through analysis, ascertain whether they reveal common ecological solutions. And if history is available for the societies in question, then the next step is to determine whether in fact, the historical sequence admits of similarities, or convergences, as well.

Steward's paper "Cultural Causality and Law: A Trial Formulation of the Development of Early Civilizations" (1949) must stand as one of the great essays in the long publishing history of the *American Anthropologist*. In this article, Steward tests the 'hydraulic society' theory of Karl Witt-fogel, using both comparative and historical analysis of the growth of civilization in Egypt, northern Peru, Mesopotamia, northern China and Meso-America. The central determinant in all five cases was found to be irrigation agriculture, which was based upon, and in turn made possible, the control of large populations in the construction and maintenance of public works. Steward and his students applied the method in a number of subsequent empirical studies, but today it no longer stands out as a distinct procedure and is understood to be a general part of any anthropological approach that is both comparative and ecological.

The most enduring part of Steward's legacy to anthropology is the theory of cultural ecology, which stimulated much of the development of modern ecological anthropology and is a part also of a tradition of materially oriented analyses in anthropology. Leslie White, of course, was also important in the growth of what has been called "cultural materialism," but the main impetus undoubtedly belongs to Julian Steward, although he would have shunned the label. Steward's influence extended beyond the students he trained at Illinois and Columbia, for he was widely read in this country and abroad. One of the best examples of the cultural ecological approach to appear in the journal during the quarter century was by a Norwegian anthropologist who had never studied with Steward: Fredrik Barth's paper "Ecologic Relationships of Ethnic Groups in Swat, North Pakistan" (1956). The article is also significant in supplying a key to the "mosaic" phenomenon that Kroeber and others had noted among pastoral nomads, and it stands as a model for later studies of herding societies.

Cultural ecology and personality and culture may be regarded as two typically American approaches in anthropology, but this was mainly a result of their virtual restriction to this country and not to their universality within it. Freudian psychology never achieved the currency in France or England that it enjoyed in the United States, and anthropologists in both countries took Durkheim's strictures on the limits of the profession quite literally. As for ecological studies, the British were too preoccupied with the study of jural norms to worry much about activity imposed by force of circumstance, and any French inclinations toward materialism were instantly swallowed by an ubiquitous academic Marxism. Moreover, in the tight little scholarly worlds of each country, there was only so much room for deviation from established theory, and I have a strong suspicion that American heterodoxies were no more welcome than Coca Cola and Yank neologisms. Whatever the causes, there never has been much of an export market for American anthropological theory. The tariff barriers on the exchange of ideas were, however, unidirectional, for American anthropologists have been remarkably on the *qui vive* for new continental theory (and loan words). This is nowhere more evident in the history of the discipline than during the 1950s, when a British-derived sociologically oriented anthropology—structural-functionalism—beame the primary direction of younger American anthropologists. There are many reasons for this other than simple diffusion of ideas, and it would be useful to briefly consider the history of the phenomenon. American anthropologists have, paradoxically, had closer associations with the discipline of sociology than have their British colleagues. It must be remembered that social anthropology preempted the field of social inquiry in Britain until the growth, largely in the red brick universities of the post-war period, of departments of sociology and anthropology. Moreover, they were usually very much in the minority and under the chairmanship of sociologists who tolerated them as one would a troublesome, but exotically interesting, pet. A certain amount of mutual influence inevitably resulted from the close association of the disciplines, bringing immediately to mind the Weberian slant picked up by Ralph Linton in the joint department at Wisconsin and by Robert Redfield through his collegial and affinal ties at Chicago. What is more notable, however, is the relative *lack* of influence of sociological method and theory upon anthropology during the decades in which they roomed together, for our rejection of most sociological theory was notable. One may conjecture that physical closeness bred intellectual distance, for the isolated little pockets of anthropologists had to struggle to maintain their identities and separateness. To have embraced Durkheim, Weber, Cooley, George Herbert Mead, Pareto, and Simmel would have constituted the erosion of a boundary and the concession of an important bargaining chip in intra-departmental politics. We did read the great social theorists, to be sure, for their relevance to anthropology was manifest, but we read them defensively.

A shift of interest to the classics of social theory began with the separation of departments, but, more important, it developed as our research moved into new areas. Structural-functionalism, or Durkheimian sociology, is based on a model of society in which norms guide actions which then feed back to reinforce the system of norms. However handy this may be as a starting point for the analysis of functioning social systems, it was less than useful when studying the shattered

remnants of American Indian society. But as a new generation of researchers went off to study societies in which social life, though
changed, still maintained a certain autonomy and vitality of its own, the
fiction of a system that seeks to perpetuate itself became of heuristic
value. Many American anthropologists undertook study in areas that
had already been investigated by British scholars, as in Africa and Melanesia. There they found not only empirical situations that loaned themselves to functional analysis, but a background of literature done in the
metier. If theories had not impelled people to read Fortes on the Tallensi
and Evans-Pritchard on the Nuer, then the very fact that they were going
to Africa for research certainly would. And all the problems dealt with
by the British Africanists, especially descent and monarchy—two very
English preoccupations—were waiting for the Americans as well.

During the 1950s and as late as the mid-1960s, many Americans went
to Oxford and Cambridge for graduate work, either for advanced training in Africa studies or as regular graduate students and degree candidates. A number of professional anthropologists went to the British
universities as exchange scholars or simply to write while on sabbatical
leave. Many came back from their year abroad with a new orientation
towards structural-functional analysis, and a slight accent. In a reverse
flow, many British anthropologists accepted visiting professorships and
permanent posts in the United States, where superior salaries prevailed
and vacancies abounded. The height of the anthropological entente between the British and American scholars was marked by a conference
sponsored by the Association of Social Anthropologists of the Common-
wealth and held at Cambridge in June 1963. From this meeting of some
dozen American anthropologists and twice that number of their British
counterparts came the series of books published as Association of Social
Anthropology monographs, under the editorship of Michael Banton.
The participants in the meeting felt themselves to be taking part in a
climactic event that marked a new beginning. Nobody was able to predict at the time that the conference marked an end, an end of the close
community of interest that had grown up among the "social anthropologists" on both sides of the ocean and the end of the primacy of structural-
functionalism. Americans still go to Britain, of course, but often on their
way to Paris. And the British scholars, in turn, have found that employment in the United States is quite as difficult to find as in Great Britain.

During the first half of our quarter century period, structural-functionalism became strongly rooted in American universities, independently of the exchange of personnel with Great Britain. The earlier per-
egrinations of A. R. Radcliffe-Brown had brought him to the University
of Chicago from 1931 to 1937, during which time he trained Fred Eggan,

Sol Tax, and others, who built the Chicago department during the postwar era. Radcliffe-Brown's students continued the tradition of their teacher, and their students, in turn, became more orthodox in their functionalism than even the grandfather. Another center of sociologically oriented anthropology was Harvard University. The establishment there of the Department of Social Relations, chaired by Talcott Parsons and including representatives from sociology, anthropology, social psychology, and political science, brought together a number of disciplines within the broad confines of a general social theory. The "general theory of action" represented Parsons' own synthesis of Weber and Durkheim, with an additional mix of Pareto, Mannheim, and Freud. It became a dominant persuasion in sociology, and filtered into anthropology through Parsons' students, including David M. Schneider, Clifford Geertz, John Roberts, and others. The Parsonian syntax caused many anthropologists to bridle at his sociology, but it is a far more sophisticated brand of functionalism than that of Radcliffe-Brown. The major problems of the school, however, were not with Radcliffe-Brown or Parsons in particular, but with functionalism in general. And it failed not because it was proven wrong but because it had exhausted its possibilities.

The *American Anthropologist* carried a large number of articles in the structural-functional vein during the decade of 1953 to 1963—indeed, it still does, but their numbers and interest are no longer dominant. One of the most important was "The Structure of Unilineal Descent Groups" by Meyer Fortes, an essay that summarized two decades of British research on African descent systems (1953). The paper presented Fortes's views on "complementary filiation," a concept that was later to become a pivotal issue in the debate with French structuralism and which can still evoke a lively argument. Fortes' article is still considered required reading by every graduate student of anthropology and is reprinted here as a classic in the discipline. Fred Eggan's article "Social Anthropology and the Method of Controlled Comparison" (1954) is in the tradition of social anthropology, but it has a uniquely American dimension in that it proposes a comparative method that seeks to find resemblances and divergences between societies that are historically, or genetically, linked. As such, one of its principal purposes is the discovery of regular processes of change, a procedure that Eggan had already tested in his studies of American Indian kinship.

The best exemplar of the Parsonian approach in anthropology to appear in the *American Anthropologist* was Clifford Geertz's "Ritual and Social Change: A Javanese Example" (1957). Aside from his substantive conclusions, the essay is particularly valuable as an illustration of the differences between the social system and the cultural system in Parsonian usage and the utility of distinguishing between the two. Geertz went beyond Parsons in applying the theory to the analysis of social change, an area in which most social scientists recognize weakness in the Parsonian system. Very much in the sociological tradition, because it was written by a sociologist, is another of our selections "The Nature of Deference and Demeanor" by Erving Goffman (1956). This is the only essay in the volume written by a non-anthropologist, but I selected it because Goffman's approach and intellectual affinities are essentially anthropological, to the extent that he attends every meeting of the American Anthropological Association. The paper is most important in that it encapsulates the essence of Goffman's interaction theory and remains thoroughly consistent with his present writings. Moreover, the essay is written with a simple, yet elegant, prose style, and is structurally splendid, one of the finest examples I have read of the scholarly form. Finally, I call the reader's attention to S. F. Nadel's paper "Witchcraft in Four African Societies: An Essay in Comparison" (1952) as an example of the one leading scholar of the British school who was trying in a systematic way to introduce a psychological dimension into studies of social structure. Significantly, Nadel's sociological orientation was toward German sociology and not the French; his antecedents belonged to Weber rather than Durkheim.

Two articles in the area of social structure, included in this volume, are marginal to the structural-functional tradition and represent rather different directions. The first is an historically important essay by Ward Goodenough under the title "A Problem in Malayo-Polynesian Social Organization" (1955). Goodenough's point of departure is George P. Murdock's reconstruction of proto-Malayo Polynesian social organization, which was postulated to have been based on bilocality, the bilateral kindred and the absence of unilineal descent. Goodenough argues that the widespread Polynesian pattern in which individual land rights were derived from kin group membership precludes the kindred as a proto-unit because its ego-centered nature prevents it from becoming an effective holder of a corporate estate. He points instead to a land-oriented kin group, which had not been adequately delineated in the literature and which he refers to as a "non-unilinear descent group." The paper was important beyond the field of Oceanian studies, for it did much to clarify bilaterality and its relation to unilineality. Moreover, Goodenough stressed the significance of the relationship between descent group and land by delineating a type of social unit in which property and residence transcend regular rules of kinship in ascribing status. The primacy of property over kinship and of situation over norm was a key feature of other, later studies of descent, including the work of Morton Fried

(1957), Mervyn Meggitt (1965), and Peter Worsley (1956).

An article by Sally Falk Moore, "Descent and Symbolic Filiation" (1964), attacks a problem in social structure using the perspectives of symbolic studies and French structuralism. Moore takes the apparent anomaly of myths of the origins of exogamic social groups from the incestuous union of brother and sister or, less frequently, parent and child, and relates them to the belief that descent flows through lineages as a mystical stream. Brother and sister in actual fact are taboo to each other, but may have a symbolic connection with each other's fertility. One one level, then, the myth is a reversal of the real world, but on another level it presents an underlying theme of the lineage as a symbolically autocthonous unit. "Kind reproduces kind in the animal and human kingdoms," writes Moore of totemism (1964:1319). This statement is a corrective of Lévi-Strauss's Le Totemisme Aujourd'hui, but the latter book clearly inspired the article.

As in evolution, successive forms co-exist and overlap in intellectual history. In just this way, the anthropological currents that would eventually displace structural-functionalism arose during a time when that school was dominant; in turn, functional thought outlived its own 'demise' and continues to be active, though not salient, to the present day. This is not the place for an autopsy of structural-functionalism, and I will only mention a few of the factors that are commonly believed to have bred disillusionment. The first was already suggested; this is that we had gone as far with functionalism as we could go. It was essentially a rather simple approach, based on a set of assumptions which, while never true, were at least useful for a time. Functionalism posited an "as if" world in which social norms and social action were isomorphic and directly complementary to one another. It assumed further that social systems were bounded, if not in fact then in theory, and that these boundaries were conditions by which systems maintained themselves. The very problem of system maintenance was based on the working proposition that a society in a slice of time could be extrapolated out to historical societies. In this way, the coherence of the parts of a system were taken to be the result of a strain toward coherence over time. This is at best a dangerous assumption, but if it turns out that this equilibrium is in good part a function of the anthropologist's mind, or his theories, then it leads to solipsism. Edmund Leach in Political Systems of Highland Burma (1954) leveled this critique at his colleagues with devastating effect, though, in balance, Leach's treatment of his empirical data were much in keeping with traditional social anthropology. Positivism is a hard habit to break, deriving as it does from our penchant for reducing the world to little nuggets of reality.

Classic functionalism was a valuable heuristic device in the days
when anthropologists were conducting their studies in small homogeneous societies in New Guinea or in outlying bush villages in Africa, but
its utility waned as the postwar world intruded into even the remotest
parts of the earth, destroying forever whatever tissues bound these
primitive worlds together. At the same time, anthropological interests
were changing, and we were shifting our locales of study to cities and'
towns, to market places and mining camps, and to the newly emergent
nations of the post-colonial world. This teeming hodge-podge of humanity seemed to defy all efforts to reduce it to bounded systems, with
uniform value-imbeddedness and internal equilibrating mechanisms.
Max Gluckman attempted in an *American Anthropologist* article titled
"The Utility of the Equilibrium Model in the Study of Social Change"
(1968) to salvage the method, but even he was forced to admit that when
rapid change takes place our descriptions become little more than historical narrative. Gluckman's colleagues at Manchester, who had long
worked in the central African areas most violently affected by the modern world, developed a series of strategies such as "event analysis" and
"network theory" to study these untidy situations. These methods took
hold in the United States as well, and the grant applications of American
graduate students make monotonous reference to the new technique of
network analysis, which they apparently believe was born in the Copper
Belt in the 1960s. The method actually saw the first light of day in the
Westinghouse Company's Hawthorne Plant in the 1930s and was described by Eliot Chapple and Conrad Arensberg in 1940 (Chapple and
Arensberg 1940), but as was noted earlier, we are prone to importing
ideas.

With the failure of the functionalist consensus in anthropology, a
number of scholars turned from the analysis of social interaction to the
study of culture as a domain of symbol and meaning. The new approaches—variously called "cognitive anthropology," "the new ethnography," "componential analysis," "ethnoscience," and the like—had in
common a preoccupation with the old problems of classification and the
relations between language, culture, and thought. They took as their
subject the means by which people of different cultures characteristically
perceive and categorize the social and natural worlds, and the rules by
which they assign meanings to certain symbols. The methods borrowed
heavily from linguistics, especially semantics, for the symbols analyzed
were generally words and one of the primary aims of the enterprise was
to discover those meanings which were correct for certain words while
incorrect for all others. These rules of classification, it was posited, are
rules by which people apprehend reality, determine cultural correctness

of interpretation of social situations, and, ultimately, are rules by which people act.

The apical ancestor of the new ethnographers was A. L. Kroeber, a truly *cultural* anthropologist, and the author of the seminal article "Classificatory Systems of Relationship" (1909). In this essay, Kroeber elaborated a series of principles by which kinship categories are terminologically merged or distinguished to produce a cognitive map of kinship that can be described by a limited number of abstract rules. The paper was generally looked upon as having chief significance for the debate as to the primacy of cultural or psychological determinants of kin terms, an issue that was as arid as it was confusing, and was read as a curio in the history of anthropology. The essentials of Kroeber's method were revived and modified, however, by Floyd Lounsbury and his students at Yale; the first results of their work were published in the linguistics journal *Language* in 1956 (Lounsbury 1956; Goodenough 1956). The Lounsbury approach, called "componential analysis," was intended to supplant the usual procedure of defining a kin term by listing all the genealogical positions to which it applies. Componential analysis went beyond this to elucidate the criteria that the speakers themselves used in conceptualizing kinship. The methodology was summarized and described by Anthony Wallace and John Atkins in their paper "The Meaning of Kinship Terms," which is reprinted in this volume (Wallace and Atkins 1960).

The method of componential analysis was clearly adaptable to domains of meaning other than kinship. Harold Conklin's paper on Hanunóo color categories (1955) actually preceded the publications on kinship, and the same author's doctoral dissertation was on the ethnobotany of that group (Conklin 1954). Formal analysis of the same kind was extended to the spheres of folk science, ritual and disease; a paper presenting a componential analysis of Tzeltal Maya terms for firewood (Metzger and Williams 1966) was viewed by many anthropologists as the ultimate application of the method. One of the areas most seriously studied by the school was ecology, although, as Charles Frake's paper "Cultural Ecology and Ethnography" clearly indicates, it is a far different cultural ecology than that pioneered by Steward (Frake 1962).

The expansion of cognitive and formal approaches into areas other than kinship provoked strong rebuttal from several anthropologists, for nobody seemed to be particularly troubled by the method until it showed imperial symptoms. Robbins Burling asked whether componential analysis was "God's truth" or "hocus-pocus," and clearly opted for the latter answer (Burling 1964). Marvin Harris took vigorous issue with the ambitious claims that, even if ethnoscience did not tell you how the natives think, it will at least tell you how they are supposed to act (Harris 1968:568-604). Denying that a behavioral code can be found anywhere but in behavior, Harris dismissed the entire method as "cultural idealism." One of the sharpest attacks on the new ethnography came from Gerald Berreman, in his paper "Anemic and Emetic Analyses in Social Anthropology," a title that suggests the tenor of the article (Berreman 1966). Berreman wrote that in their concern for methodological purity, the group was forced to study the trivial—an accusation that is often leveled at mathematical sociologists as well—and he deplored the subservience of anthropological procedures to linguistic method.

The latter is an interesting point, for social anthropologists occasionally apply the insights of other fields to their own data with very mixed results. Prime examples of this, in addition to the near reduction of ethnography to semantics, are the excesses of national character study and the new biological sociology. There seems almost to be a law by which synthesizers carry their enthusiasms into ethereal realms, leaving more cautious souls to come along later and pick up from the method whatever is useful, putting it together with what had been neglected by the overly eager pioneers. In the case of the new ethnography, reconstructive theory would call for establishing relationships between the domain of cognition and the world of sensate activity.

An even more powerful attack on traditional social anthropology was launched from France. Although "structuralism" bears certain resemblances to componential analysis in that both are formal procedures having affinities to linguistics, the theory forged by Lévi-Strauss was at once less linguistic in its methods and more sweeping in its rejection of social science positivism. Structuralism, of course, can be dated as far back as Claude Lévi-Strauss's writings on South American ethnography in the early 1940s, though its true beginnings must be found in the publication of *Les Formes Élémentaires de la Parenté* in 1949. It had limited influence, however, outside of France until the appearance of translations of most of his work in the 1960s. In England, Edmund Leach and Rodney Needham publicized, and criticized, the work of the French anthropologist, and in the United States George Homans' and David Schneider's *Marriage, Authority, and Final Causes* (1955) provided a critique that did much to impel others to turn to the original. Nonetheless, interest in the movement was slow to develop in this country, and I believe that my seminar on structuralism in 1961 at Berkeley—a course which was dubbed "The French Disease" by irreverent students—was the first offered in the United States.

The two main reasons for the slowness with which structuralism

diffused to these shores can probably be found in the regnant functionalism of the period and the unwillingness of most of us to cope with Lévi-
Strauss's elegant but difficult French. The latter difficulty was removed
with the translation into English of *Tristes Tropiques* (1961), *Structural
Anthropology* (1963), *Totemism* (1963), *The Savage Mind* (1968), *The Raw
and the Cooked* (1969), and, finally, *The Elementary Structures of Kinship*
(1969). As for functionalism, it was exactly during the period in which
most of Lévi-Strauss's work was appearing in English that interest in the
school waned. The conversion of David Schneider, one of the leading
structural-functionalists, and of Marshall Sahlins, a pillar of cultural
materialism, to French structuralism marked the dimensions of the theoretical migration that ensued.

What has been the attraction of structuralism in a discipline that was
founded in naturalism and empiricism? I suspect that the intriguing
character of Lévi-Strauss's dialectics have had much to do with the surge
of interest in this country, for he was read at a juncture in our intellectual
history that was highlighted by a growing distrust of positivism and
disbelief in the "objectivity" of social science. The profession found itself
in a theoretical dead end, and structuralism promised an alternative to
an empiricism that did not go much beyond appearances and had never
resolved the dilemma posed by the fact that the observer and what is
observed are inseparable. Moreover, there was a certain consistency
between the traditional interests of American anthropology and those of
the French school, for both dealt with culture as a set of symbols that is
sui generis and not merely an epiphenomenon or refraction of activity.
There is continuity in this respect between the work of Lévi-Strauss, the
products of componential analysis and the earlier writings of Kroeber
and his teacher Boas. Lévi-Straus himself recognized these affinities,
which should not be occasion for surprise in view of the fact that he
really learned his anthropology in the Brazilian forest and New York
City.

The awakening of deep American interest in structuralism came too
close to the end of our period to have had an extensive impact upon the
American Anthropologist. Except for the Moore article and kindred pieces
addressing structuralist issues (cf. Murphy and Kasdan 1959; Murphy
1967; Scholte 1966), there are surprisingly few essays done in the structuralist vein in the journal. This has, of course, changed since 1970, and
the full influence of structuralism on American anthropology will have
to await a centennial volume, if the world lasts that long.

My discussion of the history of anthropology during this period has
neglected three smaller subfields for the simple reason that their histories are not well reflected in the *American Anthropologist*. Although it is

satisfying to reprint the excellent summarization of taxonomy and conceptual units in archaeology by Phillips and Willey (1953), there was a sad dearth in the pages of the journal of all the developments of the past 25 years that have brought about a "new archaeology." As for linguistics, the pages of the journal during our period do not reveal the dimensions of the revolution created by Chomsky's generative grammar; and in lexico-statistics, there is little in the *American Anthropologist* on the method itself and but a few articles giving results. The one article chosen, "The Scope of Linguistics" by Carl Voegelin and Zelig Harris (1947), does not tell us of these new directions but is a summary of the state of the science at the beginning of our period. The enormous expansion of the fossil record over the past quarter century is relatively undocumented in the journal, although C. Loring Brace's vigorous defense of our Neanderthal ancestry (Brace 1962) is a valuable exception. Also of importance is Ashley Montagu's scathing attack on racial studies and on the concept of "race" itself (Montagu 1962). In an age that demanded social relevance of anthropology, he wrote:

It may be difficult for those who believe in what I. A. Richards has called "The Divine Right of Words" to accept the suggestion that a word such as "race," which has exercised so evil a tyranny over the minds of men, should be permanently dethroned from the vocabulary, but that constitutes all the more reason for trying, remembering that the meaning of a word is the action it produces. (Montagu 1962:927)

The theoretical flux within the discipline during our period was matched by profound institutional change. We entered the epoch a small and exotic branch of study with a membership that could be numbered in the hundreds and with but a dozen or so graduate schools granting advanced degrees. The great expansion of the late 1950s and the entire decade of the 1960s saw our ranks grow to the thousands, with several thousand more graduate students scattered through scores of graduate departments. During the height of academic growth, new Ph.D.s and promising candidates were beleaguered with attractive job offers, and research funds were more plentiful than applicants. By the time our period ended, however, the first effects of economic depression and inflation were joining with a cresting of the college population to flatten out the boom. Six years later, at the time of this writing, the prospects for all academia appear bleak, and the profession is searching anxiously for other outlets than teaching for its talents and energies.

The mood and climate of the campuses changed as much as did their finances. We began the period with the entry of millions of World War II veterans into our colleges and universities, but only a decade later, the younger siblings of the war group were referred to as the "silent generation." American campuses were as unpolitical as our professional association, and many people believed this to represent the shape of the future. The atmosphere changed in the early 1960s with the idealistic involvement of young people in the civil rights movement, the Peace Corps and other activities. That all was not well on the campuses, however, was indicated by the Berkeley uprising of 1964, a protest whose target was bureaucracy itself. By the late 1960s, the Vietnam War had soured the tone and quality of American political life, and caused anthropologists to question their own involvement in policies that were neither of their making nor their choice. The American Anthropological Association became a forum of political debate for the first time since World War I, and our survival of the acerbic exchanges of the late 1960s and early 1970s is a testament to the organizational entrenchment of the scholarly disciplines.

The political turmoil of the time had an interesting side-effect in the resurgence of Marxian thought in anthropology, which became interwoven with both the dialectical method underlying structuralism and the materialism of the "techno-environmental determinists." We are at an interesting juncture in the discipline of anthropology, for the present period has strong parallels to the historical situation that prevailed at the founding of the American Anthropological Association. Both times found the theoretical orientations of the profession in total disarray, a previous consensus as to aims and methods having foundered, and both times were characterized by a groping out in all directions for a new epistemology and a new common purpose. The very growth of anthropology has made for ever greater specialization and diversifications of research, and this process has joined with external political crisis to make this the most unsettled period in the history of the discipline. There has been a burgeoning of schools of thought that are all with us today—structural-functionalism, structuralism, just plain ecology, cognitive anthropologies, neo-evolutionisms, cultural materialism, and so forth—and none is dominant. Indeed, this may just be the future condition of anthropology: a pluralistic discipline tht loosely shelters a plethora of interests and which lacks a center.

There are, however, certain quite general enduring qualities that distinguish anthropology. However much specialization may have sapped the overall integrity of the four fields of the discipline, it still forms the only scholarly community that unites the cultural, biological, historic and linguistic aspects of human life. Very few of us stray outside our specialties, but most of us read the work of our colleagues in other subfields and are conditioned, albeit subtly, by their perspectives. The other distinctive characteristic of the discipline is the common enterprise of fieldwork, which joins all the varieties of cultural anthropologists with their colleagues in archaeology, linguistics, and physical anthropology. This, after all, is the praxis of anthropology, and it is in this bedrock kind of activity that our sense of the profession is formed. And if there is one aspect of fieldwork that separates it from all other forms of scholarly research, it is that we become immersed in our work in a total sense; we *live* anthropology in a direct and literal way.

One might be tempted to be pessimistic about the future of anthropology, for the doomsayers are certainly today's prophets. Let me end, instead, with a note on our lasting strength. This lies not in anthropology as science but in anthropology as a humanistic study. We set our task over a hundred years ago to chronicle and preserve the many and wonderful expressions of humanity, and we have largely succeeded in this formidable venture. Finally, in an age of growing secularization and disenchantment of life, we have become the residual heirs of the mythmakers' task, which is nothing less than to explain Man to Mankind.

Herbert Applebaum

II

Nineteenth Century Evolutionism

Introduction

Evolutionary theory can be traced to the philosophers of the enlightenment, with their belief in human progress and the possibility of human knowledge about human society. In the natural sciences, researchers sought to understand the sequence of living organisms, by relating extinct forms of life to current ones. Mechanisms of change in living forms were identified as variation, natural selection, adaptation and reproduction. The entire process was called evolution and summed up by Charles Darwin, in 1859, with the publication of his *Origin of Species*. Even before Darwin, others such as Bachofen, who wrote about kinship, and Maine, who studied the law, used an evolutionary approach to explain current institutions as developing from ancient ones. Herbert Spencer postulated that sequences existed in human societal evolution, and he offered theories to explain the sequences.

Few can argue against the idea that societies change and evolve. The more profound question is to explain the similarities and differences in the evolution of particular societies. Another problem is to develop a system of classifying societies in order to compare them. If the researcher stresses differences in societies, he will tend to view each society as unique and therefore not comparable to others. If the researcher stresses similarities, then societies can be grouped into categories and compared. Then evolutionary sequences can be established through time relations (before-and-after) and, if possible, causal relations (causal agents and effects). Evolutionary theory stresses similarities and plays down differences. It often entails abstractions from the concrete reality of living human beings in particular societies. Acceptance of evolutionary theory means that one is willing to allow for abstraction of social process for the purpose of classification. Such abstraction involves selection of signifi-

31

cant factors based on a theory of social causality. For a detailed description of this method see Steward's chapter, "Cultural Causality and Law," in this volume. For a further description of the method used by Lewis H. Morgan and his systematic collection of comparative data of kinship systems on a worldwide basis, the reader can consult Hallowell (1976:49–55).

As an organized science, anthropology began with evolutionary theory as its framework. The procedures of the evolutionists was like that of any other science. A unit of study was selected. For anthropologists, that unit of study was culture (see the chapter by Edward Tylor). Culture was viewed as a system. Cultural systems were thought to be evolving, enlarging, and producing new forms of greater complexity and organizational differentiation. This was Spencer's particular viewpoint (1912). The objectives of evolutionary theory were to formulate generalizations which could be put into a form that showed the sequential steps by which cultures developed and were transformed from one stage to another. Stages, sequence, lower, higher, and less and more advanced were the terminology of evolutionary theory.

Two nineteenth century anthropologists who were evolutionists were Edward B. Tylor (1871) and Lewis H. Morgan (1877). Both are represented in Part II. Tylor and other nineteenth century evolutionists typed and classified cultural traits. Wherever they found similar traits they assumed similar causes. Later, Boas and others were to challenge that notion, insisting that similar traits could result from dissimilar causes. While they did generalize and abstract from the life of individuals, evolutionists did not ignore the case study. Lewis Morgan's study of the Iroquois, published in 1851, was said to be the first scientific account of an Indian tribe ever given to the world (Hallowell 1976:49). Tylor also recognized the importance of the individual case as it related to the general, when he stated (see Tylor's chapter, Part II):

Sometimes we watch individuals acting for their own ends with little thought of their effect on society at large, and sometimes we have to study movements of national life as a whole, where the individuals cooperating in them are utterly beyond our observation. But seeing that collective social action is the mere resultant of many individual actions, it is clear that these two methods of enquiry (sic), if rightly followed, must be absolutly consistent.

Evolutionists, like Tylor, believed in the scientific method and the importance of basing theory on empirical evidence. There is an optimism about the ability of scientific investigators to learn the causes of social development in Tylor's article on culture (Chapter 2). Believing in the scientific method, if some social trait cannot be explained, Tylor would answer that it is because we need more data. Believing in sequences of development, if there is some dissimilarity between cultures and societies, Tylor would say that they represent differing stages in the progression of their cultures. The optimism, the belief in science, the confidence of human progress are refreshing characteristics of nineteenth century anthropology, when these early pioneers believed anything and everything was possible in their search for knowledge and explanation. It is also refreshing to note in the chapter by Tylor that, in the face of the prejudices of his era regarding non-Europeans, he regarded mankind as homogeneous in nature and eliminated hereditary varieties as an explanation for differences in culture. He also argued that the "religions of savage tribes" do not "lie too low for interest and even for respect." These early anthropologists were not as "advanced" as we moderns in their avoidance of ethnocentrism, but they were not as "primitive" as we are sometimes wont to believe.

Nineteenth century evolutionists sought to discover the sequence of societal forms as cultures and societies progressed through history. Lewis Morgan's *Ancient Society* is a prime example of such efforts, as illustrated in Chapter 3. *Ancient Society* is a remarkable effort, given the state of knowledge at the time. His sequences of evolutionary progression are based upon subsistence types, which take their form from discoveries and inventions, and upon domestic types, which take their form from family organization. He also organized political sequences, based upon forms of property and concepts of territory. Whatever one might think of the sequential order presented by Morgan, an explanation of the development of societies through subsistence, domestic institutions, and territory and property relations sounds quite modern and even scientific. Where Morgan does not sound so modern is when he believes that social institutions grow out of ideas implanted in the human mind at the beginning of time; that is, that societies evolve from some master plan.

Morgan and other nineteenth century evolutionists have been accused of being "inclined to look for a single line of development of culture" (Boas 1960:587). Yet, we find in *Ancient Society*, in a passage from Chapter 3, the following:

It is difficult, if not impossible, to find such tests of progress to mark the commencement of these several periods as will be found absolute in their application, and without exceptions upon all the continents. Neither is it necessary, for the purpose in hand, that exceptions should not exist. It will be sufficient if the principal tribes of mankind can be classified, according to the degree of their *relative* (my emphasis—H.A.) progress, into conditions which can be recognized as distinct."

Harris (1968), Bidney (1968), and Gamst and Norbeck (1976) have all commented that nineteenth century evolutionist anthropologists were aware of the role of diffusion and historical accidents as modifying agents in the progression of societies.

One cannot read *Ancient Society* and not be impressed with its scope and grandeur. It deals with the sweep of evolutionary ascent of human society, the growth and idea of government, the origin and development of the family and the growth of the idea of property. There is nothing trivial in this list. Morgan was not a Renaissance man, but he was a multifaceted one. He was a businessman and an industrialist, involved with railroads. He helped found a league for the promotion of the interests of the Iroquois. He was adopted into their nation. He was an activist on behalf of the Seneca nation. He was a member of the National Academy of Sciences. And he produced a series of profound studies of the family and of the Iroquois Confederacy. The mind that conceived the grand symmetry of *Ancient Society*, wove its intricate patterns of relationships, and handled the differentiation of stages based upon material culture was moved by a nineteenth century view of the world bequeathed by the enlightenment—hope, progress, humankind evolving toward greater heights of achievement.

Regarding Morgan's studies of the classificatory system of the family, W.H.R. Rivers wrote:

I do not know of any discovery in the whole range of science which can be more certainly put to the credit of one man than that of the classificatory system of relationship by Lewis Morgan. . . . it was he who collected the vast mass of material by which the essential characters of the system were demonstrated, and it was he who was the first to recognize the great theoretical importance of his new discovery. (Quoted in Service 1985:14)

One of the concepts evident in both of the selections by Tylor and Morgan is the notion of the psychic unity of mankind. This was seen by both men as an active agent for change and as a factor explaining the parallel evolution of societies. It was earlier formulated by Adolph Bastian (Carneiro 1973b:88), who saw certain elementary ideas arising spontaneously out of the human mind among all groups. These elementary ideas were the basic building blocks of culture. Parallel evolution was attributed to the emergence of these ideas among separate peoples. Morgan refers (Chapter 3) to the "natural logic of the human mind" as predetermining cultural stages. Tylor attributed cultural similarities to similar causes, and, while he did see the similar causes as products of thought, he also recognized that the circumstances in which humans lived must also be similar for parallelisms to take effect (Carneiro 1973b:89).

In any discussion of Lewis Morgan, it is important to mention that his work received careful attention and endorsement of Marx and Engels. Engels wrote about him (1942:5),

Morgan, in his own way . . . discovered afresh in America the materialist conception of history discovered by Marx.

This view of Morgan as a materialist no doubt stemmed from his use of subsistence technology and tool inventions as criteria for demarking the various stages of social evolution. But it ignores Morgan's other views about ideas as prime movers of history. Morgan referred to a "few germs of thought" as being responsible for the evolution of the principal institutions of mankind (1964:59). Besides material culture, Morgan attached great significance to writing, language, and family organization in the evolution of human society. Yet, one could argue that the manner in which he integrated social traits, relating them to levels of discovery and invention associated with subsistence techniques, even though they might be ascribed to origination in ideas, would cause one to classify Morgan as a materialist. Carneiro (1973b:103) argues that sometimes he was too materialistic: for example, when he relegated Polynesians to the middle level of savagery, because they did not possess two elements of material culture—pottery and the bow and arrow. Morgan did this in spite of the fact that a number of Polynesian societies were organized into chiefdoms and even kingdoms.

The period of evolutionism in anthropology was marked by bold and grand theorizing. Anthropology was born as a discipline fed by evolutionary ideas. These ideas gave it purpose and direction. Great amounts of cultural data were synthesized under its rubric and organized into patterns of great scope and sweeping social forces. True, these early anthropologists had their shortcomings. These will be dealt with in the next section. But there has been a reawakening of interest in evolution as a theory, which also will be dealt with in a subsequent section.

In general, these early evolutionary theories had one thing in common: they saw evolution as directional through time. They saw societies or cultural traits as a succession of forms moving toward some evident end. Usually the changes were judged as improvements, as progress toward something better, as something more efficient and perhaps more moral. Tylor and Morgan did recognize the possibility of retrogression in societies, but they saw it as the exception, rather than the rule. Some evolutionists, like Herbert Spencer, viewed evolution as a movement from the less complex to the more complex and to increased specialization and division of labor. This, later, was also the view of Emile Durkheim. In these later views, improvement was not so much the issue as complexity. The world has changed drastically since Morgan and Tylor were writing in the late nineteenth century. We are less hopeful, less romantic, and more cautious in our theorizing. Yet, we still have much to learn from these early pioneers and, certainly, a great deal to respect and admire in the total output of these researchers and the contribution they made in founding anthropology as a science.

Edward B. Tylor

2. The Science of Culture

Culture or Civilization, taken in its wide ethnographic sense, is that complex whole which includes knowledge, belief, art, morals, law, custom, and any other capabilities and habits acquired by man as a member of society. The condition of culture among the various societies of mankind, in so far as it is capable of being investigated on general principles, is a subject apt for the study of laws of human thought and action. On the one hand, the uniformity which so largely pervades civilization may be ascribed, in great measure, to the uniform action of uniform causes: while on the other hand its various grades may be regarded as stages of development or evolution, each the outcome of previous history, and about to do its proper part in shaping the history of the future. To the investigation of these two great principles in several departments of ethnography, with especial consideration of the civilization of the lower tribes as related to the civilization of the higher nations, the present volumes are devoted.

Our modern investigators in the sciences of inorganic nature are foremost to recognize, both within and without their special fields of work, the unity of nature, the fixity of its laws, the definite sequence of cause and effect through which every fact depends on what has gone before it, and acts upon what is to come after it. They grasp firmly the Pythagorean doctrine of pervading order in the universal Kosmos. They affirm, with Aristotle, that nature is not full of incoherent episodes, like a bad tragedy. They agree with Leibnitz in what he calls 'my axiom, that nature never acts by leaps (la nature n'agit jamais par saut),' as well as in his 'great principle, commonly little employed, that nothing happens without sufficient reason.' Nor again, in studying the structure and habits of plants and animals, or in investigating the lower functions even of man, are these leading ideas unacknowledged. But when we come to talk of the higher processes of human feeling and action, of thought and language, knowledge and art, a change appears in the prevalent tone of opinion. The world at large is scarcely prepared to accept the general study of human life as a branch of natural science, and to carry out, in a large sense, the poet's injunction to 'Account for moral as for natural things.' To many educated minds there seems something presumptuous and repulsive in the view that the history of mankind is part and parcel of the history of nature, that our thoughts, wills, and actions accord with laws as definite as those which govern the motion of waves, the combination of acids and bases, and the growth of plants and animals.

The main reasons of this state of the popular judgment are not far to seek. There are many who would willingly accept a science of history if placed before them with substantial definiteness of principle and evidence, but who not unreasonably reject the systems offered to them, as falling too far short of a scientific standard. Through resistance such as this, real knowledge always sooner or later makes its way, while the habit of opposition to novelty does such excellent service against the invasions of speculative dogmatism, that we may sometimes even wish it were stronger than it is. But other obstacles to the investigation of laws of human nature arise from considerations of metaphysics and theology. The popular notion of free human will involves not only freedom to act in accordance with motive, but also a power of breaking loose from continuity and acting without cause,—a combination which may be roughly illustrated by the simile of a balance sometimes acting in the usual way, but also possessed of the faculty of turning by itself without or against its weights. This view of an anomalous action of the will, which it need hardly be said is incompatible with scientific argument, subsists as an opinion patent or latent in men's minds, and strongly affecting their theoretic views of history, though it is not, as a rule, brought prominently forward in systematic reasoning. Indeed the definition of human will, as strictly according with motive, is the only possible scientific basis in such enquiries. . . .

Now it appears that this view of human will and conduct as subject to definite law, is indeed recognized and acted upon by the very people who oppose it when stated in the abstract as a general principle, and who then complain that it annihilates man's free will, destroys his sense of personal responsibility, and degrades him to a soulless machine. He who will say these things will nevertheless pass much of his own life in studying the motives which lead to human action, seeking to attain his wishes through them, framing in his mind theories of personal character, reckoning what are likely to be the effects of new combinations, and giving to his reasoning the crowning character of true scientific enquiry, by taking it for granted that in so far as his calculation turns out wrong, either his evidence must have been false or incomplete, or his judgment upon it unsound. . . .

The philosophy of history at large, explaining the past and predicting the future phenomena of man's life in the world by reference to general laws, is in fact a subject with which, in the present state of knowledge, even genius aided by wide research seems but hardly able to cope. Yet there are departments of it which, though difficult enough, seem comparatively accessible. If the field of enquiry be narrowed from History as a whole to that branch of it which is here called Culture, the history, not of tribes or nations, but of the condition of knowledge, religion, art, custom, and the like among them, the task of investigation proves to lie within far more moderate compass. We suffer still from the same kind of difficulties which beset the wider argument, but they are much diminished. The evidence is no longer so wildly heterogeneous, but may be more simply classified and compared, while the power of getting rid of extraneous matter, and treating each issue on its own proper set of facts, makes close reasoning on the whole more available than in general history. This may appear from a brief preliminary examination of the problem, how the phenomena of Culture may be classified and arranged, stage by stage, in a probable order of evolution. . . .

For the present purpose it appears both possible and desirable to eliminate considerations of hereditary varieties or races of man, and to treat mankind as homogeneous in nature, though placed in different grades of civilization. The details of the enquiry will, I think, prove that stages of culture may be compared without taking into account how far tribes who use the same implement, follow the same custom, or believe the same myth, may differ in their bodily configuration and the colour of their skin and hair.

A first step in the study of civilization is to dissect it into details, and to classify these in their proper groups. Thus, in examining weapons, they are to be classed under spear, club, sling, bow and arrow, and so forth; among textile arts are to be ranged matting, netting, and several grades of making and weaving threads; myths are divided under such headings as myths of sunrise and sunset, eclipse-myths, earthquake-myths, local myths which account for the names of places by some fanciful tale, eponymic myths which account for the parentage of a tribe by turning its name into the name of an imaginary ancestor; under rites and ceremonies occur such practices as the various kinds of sacrifice to the ghosts of the dead and to other spiritual beings, the turning to the east in worship, the purification of ceremonial or moral uncleanness by means of water or fire. Such are a few miscellaneous examples from a list of hundreds, and the ethnographer's business is to classify such details with a view to making out their distribution in geography and history, and the relations which exist among them. What this task is like, may be almost perfectly illustrated by comparing these details of culture with the species of plants and animals as studied by the naturalist. To the ethnographer the bow and arrow is a species, the habit of flattening children's skulls is a species, the practice of reckoning numbers by tens is a species. The geographical distribution of these things, and their transmission from region to region, have to be studied as the naturalist studies the geography of his botanical and zoological species. . . . And just as distant regions so often produce vegetables and animals which are analogous, though by no means identical, so it is with the details of the civilization of their inhabitants. How good a working analogy there really is between the diffusion of plants and animals and the diffusion of civilization, comes well into view when we notice how far the same causes have produced both at once. In district after district, the same causes which have introduced the cultivated plants and domesticated animals of civilization, have brought in with them a corresponding art and knowledge. . . . Experience leads the student after a while to expect and find that the phenomena of culture, as resulting from widely-acting similar causes, should recur again and again in the world. He even mistrusts isolated statements to which he knows of no parallel elsewhere, and waits for their genuineness to be shown by corresponding accounts from the other side of the earth, or the other end of history. . . .

To turn from the distribution of culture in different countries, to its diffusion within these countries. The quality of mankind which tends most to make the systematic study of civilization possible, is that remarkable tacit consensus or agreement which so far induces whole populations to unite in the use of the same language, to follow the same religion and customary law, to settle down to the same general level of art and knowledge. It is this state of things which makes it so far possible to ignore exceptional facts and to describe nations by a sort of general average. It is this state of things which makes it so far possible to represent immense masses of details by a few typical facts, while, these once settled, new cases recorded by new observers simply fall into their places to prove the soundness of the classification. There is found to be such regularity in the composition of societies of men, that we can drop individual differences out of sight, and thus can generalize on the arts and opinions of whole nations, just as, when looking down upon an army from a hill, we forget the individual soldier, whom, in fact, we can scarce distinguish in the mass, while we see each regiment as an organized body, spreading or concentrating, moving in advance or in retreat. . . .

That a whole nation should have a special dress, special tools and weapons, special laws of marriage and property, special moral and religious doctrines, is a remarkable fact, which we notice so little because we have lived all our lives in the midst of it. It is with such general qualities of organized bodies of men that ethnography has especially to deal. Yet, while generalizing on the culture of a tribe or nation, and setting aside the peculiarities of the individuals composing it as unimportant to the main result, we must be careful not to forget what makes up this main result. There are people so intent on the separate life of individuals that they cannot grasp a notion of the action of a community as a whole— such an observer, incapable of a wide view of society, is aptly described in the saying that he 'cannot see the forest for the trees.' But, on the other hand, the philosopher may be so intent upon his general laws of society as to neglect the individual actors of whom that society is made up, and of him it may be said that he cannot see the trees for the forest. We know how arts, customs, and ideas are shaped among ourselves by the combined actions of many individuals, of which actions both motive and effect often come quite distinctly within our view. The history of an invention, an opinion, a ceremony, is a history of suggestion and modification, encouragement and opposition, personal gain and party prejudice, and the individuals concerned act each according to his own motives, as determined by his character and circumstances. Thus sometimes we watch individuals acting for their own ends with little thought of their effect on society at large, and sometimes we have to study movements of national life as a whole, where the individuals cooperating in them are utterly beyond our observation. But seeing that collective social action is the mere resultant of many individual actions, it is clear that these two methods of enquiry, if rightly followed, must be absolutely consistent.

In studying both the recurrence of special habits or ideas in several districts, and their prevalence within each district, there comes before us ever-reiterated proofs of regular causation producing the phenomena of human life, and of laws of maintenance and diffusion according to which these phenomena settle into permanent standard conditions of society, at definite stages of culture. . . .

It being shown that the details of Culture are capable of being classified in a great number of ethnographic groups of arts, beliefs, customs, and the rest, the consideration comes next how far the facts arranged in these groups are produced by evolution from one another. It need hardly be pointed out that the groups in question, though held together each by a common character, are by no means accurately defined. To take up again the natural history illustration, it may be said that they are species which tend to run widely into varieties. And when it comes to the question what relations some of these groups bear to others, it is plain that the student of the habits of mankind has a great advantage over the student of the species of plants and animals. Among naturalists it is an open question whether a theory of development from species to species is a record of transitions which actually took place, or a mere ideal scheme serviceable in the classification of species whose origin was really independent. But among ethnographers there is no such question as to the possibility of species of implements or habits or beliefs being developed one out of another, for development in Culture is recognized by our most familiar knowledge. . . . And thus, in the other branches of our history, there will come again and again into view series of facts which may be consistently arranged as having followed one another in a particular order of development, but which will hardly bear being turned round and made to follow in reversed order. Such for instance are the facts I have here brought forward in a chapter on the Art of Counting, which tend to prove that as to this point of culture at least, savage tribes reached their position by learning and not by unlearning, by elevation from a lower rather than by degradation from a higher state.

Among evidence aiding us to trace the course which the civilization of the world has actually followed, is that great class of facts to denote which I have found it convenient to introduce the term 'survivals.' These are processes, customs, opinions, and so forth, which have been carried on by force of habit into a new state of society different from that in which they had their original home, and they thus remain as proofs and examples of an older condition of culture out of which a newer has been evolved. Thus, I know an old Somersetshire woman whose hand-loom dates from the time before the introduction of the 'flying shuttle,' which new-fangled appliance she has never even learnt to use, and I have seen her throw her shuttle from hand to hand in true classic fashion; this old woman is not a century behind her times, but she is a case of survival. . . . The serious business of ancient society may be seen to sink into the sport of later generations, and its serious belief to linger on in nursery folk-lore, while superseded habits of old-world life may be modified into new-world forms still powerful for good and evil. Sometimes old thoughts and practices will burst out afresh, to the amazement of a world that thought them long since dead or dying; here survival passes into revival, as has lately happened in so remarkable a way in the history of modern spiritualism, a subject full of instruction from the ethnographer's point of view. The study of the principles of survival has, indeed, no small practical importance, for most of what we call superstition is included within survival, and in this way lies open to the attack of its deadliest enemy, a reasonable explanation. Insignificant, moreover, as multitudes of the facts of survival are in themselves, their study is so effective for tracing the course of the historical development through which alone it is possible to understand their meaning, that it becomes a vital point of ethnographic research to gain the clearest possible insight into their nature. . . .

Progress, degradation, survival, revival, modification, are all modes of the connexion that binds together the complex network of civilization. It needs but a glance into the trivial details of our own daily life to set us thinking how far we are really its originators, and how far but the transmitters and modifiers of the results of long past ages. Looking round the rooms we live in, we may try here how far he who only knows his own time can be capable of rightly comprehending even that. . . . In fact, the books of costume, showing how one garment grew or shrank by gradual stages and passed into another, illustrate with much force and clearness the nature of the change and growth, revival and decay, which go on from year to year in more important matters of life. . . . The study of language has, perhaps, done more than any other in removing from our view of human thought and action the ideas of chance and arbitrary invention, and in substituting for them a theory of development by the co-operation of individual men, through processes ever reasonable and intelligible where the facts are fully known. Rudimentary as the science of culture still is, the symptoms are becoming very strong that even what seem its most spontaneous and motiveless phenomena will, nevertheless, be shown to come within the range of distinct cause and effect as certainly as the facts of mechanics. What would be popularly thought more indefinite and uncontrolled than the products of the imagination in myths and fables? Yet any systematic investigation of mythology, on the basis of a wide collection of evidence, will show plainly enough in such efforts of fancy at once a development from stage to stage, and a production of uniformity of result from uniformity of cause. Here, as elsewhere, causeless spontaneity is seen to recede farther and farther into shelter within the dark precincts of ignorance; like chance, that still holds its place among the vulgar as a real cause of events otherwise unaccountable, while to educated men it has long consciously meant nothing but this ignorance itself. It is only when men fail to see the line of connection in events, that they are prone to fall upon the notions of arbitrary impulses, causeless freaks, chance and nonsense and indefinite unaccountability. . . . In carrying on the great task of rational ethnography, the investigation of the causes which have produced the phenomena of culture, and of the laws to which they are subordinate, it is desirable to work out as systematically as possible a scheme of evolution of this culture along its many lines. In the following chapter, on the Development of Culture, an attempt is made to sketch a theoretical course of civilization among mankind, such as appears on the whole most accordant with the evidence. By comparing the various stages of civilization among races known to history, with the aid of archaeological inference from the remains of prehistoric tribes, it seems possible to judge in a rough way of an early general condition of man, which from our point of view is to be regarded as a primitive condition, whatever yet earlier state may in reality have lain behind it. This hypothetical primitive condition corresponds in a considerable degree to that of modern savage tribes, who, in spite of their difference and distance, have in common certain elements of civilization, which seem remains of an early state of the human race at large. If this hypothesis be true, then, notwithstanding the continual interference of degeneration, the main tendency of culture from primaeval up to modern times has been from savagery towards civilization. On the problem of this relation of savage to civilized life, almost every one of the thousands of facts discussed in the succeeding chapters has its direct bearing. Survival in Culture, placing all along the course of advancing civilization way-marks full of meaning to those who can decipher their signs, even now sets up in our midst primaeval monuments of barbaric thought and life. . . .

Nowhere, perhaps, are broad views of historical development more needed than in the study of religion. Notwithstanding all that has been written to make the world acquainted with the lower theologies, the popular ideas of their place in history and their relation to the faiths of higher nations are still of the mediaeval type. It is wonderful to contrast some missionary journals with Max Müller's Essays, and to set the unappreciating hatred and ridicule that is lavished by narrow hostile zeal on Brahmanism, Buddhism, Zoroastrism, besides the catholic sympathy with which deep and wide knowledge can survey those ancient and noble phases of man's religious consciousness; nor, because the religions of savage tribes may be rude and primitive compared with the great Asiatic systems, do they lie too low for interest and even for respect. The question really lies between understanding and misunderstanding them. Few who will give their minds to master the general principles of savage religion will ever again think it ridiculous, or the knowledge of it superfluous to the rest of mankind. Far from its beliefs and practices being a rubbish-heap of miscellaneous folly, they are consistent and logical in so high a degree as to begin, as soon as even roughly classified, to display the principles of their formation and development; and these principles prove to be essentially rational, though working in a mental condition of intense and inveterate ignorance. . . . In these investigations, however, made rather from an ethnographic than a theological point of view, there has seemed little need of entering into direct controversial argument, which indeed I have taken pains to avoid as far as possible. The connection which runs through religion, from its rudest forms up to the status of an enlightened Christianity, may be conveniently treated of with little recourse to dogmatic theology. The rites of sacrifice and purification may be studied in their stages of development without entering into questions of their authority and value, nor does an examination of the successive phases of the world's belief in a future life demand a discussion of the arguments adduced for or against the doctrine itself. The ethnographic results may then be left as materials for professed theologians, and it will not perhaps be long before evidence so fraught with meaning shall take its legitimate place. To fall back once again on the analogy of natural history, the time may soon come when it will be thought as unreasonable for a scientific student of theology not to have a competent acquaintance with the principles of the religions of the lower races, as for a physiologist to look with the contempt of past centuries on evidence derived from the lower forms of life, deeming the structure of mere invertebrate creatures matter unworthy of his philosophic study.

Not merely as a matter of curious research, but as an important practical guide to the understanding of the present and the shaping of the future, the investigation into the origin and early development of civilization must be pushed on zealously. Every possible avenue of knowledge must be explored, every door tried to see if it is open. No kind of evidence need be left untouched on the score of remoteness or complexity, of minuteness or triviality. The tendency of modern enquiry is more and more towards the conclusion that if law is anywhere, it is everywhere. To despair of what a conscientious collection and study of facts may lead to, and to declare any problem insoluble because difficult and far off, is distinctly to be on the wrong side in science; and he who will choose a hopeless task may set himself to discover the limits of discovery. One remembers Comte starting in his account of astronomy with a remark on the necessary limitation of our knowledge of the stars: we conceive, he tells us, the possibility of determining their form, distance, size, and movement, whilst we should never by any method be able to study their chemical composition, their mineralogical structure, etc. Had the philosopher lived to see the application of spectrum analysis to this very problem, his proclamation of the dispiriting doctrine of necessary ignorance would perhaps have been recanted in favour of a more hopeful view. And it seems to be with the philosophy of remote human life somewhat as with the study of the nature of the celestial bodies. The processes to be made out in the early stages of our mental evolution lie distant from us in time as the stars lie distant from us in space, but the laws of the universe are not limited with the direct observation of our senses. There is vast material to be used in our enquiry; many workers are now busied in bringing this material into shape, though little may have yet been done in proportion to what remains to do; and already it seems not too much to say that the vague outlines of a philosophy of primaeval history are beginning to come within our view.

Lewis H. Morgan

3. Ethnical Periods

The latest investigations respecting the early condition of the human race, are tending to the conclusion that mankind commenced their career at the bottom of the scale and worked their way up from savagery to civilization through the slow accumulations of experimental knowledge.

As it is undeniable that portions of the human family have existed in a state of savagery, other portions in a state of barbarism, and still other portions in a state of civilization, it seems equally so that these three distinct conditions are connected with each other in a natural as well as necessary sequence of progress. Moreover, that this sequence has been historically true of the entire human family, up to the status attained by each branch respectively, is rendered probable by the conditions under which all progress occurs, and by the known advancement of several branches of the family through two or more of these conditions.

An attempt will be made in the following pages to bring forward additional evidence of the rudeness of the early condition of mankind, of the gradual evolution of their mental and moral powers through experience, and of their protracted struggle with opposing obstacles while winning their way to civilization. It will be drawn, in part, from the great sequence of inventions and discoveries which stretches along the entire pathway of human progress; but chiefly from domestic institutions, which express the growth of certain ideas and passions.

As we re-ascend along the several lines of progress toward the primitive ages of mankind, and eliminate one after the other, in the order in which they appeared, inventions and discoveries on the one hand, and institutions on the other, we are enabled to perceive that the former stand to each other in progressive, and the latter in unfolding relations. While the former class have had a connection, more or less direct, the latter have been developed from a few primary germs of thought. Modern institutions plant their roots in the period of barbarism, into which their germs were transmitted from the previous period of savagery. They have had a lineal descent through the ages, with the streams of the blood, as well as a logical development.

Two independent lines of investigation thus invite our attention. The one leads through inventions and discoveries, and the other through primary institutions. With the knowledge gained therefrom, we may hope to indicate the principal stages of human development. The proofs to be adduced will be drawn chiefly from domestic institutions; the references to achievements more strictly intellectual being general as well as subordinate.

The facts indicate the gradual formation and subsequent development of certain ideas, passions, and aspirations. Those which hold the most prominent positions may be generalized as growths of the particular ideas with which they severally stand connected. Apart from inventions and discoveries they are the following:

I. *Subsistence,*   V. *Religion,*
II. *Government,*   VI. *House Life and Architecture,*
III. *Language,*   VII. *Property*
IV. *The Family,*

First. Subsistence has been increased and perfected by a series of successive arts, introduced at long intervals of time, and connected more or less directly with inventions and discoveries.

Second. The germ of government must be sought in the organization into gentes in the Status of savagery; and followed down, through the advancing forms of this institution, to the establishment of political society.

Third. Human speech seems to have been developed from the rudest and simplest forms of expression. Gesture or sign language, as intimated by Lucretius,[1] must have preceded articulate language, as thought preceded speech. The monosyllabical preceded the syllabical, as the latter did that of concrete words. Human intelligence, unconscious of design, evolved articulate language by utilizing the vocal sounds. This great subject, a department of knowledge by itself, does not fall within the scope of the present investigation.

Fourth. With respect to the family, the stages of its growth are embodied in systems of consanguinity and affinity, and in usages relating to marriage, by means of which, collectively, the family can be definitely traced through several successive forms.

Fifth. The growth of religious ideas is environed with such intrinsic difficulties that it may never receive a perfectly satisfactory exposition. Religion deals so largely with the imaginative and emotional nature, and consequently with such uncertain elements of knowledge, that all primitive religions are grotesque and to some extent unintelligible. This subject also falls without the plan of this work excepting as it may prompt incidental suggestions.

Sixth. House architecture which connects itself with the form of the family and the plan of domestic life, affords a tolerably complete illustration of progress from savagery to civilization. Its growth can be traced from the hut of the savage, through the communal houses of the barbarians, to the house of the single family of civilized nations, with all the successive links by which one extreme is connected with the other. This subject will be noticed incidentally.

Lastly. The idea of property was slowly formed in the human mind, remaining nascent and feeble through immense periods of time. Springing into life in savagery, it required all the experience of this period and of the subsequent period of barbarism to develop the germ, and to prepare the human brain for the acceptance of its controlling influence. Its dominance as a passion over all other passions marks the commencement of civilization. It not only led mankind to overcome the obstacles which delayed civilization, but to establish political society on the basis of territory and of property. A critical knowledge of the evolution of the idea of property would embody, in some respects, the most remarkable portion of the mental history of mankind.

It will be my object to present some evidence of human progress along these several lines, and through successive ethnical periods, as it is revealed by inventions and discoveries, and by the growth of the ideas of government, of the family, and of property.

It may be here premised that all forms of government are reducible to two general plans, using the word plan in its scientific sense. In their bases the two are fundamentally distinct. The first, in the order of time, is founded upon persons, and upon relations purely personal, and may be distinguished as a society (*societas*). The gens is the unit of this organization; giving as the successive stages of integration, in the archaic period, the gens, the phratry, the tribe, and the confederacy or tribes, which constituted a people or nation (*populus*). At a later period a coalescence of tribes in the same area into a nation took the place of a confederacy of tribes occupying independent areas. Such, through prolonged ages, after the gens appeared, was the substantially universal organization of ancient society; and it remained among the Greeks and Romans after civilization supervened. The second is founded upon territory and upon property, and may be distinguished as a state (*civitas*). The township or ward, circumscribed by metes and bounds, with the property it contains, is the basis or unit of the latter, and political society is the result. Political society is organized upon territorial areas, and deals with property as well as with persons through territorial relations. The successive stages of integration are the township or ward, which is the unit of organization; the county or province, which is an aggregation of townships or wards; and the national domain or territory, which is an aggregation of counties or provinces; the people of each of which are organized into a body politic. It taxed the Greeks and Romans to the extent of their capacities, after they had gained civilization, to invent the deme or township and the city ward; and thus inaugurate the second great plan of government, which remains among civilized nations to the present hour. In ancient society this territorial plan was unknown. When it came in it fixed the boundary line between ancient and modern society, as the distinction will be recognized in these pages.

It may be further observed that the domestic institutions of the barbarous, and even of the savage ancestors of mankind, are still exemplified in portions of the human family with such completeness that, with the exception of the strictly primitive period, the several stages of this progress are tolerably well preserved. They are seen in the organization of society upon the basis of sex, then upon the basis of kin, and finally upon the basis of territory; through the successive forms of marriage and of the family, with the systems of consanguinity thereby created; through house life and architecture; and through progress in usages with respect to the ownership and inheritance of property.

The theory of human degradation to explain the existence of savages and of barbarians is no longer tenable. It came in as a corollary from the Mosaic cosmogony, and was acquiesced in from a supposed necessity which no longer exists. As a theory, it is not only incapable of explaining the existence of savages, but it is without support in the facts of human experience.

The remote ancestors of the Aryan nations presumptively passed through an experience similar to that of existing barbarous and savage tribes. Though the experience of these nations embodies all the information necessary to illustrate the periods of civilization, both ancient and modern, together with a part of that in the Later period of barbarism, their anterior experience must be deduced, in the main, from the traceable connection between the elements of their existing institutions and inventions, and similar elements still preserved in those of savage and barbarous tribes.

It may be remarked finally that the experience of mankind has run in nearly uniform channels; that human necessities in similar conditions have been substantially the same; and that the operations of the mental principle have been uniform in virtue of the specific identity of the brain of all the races of mankind. This, however, is but a part of the explanation of uniformity in results. The germs of the principal institutions and arts of life were developed while man was still a savage. To a very great extent the experience of the subsequent periods of barbarism and of civilization have been expended in the further development of these original conceptions. Wherever a connection can be traced on different continents between a present institution and a common germ, the derivation of the people themselves from a common original stock is implied. The discussion of these several classes of facts will be facilitated by the establishment of a certain number of Ethnical Periods; each representing a distinct condition of society, and distinguishable by a mode of life peculiar to itself. The terms "Age of *Stone*," "of *Bronze*," and "of *Iron*," introduced by Danish archaeologists, have been extremely useful for certain purposes, and will remain so for the classification of objects of ancient art; but the progress of knowledge has rendered other and different subdivisions necessary. Stone implements were not entirely laid aside with the introduction of tools of iron, nor of those of bronze. The invention of the process of smelting iron ore created an ethnical epoch, yet we could scarcely date another from the production of bronze. Moreover, since the period of stone implements overlaps those of bronze and of iron, and since that of bronze also overlaps that of iron, they are not capable of a circumscription that would leave each independent and distinct.

It is probable that the successive arts of subsistence which arose at long intervals will ultimately, from the great influence they must have exercised upon the condition of mankind, afford the most satisfactory bases for these divisions. But investigation has not been carried far enough in this direction to yield the necessary information. With our present knowledge the main result can be attained by selecting such other inventions or discoveries as will afford sufficient tests of progress to characterize the commencement of successive ethnical periods. Even though accepted as provisional, these periods will be found convenient and useful. Each of those about to be proposed will be found to cover a distinct culture, and to represent a particular mode of life.

The period of savagery, of the early part of which very little is known, may be divided, provisionally, into three sub-periods. These may be named respectively the *Older*, the *Middle*, and the *Later* period of savagery; and the condition of society in each, respectively, may be distinguished as the *Lower*, the *Middle*, and the *Upper Status* of savagery.

In like manner, the period of barbarism divides naturally into three sub-periods, which will be called, respectively, the *Older*, the *Middle*, and the *Later* period of barbarism; and the condition of society in each, respectively, will be distinguished as the *Lower*, the *Middle*, and the *Upper status* of barbarism.

It is difficult, if not impossible, to find such tests of progress to mark the commencement of these several periods as will be found absolute in their application, and without exceptions upon all the continents. Neither is it necessary, for the purpose in hand, that exceptions should not exist. It will be sufficient if the principal tribes of mankind can be classified, according to the degree of their relative progress, into conditions which can be recognized as distinct.

I. Lower Status of Savagery.

This period commenced with the infancy of the human race, and may be said to have ended with the acquisition of a fish subsistence and of a knowledge of the use of fire. Mankind were then living in their original restricted habitat, and subsisting upon fruits and nuts. The commencement of articulate speech belongs to this period. No exemplification of tribes of mankind in this condition remained to the historical period.

II. Middle Status of Savagery.

It commenced with the acquisition of a fish subsistence and a knowledge of the use of fire, and ended with the invention of the bow and arrow. Mankind, while in this condition, spread from their original habitat over the greater portion of the earth's surface. Among tribes still existing it will leave in the Middle Status of savagery, for example, the Australians and the greater part of the Polynesians when discovered. It will be sufficient to give one or more exemplifications of each status.

III. Upper Status of Savagery.

It commenced with the invention of the bow and arrow, and ended with the invention of the art of pottery. It leaves in the Upper Status of Savagery the Athapascan tribes of the Hudson's Bay Territory, the tribes of the valley of the Columbia, and certain coast tribes of North and South America; but with relation to the time of their discovery. This closes the period of Savagery.

IV. Lower Status of Barbarism.

The invention or practice of the art of pottery, all things considered, is probably the most effective and conclusive test that can be selected to fix a boundary line, necessarily arbitrary, between savagery and barbarism. The distinctness of the two conditions has long been recognized, but no criterion of progress out of the former into the latter has hitherto been brought forward. All such tribes, then, as never attained to the art of pottery will be classed as savages, and those possessing this art but who never attained a phonetic alphabet and the use of writing will be classed as barbarians.

The first sub-period of barbarism commenced with the manufacture of pottery, whether by original invention or adoption. In finding its termination, and the commencement of the Middle Status, a difficulty is encountered in the unequal endowments of the two hemispheres, which began to be influential upon human affairs after the period of savagery had passed. It may be met, however, by the adoption of equivalents. In the Eastern hemisphere, the domestication of animals, and in the Western, the cultivation of maize and plants by irrigation, together with the use of adobe-brick and stone in house building have been selected as sufficient evidence of progress to work a transition out of the Lower and into the Middle Status of barbarism. It leaves, for example, in the Lower Status, the Indian tribes of the United States east of the Missouri River, and such tribes of Europe and Asia as practiced the art of pottery, but were without domestic animals.

V. Middle Status of Barbarism.

It commenced with the domestication of animals in the Eastern hemisphere, and in the Western with cultivation by irrigation and with the use of adobe-brick and stone in architecture, as shown. Its termination may be fixed with the invention of the process of smelting iron ore. This places in the Middle Status, for example, the Village Indians of New Mexico, Mexico, Central America and Peru, and such tribes in the Eastern hemisphere as possessed domestic animals, but were without a knowledge of iron. The ancient Britons, although familiar with the use of iron, fairly belong in this connection. The vicinity of more advanced continental tribes had advanced the arts of life among them far beyond the state of development of their domestic institutions.

VI. Upper Status of Barbarism.

It commenced with the manufacture of iron, and ended with the invention of a phonetic alphabet, and the use of writing in literary composition. Here civilization begins. This leaves in the Upper Status, for example, the Grecian tribes of the Homeric age, the Italian tribes shortly before the founding of Rome, and the Germanic tribes of the time of Caesar.

VII. Status of Civilization.

It commenced, as stated, with the use of a phonetic alphabet and the production of literary records, and divides into Ancient and Modern. As an equivalent, hieroglyphical writing upon stone may be admitted.

Recapitulation.

Periods.	*Conditions.*
I. *Older Period of Savagery,*	I. *Lower Status of Savagery,*
II. *Middle Period of Savagery,*	II. *Middle Status of Savagery,*
III. *Later Period of Savagery,*	III. *Upper Status of Savagery,*
IV. *Older Period of Barbarism,*	IV. *Lower Status of Barbarism,*
V. *Middle Period of Barbarism,*	V. *Middle Status of Barbarism,*
VI. *Later Period of Barbarism,*	VI. *Upper Status of Barbarism,*

VII. *Status of Civilization.*

I. *Lower Status of Savagery,*	*From the infancy of the Human Race to the commencement of the next periods*
II. *Middle Status of Savagery,*	*From the acquisition of a fish subsistence and a knowledge of the use of fire, to etc.*
III. *Upper Status of Savagery,*	*From the Invention of the Bow and Arrow, to etc.*
IV. *Lower Status of Barbarism,*	*From the Invention of the Art of Pottery, to etc.*
V. *Middle Status of Barbarism,*	*From the Domestication of animals on the Eastern hemisphere, and in the Western from the cultivation of maize and plants by Irrigation, with the use of adobe-brick and stone, to etc.*
VI. *Upper Status of Barbarism,*	*From the Invention of the process of Smelting Iron Ore, with the use of iron tools, to etc.*

VII. *Status of Civilization,*
From the Invention of a Phonetic Alphabet, with the use of writing, to the present time.

Each of these periods has a distinct culture and exhibits a mode of life more or less special and peculiar to itself. This specialization of ethnical periods renders it possible to treat a particular society according to its condition of relative advancement, and to make it a subject of independent study and discussion. It does not affect the main result that different tribes and nations on the same continent, and even of the same linguistic family, are in different conditions at the same time, since for our purpose the *condition* of each is the material fact, the *time* being immaterial.

Since the use of pottery is less significant than that of domestic animals, of iron, or of a phonetic alphabet, employed to mark the commencement of subsequent ethnical periods, the reasons for its adoption
should be stated. The manufacture of pottery presupposes village life,
and considerable progress in the simple arts.[2] Flint and stone implements are older than pottery, remains of the former having been found
in ancient repositories in numerous instances unaccompanied by the
latter. A succession of inventions of greater need and adapted to a lower
condition must have occurred before the want of pottery would be felt.
The commencement of village life, with some degree of control over
subsistence, wooden vessels and utensils, finger weaving with filaments
of bark, basket making, and the bow and arrow make their appearance
before the art of pottery. The Village Indians who were in the Middle
Status of barbarism, such as the Zuñians, the Aztecs and the Cholulans,
manufactured pottery in large quantities and in many forms of considerable excellence; the partially Village Indians of the United States, who
were in the Lower Status of barbarism, such as the Iroquois the Choctas
and the Cherokees, made it in smaller quantities and in a limited number of forms; but the Non-horticultural Indians, who were in the Status
of savagery, such as the Athapascans, the tribes of California and of the
valley of the Columbia, were ignorant of its use.[3] In Lubbock's *Pre-
Historic Times,* in Tylor's *Early History of Mankind,* and in Peschel's *Races of
Man,* the particulars respecting this art, and the extent of its distribution, have been collected with remarkable breadth of research. It was
unknown in Polynesia (with the exception of the Islands of the Tongans
and Fijians), in Australia, in California, and in the Hudson's Bay Territory. Mr. Tylor remarks that "the art of weaving was unknown in most of
the Islands away from Asia," and that "in most of the South Sea Islands
there was no knowledge of pottery."[4] The Rev. Lorimer Fison, an English
missionary residing in Australia, informed the author in answer to inquiries, that "the Australians had no woven fabrics, no pottery, and were
ignorant of the bow and arrow." This last fact was also true in general of
the Polynesians. The introduction of the ceramic art produced a new
epoch in human progress in the direction of an improved living and
increased domestic conveniences. While flint and stone implements—
which came in earlier and required long periods of time to develop all
their uses—gave the canoe, wooden vessels and utensils, and ultimately
timber and plank in house architecture,[5] pottery gave a durable vessel
for boiling food, which before that had been rudely accomplished in
baskets coated with clay, and in ground cavities lined with skin, the
boiling being affected with heated stones.[6]

Whether the pottery of the aborigines was hardened by fire or cured by the simple process of drying, has been made a question. Prof. E.T. Cox, of Indianapolis, has shown by comparing the analyses of ancient pottery and hydraulic cements, "that so far as chemical constituents are concerned it (the pottery) agrees very well with the composition of hydraulic stones." He remarks further, that "all the pottery belonging to the mound-builders' age, which I have seen, is composed of alluvial clay and sand, or a mixture of the former with pulverized fresh-water shells. A paste made of such a mixture possesses in a high degree the properties of hydraulic Puzzuolani and Portland cement, so that vessels formed of it hardened without being burned, as is customary with modern pottery. The fragments of shells served the purpose of gravel or fragments of stone as at present used in connection with hydraulic lime for the manufacture of artificial stone."⁷ The composition of Indian pottery in analogy with that of hydraulic cement suggests the difficulties in the way of inventing the art, and tends also to explain the lateness of its introduction in the course of human experience. Notwithstanding the ingenious suggestion of Prof. Cox, it is probable that pottery was hardened by artificial heat. In some cases the fact is directly attested. Thus Adair, speaking of the Gulf Tribes, remarks that "they make earthen pots of very different sizes, so as to contain from two to ten gallons, large pitchers to carry water, bowls, dishes, platters, basins, and a prodigious number of other vessels of such antiquated forms as would be tedious to describe, and impossible to name. Their method of glazing them is, they place them over a large fire of smoky pitch-pine, which makes them smooth, black and firm."⁸

Another advantage of fixing definite ethnical periods is the direction of special investigation of those tribes and nations which afford the best exemplification of each status, with the view of making each both standard and illustrative. Some tribes and families have been left in geographical isolation to work out the problems of progress by original mental effort; and have, consequently, retained their arts and institutions pure and homogeneous; while those of other tribes and nations have been adulterated through external influence. Thus, while Africa was and is an ethnical chaos of savagery and barbarism, Australia and Polynesia were in savagery, pure and simple, with the arts and institutions belonging to that condition. In like manner, the Indian family of America, unlike any other existing family, exemplified the condition of mankind in three successive ethnical periods. In the undisturbed possession of a great continent, of common descent, and with homogeneous institutions, they illustrated, when discovered, each of these conditions, and especially those of the Lower and of the Middle Status of barbarism, more elaborately and completely than any other portion of mankind. The far northern Indians and some of the coast tribes of North and South America were in the Upper Status of savagery; the partially Village Indians east of the Mississippi were in the Lower Status of barbarism, and the Village Indians of North and South America were in the Middle Status. Such an opportunity to recover full and minute information of the course of human experience and progress in developing their arts and institutions through these successive conditions has not been offered within the historical period. It must be added that it has been indifferently improved. Our greatest deficiencies relate to the last period named.

Differences in the culture of the same period in the Eastern and Western hemispheres undoubtedly existed in consequence of the unequal endowments of the continents; but the condition of society in the corresponding status must have been, in the main substantially similar.

The ancestors of the Grecian, Roman and German tribes passed through the stages we have indicated, in the midst of the last of which the light of history fell upon them. Their differentiation from the undistinguishable mass of barbarians did not occur, probably, earlier than the commencement of the Middle Period of barbarism. The experience of these tribes has been lost, with the exception of so much as is represented by the institutions, inventions and discoveries which they brought with them, and possessed when they first came under historical observation. The Grecian and Latin tribes of the Homeric and Romulian periods afford the highest exemplification of the Upper Status of barbarism. Their institutions were likewise pure and homogeneous, and their experience stands directly connected with the final achievement of civilization.

Commencing, then, with the Australians and Polynesians, following with the American Indian tribes, and concluding with the Roman and Grecian, who afford the highest exemplifications respectively of the six great stages of human progress, the sum of their united experiences may be supposed fairly to represent that of the human family from the Middle Status of savagery to the end of ancient civilization. Consequently, the Aryan nations will find the type of the condition of their remote ancestors, when in savagery, in that of the Australians and Polynesians; when in the Lower Status of barbarism in that of the partially Village Indians of America; and when in the Middle Status in that of the Village Indians, with which their own experience in the Upper Status directly connects. So essentially identical are the arts institutions and mode of life in the same status upon all the continents, that the archaic form of the principal domestic institutions of the Greeks and Romans must even now be sought in the corresponding institutions of the American aborigines, as will be shown in the course of this volume. This fact forms a part of the accumulating evidence tending to show that the principal institutions of mankind have been developed from a few primary germs of thought; and that the course and manner of their development was predetermined, as well as restricted within narrow limits of divergence, by the natural logic of the human mind and the necessary limitations of its powers. Progress has been found to be subtantially the same in kind in tribes and nations inhabiting different and even disconnected continents, while in the same status, with deviations from uniformity in particular instances produced by special causes. The argument when extended tends to establish the unity of origin of mankind.

In studying the condition of tribes and nations in these several ethnical periods we are dealing, substantially, with the ancient history and condition of our own remote ancestors.

Notes

1. Et pueros commendarunt mulierbreque saeclum
    Vocibus, et gestu, cum balbe significarent,
    Imbecillorum esse aequm miserier omnium.
                                    De Rerum Natura, lib. v, 1020.

2. Mr. Edwin B. Tylor observes that Goquet "first propounded, in the last century, the notion that the way in which pottery came to be made, was that people daubed such combustible vessels as these with clay to protect them from fire, till they found that clay alone would answer the purpose, and thus the art of pottery came into the world."—*Early History of Mankind*, p. 273. Goquet relates of Capt. Gonneville who visited the southeast coast of South America in 1503, that he found "their household utensils of wood, even their boiling pots, but plastered with a kind of clay, a good finger thick, which prevented the fire from burning them."—*Ib.* 273.

3. Pottery has been found in aboriginal mounds in Oregon within a few years past.—Foster's *Pre-Historic Races of the United States*, I, 152. The first vessels of pottery among the Aborigines of the United States seem to have been made in baskets of rushes or willows used as moulds which were burned off after the vessel hardened.—Jones's *Antiquities of the Southern Indians*, p. 461. Prof. Rau's article on *Pottery. Smithsonian Report*, 1866, p. 352.

4. *Early History of Mankind*, p. 181; *Pre-Historic Times*, pp. 437, 441, 462, 477, 533, 542.

5. Lewis and Clarke (1805) found plank in use in houses among the tribes of the Columbia River.—*Travels*, Longman's Ed., 1814, p. 503. Mr. John Keast Lord

found "cedar plank chipped from the solid tree with chisels and hatchets made of stone," in Indian houses on Vancouver's Island.—*Naturalist in British Columbia*, I, 169.

6. Tylor's *Early History of Mankind*, p. 265, *et seq.*

7. *Geological Survey of Indiana*, 1873, p. 119. He gives the following analysis: Ancient Pottery, "Bone Bank," Posey Co., Indiana.

Moisture at 212°F.,	1.00	Peroxide of Iron,	5.50
Silica,	36.00	Sulphuric Acid,	.20
Carbonate of Lime,	25.50	Organic Matter (alkalies	
Carbonate of Magnesia,	3.02	and loss),	23.60
Alumina,	5.00		100.00

8. *History of the American Indians*, Lond. ed., 1775, p. 424. The Iroquois affirm that in ancient times their forefathers cured their pottery before a fire.

Herbert Applebaum

III

The Boasian Attack—
Historical Particularism

Introduction

The central figure in the emergence of American anthropology at the turn of the century was Franz Boas—born 1858, died 1942. Born in Germany and trained in the physical sciences, Boas' first contact with nonwestern cultures was in the Arctic. He went to the Baffin Islands to test the hypothesis that geography determined culture. If ever this was true, it would surely be validated by the harsh Arctic climate. Boas returned convinced that geographic determinism was a false hypothesis. His entire career was later spent arguing against all forms of determinism as regulating human societies.

In 1896, in a paper read to the American Association for the Advancement of Science (AAAS) in Buffalo (reprinted as Chapter 4), Boas urged the renunciation of the comparative method as had been previously employed by the evolutionary anthropologists. He described it as "barren" and considered it a vain attempt to construct a systematic history of the evolution of culture. To correct what he considered shortcomings in evolutionary theory as used by anthropologists, he proposed the method of controlled comparison, where the comparative method would be restricted to geographic areas subject to similar environments and where the factor of historical contact could be accounted for and controlled.

In 1896, Boas still believed that laws existed which governed the development of society. At that time he subscribed to Bastian's concept of elementary ideas, so that identities of culture could be ascribed to the uniform workings of the human mind. Thus, similar traits could have been presumed to have arisen independently and were not necessarily proof of historical or common origin. It was a time, the late nineteenth century, when anthropologists were concerned with the origin of cultural traits and how they manifested themselves in various cultures.

Boas stressed the importance of using sound inductive methods to isolate causes of observed behavior. Thus, he recognized the difficulty of discovering the origin of the elementary ideas that Bastian had hypothesized. Boas stated that the human mind invents ideas spontaneously or accepts them whenever they are offered these ideas. The causes or origins of cultural traits could come from varied sources. For this reason, Boas argued strongly that the same cultural phenomenon may have different causes. This argument was contrary to Tylor's thinking, which placed great stress on the notion that similar traits stemmed from similar causes. Boas cited, as an example of similar traits having dissimilar origins, the case of geometric art. It could originate for technical reasons, for natural ones, or as a symbol. The same was true of masks. Like everything else about anthropology, Boas insisted that causes or origins be investigated and proven before being accepted as causes.

The heart of Boas' critique of the nineteenth century evolutionists was that he objected to the conclusion that there was one grand system according to which mankind had developed everywhere in the world. Further, he did not accept the conclusion that variations were no more than minor details in the grand, uniform scheme of social evolution. In the light of modern anthropological research, Boas' prediction, that multiple processes of development would be found in the world, seems to be borne out. Boas' insistence on the necessity for proven hypothesis and the restricting of speculative ones was an invaluable contribution to placing anthropology on a sound scientific basis.

Boas was accused of being antitheoretical. But a reading of Chapter 4 shows that he agreed that laws existed which governed the growth of human culture. As he said, customs and objects were not in themselves the object of research, but rather the reasons why such customs exist. Boas isolated three factors for explaining the origins of customs: 1. environmental conditions; 2. psychological factors; and 3. historical connections. He did not oppose larger studies comparing cultures. But he wanted to first start with limited areas, using his three-factor approach before embarking upon the larger studies embracing broader areas of the world. At the time of his address before the AAAS, he believed that the major work of investigation and research remained to be done.

Through historical particularism, Boas hoped to achieve the exhaustive analysis essential to scientific control over the variability of cultural phenomena. To him, there was no substitution for facts. Field collection alone supplied the details about interrelations of forms, ideas, psychological process, and before-after time relations. Boas believed the anthropologist must be a fieldworker, devoted to scientific objectivity. A properly trained anthropologist must interpret the world of the native through the eyes of the native. Hence, he or she must learn the native's language.

The rigor of Boas' approach to any problem was modeled upon natural science. He underscored the fact that all classifications are relative. He argued against forcing the observer's categories on the thought of the native. Boas considered classification no substitute for process, i.e., concrete behavior which actually took place. He considered classification an error practiced by the evolutionists. The correction for this error was to collect data in such detail that variations in forms and the causes of the variations could be explained. Functional analogies would not do for Boas. The history of forms must show them to be identical before they could be compared and generalized. If similar psychological processes were alike, and proven so by historical analysis, then one could reasonably assert a cause and effect relation. Coincidence must not be taken for a causal connection. Boas also stressed the relevance of context for interpretations and the necessity for quantification of data. Boas was more interested in assuring that the classificatory process was sound than he was in developing a set of concepts. For him, concepts like systematic theory were thought to get in the researcher's way by fixing the range of his thinking process.

The preoccupation with problem and method prevented Boas from developing theories regarding the dynamics of cultural growth. Boas' contribution was methodological rules. His method did not produce hard and fast rules. He constantly warned against overstepping the bounds of reasonable interpretation. And he believed that basic controls over generalizing and comparison could be reached by limiting oneself to a small geographic territory and refraining from cultural comparisons outside the limits of the territory under study.

Alfred Lewis Kroeber was the first of Boas' students at Columbia University to receive a doctorate. He could be said to have been deeply influenced by Boas in that he maintained, throughout his long and illustrious career, a historical approach to anthropology. After his "guru's" death, Kroeber went on to become a "guru" in his own right, molding and training a long list of important and famous anthropologists, including Julian Steward, who wrote the following about him (Harris 1968:338):

In spite of my views, which differ in some ways from Kroeber's, I am deeply convinced that Kroeber's five hundred odd publications are, and will be for many decades, an almost inexhaustible mine not only of information but of problems, concepts, and hypotheses which have not yet made sufficient impact upon the world of scholarship. I have tried to indicate that Kroeber frequently touched, with deep insights, many problems that searchers for causes might well heed. Some of his syntheses and interpretations could readily be classed as "hard science."

In an article in the American Anthropologist, Kroeber summed up his views, as follows (1915:283–288; summarized by Voget 1975:364)

- The aim of history is to know the relations of social facts to the whole of civilization . . .
- The material studied by history is not man, but his works . . .
- Civilization, though carried by men and existing through them, is an entity in itself, and of another order from life . . .
- A certain mental constitution of man must be assumed by the historian, but may not be used by him as a resolution of social phenomena . . .
- The person or individual has no historical value save as illustration . . .
- Geography, or physical environment, is material made use of by civilization, not a factor shaping or explaining civilization . . .
- Heredity cannot be allowed to have acted any part in history . . .
- Selection and other factors of organic evolution cannot be admitted as affecting civilization . . .
- There are no social species or standard cultural types or stages . . .
- There are no laws in history similar to the laws of physico-chemical action . . .
- History deals with conditions sine qua non, not with causes . . .
- The causality of history is teleological . . .
- In fine, the determination and methods of biological, psychological, or natural science do not exist for history, just as the results and the manner of operation of history are disregarded by consistent biological practice . . .

Item three in the list above is an important one. It presages Kroeber's concept of the superorganic. As will be evident from Chapter 5, to follow, Kroeber was essentially concerned with human beings in groups and communities, not with individuals. His concept of culture was that it was created by real human beings in the mass over long periods of history; it was not the creation of a single individual. Thus, while it came from human beings and was expressed by human beings, culture had its own characteristics, above and beyond human beings. As long as one viewed this concept of Kroeber's as a heuristic device, as a method for abstracting and analyzing concepts that stemmed from real human behavior, most social scientists would agree. It was when Kroeber seemed to suggest that culture as a superorganic phenomenon had a "life" of its own that it was challenged. Bidney (1953a), who dedicated his book *Theoretical Anthropology* to Kroeber, points out that Kroeber, like Sorokin and Spengler, viewed culture as having a transcendent reality of its own, independent of individuals or societies. In this view, culture is a transcendental, metaphysical entity which has made man what he is and to which he will conform as part of his culture, upbringing, and heritage. For others, who might be classed as humanists, humans are the efficient and final cause of their sociocultural heritage. For this latter group, culture consists of norms and ideals of behavior which humans have created and which have no existence apart from the human being and the human mind. This relationship of the individual to culture was to play an important part in American anthropology.

Besides this problem of whether the locus of culture resides in the human individual or whether it transcends individuals and has its own characteristics molding the behavior of individuals, there is another distinction about culture which the reader should keep in mind. Bidney (1953a:23–24) identifies it as a realistic vs. an idealistic approach to the concept of culture. The realists tend to conceive of culture as an attribute of human social behavior and usually define culture in terms of acquired habits, customs, and institutions. Culture so conceived is inseparable from the life of human beings in society. It is a mode of social living which has no existence independent of actual groups to which it is attributed. Examples of realistic definitions of culture may be found in writings of Tylor and Boas. Realists, however, may differ as to whether culture is to be defined entirely in social terms, to the neglect of the individual, or whether individual variations are to be considered essential to any given culture. Kroeber (see Chapter 5 and the list above) lessened the importance of the individual. For this he was criticized by other anthropologists, like Sapir (1917) and Goldenweiser (1917). To continue with Bidney's distinction of realists vs. idealists, the idealist approach to culture tends to conceive of culture as an aggregate of ideas in the minds of individuals. Other cultural anthropologists, like Kroeber and Ruth Benedict, defined culture as a pattern of behavior or a design for living. In this view, which is part of the idealistic view, culture is believed to be a conceptual construct and, therefore, an abstraction from the actual behavior. Again, Chapter 5 by Kroeber will reveal this kind of approach.

Throughout this book, the reader should keep in mind this twin duality in the approach to culture. The realistic approach and the idealistic approach—behavior on the one hand and ideas and rules on the other, as well as the individual and the superorganic—seeing the locus of culture in the concrete individual human being, on the one hand, or seeing culture as embodied in some transcendental entity like a group, a community or a civilization, on the other.

Marvin Harris stated that Robert Lowie was by far the most sophisticated advocate, and the most effective defender, of the historical-particularist position:

He possessed a capacity unique among his contemporaries, to represent that program as the embodiment of the finest flowering of empiricism, by which anthropology could win and hold a proud position among the natural sciences.
(Harris 1968:344)

Harris also remarks that Lowie provided the safest bridge between the historical-particularist position and the theory builders of the nineteenth century, the evolutionary anthropologists.

In Chapter 6, we find that even though Lowie argues against unilineal schemes to describe all evolution, he does take an evolutionary approach to the development of civilizations. He also agrees that, when full knowledge reveals an identity of cultural features, most likely similar effects were due to similar causes, an argument made by the nineteenth century evolutionists. Lowie states the following (see Chapter 6):

My instances show, then, that cultural traits may be functionally related, and this fact renders possible a parallelism, however limited, of cultural development in different parts of the globe. The field of culture, then, is not a region of complete lawlessness. Like causes produce like effects here as elsewhere, though the complex conditions with which we are grappling require unusual caution in definitely correlating phenomena.

Thus, we can see that, unlike Kroeber, Lowie did believe that social laws and cause and effect relationships could be a legitimate goal of anthropological research. A reading of Chapter 6 reveals that, whether Lowie called his approach history or evolution, he did have an evolutionary approach to the development and growth of society. Lowie postulated both convergent and parallel evolution, without either asserting that only one path is the correct one or choosing one to describe a particular process without having empirical confirmation of his hypothesis. Harris emphasizes Lowie's devotion to scientific standards and his capacity to sustain a continuous and self-correcting expansion of knowledge (1968:343). Further, emphasizing Lowie's continuity with the work of the nineteenth century evolutionists, Harris comments that there was scarcely a single paper on social organization written by Lowie that does not implicitly or explicitly begin where Morgan left off.

Lowie analyzed the classificatory kinship relations discovered by Morgan and agreed with him that they did indeed reflect the social organization of unilineal descent groups. In this type of family organization, descent is traced through one parent to the exclusion of the other. Its organization is reflected in kinship terms being "classificatory," that is, there is a lumping of relatives, such as one's father and father's brother, who are called by the same term, rather than a differentiating "description" as in our kinship terms, where father's brother is called by a different term from one's father.

Unlike Kroeber, who believed there was no general rule by which either the classificatory or the descriptive kinship terminology system could be correlated with social structure, Lowie stated that, "kinship terms have a direct relationship to cultural data" (1929b:98). With characteristic honesty, Lowie admitted that he had to change his opinion that all cultural data was unique (a position taken by other historical-particularists like Kroeber and Wissler). Lowie credited Morgan with being a pioneer in the knowledge of the social implication of kinship nomenclature (Lowie 1929b:101):

Morgan was right in the feeling that some historical conclusions could be drawn from similarities of relationship nomenclature.

Lowie also admitted the possibility of Morgan's notion of parallel evolution, stating (1929b:101–102):

When the same feature occurs in disconnected regions, we shall incline to the theory of independent development and shall inquire whether the course of evolution may have been due to the same culture determinants, i.e., in this case to the same social institutions.

Lowie goes on to argue that terms of relationship are directly correlated with such cultural phenomena as social customs regarding marriage and that kinship nomenclature is an index of tribal relationships. He points out that kinship systems, which are extremely complex, require a comparative survey of like features among neighboring tribes and, ultimately, throughout the world (1929b:175–176). This was precisely what the nineteenth century theorists like Tylor and Morgan were doing in their research. Lowie criticized the nineteenth century theorists for overlooking the significance of diffusion and borrowing and the importance of historical accidents as factors in cultural development. He also criticized them for excessive speculation when evidence and data were lacking.

Summing up Lowie's position, despite his renowned and often misunderstood statement that civilization was a thing of shreds and patches, by which he meant that it was made up of many elements and not an unplanned hodge-podge, Lowie did believe that cultures were systems and integrated wholes. He saw them as the result of history, and he was careful to describe relationships between cultural traits, without trying to ascribe causes where the data was insufficient. On this point, he differed from the nineteenth century evolutionists and criticized them for being overly speculative.

Along with his view of culture as "superorganic," Alfred L. Kroeber also saw culture as a pattern or configuration. He sometimes referred to culture as a style. As a configurationist, Kroeber believed that each culture was characterized by a cluster of traits that marked it as unique and different from other cultures. This perspective of the uniqueness of cultures was traditionally part of the Boasian viewpoint. It was also part of Boas' cultural relativity, which held that each culture, with its unique system of traits, should be treated from its own perspective rather than that of some objective criteria or that of the observer. This latter view was called ethnocentrism.

This view of cultures as configurations, as unique and particular, was adopted by one of Boas' most famous students at Columbia, Ruth Fulton Benedict. Benedict stressed the wholeness of cultures and embodied her perspective in one of the most widely read anthropological studies, *Patterns of Culture,* which has sold more than one million copies.

In Chapter 7, from *Patterns of Culture,* we find Benedict's proscription against removing cultural traits from their social context, a practice she described as creating a Frankenstein, with a head from one culture, a leg from another, a body from a third, and so forth. She said (1934:47),

We may know all about the distribution of a tribe's form of marriage, ritual dances, and puberty initiations, and yet understand nothing of the culture as a whole, which has used these elements to its own purpose. This purpose selects from among the possible traits in the surrounding regions those which it can use, and discards those which it cannot.

Benedict presents a picture of cultural possibilities as a broad range of alternatives, from which a society makes selections. However, she makes it clear that these selections are not conscious but that they evolve through history, with the culture adopting, adapting, rejecting and molding its life, and winnowing out the contradictions, until a body of custom wholly consistent and congruent with its temperament and style is achieved. Such was Benedict's picture of integrated cultures. Like personalities, they were the sum of their traits but were more than their sum in the Gestalt wholeness which related and integrated one trait with another. Benedict used the analogy of a personality life history, seeing cultures as taking on distinct characters as an integrating principle which infiltrated and pervaded every component of life. With her perspective on culture, Benedict was described in the preface to *Patterns of Culture,* written by Margaret Mead, as believing that cultures were "personalities writ large." Hence, we find that Benedict related to and was a part of two other streams of anthropological theory—that of the personality and culture perspective, in which Margaret Mead was so prominent, and that of the functionalist and structuralist schools, which, like Benedict, viewed culture as an integrated system.

Diverse sources were responsible for Benedict's study of the nature of culture. She used the stylistic approach of Kroeber, particularly with regard to art. Gestalt psychology supplied the basis for her belief in the wholeness in which cultures developed perceptions of the world. Malinowski's functionalism stressed the interrelatedness and uniqueness of culture. Boas emphasized history. Each intellectual strand in its own way contributed to a paramount concern with the nature of culture, the uniqueness of each society, and the resultant conformance of the individual due to the pressures of the culture. The rise of Gestalt psychology, functionalism, structuralism, and Boasian historicism, at the time that she was writing, in the late twenties and thirties, shaped Benedict's holistic perspective and her search for the themes by which human beings selectively regulated their aspirations and their life styles.

Franz Boas

4. The Limitations of the Comparative Method of Anthropology[1]

Modern anthropology has discovered the fact that human society has grown and developed everywhere in such a manner that its forms, its opinions and its actions have many fundamental traits in common. This momentous discovery implies that laws exist which govern the development of society, that they are applicable to our society as well as to those of past times and of distant lands; that their knowledge will be a means of understanding the causes furthering and retarding civilization; and that, guided by this knowledge, we may hope to govern our actions so that the greatest benefit to mankind will accrue from them. Since this discovery has been clearly formulated, anthropology has begun to receive that liberal share of public interest which was withheld from it as long as it was believed that it could do no more than record the curious customs and beliefs of strange peoples; or, at best, trace their relationships, and thus elucidate the early migrations of the races of man and the affinities of peoples.

While early investigators concentrated their attention upon this purely historical problem, the tide has now completely turned, so that there are even anthropologists who declare that such investigations belong to the historian, and that anthropological studies must be confined to researches on the laws that govern the growth of society.

A radical change of method has accompanied this change of views. While formerly identities or similarities of culture were considered incontrovertible proof of historical connection, or even of common origin, the new school declines to consider them as such, but interprets them as results of the uniform working of the human mind. The most pronounced adherent of this view in our country is Dr. D. G. Brinton, in Germany the majority of the followers of Bastian, who in this respect go much farther than Bastian himself. Others, while not denying the occurrence of historical connections, regard them as insignificant in results and in theoretical importance as compared to the working of the uniform

70

laws governing the human mind. This is the view of by far the greater number of living anthropologists.

This modern view is founded on the observation that the same ethnical phenomena occur among the most diverse peoples, or, as Bastian says, on the appalling monotony of the fundamental ideas of mankind all over the globe. The metaphysical notions of man may be reduced to a few types which are of universal distribution; the same is the case in regard to the forms of society, laws and inventions. Furthermore, the most intricate and apparently illogical ideas and the most curious and complex customs appear among a few tribes here and there in such a manner that the assumption of a common historical origin is excluded. When studying the culture of any one tribe, more or less close analoga of single traits of such a culture may be found among a great diversity of peoples. Instances of such analoga have been collected to a vast extent by Tylor, Spencer, Bastian, Andree, Post and many others, so that it is not necessary to give here any detailed proof of this fact. The idea of a future life; the one underlying shamanism; inventions such as fire and the bow; certain elementary features of grammatical structure—these will suggest the classes of phenomena to which I refer. It follows from these observations that when we find analogous single traits of culture among distant peoples, the presumption is not that there has been a common historical source, but that they have arisen independently.

But the discovery of these universal ideas is only the beginning of the work of the anthropologist. Scientific inquiry must answer two questions in regard to them: First, what is their origin? and second, how do they assert themselves in various cultures?

The second question is the easier one to answer. The ideas do not exist everywhere in identical form, but they vary. Sufficient material has been accumulated to show that the causes of these variations are either external, that is founded on environment—taking the term environment in its widest sense—or internal, that is founded on psychological conditions. The influence of external and internal factors upon elementary ideas embodies one group of laws governing the growth of culture. Therefore, our endeavors must be directed to showing how such factors modify elementary ideas.

The first method that suggests itself and which has been generally adopted by modern anthropologists is to isolate and classify causes by grouping the variants of certain ethnological phenomena according to external conditions under which the people live, among whom they are found, or to internal causes which influence their minds; or conversely, by grouping these variants according to their similarities. Then the correlated conditions of life may be found.

By this method we begin to recognize even now with imperfect knowledge of the facts what causes may have been at work in shaping the culture of mankind. Friedrich Ratzel and W. J. McGee have investigated the influence of geographical environment on a broader basis of facts than Ritter and Guyot were able to do at their time. Sociologists have made important studies on the effects of the density of population and of other simple social causes. Thus the influence of external factors upon the growth of society is becoming clearer.

The effects of psychical factors are also being studied in the same manner. Stoll has tried to isolate the phenomena of suggestion and of hypnotism and to study the effects of their presence in the cultures of various peoples. Inquiries into the mutual relations of tribes and peoples begin to show that certain cultural elements are easily assimilated while others are rejected, and the time-worn phrases of the imposition of culture by a more highly civilized people upon one of lower culture that has been conquered are giving way to more thorough views on the subject of exchange of cultural achievements. In all these investigations we are using sound, inductive methods in order to isolate the causes of observed phenomena.

The other question in regard to the universal ideas, namely that of their origin, is much more difficult to treat. Many attempts have been made to discover the causes which have led to the formation of ideas 'that develop with iron necessity wherever man lives.' This is the most difficult problem of anthropology and we may expect that it will baffle our attempts for a long time to come. Bastian denies that it is possible to discover the ultimate source of inventions, ideas, customs and beliefs which are of universal occurrence. They may be indigenous, they may be imported, they may have arisen from a variety of sources, but they are there. The human mind is so formed that it invents them spontaneously or accepts them whenever they are offered to it. This is the much misunderstood elementary idea of Bastian.

To a certain extent the clear enunciation of the elementary idea gives us the psychological reason for its existence. To exemplify: the fact that the land of the shadows is so often placed in the west suggests the endeavor to localize it at the place where the sun and the stars vanish. The mere statement that primitive man considers animals as gifted with all the qualities of man shows that the analogy between many of the qualities of animals and of human beings has led to the generalization that all the qualities of animals are human. In other cases the causes are not so self-evident. Thus the question why all languages distinguish between the self, the person addressed and the person spoken of, and why most languages do not carry out this sharp, logical distinction in the plural is difficult to answer. The principle when carried out consistently requires that in the plural there should be a distinction between the 'we' expressing the self and the person addressed and the 'we' expressing the self and the person spoken of, which distinction is found in comparatively few languages only. The lesser liability to misunderstandings in the plural explains this phenomenon partly but hardly adequately. Still more obscure is the psychological basis in other cases, for instance, in that of widely spread marriage customs. Proof of the difficulty of this problem is the multitude of hypotheses that have been invented to explain it in all its varied phases.

In treating this, the most difficult problem of anthropology, the point of view is taken that if an ethnological phenomenon has developed independently in a number of places its development has been the same everywhere; or, expressed in a different form, that the same ethnological phenomena are always due to the same causes. This leads to the still wider generalization that the sameness of ethnological phenomena found in diverse regions is proof that the human mind obeys the same laws everywhere. It is obvious that if different historical developments could lead to the same results, that then this generalization would not be tenable. Their existence would present to us an entirely different problem, namely, how it is that the developments of culture so often lead to the same results. It must, therefore, be clearly understood that anthropological research which compares similar cultural phenomena from various parts of the world, in order to discover the uniform history of their development, makes the assumption that the same ethnological phenomenon has everywhere developed in the same manner. Here lies the flaw in the argument of the new method, for no such proof can be given. Even the most cursory review shows that the same phenomena may develop in a multitude of ways.

I will give a few examples: Primitive tribes are almost universally divided into clans which have totems. There can be no doubt that this form of social organization has arisen independently over and over again. The conclusion is certainly justified that the psychical conditions of man favor the existence of a totemic organization of society, but it does not follow that totemic society has developed everywhere in the same manner. Dr. Washington Matthews believes that the totems of the Navaho have arisen by association of independent clans. Capt. Bourke assumes that similar occurrences gave origin to the Apache clans, and Dr. Fewkes has reached the same conclusion in regard to some of the Pueblo tribes. On the other hand, we have proof that clans may originate by division. I have shown that such events took place among the Indians of the North Pacific coast. Association of small tribes, on the one hand, and disintegration of increasing tribes, on the other, has led to results which appear identical to all intents and purposes.

To give another example: Recent investigations have shown that geometrical designs in primitive art have originated sometimes from naturalistic forms which were gradually conventionalized, sometimes from technical motives, that in still other cases they were geometrical by origin or that they were derived from symbols. From all these sources the same forms have developed. Out of designs representing diverse objects grew in course of time frets, meanders, crosses and the like. Therefore the frequent occurrence of these forms proves neither common origin nor that they have always developed according to the same psychical laws. On the contrary, the identical result may have been reached on four different lines of development and from an infinite number of starting points.

Another example may not be amiss: The use of masks is found among a great number of peoples. The origin of the custom of wearing masks is by no means clear in all cases, but a few typical forms of their use may easily be distinguished. They are used for deceiving spirits as to the identity of the wearer. The spirit of a disease who intends to attack the person does not recognize him when he wears a mask, and the mask serves in this manner as a protection. In other cases the mask represents a spirit which is personified by the wearer, who in this shape frightens away other hostile spirits. Still other masks are commemorative. The wearer personifies a deceased person whose memory is to be recalled. Masks are also used in theatrical performances illustrating mythological incidents.[2]

These few data suffice to show that the same ethnical phenomenon may develop from different sources. The simpler the observed fact, the more likely it is that it may have developed from one source here, from another there.

Thus we recogize that the fundamental assumption which is so often made by modern anthropologists cannot be accepted as true in all cases. We cannot say that the occurrence of the same phenomenon is always due to the same causes, and that thus it is proved that the human mind obeys the same laws everywhere. We must demand that the causes from which it developed be investigated and that comparisons be restricted to those phenomena which have been proved to be effects of the same causes. We must insist that this investigation be made a preliminary to all extended comparative studies. In researches on tribal societies those which have developed through association must be treated separately from those that have developed through disintegration. Geometrical designs which have arisen from conventionalized representations of natural objects must be treated separately from those that have arisen from technical motives. In short, before extended comparisons are made, the comparability of the material must be proved.

The comparative studies of which I am speaking here attempt to explain customs and ideas of remarkable similarity which are found here and there. But they pursue also the more ambitious scheme of discovering the laws and the history of the evolution of human society. The fact that many fundamental features of culture are universal, or at least occur in many isolated places, interpreted by the assumption that the same features must always have developed from the same causes, leads to the conclusion that there is one grand system according to which mankind has developed everywhere; that all the occurring variations are no more than minor details in this grand uniform evolution. It is clear that this theory has for its logical basis the assumption that the same phenomena are always due to the same causes. To give an instance: We find many types of structure of family. It can be proved that paternal families have often developed from maternal ones. Therefore, it is said, all paternal families have developed from maternal ones. If we do not make the assumption that the same phenomena have everywhere developed from the same causes, then we may just as well conclude that paternal families have in some cases arisen from maternal institutions; in other cases in other ways. To give another example: Many conceptions of the future life have evidently developed from dreams and hallucinations. Consequently, it is said, all notions of this character have had the same origin. This is also true only if no other causes could possibly lead to the same ideas.

We have seen that the facts do not favor at all the assumption of which we are speaking; that they much rather point in the opposite direction. Therefore we must also consider all the ingenious attempts at constructions of a grand system of the evolution of society as of very doubtful value, unless at the same time proof is given that the same phenomena must always have had the same origin. Until this is done, the presumption is always in favor of a variety of courses which historical growth may have taken.

It will be well to restate at this place one of the principal aims of anthropological research. We agreed that certain laws exist which govern the growth of human culture, and it is our endeavor to discover these laws. The object of our investigation is to find the *processes* by which certain stages of culture have developed. The customs and beliefs themselves are not the ultimate objects of research. We desire to learn the reasons why such customs and beliefs exist—in other words, we wish to discover the history of their development. The method which is at present most frequently applied in investigations of this character compares the variations under which the customs or beliefs occur and endeavors to find the common psychological cause that underlies all of them. I have stated that this method is open to a very fundamental objection.

We have another method, which in many respects is much safer. A detailed study of customs in their relation to the total culture of the tribe practicing them, in connection with an investigation of their geographical distribution among neighboring tribes, affords us almost always a means of determining with considerable accuracy the historical causes that led to the formation of the customs in question and to the psychological processes that were at work in their development. The results of inquiries conducted by this method may be three-fold. They may reveal the environmental conditions which have created or modified cultural elements; they may clear up psychological factors which are at work in shaping the culture; or they may bring before our eyes the effects that historical connections have had upon the growth of the culture.

We have in this method a means of reconstructing the history of the growth of ideas with much greater accuracy than the generalizations of the comparative method will permit. The latter must always proceed from a hypothetical mode of development, the probability of which may be weighed more or less accurately by means of observed data. But so far I have not yet seen any extended attempt to prove the correctness of a theory by testing it at the hand of developments with whose histories we are familiar. Forcing phenomena into the strait-jacket of a theory is opposed to the inductive process by which the actual relations of definite phenomena may be derived. The latter is no other than the much ridiculed historical method. Its way of proceeding is, of course, no longer that of former times when slight similarities of culture were considered proofs of relationships, but it duly recognizes the results obtained by comparative studies. Its application is based, first of all, on a well-defined, small geographical territory, and its comparisons are not extended beyond the limits of the cultural area that forms the basis of the study. Only when definite results have been obtained in regard to this area is it permissible to extend the horizon beyond its limits, but the greatest care must be taken not to proceed too hastily in this, as otherwise the fundamental proposition which I formulated before might be overlooked, viz: that when we find an analogy of single traits of culture among distant peoples the presumption is not that there has been a common historical source, but that they have arisen independently. Therefore the investigation must always demand continuity of distribution as one of the essential conditions for proving historical connection, and the assumption of lost connecting links must be applied most sparingly. This clear distinction between the new and the old historical methods is still often overlooked by the passionate defenders of the comparative method. They do not appreciate the difference between the indiscriminate use of similarities of culture for proving historical connection and the careful and slow detailed study of local phenomena. We no longer believe that the slight similarities between the cultures of Central America and of eastern Asia are sufficient and satisfactory proof of a historical connection. On the other hand, no unbiased observer will deny that there are very strong reasons for believing that a limited number of cultural elements found in Alaska and in Siberia have a common origin. The similarities of inventions, customs and beliefs, together with the continuity of their distribution through a limited area, are satisfactory proof of the correctness of this opinion. But it is not possible to extend this area safely beyond the limits of Columbia River in America and northern Japan in Asia. This method of anthropological research is represented in our country by F. W. Putnam and Otis T. Mason; in England by E. B. Tylor; in Germany by Friedrich Ratzel and his followers.

It seems necessary to say a word here in regard to an objection to my arguments that will be raised by investigators who claim that similarity of geographical environment is a sufficient cause for similarity of culture, that is to say, that, for instance, the geographical conditions of the plains of the Mississippi basin necessitate the development of a certain culture. Horatio Hale would even go so far as to believe that similarity of form of language may be due to environmental causes. Environment has a certain limited effect upon the culture of man, but I do not see how the view that it is the primary molder of culture can be supported by any facts. A hasty review of the tribes and peoples of our globe shows that people most diverse in culture and language live under the same geographical conditions, as proof of which may be mentioned the ethnography of East Africa or of New Guinea. In both these regions we find a great diversity of customs in small areas. But much more important is this: Not one observed fact can be brought forward in support of this hypothesis which cannot be much better explained by the well known facts of diffusion of culture; for archaeology as well as ethnography teach us that intercourse between neighboring tribes has always existed and has extended over enormous areas. In the Old World the products of the Baltic found their way to the Mediterranean and the works of art of the eastern Mediterranean reached Sweden. In America the shells of the ocean found their way into the innermost parts of the continent and the obsidians of the West were carried to Ohio. Intermarriages, war, slavery, trade, have been so many sources of constant introduction of foreign cultural elements, so that an assimilation of culture must have taken place over continuous areas. Therefore, it seems to my mind that where among neighboring tribes an immediate influence of environment cannot be shown to exist, the presumption must always be in favor of historical connection. There has been a time of isolation during which the principal traits of diverse cultures developed according to the previous culture and the environment of the tribes. But the stages of culture representing this period have been covered with so much that is new and that is due to contact with foreign tribes that they cannot be discovered without the most painstaking isolation of foreign elements.

The immediate results of the historical method are, therefore, histories of the cultures of diverse tribes which have been the subject of study. I fully agree with those anthropologists who claim that this is not the ultimate aim of our science, because the general laws, although implied in such a description, cannot be clearly formulated nor their relative value appreciated without a thorough comparison of the manner in which they become manifest in different cultures. But I insist that the application of this method is the indispensable condition of sound progress. The psychological problem is contained in the results of the historical inquiry. When we have cleared up the history of a single culture and understand the effects of environment and the psychological conditions that are reflected in it we have made a step forward, as we can then investigate in how far the same causes or other causes were at work in the development of other cultures. Thus by comparing histories of growth general laws may be found. This method is much safer than the comparative method, as it is usually practiced, because instead of a hypothesis on the mode of development actual history forms the basis of our deductions.

The historical inquiry must be considered the critical test that science must require before admitting facts as evidence. By its means the comparability of the collected material must be tested, and uniformity of processes must be demanded as proof of comparability. Furthermore, when historical connection between two phenomena can be proved, they must not be admitted as independent evidence.

In a few cases the immediate results of this method are of so wide a scope that they rank with the best results that can be attained by comparative studies. Some phenomena have so immense a distribution that the discovery of their occurrence over very large continuous areas proves at once that certain phases of the culture in these areas have sprung from one source. Thus are illuminated vast portions of the early history of mankind. When Edward S. Morse showed that certain methods of arrow release are peculiar to whole continents it became clear at once that the common practice found over a vast area must have had a common origin. When the Polynesians employ a method of fire making consisting in rubbing a stick along a groove, while almost all other peoples use the fire drill, it shows their art of fire making has a single origin. When we notice that the ordeal is found all over Africa in certain peculiar forms, while in those parts of the inhabited world that are remote from Africa it is found not at all or in rudimentary forms only, it shows that the idea as practiced in Africa had one single origin.

The great and important function of the historical method of anthropology is thus seen to lie in its ability to discover the processes which in definite cases led to the development of certain customs. If anthropology desires to establish the laws governing the growth of culture it must not confine itself to comparing the results of the growth alone, but whenever such is feasible it must compare the processes of growth, and these can be discovered by means of studies of the cultures of small geographical areas.

Thus we have seen that the comparative method can hope to reach the results for which it is striving only when it bases its investigations on the historical results of researches which are devoted to laying clear the complex relations of each individual culture. The comparative method and the historical method, if I may use these terms, have been struggling for supremacy for a long time, but we may hope that each will soon find its appropriate place and function. The historical method has reached a sounder basis by abandoning the misleading principle of assuming connections wherever similarities of culture were found. The comparative method, notwithstanding all that has been said and written in its praise, has been remarkably barren of definite results, and I believe it will not become fruitful until we renounce the vain endeavor to construct a uniform systematic history of the evolution of culture, and until we begin to make our comparisons on the broader and sounder basis which I ventured to outline. Up to this time we have too much reveled in more or less ingenious vagaries. The solid work is still all before us.

Notes

1. Paper read at the meeting of the A. A. A. S. at Buffalo. *Science*, N.S., vol. 4 (1896), pp. 901–908.

2. See Richard Andree. *Ethnographische Parallelen und Vergleiche*. Neue Folge (Leipzig, 1889), pp. 107 ff.

Alfred L. Kroeber

5. The Nature of Culture

What Culture Is

What culture is can be better understood from knowledge of what forms it takes and how it works than by a definition. Culture is in this respect like life or matter: it is the total of their varied phenomena that is more significant than a concentrated phrase about them. And again as with life and with matter, it is true that when we are dealing with the actual manifestations we are less often in doubt as to whether a phenomenon is or is not cultural than we are in deciding on what is includable in the concept of culture when we reason abstractly about it. Nevertheless, it will be worth while to consider some definitions briefly.

Tylor says that "culture or civilization is that complex whole which includes knowledge, belief, art, morals, law, customs, and any other capabilities and habits acquired by man as a member of society." Linton equates culture with "social heredity." Lowie calls it "the whole of social tradition." All three statements use the term "social" or "society," but in an attributive or qualifying sense. We can accept this: society and culture, social and cultural, are closely related concepts. There can obviously be no culture without a society—much as there can be no society without individuals. The converse—no society without culture—holds for man: no cultureless human society is known; it would even be hard to imagine. But it does not hold on the subhuman level. As we have seen, ants and bees do have genuine societies without culture, as well as without speech. Less integrated and simpler associations are frequent among animals. Even a pair of nesting birds rearing their young constitute a society, though a small and temporary one. Accordingly, so far as man is concerned, culture always has society as a counterpart; it rests on, and is carried by, society. Beyond the range of man there are societies, but no cultures. Cultural phenomena thus characterize man more specifically than his social manifestations characterize him, for these latter he shares with vertebrate and invertebrate animals.

Roughly, then, we can approximate what culture is by saying it is that

80

which the human species has and other social species lack. This would include speech, knowledge, beliefs, customs, arts and technologies, ideals and rules. That, in short, is what we learn from other men, from our elders or the past, plus what we may add to it. That is why Tylor speaks of "capabilities and habits acquired by man," and what Lowie means when he says "the whole of social tradition," or Linton by "social heredity." The last term is unfortunate because heredity now denotes in biology precisely what is received organically or genetically to the exclusion of what is acquired socially or culturally. But if we substitute for "heredity" the more noncommittal near-synonym "inheritance," the phrase then conveys much the same meaning as Lowie's "social tradition."

The terms "social inheritance" or "tradition" put the emphasis on how culture is acquired rather than on what it consists of. Yet a naming of all the kinds of things that we receive by tradition—speech, knowledges, activities, rules, and the rest—runs into quite an enumeration. We have already seen that things so diverse as hoeing corn, singing the blues, wearing a shirt, speaking English, and being a Baptist are involved. Perhaps a shorter way of designating the content of culture is the negative way of telling what is excluded from it. Put this way around, culture might be defined as all the activities and nonphysiological products of human personalities that are not automatically reflex or instinctive. That in turn means, in biological and psychological parlance, that culture consists of conditioned or learned activities (plus the manufactured results of these); and the idea of learning brings us back again to what is socially transmitted, what is received from tradition, what "is acquired by man as a member of societies." So perhaps *how it comes to be* is really more distinctive of culture than what it *is*. It certainly is more easily expressed specifically.

In one sense culture is both superindividual and superorganic. But it is necessary to know what is meant by these terms so as not to misunderstand their implications. "Superorganic" does not mean nonorganic, or free of organic influence and causation; nor does it mean that culture is an entity independent of organic life in the sense that some theologians might assert that there is a soul which is or can become independent of the living body. "Superorganic" means simply that when we consider culture we are dealing with something that is organic but which must also be viewed as something more than organic if it is to be fully intelligible to us. In the same way when we say that plants and animals are "organic" we do not thereby try to place them outside the laws of matter and energy in general. We only affirm that fully to understand organic beings and how they behave, we have to recognize certain kinds of phenomena or properties—such as the powers of reproduction, assimilation, irritability—as added to those which we encounter in inorganic substances. Just so, there are certain properties of culture—such as transmissibility, high variability, cumulativeness, value standards, influence on individuals—which it is difficult to explain, or to see much significance in, strictly in terms of the organic composition of personalities or individuals. These properties or qualities of culture evidently attach not to the organic individual man as such, but to the actions and the behavior products of societies of men—that is, to culture.

In short, culture is superorganic and superindividual in that, although carried, participated in, and produced by organic individuals, it is acquired; and it is acquired by learning. What is learned is the existent culture. The content of this is transmitted between individuals without becoming a part of their inherent endowment. The mass or body of culture, the institutions and practices and ideas constituting it, have a persistence and can be conceived as going on their slowly changing way "above" or outside the societies that support them. They are "above" them in that a particular culture, a particular set of institutions, can pass to other societies; also in that the culture continuously influences or conditions the members of the underlying society or societies—indeed, largely determines the content of their lives. Further, particular manifestations of cultures find their primary significance in other cultural manifestations, and can be most fully understood in terms of these manifestations; whereas they cannot be specifically explained from the generic organic endowment of the human personality, even though cultural phenomena must always conform to the frame of this endowment.

An illustration may make this superorganic quality more vivid. A religion, say Roman Catholicism or Mohammedanism, is of course a piece of culture, and a typical piece or sample. Obviously Catholicism exists only in so far as there are Catholics; that is, when and where there are human individuals who have acquired the faith. Once established, however, the Catholic hierarchy, beliefs, rituals, habits, and attitudes can also be viewed as going on century after century. Popes, bishops, communicants succeed one another; the church persists. It certainly possesses a continuity and an influence of its own: it affects not only its adherents but the course of history. On a smaller scale, or for shorter periods, the same thing holds for smaller segments of culture—institutions, beliefs, or customs down to short-lived trivialities of fashion and etiquette. On a larger and more general scale, the same holds for the totality of human culture since it first began to develop. Big or little, then, culture affects human action. It is the accident of what culture happens to be in Occidental countries toward the middle of the twentieth century which determines that when I get up in the morning I put on a shirt and pants and not a chlamys or a toga or just a breech-clout. Can we call this contemporary Western culture the cause of my shirt-wearing? In ordinary parlance, we might; the specific custom can certainly not be derived from anything in human hereditary constitution. Dialectically, the cultural causation might be challenged; it depends on logical definitions. But everyone will agree at least that the concrete cultural fact of habitual shirt-wearing is specifically related to or conditioned by other cultural facts, such as antecedent dress styles, manners, laws, or religion.

Again, the English language is a piece of culture. The faculty of speaking and understanding some or any language is organic: it is a faculty of the human species. The sounds of words are of course made by individual men and women, and are understood and reacted to by individuals, not by the species. But the total aggregation of words, forms, grammar, and meanings which constitute the English language are the cumulative and joint product of millions of individuals for many centuries past. No one of us creates or invents for himself the English he speaks. He talks it as it comes to him, ready-made, from his millions of predecessors and from his elders and age mates. English is obviously super-individual in the sense that it is something enormously bigger and more significant than the speech of any individual man, and in that it influences his speaking infinitely more than his speaking can hope to contribute to or influence the English language. And English is superorganic in that its words and meanings are not direct outflows or consequences of men's (sic) being human organisms—else all men would spontaneously talk as much alike as they walk alike. Instead, how they talk depends overwhelmingly on how the societies in which they were raised talked before.

A piece of culture such as the English language is therefore a historical phenomenon. This means that its specific features cannot be adequately explained by the organic features of our species—nor of a race—but are most intelligible in the light of the long, complex, and locally varied history of the institution we call English speech. In short, a cultural fact is always a historical fact; and its most immediate understanding, and usually the fullest understanding of it to which we can attain, is a historical one. To a large degree calling culture superorganic or superindividual means that it yields more readily to historical interpretation than to organic or psychosomatic explanations.

A simile that may further help the realization of what culture is and how it works is that of a coral reef. Such a reef may be miles long and inhabited by billions of tiny polyp animals. The firm, solid part of the reef consists of calcium carbonate produced by the secretions of these animals over thousands of years—a product at once cumulative and communal and therefore social. What is alive and organic in the reef is these innumerable little animals on its ocean-fronting surface. Without their ancestors, there would have been no reef. But the reef now exists independently of the living polyps, and would long continue to endure even if every polyp were killed by, say, a change in ocean temperature or salinity. It would still break the surf, would now and then wreck ships, and would bar off quiet water behind. While a coral reef is the accumulated precipitate of dead polyps, it is also a phenomenon affording to millions of living polyps a base and a foothold, and a place to thrive.

This parallel is incomplete. It breaks down in that a reef is actual physical matter, whereas only the artifacts and the manufactures of culture are material or physical, most of culture consisting of ideas and behaviors. Also, a reef determines that and where new polyps are to live, but not how they will live, not the specific way of many possible ways in which they will function, which on the contrary is just what culture does largely determine for men. Yet the simile is valid and suggestive on one point: the minute role played by the individual polyp or human being in proportion, respectively, to the mass of reef or of culture. Each of us undoubtedly contributes something to the slowly but ever changing culture in which we live, as each coral contributes his gram or two of lime to the Great Barrier Reef. In the main, though, it is our culture that directs and outlines the kind of life we can lead. There is left to our individual gifts and temperaments the relative success and happiness we attain in life; and to our own volition, the alternative choices provided by our culture—the choice, perhaps, between being doctor, lawyer, or merchant chief; or whether our next drink shall be water, beer, tea, or milk. Even this last set of choices would not be wholly free to the individual if he were a participant in strict Methodist or Mohammedan culture; and in old China the beer would not be available and the milk considered too nasty to want.

At any rate, the comparison may be of aid toward seeing things in perspective; with a consequence, perhaps, of somewhat deepened personal humility in the face of the larger world and human history.

Robert H. Lowie

6. The Determinants of Culture

Psychology, racial differences, geographical environment, have all proved inadequate for the interpretation of cultural phenomena. The inference is obvious. Culture is a thing *sui generis* which can be explained only in terms of itself. This is not mysticism but sound scientific method. The biologist, whatever metaphysical speculations he may indulge in as to the ultimate origin of life, does not depart in his workaday mood from the principle that every cell is derived from some other cell. So the ethnologist will do well to postulate the principle, *Omnis cultura ex cultura*.[1] This means that he will account for a given cultural fact by merging it in a group of cultural facts or by demonstrating some other cultural fact out of which it has developed. The cultural phenomenon to be explained may either have an antecedent within the culture of the tribe where it is found or it may have been imported from without. Both groups of determinants must be considered.

The extraneous determinants of culture summed up under the heading of 'diffusion' or 'contact of peoples' have been repeatedly referred to in the preceding pages. A somewhat detailed examination seems desirable, for it is difficult to exaggerate their importance.

"Civilization," says Tylor, "is a plant much oftener propagated than developed;"[2] and the latest ethnographic memoir that comes to hand voices the same sentiment: "It is and has always been much easier to borrow an idea from one's neighbors than to originate a new idea; and transmission of cultural elements, which in all ages has taken place in a great many different ways, is and has been one of the greatest promoters of cultural development."[3]

A stock illustration of cultural assimilation is that of the Japanese, who in the nineteenth century adopted our scientific and technological civilization ready-made, just as at an earlier period they had acquired wholesale the culture of China. It is essential to note that it is not always the people of lower culture who remain passive recipients in the process of diffusion. This is strikingly shown by the spread of Indian corn. The white colonist "did not simply borrow the maize seed and then in con-

85

formity with his already established agricultural methods, or on original lines, develop a maize culture of his own," but "took over the entire material complex of maize culture" as found among the aborigines.[4] The history of Indian corn also illustrates the remarkable rapidity with which cultural possessions may travel over the globe. Unknown in the Old World prior to the discovery of America, it is mentioned as known in Europe in 1539 and had reached China between 1540 and 1570.[5]

The question naturally arises here, whether this process of diffusion, which in modern times is a matter of direct observation, could have been of importance during the earlier periods of human history when means of communication were of a more primitive order. So far as this point is concerned, we must always remember that methods of transportation progressed very slightly from the invention of the wheeled cart until the most recent times. As Montelius suggests, the periods of 1700 B.C. and 1700 A.D. differed far less in this regard than might be supposed on superficial consideration. Yet we know the imperfection of facilities for travel did not prevent dissemination of culture in historic times.

The great Swedish archaeologist has, indeed, given us a most fascinating picture of the commercial relations of northern Europe in earlier periods and their effect on cultural development.[6] We learn with astonishment that in the ninth and tenth centuries of our era, trade was carried on with great intensity between the North of Europe and the Mohammedan culture sphere since tens of thousands of Arabic coins have been found on Swedish soil. But intercourse with remote countries dates back to a far greater antiquity. One of the most powerful stimuli of commercial relations between northern and southern Europe was the desire of the more southern populations to secure amber, a material confined to the Baltic region and occurring more particularly about Jutland and the mouth of the Vistula. Amber beads have been found not only in Swiss pile-dwellings[7] but also in Mycenaean graves of the second millennium B.C. Innumerable finds of amber work in Italy and other parts of southern Europe prove the importance attached to this article, which was exchanged for copper and bronze. The composition of Scandinavian bronzes indicates that their material was imported not from England but from the faraway regions of central Europe. That bronze was not of indigenous manufacture is certain because tin does not occur in Sweden at all while the copper deposits of northern Scandinavia remained untouched until about 1500 years after the end of the Bronze Age. Considering the high development of the bronze technique in Scandinavia and the fact that every pound of bronze had to be imported from without, it would be difficult to exaggerate the extent of contact with the southern populations. But intercourse was not limited to the

South. For example, Swedish weapons and implements have been discovered in Finland. Again, crescent-shaped gold ornaments of Irish provenance have been found in Denmark, while a Swedish rock-painting represents with painstaking exactness a type of bronze shield common at a certain prehistoric period of England.

Montelius shows that historical connections of the type so amply attested for the Bronze Age also obtained in the preceding Neolithic era. Swedish hammers of stone dating back to the third pre-Christian millennium and flint daggers have been found in Finland, and earthenware characteristic of Neolithic Scandinavia also turns up on the Baltic coast of Russia. Stone burial cists with a peculiar oval opening at one end occur in a limited section of southwestern Sweden and likewise in England. Since such monuments have been discovered neither in other parts of Sweden nor in Jutland or the Danish islands, they point to a direct intercourse between Britain and western Sweden at about 2,000 B.C. A still older form of burial unites Scandinavia with other parts of the continent. Chambers built up of large stones set up edgewise and reaching from the floor to the roof, the more recent ones with and the older without a long covered passage, are highly characteristic of Sweden, Denmark, the British Isles, and the coasts of Europe from the Vistula embouchure to the coasts of France and Portugal, of Italy, Greece, the Crimea, North Africa, Syria, and India. Specific resemblances convince the most competent judges that some, at least, of these widely diffused 'dolmens' are historically connected with their Swedish equivalents, and since the oldest of these Northern chambers go back 3,000 years before our era, we thus have evidence of cultural diffusion dating back approximately five millennia.

It is highly interesting to trace under Montelius' guidance the development of culture as it seems to have actually taken place in southern Sweden. Beginning with the earliest periods, we find the coastal regions inhabited by a population of fishermen and hunters. At a subsequent stage coarse pottery appears with articles of bone and antler, and there is evidence that the dog has become domesticated. In the later Neolithic era perfectly polished stone hammers and exquisitely chipped flint implements occur, together with indications that cattle, horses, sheep and pigs are domesticated and that the cultivation of the soil has begun. Roughly speaking, we may assume that the culture of Scandinavia at the end of the Stone Age resembled in advancement that of the agricultural North American and Polynesian tribes as found by the first European explorers. We may assume a long period of essentially indigenous cultural growth followed towards its close by intimate relations with alien populations. Nevertheless, it was the more extensive contact of the

Bronze period that rapidly raised the ancestral Swedes to a cultural position high above a primitive level, with accentuation of agriculture, the use of woolen clothing, and a knowledge of metallurgy. It was again foreign influence that later brought the knowledge of iron and in the third century of our era transformed the Scandinavians into a literary people, flooded their country with art products of the highest then existing Roman civilization, and ultimately introduced Christianity.

The case of Scandinavian culture is fairly typical. We have first a long-continued course of leisurely and relatively undisturbed development, which is superseded by a tremendously rapid assimilation of cultural elements from without. Through contact with tribes possessing a higher civilization the ancient Scandinavians came to participate in its benefits and even to excel in special departments of it, such as bronze work, which from lack of material, they would have been physically incapable of developing unaided. Diffusion was the determinant of Scandinavian cultural progress from savagery to civilization.

It is obvious that this insistence on contact of peoples as a condition of cultural evolution does not solve the ultimate problem of the origin of culture. The question naturally obtrudes itself: If the Scandinavians obtained their civilization from the Southeast, how did the Oriental cultures themselves originate? Nevertheless, when we examine these higher civilizations of the Old World, we are again met with indubitable evidence that one of the conditions of development is the contact of peoples and the consequent diffusion of cultural elements. This appears clearly from a consideration of the ancient civilizations of Egypt, Babylonia, and China.

We now have abundant evidence for a later Stone Age in Egypt with an exceptionally high development of the art of chipping, as well as specimens of pottery and other indications of a sedentary mode of life. About 5,000 b.c. this undisturbed evolution began to suffer from a series of migrations of West Asiatic tribes, bringing in their wake a number of cultivated plants and domesticated animals, as well as various other features which possibly included the art of smelting copper, while the ceramic ware of the earlier period agrees so largely with that of Elam in what is now southern Persia that a cultural connecton seems definitely established.

If from Egypt we turn to the most probable source of alien culture elements found there, *viz.*, to the region of Mesopotamia, possibly the oldest seat of higher civilization in Asia, we find again that the culture of Babylonia under the famous lawgiver Hammurabi (about 2,000 b.c.) is not the product of purely indigenous growth but represents the resultant of at least two components, that of the Sumerian civilization of southern Babylonia and the Accadian culture of the North. It is certain that the Accadians adopted the art of writing from the Sumerians and were also stimulated by this contact in their artistic development. The evolution of Sumerian civilization is lost in obscurity but on the basis of well-established historical cases we should hesitate to assign to them an exclusively creative, and to other populations an exclusively receptive, rôle. We may quite safely assume that the early splendor of Sumerian civilization was also in large part due to stimuli received through foreign relations. That cultural elements of value may be borrowed from an inferior as well as from a higher level, has already been exemplified by the case of maize. It is also, among other things, illustrated by the history of the Chinese.

The Chinese have generally been represented as developing in complete isolation from other peoples. This traditional conception, however, breaks down with more intimate knowledge. Dr. Laufer has demonstrated that Chinese civilization, too, is a complex structure due to the conflux of distinct cultural streams. As an originally inland people inhabiting the middle and lower course of the Yellow River, they gradually reached the coast and acquired the art of navigation through contact with Indo-Chinese seafarers. Acquaintance with the northern nomads of Turkish and Tungus stock led to the use of the horse, donkey and camel, as well as the practice of felt and rug weaving, possibly even to the adoption of furniture and the iron techniques.[8] Most important of all, it appears that essentials of agriculture, cattle-raising, metallurgy and pottery, as well as less tangible features of civilization are common to ancient China and Babylonia, which forces us to the conclusion that both the Chinese and Babylonian cultures are ramifications from a common Asiatic substratum. It would be idle to speculate as to the relative contributions of each center to this ancient cultural stock. The essential point is that the most ancient Asiatic civilizations of which we have any evidence already indicate close contact of peoples and the dispersal of cultural elements.

Contact of peoples is thus an extraordinary promoter of cultural development. By the free exchange of arts and ideas among a group of formerly independent peoples, a superiority and complexity is rendered possible which without such diffusion would never have occurred. The part played in this process by the cruder populations must not be underestimated. They may contribute both actively and passively; actively, by transmitting knowledge independently acquired, as in the case of the felt technique the Chinese learned from the northern nomads; passively, by forming a lower caste on which the economic labors devolve and thus liberating their conquerors for an enlarged activity in the less utilitarian spheres of culture.

Nevertheless, before peoples can communicate their cultures to others with whom they come into contact, they must first evolve these cultures. The question thus remains, What determines this evolution? In order to gain a proper perspective in this matter, we must for a moment consider the progress of human civilization as a whole. Archaeological research shows that the modern era of steel and iron tools was preceded by an age of bronze and copper implements, which in turn was preceded by a stone age subdivided into a more recent period of polished, and an earlier of merely chipped, stone tools. Now the chronological relations of these epochs are extremely suggestive. The very lowest estimate by any competent observer of the age of Palaeolithic man in Europe sets it at 50,000 years;[9] since this is avowedly the utmost minimum value that can be assigned on geological grounds, we may reasonably assume twice that figure for the age of human culture generally. Using the rough estimate permissible in discussions of this sort, we may regard the end of the Palaeolithic era as dating back about 15,000 years ago. In short, for more than eight-tenths of its existence, the human species remained at a cultural level at best comparable with that of the Australian. We may assume that it was during this immense space of time that dispersal over the face of the globe took place and that isolation fixed the broader diversities of language and culture, over and above what may have been the persisting cultural sub-stratum common to the earliest undivided human group. The following Neolithic period of different parts of the globe terminated at different times and had not been passed at all by most of the American aborigines and the Oceanians at the time of their discovery. However, from the broader point of view here assumed, it was not relieved by the age of metallurgy until an exceedingly recent past. The earliest estimate I have seen does not put the event back farther than 6000 B.C. even in Mesopotamia. During nine-tenths of his existence, then, man was ignorant of the art of smelting copper from the ore. Finally, the iron technique does not date back 4,000 years; it took humanity ninety-six hundredths of its existence to develop this art.

We may liken the progress of mankind to that of a man a hundred years old, who dawdles through kindergarten for eighty-five years of his life, takes ten years to go through the primary grades, then rushes with lightning rapidity through grammar school, high school and college. Culture, it seems, is a matter of exceedingly slow growth until a certain 'threshold' is passed, when it darts forward, gathering momentum at an unexpected rate. For this peculiarity of culture as a whole, many miniature parallels exist in special subdivisions of culture history. Natural science lay dormant until Kepler, Galileo and Newton stirred it into unexampled activity, and the same holds for applied science until about a century ago.

This discontinuity of development receives strong additional illustration from a survey of special subdivisions of ancient culture. Though the Palaeolithic era certainly preceded the later Stone Age, archaeologists have hitherto failed to show the steps by which the latter could develop out of the earlier. This gap may, of course, be due merely to our lack of knowledge. Yet when we take subdivisions of the Palaeolithic period, the same fact once more confronts us. There is no orderly progression from Solutrean to Magdalenian times. The highly developed flint technique of the former dwindles away in the latter and its place is taken by what seems a spontaneous generation of bone and ivory work, with a high development of realistic art.

In view of the evidence, it seems perfect nonsense to say that early European civilization, by some law inherent in the very nature of culture, developed in the way indicated by archaeological finds. Southern Scandinavia could not possibly have had a bronze age without alien influence. In this case, discontinuity was the result of cultural contact. It may be that the lack of definite direction observed throughout the Stone age may in part be due to similar causes, the migrations and contact of different peoples, as Professor Sollas suggests. But it is important to note that discontinuity is a necessary feature of cultural progress. It does not matter whether we can determine the particular point in the series at which the significant trait was introduced. It does not matter whether, as I have suggested in the discussion of racial features, the underlying *causes* of the phenomena proceed with perfect continuity. Somewhere in the observed cultural *effects* there is the momentous innovation that leads to a definite break with the past. From a broad point of view, for example, it is immaterial whether the doctrine of evolution clings to the name of the younger or the elder Darwin, to Lamarck or St. Hilaire; the essential thing is that somehow the idea originated, and that when it had taken root it produced incalculable results in modern thought.

If culture, even when uninfluenced by foreign contact, progresses by leaps and bounds, we should naturally like to ascertain the determinants of such 'mutations.' In this respect, the discontinuity of indigenous evolution differs somewhat from that connected with cultural development due to diffusion. It was absolutely impossible that Scandinavia should produce bronze in the absence of tin. But *a priori* it is conceivable that an undisturbed culture might necessarily develop by what biologists call 'orthogenetic evolution', *i.e.*, in a definite direction through definite stages. This is, indeed, what is commonly known as the classical scheme of cultural evolution, of which men like Morgan are the protagonists. Now, how do the observed facts square with this theoretical possibility?

As Professor Boas and American ethnologists generally have maintained,[10] many facts are quite inconsistent with the theory of unilinear evolution. That theory can be tested very simply by comparing the sequence of events in two or more areas in which independent development has taken place. For example, has technology in Africa followed the lines ascertained for ancient Europe? We know today that it has not. Though unlike southern Scandinavia, the Dark Continent is not lacking in copper deposits, the African Stone Age was not superseded by a Copper Age, but directly by a period of Iron. Similarly, I have already pointed out that the possession of the same domesticated animals does not produce the same economic utilization of them while the Tungus rides his reindeer, other Siberians harness their animals to a sledge; the Chinaman will not milk his cattle, while the Zulu's diet consists largely of milk. That a particular innovation occurred at a given time and place is, of course, no less the result of definite causes than any other phenomenon of the universe. But often it seems to have been caused by an accidental complex of conditions rather than in accordance with some fixed principle.

For example, the invention of the wheel revolutionized methods of transportation. Now, why did this idea develop in the Old World and never take root among the American Indians? We are here face to face with one of those ultimate data that must simply be accepted like the physicist's fact that water expands in freezing while other substances contract. So far as we can see, the invention might have been made in America as well as not; and for all we know it would never have been made there until the end of time. This introduces a very important consideration. A given culture is, in a measure, at least, a unique phenomenon. In so far as this is true it must defy generalized treatment, and the explanation of a cultural phenomenon will consist in referring it back to the particular circumstances that preceded it. In other words, the explanation will consist in a recital of its past history; or, to put it negatively, it cannot involve the assumption of an organic law of cultural evolution that would necessarily produce the observed effect.

Facts already cited in other connections may be quoted again by way of illustration. When a copper implement is fashioned not according to the requirements of the material, but in direct imitation of preëxisting stone patterns, we have an instance of cutural inertia: it is only the past history of technology that renders the phenomena conceivable. So the unwieldly Chukchee tent, which adheres to the style of a pre-nomadic existence, is explained as soon as the past history of the tribe comes to light.

Phenomena that persist in isolation from their original context are technically known as 'survivals', and form one of the most interesting chapters of ethnology. One or two additional examples will render their nature still clearer. The boats of the Vikings were equipped for rowing as well as for sailing. Why the superfluous appliances for rowing, which were later dropped? As soon as we learn that the Norse boats were originally rowboats and that sails were a later addition, the rowing equipment is placed in its proper cultural setting and the problem is solved. Another example may be offered from a different phase of life. Among the Arapaho Indians there is a series of dance organizations graded by age. Membership is acquired by age-mates at the same time, each receiving the requisite ceremonial instructions from some other man who passed through the dance in his day. These older men, who are paid for their services by the candidates, may belong to any and all of the higher organizations. Oddly enough, each group of dancers is assisted by a number of 'elder brothers', all of whom rank them by *two* grades in the series of dancers. This feature is not at all clear from the Arapaho data alone. When, however, we turn to the Hidatsa Indians, with whom there is evidence this system of age-societies originated, we find that here the youngest group of men does not buy instructions from a miscellaneous assemblage of older men, but buys the dance outright from the whole of the second grade; this group, in order to have the privilege of performing a dance, must buy that of the third grade, and so on. In all these purchases the selling group seeks to extort the highest possible price while the buyers try to get off as cheaply as possible and are aided by the second higher group, *i.e.*, the group just ranking the sellers. Here the sophomore-senior versus freshman-junior relationship is perfectly intelligible; both the freshman and the junior, to pursue the analogy, bear a natural economic hostility against the sophomore, and vice versa. The Arapaho usage is intelligible as a survival from this earlier Hidatsa condition.

Our own civilization is shot through with survivals, so that further illustrations are unnecessary. They suggest, however, another aspect of our general problem. Of course, in every culture different traits are linked together without there being any essential bond between them. An illustration of this type of association is that mentioned by Dr. Laufer for Asiatic tribes, *viz.*, that all nations which use milk for their diet have epic poems, while those which abstain from milk have no epic literature. This type of chance association, due to historical causes, has been discussed by Dr. Wissler[11] and Professor Czekanowski.[12] But survivals show that there may be an *organic* relation between phenomena that have become separated and are treated as distinct by the descriptive ethnologist. In such cases, one trait is the determinant of the other, possibly as the actual preceding cause, possibly as part of the same phenomenon in the sense in which the side of a triangle is correlated with an angle.

A pair of illustrations will elucidate the matter. Primitive terms of relationship often reveal characteristic differences of connotation from their nearest equivalents in European languages. On the other hand, they are remarkably similar not only among many of the North American Indians but also in many other regions of the globe, such as Australia, Oceanica, Africa. The most striking peculiarity of this system of nomenclature lies in the inclusiveness of certain terms. For example, the word we translate as 'father' is applied indiscriminately to the father, all his brothers, and some of his male cousins; while the word for 'mother' is correspondingly used for the mother's sisters and some of their female cousins. On the other hand, paternal and maternal uncle or aunt are rigidly distinguished by a difference in terminology. As Morgan divined and Tylor clearly recognized, this system is connected with the one-sided exogamous kin organization by which an individual is reckoned as belonging to the exogamous social group of one, and only one, of his parents. The terminology that appears so curious at first blush then resolves itself very simply into the method of calling those members of the tribe who belong to the father's social group and generation by the same term as the father, while the maternal uncles, who must belong to another group because of the exogamous rule, are distinguished from the father. In short, the terminology simply expresses the existing social organization. In a world-wide survey of the field Tylor found that the number of peoples who use the type of nomenclature I have described and are divided into exogamous groups, is about three times that to be expected on the doctrine of chances: in other words, the two apparently distinct phemonema are causally connected.[13] This interpretation has recently been forcibly advocated by Dr. Rivers, and I have examined the North American data from this point of view. It developed, as a matter of fact, that practically all the tribes with exogamous 'clans', *i.e.*, matrilineal kin groups, or exogamous 'gentes', *i.e.*, patrilineal kin groups, had a system of the type described, while most of the tribes lacking such groups also lacked the nomenclature in question. Accordingly, it follows that there is certainly a functional relation between these phenomena, although it is conceivable that both are functionally related to still other phenomena, and that the really significant relationship remains to be determined.

As a linked illustration, the following phenomena may be presented. Among the Crow of Montana, the Hopi of Arizona, and some Melanesian tribes, the same term is applied to a father's sister and to a father's sister's daughter; indeed, among the Crow and the Hopi the term is extended to all the female descendants through females of the father's sister *ad infinitum*. Such a usage is at once intelligible from the tendency to call females of the father's group belonging to his and younger generations by a single term, regardless of generation, *if* descent is reckoned through the mother, for in that case, and that case only, will the individuals in question belong to the same group. And the fact is that in each of the cases mentioned, group affiliation is traced through the mother, while I know of not a single instance in which paternal descent coexists with the nomenclatorial disregard of generations in the form described.

My instances show, then, that cultural traits may be functionally related, and this fact renders possible a parallelism, however limited, of cultural development in different parts of the globe. The field of culture, then, is not a region of complete lawlessness. Like causes produce like effects here as elsewhere, though the complex conditions with which we are grappling require unusual caution in definitely correlating phenomena. It is true that American ethnologists have shown that in several instances like phenomena can be traced to diverse causes; that, in short, unlike antecedents converge to the same point. However, at the risk of being anathematized as a person of utterly unhistorical mentality, I must register my belief that this point has been overdone and that the continued insistence on it by Americanists is itself an illustration of cultural inertia. Indeed, the vast majority of so-called convergencies are not genuine, but false analogies due to our throwing together diverse facts from ignorance of their true nature, just as an untutored mind will class bats with birds, or whales with fish. When, however, rather full knowledge reveals not superficial resemblance but absolute identity of cultural features, it would be miraculous, indeed, to assume that such equivalence somehow was shaped by different determinants. When a Zulu of South Africa, an Australian, and a Crow Indian all share the mother-in-law taboo imposing mutual avoidance on the wife's mother and the daughter's husband, with exactly the same psychological correlate, it is, to my mind, rash to decree without attempt to produce evidence that this custom must, in each case, have developed from entirely distinct motives. To be sure, this particular usage has not yet, in my opinion, been satisfactorily accounted for. Nevertheless, in contradistinction to some of my colleagues and to the position I myself once shared, I now believe that it is pusillanimous to shirk the real problem involved, and that in so far as any explanation admits the problem, any explanation is preferable to the flaunting of fine phrases about the unique character of cultural phenomena. When, however, we ask what sort of explanation could be given, we find that it is by necessity a *cultural* explanation. Tylor, *e.g.*, thinks that the custom is correlated with the social rule that the husband takes up his abode with the wife's relatives and that the taboo merely marks the difference between him and the rest of the family. We have here clearly one cultural phenomenon as the determinant of another.

It is not so difficult as might at first appear to harmonize the principle that a cultural phenomenon is explicable only by a unique combination of antecedent circumstances with the principle that like phenomena are the product of like antecedents. The essential point is that in either case we have past history as the determinant. It is not necessary that certain things should happen; but if they do happen, then there is at least a considerable likelihood that certain other things will also happen. Diversity occurs where the particular thing of importance, say the wheel, has been discovered or conceived in one region but not in another. Parallelism tends to occur when the same significant phenomenon is shared by distinct cultures. It remains true that in culture history we are generally wise after the event. *A priori*, who would not expect that milking must follow from the domestication of cattle?

When we find that a type of kinship terminology is determined by exogamy or matrilineal descent, we have, indeed, given a cultural explanation of a cultural fact; but for the ultimate problems how exogamy or maternal descent came about, we may be unable to give a solution. Very often we cannot ascertain an anterior or correlated cultural fact for another cultural fact, but can merely group it with others of the same kind. Of this order are many of the parallels that figure so prominently in ethnological literature. For example, that primitive man everywhere believes in the animation of nature seems an irreducible datum which we can, indeed, paraphrase and turn hither and thither for clearer scrutiny but can hardly reduce to simpler terms. All we can do is to merge any particular example of such animism in the general class after the fashion of all scientific interpretation. That certain tendencies of all but universal occurrence are characteristic of culture, no fair observer can deny, and it is the manifest business of ethnology to ascertain all such regularities so that as many cultural phenomena as possible may fall into their appropriate categories. Only those who would derive each and every trait similar in different communities of human beings from a single geographical source can ignore such general characteristics of culture, which may, in a sense, be regarded as determinants of specific cultural data or rather, as the principles of which these are particular manifestations.

Recently I completed an investigation of Plains Indian societies begun on the most rigorous of historical principles, with a distinct bias in favor of the unique character of cultural data. But after smiting hip and thigh the assumption that the North American societies were akin to analogous institutions in Africa and elsewhere, I came face to face with the fact that, after all, among the Plains Indians, as among other tribes, the tendency of age-mates to flock together had formed social organizations and thus acted as a cultural determinant.

Beyond such interpretative principles for special phases of civilization, there are still broader generalizations of cultural phenomena. One has been repeatedly alluded to under the caption of cultural inertia, or survival—the irrational persistence of a feature when the context in which it had a place has vanished. But culture is not merely a passive phenomenon but a dynamic one as well. This is strikingly illustrated in the assimilation of an alien cultural stimulus. As I have already pointed out, it is not sufficient to bring two cultures into contact in order to have a perfect cultural interpenetration. The element of selection enters in a significant way. Not everything that is offered by a foreign culture is borrowed. The Japanese have accepted our technology but not our religion and etiquette. Moreover, what is accepted may undergo a very considerable change. While the whole range of phenomena is extremely wide and cannot be dismissed with a few words, it appears fairly clear that generally the preëxisting culture at once seizes upon a foreign element and models it in accordance with the *native* pattern. Thus, the Crow Indians, who had had a pair of rival organizations, borrowed a society from the Hidatsa where such rivalry did not exist. Straightway, the Crow imposed on the new society their own conception, and it became the competitor of another of their organizations. Similarly the Pawnee have a highly developed star cult. Their folklore is in many regards similar to that of other Plains tribes, from which some tales have undoubtedly been borrowed. Yet in the borrowing these stories became changed and the same episodes which elsewhere relate to human heroes now receive an astral setting. The preëxisting cultural pattern synthesizes the new element with its own preconceptions.

Another tendency that is highly characteristic of all cultures is the rationalistic explanation of what reason never gave rise to. This is shown very clearly in the justification of existing cultural features or of opinions acquired as a member of a particular society. Hegel's notion that whatever exists is rational and Pope's 'whatever is, is right' have their parallels in primitive legend and the literature of religious and political partisanship. In the special form of justification employed we find again the determining influence of the surrounding cultural atmosphere. Among the Plains Indians almost everything is explained as the result of supernatural revelation; if a warrior has escaped injury in battle it is because he wore a feather bestowed on him in a vision; if he acquires a large herd of horses it is in fulfilment of a spiritistic communication during the fast of adolescence. In a community where explanations of this type hold sway, we are not surprised to find that the origin of rites, too, is almost uniformly traced to a vision and that even the most trivial alteration in ceremonial garb is not claimed as an original invention but ascribed to supernatural promptings. Thus, the existing culture acts doubly as the determinant of the explanation offered for a particular cultural phenomenon. It evokes the search for its own *raison d'être;* and the type of interpretation called forth conforms to the explanatory pattern characteristic of the culture involved.

Culture thus appears as a closed system. We may not be able to explain all cultural phenomena or at least not beyond a certain point; but inasmuch as we *can* explain them at all, explanation must remain on the cultural plane.

What are the determinants of culture? We have found that cultural traits may be transmitted from without and in so far forth are determined by the culture of an alien people. The extraordinary extent to which such diffusion has taken place proves that the actual development of a given culture does not conform to innate laws necessarily leading to definite results, such hypothetical laws being overridden by contact with foreign peoples. But even where a culture is of relatively indigenous growth comparison with other cultures suggests that one step does not necessarily lead to another, that an invention like the wheel or the domestication of an animal occurs in one place and does not occur in another. To the extent of such diversity we must abandon the quest for general formulae of cultural evolution and recognize as the determinant of a phenomenon the unique course of its past history. However, there is not merely discontinuity and diversity but also stability and agreement in the sphere of culture. The discrete steps that mark culture history may not determine one another, but each may involve as a necessary or at least probable consequence other phenomena which in many instances are simply new aspects of the same phenomenon, and in so far forth one cultural element as isolated in description is the determinant or correlate of another. As for those phenomena which we are obliged to accept as realities without the possibility of further analysis, we can, at least, classify a great number of them and merge particular instances in a group of similar facts. Finally, there are dominant characteristics of culture, like cultural inertia or the secondary rationalization of habits acquired irrationally by the members of a group, which serve as broad interpretative principles in the history of civilization.

In short, as in other sciences, so in ethnology there are ultimate, irreducible facts, special functional relations, and principles of wider scope that guide us through the chaotic maze of detail. And as the engineer calls on the physicist for a knowledge of mechanical laws, so the social builder of the future who should seek to re-fashion the culture of his time and add to its cultural values will seek guidance from ethnology, the science of culture, which in Tylor's judgment is 'essentially a reformer's science.'

Notes

1. Rivers, W.H.R. Kinship and Social Organization, London, 1914, p. 92.

2. Tylor, Edward B. Primitive Culture; Researches into the Development of Mythology, Philosophy, Religion, Languages, Art and Custom. 2 vols, New York, 1889, vol. I, p, 53.

3. Hatt, Gudmund. Moccasins and their Relation to Arctic Foot-Wear, Memoirs, American Anthropological Association, vol. 3, no. 3, 1916, p. 246.

4. Wissler, Clark. Aboriginal Maize Culture, etc., pp. 656–661.

5. Boas, Franz. Mind of Primitive Man, p. 167.

6. Montelius, O. Der Handel in der Vorzeit, Praehistorische Zeitschrift, II, 1910, pp. 249–291; Id., A Guide to the National Historical Museum, Stockholm.

7. Forrer, Robert. Urgeschichte des Europäers, etc., p. 197.

8. Laufer, Berthold. Chinese Pottery of the Han Dynasty. Leiden, 1909, pp. 212–236.

9. Obermaier, Hugo. Der Mensche der Vorzeit, p. 337.

10. Boas, Franz. Mind of Primitive Man, p. 182 et seq.

11. Wissler, Clark. Material Cultures of the North American Indians, American Anthropologist, N.S. vol. 16, 1914, pp. 447–505, pp. 487–489.

12. Czekanowski, Jan. Objektive Kriterien in der Ethnologie, Korrespondenzblatt der Deutschen Gesellschaft für Anthropologie, Ethnologie und Urgeschichte, 1911, XLII, pp. 71–75.

13. Tylor, E. B. On a Method of Investigating the Development of Institutions; applied to Laws of Marriage and Descent, Journal of the Anthropological Institute, vol. 18, 1889, pp. 245–272, esp. p. 264.

Ruth Benedict

7. The Integration of Culture

The diversity of cultures can be endlessly documented. A field of human behaviour may be ignored in some societies until it barely exists; it may even be in some cases unimagined. Or it may almost monopolize the whole organized behaviour of the society, and the most alien situations be manipulated only in its terms. Traits having no intrinsic relation one with the other, and historically independent, merge and become inextricable, providing the occasion for behaviour that has no counterpart in regions that do not make these identifications. It is a corollary of this that standards, no matter in what aspect of behaviour, range in different cultures from the positive to the negative pole. We might suppose that in the matter of taking life all peoples would agree in condemnation. On the contrary, in a matter of homicide, it may be held that one is blameless if diplomatic relations have been severed between neighbouring countries, or that one kills by custom his first two children, or that a husband has right of life and death over his wife, or that it is the duty of the child to kill his parents before they are old. It may be that those are killed who steal a fowl, or who cut their upper teeth first, or who are born on a Wednesday. Among some peoples a person suffers torments at having caused an accidental death; among others it is a matter of no consequence. Suicide also may be a light matter, the recourse of anyone who has suffered some slight rebuff, an act that occurs constantly in a tribe. It may be the highest and noblest act a wise man can perform. The very tale of it, on the other hand, may be a matter for incredulous mirth, and the act itself impossible to conceive as a human possibility. Or it may be a crime punishable by law, or regarded as a sin against the gods.

The diversity of custom in the world is not, however, a matter which we can only helplessly chronicle. Self-torture here, head-hunting there, prenuptial chastity in one tribe and adolescent license in another, are not a list of unrelated facts, each of them to be greeted with surprise wherever it is found or wherever it is absent. The tabus on killing oneself or another, similarly, though they relate to no absolute standard, are not therefore fortuitous. The significance of cultural behaviour is not exhausted when we have clearly understood that it is local and man-made and hugely variable. It tends also to be integrated. A culture, like an individual, is a more or less consistent pattern of thought and action. Within each culture there come into being characteristic purposes not necessarily shared by other types of society. In obedience to these purposes, each people further and further consolidates its experience, and in proportion to the urgency of these drives the heterogeneous items of behaviour take more and more congruous shape. Taken up by a well-integrated culture, the most ill-assorted acts become characteristic of its peculiar goals, often by the most unlikely metamorphoses. The form that these acts take we can understand only by understanding first the emotional and intellectual mainsprings of that society.

Such patterning of culture cannot be ignored as if it were an unimportant detail. The whole, as modern science is insisting in many fields, is not merely the sum of all its parts, but the result of a unique arrangement and interrelation of the parts that has brought about a new entity. Gunpowder is not merely the sum of sulphur and charcoal and saltpeter, and no amount of knowledge even of all three of its elements in all the forms they take in the natural world will demonstrate the nature of gunpowder. New potentialities have come into being in the resulting compound that were not present in its elements, and its mode of behaviour is indefinitely changed from that of any of its elements in other combinations.

Cultures, likewise, are more than the sum of their traits. We may know all about the distribution of a tribe's form of marriage, ritual dances, and puberty initiations, and yet understand nothing of the culture as a whole which has used these elements to its own purpose. This purpose selects from among the possible traits in the surrounding regions those which it can use, and discards those which it cannot. Other traits it recasts into conformity with its demands. The process of course need never be conscious during its whole course, but to overlook it in the study of the patternings of human behaviour is to renounce the possibility of intelligent interpretation.

This integration of cultures is not in the least mystical. It is the same process by which a style in art comes into being and persists. Gothic architecture, beginning in what was hardly more than a preference for altitude and light, became, by the operation of some canon of taste that developed within its technique, the unique and homogeneous art of the thirteenth century. It discarded elements that were incongruous, modified others to its purposes, and invented others that accorded with its taste. When we describe the process historically, we inevitably use animistic forms of expression as if there were choice and purpose in the growth of this great art-form. But this is due to the difficulty in our language-forms. There was no conscious choice, and no purpose. What was at first no more than a slight bias in local forms and techniques expressed itself more and more forcibly, integrated itself in more and more definite standards, and eventuated in Gothic art.

What has happened in the great art-styles happens also in cultures as a whole. All the miscellaneous behaviour directed toward getting a living, mating, warring, and worshipping the gods, is made over into consistent patterns in accordance with unconscious canons of choice that develop within the culture. Some cultures, like some periods of art, fail of such integration, and about many others we know too little to understand the motives that actuate them. But cultures at every level of complexity, even the simplest, have achieved it. Such cultures are more or less successful attainments of integrated behaviour, and the marvel is that there can be so many of these possible configurations.

Anthropological work has been overwhelmingly devoted to the analysis of culture traits, however, rather than to the study of cultures as articulated wholes. This has been due in great measure to the nature of earlier ethnological descriptions. The classical anthropologists did not write out of first-hand knowledge of primitive people. They were armchair students who had at their disposal the anecdotes of travellers and missionaries and the formal and schematic accounts of the early ethnologists. It was possible to trace from these details the distribution of the custom of knocking out teeth, or of divination by entrails, but it was not possible to see how these traits were embedded in different tribes in characteristic configurations that gave form and meaning to the procedures.

Studies of culture like *The Golden Bough* and the usual comparative ethnological volumes are analytical discussions of traits and ignore all the aspects of cultural integration. Mating or death practices are illustrated by bits of behaviour selected indiscriminately from the most different cultures, and the discussion builds up a kind of mechanical Frankenstein's monster with a right eye from Fiji, a left from Europe, one leg from Tierra del Fuego, and one from Tahiti, and all the fingers and toes from still different regions. Such a figure corresponds to no reality in the past or present, and the fundamental difficulty is the same as if, let us say, psychiatry ended with a catalogue of the symbols of which psychopathic individuals make use, and ignored the study of patterns of symptomatic behavior—schizophrenia, hysteria, and manic-depressive disorders—into which they are built. The rôle of the trait in the behaviour of the psychotic, the degree to which it is dynamic in the total personality, and its relation to all other items of experience, differ completely. If we are interested in mental processes, we can satisfy ourselves only by relating the particular symbol to the total configuration of the individual. There is as great an unreality in similar studies of culture. If we are interested in cultural processes, the only way in which we can know the significance of the selected detail of behaviour is against the background of the motives and emotions and values that are institutionalized in that culture. The first essential, so it seems today, is to study the living culture, to know its habits of thought and the functions of its institutions, and such knowledge cannot come out of post-mortem dissections and reconstructions.

The necessity for functional studies of culture has been stressed over and over again by Malinowski. He criticizes the usual diffusion studies as post-mortem dissections of organisms we might rather study in their living and functioning vitality. One of the best and earliest of the full-length pictures of a primitive people which have made modern ethnology possible is Malinowski's extended account of the Trobriand Islanders of Melanesia. Malinowski, however, in his ethnological generalizations is content to emphasize that traits have a living context in the culture of which they are a part, that they function. He then generalizes the Trobriand traits—the importance of reciprocal obligations, the local character of magic, the Trobriand domestic family—as valid for the primitive world instead of recognizing the Trobriand configuration as one of many observed types, each with its characteristic arrangements in the economic, the religious, and the domestic sphere.

The study of cultural behaviour, however, can no longer be handled by equating particular local arrangements with the generic primitive. Anthropologists are turning from the study of primitive culture to that of primitive cultures, and the implications of this change from the singular to the plural are only just beginning to be evident.

The importance of the study of the whole configuration as over against the continued analysis of its parts is stressed in field after field of modern science. Wilhelm Stern has made it basic in his work in philosophy and psychology. He insists that the undivided totality of the person must be the point of departure. He criticizes the atomistic studies that have been almost universal both in introspective and experimental psychology, and he substitutes investigation into the configuration of personality. The whole *Struktur* school has devoted itself to work of this kind of various fields. Worringer has shown how fundamental a difference this approach makes in the field of aesthetics. He contrasts the highly developed art of two periods, the Greek and the Byzantine. The older criticism, he insists, which defined art in absolute terms and identified it with the classical standards, could not possibly understand the processes of art as they are represented in Byzantine painting or mosaic. Achievement in one cannot be judged in terms of the other, because each was attempting to achieve quite different ends. The Greeks in their art attempted to give expression to their own pleasure in activity; they sought to embody their identification of their vitality with the objective world. Byzantine art, on the other hand, objectified abstraction, a profound feeling of separation in the face of outside nature. Any understanding of the two must take account, not only of comparisons of artistic ability, but far more of differences of artistic intention. The two forms were contrasting, integrated configurations, each of which could make use of forms and standards that were incredible in the other.

The *Gestalt* (configuration) psychology has done some of the most striking work in justifying the importance of this point of departure from the whole rather than from its parts. *Gestalt* psychologists have shown that in the simplest sense-perception no analysis of the separate percepts can account for the total experience. It is not enough to divide perceptions up into objective fragments. The subjective framework, the forms provided by past experience, are crucial and cannot be omitted. The 'wholeness-properties' and the 'wholeness-tendencies' must be studied in addition to the simple association mechanisms with which psychology has been satisfied since the time of Locke. The whole determines its parts, not only their relation but their very nature. Between two wholes there is a discontinuity in kind, and any understanding must take account of their different natures, over and above a recognition of the similar elements that have entered into the two. The work in *Gestalt* psychology has been chiefly in those fields where evidence can be experimentally arrived at in the laboratory, but its implications reach far beyond the simple demonstrations which are associated with its work.

In the social sciences the importance of integration and configuration was stressed in the last generation by Wilhelm Dilthey. His primary interest was in the great philosophies and interpretations of life. Especially in *Die Typen der Weltanschauung* he analyzes part of the history of thought to show the relativity of philosophical systems. He ses them as great expressions of the variety of life, moods, *Lebensstimmungen,* integrated attitudes the fundamental categories of which cannot be resolved one into another. He argues vigorously against the assumption that any one of them can be final. He does not formulate as cultural the different attitudes he discusses, but because he takes for discussion great philosophical configurations, and historical periods like that of Frederick the Great, his work has led naturally to more and more conscious recognition of the rôle of culture.

This recognition has been given its most elaborate expression by Oswald Spengler. His *Decline of the West* takes its title not from its theme of destiny ideas, as he calls the dominant patterning of a civilization, but from a thesis which has no bearing upon our present discussion, namely, that these cultural configurations have, like any organism, a span of life they cannot overpass. This thesis of the doom of civilizations is argued on the basis of the shift of cultural centres in Western civilization and the periodicity of high cultural achievement. He buttresses this description with the analogy, which can never be more than an analogy, with the birth- and death-cycle of living organisms. Every civilization, he believes, has its lusty youth, its strong manhood, and its disintegrating senescence.

It is this latter interpretation of history which is generally identified with *The Decline of the West*, but Spengler's far more valuable and original analysis is that of contrasting configurations in Western civilization. He distinguishes two great destiny ideas: the Apollonian of the classical world and the Faustian of the modern world. Apollonian man conceived of his soul 'as a cosmos ordered in a group of excellent parts.' There was no place in his universe for will, and conflict was an evil which his philosophy decried. The idea of an inward development of the personality was alien to him, and he saw life as under the shadow of catastrophe always brutally threatening from the outside. His tragic climaxes were wanton destructions of the pleasant landscape of normal existence. The same event might have befallen another individual in the same way and with the same results.

On the other hand, the Faustian's picture of himself is as a force endlessly combating obstacles. His version of the course of individual life is that of an inner development, and the catastrophes of existence come as the inevitable culmination of his past choices and experiences. Conflict is the essence of existence. Without it personal life has no meaning, and only the more superficial values of existence can be attained. Faustian man longs for the infinite, and his art attempts to reach out toward it. Faustian and Apollonian are opposed interpretations of existence, and the values that arise in the one are alien and trivial to the other.

The civilization of the classical world was built upon the Apollonian view of life, and the modern world has been working out in all its institutions the implications of the Faustian view. Spengler glances aside also at the Egyptian, 'which saw itself as moving down a narrow and inexorably prescribed life-path to come at last before the judges of the dead,' and at the Magian with its strict dualism of body and soul. But his great subjects are the Apollonian and the Faustian, and he considers mathematics, architecture, music, and painting as expressing these two great opposed philosophies of different periods of Western civilization.

The confused impression which is given by Spengler's volumes is due only partially to the manner of presentation. To an even greater degree it is the consequence of the unresolved complexities of the civilizations with which he deals. Western civilizations, with their historical diversity, their stratification into occupations and classes, their incomparable richness of detail, are not yet well enough understood to be summarized under a couple of catchwords. Outside of certain very restricted intellectual and artistic circles, Faustian man, if he occurs, does not have his own way with our civilization. There are the strong men of action and the Babbitts as well as the Faustians, and no ethnologically satisfactory picture of modern civilization can ignore such constantly recurring types. It is quite as convincing to characterize our cultural type as thoroughly extrovert, running about in endless mundane activity, inventing, governing, and as Edward Carpenter says, 'endlessly catching its trains,' as it is to characterize it as Faustian, with a longing for the infinite.

Anthropologically speaking, Spengler's picture of world civilizations suffers from the necessity under which he labours of treating modern stratified society as if it had the essential homogeneity of a folk culture. In our present state of knowledge, the historical data of western European culture are too complex and the social differentiation too thoroughgoing to yield to the necessary analysis. However suggestive Spengler's discussion of Faustian man is for a study of European literature and philosophy and however just his emphasis upon the relativity of values, his analysis cannot be final because other equally valid pictures can be drawn. In the retrospect it may be possible to characterize adequately a great and complex whole like Western civilization, but in spite of the importance and the truth of Spengler's postulate of incommensurable destiny ideas, at the present time the attempt to interpret the Western world in terms of any one selected trait results in confusion.

It is one of the philosophical justifications for the study of primitive peoples that the facts of simpler cultures may make clear social facts that are otherwise baffling and not open to demonstration. This is nowhere more true than in the matter of the fundamental and distinctive cultural configurations that pattern existence and condition the thoughts and emotions of the individuals who participate in those cultures. The whole problem of the formation of the individual's habit-patterns under the influence of traditional custom can best be understood at the present time through the study of simpler peoples. This does not mean that the facts and processes we can discover in this way are limited in their application to primitive civilizations. Cultural configurations are as compelling and as significant in the highest and most complex societies of which we have knowledge. But the material is too intricate and too close to our eyes for us to cope with it successfully.

The understanding we need of our own cultural processes can most economically be arrived at by a détour. When the historical relations of human beings and their immediate forbears in the animal kingdom were too involved to use in establishing the fact of biological evolution, Darwin made use instead of the structure of beetles, and the process, which in the complex physical organization of the human is confused, in the simpler material was transparent in its cogency. It is the same in the study of cultural mechanisms. We need all the enlightenment we can obtain from the study of thought and behaviour as it is organized in the less complicated groups.

I have chosen three primitive civilizations to picture in some detail. A few cultures understood as coherent organizations of behaviour are more enlightening than many touched upon only at their high spots. The relation of motivations and purposes to the separate items of cultural behaviour at birth, at death, at puberty, and at marriage can never be made clear by a comprehensive survey of the world. We must hold ourselves to the less ambitious task, the many-sided understanding of a few cultures.

Herbert Applebaum

IV

Integration of Cultures—Structuralism and Functionalism

Introduction

During the period when Boas was the dominant figure in American anthropology, A.R. Radcliffe-Brown and Bronislaw Malinowski were the inspirations for British anthropology. They not only trained most of the outstanding British anthropologists but came to the United States and influenced many Americans, as well. Radcliffe-Brown taught at the University of Chicago, and Malinowski taught at Yale.

Structuralism and functionalism received its modern expression initially by a French sociologist and anthropologist, Emile Durkheim. Durkheim (1960) credited Montesquieu and Rousseau with laying the foundations of social science and with formulating the essentials of functional analysis. Durkheim's exploration of the relationship between the individual and society came with his study of suicide (1951). He correlated three patterns in suicide with three kinds of individual-social relationships.

In a work on the division of labor, Durkheim (1949) continued his investigation of social integration to show how a functional differentiation of tasks contributed to the emergence of human personality. As specialization of labor proceeds, Durkheim ascertained, the individual is drawn into a more interdependent relation with others, creating an organic bond of solidarity, linking the individual and society. The organic solidarity of complex societies contrasts with the mechanical bonding of nonindustrial societies. Persons living in societies with simple division of labor are subject to the collective restraints and will of the entire community. Deviance is punished by accusations of witchcraft or expulsion and is personal and face-to-face. In complex societies, social constraints are impersonal, bureaucratic, and the subject of laws, courts and police forces. Both organic and mechanical solidarity operates in any social order, but organic solidarity increases with functional differentiation of labor and is most characteristic of industrial societies.

Like Kroeber, Durkheim defined social phenomenon as a thing in itself, obedient to its own structural laws and independent of human beings. The units of this social reality of Durkheim's were "social facts." For Durkheim, gathering social facts should be approached without preconceptions or speculations about the basics of human nature. Durkheim argued against the Bastian notion of the psychic universals of human nature and against the method of explaining social phenomena as a construction suited to the expression of human nature. Instead, he viewed social phenomenon as a separate dimension of reality. A social fact is to be explained in terms of the efficient cause which produced it and the function which it fulfills. Social facts, in Durkheim's view, derive from social consciousness, distinct from individual consciousness. A social fact is rooted in collectively engendered sentiments and finds expression in collective representations and collective symbols. Social facts exist for a purpose, or function, and to understand them one has to see what the social fact accomplished in establishing the social order. Durkheim expresses the relation between the individual and society in this way (Durkheim 1938:102; quoted in Voget 1975:483):

When the individual has been eliminated, society alone remains. We must, then, seek the explanation of social life in the nature of society itself. It is quite evident that, since it infinitely surpasses the individual in time as well as in space, it is in a position to impose upon him ways of acting and thinking which it has consecrated with its prestige. This pressure, which is the distinctive property of social facts, is the pressure which the totality exerts on the individual.

Durkheim went on to study religion and offer a theory of its origins, based on its social function rather than on individual consciousness. He sought to find the origin of religion in the study of totemism, the most elemental and original of all religious expression (Durkheim 1947:89). After identifying totemism and, in extension, religion, he sought to relate it to the ideas, symbols, and ceremonies which religions use to express the collective sentiment.

For Durkheim, any social type contained and expressed truths concerning basic relationships, conceptualizations, and generalizations about human society. Thus, a particular social type could serve as a basic case study for all other cases of that social type. Durkheim's method, quite similiar to that of Boas, Benedict, and Mead, was a case study approach with a detailed analysis of social units. Such in-depth procedure would uncover more valid meaning than could be achieved, so Durkheim believed, than a superficial cross-cultural comparison of items wrested from their contexts, the procedure used by exponents of the comparative, evolutionary method. This procedure, the case study method, was also adopted by Malinowski, the functionalist, and Radcliffe-Brown, the structuralist. Indeed, Malinowski relied upon his most extended study, that of the Trobriand Islanders, to produce a vast literature on the nature of society; and he was criticized for overgeneralizing from that one particular case. Functionalism, which co-existed with Boasian historical-particularism, both departed and converged with the latter in method and perspective. The participant-observation method, espoused by Boas, probably reached its greatest heights and achievements in the hands of Malinowski. The integrated nature of culture, theorized by Boas, Benedict, and Lowie, was one of the firm foundations of Malinowski's functionalism, which saw society as composed of a bundle of interrelated institutions. Where Boas and Malinowski parted company was on the question of history. Malinowski saw no use for history, believing that one need not know the history of society in order to understand how it functioned. Whereas, Boas believed that history, with its unique combination of internal development, borrowings, and accidents provided an explanation for the current workings of a society or culture.

Bronislaw Malinowski was born in Poland in 1884 and died in the United States, in 1942, while he was a professor of anthropology at Yale University. Like Boas, he came to anthropology from the physical sciences. He took his doctorate in 1908 in physics and mathematics. He was inspired to take up anthropology as a career after he read James Frazer's GOLDEN BOUGH. In 1914, he went to Melanesia, where he studied the Trobriand Islanders. Thus began a career that marked him as an outstanding ethnographer and a theoretical innovator in economics, the family, psychology, law, and social organization.

Malinowski based his notion of society on institutions—the family, law, religion, economics, education, political. Institutions existed in human societies to fulfill human needs. Anything that satisfied a need had a function. Needs, social activities, purpose, function, and social institutions were intertwined in Malinowski's concept of an integrated society in which the institution was the key unit in his general theory of culture. Institutionalized people operated according to specific norms, which were fortified by social and legal sanctions. Institutionalized groups carry out mutually beneficial activities through the use of resources allocated by society to the various institutions operating within it. The institution is, for Malinowski, the primary unit of study, to which specific cultural elements—traits, customs, ideas, norms, rules—are related. The institutional context gives meaning and functional significance to individual activities. Malinowski postulated the idea that as an organized system of purposeful activities, institutions universally followed the same structure (1960:53).

Behind all institutional structures are seven basic needs, according to Malinowski—metabolism, reproduction, bodily comforts, safety, movement, growth, and health. Basic needs require human beings to form a number of primary institutions for carrying out basic activities: food getting, forming kinship groups, satisfying body comforts, survival defenses, release of motor tensions, training for institutional roles, and maintenance of health. These basic needs require a cultural form before they can be satisfied. Cultural forms take shape around four basic mechanisms: 1. technology and production (economic institution), 2. norms (legal institution), 3. knowledge and skills (educational institution), and 4. power (political institution). The various institutions and the activities carried out within them also served to foster integration of a culture, based on seven categories of integration—reproduction, territorial, physiological, voluntary associations, occupational and professional, rank and status, and community unity. Each of these last principles can be found in all societies but with different emphasis and different institutional arrangements.

Malinowski's categories were broad and far-reaching, so that he touched upon elements that were found in the perspectives of Durkheim, Boas, Freud, Radcliffe-Brown, Benedict, and Mead. By basing himself upon physiological and biopsychological needs, Malinowski lent a universal character to his theory of culture. These needs could not be satisfied directly but only through cultural institutions, which then permitted Malinowski to identify specific, unique, and particular forms of cultural and societal formations set up to satisfy these needs. And functionalism is the way each institution operates in its own particularly cultural way to fulfill these human needs. Thus, there is both the collective and individual expression of human culture in Malinowski functionalism.

For Malinowski, culture was raised on human needs and served those needs. This was why culture existed. Social structuralists, on the other hand, viewed humans as once removed from primary survival requirements. Survival needs were transmuted into social needs; hence, analysis should begin and center on the functional needs of society and not that of the individual. This issue, does culture exist for humans or do humans exist for culture? is a dichotomy and an issue of debate which continues into the present period, as will be seen later in this book.

It was Malinowski's judgment that, if the analysis of culture were to contribute anything, it was to find a way to unite the individual and the group in a theoretical context. This was the role of functionalism. The individual and society were at opposite ends but were not separated. Individuals supplied a common human biopsychological make up and a personal concern for their own activities. Society supplied traditional beliefs, customs, norms, sanctions, and material apparatus which individuals must cope with and use in cooperation with other human beings. Concern for analysis of individuals meant concern with drive, feeling, and cognitive awareness of each individual's share of his or her heritage. Through uniformity of their mental and emotional processes, each person contributes a need impulse to institutions. It is this very individual need which limits the number of institutions and allows a measure of typing of social behavior, despite the infinite variations in beliefs, ideas, and opinions.

In Malinowski's theory, the linkage between biological needs and cultural institutions forges a double bond which limits individual freedom and variation. Biology leads to some determinism based on the necessities for survival. But, since cultural instrumentalities are required for satisfaction of needs, there is also some cultural determinism, based on traditional customs and rules. Biological and cultural determinism are greater wherever technological efficiency is lower, as in nonindustrial cultures. Malinowski recognized that, while culture molded the individual, many individuals evaded the press of culture. He had no deep theoretical interest in free will or the individual versus culture. He was fundamentally concerned with forces operating to produce the uniformity essential to the maintenance of social and cultural systems. Thus, functionalism has come to be associated with equilibrium theory, since it focuses on those aspects of a society which foster continuity and permanence. That is why when the world was undergoing rapid changes after World War II, there was a decline in interest in functionalism, since it did not address the issues of dynamics and change.

Alfred R. Radcliffe-Brown was born in England in 1881 and died in 1955. He attended Cambridge where W.H.R. Rivers was one of his teachers. He was influenced to some degree by James Frazer but to a larger extent by Comte and Durkheim. He did major fieldwork in the Andaman Islands between 1906 and 1908. Later, he did fieldwork in Australia between 1910 and 1912. His fieldwork was more survey oriented than participant observation.

Radcliffe-Brown's orientation was the study of social structure which could yield nomothetic laws governing social behavior. He sought to determine how the parts, institutions, roles, and other cultural traits maintained the equilibrium and wholeness of a society. He was attracted to Durkheim's notion of the integrated society and Durkheim's argument that social facts required explanation in terms of social laws, not in the psychology of individuals. In this respect, he differed from Malinowski, who related his concept of society as dealing ultimately with the needs of individuals and their bio-psychological underpinnings. Radcliffe-Brown was emphatic in his differentiation from Malinowski's functionalism (see Chapter 9). He was also emphatic in his view that anthropology was a science and that it should seek the discovery of laws and generalizations based on the comparative study of different cultures. Thus, he separated himself from Boasian anthropology, as he had from the Malinowskian viewpoint.

Radcliffe-Brown used the analogy of society as an organism. In Chapter 9, he states that social structures are like organisms in that they are not only made up of individual parts, but, like the cells in a human organism, the parts are united as the result of a particular structure. He adds, "So the social phenomena which we observe in any human society are not the immediate result of the nature of individual human beings, but are the result of the social structure by which they are united" (1952:190–191).

Radcliffe-Brown pointed to a distinction between functional consistency and logical consistency as important for an understanding of the nature of social integration. Logical consistency is associated with the coherence of values, norms, and ideas. Functional consistency involves the coherence of institutions and social units. Functional consistency was considered by Radcliffe-Brown to be one of the laws of social structure. It involved the establishment of a formal structure with a set of relationships operating between individuals and groups. Coherence within the structural system is brought about through the education, training, and acculturation of individuals to accept certain rights and duties. Legal, moral, and religious sanctions are used to preserve the integrity of the structure. The conformity of societies to general functional requirements, or laws of social survival, underline the adaptive quality of human society.

Rather than looking for the rise and fall of civilizations, or conflicts and contradictions in a society, Radcliffe-Brown stressed the positive forces which assured social harmony, growth, and survival. Such was also the emphasis of Malinowski. Exploring the structuring of society highlighted the positive and integrative processes of social life, rather than seeds of destruction that might be embedded in the system.

Conflicts of interest and contradictions exist in any social system, but they can be accommodated by rules that minimize tensions. Thus, Radcliffe-Brown explained the "joking relationship" in societies as an example of the way social conflict could be stabilized by ritualization of aggression (1952:90–105). Through a system of ritualized hostility and disrespect, the joking relationship draws attention to social nonconformity and allows hostility to be played out, without threatening the formal structure. The joking relationship relaxes tensions accompanying formal relationships by bringing into play social rules which require a friendly demeanor over the underlying hostility and a system of mutual obligations despite the personal conflict. Anyone who has observed or been involved in joshing and friendly insults in a work group or a street gang would recognize this kind of behavior.

Radcliffe-Brown presented a theoretical portrait of society as unified by two kinds of structural features. First are those laws to which all societies conform in their structural and functional consistency, the use of moral and jural obligations to regulate social relationships, and the notion of corporate continuity. Second are the structural principles by which individual societies achieve these larger, broader first principles. Some structural laws, like the formation of dyadic relationships, Radcliffe-Brown considered universal. Others, like the lineage principle, he considered specific for certain types of societies. Thus, this theoretical system contained both the broad principles underlying all societies and the stylistic distinction which differentiated one society from another. The effects of social functions permeated both subordinate and higher levels of organization, with the higher levels supplying the principles by which the different levels were integrated.

The thrust of Radcliffe-Brown's perspective on society was to look at the overall morphology, the skeleton of society. It was that aspect of society which was lasting, regardless of those who entered and left the institutions which made it up. Understanding a social system, for Radcliffe-Brown, was understanding its structural principles. Once structure was determined, then one could relate the contribution of the parts to the system in accordance with its laws and structural principles. This viewpoint was reminiscent of the Gestalt view which Benedict employed.

The structural analysis proposed by Radcliffe-Brown, with its focus on integrative processes, tends to restrict analysis to description and those aspects of society which give it consistency. In such a view, one could describe relationships stemming from structural principles, but causal explanations proved to be elusive. The unit of study, function, dissolved the need for causal determinations, since the parts of the structure were seen as interrelated and reciprocal, and final cause was ultimately located in the totality of needs associated with the entire social structure. Covariation could be established by statistical methods, but it did not explain the nature nor the cause of the relationship. The issue of variation and change continued to nag at the structural/functionalists, and, when their analysis was no longer in step with rapidly changing social conditions, social scientists, including anthropologists, sought other theoretical paths.

Bronislaw Malinowski

8. The Group and the Individual in Functional Analysis

Funtionalism differs from other sociological theories more definitely, perhaps, in its conception and definition of the individual than in any other respect.[1] The functionalist includes in his analysis not merely the emotional as well as the intellectual side of mental processes, but also insists that man in his full biological reality has to be drawn into our analysis of culture. The bodily needs and environmental influences, and the cultural reactions to them, have thus to be studied side by side. . . .

In this brief preamble we have already insisted that the individual must be studied as a biological reality. We have indicated that the physical world must be part of our analysis, both as the natural milieu and as the body of tools and commodities produced by man. We have pointed out that individuals never cope with, or move within, their environment in isolation, but in organized groups, and that organization is expressed in traditional charters, which are symbolic in essence.

The Individual Organism under Conditions of Culture

Taking man as a biological entity it is clear that certain minima of conditions can be laid down which are indispensable to the personal welfare of the individual and to the continuation of the group. All human beings have to be nourished, they have to reproduce, and they require the maintenance of certain physical conditions: ventilation, temperature within a definite range, a sheltered and dry place to rest, and safety from the hostile forces of nature, of animals, and of man. The physiological working of each individual organism implies the intake of food and of oxygen, occasional movement, and relaxation in sleep and recreation. The process of growth in man necessitates protection and guidance in its early stages and, later on, specific training.

We have listed here some of the essential conditions to which cultural activity, whether individual or collective, has instrumentally to conform.

It is well to recall that these are only minimum conditions—the very manner in which they are satisfied in culture imposes certain additional requirements. These constitute new needs, which in turn have to be satisfied. The primary—that is, the biological—wants of the human organism are not satisfied naturally by direct contact of the individual organism with the physical environment. Not only does the individual depend on the group in whatever he achieves and whatever he obtains, but the group and all its individual members depend on the development of a material outfit, which in its essence is an addition to the human anatomy, and which entails corresponding modifications of human physiology.

In order to present our argument in a synoptic manner, let us concisely list in Column A of Table 8-1 the basic needs of the individual. Thus "Nutrition (metabolism)" indicates not only the need for a supply of food and of oxygen, but also the conditions under which food can be prepared, eaten, digested, and the sanitary arrangements which this implies. "Reproduction" obviously means that the sexual urges of man and woman have to be satisfied, and the continuity of the group maintained. The entry "Bodily comforts" indicates that the human organism can be active and effective only within certain ranges of temperature; that it must be sheltered from dampness and drafts; that it must be given opportunities for rest and sleep. "Safety" again refers to all the dangers lurking in the natural environment, both for civilized and primitive: earthquakes and tidal wave, snowstorms and excessive insolation; it also indicates the need of protection from dangerous animals and human foes. "Relaxation" implies the need of the human organism for a rhythm of work by day and sleep at night, of intensive bodily exercise and rest, of seasons of recreation alternating with periods of practical activity. The entry "Movement" declares that human beings must have regular exercise of muscles and nervous system. "Growth" indicates the fact that the development of the human organism is culturally directed and redefined from infancy into ripe age.

It is clear that the understanding of any one of these entries of Column A brings us down immediately to the analysis of the individual organism. We see that any lack of satisfaction in any one of the basic needs must necessarily imply at least temporary maladjustment. In more pronounced forms, nonsatisfaction entails ill-health and decay through malnutrition, exposure to heat or cold, to sun or moisture; or destruction by natural forces, animals, or man. Psychologically the basic needs are expressed in drives, desires, or emotions, which move the organism to the satisfaction of each need through systems or linked reflexes.

The science of culture, however, is concerned not with the raw materi-

Bronislaw Malinowski

al of anatomical and physiological endowment in the individual, but with the manner in which this endowment is modified by social influences. When we inquire how the bodily needs are satisfied under conditions of culture, we find the systems of direct response to bodily needs which are listed in Column B. And here we can see at once the complete dependence of the individual upon the group: each of these cultural responses is dependent upon organized collective activities, which are carried on according to a traditional scheme, and in which human beings not merely co-operate with one another but continue the achievements, inventions, devices, and theories inherited from previous generations. . . .

Table 8–1
Synoptic Survey of Biological and Derived
Needs and Their Satisfaction in Culture

A	B	C	D	E	F
Basic Needs (Individual)	Direct Responses (Organized, i.e., Collective)	Instrumental Needs	Responses to Instrumental Needs	Symbolic and Integrative Needs	Systems of Thought and Faith
Nutrition (metabolism	Commissariat	Renewal of cultural apparatus	Economics	Transmission of experience by means of precise, consistent principles	Knowledge
Reproduction	Marriage and family				
Bodily comforts	Domicile and dress	Charters of behavior and their sanctions	Social control		
Safety	Protection and defense			Means of intellectual, emotional, and pragmatic control of destiny and chance	Magic Religion

Table 8–1, Cont.

A	B	C	D	E	F
Basic Needs (Individual)	Direct Responses (Organized, i.e., Collective)	Instrumental Needs	Responses to Instrumental Needs	Symbolic and Integrative Needs	Systems of Thought and Faith
Relaxation	Systems of play and repose	Renewal of personnel	Education		
Movement	Set activities and systems of communication				
Growth	Training and apprenticeship	Organization of force and compulsion	Political organization	Communal rhythm of recreation, exercise, and rest	Art sports Games Ceremonial

The Instrumental Imperatives of Culture

In glancing at our chart and comparing Columns A and B, we recognize that the first represents the biological needs of the individual organism which must be satisfied in every culture. Column B describes briefly the cultural responses to each of these needs. Culture thus appears first and foremost as a vast instrumental reality—the body of implements and commodities, charters of social organization, ideas and customs, beliefs and values—all of which allow man to satisfy his biological requirements through co-operation and within an environment refashioned and readjusted. The human organism, however, itself becomes modified in the process and readjusted to the type of situation provided by culture. In this sense culture is also a vast conditioning apparatus, which through training, the imparting of skills, the teaching of morals, and the development of tastes amalgamates the raw material of human physiology and anatomy with external elements, and through this supplements the bodily equipment and conditions the physiological processes. Culture thus produces individuals whose behavior cannot be understood by the study of anatomy and physiology alone, but has to be studied through the analysis of cultural determinism—that is, the processes of conditioning and molding. At the same time we see that from the very outset the existence of groups—that is, of individuals organized for co-operation and cultural give and take—is made indispensable by culture.

Notes

1. When I speak of "functionalism" here I mean the brand which I have produced and am cultivating myself. My friend, Professor R. H. Lowie of Berkeley, has in his last book, *The History of Ethnological Theory* (1937), introduced the distinction between "pure" and "tempered" functionalism—my brand being the pure one. Usually Professor Radcliffe-Brown's name is linked with mine as a representative of the functional school. Here the distinction between "plain" and "hyphenated" functionalism might be introduced. Professor Lowie has, in my opinion, completely misunderstood the essence of "pure" functionalism. The substance of this article may serve as a corrective. Professor Radcliffe-Brown is, as far as I can see, still developing and deepening the views of the French sociological school. He thus has to neglect the individual and disregard biology. In this article functionalism "plain and pure" will be briefly outlined with special reference to the problem of the group and the individual.

Alfred R. Radcliffe-Brown

9. On Social Structure[1]

It has been suggested to me by some of my friends that I should use this occasion to offer some remarks about my own point of view in social anthropology; and since in my teaching, beginning at Cambridge and at the London School of Economics thirty years ago, I have consistently emphasised the importance of the study of social structure, the suggestion made to me was that I should say something on that subject.

I hope you will pardon me if I begin with a note of personal explanation. I have been described on more than one occasion as belonging to something called the 'Functional School of Social Anthropology' and even as being its leader, or one of its leaders. This Functional School does not really exist; it is a myth invented by Professor Malinowski. He has explained how, to quote his own words, 'the magnificent title of the Functional School of Anthropology has been bestowed by myself, in a way on myself, and to a large extent out of my own sense of irresponsibility'. Professor Malinowski's irresponsibility has had unfortunate results, since it has spread over anthropology a dense fog of discussion about 'functionalism'. Professor Lowie has announced that the leading, though not the only, exponent of functionalism in the nineteenth century was Professor Franz Boas. I do not think that there is any sense, other than the purely chronological one, in which I can be said to be either the follower of Professor Boas or the predecessor of Professor Malinowski. The statement that I am a 'functionalist' would seem to me to convey no definite meaning.

There is no place in natural science for 'schools' in this sense, and I regard social anthropology as a branch of natural science. Each scientist starts from the work of his predecessors, finds problems which he believes to be significant, and by observation and reasoning endeavours to make some contribution to a growing body of theory. Co-operation amongst scientists results from the fact that they are working on the same or related problems. Such co-operation does not result in the formation of schools, in the sense in which there are schools of philosophy or of painting. There is no place for othodoxies and heterodoxies in science. Nothing is more pernicious in science than attempts to establish adherence to doctrines. All that a teacher can do is to assist the student in learning to understand and use the scientific method. It is not his business to make disciples.

I conceive of social anthropology as the theoretical natural science of human society, that is, the investigation of social phenomena by methods essentially similar to those used in the physical and biological sciences. I am quite willing to call the subject 'comparative sociology', if anyone so wishes. It is the subject itself, and not the name, that is important. As you know, there are some ethnologists or anthropologists who hold that it is not possible, or at least not profitable, to apply to social phenomena the theoretical methods of natural science. For these persons social anthropology, as I have defined it, is something that does not, and never will, exist. For them, of course, my remarks will have no meaning, or at least not the meaning I intend them to have.

While I have defined social anthropology as the study of human society, there are some who define it as the study of culture. It might perhaps be thought that this difference of definition is of minor importance. Actually it leads to two different kinds of study, between which it is hardly possible to obtain agreement in the formulation of problems.

For a preliminary definition of social phenomena it seems sufficiently clear that what we have to deal with are relations of association between individual organisms. In a hive of bees there are the relations of association of the queen, the workers and the drones. There is the association of animals in a herd, of a mother-cat and her kittens. These are social phenomena; I do not suppose that anyone will call them cultural phenomena. In anthropology, of course, we are only concerned with human beings, and in social anthropology, as I define it, what we have to investigate are the forms of association to be found amongst human beings.

Let us consider what are the concrete, observable facts with which the social anthropologist is concerned. If we set out to study, for example, the aboriginal inhabitants of a part of Australia, we find a certain number of individual human beings in a certain natural environment. We can observe the acts of behaviour of these individuals, including, of course, their acts of speech, and the material products of past actions. We do not observe a 'culture', since that word denotes, not any concrete reality, but an abstraction, and as it is commonly used a vague abstraction. But direct observation does reveal to us that these human beings are connected by a complex network of social relations. I use the term 'social structure' to denote this network of actually existing relations. It is this that I regard it as my business to study if I am working, not as an ethnologist or psychologist, but as a social anthropologist. I do not mean that the study of social structure is the whole of social anthropology, but I do regard it as being in a very important sense the most fundamental part of the science.

My view of natural science is that it is the systematic investigation of the structure of the universe as it is revealed to us through our senses. There are certain important separate branches of science, each of which deals with a certain class or kind of structures, the aim being to discover the characteristics of all structures of that kind. So atomic physics deals with the structure of atoms, chemistry with the structure of molecules, crystallography and colloidal chemistry with the structure of crystals and colloids, and anatomy and physiology with the structures of organisms. There is, therefore, I suggest, place for a branch of natural science which will have for its task the discovery of the general characteristics of those social structures of which the component units are human beings.

Social phenomena constitute a distinct class of natural phenomena. They are all, in one way or another, connected with the existence of social structures, either being implied in or resulting from them. Social structures are just as real as are individual organisms. A complex organism is a collection of living cells and interstitial fluids arranged in a certain structure; and a living cell is similarly a structural arrangement of complex molecules. The physiological and psychological phenomena that we observe in the lives of organisms are not simply the result of the nature of the constituent molecules or atoms of which the organism is built up, but are the result of the structure in which they are united. So also the social phenomena which we observe in any human society are not the immediate result of the nature of individual human beings, but are the result of the social structure by which they are united.

It should be noted that to say we are studying social structures is not exactly the same thing as saying that we study social relations, which is how some sociologists define their subject. A particular social relation between two persons (unless they be Adam and Eve in the Garden of Eden) exists only as part of a wide network of social relations, involving many other persons, and it is this network which I regard as the object of our investigations.

I am aware, of course, that the term 'social structure' is used in a number of different senses, some of them very vague. This is unfortunately true of many other terms commonly used by anthropologists. The choice of terms and their definitions is a matter of scientific convenience, but one of the characteristics of a science as soon as it has passed the first formative period is the existence of technical terms which are used in the same precise meaning by all the students of that science. By this test, I regret to say, social anthropology reveals itself as not yet a formed science. One has therefore to select for oneself, for certain terms, definitions which seem to be the most convenient for the purpose of scientific analysis.

There are some anthropologists who use the term social structure to refer only to persistent social groups, such as nations, tribes and clans, which retain their continuity, their identity as individual groups, in spite of changes in their membership. Dr. Evans-Pritchard, in his recent admirable book on the Nuer, prefers to use the term social structure in this sense. Certainly the existence of such persistent social groups is an exceedingly important aspect of structure. But I find it more useful to include under the term social structure a good deal more than this.

In the first place, I regard as a part of the social structure all social relations of person to person. For example, the kinship structure of any society consists of a number of such dyadic relations, as between a father and son, or a mother's brother and his sister's son. In an Australian tribe the whole social structure is based on a network of such relations of person to person, established through genealogical connections.

Secondly, I include under social structure the differentiation of individuals and of classes by their social role. The differential social positions of men and women, of chiefs and commoners, of employers and employees, are just as much determinants of social relations as belonging to different clans or different nations.

In the study of social structure the concrete reality with which we are concerned is the set of actually existing relations, at a given moment of time, which link together certain human beings. It is on this that we can make direct observations. But it is not this that we attempt to describe in its particularity. Science (as distinguished from history or biography) is not concerned with the particular, the unique, but only with the general, with kinds, with events which recur. The actual relations of Tom, Dick and Harry or the behaviour of Jack and Jill may go down in our field note-books and may provide illustrations for a general description. But what we need for scientific purposes is an account of the form of the structure. For example, if in an Australian tribe I observe in a number of instances the behaviour towards one another of persons who stand in the relation of mother's brother and sister's son, it is in order that I may be able to record as precisely as possible the general or normal form of this relationship, abstracted from the variations of particular instances, though taking account of those variations.

This important distinction, between structure as an actually existing concrete reality, to be directly observed, and structural form, as what the field-worker describes, may be made clearer perhaps by a consideration of the continuity of social structure through time, a continuity which is not static like that of a building, but a dynamic continuity, like that of the organic structure of a living body. Throughout the life of an organism its structure is being constantly renewed; and similarly the social life constantly renews the social structure. Thus the actual relations of persons and groups of persons change from year to year, or even from day to day. New members come into a community by birth or immigration; others go out of it by death or emigration. There are marriages and divorces. Friends may become enemies, or enemies may make peace and become friends. But while the actual structure changes in this way, the general structural form may remain relatively constant over a longer or shorter period of time. Thus if I visit a relatively stable community and revisit it after an interval of ten years, I shall find that many of its members have died and others have been born; the members who still survive are now ten years older and their relations to one another may have changed in many ways. Yet I may find that the kinds of relations that I can observe are very little different from those observed ten years before. The structural form has changed little.

But, on the other hand, the structural form may change, sometimes gradually, sometimes with relative suddenness, as in revolutions and military conquests. But even in the most revolutionary changes some continuity of structure is maintained.

I must say a few words about the spatial aspect of social structure. It is rarely that we find a community that is absolutely isolated, having no outside contact. At the present moment of history, the network of social relations spreads over the whole world, without any absolute solution of continuity anywhere. This gives rise to a difficulty which I do not think that sociologists have really faced, the difficulty of defining what is meant by the term 'a society'. They do commonly talk of societies as if they were distinguishable, discrete entities, as, for example, when we are told that a society is an organism. Is the British Empire a society or a collection of societies? Is a Chinese village a society, or is it merely a fragment of the Republic of China?

If we say that our subject is the study and comparison of human societies, we ought to be able to say what are the unit entities with which we are concerned.

If we take any convenient locality of a suitable size, we can study the structural system as it appears in and from that region, i.e. the network of relations connecting the inhabitants amongst themselves and with the people of other regions. We can thus observe, describe, and compare the systems of social structure of as many localities as we wish. To illustrate what I mean, I may refer to two recent studies from the University of

Chicago, one of a Japanese village, Suye Mura, by Dr. John Embree, and the other of a French Canadian community, St. Denis, by Dr. Horace Miner.

Closely connected with this conception of social structure is the conception of 'social personality' as the position occupied by a human being in a social structure, the complex formed by all his social relations with others. Every human being living in society is two things: he is an individual and also a person. As an individual, he is a biological organism, a collection of a vast number of molecules organised in a complex structure, within which, as long as it persists, there occur physiological and psychological actions and reactions, processes and changes. Human beings as individuals are objects of study for physiologists and psychologists. The human being as a person is a complex of social relationships. He is a citizen of England, a husband and a father, a bricklayer, a member of a particular Methodist congregation, a voter in a certain constituency, a member of his trade union, an adherent of the Labour Party, and so on. Note that each of these descriptions refers to a social relationship, or to a place in a social structure. Note also that a social personality is something that changes during the course of the life of the person. As a person, the human being is the object of study for the social anthropologist. We cannot study persons except in terms of social structure, nor can we study social structure except in terms of the persons who are the units of which it is composed.

If you tell me that an individual and a person are after all really the same thing, I would remind you of the Christian creed. God is three persons, but to say that He is three individuals is to be guilty of a heresy for which men have been put to death. Yet the failure to distinguish individual and person is not merely a heresy in religion; it is worse than that; it is a source of confusion in science.

I have now sufficiently defined, I hope, the subject-matter of what I regard as an extremely important branch of social anthropology. The method to be adopted follows immediately from this definition. It must combine with the intensive study of single societies (i.e. of the structural systems observable in particular communities) the systematic comparison of many societies (or structural systems of different types). The use of comparison is indispensable. The study of a single society may provide materials for comparative study, or it may afford occasion for hypotheses, which then need to be tested by reference to other societies; it cannot give demonstrated results.

Our first task, of course, is to learn as much as we can about the varieties, or diversities, of structural systems. This requires field research. Many writers of ethnographical descriptions do not attempt to give us any systematic account of the social structure. But a few social anthropologists, here and in America, do recognise the importance of such data and their work is providing us with a steadily growing body of material for our study. Moreover, their researches are no longer confined to what are called 'primitive' societies, but extend to communities in such regions as Sicily, Ireland, Japan, Canada and the United States.

If we are to have a real comparative morphology of societies, however, we must aim at building up some sort of classification of types of structural systems. That is a complex and difficult task, to which I have myself devoted attention for thirty years. It is the kind of task that needs the co-operation of a number of students and I think I can number on my fingers those who are actively interested in it at the present time. Nevertheless, I believe some progress is being made. Such work, however, does not produce spectacular results and a book on the subject would certainly not be an anthropological best-seller.

We should remember that chemistry and biology did not become fully formed sciences until considerable progress had been made with the systematic classification of the things they were dealing with, substances in the one instance and plants and animals in the other.

Besides this morphological study, consisting in the definition, comparison and classification of diverse structural systems, there is a physiological study. The problem here is: How do structural systems persist? What are the mechanisms which maintain a network of social relations in existence, and how do they work? In using the terms morphology and physiology, I may seem to be returning to the analogy between society and organism which was so popular with medieval philosophers, was taken over and often misused by nineteenth century sociologists, and is completely rejected by many modern writers. But analogies, properly used, are important aids to scientific thinking and there is a real and significant analogy between organic structure and social structure.

In what I am thus calling social physiology we are concerned not only with social structure, but with every kind of social phenomenon. Morals, law, etiquette, religion, government, and education are all parts of the complex mechanism by which a social structure exists and persists. If we take up the structural point of view, we study these things, not in abstraction or isolation, but in their direct and indirect relations to social structure, i.e. with reference to the way in which they depend upon, or affect, the social relations between persons and groups of persons. I cannot do more here than offer a few brief illustrations of what this means.

Let us first consider the study of language. A language is a connected set of speech usages observed within a defined speech-community. The existence of speech-communities and their sizes are features of social structure. There is, therfore, a certain very general relation between social structure and language. But if we consider the special characteristics of a particular language—its phonology, its morphology and even to a great extent its vocabulary—there is no direct connection of either one-sided or mutual determination between these and the special characteristics of the social structure of the community within which the language is spoken. We can easily conceive that two societies might have very similar forms of social structure and very different kinds of language, or vice versa. The coincidence of a particular form of social structure and a particular language in a given community is always the result of historical accident. There may, of course, be certain indirect, remote interactions between social structure and language, but these would seem to be of minor importance. Thus the general comparative study of languages can be profitably carried out as a relatively independent branch of science, in which the language is considered in abstraction from the social structure of the community in which it is spoken.

But, on the other hand, there are certain features of linguistic history which are specifically connected with social structure. As structural phenomena may be instanced the process by which Latin, from being the language of the small region of Latium, became the language of a considerable part of Europe, displacing the other Italic languages, Etruscan, and many Celtic languages; and the subsequent reverse process by which Latin split up into a number of diverse local forms of speech, which ultimately became the various Romance languages of today.

Thus the spread of language, the unification of a number of separate communities into a single speech-community and the reverse process of subdivision into different speech-communities, are phenomena of social structure. So also are those instances in which, in societies having a class structure, there are differences of speech usage in different classes.

I have considered language first, because linguistics is, I think, the branch of social anthropology which can be most profitably studied without reference to social structure. There is a reason for this. The set of speech usages which constitute a language does form a system, and systems of this kind can be compared in order to discover their common general, or abstract, characters, the determination of which can give us laws, which will be specifically laws of linguistics.

Let us consider very briefly certain other branches of social anthropology and their relation to the study of social structure. If we take the social life of a local community over a period, let us say a year, we can observe a certain sum total of activities carried out by the persons who compose it. We can also observe a certain apportionment of these activities, one person doing certain things, another doing others. This apportionment of activities, equivalent to what is sometimes called the social division of labour, is an important feature of the social structure. Now activities are carried out because they provide some sort of 'gratification', as I propose to call it, and the characteristic feature of social life is that activities of certain persons provide gratifications for other persons. In a simple instance, when an Australian blackfellow goes hunting, he provides meat, not only for himself, but for his wife and children and also for other relatives to whom it is his duty to give meat when he has it. Thus in any society there is not only an apportionment of activities, but also an apportionment of the gratifications resulting therefrom, and some sort of social machinery, relatively simple or, sometimes, highly complex, by which the system works.

It is this machinery, or certain aspects of it, that constitutes the special subject-matter studied by the economists. They concern themselves with what kinds and quantities of goods are produced, how they are distributed (i.e. their flow from person to person, or region to region), and the way in which they are disposed of. Thus what are called economic institutions are extensively studied in more or less complete abstraction from the rest of the social system. This method does undoubtedly provide useful results, particularly in the study of complex modern societies. Its weaknesses become apparent as soon as we attempt to apply it to the exchange of goods in what are called primitive societies.

The economic machinery of a society appears in quite a new light if it is studied in relation to the social structure. The exchange of goods and services is dependent upon, is the result of, and at the same time is a means of maintaining a certain structure, a network of relations between persons and collections of persons. For the economists and politicians of Canada the potlatch of the Indians of the north-west of America was simply wasteful foolishness and it was therefore forbidden. For the anthropologist it was the machinery for maintaining a social structure of lineages, clans and moities, with which was combined an arrangement of rank defined by privileges.

Any full understanding of the economic institutions of human societies requires that they should be studied from two angles. From one of these the economic system is viewed as the mechanism by which goods of various kinds and in various quantities are produced, transported and transferred, and utilised. From the other the economic system is a set of relations between persons and groups which maintains, and is maintained by, this exchange or circulation of goods and services. From the latter point of view, the study of the economic life of societies takes its place as part of the general study of social structure.

Social relations are only observed, and can only be described, by reference to the reciprocal behaviour of the persons related. The form of a social structure has therefore to be described by the patterns of behaviour to which individuals and groups conform in their dealings with one another. These patterns are partially formulated in rules which, in our own society, we distinguish as rules of etiquette, of morals and of law. Rules, of course, only exist in their recognition by the members of the society; either in their verbal recognition, when they are stated as rules, or in their observance in behaviour. These two modes of recognition, as every field-worker knows, are not the same thing and both have to be taken into account.

If I say that in any society the rules of etiquette, morals and law are part of the mechanism by which a certain set of social relations is maintained in existence, this statement will, I suppose, be greeted as a truism. But it is one of those truisms which many writers on human society verbally accept and yet ignore in theoretical discussions, or in their descriptive analyses. The point is not that rules exist in every society, but that what we need to know for a scientific understanding is just how these things work in general and in particular instances.

Let us consider, for example, the study of law. If you examine the literature on jurisprudence you will find that legal institutions are studied for the most part in more or less complete abstraction from the rest of the social system of which they are a part. This is doubtless the most convenient method for lawyers in their professional studies. But for any scientific investigation of the nature of law it is insufficient. The data with which a scientist must deal are events which occur and can be observed. In the field of law, the events which the social scientist can observe and thus take as his data are the proceedings that take place in courts of justice. These are the reality, and for the social anthropologist they are the mechanism or process by which certain definable social relations between persons and groups are restored, maintained or modified. Law is a part of the machinery by which a certain social structure is maintained. The system of laws of a particular society can only be fully understood if it is studied in relation to the social structure, and inversely the understanding of the social structure requires, amongst other things, a systematic study of the legal institutions.

I have talked about social relations, but I have not so far offered you a precise definition. A social relation exists between two or more individual organisms when there is some adjustment of their respective interests, by convergence of interest, or by limitation of conflicts that might arise from divergence of interests. I use the term 'interest' here in the widest possible sense, to refer to all behaviour that we regard as purposive. To speak of an interest implies a subject and an object and a relation between them. Whenever we say that a subject has a certain interest in an object we can state the same thing by saying that the object has a certain value for the subject. Interest and value are correlative terms, which refer to the two sides of an asymmetrical relation.

Thus the study of social structure leads immediately to the study of interests or values as the determinants of social relations. A social relation does not result from similarity of interests, but rests either on the mutual interest of persons in one another, or on one or more common interests, or on a combination of both of these. The simplest form of social solidarity is where two persons are both interested in bringing about a certain result and co-operate to that end. When two or more persons have a *common interest* in an object, that object can be said to have a *social value* for the persons thus associated. If, then, practically all the members of a society have an interest in the observance of the laws, we can say that the law has a social value. The study of social values in this sense is therefore a part of the study of social structure.

It was from this point of view that in an early work I approached the study of what can conveniently be called ritual values, i.e. the values expressed in rites and myths. It is perhaps again a truism to say that religion is the cement which holds society together. But for a scientific understanding we need to know just how it does this, and that is a subject for lengthy investigations in many different forms of society.

As a last example let me mention the study of magic and witchcraft, on which there is an extensive anthropological literature. I would point to Dr. Evans-Pritchard's work on the Zande as an illuminating example of what can be done when these things are systematically investigated in terms of the part they play in the social relations of the members of a community.

From the point of view that I have attempted briefly to describe, social institutions, in the sense of standardised modes of behaviour, constitute the machinery by which a social structure, a network of social relations, maintains its existence and its continuity. I hesitate to use the term 'function', which in recent years has been so much used and misused in a multitude of meanings, many of them very vague. Instead of being used, as scientific terms ought to be, to assist in making distinctions, it is now used to confuse things that ought to be distinguished. For it is often employed in place of the more ordinary words 'use' 'purpose', and 'meaning'. It seems to me more convenient and sensible, as well as more scholarly, to speak of the use or uses of an axe or digging stick, the meaning of a word or symbol, the purpose of an act of legislation, rather than to use the word function for these various things. 'Function' has been a very useful technical term in physiology and by analogy with its use in that science it would be a very convenient means of expressing an important concept in social science. As I have been accustomed to use the word, following Durkheim and others, I would define the social function of a socially standardised mode of activity, or mode of thought, as its relation to the social structure to the existence and continuity of which it makes some contribution. Analogously, in a living organism, the physiological function of the beating of the heart, or the secretion of gastric juices, is its relation to the organic structure to the existence or continuity of which it makes its contribution. It is in this sense that I am interested in such things as the social function of the punishment of crime, or the social function of the totemic rites of Australian tribes, or of the funeral rites of the Andaman Islanders. But this is not what either Professor Malinowski or Professor Lowie means by functional anthropology.

Besides these two divisions of the study of social structure, which I have called social morphology and social physiology, there is a third, the investigation of the processes by which social structures change, of how new forms of structures come into existence. Studies of social change in the non-literate societies have necessarily been almost entirely confined to one special kind of process of change, the modification of the social life under the influence or domination of European invaders or conquerors.

It has recently become the fashion amongst some anthropologists to treat changes of this kind in terms of what is called 'culture contact'. By that term we can understand the one-sided or two-sided effects of interaction between two societies, groups, classes or regions having different forms of social life, different institutions, usages and ideas. Thus in the eighteenth century there was an important exchange of ideas between France and Great Britain, and in the nineteenth century there was a marked influence of German thought on both France and England. Such interactions are, of course, a constant feature of social life, but they need not necessarily involve any marked change of social structure.

The changes that are taking place in the non-literate peoples of Africa are of a very different kind. Let us consider an African colony or possession of a European nation. There is a region that was formerly inhabited by Africans with their own social structure. Europeans, by peaceful or forceful means, establish control over the region, under what we call a 'colonial' regime. A new social structure comes into existence and then undergoes development. The population now includes a certain number of Europeans—government officials, missionaries, traders and in some instances settlers. The social life of the region is no longer simply a process depending on the relations and interactions of the native peoples. There grows up a new political and economic structure in which the Europeans, even though few in numbers, exercise dominating influence. Europeans and Africans constitute different classes within the new structure, with different languages, different customs and modes of life, and different sets of ideas and values. A convenient term for societies of this kind would be 'composite' societies; the term 'plural' societies has also been suggested. A complex example of a composite society is provided by the Union of South Africa with its single political and economic structure and a population including English-speaking and Afrikaans-speaking peoples of European descent, the so-called 'coloured people' of the Cape Province, progeny of Dutch and Hottentots, the remaining Hottentots, the 'Malays' of Cape Town, descendants of persons from the Malay Archipelago, Hindus and Mohammedans from India and their descendants, and a number of Bantu tribes who constitute the majority of the population of the Union taken as a whole.

The study of composite societies, the description and analysis of the processes of change in them, is a complex and difficult task. The attempt to simplify it by considering the process as being one in which two or more 'cultures' interact, which is the method suggested by Malinowski in his Introduction to Memorandum XV of the International Institute of African Language and Culture on 'Methods of Study of Culture Contact in Africa' (1938), is simply a way of avoiding the reality. For what is happening in South Africa, for example, is not the interaction of British culture, Afrikander (or Boer) culture, Hottentot culture, various Bantu cultures and Indian culture, but the interaction of individuals and groups within an established social structure which is itself in process of change. What is happening in a Transkeian tribe, for example, can only be described by recognising that the tribe has been incorporated into a wide political and economic structural system.

For the scientific study of primitive societies in conditions in which they are free from the domination by more advanced societies which result in these composite societies, we have unfortunately an almost complete lack of authentic historical data. We cannot study, but can only speculate about, the processes of change that took place in the past of which we have no record. Anthropologists speculate about former changes in the societies of the Australian aborigines, or the inhabitants of Melanesia, but such speculations are not history and can be of no use in science. For the study of social change in societies other than the composite societies to which reference has been made we have to rely on the work of historians dealing with authentic records.

You are aware that in certain anthropological circles the term 'evolutionary anthropologist' is almost a term of abuse. It is applied, however, without much discrimination. Thus Lewis Morgan is called an evolutionist, although he rejected the theory of organic evolution and in relation to society believed, not in evolution, but in progress, which he conceived as the steady material and moral improvement of mankind from crude stone implements and sexual promiscuity to the steam engines and monogamous marriage of Rochester, N.Y. But even such anti-evolutionists as Boas believe in progress.

It is convenient, I think, to use the term 'progress' for the process by which human beings attain to greater control over the physical environment through the increase of knowledge and improvement of techniques by inventions and discoveries. The way in which we are now able to destroy considerable portions of cities from the air is one of the latest striking results of progress. Progress is not the same thing as social evolution, but it is very closely connected with it.

Evolution, as I understand the term, refers specifically to a process of emergence of new forms of structure. Organic evolution has two important features: (1) in the course of it a small number of kinds of organisms have given rise to a very much larger number of kinds; (2) more complex forms of organic structure have come into existence by development out of simpler forms. While I am unable to attach any definite meaning to such phrases as the evolution of culture or the evolution of language, I think that social evolution is a reality which the social anthropologist should recognise and study. Like organic evolution, it can be defined by two features. There has been a process by which from a small number of forms of social structure, many different forms have arisen in the course of history; that is, there has been a process of diversification. Secondly, throughout this process more complex forms of social structure have developed out of, or replaced, simpler forms.

Just how structural systems are to be classified with reference to their greater or less complexity is a problem requiring investigation. But there is evidence of a farily close correlation between complexity and another feature of structural systems, namely, the extent of the field of social relations. In a structural system with a narrow total social field, an average or typical person is brought into direct and indirect social relations with only a small number of other persons. In systems of this type we may find that the linguistic community—the body of persons who speak one language—numbers from 250-500, while the political community is even smaller, and economic relations by the exchange of goods and services extend only over a very narrow range. Apart from the differentiation by sex and age, there is very little differentiation of social role between persons or classes. We can contrast with this the systems of social structure that we observe today in England or the United States. Thus the process of human history to which I think the term social evolution may be appropriately applied might be defined as the process by which wide-range systems of social stucture have grown out of, or replaced, narrow-range systems. Whether this view is acceptable or not, I suggest that the concept of social evolution is one which requires to be defined in terms of social structure.

There is no time on this occasion to discuss the relation of the study of social structure to the study of culture. For an interesting attempt to bring the two kinds of study together I would refer you to Mr. Gregory Bateson's book *Naven*. I have made no attempt to deal with social anthropology as a whole and with all its various branches and divisions. I have endeavoured only to give you a very general idea of the kind of study to which I have found it scientifically profitable to devote a considerable and steadily increasing proportion of time and energy. The only reward that I have sought I think I have in some measure found—something of the kind of insight into the nature of the world of which we are part that only the patient pursuit of the method of natural science can afford.

Notes

1.   Presidential Address to the Royal Anthropological Institute. Reprinted from the *Journal of the Royal Anthropological Institute*, Vol. LXX, 1940.

Herbert Applebaum

V

Psychological Anthropology

Introduction

With the introduction of psychoanalysis, attempts were made to find the meaning of culture in psychological processes. The first attempt was made by Freud himself in 1913 in his work *Totem and Taboo*. W. H. R. Rivers (1920), a British psychologist, used the Freudian concepts of repression and of the unconscious to explain the operation of wartime psychosis observed in soldiers. C. G. Seligman and his wife, Brenda, applied psychiatic concepts to human behavior in their study of incest. Malinowski, through his association with Rivers and Seligman, studied Freudian theory and accepted its basic tenets about the nature of psychological processes. However, when in the Trobriands, a matrilineal kinship society, Malinowski observed that hostility was directed toward the mother's brother, rather than the father, and incestuous desires of males focused on the sister rather than the mother. Accordingly, Malinowski disputed the universality of Freud's classic Oedipal complex. Malinowski owed much to Freudian psychology in his perceptive deductions and hypotheses regarding incest, family solidarity, and conflict control (Voget 1975:433–434).

Since the Freudian system was too systematized for Boas, and given the behavioristic orientation of Boasian anthropologists, a spotty penetration of psychological theory into American anthropology resulted. In the 1920s, Edward Sapir (1949:544–559) pointed to the importance of the unconscious patterning of behavior and the role of the individual in the transmitting of culture from one generation to another. The search for psychological typologies for culture, raised by Sapir, was communicated to Ruth Benedict and Margaret Mead. Benedict's *Patterns of Culture* reflects the use of psychological types—Appolonian, Dionysian, Paranoid—to characterize entire cultures. And Margaret Mead's *Coming of*

137

Age in Samoa was one of the first attempts to apply psychological theory to behavior based on a cross-cultural comparison. Included in Chapter 11 are the introductions to Mead's seminal studies in the relationship of psychology to culture—*Coming of Age In Samoa* and *Growing Up in New Guinea*.

The study of personality and culture was well underway in the 1930s, when Abram Kardiner gathered a core of American anthropologists around him at Columbia University. They included Ralph Linton, Cora Du Bois, James West, Clyde Kluckhohn, and Ruth Benedict. Psychological anthropology, as espoused by Kardiner and developed by those who followed him, is based on the idea that psychological dimensions in human beings are essential components of culture and human behavior. It was believed that the integration of cultures depended on how well suited the personality characteristics of people living within the culture were to the values and ideals of the society. This focus coincided with the rise of structural/functionalism, which also sought to find those elements in society which gave it cohesion and integration. The structural/ functionalists concentrated on institutions. The psychological anthropologists concentration on *enculturation*. Enculturation is the process of becoming competent in one's culture. In contrast to socialization, which usually apples to the childhood years, enculturation is thought of as continuing throughout one's life (Garbarino 1983).

Kardiner defined psychology as "the science of adaptation, its determinants, its modalities and motivations, and of the mental and emotional phenomena that accompany the vicissitudes of adaptation" (1981:5). Kardiner saw the individual as standing midway between institutions, which mold and direct his adaptation to the world, and his biological needs, which press for gratification. This viewpoint places heavy emphasis on institutions and stresses the significant role they play in creating the adaptive systems of the individual (Voget 1975:441–442).

Kardiner, following Freud, placed strong emphasis on the importance of ego formation. Overdevelopment of either the id (the instinctual aspect of personality) or the superego (the social constraints on personality) could lead to out-of-control emotionalism in the first case or strong patterns of guilt and fear in the second. Approaching the problem of ego formation and following Freud, Kardiner singled out:

1. The predominant influence of early experience on character formation;
2. Social norms as barriers to impulse gratification;
3. Frustrative reactions prominent in the unconscious; and
4. The release of unconscious impulse in symbolic behavior.

Like Malinowski, Kardiner correlated the role of institutions with primary biological needs. The psychoanalytic focus drew a picture of cultural institutions that were both repressive and restraining and also means for the release of impulse frustration. Application of psychoanalysis to culture carried the hazard of psychological reductionism, that culture would be seen, at its base, as psychological mechanisms or personality types. Boas warned against the reductionism that would derive culture from personality types rather than the historical process. This was turning the process on its head. Boas states in his Foreword to *Coming of Age in Samoa* (1928) that Mead's work confirms "the suspicion long held by anthropologists, that much of what we ascribe to human nature is no more than a reaction to the restraints put upon us by our civilization."

One of the key concepts of Kardiner, later used by Benedict, Mead, DuBois, Gorer, and others in their personality and culture studies, was the notion of "basic personality structure." Kardiner makes the claim for "basic personality structure" that it provides the derivation for institutions (1981:29). Kardiner creates for his basic personality structure the amazing capacity to "invent" institutions. His definition of institutions is so broad and loose as to make of it almost any kind of behavior pattern. This is quite different from Malinowski's or Radcliffe-Brown's notion of institutions, both of whom defined institutions as organized activity, which incorporated a hierarchy of personnel, had rules and procedures, and occupied a strategic segment of a social system through its use of resources and exercise of power and influence.

Kardiner's argument about the formation and origin of basic personality structures becomes circular when he presents a list of "key situations which influence personality formation" (1981:26). The list includes maternal care, induction of affectivity, early disciplines, sexual disciplines, institutionalized sibling attitudes, induction into work, puberty, marriage, character of participation in society, factors that keep the society together, projective systems, reality systems, arts, craft and techniques, and techniques of production. This is a mixed bag that includes very specific items, like induction into work with broad, abstract items like "factors" that keep the society together. It also includes "institutionalized attitudes." Thus, basic personality structure can give rise to and even "invent" institutions, but it is, in turn, created by existing institutions. Reminiscent of functional analysis, where certain parts of a society are said to hold it together, this integration approach does not deal with which parts are more significant than others or how the parts are interrelated.

Kardiner advocated the method of biographies to arrive at the basic personality structure in a society. He said that many biographies were needed, which took into account the variety of sex, age, status, and other social variables. The biographies would be sought within a theoretical viewpoint that drew from anthropology, psychoanalysis, and psychology. This viewpoint included the notion that human behavior is predominantly learned; that behavior is similar depending on sex, age, and status; that all societies have an ideal adult behavior; that habits are formed through punishment and reward; that patterns learned early in life are crucial; that learning in childhood consists of modifications of biological drives; that parents reward and punish children; that the most powerful drives are unconscious and unverbalized; that social institutions reflect the wishes and primary needs of the population; and that in a homogeneous and integrated culture there are patterns of behavior that are consistent and mutually reinforce each other.

Kardiner relates his concept of basic personality structure to the concept of national character. He complains about the notion of national character, saying that a group can no more have a national character than it can have a national pair of lungs, that is, its members cannot share a personality trait in common. But basic personality structure, in the way Kardiner handles it, involves the manner in which personalities and character traits are created in a particular society. By focusing on how personality is formed in a particular culture, Kardiner can thus relate personality to institutionalized processes. While he does exhibit a poor understanding of the nature of institutions, the value of his approach is that it enabled investigators to seek correlations between behavioral patterns and cultural process. And this was the thrust of the early work by Margaret Mead.

Margaret Mead (1901–1978) was one of Benedict's students. Her early work was involved with the study of personality and culture, with an emphasis on the individual and the importance of the enculturation process. She was especially interested in problems of adolescence, preadolescence, and preschool age children, believing that human character is molded in these early years by society. She was particularly keen to show that traits found in western cultures were not universal and that diverse cultures produce diverse character traits.

Like Benedict, one of Mead's major interests was in pattern. While she dealt with the psychology of the individual, it was the relationship between the individual and cultural pattern that was important. This importance of pattern was brought home to her during her research in Samoa, where she observed individual behavior constantly absorbed with how it fit into the pattern of the culture. Child rearing was also her concern, since it was part of the process by which people incorporate the pattern of society and become cultured beings. She used personality and differences to heighten awareness of cultural pattern, its complexity, and the relationship between it and deviation (McDowell 1980:283).

While discussing the development of personality and social structure or the interaction between the two, Mead emphasized process and system. She perceived human cultures as complex systems composed of a varity of elements: social, economic, political, ideology, and personality structure, combined in a web of interconnectedness. Even in her early work, she stated that "cultures must be treated, not as chance arrays of essentially unrelated traits, but as highly integrated systems" (1938:5). We observe here the influence of Benedict and Boas, who both stressed the wholeness of cultures, and also the influence of functionalism, which emphasized the interconnectedness of social structure. However, Mead, unlike Radcliffe-Brown and Durkheim, never failed to stress the importance of the individual. And she never failed to point to the permutations possible between the ideal behavior patterns of a culture and the deviations from it in real behavior. Another of her primary interests, even in her early work, was the influence of Western contact and colonialization on small-scale societies and the consequent changes it effected (McDowell 1980:284).

Mead's work has great appeal for modern women's rights organizations. Speaking not as a N.O.W. (National Organization for Women) woman, but as a social scientist, she appealed to the abolition of the social image of masculine and feminine and for a society open to all temperaments and the individuality of behavior based on complex cultural influences. After comparing temperamental preferences in three New Guinea societies—Arapesh, Mundugumor, and Tchambuli—she concluded (1950:280):

The material suggests that we may say that many, if not all, of the personality traits which we have called masculine or feminine are as lightly linked to sex as are the clothing, the manners, and the form of head-dress that a society at a given period assigns to either sex. When we consider the behaviour of the typical Arapesh man or woman as contrasted with the behaviour of the typical Mundugumor man or woman, the evidence is overwhelmingly in favour of the strength of social conditioning. . . . Only to the impact of the whole of the integrated culture upon the growing child can we lay the formation of the contrasting types. . . . The differences between individuals who are members of different cultures, like the differences between individuals within a culture, are almost entirely to be laid to differences in conditioning, especially during early childhood, and the form of this conditioning is culturally determined.

Mead's attempt to minimize the importance of maleness and femaleness as a biological given brought criticism from those who could only
see sexual dimorphism. But in the Preface to what she called her "most
misunderstood book" (1950), Mead said that she did not deny sex differences, but that sex differences, from a biological perspective, could not
account for the behavior expected of the sexes in various cultures. Mead
believed that the correlation between the biological basis of sexual dimorphism and cultural distinctions were exaggerated. This is an issue
that has resurfaced with the rise of sociobiology, which will be discussed
later in the book. Mead argued that cultural distinctions between males
and females were artificial and should be modified to correlate the cultural with an equitable distribution of opportunities in society based on
individual talents and temperaments (Voget 1975:411).

One final note regarding Margaret Mead's perspective. Despite her
mentor's doubts about the comparative method, Mead stressed the importance of comparative material. She saw it as a means to highlight
cultural variation and to evolve theories and generalizations about human behavior. *Sex and Temperament* was a striking illustration.

The integration of culture, which Mead stressed, and the commonal-
ities in cultures have been continuing theoretical lures for anthropologists. Clyde Kluckhohn (1905–1960) sought to answer the question of
uniformities in culture by relating culture to variables associated with
human nature and the requirements of social living. Kluckhohn, like
Kroeber, Mead, and Benedict, was also interested in the concept of
pattern. He saw pattern, as Kroeber did, as an abstraction from a number of concrete instances. Kluckhohn, like Kroeber, ruled out actual
behavior from his concept of culture. Culture was, for him, a form or
pattern or design, an abstraction from concrete behavior, but not behavior in itself. Cultural data fell into three classes: 1. ideal behavior; 2. the
conceptions people had about behavior; and 3. actual behavior as objectively determined through observation and scientific inquiry.

The conception of culture as a logical construct reflected a growing
interest in values as the basis for cultural integration. The view of culture
as a construct also coincided with the growth of psychologizing of culture. For Kluckhohn, the important relations were not between concrete
actors and events but in the mental relations, or patterns, which unified
actors and events. For this reason, Kluckhohn pointed to the ideal patterns as more important for discovering the structure of a culture than
the actual behavior patterns. This is discussed by Kluckhohn in Chapter 12, taken from an article in the American Anthropologist (1943:414–
415).

Another theoretical interest of Clyde Kluckhohn was in *values* as integral to the character of a people and their cultural patterns. With his study of values, Kluckhohn sought linkages with sister disciplines, notably psychology and sociology. He also participated in Kardiner's seminars at the New York Psychoanalytic Institute. Kluckhohn stressed the unconscious as basic to enculturated behavior. He referred to the overt and covert culture, locating the essence of culture in a socio-psychological configuration of intuitive values and premises:

A cultural configuration may be defined as a principle of the covert culture—either a way of doing a variety of things (a means) or an end (a culturally defined goal). Since configurations are part of the covert culture they are unstated premises. (Quoted in Voget 1975:416)

Values were seen by Kluckhohn as a mental construct, just like culture and social structure. Kluckhohn extended his concept of value orientation to include a world view.

In summary, Kluckhohn's concept of the integrative nature of culture was that it contained a fundamental structure and organization which was related to psychological processes operating within a value context. The nature of culture appeared to the observer like a stream of behavior which took its form and order from the covert value premises and categories shared by members of the society. Culture was not behavior, as such, but mental constructs and ideas about what was considered ideal behavior. Many of the modern mentalist concepts of culture contain a basic orientation to culture similar to that of Clyde Kluckhohn.

The challenge of any social science theory is to find instruments of scientific precision with which to test one's theories. John and Beatrice Whiting, in collaboration with others, like Irvin Child, believed they found such an instrument in the Human Relations Area Files of Yale University. These files were developed by George P. Murdock, who believed that, while Boas had avoided generalizations and cross-cultural comparisons at the beginning of the century because of insufficient data gathering, by midcentury this was no longer the case. Murdock wanted a return to theory building. Using categories similar to those suggested by Clark Wissler as universals of culture, he compiled a cross-cultural survey, called the Human Relations Area Files (HRAF). These files made available ethnographic data from societies and cultures throughout the world. HRAF lent itself to hypothesis testing and statistical correlations, without the need for fieldwork. The files are constantly updated with data and ethnographic material and, while established at Yale, have been made available to universities throughout the United States and in many foreign countries. The benefits of a coded, cross-indexed, data retrieval system are the enormous volume of information and speed of access which the researcher can use. Problems include the fact that aspects of culture are taken out of cultural context, the materials are uneven in coverage, and maintaining adequate controls for diffusion and independence of cases. There is also the problem of the reliability and replicability of the ethnographer's data, particularly if they are not quantified. Nevertheless, the HRAF data have proved to be a valuable contribution to the anthropological enterprise.

Whiting and Child (1953), using psychoanalytical theory as a basis for their hypotheses, also related them to behavior theory to derive a general theory to explain the relationship between the individual and culture. As stated on the last page of Chapter 13, John and Beatrice Whiting hope to develop hypotheses designed to be true for all peoples at all times, and they are convinced that child rearing is the key to understanding personality and culture. They are also convinced that in their search for testable hypotheses they need the collaboration of anthropologists, ethologists, psychologists, and other behavioral scientists. And they also need the help and assistance of people in host countries where research is carried out.

In their seminal study, Whiting and Child (1953) selected five systems of behavior to test behavioral correlates cross-culturally. They were looking for universals and turned to experiences common to infants everywhere—the oral, anal, sexual, dependency, and aggression response systems. Rating of the cultural practices was projected on an indulgence-severity continuum; that of effect on a satisfaction-anxiety continuum. Focus on satisfaction and anxiety was thought to probe the dynamics of motivation and the way cultures might influence personality integration. In their broader intentions, Whiting and Child hoped to uncover the psychological linkages binding the individual to culture. The dynamics of this relationship, according to Whiting and Child, was to be found in child training. Personality organization, stemming from common childhood experiences, was central to cultural integration, since motivation and punishment/reward systems are reflected in the symbolism of cultures (Voget 1975:471).

Whiting and Child postulated that indulgence in one of the five primary systems—oral, anal, sexual, dependence, and aggression—would increase the likelihood of satisfaction in that system in adulthood, whereas early punishment would increase the likelihood of anxiety and conflict in that system later in life. After making appropriate statistical studies from the HRAF data, Whiting and Child concluded that the positive case was not proved but that the negative was generally substantiated. The most conclusive evidence for negative fixation came from the oral, dependence, and aggression systems, which suggested that Freudian theory exaggerated the strength of the anal and sexual drives (Garbarino 1983:69).

In the light of the Whiting and Child study, it appeared that the concept of the modal personality no longer could be maintained, even for the simpler societies. This led to increased concern with the concept of choice, something that Margaret Mead had noted in her study of the Manus, whom she said operated not as culturally unconscious automatons but as strategists. She said they were disposed to accept innovations and changes in their culture where they could perceive a personal gain 1956).

There was a waning of culture and personality theories after the second World War, which was followed by the emergence of a more comprehensive perspective under the heading of cognitive theory. These new perspectives no longer admitted personality organization or Kardiner's basic personality concept as the central variable for explaining culture and cultural differences. Instead personality and culture was placed alongside a number of other variables to account for the pattern and direction of social organization. This, indeed, is reflected in the reading by the Whitings (Chapter 13, Figure 13-1), where we see child learning related to both individual needs and behavioral and expressive systems, as well as environment, history, and maintenance systems that include social structure and institutional organizations.

Summing up this introduction to psychological anthropology, we see that the use of psychology and psychoanalytic theory in anthropology was a logical extension of both historical-particularism and functionalism. It related to the notion of Boas and Bastian before him, about the psychic unit of mankind, which would provide a clue to the origins of cultural patterns. It related to the functionalism of Malinowski, who related institutions to individuals by theorizing that the function of institutions was to satisfy the biopsychological needs of individuals. Edward Sapir, Ruth Benedict, Abram Kardiner, and Margaret Mead were all instrumental in the thirties and early forties in introducing individual psychology into anthropological theory. However, it was not the individual as an entity that engaged their interest but the person replicating the psychological patterning of culture.

Psychological anthropology established connections between the historical and functional perspectives by dealing both with problems of maintenance of the social system and with change. It related personality structure both to the security of functional integration and to the anxiety of change and dynamics in the social system. In Kluckhohn's hands, it drew individual personality formation to social values, and, in Jules Henry's hands (1959), it centered human evolutionary development in the ability of human personality to use adaptive techniques to discharge the stresses of the sociocultural environment. Psychological anthropology also provided links between psychoanalytic theory and behavioral data, so that investigators like Margaret Mead could test psychoanalytic theory through cross-cultural evidence. Psychological theory took its place alongside functionalism and social structure when Murdock was formulating his inventory of cultural traits to be cross-filed in his Human Relations Area Files. Finally, one of the important contributions of psychological anthropology has been to identify cultural variables which had remained hidden because there is a cultural blindness when all one knows about human personality is based only on one's own cultural world.

Abram Kardiner

10. The Technique of Psychodynamic Analysis

Psychology can be of use to the social sciences only if its use can be reduced to a technique which is verifiable, teachable, and can be corrected or changed in the face of new evidence. Systematized opinions in technical language are no more binding in psychology than in any other field. Generalizations which codify the obvious are not techniques capable of yielding new information.

The predecessor of this book was an adventure in technique. This technique was the outgrowth of a few simple observations. After a culture like that of Tanala had been presented in detail, certain correspondences were noted. In Tanala the relation of the individual to the ancestral gods seemed strikingly like the relation of the child to the parent in this culture. There was the same emphasis on obedience. The first conclusion was that obedience to a duty was universal. We found as we studied the same correlation in Marquesas that this was not so, and correspondingly discovered that in Marquesas there was no emphasis on childhood obedience. The folklore in Tanala showed a typical father-son relationship, in which jealousy was repressed and a passive feminine attitude appeared in its place. In Marquesas myths father-hatred was absent, and in lieu of this father hatred there was strong fear, hatred, and distrust of the woman. In other words, according as the experiences varied, so did the products of the *projective systems* in folklore and religion. This gave us our first clue, and the same procedure was used on more and more phenomena.

As we proceeded we found it necessary to have a cultural unit to describe the various practices and customs, and for this purpose the concept *institution* could be used operationally. The insitutions were therefore treated as the vehicle through which specific influences were brought to bear on the growing individual. If therefore we again look at the correlation in the previous paragraph, we find that if childhood disciplines constitute one order of institutions then religion and folklore

147

comprise another. We called the former primary and the latter secondary. Also there was something created in the individual by his childhood experiences which formed the basis for the projective systems subsequently used to create folklore and religion. The group of nuclear constellations in the individual was designated the *basic personality structure*. This concept proved to be only a refinement of a concept long since used descriptively by Herodotus and Caesar and known as *national character*. The term *basic personality structure* was chosen to obviate the lack of clarity in the terms group, national, or social character, because a group can no more have a common character than it can have a common soul or pair of lungs. Moreover the constellations identified in basic personality structure were not finished character traits, but a matrix in which these character traits develop. For example, in Alor we find distrust as a permanent feature of basic personality; but this distrust may show itself in any number of different character traits. What was new and important about this concept was not its name, but the technique of its derivation and the introduction of a genetic viewpoint into sociology. The concept of basic personality structure thus became a powerful operational implement, for through it we acquired a precise means of delineating the interrelationship of various social practices through their compatibility or incompatibility with certain constant identifiable human needs and drives.

Whereas this operational scheme was made possible by the ability to identify remote derivations of basic experiences through the use of projections, further experience with new cultures and new material in the form of biographies showed this scheme to be oversimplified and decidedly incomplete.

The first difficulty arose in connection with the use of the concept *institution*. This concept was originally defined to connote "a fixed mode of thought or behavior which can be communicated, which enjoys common acceptance and the infringement of or deviation from which creates some disturbance in the individual or group." This definition did not work in practice. It was found that in some societies (e.g., Alor) some of the most important sources of projective systems were not institutionalized but were related to other practices which were. Poor maternal care in Alor was an accident resulting from the mother's having to work all day in her fields. The basic institution is that the mother works in the fields all day; the neglect of the children is not institutionalized, though almost universal. There are no sanctions against good care of the children. We can therefore amend the concept primary institution to read: *primary institution or related practices, whether institutionalized or not.* To substitute the word *practices* for institutions would not be any more satisfactory than either *institutions* or *mores*. Moreover the latter terms would imply the backing by a specific rationale, which, though often the case, is not universal. Institutions should be defined to mean what people do, think, believe, or feel. Their locus is within the human personality; and they have an accommodative or adaptive function. In connection with primary institutions, the question frequently arose concerning their origin. This question could never be answered. Linton[1] pointed out that this question was not pertinent to the present endeavor. The primary institution is treated as the taking-off point for the individual, not for the culture. The origin of an institution has nothing to do with the effect it creates on the growing individual.

A second technical difficulty arose in connection with the identification of the products of the projective systems, called secondary institutions. Here much confusion arose because many institutions could not be classified as either primary or secondary. This fact alone, that there were institutions outside and independent of the projective system, indicates either that our formulation of the determinants of basic personality structure is incomplete or that institutions exist outside its range. This is very likely to be the case with institutions or practices of purely rational origin.

The important point about this classification into primary and secondary institutions is that it is closely bound to the concept of basic personality structure. It means that institutions cannot be compared with each other or establish relations with each other directly. This relationship is mediated by the personality.

In the earlier work we had no opportunity to check the validity of basic personality against actual biographical material and social changes. The only cultures that have a long recorded history and plenty of biographical material are the oriental cultures and our own. But these could not be confidently approached until certain elementary problems had been solved.

The use of the concept of basic personality structure therefore includes the following questions: (1) What are the key integrational systems and their institutional background? (2) Are the effects of normative institutions the only sources of basic personality structure? (3) How can the concept be tested against biographies and how could the inevitable variations of personal character in the same culture be reconciled with it? (4) What are the effects of knowledge empirically derived and verified by criteria outside the range of the "common sense" of the culture upon institutions of projective origin? In other words, what are the relations of scientific knowledge to the basic personality? The last is of course significant for the study of our own society, where science has so evidently altered the social utility of the projective systems employed in religion.

The Key Integrational Systems

Any selection of key situations which influence personality formation is bound to be incomplete. We are prejudiced in our selection by our experience with individuals in our society and particularly by the constellations which predominate in neuroses. This is admittedly a bias. We have already surveyed a sufficient number of cultures to know that constellations important in our society are not universal, and some situations in our society are overlooked because they do not act as impediments to development in our culture but do in others. If we had no opportunity to examine any culture other than our own, we would never surmise that maternal care and nurture are exceedingly important to the cohesiveness of the society and so would never look to maternal care as a key situation. This we can learn only by comparison with other cultures where maternal care is inadequate. By this time we have studied ten cultures intensively and have a sufficient number of contrasts to indicate a workable list.[2]

Maternal care
  Constancy of attention—or abandonment
  Feeding regularity
  Surrogate parents—activities of
  Help in learning processes—walking, talking
  Pre-walking and post-walking care
  Weaning—age, methods
  Sphincter control—when inducted, associated ideas (cleanliness, obedience, etc.)
Induction of affectivity
  Solicitation of response; handling, play, fondling
  Maternal attitudes to child—care or neglect, honesty to children or practice of deception
  Insistence on obedience and presence or absence of reward systems—superego formation
Early disciplines
  Consistency
  Punishment—reward systems—when punishment is inflicted, place of choice for inflicting bodily pain, etc.
Sexual disciplines
  Masturbation, interdicted or permitted, attitudes of elders—neglect, ridicule, castration threats, tolerance, or used as placebo
  Playing with opposite sex—permitted openly or tacitly, attitude of elders

Institutionalized sibling attitudes
  Rivalries encouraged or suppressed
  Aggression—controls
Introduction into work
  Age—duties, rewards, degree of participation
  Differences between sexes
  Attitudes to work—division of economic responsibilities
Puberty
  Alteration of participation in society
  Premature or deferred
  Parental aid in preparation for marital status
Marriage
  Mating mores
    Difficulties in mating created by parents
  Position of woman, freedom of choice
  Economic status requirements
  Fidelity requirements, freedom of divorce
Character of participation in society
  Status differentiation
  Function differentiation
  Life goals
Factors that keep the society together
  Superego formation
  Cooperative and antagonistic phases
  Permitted and controlled activities—sanctions
Projective systems
  Religion
  Folklore
Reality systems, derived from empirical or projective sources
Arts, crafts, and techniques
Techniques of production
  Differentiation of function
  Participation in distributed products—status differentiation, degrees and
    controls or prestige

The technique of applying these principles can be illustrated by taking a particular combination of conditions. Society A is one in which the mother cares diligently for the infant for two weeks after birth, and thereafter only two hours in the morning and two hours in the evening, the rest of her time being spent in the gardens raising vegetable food. For the major portion of the day the care of the infant is left to older siblings or others. The child probably is given enough food, but many tensions are unsatisfied for long periods. No systematic teaching of talking or walking occurs. The child shifts for itelf. It is masturbated to keep it quiet. Add to this, teasing and later deliberate misrepresentation. To this situation someone may say: "What does a child or infant know, and therefore what difference does it make? It gets enough food, doesn't it?" This view overlooks the fact that the infant has no ready-made reactions; that by the conditions described a specific environment is created for the child; that its needs and tensions are constant, and if they are relieved with little effort or discomfort on the part of the child, one integrational system will follow; while if the tensions are unrelieved, the resulting constellation will be different. The child will eventually develop a definite attitude to the parent, to itself, and to the tensions which cause it so much discomfort. These attitudes are adapted to the particular conditions and tend to become habitual, automatic, and compounded. Moreover the constellations formed under these conditions can be predicted with a fair degree of accuracy. The constellations thus created will not all be alike, but the range can be predicted.

A child under these conditions cannot develop an undivided feeling or attitude to the mother. He must feel some hatred, some distrust, some isolation, a sense of having no one whom he can positively count on. Moreover the functions which develop under the influence of good care, confidence in himself, interest in the outer world, enterprise—these will all suffer. Sexuality is stimulated, but it is detached from the image of an affectionate person who stimulates it.

The next question that arises is whether these attitudes need remain permanent. They need not, if other factors are introduced into the child's life which would tend to counteract them. However if they are not counteracted, they tend to continue. If the child as he grows encounters influences which tend to reinforce these reactions, by the time he is an adult they constitute his character. By that time there is formed a definite pattern (for perceiving human relationships and dealing with them) which is totally unconscious, and a definite and specific system of projections is likely to spring from these early experiences. When adult he may invent a story, a pure fabrication, in which we may detect the operation of these constellations formed in childhood. These constellations may be recovered in dreams in distorted forms.

We have had up to this point a series of inferences about the probable effects of certain formative institutions. How can this guess be substantiated or contradicted? If our hypothesis is correct, namely that these conditions in childhood become consolidated and form a basis for subsequent projective use, then we can expect to find some evidence of it in all projective systems—religious, folklore, and perhaps other institutions. In other words, if we know how the basic personality is established, we can make certain predictions about the institutions this personality is likely to invent. If we follow the particular personality created by the above mentioned conditions, we expect to find folk tales dealing with parental hatred, with desertion by parents; we expect to find a religion devoid of any concepts dealing with reward for good deeds or punishment for bad ones. We expect no emphasis on the idea of reinstatement into the good graces of the deity through suffering. We expect no idealization of the deity.

The utility of the concept of basic personality structure does not end here. We find institutions other than folklore and religion derived from that same source. If we could do no more than predict types of religion and folklore, the usefulness of this procedure would be very limited and would be entirely inadequate for our society where the projective systems have been largely deflected from use in religion. Since the personality has in it elements of distrust toward parents, we could not expect this lack of trust to be limited to the parents, but extended to others. When the whole chain of elements entering into this particular integrational system is completed, we would also expect to find bad relations between the sexes, frequency of divorce, and also institutionalized obstacles against divorce.

The more the ethnographer tells us about the traits of these people, the greater the number of institutions that we can place as derivatives of this *basic personality structure*. For example, we hear that the people discussed above have no interest in the arts and their skills rate very low. We also hear that they surrender easily to illness. These traits fall easily into place once we know the basic personality structure; but these particular traits *could not be predicted*, and there are likely to be some that cannot be accounted for even when we know the basic personality.

We cannot therefore maintain that the prediction value of the concept of the basic personality structure is its chief merit; we do not know the possibilities of early conditionings accurately enough to make predictions on a large scale. We may be able to do so when we have comparative studies on about fifty cultures, and even then original and unique details are likely to surprise us.

The chief merit of this concept is that it offers us a basis for examining the structuralizations in society and for relating institutions to each other, not directly but through the medium of the individuals who compose it.

This is as far as our procedure can take us, given only the accurate description of institutions. Conclusions made from this source alone can have but the status of guesses, more or less approximate. There is another way not only to check on our conclusions but to furnish us with a fresh source of information—that is, the biographies of the individuals in the society.

What Additional Factors Enter into Basic Personality Structure?

If we were to stop our consideration of basic personality structure with those systems which, though they originate in actual experience, become the unconscious basis for projective systems, we could be justly accused of omitting several very important sources of "learning," which play a prominent role in the adaptation of the individual. There is a large contingent of data imparted to the child by direct tuition.[3] To this group belong all explanations about the outer world, how to deal with it, and the relations of man to it, and the conventionalized attitudes which govern the relations of people to each other. These systems are consciously inducted, much of their content being subject to demonstrations of a kind, and in some instances are modifiable.

The introduction of this category of "learned" systems brings with it unavoidable difficulty. In the previous section we described an aspect of common sense derived from actual experiences in interpersonal relationships which form the basis of projective systems, some of which are used to explain the outer world. Now we introduce a system taught directly. These two systems cannot possibly be incompatible if they are used to explain the outer world. If they were, one would tend to disappear, and the system eliminated would of necessity be the one most amenable to change, the conscious system. More likely than not a taught system at complete variance with the projective system could not be accepted. This simple idea can be illustrated as follows: Suppose that a missionary attempts to convey to a primitive people the idea of redemption through suffering and atonement. This is presented as a bit of reality, and hence it is "taught" as such. Whether or not this idea has any significance to a primitive man depends on whether it has a certain plausibility according to his own experience. If he has not himself experienced the logical sequence of committing an act interpreted as a misdeed, being punished for it, and then being reinstated, the proposition as stated must remain meaningless. For it is merely a projection, rationalization, and generalization from the basic experience.

What we are saying therefore is that the entire projective system tends to exercise a polarizing influence over all taught reality systems that are presented to the individual; there are bound to be inconsistencies and exceptions.[4] But all aspects of the reality systems do not by any means fall under the influence of the system. One can in fact establish a series in which the projective system has less and less influence. It naturally has the least influence on manipulation of crafts and techniques. But other systems, which are taught also, fall decidedly under the influence of the projective system. Let us take two instances, one in which a drive is involved and another in which no drive is concerned. The first can be taken from a very common injunction in both primitive and civilized society. It is the proposition: "If you masturbate then you will become insane" (or some other dire consequence). For the moment we are less concerned about the disposition of the somatically determined tensions than we are about the form in which the injunction is implemented. The consequence of insanity is stated as a fact, which is a ready-made rationalization to justify the prohibition. The impulse to masturbate is thus accompanied by an anxiety which is channelized into a specific direction. The danger is made to appear as a real danger, for if it did not arouse terror it would hardly act as a deterrent.

This reality aspect occupies an important place in the conflict which centers about masturbation. If the activity in question is abandoned, it may undergo repression, and the only manifestation of its existence may be the anxiety about insanity. This can be represented graphically thus:

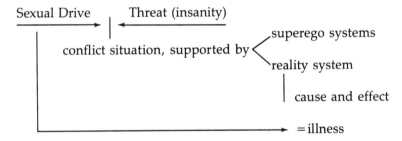

Thus the fear of illness may emerge as the only manifestation of the original impulse to satisfy a somatic sexual tension. The place of the reality aspect (masturbation causes insanity) is therefore shown to be related to the superego (conscience) systems created in a society.

This is an opportune place to discuss how extensively such an idea as the one described above can become systematized. This belief about the pernicious effects of masturbation persisted until about a half century ago. Before the advent of bacteriology almost every illness was attributed to masturbation, and long treatises based on "scientific" empirical observations were written in proof. This is an illustration of scientific rationalization. The unknown factor in this complex rationalization is the unconscious insistence that masturbation should be punished. The scientific data were merely organized to support this assumption.

There are other types of reality systems taught by direct induction which are unrelated to any drive. The Pomo and Navaho are both taught at an early age to bury excreta lest they be used as bait. This is an anxiety which can cling to the individual for a lifetime. But it is natural to assume that an anxiety of this kind would be reinforced by strong interpersonal tensions. In childhood, however, this belief becomes a part of the reality system, and the anxiety is controlled by appropriate defenses and precautions which become institutionalized. Thus the excretory function becomes associated with a special set of ideas laden with anxiety. These ideas are different from those we encountered in Tanala, where the associated idea was neither cleanliness nor fear of poisoning, but obedience. Several tension-release systems depend on which of these ideas becomes associated with the excretory function. The anxiety system just described can be represented thus:

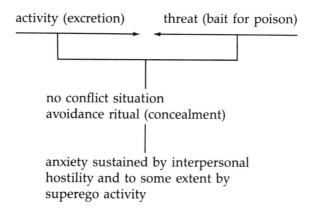

activity (excretion)   threat (bait for poison)

no conflict situation
avoidance ritual (concealment)

anxiety sustained by interpersonal
hostility and to some extent by
superego activity

A system like the one described can outlive by centuries the original circumstances that gave it origin, whose meaning can no longer be reconstructed. Among certain tribes of the Navaho the practice of concealing excreta has disappeared owing to the influence of whites. It would be interesting to know whether the disappearance was facilitated by the diminution of interpersonal hostilities and mutual suspicion.

In relation to these systems the question of the place of primitive taboo systems arises. The taboo systems may differ in origin. For the greater part they are taught as a part of the external reality system, in much the same way as we are taught to avoid a live electric wire. The relation of taboo systems to the culture as a whole cannot be precisely defined. We would expect them to be compatible with the basic personality structure. At the same time, as in our culture, many taboos are likely to persist in spite of the fact that no precise relationship to basic personality structure can be established.

In this hierarchy of systems in the basic personality structure there are the purely rational or scientific systems, subject to direct demonstration and discarded when proven wrong. This hierarchy of systems in basic personality structure can be arranged as follows:

1. Projective systems based on experience with the aid of rationalizations, generalizations, systematization and elaboration. To this category belongs the security system of the individual and superego systems, that is, those dealing with conscience and ideals.
2. Learned systems connected with drives.
3. Learned systems in which no drives are involved but ideas associated with activities.
   Groups 2 and 3 lay the basis for specific psychosomatic tension release routes.
4. Taboo systems, all learned as part of reality.[5]
5. Pure empirical reality systems, subject to demonstration.
6. Value systems and ideologies (which cut across all the previous systems).

At this point it is important to decide the position of *value systems*. They cannot be placed in any of the categories above. Some value systems belong to ideals, for example, honesty; some value systems derive from ideas associated with activities and hence directly taught, for example, cleanliness. Others derive from a social complex which precipitates our qualities having a high value at one time and not at another. Such a value is "freedom," which can never be defined in absolute terms but only in relation to the particular conditions which create an issue about it. No Comanche or Alorese would have any conception of freedom in the sense in which it is commonly used today in our society.

The question of ideologies presents the same difficulties as value systems. They are compounds of projective systems, in the interest of which empirical evidence is mobilized, and have therefore the same structure as rationalizations.

These are all constituents of the basic personality structure but they are not homogeneous; they vary in the degree of conscious representability and in the degree to which they are modifiable. Group 1 is completely unconscious and can only be identified through its projective manifestations, from which source it can be traced back to the institutions which gave it origin. This system is least susceptible to modification except by way of the institutions which gave it origin. All the other systems are subject to validation by some kind of empirical demonstration. Group 5 is subject to direct demonstration; the others are held in place by a chain of rationalizations of which the following is typical. A native of Alor tells us that his younger brother falls ill and is given appropriate medicine. The boy does not recover. His father, a seer, divines that he has failed to get well because a pair of carabao horns was stolen from the hearth. The carabao horns are replaced and the boy gets well. This is a closed system of rationalizations that cannot be beaten. If the boy had failed to get well with the replacement of the horns, some other explanation would have been offered. The manner in which these rationalizations are defended by the natives is fantastic in its tenacity. The commonest of all rationalizations used is that "everything was done right, but it was too late." This leaves the system intact. Why are these systems maintained on such "flimsy evidence" concerning their efficacy? Because they cannot be readily replaced and because a bad system has better anxiety-staying powers than no system at all. Systems like this present a never-ending, vicious logical cycle.

The viability and modifiability of these systems (1 to 5) is indicated in the order they are presented. This order is important in attempting to evaluate the extent to which diffusion of culture can take place. The most easily diffused are the manipulative and purely empirically derived reality systems, and manipulative techniques whose utility value is directly discernible. The least modifiable are those systems which are unconscious and those in which only parts are conscious, the rest being maintained by deep-rooted emotional interests.

Notes

1. In seminar at Columbia University.

2. Marquesan, Tanala, Comanche, Pomo, Alor, Navaho, Plainville, Tapirapen, Sikh, and Ojibwa.

3. A recent effort to account for social dynamics on the basis of direct learning processes has been made by J. W. M. Whiting, *On Becoming a Kwoma* (New Haven, Yale University Press, 1942). This approach would be valid if man did not *integrate experience*. It therefore presents a one-dimensional picture of mental processes on the basis of which no dynamic of social stability or change can be formulated.

4. To this point we can add a comment of Dr. Robert K. Merton: "It is not, of course, only the projective systems which polarize reality systems. Patterned experiences, differing according to social class, will also make certain beliefs 'meaningless' and 'unacceptable.' A particular type of belief in redemption through suffering and atonement will not spread among the upper social strata of a society, but will have rapid diffusion among the lower strata of the same society. It can also be shown that certain social and economic views or certain scientific systematizations spread rapidly at one time and slowly at another because they are compatible with the generalized personal experience of certain

segments of the population. I have found, for example, among 17th century physical scientists, that the Puritan projective system patently exercised a selective influence, such that an undue proportion of these scientists derived from Puritan circles. . . . The English century of genius is not unrelated to Puritanism." (Personal communication.)

5. The inclusion of taboo systems was suggested by Dr. Linton.

Margaret Mead

11. Introduction: Coming of Age in Samoa Introduction: Growing up in Manus Society

Introduction: Coming of Age in Samoa

During the last hundred years parents and teachers have ceased to take childhood and adolescence for granted. They have attempted to fit education to the needs of the child, rather than to press the child into an inflexible educational mould. To this new task they have been spurred by two forces, the growth of the science of psychology, and the difficulties and maladjustments of youth. Psychology suggested that much might be gained by a knowledge of the way in which children developed, of the stages through which they passed, of what the adult world might reasonably expect of the baby of two months or the child of two years. And the fulminations of the pulpit, the loudly voiced laments of the conservative social philosopher, the records of juvenile courts and social agencies all suggested that something must be done with the period which science had named adolescence. The spectacle of a younger generation diverging ever more widely from the standards and ideals of the past, cut adrift without the anchorage of respected home standards or group religious values, terrified the cautious reactionary, tempted the radical propagandist to missionary crusades among the defenceless youth, and worried the least thoughtful among us.

In American civilisation, with its many immigrant strains, its dozens of conflicting standards of conduct, its hundreds of religious sects, its shifting economic conditions, this unsettled, disturbed status of youth was more apparent than in the older, more settled civilisation of Europe. American conditions challenged the psychologist, the educator, the social philosopher, to offer acceptable explanations of the growing children's plight. As to-day in post-war Germany, where the younger generation has even more difficult adjustments to make than have our own children, a great mass of theorising about adolescence is flooding the book shops; so the psychologist in America tried to account for the restlessness of youth. The result was works like that of Stanley Hall on "Adolescence," which ascribed to the period through which the children were passing, the causes of their conflict and distress. Adolescence was characterised as the period in which idealism flowered and rebellion against authority waxed strong, a period during which difficulties and conflicts were absolutely inevitable.

The careful child psychologist who relied upon experiment for his conclusions did not subscribe to these theories. He said, "We have no data. We know only a little about the first few months of a child's life. We are only just learning when a baby's eyes will first follow a light. How can we give definite answers to questions of how a developed personality, about which we know nothing, will respond to religion?" But the negative cautions of science are never popular. If the experimentalist would not commit himself, the social philosopher, the preacher and the pedagogue tried the harder to give a short-cut answer. They observed the behaviour of adolescents in our society, noted down the omnipresent and obvious symptoms of unrest, and announced these as characteristics of the period. Mothers were warned that "daughters in their teens" present special problems. This, said the theorists, is a difficult period. The physical changes which are going on in the bodies of your boys and girls have their definite psychological accompaniments. You can no more evade one than you can the other; as your daughter's body changes from the body of a child to the body of a woman, so inevitably will her spirit change, and that stormily. The theorists looked about them again at the adolescents in our civilisation and repeated with great conviction, "Yes, stormily."

Such a view, though unsanctioned by the cautious experimentalist, gained wide currency, influenced our educational policy, paralysed our parental efforts. Just as the mother must brace herself against the baby's crying when it cuts its first tooth, so she must fortify herself and bear with what equanimity she might the unlovely, turbulent manifestations of the "awkward age." If there was nothing to blame the child for, neither was there any programme except endurance which might be urged upon the teacher. The theorist continued to observe the behaviour of American adolescents and each year lent new justification to his hypothesis, as the difficulties of youth were illustrated and documented in the records of schools and juvenile courts.

But meanwhile another way of studying human development had

been gaining ground, the approach of the anthropologist, the student of man in all of his most diverse social settings. The anthropologist, as he pondered his growing body of material upon the customs of primitive people, grew to realise the tremendous rôle played in an individual's life by the social environment in which each is born and reared. One by one, aspects of behaviour which we had been accustomed to consider invariable complements of our humanity were found to be merely a result of civilisation, present in the inhabitants of one country, absent in another country, and this without a change of race. He learned that neither race nor common humanity can be held responsible for many of the forms which even such basic human emotions as love and fear and anger take under different social conditions.

So the anthropologist, arguing from his observations of the behaviour of adult human beings in other civilisations, reaches many of the same conclusions which the behaviourist reaches in his work upon human babies who have as yet no civilisation to shape their malleable humanity.

With such an attitude towards human nature the anthropologist listened to the current comment upon adolescence. He heard attitudes which seemed to him dependent upon social environment—such as rebellion against authority, philosophical perplexities, the flowering of idealism, conflict and struggle—ascribed to a period of physical development. And on the basis of his knowledge of the determinism of culture, of the plasticity of human beings, he doubted. Were these difficulties due to being adolescent or to being adolescent in America?

For the biologist who doubts an old hypothesis or wishes to test out a new one, there is the biological laboratory. There, under conditions over which he can exercise the most rigid control, he can vary the light, the air, the food, which his plants or his animals receive, from the moment of birth throughout their lifetime. Keeping all the conditions but one constant, he can make accurate measurement of the effect of the one. This is the ideal method of science, the method of the controlled experiment, through which all hypotheses may be submitted to a strict objective test.

Even the student of infant psychology can only partially reproduce these ideal laboratory conditions. He cannot control the pre-natal environment of the child whom he will later subject to objective measurement. He can, however, control the early environment of the child, the first few days of its existence, and decide what sounds and sights and smells and tastes are to impinge upon it. But for the student of the adolescent there is no such simplicity of working conditions. What we wish to test is no less than the effect of civilisation upon a developing human being at the age of puberty. To test it most rigorously we would have to construct various sorts of different civilisations and subject large numbers of adolescent children to these different environments. We would list the influences the effects of which we wished to study. If we wished to study the influence of the size of the family, we would construct a series of civilisations alike in every respect except in family organisation. Then if we found differences in the behaviour of our adolescents we could say with assurance that size of family had caused the difference, that, for instance, the only child had a more troubled adolescence than the child who was a member of a large family. And so we might proceed through a dozen possible situations—early or late sex knowledge, early or late sex-experience, pressure towards precocious development, discouragement of precocious development, segregation of the sexes or coeducation from infancy, division of labour between the sexes or common tasks for both, pressure to make religious choices young or the lack of such pressure. We would vary one factor, while the others remained quite constant, and analyse which, if any, of the aspects of our civilisation were responsible for the difficulties of our children at adolescence.

Unfortunately, such ideal methods of experiment are denied to us when our materials are humanity and the whole fabric of a social order. The test colony of Herodotus, in which babies were to be isolated and the results recorded, is not a possible approach. Neither is the method of selecting from our own civilisation groups of children who meet one requirement or another. Such a method would be to select five hundred adolescents from small families and five hundred from large families, and try to discover which had experienced the greatest difficulties of adjustment at adolescence. But we could not know what were the other influences brought to bear upon these children, what effect their knowledge of sex or their neighbourhood environment may have had upon their adolescent development.

What method then is open to us who wish to conduct a human experiment but who lack the power either to construct the experimental conditions or to find controlled examples of those conditions here and there throughout our own civilisation? The only method is that of the anthropologist, to go to a different civilisation and make a study of human beings under different cultural conditions in some other part of the world. For such studies the anthropologist chooses quite simple peoples, primitive peoples, whose society has never attained the complexity of our own. In this choice of primitive peoples like the Eskimo, the Australian, the South Sea islander, or the Pueblo Indian, the anthropologist is guided by the knowledge that the analysis of a simpler civilisation is more possible of attainment.

In complicated civilisations like those of Europe, or the higher civilisations of the East, years of study are necessary before the student can begin to understand the forces at work within them. A study of the French family alone would involve a preliminary study of French history, of French law, of the Catholic and Protestant attitudes towards sex and personal relations. A primitive people without a written language present a much less elaborate problem and a trained student can master the fundamental structure of a primitive society in a few months.

Furthermore, we do not choose a simple peasant community in Europe or an isolated group of mountain whites in the American South, for these people's ways of life, though simple, belong essentially to the historical tradition to which the complex parts of European or American civilisation belong. Instead, we choose primitive groups who have had thousands of years of historical devleopment along completely different lines from our own, whose language does not possess our Indo-European categories, whose religious ideas are of a different nature, whose social organisation is not only simpler but very different from our own. From these contrasts, which are vivid enough to startle and enlighten those accustomed to our own way of life and simple enough to be grasped quickly, it is possible to learn many things about the effect of a civilisation upon the individuals within it.

So, in order to investigate the particular problem, I chose to go not to Germany or to Russia, but to Samoa, a South Sea island about thirteen degrees from the Equator, inhabited by a brown Polynesian people. Because I was a woman and could hope for greater intimacy in working with girls rather than with boys, and because owing to a paucity of women ethnologists our knowledge of primitive girls is far slighter than our knowledge of boys, I chose to concentrate upon the adolescent girl in Samoa.

But in concentrating, I did something very different from what I would do if I concentrated upon a study of the adolescent girl in Kokomo, Indiana. In such a study, I would go right to the crux of the problem; I would not have to linger long over the Indiana language, the table manners or sleeping habits of my subjects, or make an exhaustive study of how they learned to dress themselves, to use the telephone, or what the concept of conscience meant in Kokomo. All these things are the general fabric of American life, known to me as investigator, known to you as readers.

But with this new experiment on the primitive adolescent girl the matter was quite otherwise. She spoke a language the very sounds of which were strange, a language in which nouns became verbs and verbs nouns in the most sleight-of-hand fashion. All of her habits of life were different. She sat cross-legged on the ground, and to sit upon a chair made her stiff and miserable. She ate with her fingers from a woven plate; she slept upon the floor. Her house was a mere circle of pillars, roofed by a cone of thatch, carpeted with water-worn coral fragments. Her whole material environment was different. Cocoanut palm, breadfruit, and mango trees swayed above her village. She had never seen a horse, knew no animals except the pig, dog and rat. Her food was taro, breadfruit and bananas, fish and wild pigeon and half-roasted pork, and land crabs. And just as it was necessary to understand this physical environment, this routine of life which was so different from ours, so her social environment in its attitudes towards children, towards sex, towards personality, presented as strong a contrast to the social environment of the American girl.

I concentrated upon the girls of the community. I spent the greater part of my time with them. I studied most closely the households in which adolescent girls lived. I spent more time in the games of children than in the councils of their elders. Speaking their language, eating their food, sitting barefoot and cross-legged upon the pebbly floor, I did my best to minimise the differences between us and to learn to know and understand all the girls of three little villages on the coast of the little island of Taū, in the Manu'a Archipelago.

Through the nine months which I spent in Samoa, I gathered many detailed facts about these girls, the size of their families, the position and wealth of their parents, the number of their brothers and sisters, the amount of sex experience which they had had. All of these routine facts are summarised in a table in the appendix. They are only the barest skeleton, hardly the raw materials for a study of family situations and sex relations, standards of friendship, of loyalty, of personal responsibility, all those impalpable storm centres of disturbances in the lives of our adolescent girls. And because these less measurable parts of their lives were so similar, because one girl's life was so much like another's, in an uncomplex, uniform culture like Samoa, I feel justified in generalising although I studied only fifty girls in three small neighboring villages.

In the following chapters I have described the lives of these girls, the lives of their younger sisters who will soon be adolescent, of their brothers with whom a strict taboo forbids them to speak, of their older sisters who have left puberty behind them, of their elders, the mothers and fathers whose attitudes towards life determine the attitudes of their children. And through this description I have tried to answer the question which sent me to Samoa: Are the disturbances which vex our adolescents due to the nature of adolescence itself or to the civilisation? Under different conditions does adolescence present a different picture?

Also, by the nature of the problem, because of the unfamiliarity of this simple life on a small Pacific island, I have had to give a picture of the whole social life of Samoa, the details being selected always with a view to illuminating the problem of adolescence. Matters of political organisation which neither interest nor influence the young girl are not included. Minutiae of relationship systems or ancestor cults, genealogies and mythology, which are of interest only to the specialist, will be published in another place. But I have tried to present to the reader the Samoan girl in her social setting, to describe the course of her life from birth until death, the problems she will have to solve, the values which will guide her in her solutions, the pains and pleasures of her human lot cast on a South Sea island.

Such a description seeks to do more than illuminate this particular problem. It should also give the reader some conception of a different and contrasting civilisation, another way of life, which other members of the human race have found satisfactory and gracious. We know that our subtlest perceptions, our highest values, are all based upon contrast; that light without darkness or beauty without ugliness would lose the qualities which they now appear to us to have. And similarly, if we would appreciate our own civilisation, this elaborate pattern of life which we have made for ourselves as a people and which we are at such pains to pass on to our children, we must set our civilisation over against other very different ones. The traveller in Europe returns to America, sensitive to nuances in his own manners and philosophies which have hitherto gone unremarked, yet Europe and America are parts of one civilisation. It is with variations within one great pattern that the student of Europe to-day or the student of our own history sharpens his sense of appreciation. But if we step outside the stream of Indo-European culture, the appreciation which we can accord our civilisation is even more enhanced. Here in remote parts of the world, under historical conditions very different from those which made Greece and Rome flourish and fall, groups of human beings have worked out patterns of life so different from our own that we cannot venture any guess that they would ever have arrived at our solutions. Each primitive people has selected one set of human gifts, one set of human values, and fashioned for themselves an art, a social organisation, a religion, which is their unique contribution to the history of the human spirit.

Samoa is only one of these diverse and gracious patterns, but as the traveller who has been once from home is wiser than he who has never left his own door step, so a knowledge of one other culture should sharpen our ability to scrutinise more steadily, to appreciate more lovingly, our own.

And, because of the particular problem which we set out to answer, this tale of another way of life is mainly concerned with education, with the process by which the baby, arrived cultureless upon the human scene, becomes a full-fledged adult member of his or her society. The strongest light will fall upon the ways in which Samoan education, in its broadest sense, differs from our own. And from this contrast we may be able to turn, made newly and vividly self-conscious and self-critical, to judge anew and perhaps fashion differently the education we give our children.

Introduction: Growing up in Manus Society

The way in which each human infant is transformed into the finished adult, into the complicated individual version of his city and his century is one of the most fascinating studies open to the curious minded. Whether one wishes to trace the devious paths by which the unformed baby which was oneself developed personality, to prophesy the future of some child still in pinafores, to direct a school, or to philosophise about the future of the United States—the same problem is continually in the foreground of thought. How much of the child's equipment does it bring with it at birth? How much of its development follows regular laws? How much or how little and in what ways is it dependent upon early training, upon the personality of its parents, its teachers, its playmates, the age into which it is born? Is the framework of human nature so rigid that it will break if submitted to too severe tests? To what limits will it flexibly accommodate itself? Is it possible to rewrite the conflict between youth and age so that it is less acute or more fertile of good results? Such questions are implicit in almost every social decision—in the mother's decision to feed the baby with a spoon rather than force it to drink from a hated bottle, in the appropriation of a million dollars to build a new manual training high school, in the propaganda plans of the Anti-Saloon League or of the Communist party. Yet it is a subject about which we know little, towards which we are just developing methods of approach.

But when human history took the turn which is symbolised in the story of the confusion of tongues and the dispersion of peoples after the Tower of Babel, the student of human nature was guaranteed one kind of laboratory. In all parts of the world, in the densest jungle and on the small islands of the sea, groups of people, differing in language and customs from their neighbours, were working out experiments in what could be done with human nature. The restless fancy of many men was drawing in diverse ways upon their historical backgrounds, inventing new tools, new forms of government, new and different phrasings of the problem of good and evil, new views of man's place in the universe.

By one people the possibilities of rank with all its attendant artificialities and conventions were being tested, by a second the social consequences of large scale human sacrifice, while a third tested the results of a loose unpatterned democracy. While one people tried out the limits of ceremonial licentiousness, another exacted season-long or year-long continence from all its members. Where one people made their dead their gods, another chose to ignore the dead and rely instead upon a philosophy of life which viewed man as grass that grows up in the morning and is cut down forever at nightfall.

Within the generous lines laid down by the early patterns of thought and behaviour which seem to form our common human inheritance, countless generations of men have experimented with the possibilities of the human spirit. It only remained for those of inquiring mind, alive to the value of these hoary experiments, to read the answers written down in the ways of life of different peoples. Unfortunately we have been prodigal and blind in our use of these priceless records. We have permitted the only account of an experiment which it has taken thousands of years to make and which we are powerless to repeat, to be obliterated by firearms, or alcohol, evangelism or tuberculosis. One primitive people after another has vanished and left no trace.

If a long line of devoted biologists had been breeding guinea pigs or fruit flies for a hundred years and recording the results, and some careless vandal burnt the painstaking record and killed the survivors, we woud cry out in anger at the loss to science. Yet, when history, without any such set purpose, has presented us with the results of not a hundred years' experiment on guinea pigs, but a thousand years' experiment on human beings, we permit the records to be extinguished without a protest.

Although most of these fragile cultures which owed their perpetuation not to written records but to the memories of a few hundred human beings are lost to us, a few remain. Isolated on small Pacific islands, in dense African jungles or Asiatic wastes, it is still possible to find untouched societies which have chosen solutions of life's problems different from our own, which can give us precious evidence on the malleability of human nature.

Such an untouched people are the brown sea-dwelling Manus of the Admiralty Islands, north of New Guinea. In their vaulted, thatched houses set on stilts in the olive green waters of the wide lagoon, their lives are lived very much as they have been lived for unknown centuries. No missionary has come to teach them an unknown faith, no trader has torn their lands from them and reduced them to penury. Those white men's diseases which have reached them have been few enough in number to be fitted into their own theory of disease as a punishment for evil done. They buy iron and cloth and beads from the distant traders; they have learned to smoke the white man's tobacco, to use his money, to take an occasional dispute into the District Officer's Court. Since 1912 war has been practically abolished, an enforced reformation welcome to a trading, voyaging people. Their young men go away to work for two or three years in the plantations of the white man, but come back little changed to their own villages. It is essentially a primitive society without written records, without economic dependence upon white culture, preserving its own canons, its own way of life.

The manner in which human babies born into these water-dwelling communities, gradually absorb the traditions, the prohibitions, the values of their elders and become in turn the active perpetuators of Manus culture is a record rich in its implications for education. Our own society is so complex, so elaborate, that the most serious student can, at best, only hope to examine a part of the educational process. While he concentrates upon the method in which a child solves one set of problems, he must of necessity neglect the others. But in a simple society, without division of labour, without written records, without a large population, the whole tradition is narrowed down to the memory capacities of a few individuals. With the aid of writing and an analytic point of view, it is possible for the investigator to master in a few months most of the tradition which it takes the native years to learn.

From the vantage point of a thorough knowledge of the cultural background, it is then possible to study the educational process, to suggest solutions to educational problems which we would never be willing to study by experimentation upon our own children. But Manus has made the experiment for us; we have only to read the answer.

I made this study of Manus education to prove no thesis, to support no preconceived theories. Many of the results came as a surprise to me. This description of the way a simple people, dwelling in the shallow lagoons of a distant south sea island, prepare their children for life, is presented to the reader as a picture of human education in miniature. Its relevance to modern educational interest is first just that it is such a simplified record in which all the elements can be readily grasped and understood, where a complex process which we are accustomed to think of as written upon too large a canvas to be taken in at a glance, can be seen as through a painter's diminishing glass. Furthermore in Manus certain tendencies in discipline or accorded license, certain parental attitudes, can be seen carried to more drastic lengths than has yet occurred within our own society. And finally these Manus people are interesting to us because the aims and methods of Manus society, although primitive, are not unlike the aims and methods which may be found in our own immediate history.

We shall see how remarkably successful the Manus people are in instilling into the smallest child a respect for property; how equally remarkable is the physical adjustment which very young children are taught to make. The firm discipline combined with the unflagging solicitude which lie back of these two conspicuous Manus triumphs, contradict equally the theory that a child should be protected and sheltered and the theory that he should be thrown into the waters of experience to "sink or swim." The Manus world, slight frameworks of narrow boards above the changing tides of the lagoon, is too precarious a place for costly mistakes. The successful fashion in which each baby is efficiently adapted to its dangerous way of life is relevant to the problems which parents here must face as our mode of life becomes increasingly charged with possibilities of accident.

Perhaps equally illuminating are the Manus mistakes, for their efficiency in training dexterous little athletes and imbuing them with a thorough respect for property is counterbalanced by their failure in other forms of discipline. The children are allowed to give their emotions free play; they are taught to bridle neither their tongues nor their tempers. They are taught no respect for their parents; they are given no pride in their tradition. The absence of any training which fits them to accept graciously the burden of their tradition, to assume proudly the rôle of adults, is conspicuous. They are permitted to frolic in their ideal playground without responsibilities and without according either thanks or honour to those whose unremitting labour makes their long years of play possible.

Those who believe that all children are naturally creative, inherently imaginative, that they need only be given freedom to evolve rich and charming ways of life for themselves, will find in the behaviour of Manus children no confirmation of their faith. Here are all the children of a community, freed from all labour, given only the most rudimentary schooling by a society which concerns itself only with physical proficiency, respect for property and the observance of a few tabus. They are healthy children; a fifty per cent infant death rate accomplishes that. Only the most fit survive. They are intelligent children; there are only three or four dull children among them. They have perfect bodily coordination; their senses are sharp, their perceptions are quick and accurate. The parent and child relationship is such that feelings of inferiority and insecurity hardly exist. And this group of children are allowed to play all day long, but, alas for the theorists, their play is like that of young puppies or kittens. Unaided by the rich hints for play which

children of other societies take from the admired adult traditions, they
have a dull, uninteresting child life, romping good humouredly until
they are tired, then lying inert and breathless until rested sufficiently to
romp again.

The family picture in Manus is also strange and revealing, with the
father taking the principle rôle, the father the tender solicitous indulgent
guardian, while the mother takes second place in the child's affection.
Accustomed as we are to the family in which the father is the stern and
distant dictator, the mother the child's advocate and protector, it is provocative to find a society in which father and mother have exchanged
parts. The psychiatrists have laboured the difficulties under which a
male child grows up if his father plays patriarch and his mother madon-
na. Manus illustrates the creative part which a loving tender father may
play in shaping positively his son's personality. It suggests that the
solution of the family complex may lie not in the parents assuming no
rôles, as some enthusiasts suggest, but in their playing different ones.

Besides these special points in Manus educational practice, there is
also a curious analogy between Manus society and America. Like America, Manus has not yet turned from the primary business of making a
living to the less immediate interest of the conduct of life as an art. As in
America, work is respected and industry and economic success is the
measure of the man. The dreamer who turns aside from fishing and
trading and so makes a poor showing at the next feast, is despised as a
weakling. Artists they have none, but like Americans, they, richer than
their neighbours, buy their neighbours' handiwork. To the arts of leisure, conversation, story telling, music and dancing, friendship and
love making, they give scant recognition. Conversation is purposeful,
story telling is abbreviated and very slightly stylised, singing is for
moments of boredom, dancing is to celebrate financial arrangements,
friendship is for trade, and love making, in any elaborate sense, is
practically unknown. The ideal Manus man has no leisure; he is ever up
and about his business turning five strings of shell money into ten.

With this emphasis upon work, upon the accumulation of more and
more property, the cementing of firmer trade alliances, the building of
bigger canoes and bigger houses, goes a congruent attitude towards
morality. As they admire industry, so do they esteem probity in business
dealings. Their hatred of debt, their uneasiness beneath undischarged
economic obligations is painful. Diplomacy and tact are but slightly
valued; obstreperous truthfulness is the greater virtue. The double standard permitted very cruel prostitution in earlier days; the most rigorous
demands are still made upon the virtue of Manus women. Finally their
religion is genuinely ethical; it is a spiritualistic cult of the recently dead

ancestors who supervise jealously their descendants' economic and sexual lives, blessing those who abstain from sin and who labour to grow
wealthy, visiting sickness and misfortune on violators of the sexual code
and on those who neglect to invest the family capital wisely. In many
ways, the Manus ideal is very similar to our historical Puritan ideal,
demanding from men industry, prudence, thrift and abstinence from
worldly pleasures, with the promise that God will prosper the virtuous
man.

In this stern workaday world of the adult, the children are not asked
to play any part. Instead they are given years of unhampered freedom by
parents whom they often bully and despise for their munificence. We
often present our children with this same picture. We who live in a
society where it is the children who wear the silk while the mothers
labour in calico, may find something of interest in the development of
these primitive young people in a world that is so often like a weird
caricature of our own, a world whose currency is shells and dogs' teeth,
which makes its investments in marriages instead of corporations and
conducts its overseas trade in outrigger canoes, but where property,
morality and security for the next generation are the main concerns of its
inhabitants.

This account is the result of six months' concentrated and uninter-
rupted field work. From a thatched house on piles, built in the centre of
the Manus village of Peri, I learned the native language, the children's
games, the intricacies of social organisation, economic custom and religious belief and practice which formed the social framework within
which the child grows up. In my large living room, on the wide veran-
dahs, on the tiny islet adjoining the houses, in the surrounding lagoon,
the children played all day and I watched them, now from the midst of a
play group, now from behind the concealment of the thatched walls. I
rode in their canoes, attended their feasts, watched in the house of
mourning and sat severely still while the mediums conversed with the
spirits of the dead. I observed the children when no grown-up people
were present, and I watched their behaviour towards their parents.
Within a social setting which I learned to know intimately enough not to
offend against the hundreds of name tabus, I watched the Manus baby,
the Manus child, the Manus adolescent, in an attempt to understand the
way in which each of these was becoming a Manus adult.

Clyde Kluckhohn

12. Covert Culture and Administrative Problems[1]

During the last eight years the U.S. Indian Service has made tremendous strides in the application of social science skills. In no field of administration has anthropology's master concept, culture, been so basic to planning and to action. It would be too much to expect that culture should, in so short a space of time, have become part of the thinking of every member of this organization. Within the last two years I have encountered a teacher in an Indian school who was baffled when a Navaho high school boy refused to ask an attractive girl to fox-trot. ("Sometimes they seem just as bright as white students, and then something like this happens that makes me feel they are just dumb animals.") When I suggested that perhaps they were members of the same clan, the teacher failed to see how this could be related to their "stupid" behavior, and when I asked her how she would feel about getting into bed with her brother, she seemed more indignant than enlightened. Similarly, when a newly arrived teacher volunteered the generalization that Navaho first grade girls were intelligent and friendly, but the boys slow and uncooperative, pottery-making turned out to be the activity in which the two sexes had been compared! However, such obtuseness survives only in the face of consistent propaganda for cultural relativity in *Indian Education*, instruction by anthropologists in summer schools, and almost every other educative device which an enlightened administration can provide. There can be no doubt that the top administrative group are sensitively aware that *social* heredity is a major determinant of the habits and goals characteristic of different societies. Likewise, there is now full realization that not merely are there culturally patterned ways of feeling and reacting but that members of the society are not neutrally but affectively oriented to culture traits and culture patterns. Rational, irrational, and non-rational elements in human action are explicitly recognized. Most administrators of Indian groups know that people will often respond in terms of "the logic of the sentiments." Finally, as the more recent handling of the Navaho stock reduction program has demonstrated, the administrative process is carried out with discriminating acceptance of the theorem of interdependence. It has been realized that the technological basis of Navaho society could not be altered without ramified consequences for many other sectors of the culture.

These are large gains. If performance is often still not above criticism, this is at least as much the result of the inadequacy of the data and analytical skills which anthropology (and other social sciences) are as yet able to supply as of any administrative ineptness. In fact, the Indian Service has kept amazingly abreast of social science theory, and the whole anthropological profession, in my judgment, owes an immense debt of gratitude to Commissioner Collier and his associates for the most whole-hearted application of anthropological knowledge which has thus far been put to the test by any administrative agency.

Further progress will be largely contingent upon further development of less superficial and more systematic anthropological theory. New conceptual refinements will suggest new observations and the re-sifting of already accumulated data for illuminations which will have practical implications. In no aspect of theory are the frontiers being pushed back so rapidly as in that of structural analysis. Professor Boas has shown abundant awareness that cultures have organization as well as content, but the beginnings of an articulate terminology for describing structural phenomena have been largely provided by such anthropologists as Sapir, Linton, Benedict, Mead, Warner, Bateson, and Hallowell.

There are, first of all, the more concrete types of patterning. These are the observed regularities of word and deed—a determinate sequence of action-events or word-events which could not be predicted on the basis of functional connection alone, their association depends primarily upon cultural selectivity. All patterning implies "an exactness of relationship, irrespective of dimensions." Thus Navaho bows used in shooting and the miniature replicas (of varying sizes and materials) used in several Navaho chants are distinct culture traits. But all conform to the same general pattern. The problem of pattern is the problem of symmetry, of constancies of form irrespective of wide variations in concrete actualization.

At this level, a major dichotomy may be distinguished, that of ideal and behavioral patterns.[2] This is essentially the familiar contrast between rules and practices, but the inclusion of the term "pattern" is useful insofar as we are reminded that we are dealing not merely with regularities but with structural regularities—with a predictable conjunction of words and acts in a fixed order. The concepts of ideal and behavioral pattern bear some similarity to Sumner's distinction between mores and folkways. This distinction was one of the earliest systematic discriminations of cultural structure and has proven of considerable utility. But the focal issue is that of *degree* of sanction, and this must often be decided upon grounds which are unusually arbitrary. Moreover, it is not always clear whether a more or a folkway is established upon basis of behavioral or normative modalities. Finally, mores and folkways tend to imply a static culture, whereas ideal and behavioral patterns are conceptual instruments helpful in dealing with culture change. If we describe the ideal patterns we answer the question: what are the cultural standards? When we have also described the behavioral patterns, we can rigorously contrast the extent of conformance to the ideal patterns.

Another popular dichotomy with which there are points of resemblance is that between "formal organization" and "informal organization" which Roethlisberger[3] and Barnard[4] have applied in industry with such success. At first glance these might be regarded as special cases of ideal and behavioral patterns respectively. While there is a rough equivalence between ideal patterns and those schemata for communication, etc., which constitute a formal organization, the categories are by no means identical. For example, there are ideal patterns for the communication and interaction which take place within an informal organization.

Having indicated certain differences from other partially similar concepts, let me now try to define ideal and behavioral patterns by saying what they do and do not denote. The term "ideal" is unfortunate, for it has the connotation for many of "ideals" in the sense of quasi-mystical and unattainable goals. The contrast intended, however, is not so much that between "ideals" and conduct as between standards and conduct. Behavioral patterns are modes of conduct; ideal patterns, modes of standards. If we shift our interest from behavioral to ideal patterns we are, to some extent, making the transition from the regular to the regulative. The word "ideal" also breeds confusion by suggesting to some an equation with words as opposed to overt non-linguistic acts. But a behavioral pattern can consist of either verbal or non-verbal acts. For instance, there are no "ideal patterns" for Navaho witchcraft because all witch acts are disapproved. The culture does, however, encompass behavioral idea patterns which state how witches are believed to operate.

The test of an ideal pattern is: does there exist a normative demand on the part of some considerable proportion of the society that individuals will conform to a standard so that non-conformity tends to be punished by organized or diffuse sanctions? To call such standards "patterns of expectancy" would seem to be a mistake, for behavioral patterns are also "expected" in the sense of being anticipated by the participants in the culture. Perhaps "sanctioned pattern" or "regulatory pattern" would be a preferable usage. For the peripheral category of those patterns which embody "ideals" in the vulgar sense one may suggest the term "utopian patterns." Thus the "ideals" set forth in the Sermon on the Mount[5] are not patterns to which conformity is really expected by most groups in the "Christian world" today; literal conformity evokes amazement or suspicion of "queerness," and non-conformity remains almost totally unpunished.

Of the general principle of pattern, good use has been made in the Indian Service. Thus MacGregor prevented the needless destruction of houses in which death had occurred by introducing the familiar pattern of fumigation into this context. But, although any good executive is intuitively aware of the differences between "theory" and "practice," Indian administrators are perhaps insufficiently aware of the utility of systematically making the discrimination between sanctioned and behavioral patterns. Particularly since many ethnographies consist almost exclusively of descriptions of the sanctioned patterns of a culture, the administrator who is conscientiously striving for an anthropological orientation runs the danger of taking the sanctioned patterns at their face value, i.e., as an adequate statement of the whole of the culture. He is then perplexed at the deviations, at the fact that a policy oriented toward such formulas often gives rise to as many administrative difficulties as one which neglects culture entirely. The opposite error is also not infrequent. The "tough-minded" superintendent says, "I don't want to know what these Indians say they do. I want to know what they actually do." But the fact that there is never complete correspondence between sanctioned pattern and behavioral pattern does not prove that the sanctioned patterns are unimportant. This observation shows merely that a sanctioned pattern is only one of a number of the determinants of any action. As a matter of fact, one of the most objective indices of the extent of acculturation, of the existent rate of culture change, of the intensity of strains to which individuals in a group are subjected is the range, degree, and number of deviations of conduct from the culturally approved standards.

Although application of the theory of patterns is not yet as systematic or explicit as would be desirable, there is awareness of these patterns of the overt culture. Sanctioned and behavioral patterns are abstractions of the first order. They are what logicians would call "class constructs," and are arrived at mainly by induction from direct observation. But when we turn to phenomena of patterning in the covert culture, we have to deal with second order abstractions, with "analytical abstractions." These are not inductive generalizations but inferential constructs. They are principles which the investigator introduces to "explain" connections between constellations of data which have no obvious connection in the world of direct observation. They start from data, and they must be validated by a return to the data, but they unquestionably rest upon systematic extrapolations. This need not alarm us unduly. No one has ever seen "gravitation." One sees bodies fall—all sorts of bodies, falling under different conditions. "Gravitation" is a convenient conceptual construct which "orders" phenomena having a wide range in the concrete.

As yet, social science has hardly done more than grope toward a coherent theory of the forms of the covert culture. It can be said, however, that there is increasing recognition of the premise that "there is more to any culture than meets the eye." A contrast of "overt culture" with something else which is not consistently named is a current which runs all through the later writings of Sapir. He says, for example, ". . . culture . . . cannot be adequately defined by a description of those more colorful patterns of behavior in society which lie open to observation."[6] The problem is strictly analogous to that of understanding the individual. A well-known clinical psychologist has recently distinguished three classes of information needed in a case history: 1) what the person can tell about himself and is willing to tell; 2) what he knows but is reticent or resistive about; 3) what he does not know about himself but is still a highly relevant part of his personality. In the case of the individual, this last class of data can be obtained by psychoanalytic methods, by free association tests and the like, and by the Rohrschach and various other projective techniques.

What Linton has specifically designated as the covert culture is, as the name necessarily implies, precisely that sector of the culture of which the members of the society are unaware or minimally aware. "Covert," then, refers primarily to the culture carriers, although this part of culture is also inevitably submerged or covert at first from the point of view of the investigator and only later inferred out. Professor Linton, who has never published the theory of covert culture which he has helped develop in his lectures, kindly permits me to quote a statement[7] from him:

I begin by taking the widest definition of culture as established by uncritical but scientific anthropological usage. A culture thus includes the implements and objects used by any society, the behavior of its members, and the habit patterns, knowledge, value system, and attitudes shared by these members. The concept thus includes phenomena of three distinct orders: material (tools and objects); kinesthetic (overt behavior); and psychological (habit patterns, etc.). I use the term overt culture to refer to phenomena of the first two categories, which are directly observable and recordable, in most cases by impersonal, mechanical means. Covert culture, as I use the term, refers to the phenomena of the psychological order as a whole, the existence of these phenomena being deducible only from their manifestations in phenomena of the first two orders. Thus, from the repetitive behavior of the individual in response to a particular repetitive stimulus, one deduces the existence within the individual of some condition which leads him to make the same response to the same stimulus, i.e., a habit. The difference between overt and covert is thus very much that between tangible and intangible. For example, both speech and music I should class as elements of overt culture.

To this I should like to add only the emphasis that speaking of "covert *culture*" is necessary because we are, after all, dealing with and interested in the social heredity of a particular human group.

In the remainder of this paper I shall discuss only one aspect of the covert culture: the implicit or suppressed premises which tend to be characteristic of members of a certain group. These unconscious assumptions I have called, for want of a more satisfactory term, "cultural configurations." If there appears to be a single dominant master configuration, this may be designated as "the integrating principle of the culture" or as "the ethos of the society."

A cultural configuration may be defined as a principle of the covert culture—either a way of doing a variety of things (a means) or an end (a culturally defined goal). Since configurations are part of the *covert* culture they are *unstated* premises. One is tempted to say that configurations are cultural principles of which there is characteristically no sustained and systematic awareness on the part of most members of a society. This statement, however, would give a special and narrow sense to "awareness." It must mean "awareness with respect to customary or even habitual verbalization." The members of the society are, of course, aware in the sense that they make choices with the configurations as unconscious but determinative backgrounds.

The distinction between the configurations and those cultural premises which are explicitly stated in idea patterns is that of polar concepts, not of the all-or-none type. Reality, and not least cultural reality, appears to be a continuum rather than a set of neat, water-tight compartments which await our discovery. But we can seldom cope with the continuum as a whole, and the isolation and naming of certain contrastive sections of the continuum is highly useful. It follows, however, that the theoretical structure does not collapse with the production of doubtful or transitional cases. In a highly self-conscious culture like our own which makes a business of studying itself, the proportion of the culture which is literally covert in the sense of never having been stated explicitly by any member of the society may be small. Yet only a trifling per cent of American citizens could state even those implicit premises of our culture which have been dissected out by social scientists. I remember an astute remark by Professor Lloyd Warner: "If you could bring an Australian aborigine who had been fully socialized in his own culture and then trained in social science to the American scene, he would perceive all sorts of patterned regularities of which our sociologists are completely unaware."

In the case of less sophisticated and self-conscious societies, the unconscious assumptions characteristically made by individuals socialized by approximately the same social controls will bulk large. These are what Whorf has called, with special reference to grammatical categories, "background phenomena." What he says of language applies to many other aspects of culture: ". . . our psychic make-up is somehow adjusted to disregard whole realms of phenomena that are so all-pervasive as to be irrelevant to our daily lives and needs . . . the phenomena of a language are to its own speakers largely . . . outside the critical consciousness and control of the speaker. . . ." Such an insight is far from irrelevant to the problems of the Indian Service. It is an induction from wide experience that sometimes a program which has been carefully thought through for its possible continuities with the cultural inventory and even for its interdigitation with first-order patterns sometimes fails to work out. This is very probably because, as Sapir says, the innovations do not "configurate correctly with the unconscious system of meanings characteristic of the given culture."[8] Undoubtedly this is the explanation of the unexpected consequences of certain earlier attempts at acculturation on the part of governmental and missionary groups to which La Barre[9] has drawn attention:

Thus, ironically, the intended modes of deculturalizing the Indian have contributed pre-eminently to the reinvigoration of a basically aboriginal religion.

Likewise, this conceptual framework enables us to understand certain results almost universally regarded as unsatisfactory, of the adoption by Indians of *parts* of our value system (that is, sanctioned patterns and configurations of the covert culture) without also taking over the other sanctioned patterns and configurations which to some degree act as limiting and integrating controls. Keesing [10] has commented:

Among such groups as the Menominie "rugged individualism" can be observed actually operating minus the multitudinous disciplines and control which the ordinary white American absorbs more or less unconsciously.

The administrator is often deceived by the tangible and readily observable changes in culture content. He sees Hopi men dressed like white men in their own region, skillfully driving trucks and otherwise manifesting adaptation to our technology, and makes very mistaken inferences as to the degree of acculturation among the Hopi. Actually, the tenacity of cultural structure, and especially of the covert structure, is one of the widest and most useful generalizations with which anthropology can provide the administrator. As Boas well says, "In comparison to changes of content of culture the configuration has often remarkable permanency."[11] Sapir has made the same induction as to the conservatism of organizational principles in language.[12]

Notes

1. This paper has had the benefit of helpful criticisms and suggestions from Ralph Linton, Florence Kluckhohn, and Otis Lee.

2. For a fuller discussion of ideal and behavioral patterns and suggested subcategories (alternative, compulsory, preferred, typical, and restricted ideal patterns; major, minor, conformant, and deviant behavioral patterns) see Clyde Kluckhohn, *Patterning as Exemplified in Navaho Culture* (*Language, Culture, and Personality*, Menasha, Wis., 1941), pp. 109–130. The theoretical aspects of the present paper are to be regarded as an extension and modification of the conceptual scheme set forth in the earlier paper. See also *Anent Patterns and "Flexible Methods,"* pp. 328, *American Anthropologist*, 1943.

3. F. Roethlisberger, *Management and Morale* (Cambridge, Mass., 1941).

4. C. I. Barnard, *The Functions of the Executive* (Cambridge, Mass., 1938).

5. This illustration and the term "utopian patterns" were first suggested to me by my colleague, Talcott Parsons.

6. Article, *Language*, Encyclopaedia of the Social Sciences, vol. IX, p. 157.

7. Personal communication of Nov. 30, 1942.

8. Article, *Fashion*, Encyclopaedia of the Social Sciences, vol. VI, p. 141.

9. W. La Barre, *The Peyote Cult* (Yale Publications in Anthropology, New Haven, 1938), p. 55.

10. Felix Keesing, *The Menomini Indians of Wisconsin* (Memoirs of the American Philosophical Society, vol. 10, Philadelphia, 1939), pp. 246–247.

11. Introduction to Ruth Benedict, *Patterns of Culture* (New York, 1934), p. xiii.

12. *Language* (New York, 1921), pp. 57–58.

John and Beatrice Whiting

13. A Strategy for Psychocultural Research

Our approach to psychological anthropology can best be introduced by using a genealogical metaphor. Our totemic ancestors are William Graham Sumner, Sigmund Freud, Bronislaw Malinowski, Ivan Petrovich Pavlov and Franz Boaz.

The Sumner lineage provided us with a number of basic notions, the most important of which is that culture has evolved by a process of trial and error rather than by a rational plan. As Sumner puts it in the opening paragraph of his *Folkways* (1906), "Men begin with acts, not with thoughts. Every moment brings necessities which must be satisfied at once. Need was the first experience, and it was followed at once by a blundering effort to satisfy it." This materialist approach lead us in the development of our theory to start with the environment and history and to end with magic, art and religion. It led us to prefer Marx to Weber and Pavlov to Piaget. "The maintenance mores are basic" is the phrase we learned to express our commitment to a materialist theory of social change.

Sumner went on to say in his "charter" statement (*Folkways*, p. 3): "From recurrent needs arise habits for the individual and customs for the group." The assumption of the equivalence between custom and habit made it possible for us to use theories of learning, developed by psychologists to explain individual behavior, to interpret the customary behavior of a group (Whiting and Child 1953).

G. P. Murdock was a member of the Sumner lineage of our parental generation—he was a teacher and thesis director for both of us. From him we learned many things but perhaps the most important was the cross-cultural method. Starting with Sumner's voluminous notes on the peoples of the world, Murdock developed the Human Relations Area Files, set standards for proper use of ethnographic materials to test hypotheses on world wide samples, and published in the Ethnographic Atlas (*Ethnology*, 1962–1966) coded materials on over one thousand societies describing such items as subsistence patterns, social organization, settlement pattern, division of labor, political organization and religious beliefs. Many of the studies that we will describe below made use of coded material from the Ethnographic Atlas, drew on the Human Relations Area files to make judgments of our own, and used the cross cultural method to test our hypotheses.

The materialist, evolutionary and cross-cultural approach of Sumner and Murdock was strongly opposed by the American Historical School whose leading figure was Franz Boaz and whose student, Leslie Spier, was one of our teachers. He imbued in us the importance of careful fieldwork and of historical processes, such as diffusion and borrowing, migration, and invention as principles by which the beliefs, values and techniques of a particular culture can be explained. He was critical of "grand theories" which include British evolutionists such as Tylor and Frazer and particularly critical of the French "sociological" school as represented by Durkheim. Perhaps the most important lesson that we learned from him was that, if you describe something about a culture, you must be sure that you know how it works. We spent one summer together while Bea was working with the Paiute gathering material for her thesis and John was coding ethnographies for the cross-cultural material files and editing some of Bea's field notes on material culture. One of these concerned a deadfall rabbit trap. John had read the description and approved it but when Leslie read it he called Bea in to ask her to please explain how it could possible work. Bea passed the buck to John and we both had to agree that any Paiute who made a trap as we described it would probably go hungry. This lesson has stood us in good stead. Child rearing practices and women's daily routines must be described so that they will "catch the rabbit."

Bronislaw Malinowski was another teacher who had a strong influence on our thinking. A British functionalist, he emphasized the importance of explaining customs in terms of individual and social needs. Malinowski came to Yale the year John came back from New Guinea and was writing his thesis on the Kwoma. We were asked to his house one evening so John could read a draft of one of his chapters out loud. He had asked a group of his non-anthropological friends to listen and criticize. Their criticisms were devastating—almost as traumatic as when Murdock told each of us in turn that the first drafts of our theses were excruciatingly bad, or when Spier told us our rabbit trap wouldn't work.

The Institute of Human Relations which flowered during our careers as graduate students and with which we were both affiliated brought us in contract with learning and behavior theory through Clark Hull, Neal Miller, Don Marquis, Hobart Mowrer and Bob Sears. The assumption of this school that drive reduction was a necessary condition for learning was quite compatible with the materialism of Sumner and Murdock, the practicality of Spier, and the functional approach of Malinowski. But more important than this particular theory of learning and behavior, we learned from them how to formulate and test hypotheses, the meaning of probability statistics, and the value of the experimental method. We spent one summer running white rats through a maze for a study of "habit progression and regression" that we carried out with Hobart Mowrer (1943). From Hull in particular we learned the importance of distinguishing between coherence and correspondence truth and, hence, the difference between proving a hypotheses and testing it. Like a theorem in geometry, the proof of a hypothesis consists of showing that it logically follows from and does not contradict other assumptions in the theory. The *test* consists of observing whether empirical reality does or does not correspond to that which is stated in the hypothesis. From Hull we also learned that science progresses from the creative acts that follow when a hypothesis is disconfirmed in such a way that theory must be revised. To jeopardize assumptions that are taken for granted is more productive and exciting than to illustrate them.

The Freudian lineage, as well as the Pavlovian, was strongly represented at the Institute of Human Relations. We learned psychoanalytic theory from John Dollard through lectures, seminars and informal discussions. The most important learning experience came from our personal analyses. We both received fellowships for this purpose. Our analyst was Earl Zinn. We discovered that the meaning of unconscious motivation and the way in which one can delude oneself by various defensive maneuvers could be more profoundly understood when they were illustrated from one's own life than from a text book case.

The psychoanalytic assumption that early experience had a determining effect on the development of personality was responsible for our interest in child rearing. A concerted effort was being made at the Institute to redefine the basic concepts of Freudian theory in such a way that they could be subjected to empirical test. This was done by integrating them with the concepts and principles of both learning and behavior theory and those of cultural anthropology. The Freudian principle of displacement was described as a special case of stimulus generalization as defined by Pavlov. Identification, a psychoanalytic concept, was related to imitation, a concept from the field of learning. The magico-religious beliefs reported by anthropologists were interpreted as manifestations of various mechanisms of defense proposed by Freud. Both of us participated in this enterprise.

The lineages we have mentioned thus far represent the materialistic, practical, functional and scientific hypothesis testing approaches to psychological anthropology. It was Edward Sapir who represented for us the more subtle and humanistic point of view. He stressed the importance of knowing the native language for understanding culture. His stress on the importance of metaphor anticipates the position of the present symbolic school. His explication of the phonemic analysis of language was a model for the emic approach developed in ethnoscience. He also speculated on the relationship between culture and personality and made suggestions that were much more subtle and persuasive than the ethnologically naive approach of Freud in his attempt to explain *Totem and Taboo* (1938). Although others soon followed his lead, Sapir inspired us to isolate the expressive-projective domain of magic, religion and art as a potential index of the modal personality of a culture.

The influence of our various intellectual forebears guided our subsequent research and eventually lead us to formulate the model presented in Figure 13–1. This model serves as a guide for our thinking. It enables us to relate the various studies that we undertake and have undertaken so their results are more cumulative than might otherwise be the case. It also enables us to relate our research to those of others in the field of psychological anthropology. It is for us a cognitive map for psychocultural research.

Over the years we have elaborated this model and the variables whose interrelationship forms the basis for our theories and governs our research. Figure 13–1 is its most recent form. The arrows should not be interpreted as irreversible indicators of causal relations. They represent assumptions about the direction of causality but they do *not* imply that in some, if not many, instances the true direction of causation is the reverse, or that there are not feedback loops or that steps in the assumed sequence may not be skipped. On the basis of this model we have formulated hypotheses which we have attempted to test using published ethnographic descriptions of societies and data from field work which we have designed in collaboration with our colleagues and students. Our pleasure comes from testing these hypotheses, finding them probable or improbable, revising them and repeating the process. We are most satisfied when one of our projects follows logically from the preceding ones and when our hypotheses are interrelated in a coherent manner.

We have attempted to test hypotheses both across and within societies. In the former case we have treated societies as units of analysis, have rated them on sets of variables and made tests of association between the variables. In many instances there are the same variations within as across societies thus enabling us to replicate our findings by

Figure 13-1

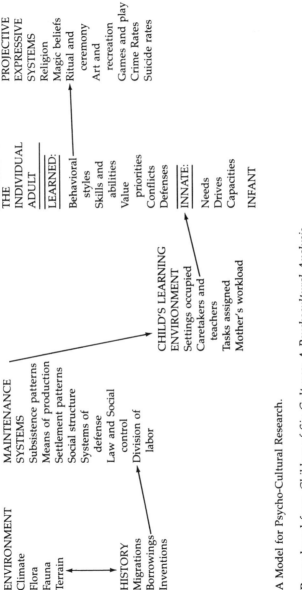

ENVIRONMENT	MAINTENANCE	CHILD'S LEARNING	THE	PROJECTIVE
Climate	SYSTEMS	ENVIRONMENT	INDIVIDUAL	EXPRESSIVE
Flora	Subsistence patterns	Settings occupied	ADULT	SYSTEMS
Fauna	Means of production	Caretakers and	LEARNED:	Religion
Terrain	Settlement patterns	teachers	Behavioral	Magic beliefs
	Social structure	Tasks assigned	styles	Ritual and
	Systems of	Mother's workload	Skills and	ceremony
	defense		abilities	Art and
	Law and Social		Value	recreation
HISTORY	control		priorities	Games and play
Migrations	Division of		Conflicts	Crime Rates
Borrowings	labor		Defenses	Suicide rates
Inventions			INNATE:	
			Needs	
			Drives	
			Capacities	
			INFANT	

A Model for Psycho-Cultural Research.

Reproduced from *Children of Six Cultures: A Psychocultural Analysis.*

case studies. As an example, cultures can be characterized as either monogamous or polygynous but there are no so-called polygynous societies in which monogamous families cannot be found. All of our findings are of necessity based on correlational studies. Since when one is working with human beings it is difficult to devise appropriate experiments, one is forced to search in his own and other societies for naturally occurring variations in the life experiences of individuals and attempt to assess their influence on behavior and related aspects of culture. We have found it wise, whenever possible, to pretest all of our hypotheses on published ethnographic data. If hypothesized associations look promising we try to turn to the detailed analysis of type cases and to testing the hypotheses in societies which are particularly suited because of variation in the predictor variables.

To illustrate this method let us take one of our current hypotheses: children brought up by mothers who make a substantial contribution to the subsistence of the family will be more concerned with the welfare of others than children brought up by mothers who do not make such a contribution. To test this theory across cultures on the basis of published data two sets of judges are needed. One set reads the ethnographies of a sample of societies distributed around the world and rates the mothers' reported contribution to the subsistence economy; the other set reads the same sources and rates the children on their tendency to help others and take responsibility for the welfare of others. Neither set of judges should know the hypothesis to be tested. If this evidence supports the hypothesis, a field study can be designed to investigate the relation of these variables within a society. The field study can identify a sample of women, estimate their contribution to subsistence, and record the rate of helpful and responsible behavior observed in their children. If the hypothesis holds up within this society we have further evidence for its validity.

Few of our studies encompass the entire model. Most of them have focused on a segment. In this chapter we will give examples of some of the studies, attempting at the same time to indicate how they are related historically. The original version of the model appeared in *Child Training and Personality*, the collaborative work of John Whiting and Irvin Child (1953, p. 310). This cross-cultural study explored the relation between a child's learning environment as measured by reported child training practices and one of the projective systems, theories of disease. The hypotheses relating these two sets of variables were derived from psychoanalytic and learning theories. The ethnographic accounts of seventy-five societies were read, analyzed and rated as to the parental treatment of critical issues during the Freudian stages of psychosexual development (oral, anal, and phallic) and parental behavior concerning two other problems which seemed of universal concern, training for independence and the management of aggression. Raters made judgments of the socialization practices surrounding these issues. They included assessments of (1) the initial indulgence or permissiveness associated with the behavior system; (2) the age at the onset of socialization; (3) the severity of socialization; and (4) the technique of punishment characteristically used by parents and other socializing agents. Two other raters made judgments of the society's most common explanations for illness, classifying them according to their relevance to these five behavior systems. For example the belief in magical poisoning was classified as an oral theory of disease.

Although the main thrust of this study was the relationship between an aspect of a child's learning environment and one type of projective system, the chapter on guilt considered the relation of social structure to child training practices and initiated another chain of studies. In the discussion of the possible origins of guilt, residence rules (whether a newly married couple set up residence independently of either set of parents, i.e., neolocal; or with the husband's family, i.e., patrilocal; or the wife's family, i.e., matrilocal) and forms of marriage (sororal polygyny, polygyny, monogamy) were explored as index measures of the relative role of parents, relatives and nonrelatives in the training of children (ibid., pp. 250–55. See also "Sorcery, Sin and Superego: A Cross-Cultural Study of Some Mechanisms of Social Control," J. Whiting 1959). The cross-cultural work of George Peter Murdock on social structure (Murdock 1949) gave impetus to the analysis of the effect of these variables on a child's learning environment. Further exploration of the relation of social structure to child training practices was presented in 1951 by Murdock and Whiting at a conference on the problems of infancy and childhood (Murdock and Whiting 1951). The most interesting finding concerned the relative severity of parental training in the five areas of socialization rated in the Whiting and Child study. Societies with sororal polygyny were judged to be less severe in their training than societies with non-sororal polygyny or monogamy. This was interpreted as reflecting the cooperation of the cowives (who are sisters) in the first type of household. These women, because they had worked out their interpersonal relations and rivalries in childhood, were able to help each other and share the care of each other's children and hence could give them more attention and postpone socialization. Since they could share their workload, these women seemed to be under less pressure than women in monogamous households where there were no other adult females or in non-sororal polygynous families where the women were rivalrous and had no long established pattern for working out these rivalries.

These findings in turn led to the expansion of the model and to the exploration of the influence of the maintenance systems, particularly economic and social structure variables on child training practices.

Two important decisions about our future research in culture and personality were the result of Irvin Child and John Whiting's collaboration in writing *Child Training and Personality*. In the first place the issues centering around the Freudian concept of psychosexual development appeared to be of less universal concern than others which could be identified: toilet training was seldom mentioned in the literature as being any problem at all. Weaning from the breast was usually not nearly so important as weaning from the back or training for independence. The socialization of sex turned out to be dealt with by rules governing premarital sex behavior in late childhood and adolescence rather than during early childhood. Training for aggression was, as expected, a universal problem as was training for independence. Parents in most cultures were more concerned with interpersonal relations than with body functions. It was clear that a different set of variables was needed to describe the most important feature of the child's learning environment.

Irvin Child, together with Margaret Bacon and Herbert Barry set out to work on a new analytic framework for analyzing child training practices using a combination of Henry Murray's theory of personality (1938) and the theory of learning of Hull (1943) and Miller and Dollard (1941). They developed the well known "Barry, Bacon and Child code" (1967). In this code infant indulgence was reanalyzed but, more importantly, independence training was broken down into six categories: responsibility, nurturance, self-reliance, achievement, obedience, and general independence.

Second, as a result of combing the ethnographic sources, John Whiting and Irvin Child were convinced that the accounts of child life and socialization were inadequate and that special field work should be undertaken by researchers who were particularly interested in children and were willing to attempt to collect comparable data on a sample of societies which represented the variety of cultures existing in the world. With the help of Professor Robert Sears, the Social Science Research Council, and the Ford Foundation a field study was planned with a goal of studying the child's learning environment and the socialization practices in six societies. The field teams were committed to collecting data according to an agreed upon design developed by Irvin Child, William Lambert and John Whiting in collaboration with a group of consultants (see *Field Guide for the Study of Socialization,* Whiting et al. 1966). This field work was carried out from 1954 to 1956 in six societies and has been reported in a series of monographs (B. Whiting 1963: Minturn and Lambert 1964; Whiting and Whiting 1975). Some of the results will be discussed later.

Returning to our model, the next important analysis of the relation of child training to the maintenance systems appeared in Bacon, Barry and Child's paper on the relation of subsistence economy to their new ratings (1959). They reported that in societies with a high accumulation of property children were pressured to be responsible, obedient and nurturant while in societies with low accumulation of property pressure was exerted on children to be self-reliant and achievement oriented. Our most recent publication on the six culture study has included a follow up on the paper (Whiting and Whiting 1975). The hypotheses concerning the relation of a mother's workload to children's responsibility and nurturance suggested at the beginning of this chapter was tested with positive results.

The revision of the Bacon, Barry and Child hypothesis focused on the workload of the mother rather than on the accumulation of property as the more important predictor variable. In fact, in what might be considered the most complex and highly accumulating society in our sample, Orchard Town, New England, U.S.A., children scored comparatively low on nurturance and responsibility as measured by our code. The mothers of Orchard Town were also judged to have the lightest workload.

The extensive study of type cases has been invaluable in revising this theory and identifying new predictor variables. In the Bacon, Barry and Child sample societies which scored highest in pressure toward responsibility and nurturance were the subsaharan African groups who combined agriculture and herding (Barry, Child and Bacon 1959; Whiting and Whiting 1971). Since one of our societies in the six culture study, the Gusii of Kenya (LeVine and LeVine 1966) fit this description, we were able to analyze in detail the learning environment and the training children received. We were able to assess the mother's workload and the animal husbandry, farm work, child care and housework expected of children between the ages of three and eleven.

However, our sample of families in Gusii was not large enough to test many of our hypotheses on the basis of within culture differences and we could only compare Gusii as a unit with the other five cultures. In order to carry out a within culture test we are now engaged in a field study of a Kikuyu village in Kenya where we are able to assess the differences in the workload of various mothers in the village, the work required of their children, and compare the children's responsibility as observed in social interaction in naturally occurring situations.

In the Barry, Bacon and Child sample the hunter and gathering societies ranked comparatively low in reported socialization pressure toward nurturance and responsibility and high in pressure toward self reliance and achievement (1959). As in the case of the Gusii we have been able to profit by analyzing detailed data from one of these societies, the Kung Bushmen of The Kalahari Desert in South Africa. Patricia Draper, who had previously worked with us on a cross-cultural study of children's chores, spent eighteen months living with the Bushmen observing parental and child behavior. It is clear from her data that the workload of these women is far lighter than that of the agriculturalists and the children are not expected to do any real work until their teens (Draper 1972). The nature of the settlement camp and the spacing of children makes the use of child nurses to help busy mothers less important. The children spend time playing and practicing skills and are not overtly supervised or directed in their activities. These are the practices which have contributed to their high score in pressure toward self-reliance and achievement.

In our present work in Kenya we hope to be able to continue our comparative study of the influence of the economy on a child's learning environment, not only by comparing the herding cultures (Masai and Samburu) with the groups who combine herding and agriculture (Kipsigis, Luo, and Gusii) and with the more intensive agriculturalists (Kikuyu and Luhyua) but also with groups who are moving into a wage earning economy and successful white collar workers who are urban dwellers.

The progression of our research in this area best exemplifies the strategy which we try to follow, namely, working back and forth between the macro cross-cultural level and the micro level, the detailed study of type cases, if possible making comparisons within a geographic area, and finally the study of individual differences within a society. We have attempted to replicate the associations we find between custom complexes on each of these levels. We favor beginning on the macro level, if possible, using the extensive cross cultural ratings which have grown out of the library research of George Peter Murdock and his followers (see *Ethnology* 1962–1966). If our hypotheses seem to work on this macro level, wherever possible we turn to the analysis of the best field research type cases or best of all organize the field work ourselves. Finally, we attempt to do a test of the hypothesis within a culture if there is sufficient individual variation in the independent variables. Obviously such strategy requires team work, and the more collaboration among researchers in exploring similar hypotheses the more fruitful the results.

Returning to our model, we have developed another promising set of hypotheses about the relation of family structure variables to characteristics of the child's learning environment and a child's behavior. As mentioned above, the first findings in this area were reported by Murdock and Whiting in 1951. Following these leads, John Whiting with his interest in the origins of guilt and self-control began exploring the effect of family form, household structure and mother-father-child sleeping arrangements on the development of identification and conflicts in sex identity. This research spans the entire model. Temperature and diet, *environment*, are hypothesized as being associated with household type and sleeping arrangements, *maintenance systems* (J. Whiting, 1964), the degree of salience of the father during infancy and childhood, *child's learning environment* (Burton and Whiting 1961), sex identity conflict and behavior styles, *the individual adult* (Carlsmith 1964, 1973), and magical beliefs as exemplified in theories of disease, ritual as exemplified by initiation ceremonies (Whiting, Kluckhohn and Anthony 1958), and the practice of couvade (Munroe, Munroe and Whiting 1973) and crime rates (B. Whiting 1965), *the projective-expressive systems*. It is impossible here to discuss these theories in detail or to describe the type of field work and the collaboration which is involved in this series of hypotheses. It has been recently summarized by one of the authors. (J. Whiting 1973). Again, this research follows not only the model presented in Figure 13–1 but our research strategy. The original research relating child training practices to theories of disease and sorcery was cross-cultural (Whiting and Child 1953). Similarly the early research on the relation of climate, diet and social structure and household type was cross-cultural followed by field work by the staff of the Laboratory of Human Development at Palfrey House, Harvard, among a group of Barbadians in Central Square, Cambridge (D' Andrade 1962, 1973; Longabaugh 1962, 1973; Tancock 1961), followed by John Herzog's field work in the Barbados (1968) and the Munroe's field work among the Black Carib in British Honduras (Munroe and Munroe 1971, 1973) and other couvade practicing males, in this case a sample of fathers in the Boston area (Munroe and Munroe 1973). This field work was followed by new cross-cultural research, followed by extensive field work in Kenya, the analysis of which is still in process (Daniels 1970; Herzog 1973).

It should be noted again that research of this type involves team work and in the present world is greatly aided by the help of local students and scholars in any of the host countries which offer settings suited for testing the hypotheses. It should also be stressed that ideally the selection of field sites should be based on the presence and/or absence of important variables which are components of one's hypotheses. Thus if

one has theories about the custom complexes associated with the practice of circumcision rites at puberty, male bonding and sex identity
conflict, a field site such as Kenya which has groups of people some of
whom have all the associated characteristics, some of whom have some
but not all and some of whom have none, is an ideal place. The value of
collaborative work in the field with Kenyan students and colleagues has
been well documented by our research in this host country.[1]

It will be noted that in the studies of sex identity conflict environmental factors including climate and flora and fauna appear for the first time
as predictor variables. Two particular studies have focused on their effect
on social structure and settlement patterns and hence on a child's learning environment, particularly on the relative salience of the father in
infancy and early and late childhood (*Ethos* 1 (4) Winter 1973 passim).
Children in divergent cultures grow up in houses which include a variety of human beings. As infants and young children they are in intimate
contact with different categories of people. Since both psychoanalytic
and behavioral psychology postulate different outcomes as a result of
these experiences, some of our studies have focused upon the amount of
contact between various categories of people. Among the most intimate
relations are those between persons who sleep together. Investigation of
sleeping arrangements in various parts of the world indicate that there
were four main types which occurred with frequency in a world sample
of societies; husband and wife might share a bed and the infant sleep in a
crib or cradle, the wife and baby might sleep together and the husband
sleep in a separate bed in the same room, in a different room, or in a
different house, the husband and wife and baby could all share the same
bed, or all three could sleep in separate beds. Analysis of the distribution
of these sleeping arrangments indicated that they were associated with
climate and that temperature appeared to be the predictor variable
(J. Whiting 1964, p. 514). When the winter temperature falls below
freezing husband and wife most frequently sleep together and the baby
is wrapped well and put in a separate cradle or crib. In societies where
the winter temperature does not fall below 68°F the mother and the baby
most frequently share a bed and the father sleeps alone. When the
mother and infant share a bed it is possible for the baby to have access to
his mother's breast with little effort. If on the other hand he is in a
separate bed he has to cry in order to summon his mother, and if the bed
is in a separate room his crying might need to be loud and prolonged.
The body contact with the mother and easy access to her breast most
frequently terminates when the mother becomes pregnant with a new
child or when the new child is born.

Recent changes in our own society suggest that invention and the borrowing of technology can change existing patterns. Although psychoanalysts' warnings about the Oedipal complex and pediatricians warning about smothering the child or disturbing his sleep have in the past discouraged mothers from taking their babies into bed with them, there are indications of changing patterns among U. S. middle-class mothers. Many of these mothers who are breast feeding find it most convenient not to have to get up during the night, and hence they allow the infant to sleep in the parental bed. Associated with this change is the improvement of our modern heating facilities so that the temperature of the sleeping room may be kept warm enough during the winter months for the infant to be comfortable in the parental bed without extensive swaddling or close wrapping. Of equal importance for this culture change may be the invention of leakproof rubber pants which make the infant's presence less irritating to both mother and father (B. Whiting 1973).

Temperature not only effects body contact during the night but also during the day. A search of the ethnographic literature on over two hundred societies indicated that in about sixty judges could rate the amount of physical contact between a baby and its mother or surrogate caretaker during the day (J. Whiting 1971). In some societies the baby was carried or propped up in a cradleboard or wrapped in thick clothing or placed in some other type of container; in others it had more physical contact with the mother during the day; and in still others he was judged to be in direct physical contact most of the day, carried by his mother or surrogate mother with no clothing or only light clothing separating him from his caretaker's skin. With few notable exceptions, the Eskimo and the Yahgan of Patagonia, this latter type of close physical contact again is associated with climate. Forty of the forty-eight societies lying in the tropics between latitude 20 degrees north and 20 degrees south were reported to have close and frequent contact between mother and infant, whereas twenty-nine out of thirty-seven societies situated in the temperate and frigid zones used heavy swaddling or strapped the baby into cradleboards or crib-like containers. It is our hypothesis that close physical contact may have lasting effects on reactions to physical stress, physical growth (Landauer and Whiting 1964; Gunders and Whiting 1968; Whiting, Landauer and Jones 1968) and on styles of communication (J. Whiting 1971).

For the infant and young child who is dependent on caretakers and stays near home, the structure of the house determines the persons who are around during the day and night which in turn is associated with the size of the dwelling in which his mother lives. In areas of the world lacking large timber, before the importation or manufacture of building materials it was difficult to build large houses (Whiting and Ayres 1968). Families either lived in close intimate contact within one small structure or built separate huts which served as separate bedrooms or living quarters. In sub-Saharan agricultural areas of East Africa, for example, the husband often had a hut of his own in which he might sleep and eat with his elder sons. Furthermore, if he was polygynously married each wife had a hut of her own. As a consequence of this arrangement the younger children were not in intimate contact with their fathers. Our recent research in a Kikuyu village in Kenya suggests how new technology can effect this pattern. One of the traditional Kikuyu's woman's most time consuming burdensome chores was providing water for her family, often walking for over a mile twice a day and carrying five to eight gallons of water on her back. With the importation of metal roofing and barrels, it was possible to rig up a system whereby rain which fell on a metal roof could be collected in rain barrels. Traditional Kikuyu houses were circular in floor plan with mud and wattle walls and thatched roofs. Circular tin roofs were impractical and hence when families could afford the metal the house plan became rectangular. This made it possible to include more rooms under the same roof. As a result the husband often abandoned his separate hut and moved into a room in the new house. In some cases he even put his polygynous wives under one roof since it was cheaper to build one metal-roofed house than two (B. Whiting 1974).

In our research in the Kikuyu village over the last six years we have monitored changes in house types and sleeping arrangements. We have discovered that with the introduction of the rectangular house and tin roofs there is also an increase in use of the master bedroom reserved for the father, mother and infant—older children being relegated to another bedroom. The new house often also houses the kitchen and a livingroom for receiving guests. These shifts in architecture have the effect of increasing the contact between the father and his young children, a variable which we postulate has important effects on the child's learning environment.

The effect of environment and history is obvious on a more macro level and has been documented by anthropologists for many years. Agriculture cannot easily exist in desert land, nor can industry exist where there is no source of power. People cannot live in large aggregations unless there is enough water and food. If large numbers of people live together there must be formalized ways of solving conflict (B. Whiting 1950). The larger the aggregate of people, the more specialized the status and roles (Murdock 1949). Thus economy, settlement pattern, social and political structure, and the legal system are all directly influenced by climate, terrain, flora, fauna and technological knowledge.

For psychological anthropology the importance of these environmental factors stems primarily from their effect on the maintenance systems, the economy, settlement pattern and social structure factors which determine the division of labor, and the status and role of the adults. These are the variables which influence parental behavior and are so often overlooked in the study of child development because there is comparatively little variation in Western societies where most of our psychological theories have been developed. One of the important functions of psychological anthropology is to identify these hidden variables which have been obscured because there is a cultural blindness (J. Whiting 1954; B. Whiting 1973). Although child psychologists have paid lip service to social structure and economic variables they have summarized them in the concept of SES (social economic class) and have spent too little time exploring the independent effect of the elements hidden in this concept (B. Whiting 1973).

In conclusion we would like to describe one of our most promising present research projects which represents our effort to develop better instruments for evaluating personality. In the six culture study we decided to use observed behavior as our dependent variable. (Whiting and Whiting 1975). Our decision in 1955 to invest the innumerable man hours required to observe, record, code, and analyze samples of individual children's behavior as it occurred in natural settings, grew out of a dissatisfaction with projective tests. As mentioned earlier one of the great problems in the study of the effect of culture on personality has been the problem of measurement. How does one assess and compare personality types? In the six culture study, although we attempted to study and describe the projective-expressive systems of each society, we did not attempt to collect data on an individual's perceptions of these systems and hence had no measures for "modal personality." The samples of behavior collected by the field teams on twenty-four children, age three to eleven, in each of the societies were analyzed in terms of the nine behavior systems which were selected for attention by Irvin Child, William Lambert and John Whiting (Whiting and Whiting 1975). All of the behavior was recorded and coded in terms of interacts—exchanges between individuals, which could be considered to be oriented toward helping, being responsible, hurting, roughhousing, seeking help and physical contact, seeking competition and dominance, and seeking friendly interaction. Comparisons between children were made both within societies and across the six. We were interested in exploring the degree to which the behavior of children brought up in diverse cultures was similar or different. We explored for universals which could be explained by sex, age, sibling order and culture type. In our attempt to assess the particular role of culture in influencing children's behavior, we turned to our model exploring economic factors, the division of labor, settlement patterns, social structure, the settings occupied by children, the persons responsible for their training, the tasks assigned to children, and the child training practices observed and reported by mothers.

Although the culture of the society in which one grew up had a significant effect on behavior, we found there were indeed universals. There were similar differences between boys and girls in all six cultures, most of which seem to be attributable to the similarity of the role of adult woman in all cultures (Whiting and Edwards 1973; Whiting and Whiting 1975). We found consistent changes in behavior with age: we found the youngest children in all six societies shared behavioral characteristics; and we found one of the most important predictors of a child's behavior was the status and age of the person with whom he interacted. Thus, in all cultures children tend to offer help, support, and entertainment to infants, they tend to seek help, information, physical proximity and friendly interaction and support from adults. Aggressive behavior was most frequent between peers. If one interprets personality to be the tendency to behave in certain ways regardless of the specific setting, it seems reasonable to suppose that habits associated with the settings one occupies most frequently will influence one's "personality." Thus we would predict from our findings that one of the important effects of culture is in determining the type of settings an individual is most apt to frequent. A child growing up in an isolated nuclear family with one or two other siblings is high on seeking behavior and sociability as his interaction with adults is frequent; he will be comparatively low on nurturant behavior since the chances are that when he is at an age when in other societies he would be expected to help care for an infant sibling, there will not be any infants in his family. Children growing up in families where there are infant siblings and where their mothers are busy and need help, will be more apt to offer help and support to others because of the habits established in their role as child nurses. They will have less experience in exclusive face to face interaction with adults (Whiting and Whiting 1975), and fewer seeking behaviors focused on them.

One aspect of our present work in Kenya is a follow up on these findings focused on further exploration of the effect of setting on the behavior of parents and children, where setting is conceived as including the physical space in which customary behavior takes place, the cast of characters with whom one frequently interacts and the activities one customarily performs. Again Kenya offers unusual opportunities for research. Thomas Weisner and the authors have identified a group of mothers and children who spend some time in both the country and the city (Weisner 1973; B. Whiting 1969) and we are able to train Kenyan students to observe these adults and children as they interact in both settings. With modernization, family and household structure are in rapid transition so that it is possible in various communities in Kenya to contrast children who are growing up in divergent settings but who are not, as is so often the case when we work in our own society, members of a depressed minority. Observational studies are facilitated by the fact that much of the daily living in Kenya occurs outside the house and hence observers are less obtrusive than in U.S. society.

We would like to stress the need for cooperation in this type of exploration of the relation of culture and personality. If we are to make headway in understanding the interaction, we need the collaboration of anthropologists, ethologists, psychologists and other behavioral scientists. We need the assistance of students and scholars in host countries, and we need to be willing to collect data for each other and replicate each other's findings. If we are to develop theories which are valid they must stand up to repeated tests on many samples of individuals in various parts of the world.

All our work has been directed toward developing and testing general principles that apply across cultures and/or across individuals within a culture. Because of this preoccupation we have been accused of neglecting the unique and idiosyncratic. There are many who prefer a more humanistic approach to psychological anthropology. Their goal is to discover and portray the subtleties of metaphor, the complexities of structure and ritual, and the unique "emic" meanings of each culture. To these individuals the fact that snowflakes are octagonal and will melt if the temperature rises above freezing is of little interest compared to the beauty and uniqueness of each flake. Although we are committed to the hypothesis jeopardizing, snowflake melting approach, we depend on the careful and insightful dscriptions of cultures and peoples by those ethnographers with a more humanistic orientation. Likewise, it is true they often use the findings of science to interpret the individual case.

We remain dedicated to developing and testing hypotheses designed to be true for all peoples at all times. We are also interested in explaining the individual, culture, and the interaction between them. And we remain convinced that child rearing involves more than the simple and intentional transmission of culture.

Unless otherwise noted, all the research reported in this paper has been financed by a grant from United States Public Health MH 01096–19.

Notes

1. This research has been conducted under the auspices of the Child Development Research Unit in the Department of Education in the University of Nairobi, financed by a grant from the Carnegie Corporation.

Herbert Applebaum

VI

Twentieth Century Evolution and Ecological Anthropology

Introduction

A notable shift began to take place in American anthropology in the late 1950s and 1960s. This was a renewed interest in the search for generalizations, causal regularities, and nomothetic explanations for social phenomena. Prominent in this upsurge in the search for general theory were those seeking causality based on an evolutionary perspective and a techno-environmental or ecological perspective. In Julian Steward, both these themes were united. He was a student of both Kroeber and Lowie.

Julian Steward did not seek to revitalize classical evolutionary theory nor to attempt a general synthesis of cultural evolution. He termed himself a "multilinear evolutionist." He was primarily concerned with specific lines of development in specific societies or groups of societies which shared what he termed a "cultural core." His cultural core was a "constellation of features which are most closely related to subsistence activities and economic arrangements. The core includes such social, political and religious patterns as are empirically determined to be closely connected with these arrangements" (1955a:37). Thus, Steward suggests that cultures evolving in riverine valleys, surrounded by arid regions, such as the Nile, the Tigris-Euphrates and the Indus valleys, shared a common culture core. They displayed such traits as irrigation agriculture, city-states, and a temple-centered religious system. Although they may differ in specifics, it was Steward's view that they would tend to follow the same evolutionary sequences. Cultures evolving in tropical forest zones, or in central deserts, will have different sequences because their ecologically based cores will differ. Steward's perspective is that a culture may follow any one of several distinct lines of development, rather than a single sequence or a universally prescribed one. Steward called his formulation multilinear evolution, as compared to the unilineal evolutionism of the nineteenth century evolutionary anthropologists.

Steward attributes the convergence he discovered in the Old and New World to cultural interaction with the environment (see Chapter 14). While he never claimed that environment was determinative, as evidenced by the variety of human responses to ecological constraints, he argued that human societies must react to their ecology; they cannot ignore it. In the course of adapting to ecology, humans introduce culture. Seeing culture as a means of adaptation to environment, Steward proposed the study of cultural ecology—the relationships among environment, human beings, and culture.

As mentioned before, Steward concentrated on cultural cores—those institutions and techniques most closely associated with environmental adaptation. Cultures having similar core features belong to the same cultural types and are assumed to have the same structural and functional interrelationships. Placed on a continuum of social complexity, Steward traced levels of sociocultural complexity. By identifying levels of sociocultural complexity and integration, Steward believed that he could isolate like units to be compared. He used categories like family level to correspond to band organization, multifamily level to correlate with tribe and chiefdom, and state level to correlate with empires and urban organization. Each level had a different means of organizing and integrating the culture through kinship, economic institution, political and police forces, bureaucracies, religious hierarchies, and various forms of monarchies and priesthoods.

Steward proposed a culture area formulation, based on cultural types according to ecological adaptations and historical developments. He worked out a scheme for South America based on adaptations and level of sociocultural complexity. His categories included four areas: Marginal, Tropical Forest, Circum-Caribbean, and Andean. They were used as the basis for his *Handbook of South American Indians,* a monumental accomplishment, contained in six volumes.

It was through cultural ecology and the work of Julian Steward, as well as that of V. G. Childe and Leslie White, that evolutionary theory became respectable again in American anthropology. Steward's ecological and evolutionary approach forged new links between the environment, technology, economics, social organization, settlement patterns, demography, and history. Population density and settlement patterns were a basic part of his explanation of patrilineal hunting bands (1955a) and the evolution of Pueblo society (1955b). Steward argued that an increase in population density attributable to growing ecological pressures promoted the rise of clan organization in the Pueblo region. He drew up archaeological materials to demonstrate an increase in the ratio of dwelling units to ceremonial kivas. The population-productivity ratio was also key to his interpretation of the rise and disintegration of ancient states and empires (1949a; Chapter 14).

Leslie White (1900–1975) had been trained in the Boasian cultural-relativist and historical-particularist school. A professor at the University of Michigan, White had found the Boasian school confining and unable to provide answers for causal explanations. He restudied the ideas of Tylor and Morgan and concluded that evolutionism as propounded by them was not wrong, only that their data was inadequate. White believed that cultural evolution was just as valid and just as demonstrable as biological evolution. He believed, as Herbert Spencer did before him (1897a:3, 331), that societies exhibited change from simple to complex, with increased specialization and differentiation of social groups. White sought to find a unit of study that was subject to quantification and that was universal and not culture-bound. That standard was *energy*.

In his article "Energy and the Evolution of Culture" (1943), White posited that energy was the key factor in societal development. He argued that the amount of energy available per capita, per annum was a determining factor in the level of cultural evolution at any given time and place. As increased amounts of energy was put to work, the efficiency of the instruments of development was increased. He compared cultural systems to biological systems and found that increased concentrations of energy result in greater complexity, specialization, and more differentiation.

White believed that the main problem with Morgan was his lack of substantiating data, which White believed was then available by the 1950s and 1960s. He divided social and cultural phenomena into three major levels. The most basic was the technological level, where the process of change begins in society. The second is the sociological order, which includes groups and institutions, such as the family, the law, and the state. Finally, there is the ideological order, which includes the value system and belief system in a society. White saw the institutional order of a society as a mediating factor between the technological base of a society and its ideology. Changes in the available energy level originate with a new discovery or invention and become translated into a new type of technology. This new technology eventually affects the institutions of the society and its ideology and value system. Finally, the entire society, as an integrated social system, changes and reaches a new evolutionary level.

White saw anthropology as the science of culture. He called it culturology (1959a:231). He saw three processes operating in the human social organism—historical, evolutionary, and formal-functional. If anthropology was to be a science, in White's view, it should interpret its data in the light of these three fundamental processes. The historical is concerned with the chronological sequence of events, unique in time and place. The particularity of events negates the recurrence of the same sequence with the same individuals. The formal-functional process deals with similarities in forms or structures which arise out of functional necessities to maintain the social system. The scientist who is interested in functional relations is not concerned with the particulars of history. The evolutionist investigates the sequencing and appearance of forms and structures of societies.

White argues that each scientist concerned with each one of the three basic processes is involved with a different problem and seeks a different set of data. Each process represents a different level of explanation. However, for White, the interpretation supplied by the evolutionist is more basic and more fundamental than that supplied by either the historian or the functionalist. This was so because the evolutionist grasps and interprets events in their wholeness and entirety, using space-time properties and relations, whereas the historian or the functionalist each deals with only one aspect—the temporal or the formal. Every science, in seeking a precise and comprehensive perspective, had moved to the evolutionary position, and White called upon anthropologists to do likewise and thereby advance the maturity of their discipline (Voget 1975:377; White 1945b:243).

Ronald Cohen, in Chapter 16, reviews the major ideas of social evolution. Cohen links and differentiates social and biological evolution. He finds that the processes identified with biological or natural evolution can be found in social evolution—variation, adaptation, retention, reproduction, and directionality. But there are significant differences. In human evolution there is human intervention and rational selection. There is also acquired characteristics, since the psycho-cultural inheritance is passed on from generation to generation. In natural evolution, variation is by chance. There is a fatalism, no choice; there is only the chance that one variation will be more adaptable to the natural environment than the previous norm and will outproduce it.

In human evolution, transmission of culture does not occur through biologically programmed genes. In language and writing, the social inheritance is preserved and shared through individuals possessing values, thoughts, and ideas. Human efforts create and preserve cultural inheritance through the roles and behavior they exhibit in social institutions. In social evolution, there are the limiting conditions of biology and historical circumstance, but social evolution involves the active, self-determination of humans cultivating the potentialities of human nature and the ecological environment. Thus, social evolution is not hit-and-miss but sought after and planned for. Unplanned, accidental, and chance events are also part of social evolution. But humans are aware of how their societies function, and they do attempt to plan their social life, even though their plans are not always, or often, realized.

Progress and direction are two issues associated with social evolution. While we can look back and perceive direction, we can never be sure of the future. Anthropologists have been careful not to equate evolution with progress. Social evolution appears to advance from the less complex to the more complex, from the less efficient to the more efficient, from harnessing less energy to harnessing more energy. But sometimes, social systems do go into decline after reaching a peak—the Roman Empire, Mayan civilization, Egyptian and Babylonian civilizations, West African empires, and so on. The fate of human society is that, although social evolution is limited and nonrandom, up to now human beings have difficulty predicting or even determining the directionality of their evolution. Both accidental and deterministic social events are two inseparable elements in the process of social evolution. Though past and present limits are knowable, the future of social evolution is not.

We normally think of a theory as a set of general propositions from which specific hypotheses can be postulated and tested. Evolution cannot be tested. It can be observed and described. Evolution can be an orientation or a philosophy. Evolution does not tell why certain variables enable us to predict change or its direction. The categories used to classify societies on an evolutionary scale vary with the viewpoint of the classifier. Each classification will reveal its own transformational pattern. One may choose to classify societies on the basis of harnessing energy or levels of technology, degrees of urbanization, levels of political hierarchy, existence of classes, or modes of subsistence and production. Each classification reveals its own insights. A comprehensive list of social units might be drawn up to place societies on an evolutionary scale. All such scales are rough and general and inevitably abstract from the particular of each society.

In summary, social evolution differs from biological evolution in that it involves intentions, revolutions, contending interests, and choices. While social and natural evolution display similarities, such as variation, adaptation, retention, reproduction, and directionality—similarities of process—they are dissimilar in content. Social evolution takes place through conscious and unconscious learning, based on language and acquired culture. Biological evolution is genetic and without consciousness. The difference between the two is what is truly human.

Ecological anthropology is concerned with the relationship between human beings and their physical environment. The environment contains, not only the physical means of plant and animal life necessary for human subsistence, but rivers, lake waters, and climate, as well as the technology and material instruments created by human beings for utilizing the materials available in the natural environment. At the base of every culture are the tools, machines, techniques, and practices relating human existence to the material conditions of specific habitats. Through its technology, each culture interacts with its physical environment to obtain food, fuels, and other forms of usable energy. Technology and culture provide communities with protection against predators, disease, climactic extremes, and neighboring populations, all of which are considered part of the environment by ecologists. Ecological anthropology is concerned with the regulation of populations in relation to geographical space, the use of natural resources, and the disposal of human and industrial waste products. Demographic factors like age and sex compositions are also investigated by ecologists, since they affect the relationship between a cultural system and its environment by affecting population growth rates.

In a review of ecological anthropology, Benjamin Orlove (1980:235–273), identifies three stages in the development of ecological anthropology.

The first stage was dominated by the work of Julian Steward and Leslie White. Both White and Steward sought to correlate similarities in cultures which could be explained on the basis of similar environmental conditions. Geographical determinism was avoided by defining environment in a broad sense to include social and technological features. Emphasis was placed on geographic and historical separateness to exclude the influence of diffusion. Both White and Steward saw the environment as something to which cultures adapted through the use of tools, technology, and knowledge—in a word, culture. This cultural adaptation was an evolutionary process of development and growth or decline. Steward emphasized his "cultural core," and White stressed his "harnessing of energy" as the driving force for development and growth.

The second stage in ecological anthropology was neofunctionalism and neoevolutionism. The neoevolutionists were interested in *origins*— the origin of agriculture, the origin of the state, the origins of class society (Fried 1967; Carneiro 1970; Service 1975; Flannery 1972). The neofunctionalists took the position that social organization and culture were functional adaptations which permitted populations to exploit their environments successfully, without exceeding the carrying capacity of their ecological resources (Vayda and Rappaport 1968; Harris 1975; Hardesty 1977). Functional ecologists used the concept of negative feedback to explain cultural stability. Recognizing that functional explanations were not causal, they isolated variables which acted to maintain a balance between populations and resources. One example is the potlatch of American Indians of the Northwest American Coast. The potlatch is a system in which chiefs compete with each other to give away goods.

Functional ecological theory views this system as a means for distributing food between the wealthy and poor communities. Kwakiutl chiefs, though motivated by their own status-prestige and validating their rank, triggered exchanges of food and wealth that made up for periodic deficiencies in the subsistence of localized numayms and tribes invited to the potlatch (Piddocke 1965). According to Sweet (1965), camel raiding in North Arabia could be viewed as a cultural convention for redistributing camel resources among those suffering losses due to drought and disease.

What seemed to be true for redistribution of camels among North Arabian Bedouins, seemingly held true for pig reduction and sacrifice among the Tsembaga of New Guinea. Taking a broad ecosystems approach, Rappaport (1967) found that the ritual sacrifice of pigs served as a feedback system governing the relations of men to men, men to pigs, and men to garden and forest crops. This self-regulation ritual was called *kaiko*. The ceremony was held when the pig population had grown to such proportions that their feeding reached the limit of economic utility. It was no longer possible to tolerate their numbers, given the amount of extra work in fencing, having to divert food from humans to pigs, or tolerating the interpersonal conflicts when pigs overran neighbor's gardens.

Cybernetics, with its emphasis on self-regulatory processes, has been used as a model by cultural ecologists for uniting humans, animals, plants, and the physical environment. In this view, the activities of humans in the environment is seen as part of a calorimetric system, with the energy inputs and takeout measured for efficiency. Lee (1969) did an analysis of !Kung Bushmen regarding their food output per person as compared with their body requirements for calories. Rappaport compiled quantitative data on the Tsembaga regarding pigs, food intake, labor, and product to estimate that their land could support between 270 and 320 people. In 1963 their number was 204, which indicated that they were not living up to their ecological potential. The cattle complex of India was reviewed by Harris (1966) and calculated to have an important ecological and economic input, expressed in milk production, traction, fertilizer, fuels, and meat and hide products. This often has been overlooked in attacks on the sacred status of cattle in India. Models of feedback systems do not include conscious intent by those within such systems to see them as restoring ecological equilibrium. The Tsembaga and the Kwakiutl are unaware, presumably, of the relation of their ceremonials to the restorative consequences of the killing of pigs in the former or the potlatch in the latter. The Tsembaga do not kaiko and the Kwakiutl do not potlatch for ecological reasons, but rather for cultural ones. It could be argued that unconscious mechanisms have the advantage of serving as an adaptive mechanism, while conscious choice of individuals might be maladaptive. Thus, a New Guinea man may wish to maintain large pig herds or a Kwakiutl Chief may want to increase his stock of resources. However, the prestige systems of the Tsembaga and the Kwakiutl act to offset individual desires in favor of the needs of the community. The rituals act like a thermostat, regulating the system and keeping it in balance.

Functionalist ecological explanations are appealing because they appear to be scientific. However, accurate measurements do not presently exist. Lee's and Rappaport's data were rough estimates. Ecological explanations of a functional nature require precise measurements over a long period of time. To date, they have not been developed.

The third stage in ecological anthropology identified by Orlove is the *processual* stage. This is a reaction to functional ecology. Using a historical framework, processual ecologists hope to focus on mechanisms of change, incorporating into their analysis conflict, as well as cooperation.

Ecological anthropologists with a processual orientation object to functionalist explanations that leave out conscious human choice. They use decision-making models which explain change based on choices. In processual analysis, adaptive strategies are not unconscious systems working themselves out but conscious choices of actors seeking goals. Culture and ideology are seen as proximate causes shaping human action. They use the research of cognitive anthropologists, concentrating on emic views, on the ways human populations perceive and classify their own environments. The argument is that humans can only utilize what they can conceive.

In addition to the three stages identified by Orlove, ecological anthropologists have studied hazards and how populations and communities react to them (Vayda and McCay 1975:293–306). Hazards include both physical and social threats to the health and survival of organisms, including humans. Hazards require an adaptive response, requiring resources to be deployed to cope with immediate problems, as well as providing for resources in the future. There are geophysical hazards like earthquakes, hurricanes, tornadoes, droughts, frosts, and floods. And there are human-made hazards like pollution, oil spills, chemical dumps, starvation, and waste dumps. There are also human hazards based on human predation—terrorism, assassination, kidnapping, hijacking, wars, religious persecution, jailings, torture, and violations of persons. Ecological anthropologists studying hazards become applied anthropologists, dealing with urgent problems facing people and communities in all parts of the world.

In summing up ecological anthropology, it can be seen that with its stress on subsistence activities, food getting, and the physical environment, it is materialist in its orientation. While functionalists stress systems operating independently of individual human beings, the processualists emphasize choice and decision making and the way people view and classify their environment. Thus, they add the cognitive factor to ecological studies. Finally, with the study of environmental hazard, ecological anthropologists become involved with applied, as well as theoretical, research regarding the linkages between humans and their environment.

Julian H. Steward

14. Cultural Causality and Law: A Trial Formulation of the Development of Early Civilizations

I. Methodological Assumptions

It is about three-quarters of a century since the early anthropologists and sociologists attempted to formulate cultural regularities in generalized or scientific terms. The specific evolutionary formulations of such writers as Morgan[1] and Tylor[2] and the functional or sociological formulations of Durkheim and others were largely repudiated by the 20th century anthropologists, especially by those of the so-called "Boas" school, whose field work tested and cast doubt on their validity. Today, despite an enormous and ever-increasing stock-pile of cultural data, little effort has been made to devise new formulations or even to develop a methodology for doing so, except as White and Childe have kept alive the tradition of Morgan, as Radcliffe-Brown and Redfield have continued in the spirit of Durkheim, and as Malinowski has attempted to reconcile diverse schools of anthropology through a "scientific theory of culture."

Reaction to evolutionism and scientific functionalism has very nearly amounted to a denial that regularities exist; that is, to a claim that history never repeats itself. While it is theoretically admitted that cause and effect operate in cultural phenomena, it is considered somewhat rash to mention causality, let alone "law," in specific cases. Attention is centered on cultural differences, particulars, and peculiarities, and culture is often treated as if it developed quixotically, without determinable causes, or else appeared full-blown.

It is unfortunate that the two approaches are so widely thought of as theoretically irreconcilable rather than as expressions of different purposes or interests. The 19th century writers had the perfectly legitimate purpose of making scientific generalizations from what they considered recurrent cultural patterns, sequences, and processes in different cultures, while the more recent school has the equally legitimate purpose of examining the distinctive or nonrecurrent features of cultures. As all cultures, though unique in many respects, nonetheless share certain traits and patterns with other cultures, an interest in either or both is entirely defensible. In fact, the analyses of cultural particulars provide the data necessary for any generalizations. If the 19th century formulations were wrong, it was not because their purpose was inadmissible or their objective impossible, but because the data were inadequate and insufficient, the methodology weak, and the application of the schemes too broad.

In spite of a half century of skepticism concerning the possibility of formulating cultural regularities, the conviction is widely held that the discovery of cultural laws is an ultimate goal of anthropology, to be attained when fact-collecting and detailed analyses of particular cultures and sequences are sufficiently advanced. White[3] has already offered some general formulations concerning the relationship of energy to cultural development, and he has argued for the importance of formulations of all kinds. Even some members of the so-called "Boas" school expressly advocate a search for regularities. Lowie, for example, remarks that cultural phenomena "do point toward certain regularities, and these it is certainly our duty to ascertain as rigorously as possible."[4] Lesser cites several trial formulations of regularities, which have been made by various persons, including Boas, and calls for more explicit statement of the regularities which, in the course of his work and thinking, every social scientist assumes to exist.[5] The author has attempted to formulate regularities pertaining to the occurrence of patrilineal bands among hunting and gathering tribes[6] and has suggested others that may occur in the origin and development of clans.[7] In reality, hundreds of formulations appear in the literature—for example, correlations of kinship terminologies with forms of social organization—and the possibility of recognizing the general in the particular is implicit in the very terminology of anthropology. The routine use of such concepts, or typological categories, as "clans," "castes," "classes," "priests," "shamans," "men's tribal societies," "cities," and the like are tacit recognition that these and scores of other features are common to a large number of cultures, despite the peculiarities of their local patterning.

The present need is not to achieve a world scheme of culture development or a set of universally valid laws, though no doubt many such laws can even now be postulated, but to establish a genuine interest in the scientific objective and a clear conceptualization of what is meant by regularities. It does not matter whether the formulations are sequential (diachronic) or functional (synchronic), on a large scale or a small scale. It is more important that comparative cultural studies should interest themselves in recurrent phenomena as well as in unique phenomena, and that anthropology explicitly recognize that a legitimate and ultimate objective is to see through the differences of cultures to the similarities, to ascertain processes that are duplicated independently in cultural sequences, and to recognize cause and effect in both temporal and functional relationships. Such scientific endeavor need not be ridden by the requirement that culture laws or regularities be formulated in terms comparable to those of the biological or physical sciences, that they be absolutes and universals, or that they provide ultimate explanations. Any formulations of cultural data are valid provided the procedure is empirical, hypotheses arising from interpretations of fact and being revised as new facts become available.

1. *There must be a typology of cultures, patterns, and institutions.* Types represent abstractions, which disregard peculiarities while isolating and comparing similarities. To use Tylor's classic example, the mother-in-law tabu and matrilocal residence, though in each case unique in their local setting, are recurrent types, the cause and effect relationships of which may be compared and formulated. Anthropological terminology demonstrates that hundreds of types of culture elements, patterns, and total configurations are recognized, despite the peculiarities attaching to each in its local occurrence.

2. *Causal interrelationship of types must be established in sequential or synchronic terms, or both.* Any reconstruction of the history of a particular culture implies, though it may not explicitly state, that certain causes produced certain effects. Insights into causes are deeper when the interrelationships of historical phenomena are analyzed functionally. Functional analysis of archeological data has not been lacking, though archeology has used an atomistic and taxonomic approach[8] far more than has conventional history. Gordon Childe[9] is exceptional in his effort to treat archeological materials functionally. Wittfogel[10] has been outstanding in his use of historical data to make functional-historical analyses of the socio-economic structure of early civilizations.

   Where historical data are not available, only the synchronic approach to cause and effect is possible. Radcliffe-Brown, Redfield, and Malinowski, despite important differences in their thinking, are distinctive for their functional analyses.

3. *The formulation of the independent recurrence of synchronic and/or sequential interrelationships of cultural phenomena is a scientific statement of cause and effect, regularities, or laws.* The particularists, though conceding that such formulations are theoretically possible and even desirable, are inclined to hold that in practice it is virtually impossible to isolate identifiable cause-and-effect relationships that operate in independent cases. Similarities between cultures are interpret-

ed as the result of a single origin and diffusion, provided the obstacles to diffusion do not seem too great. If the obstacles are very great, differences are emphasized. Thus, most American anthropologists explain similarities between the early civilizations of the New World as a case of single origin and diffusion, but, impressed by the obstacles to trans-oceanic culture contacts, they stress the dissimilarities between the civilizations of the Old and New Worlds. Some writers, however, like Elliot-Smith, Perry, and Gladwin[11] recognize the similarities between the two hemispheres and, unimpressed by barriers to diffusion, use the similarities as proof of single world origin.

The use of diffusion to avoid coming to grips with problems of cause and effect not only fails to provide a consistent approach to culture history, but it gives an explanation of cultural origins that really explains nothing. Diffusion becomes a mechanical and unintelligible, though universal, cause, and it is employed, as if in contrast to other kinds of causes, to account for about ninety per cent of the world's culture. One may fairly ask whether, each time a society accepts diffused culture, it is not an independent recurrence of cause and effect. Malinowski[12] states: "Diffusion . . . is not an act, but a process closely akin in its working to the evolutionary process. For evolution deals above all with the influence of any type of 'origins'; and origins do not differ fundamentally whether they occur by invention or by diffusion."[13] For example, the civilizations of the Andes and Mexico were based on dense, sedentary populations, which in turn were supported by intensive irrigation farming. In both cases, the early societies were integrated by a theocratic hierarchy, which controlled communal endeavor and enlisted labor for the construction of religious centers. It is not sufficient to say that the agricultural, social, and religious institutions merely diffused as a unit, for that would be merely stating distributions in historical terms but failing to explain process. Incipient farming appeared first, and it diffused before the other complexes developed. The latter have a functional dependence on intensive farming. They could not have been accepted anywhere until it developed, and in the course of its development similar patterns would undoubtedly have emerged, whether or not they were diffused. The increasing population and the growing need for political integration very probably would have created small states in each area, and these states would almost certainly have been strongly theocratic, because the supernatural aspects of farming—for example, fertility concepts, the need to reckon seasons and to forecast the rise and fall of rivers, and the like—would have placed power in the hands of religious leaders. Diffusion may have hastened the development of theocratic states, but in each case the new developments were within determinable limits, and independently involved the same functional or cause-and-effect relationships.

It is true, of course, that many peculiar features common to New World civilizations do not represent a logical outgrowth of basic patterns and that they can be disposed of with the superficial explanation that they diffused. Thus, the wide distribution of such concepts as the plumed serpent or the jaguar god, or of such constructions as terraced pyramids, may be explained in this manner, though deeper analysis might reveal the reasons for their wide acceptance. In general, it is the rather arbitrary, specific, or stylized features, that is, those features which have the least functional dependence on the basic patterns, that provide the greatest evidence of diffusion. These, in other words, are the particulars, which distinguish tribes or areas and which obscure regularities.

Another means of denying the possibility of isolating cultural regularities is to stress that the complexity or multiplicity of the antecedents or functional correlates of any institution makes it virtually impossible to isolate the true causes of the institution; convergent evolution rather than parallel evolution is generally used to explain similarities that seem not to be the result of diffusion. The answer to this is simply that in dealing with cultural phenomena, as in dealing with all the complex phenomena of nature, regularities can be found only by looking for them, and they will be valid only if a rigorous methodology underlies the framing of hypotheses.

It is not necessary that any formulation of cultural regularities provide an ultimate explanation of culture change. In the physical and biological sciences, formulations are merely approximations of observed regularities, and they are valid as working hypotheses despite their failure to deal with ultimate realities. So long as a cultural law formulates recurrences of similar interrelationships of phenomena, it expresses cause and effect in the same way that the law of gravity formulates but does not ultimately explain the attraction between masses of matter. Moreover, like the law of gravity, which has been greatly modified by the theory of relativity, any formulation of cultural data may be useful as a working hypothesis, even though further research requires that it be qualified or reformulated.

Cultural regularities may be formulated on different levels, each in its own terms. At present, the greatest possibilities lie in the purely cultural or super-organic level, for anthropology's traditional primary concern with culture has provided far more data of this kind. Moreover, the greater part of culture history is susceptible to treatment only in superorganic terms. Both sequential or diachronic formulations and synchronic formulations are super-organic, and they may be functional to the extent that the data permit. Redfield's tentative formulation[14] that urban culture contrasts with folk culture in being more individualized, secularized, heterogeneous, and disorganized is synchronic, superorganic, and functional. Morgan's evolutionary schemes[15] and White's formulation concerning the relationship of energy to cultural development[16] are sequential and somewhat functional. Neither type, however, is wholly one or the other. A time-dimension is implied in Redfield's formulation, and synchronic, functional relationships are implied in White's.

Superorganic formulations do not, of course, provide the deeper explanations of culture change that may come from a psychological level or a biological level. Research on these latter levels may profitably run concurrently with the other, but for the present their formulations will be more applicable to synchronic, functional studies than to sequential ones. Thus, to advocate search for regularities in cultural terms is not at all in conflict with those who state that "culture does not exist apart from the individual, its human carrier." To hope for basic and ultimate explanations of behavior that will interrelate cultural, psychological, neurological, physiological, and even physical phenomena is not to deny the desirability of doing what now seems possible and, in view of anthropology's traditional and primary concern with culture, of doing first things first.

The present statement of scientific purpose and methodology rests on a conception of culture that needs clarification. *If the more important institutions of culture can be isolated from their unique setting so as to be typed, classified and related to recurring antecedents or functional correlates, it follows that it is possible to consider the institutions in question as the basic or constant ones, whereas the features that lend uniqueness are the secondary or variable ones.* For example, the American high civilizations had agriculture, social classes, and a priest-temple-idol cult. As types, these institutions are abstractions of what was actually present in each area, and they do not take into account the particular crops grown, the precise patterning of the social classes, or the conceptualization of deities, details of ritual, and other religious features of each culture center. The latter are secondary and variable so far as the institutions in question are concerned. In a more comprehensive analysis, however, they would serve to distinguish subtypes, which would require more specific formulations.

This conception of culture is in conflict with an extreme organic view, which regards culture as a closed system in which all parts are of equal importance and are equally fixed. It holds that some features of culture are more basic and more fixed than others and that the problem is to ascertain those which are primary and basic and to explain their origin and development. It assumes that, although the secondary features must be consistent and functionally integrated with the primary ones, it is these that are more susceptible to fortuitous influences from inside or outside the culture, that change most readily, and that acquire such a variety of aspects that they give the impression that history never repeats itself.[17]

For the present, it is not necessary to state criteria for ascertaining the primary features. In general, they are the ones which individual scientists are most interested in studying and which the anthropological record shows to have recurred again and again in independent situations. A procedure which attempts to give equal weight to all features of culture amounts to a negation of typing and of making formulations, for it must include all the unique features, which obscure similarities between cultures.

II. Eras in the Development of Early Civilizations

The present section deals with the development of early agricultural civilizations in Northern Peru (the sequences are longest and best known in this part of Peru, thanks to the Viru Valley project of the Institute of Andean Research), Mesoamerica (Mexico and the Maya area), Mesopotamia, Egypt, and China. These areas were chosen because they were the cradles of civilization and because their exploitation by a pre-metal technology seems to have entailed similar solutions to similar problems and consequently to have caused similar developmental sequences. The environments are arid or semiarid, which, contrary to a common belief, did not impose great difficulties and thereby stimulate cultural development. Instead, they facilitated culture growth because they were easily tilled by digging-stick and irrigation farming. The tropical rain forests, the northern hardwood forests, and the sodded plains areas, on the other hand, were exploited only with the greatest difficulty by people who lacked iron tools.

The procedure to be followed is first to establish a tentative developmental typology or sequence in which the smaller periods are grouped into major eras, which have similar diagnostic features in each area. This requires considerable revision of current terminology, for no two authors use quite the same criteria for major stages of development. Americanists, who have discussed some of these problems together, are now using such terms as Formative, Developmental, Classical, Florescent, and Empire and Conquest, and they are attempting to reach an understanding about the cultural typology implied by these terms. Old World writers still cling largely to such entrenched terms as Mesolitic, Neolithic, Chalcolithic, Ceramolithic, Bronze, and Dynastic, thereby emphasizing technological features of minor developmental significance. Gordon Childe's use of Neolithic Barbarism, Higher Barbarism of the Copper Age, Urban Revolution, and Early Bronze Age, which incorporate some terms from L.H. Morgan, indicates that his thinking is somewhat closer to that of the Americanists, but his terminology and his period markers still fail to be very comparable to those of the latter.

The second step in the following procedure (next section) is to suggest cause-and-effect relationships between the cultural phenomena of the successive eras and to formulate as basic regularities those relationships which are common to all areas. These formulations are offered primarily as an illustration of the generalizing approach to cultural data. Tentative and preliminary, they would have served their purpose if they stimulated students of culture development to interest themselves in the same problems, to use comparable methods, and to present their findings in comparable terms—in short, to talk one another's language.[18]

Chart 14–1 groups the periods of each center into eras that have the same general features. Periods in the same relative position, consequently, were similar but were not contemporaneous. Chart 14–2 places the eras of each center on an absolute time-scale, which is fairly precise for the periods of written history but much less accurate for the early periods. The margin of error in dating these early periods does not, however, greatly affect the functional analysis of cultural development.

Pre-agricultural Era

This era includes all the Old World paleolithic and mesolithic periods, which lacked farming, and the New World pre-agricultural periods. To judge by the simple remains of these periods as well as by the recent hunting-and-gathering cultures, the technologies were devoted principally to satisfying biological needs for food, clothing, and shelter. Pottery, basketry, loom-weaving, metallurgy, permanent houses, and boat and animal transportation were probably absent until they were borrowed to a limited degree from higher centers. Social patterns were based on kinship, age, and sex, but they varied greatly as they became adapted to local conditions. Warfare was restricted to blood feuds, revenge for witchcraft, and perhaps in some areas retaliation against trespass.

Incipient agriculture

This era cannot be dated exactly, and it is known through very few finds. It must have been very long, passing through several stages,

Julian H. Steward

CHART 14–1. ARCHEOLOGICAL AND HISTORICAL PERIODS GROUPED IN MAJOR ERAS

ERAS	MESOPO-TAMIA SYRIA ASSYRIA	EGYPT	CHINA	MESOAMERICA		N. PERU
				MEXICO	MAYA AREA	
Industrial Revolution	Euro-American 19th and 20th century economic and political empires					
Iron Age Culture	Influences from Greece, Rome; later from north and central Europe Spanish Conquest in New World destroys native empires					
Cyclical Conquests	Kassites Hammurabi Dyn. Accad	Hyksos New Empire	Ming Sui, Tang Ch'in, Han			Inca
Dark Ages	Invasions	First Inter-mediate	Warring states			Local states
Initial Conquest	Royal tombs Ur Early Dyn. Sumer	Pyramid Age Early Dynastic Semainian	Chou	Aztec Toltec	Mexican Absorp-tion	Tiahuanaco
Regional Florescence	Jedmet Nasr Warkan-Tepe-Gawra Obeidian	Gerzian	Shang "Hsia"	Teoti-huacan	Initial Series or Classical	Mochica Gallinazo
Formative	Halafian Samarran Hassunan Mersian	Amratian Badarian Merimdean Fayumian	Yang Shao Pre-Yang Shao	Archaic or Middle Periods Zacatenco	Formative or Old Em-pire Mamom	Salinar Chavin-Cupisnique
Incipient Agriculture	Tahunian Natufian	Tasian	Plain Pottery?	?	?	Cerro Prieto
Hunting and Gathering	Paleolithic and Mesolithic			Pre-Agriculture		

which began when the first cultivation of plant domesticates supplemented hunting and gathering, and ended when plant and animal breeding was able to support permanent communities. To judge by what are the earliest-known evidences of domestication in Mesopotamia and Peru, technologies made little advance over those of the previous era until settled village life was fully achieved.

CHART 14–2. ABSOLUTE CHRONOLOGY OF THE MAJOR ERAS

	MESOPO-TAMIA	EGYPT	INDIA	CHINA	N. ANDES	MESO-AMERICA
2000						
					Spanish Conquest	
					Cyclical Conquests	Cyclical Conquests
1000				Cyclical Conquests		
					Regional Florescence	Regional Florescence
		Cyclical Conquests	Cyclical Conquests			
A.D. B.C.	Cyclical Conquests					Formative
					Formative	
				Dark Ages		
1000				Initial Conquests		Incipient Agriculture?
					Incipient Agriculture	
		Dark Ages	Dark Ages			Hunting and Gathering
			Initial	Regional Florescence		
2000	Dark Ages	Initial Conquests	Conquests		Hunting and Gathering	
	Initial Conquests			Formative		
			Regional Florescence			
3000	Regional Florescence	Regional Florescence		Incipient Agriculture		
4000		Formative	Formative			
	Formative					
5000			Incipient Agriculture			
	Incipient Agriculture	Incipient Agriculture		Hunting and Gathering		
6000						
7000		Hunting and Gathering	Hunting and Gathering			
8000	Hunting and Gathering					
9000						

Peru: Cerro Prieto.
Culture: farming based on beans; twined weaving; ceramics absent; semi-subterranean houses.
Mesoamerica: As the earliest-known agricultural periods of Mesoamerica appear to have had technologies and temple mounds, which elsewhere characterized the Formative Era, it is generally believed (Morley[19] excepted) that the cultures of these periods were introduced full-blown from elsewhere. Theoretically, however, it would seem that remains of simpler agricultural peoples should antedate the fairly developed theocratic communities in Mesoamerica.
Mesopotamia: Natufian, Tahunian.
Culture: probably domesticated millet or wheat and perhaps domesticated animals. Pottery and polished stone lacking.
Egypt: Tasian.
Culture: possibly domesticated plants. Pottery present.
China: Period of Plain Pottery. This period is considered to be the first phase of neolithic China, though the presence of domesticated plants or animals is doubtful.

Formative Era of basic technologies and folk culture

The Formative Era is so named because the principal technologies—basketry, pottery, weaving, metallurgy, and construction—appeared and the patterns of community culture took form at this time. It was an era of population growth, area expansion of cultures and peoples, comparative peace, and wide diffusion of culture between centers of civilization.

The principal domesticated plants were brought under intensive cultivation, and irrigation was begun on a community scale. In the Old World, the more important domesticated animals, except the horse, were present from early in the Era. In the New World, the absence of suitable wild species for domestication limited such animals to the dog, and, in the Andes, to the llama and alpaca.

Food production was on a subsistence basis, except as a share was provided for the ruling class. Increasingly efficient farming released considerable labor for the satisfaction of socially derived needs; that is, craft production of finer goods and construction of religious edifices for the theocracy made rapid progress during each period.

The sociopolitical unit seems to have been the small local community. The clustering of rooms in house units suggests that lineage or kingroups were the basis of society. One to several such units were associated with a ceremonial center, which served as the nucleus and integrating factor of a dispersed community. Control of irrigation, which was on a local scale, was one of the more important practical functions of the religious leaders. Warfare was probably limited to raids and contributed little either to social structure or to expansion of the state.

Peru: Chavín-Cupisnique, Salinar.

Technologies: domesticated maize, manioc, beans, gourds, peanuts; small-scale irrigation; llamas. Pottery; metallurgy in gold, copper (?); loom-weaving in cotton; twined baskets; surface adobe houses; balsa (reed bundle) boats.

Social: dispersed communities, evidently centering in religious mounds and temples. Feline, condor, and serpent deities. Theocratic control of society; rulers accorded status burial.

Mesoamerica: Armillas'[20] and Kidder's[21] Formative; in Mexico, Vaillant's Middle Periods[22], in Yucatan, Thompson's Formative[23] and Morley's Pre-Maya.[24] These include Zacatenco and Ticomán in highland Mexico, Lower Tres Zapotes on the east coast, Mamom and Chicanel in lowland Guatemala, Miraflores in highland Guatemala, and Playa de los Muertos in Honduras.

Technologies: probably domesticated maize, manioc, and other plants; local irrigation. Pottery; loom-weaving, probably in cotton; basketry (?); no metallurgy. Wattle-and-daub houses in Guatemala.

Social: Small, scattered settlements. Female figurines suggest a fertility cult. Temple mounds; funerary architecture; and beginnings of intellectual development, as evidenced by calendrical stelae of the Maya area, which appeared at the end of the era.

Mesopotamia: Childe's[25] Higher Barbarism of the Copper Age and beginnings of his Urban Revolution; beginnings of Albright's[26] Chalcolithic. In Mesopotamia: Sialk I, Mersian, Hassunan, Samarran, and Halafian.

Technologies: domesticated plants, probably wheat, barley, millet, and others; cattle, sheep, goats, pigs; some irrigation. Pottery; loom-weaving, probably in flax; basketry; metallurgy in gold and copper; possibly the wheel; rectangular, adobe houses.

Social: villages have local shrines. Religion involves female and animal figurines; male and female gods are represented.

Egypt: Faiyumian, Merimdean, Badarian, Amratian.

Technologies: wheat, barley; cattle, pigs, sheep, goats. Pottery; metallurgy in gold and copper; loom-weaving in linen; coiled basketry. Semi-subterranean, circular houses. Balsa (papyrus bundle) boats.

Social: clans or kin groups (?); captive slaves (?); female and animal figurines in religion; dog-sacrifice in burials.

China: Neolithic (Pre-Yang Shao, Yang Shao).

Technologies: millet, sorghum (?), rice, wheat; pigs; probably well-and-ditch irrigation. Pottery; loom-weaving in hemp (?); basketry; metallurgy in copper.

Social: small, semi-permanent settlements of circular pit-houses, possibly based on matrilineal lineages. Religion evidenced by pottery phalli; possibly human sacrifice and cannibalism.

Era of Regional Development and Florescence

This era was marked by the emergence and florescence of regionally distinctive cultures. No new basic technologies were invented, but irrigation works were enlarged, thus releasing a larger portion of the population to develop arts and crafts and to further intellectual interests. Multi-community states arose.

States were still strongly theocratic, but inter-state competition and state expansion seem to have entailed some militarism. A class-structured society, which was foreshadowed in the previous era, now became fully established. The ruling class appears to have been predominantly theocratic, but it was likely that some status was accorded successful warriors. The priesthood now had sufficient leisure to develop astronomy, mathematics, and writing (these were little developed in Peru). The largest religious edifices were built, and the finest art and manufactures of any era were produced toward the end of this era, each region producing distinctive styles. These products were made by special artisans and were dedicated principally to the upper classes and to the temples. Trade attained important proportions, and improved transportational devices were introduced.

Peru: Willey's[27] Regional Classical; Strong's[28] Late Formative and Florescent; Bennett's[29] late Early Periods. Gallinazo and Mochica (Nazca in south Peru).

Technologies: maize, manioc, potatoes, sweet potatoes, calabashes, pumpkins, peanuts; llamas, alpacas. Inter-valley irrigation.

Social: large communities; population maximum; largest mounds, temples; fanged deity, and gods of agriculture, fishing, celestial phenomena, and places. Ruler was warrior-god. Hilltop forts were built. Regional states (entire valley or several valleys?). War captives, human sacrifice, human trophies. Status burial for the upper class.

Roads; probably llama-packing; ocean-going balsa boats with sails (?); trade.

Ideographic writing on beans (?); quipus. Finest art of all eras.

Mesoamerica: Armillas'[30] Florescent; Kidder's[31] Classical; Thompson's[32] Initial Series; Morley's[33] Old Empire. These include: Middle and

Upper Tres Zapotes on the east coast; Teotihuacan and Monte Alban II and III in Mexico; Esperanza in highland Guatemala; and Tsakol and Tepeu in lowland Guatemala.

Technology: local irrigation, chinampas, and terracing in agriculture.

Social: dispersed settlements; local theocratic states that controlled all settlements of a valley or other natural regions. Population maximum (?).[34] Largest mounds and temples. Priestly hierarchy. Gods of rain, water, jaguar, serpent, quetzal. Child sacrifice (?); possibly ancestor worship (as evidenced by figurine portraits in Mexico, status burial in Guatemala). Militarism evidently restricted to raids, with some captive-taking.

Roads and causeways; widespread trade; (toy wheel).

Phonetic writing, mathematics, astronomy. Finest art of all eras.

Mesopotamia: Latter part of Albright's[35] Chalcolithic; Childe's[36] Urban Revolution and Early Bronze Age. These include: Obeidian (Al'Ubaid), Warkan-Tepe Gawra, and Jedmet Nasr.

Techologies: wheat, barley, millet, date palm, figs, grapes, sesame, onions, garlic, lettuce, melons, chick peas, horse beans; drained fields, large-scale irrigation. Wheel-made ceramics.

Social: urbanization began. Multi-community states, which were essentially theocratic, though rulers had also war power. Large palace-temples. Gods of agriculture. Some pressures or infiltration by foot-nomads.

Horse (?), chariot and four-wheeled wagon; balsa (reed bundle) boats; widespread trade.

Phonetic writing, mathematical systems, astronomy.

Egypt: Gerzian.

Technologies: farming as in Formative Era, though probably increased irrigation. Rectangular, above-ground, adobe houses.

Social: Tendency to urbanization; multi-community states, each with an associated animal god and under the rule of heads of principal lineages (?). Some warfare implements expansion of state. Status burial shows a cult of the dead.

Sailing vessels; ass; considerable trade.

Beginnings of writing; calendrical and numerical systems.

Possibly the Semainian period and the beginnings of the Early Dynastic periods should be included in the Era of Regional Florescence in Egypt, for the temple cult appeared, class differentiation became definite, and phonetic writing, a calendrical system, and mathematics were developed. These features, however, continued to develop with little interruption into the era of Conquest and Empire.

China: "Hsia" (Black Pottery period) and Shang Dynasty.

Technologies: wheat, millet, rice, pig, cattle, sheep, in north; buffalo and chicken in south. Beginnings of public works in form of dikes; otherwise, local well-and-ditch irrigation were practiced. Bronze manufactures. Horse and chariot. Weaving in silk.

Social: local state, Wittfogel's "feudal" type, under which serfs cultivated the local ruler's land. Divine monarch; status burial in deep grave. Use of oracle bones to forecast rain and for other divination; dragon deity; human and animal sacrifice. Warfare arising from conflict over grazing lands[37] and from pressure of herding nomads.

Picture and ideographic writing. Finest esthetic expressions, especially in bronzes.

Cyclical Conquests

The diagnostic features of this era are the emergence of large-scale militarism, the extension of political and economic domination over large areas or empires, a strong tendency toward urbanization, and the construction of fortifications. In the social structure, priest-warriors constituted the ruling groups, usually under a divine monarch, whose importance is revealed in elaborate status burial. Social classes now tended to become frozen into hereditary classes, in contrast to society of the previous era, which probably permitted individuals some upward mobility through personal achievements. Gods of war became prominent in the pantheon of deities.

There were no important technological changes. Bronze appeared in Peru, Mesopotamia, and Egypt and was used for weapons and ornaments, but it contributed little to the production of food or other goods. Iron, though not an iron-age culture, appeared in China. The principal change in manufactures was a strong trend toward standardization and mass production, with a concomitant sacrifice of esthetic freedom and variety. Large-scale trade within the empires, and even beyond, brought the beginnings of a special commercial class, but coinage and an efficient monetary system were not yet developed.

Peru: Willey's Expansion and Conquest; Strong's Fusion and Imperial periods; Bennett's Tiahuanaco, Late Periods, and Inca.

Technologies: as before, except that bronze was used for ornaments, weapons, and a few tools. By the Inca period, there was standardized, mass production.

Social: planned urban centers were constructed, and they drew off much population from the local communities. Under the Inca, social classes were finally frozen in a caste system, headed by the divine royal family. A priesthood and bureaucracy ruled the state, and placed levies on the commoners, but the local folk culture persisted. An ancestor cult occurred along with agricultural, place, and animal gods. The state was enlarged by wars of conquest, which perhaps started in the previous era and originated from population pressures. Populations were moved from place to place by imperial command.

Mesoamerica: Armillas' Militaristic Period (in Mexico, Toltec, Aztec, Monte Albán V, Tzintzuntzan Tarascan; and, in Yucatan, Mexican Absorption). Thompson's Mexican Period and Morley's New Empire in Yucatan. Kidder's Amatle and Pamplona in highland Guatemala.

Technologies: as before, except that metallurgy in copper and gold appeared, being used mainly for ornaments. There was extensive trade, and money, in the form of cacao beans, was used during the Aztec period.

Social: The population was increasingly concentrated in defensible sites, and special forts were constructed. Larger and larger areas were drawn into empires, and wealth was concentrated through tribute in the hands of the ruling classes. The king-priest had great military power. There were military classes, warrior societies, and slaves. Great population movements are evident in the inroads of Chichimecs into the Valley of Mexico, the Nahuatl migrations to Central America, and the Mexican invasion of Yucatan. Warfare was intensified, gods of war entered the pantheon, and human sacrifice became a major feature of religion.

Mesopotamia: Early Dynastic Sumerians to Dynasty of Accad.

Technologies: bronze was used for weapons, ornaments, and a few tools. There was standardized mass production, especially of goods used by commoners, and widespread trade, mainly for luxury items.

Social: Urban communities attained great size and served as military, political, religious, and commercial centers. The king combined religious and military leadership and controlled multicommunity states. Statuses were strongly differentiated: the king, representing the god (sometimes a war god), was supreme; priests and nobles tended to have hereditary status; farmers, artisans, and wage-earners were either attached to the temple or else worked on privately-owned lands; captives became slaves. Soldiers sometimes gained status. Gods included agricultural and local deities; the cult of the dead attained some importance, as shown in status burials.

Egypt: Early Dynasties, I-IV.

Technologies: Bronze was used for weapons and ornaments, and there was evidence of mass production and extensive trade.

Social: Planned cities were built. The god-king became the military and political head of large states, which were expanded through warfare, and he eclipsed the power of the priesthood. Social structure became rigid, hereditary nobles controlling great wealth. Warfare, probably originating in population pressures and dislocations throughout the Near East, was waged to create empires and to ward off invasions.

Theology was based on a pantheon of general gods, such as the Sun, on local animal gods, and on a cult of the dead. The last, combined somewhat with the first two, became predominant, as evidenced by the divine power of the king and by his status burial in pyramids.

China: Chou through Ming Dynasties. The culture center shifts south from the Yellow River to the Yangtze River,[38] while conquests, starting with the Chou Dynasty, culminate in Wittfogel's type of oriental absolute state[39] by the T'ang Dynasty.

Technologies: irrigation and water works develop under state control and become large scale under the Warring States; plow and fertilizer. Iron, glass, and other technologies diffuse from the west.

Social: the Chou Dynasty initiates the era of conquests. A divine ruler and bureaucracy control a state which is stratified into hereditary nobles with military and economic power, merchants, serfs, and some slaves. Cities develop as administrative, religious, and commercial centers.

III. Trial Formulation of Developmental Regularities of Early Civilizations

At the present time the difficulties in making any formulation of the development of early civilizations in the five principal centers of the world are obviously very great. Data on early periods are incomplete, not only because research has been limited but also because it has been directed toward special and restricted problems. Archeology has, until recently, paid comparatively little attention to settlement patterns, demographic trends, and sociological implications of its materials. Historians on the whole are more interested in the fate of particular societies than in culture and its development, and anthropologists have made comparatively little use of the data of written history. These difficulties mean primarily that any present formulation must be highly tentative.

The successive eras in each of the five principal centers of early civilizations appear to have had similar diagnostic features which, arranged chronologically, might be considered as a superficial formulation of regularities. Such a formulation, however, would fail to provide a satisfactory and generally valid functional explanation of cause-and-effect relationships between phenomena. To provide deeper explanations, it is necessary to make cause-and-effect relationships as explicit as possible and to test the explanations offered for the sequence in each center by the data of other centers. This purpose is consistent with the comparative approach of anthropology, and it is far more important to achieve a common sense of problem than to construct enduring formulations.

The formulation here offered excludes all areas except the arid and semiarid center of ancient civilizations. In the irrigation areas, environment, production, and social patterns had similar functional and developmental interrelationships. The productivity of farming was limited only by the amount of water that could be used in irrigation. Metal tools and animal-drawn ploughs, though essential to maximum efficiency of farming in forest or grassland areas, could not increase the yield of irrigation areas beyond the limits imposed by water supply.

Early civilizations occurred also in such tropical rain-forest areas as southern Asia and Yucatan. Yucatan appears to fit the formulation made for the more arid areas to the extent that its sequences were very similar to those of Mesoamerica generally. Farming in Yucatan, however, required slash-and-burn rather than irrigation techniques, and the rural population must have been very scattered. It is possible, therefore, that the Maya were able to develop a high civilization only because they enjoyed an unusually long period of peace; for their settlement pattern would seem to have been too vulnerable to warfare. Yucatan, consequently, should perhaps be excluded from the present formulation. In southeastern Asia, the environment is extremely humid, presenting the difficulties of rain forests and also requiring large drainage projects. And in both areas, the civilizations appear to have been later than and in part derived from those of the irrigation areas.

The Era of Incipient Agriculture in the irrigation centers is very little known, but evidence from Peru, Mesopotamia, and Egypt suggests that it lasted a very long time. Farming was at first supplementary to hunting and gathering, and the social groups were consequently small and probably seminomadic. Technologies differed little from those of the earlier hunting and gathering periods. By the end of this era, farming supported permanent communities, and new technologies began to appear.

A local community, or "folk," culture[40] took form during the next era. The principal crops and animals were brought under domestication, but irrigation was undertaken only on a small, local scale. In subsequent eras, agricultural production increased as irrigation works were developed, the only limit being available land and water, especially the latter. The animal-drawn plough, which appeared in the Old World much later, during the Era of Cyclical Conquests, and which was unknown in prehistoric America, no doubt released a certain portion of the population from farm work but neither it nor iron tools, which appeared still later, could increase production beyond the limits of water supply. Population consequently increased as irrigation works were developed to their maximum. For this reason, the Old World possession of draught animals and the plough does not affect the present formulation.

During the Formative Era, all centers of civilization developed ceramics, loom-weaving, basketry, metallurgy (except Mesoamerica), and the construction of houses and religious edifices. These technologies soon came to be used for two kinds of goods: first, objects that served the simple, domestic—that is, essentially biological—needs of the common folk; second, highly elaborate, stylized goods that served the socially derived needs as well as the more basic needs of the theocratic class. In simple form, some of these technologies spread beyond the areas of irrigation.

Subsequent to the Formative Era, no very important technological advances were made until the Iron Age. Metallurgy ran through similar sequences everywhere (except in Mesoamerica), starting with work in copper and gold and finally achieving bronze. Copper and tin were so rare that the use of bronze was largely limited to ornaments and weapons, while tools of stone, bone, wood, and shell were used for daily chores. Improvement in the other technologies consisted of embellishments and refinements that enhanced their esthetic qualities and produced varied products; but there were no important new inventions.

Transportation improved in successive eras. Domesticated animals were first probably used for packing in all centers except in Mesoamerica, which lacked species suitable for domestication. Wheeled vehicles appeared in the Old World during the Era of Regional Florescence. The wheel was evidently used in toys during the same era in Mesoamerica,[41] but its failure to be used in transportation perhaps may be explained by the absence of draught animals. The importance of transportation increased as states grew larger and as trade expanded. Although draught animals and wheels, which were used on war chariots before they were used on carts and wagons, gave the Old World some technical advantage, every New World center developed roads, boats, and canals to a degree of efficiency which enabled them to achieve states as large as those of the Old World.

The general sequence of social, religious, and military patterns ran a similar course in each center of civilization, and a generally valid formulation is possible. Certain problems which cannot yet be answered will be stated subsequently.

In the Era of Incipient Agriculture it is reasonable to suppose that sociopolitical groups were as varied in nature as they are today among the hunting and gathering people of arid areas.

At the beginning of the Formative Era, the sociopolitical unit was a small house cluster, which probably consisted of a kin group or lineage. As population increased, new clusters evidently budded off and established themselves in unsettled lands. In the course of time, as flood plains became densely settled and as need arose to divert water through canals to drier land, collaboration on irrigation projects under some coordinating authority became necessary. That the need was met by the rise to power of a theocratic class is shown by the appearance toward the end of the Formative Era of evidence of religious domination of society, for example, ceremonial centers, such as mounds and temples, and a large number of religious objects. Farming required careful reckoning of the seasons, considerable ritual, and worship of agricultural gods, tasks which necessitated a special priesthood. During the Formative Era, a small number of house clusters were dispersed around a ceremonial center and were ruled by a priesthood. The priesthood provided centralized control of irrigation and new patterns of group religion. Society became differentiated into theocratic and common classes.

In the Formative Era, state warfare was probably of minor importance. There is little archeological evidence of militarism, and it is likey that warfare was limited to raids. As long as there was ample land for the expanding population, competition for terrain cannot have been important. Because pastoral nomads during this era were unmounted and probably had not become very numerous, they cannot have been a great threat. In the Near East, they probably had asses, cattle, sheep and goats, but did not ride horses and camels until the Iron age,[42] and horse riding did not appear in China until the Era of the Dark Ages or Warring States.

The precise patterning, content, and history of religion, which supplied the socially integrating factor, varied with each center of civilization. In some centers, such as Egypt, China, Peru, and Guatemala, elaborate burials for certain individuals suggest a cult of the dead or ancestor worship, which elevated these persons to the status of god-priests while living and to the status of gods after death. Other kinds of gods are represented by animal, place, and fertility deities. In some instances, the priesthood may have developed from an earlier class of shamans.

The particular religious patterns of each center arose from complex factors of local development and diffusion, and they gave local distinctiveness to the cultures. In terms of the present formulation, however, these differences are secondary in importance to the fact that in all cases a national religion and a priestly class developed because increasing populations, larger irrigation works, and greater need for social coordination called upon religion to supply the integrating factor. The very great importance of religion at the end of the Formative Era is proved by the effort devoted to the construction of temple mounds, temples, palaces, and tombs, and to the special production of religious ornaments, sculpture, and various material appurtenances of the priesthood and temples. It was the priesthood which, devoting full time to religious matters, now laid the foundations of astronomy, writing, and mathematics in all centers.

The Era of Regional Florescence fulfilled the potentialities of the Formative Era. Communities were welded into small states, which, however, continued to be essentially theocratic, for archeological remains of this era are predominantly of a religious nature. The largest mounds, temples, and tombs (mortuary pyramids and burial mounds) of any eras were constructed. Intellectual trends were fulfilled in the development of phonetic writing, numerical systems, and accurate calendars. Even Peru, which never achieved developed writing, may have used an ideographic system at this time.[43] Ceramics, metallurgy, weaving, work in precious stones, and sculpture attained their highest peak of esthetic expression and their most distinctive local stylization.

The relation of militarism to the enlargement of irrigation works and the expansion of states during the Era of Regional Florescence is not clear. Population, irrigation works, and states all increased in size until the end of the era. In Mesoamerica, it is generally believed[44] that the states were peaceful and theocratic, and Cook[45] believes that population reached its maximum at this time, decreasing in the subsequent era. In this case, a priesthood without the backing of armed force was able to create multi-community states, though the extent of irrigation works at this time is not well-known. In other areas, it appears that some militarism was present in the Era of Regional Florescence, and that without warfare the rulers could not have increased the size of states and thereby of irrigation works. In northern Peru, warfare was definitely present in the Era of Regional Florescence, and in China, warfare, arising from conflicts over grazing lands[46] enabled local rulers to extend their authority over subject states,[47] perhaps facilitating the enlargement of irrigation works. Irrigation, however, did not attain maximum size in China until true empires appeared in the following era of Cyclical Conquests.[48] Thus, in China the population maximum came only when militarism achieved empire-wide irrigation projects. In Mesopotamia and Egypt, warfare also appeared during the Era of Regional Florescence, and it was no doubt instrumental in enlarging states but true kingdoms or empires did not appear until the following era. The relation of irrigation and population to warfare and state size in Egypt are not clear, but if Childe[49] is correct in believing that warfare resulted from competition for lands as well as from the pressures of nomads, it would seem that population limits may have been reached.

This seeming contradiction cannot be resolved at present, but it may be suspected either that Mesoamerica had unusually powerful priests or else that the population maximum was not really reached until after the Era of Regional Florescence, when militarism increased the size of states and consequently of irrigation works. In all centers, a temporary decrease of population probably followed the initiation of large-scale warfare.

Social structure seems to have been very similar in all centers of civilization. The local community retained its folk culture, that is, its social structure, local shrines, agricultural practices, and the like, and its members constituted the commoners. Rulers were predominantly priests, though they began to acquire some military functions. It is possible that war achievements gave status to special individuals and that war captives formed a slave class, but as the existence of true economic slavery in native America is in doubt, the social role of captives and the problem of the origin and nature of slavery are open problems which are excluded from consideration here.

The Era of Cyclical Conquests was one of comparatively few culture changes, except those produced by warfare. It initiated a succession of empires and then local states or dark ages that alternated in a fairly stereotyped pattern until the Iron Age and Industrial Era brought cultural influences from other areas. In each center, large scale warfare, which probably originated from internal population pressures, from competition for resources, and from the pressures of outside nomads, was an instrument in creating true empires and starting dynasties. As the empires grew, irrigation works were increased to the limits of water supply and population also increased. After reaching a peak, marked by a temporary florescence of culture, population pressure and abuse of the common people brought rebellion, which destroyed the empires and returned society to local states and a period of dark ages. Irrigation works were neglected and population decreased. New conquests initiated another cycle.

The cyclical phenomena are strikingly illustrated in China[50] where, during 1500 years of the Era of Cyclical Conquests, each of the four major peaks of empires and dynasties coincided with a population peak.[51] These were separated by periods of internal strife and local autonomy. The series of empires in the Near East, which began in Mesopotamia with the early Dynasty of Sumer and in Egypt with the Dynastic period, ran through cycles generally comparable with those of China and lasted until the northern Mediterranean states of the Iron Age brought portions of the Near East under periodic conquests. In Peru, the widespread Tiahuanaco culture and the later Inca Empire probably represent two cycles of empire growth, while in Mexico, the first cycle, that of the Aztec conquests, had not run its course when the Spaniards conquered America.

In the Era of Conquest, militarism produced several important social changes. Towns, which previously had been ceremonial, administrative, and trading centers, now became large walled cities, and special forts were built to afford refuge to the dispersed farm settlements. A true military class appeared in the social hierarchy, and warrior-priests ruled the states and empires. War gods became prominent in the pantheons of state deities.

In this era, all aspects of culture were increasingly regimented at the expense of creative effort. There were sharpened differences in social classes, such as nobles, priests, warriors, commoners, slaves, and stronger differentiation of occupational groups. Laws were codified, learning was systematized (astronomy, theology, mathematics, medicine, writing), art became standardized, and goods were mass-produced by specialists.

Specialized production of commodities and wide-spread trade laid a basis for commercialism, but a free commercial class, factory production, and wage labor could not emerge until economy achieved a strong monetary basis, private property, and specialized cash crops, and until trade was disengaged from the system of state tribute and freed from state control. Though foreshadowed everywhere, this did not occur in the Near East until the Iron Age. In China, the development of private property in land and a system of money and taxation was not sufficient to free economy from the control of powerful states, which existed by virtue of grain taxes which their water works made possible.[52] In the New World, this era was not reached until the Spanish Conquest.

The developments of the Iron Age and the Industrial Era are beyond the scope of the present inquiry. Iron appeared in China in the Era of Cyclical Conquests, but it did not revolutionize the patterns of basic production and social structure as it did in the forested areas of the northern Mediterranean.

IV. Summary and Conclusions

The above analysis may be briefly summarized.

In arid and semi-arid regions, agriculture may be carried on by means of flood-plain and irrigation farming, which does not require metal tools. As irrigation works are developed, population will increase until the limits of water are reached. Political controls become necessary to manage irrigation and other communal projects. As early societies were strongly religious, individuals with supernatural powers—lineage heads, shamans, or special priests—formed a theocratic ruling class, which governed first multi-house-cluster communities and later multi-community states.

The increasing productivity of farming released considerable labor from subsistence activities, and new technologies were developed—basketry, loom-weaving, pottery, metallurgy, domestic and religious construction, and transportational facilities. Products made for home use were simple and utilitarian; those made for the theocratic class and for religious purposes became increasingly rich and varied, and they required an increasing proportion of total productive efforts.

When the limits of agricultural productivity under a given system of irrigation were reached, population pressures developed and interstate competition for land and for produce of all kinds began. The resulting warfare led to the creation of empires, warrior classes, and military leaders. It also led to enlargement of irrigation works and to a further increase of population. But the powerful military empires regimented all aspects of culture, and few new inventions were made. Consequently, each culture entered an era of rising and falling empires, each empire achieving a peak of irrigation, population, and political organization and a temporary florescence, but giving way to a subsequent period of dark ages.

The Iron Age gave the Old World a revolutionary technology, but, as iron tools cannot increase water supply, the irrigation areas were little affected, except as they fell under the empires of the north Mediterranean. Iron Age cultures developed in the forested areas of Europe, which had been exploited only with difficulty under the old technology. The New World never reached an Iron Age in precolumbian times. Instead, the Spanish Conquest brought it an Iron Age culture from the Old World, and native culture development was abruptly ended just after it had entered the Era of Cyclical Conquests.

The above formulation is rough, cursory, and tentative. It applies only to the early centers of world civilization. The eras are not "stages," which in a world evolutionary scheme would apply equally to desert, arctic, grassland, and woodland areas. In these other kinds of areas, the functional interrelationship of subsistence patterns, population, settlements, social structure, cooperative work, warfare, and religion had distinctive forms and requires special formulations.

The principal grounds for questioning the present formulation will, I suspect, be that diffusion between the centers of civilization in each hemisphere can be demonstrated. The relative chronology of the eras (Chart 14–2) fits a diffusionist explanation perfectly. The essential question, however, is just what diffusion amounts to as an explanation. There is no doubt about the spread of domesticated plants and animals and little doubt about the diffusion of many technologies, art styles, and details of both material and non-material culture. Proof of diffusion, however, lies in the unique qualities of secondary features, not in the basic types of social, economic, and religious patterns. The latter could be attributed to diffusion only by postulating mass migration or far-flung conquests.

If people borrow domesticated plants and agricultural patterns, it is evident that population will increase in favorable areas. How shall dense, stable populations organize their sociopolitical relations? Obviously, they will not remain inchoate mobs until diffused patterns have taught them how to live together. (And even diffused patterns had to originate somewhere for good and sufficient reasons.) In densely settled areas, internal needs will produce an orderly interrelationship of environment, subsistence patterns, social groupings, occupational specialization, and over-all political, religious, and perhaps military integrating factors. These interrelated institutions do not have unlimited variability, for they must be adapted to the requirements of subsistence pattterns established in particular environments; they involve a cultural ecology. Traits whose uniqueness is proof of their diffusion are acceptable if they are congruent with the basic socio-economic institutions. They give uniqueness and local color, and they may help crystallize local patterns in distinctive ways, but they cannot per se produce the underlying conditions of or the need for greater social and political organization. It is therefore possible to concede wide diffusion of particulars within the hemispheres and even between the hemispheres without having to rely upon diffusion as the principal explanation of cultural development.

We have attempted here to present a conception of culture and a methodology for formulating the regularities of cultural data which are consistent with scientific purpose. The data are those painstakingly gathered and arranged spacially and temporally by culture history. Thorough attention to cultural differences and particulars is necessary if typology is to be adequate and valid, but historical reconstructions need not be the sole objective of anthropology. Strong observed that "The time is coming when the rich ethnological and archeological record of the New World can be compared in full detail and time perspective with similar records from Europe, Egypt, Mesopotamia, India, China, and Siberia. When such comparative data are in hand the generalizations that will emerge may well revolutionize our concept of culture history and culture process over the millennia."[53] Any generalizations or formulations must be subject to frequent revision by new data, for as Kroeber remarks,[54] "Detailed case-by-case analyses are . . . called for if interpretations are not to become vitiated over generalizations which more and more approach formulas." At the same time, it is obvious that the minutiae of culture history will never be completely known and that there is no need to defer formulations until all archeologists have laid down their shovels and all ethnologists have put away their notebooks. Unless anthropology is to interest itself mainly in the unique, exotic, and non-recurrent particulars, it is necessary that formulations be attempted no matter how tentative they may be. It is formulations that will enable us to state new kinds of problems and to direct attention to new kinds of data which have been slighted in the past. Fact-collecting of itself is insufficient scientific procedure; facts exist only as they are related to theories, and theories are not destroyed by facts—they are replaced by new theories which better explain the facts. Therefore, criticisms of this paper which concern facts alone and which fail to offer better formulations are of no interest.

Notes

1. Morgan, 1877.
2. Tylor, 1865, 1871.
3. White, 1943.
4. Lowie, 1936, pp. 3, 7.
5. Lesser, 1930.
6. Steward, 1936.
7. *Idem.*, 1937.
8. *See* Steward and Setzler, 1938.
9. Childe, 1934, 1946.
10. Wittfogel, 1935, 1938, 1939–1940.
11. Gladwin, 1947.
12. Malinowski, 1944, pp. 214–215.
13. *See also* Wittfogel, 1939–1940, pp. 175–176.
14. Redfield, 1941.
15. Morgan, 1877.
16. White, 1943.
17. This proposition has been developed in detail in Steward, 1940; pp. 479–498; 1938: pp. 1–3, 230–262.

18. Cultural historical data are from the following sources, unless otherwise cited. Northern Peru: Bennett, 1946; Kroeber, 1940, 1944; Strong, 1947; Wiley, 1948. Mesoamerica: Armillas, 1948; Kidder, Jennings, and Shook, 1946; Morley, 1946; Thompson, 1943, 1945; Vaillant, 1944. Mesopotamia and Egypt: Childe, 1934, 1946; Albright, 1946. China: Bishop, 1942; Creel, 1937a, 1937b; Wittfogel, 1935, 1938, 1939–40, 1946.

19. Morley, 1944.

20. Armillas, 1948.

21. Kidder, 1946.

22. Vaillant, 1944.

23. Thompson, 1943, 1945.

24. Morley, 1946.

25. Childe, 1946.

26. Albright, 1946.

27. Willey, 1948.

28. Strong, 1947.

29. Bennett, 1946.

30. Armillas, 1948.

31. Kidder, 1946.

32. Thompson, 1943, 1945.

33. Morley, 1947.

34. Cook, 1947.

35. Albright, 1946.

36. Childe, 1946.

37. Creel, 1937b, p. 184.

38. Chi, 1936.

39. Wittfogel, 1935.

40. This may be considered to have had the general characteristics of Redfield's "Folk Society" (1947).

41. Ekholm, 1946.

42. Albright, 1946, pp. 120–123.

43. Larco Hoyle, 1946, p. 175.

44. Armillas, 1948; Kidder *et al.*, 1946; Thompson, 1943, 1945; Morley, 1946.

45. Cook, 1947.

46. Creel, 1937, p. 184.

47. Bishop, 1942, p. 20.
48. Chi, 1936; Wittfogel, 1938, 1939–1940.
49. Childe, 1946.
50. Wittfogel, 1938, 1946.
51. Ta Chen, 1946, pp. 4–6.
52. Wittfogel, 1935, 1939–1940.
53. Strong, 1943, p. 34.
54. Kroeber, 1940, p. 477.

Leslie A. White

15. Energy and the Evolution of Culture

The purpose of culture is to serve the needs of man. These needs are of two kinds: (1) those which can be served or satisfied by drawing upon resources within the human organism alone. Singing, dancing, myth-making, forming clubs or associations for the sake of companionship, etc., illustrate this kind of needs and ways of satisfying them. (2) The second class of needs can be satisfied only by drawing upon the re-sources of the external world, outside the human organism. Man must get his food from the external world. The tools, weapons, and other materials with which man provides himself with food, shelter from the elements, protection from his enemies, must likewise come from the external world. The satisfaction of spiritual and esthetic needs through singing, dancing, myth-making, etc., is possible, however, only if man's bodily needs for food, shelter, and defense are met. Thus the whole cultural structure depends upon the material, mechanical means with which man articulates himself with the earth. Furthermore, the satisfac-tion of human needs from "inner resources" may be regarded as a constant, the satisfaction of needs from the outer resources a variable. Therefore, in our discussion of cultural development we may omit con-sideration of the constant factor and deal only with the variable—the material, mechanical means with which man exploits the resources of nature.

The articulation-of-man-with-the-earth process may be analyzed and resolved into the following five factors: (1) the human organism, (2) the habitat, (3) the amount of energy controlled and expended by man, (4) the ways and means in which energy is expended, and (5) the human-need-serving product which accrues from the expenditure of energy. This is but another way of saying that human beings, like all other living creatures, exploit the resources of their habitat, in one way or another in order to sustain life and to perpetuate their kind.

Of the above factors, we may regard the organic factor as a constant. Although peoples obviously differ from each other physically, we are not able to attribute differences in culture to differences in physique (or "mentality"). In our study of culture, therefore, we may regard the human race as of uniform quality, i.e., as a constant, and, hence, we may eliminate it from our study.

No two habitats are alike; every habitat varies in time. Yet, in a study of culture as a whole, we may regard the factor of habitat as a constant: we simply reduce the need-serving, welfare-promoting resources of all particular habitats to an average. (In a consideration of particular manifestations of culture we would of course have to deal with their respective particular habitats.) Since we may regard habitat as a constant, we exclude it, along with the human organism, from our study of the development of culture.

This leaves us, then, three factors to be considered in any cultural situation: (1) the amount of energy per capita per unit of time harnessed and put to work within the culture, (2) the technological means with which this energy is expended, and (3) the human need-serving product that accrues from the expenditure of energy. We may express the relationship between these factors in the following simple formula: $E \times T = P$, in which E represents the amount of energy expended per capita per unit of time, T the technological means of its expenditure, and P the magnitude of the product per unit of time. This may be illustrated concretely with the following simple example: A man cuts wood with an axe. Assuming the quality of the wood and the skill of the workman to be constant, the amount of wood cut in a given period of time, an hour say, depends, on the one hand upon the amount of energy the man expends during this time: the more energy expended, the more wood cut. On the other hand, the amount of wood cut in an hour depends upon the kind of axe used. Other things being equal, the amount of wood cut varies with the quality of the axe: the better the axe the more wood cut. Our workman can cut more wood with an iron, or steel, axe than with a stone axe.

The efficiency with which human energy is expended mechanically depends upon the bodily skills of the persons involved, and upon the nature of the tools employed. In the following discussion we shall deal with skill in terms of averages. It is obvious, of course, that, other things being equal, the product of the expenditure of human energy varies directly as the skill employed in the expenditure of this energy. But we may reduce all particular skills, in any given situation, to an average, which, being constant may be eliminated from our consideration of culture growth. Hereafter, then, when we concern ourselves with the efficiency with which human energy is expended mechanically, we shall be dealing with the efficiency of tools only.

With reference to tools, man can increase the efficiency of the expenditure of his bodily energy in two ways: by improving a tool, or by substituting a better tool for an inferior one. But with regard to any given kind of tool, it must be noted that there is a point beyond which it cannot be improved. The efficiency of various tools of a certain kind varies; some bows are better than others. A bow, or any other implement, may vary in efficiency between 0 per cent and 100 per cent. But there is a maximum, theoretically as well as actually, which cannot be exceeded. Thus, the efficiency of a canoe paddle can be raised or lowered by altering its length, breadth, thickness, shape, etc. Certain proportions or dimensions would render it useless, in which case its efficiency would be 0 per cent. But, in the direction of improvement, a point is reached, ideally as well as practically, when no further progress can be made—any further change would be a detriment. Its efficiency is now at its maximum (100 per cent). So it is with a canoe, arrow, axe, dynamo, locomotive, or any other tool or machine.

We are now ready for some generalizations about cultural development. Let us return to our formula, but this time let us write it $E \times F = P$, in which E and P have the same values as before—E, the amount of energy expended; P the product produced—while F stands for the efficiency of the mechanical means with which the energy is expended. Since culture is a mechanism for serving human needs, cultural development may be measured by the extent to which, and the efficiency with which, need-serving goods or services are provided. P, in our formula, may thus stand for the total amount of goods or services produced in any given cultural situation. Hence P represents the status of culture, or, more accurately, the degree of cultural development. If, then, F, the efficiency with which human energy is expended, remains constant, the P, the degree of cultural development, will vary as E, the amount of energy expended per capita per year varies:

$$\frac{E_1 \times F}{E_2 \times F} = \frac{P_1}{P_2}$$

Thus we obtain the first important law of cultural development: *Other things being equal, the degree of cultural development varies directly as the amount of energy per capita per year harnessed and put to work.*

Secondly, if the amount of energy expended per capita unit of time remains constant, then P varies as F:

$$\frac{E \times F_1}{E \times F_2} = \frac{P_1}{P_2}$$

and we get the second law of cultural development: *Other things being equal, the degree of cultural development varies directly as the efficiency of the technological means with which the harnessed energy is put to work.*
It is obvious, of course, that E and F may vary simultaneously, and in the same or in opposite directions. If E and F increase simultaneously P will increase faster, naturally, than if only one increased while the other remained unchanged. If E and F decrease simultaneously P will decrease more rapidly than if only one decreased while the other remained constant. If E increases while F decreases, or vice versa, then P will vary or remain unchanged, depending upon the magnitude of the changes of these two factors and upon the proportion of one magnitude to the other. If an increase in E is balanced by a decrease in F, or vice versa, then P will remain unchanged. But should E increase faster than F decreases, or vice versa, then P would increase; if E decreases faster than F increases, or vice versa, then P would decrease.
We have, in the above generalizations *the* law of cultural evolution: *culture develops when the amount of energy harnessed by man per capita per year is increased; or as the efficiency of the technological means of putting this energy to work is increased; or, as both factors are simultaneously increased.*
All living beings struggle to live, to perpetuate their respective kinds. In the human species the struggle for survival assumes the cultural form. The human struggle for existence expresses itself in a never-ending attempt to make of culture a more effective instrument with which to provide security of life and survival of the species. And one of the ways of making culture a more powerful instrument is to harness and to put to work within it more energy per capita per year. Thus, wind, and water, and fire are harnessed; animals are domesticated, plants cultivated; steam engines are built. The other way of improving culture as an instrument of adjustment and control is to invent new and better tools and to improve old ones. Thus energy for culture-living and culture-building is augmented in quantity, is expended more efficiently, and culture advances.
Thus we know, not only *how* culture evolves, but *why,* as well. The urge, inherent in all living species, to live, to make life more secure, more rich, more full, to insure the perpetuation of the species, seizes

upon, when it does not produce, better (i.e., more effective) means of living and surviving. In the case of man, the biological urge to live, the power to invent and to discover, the ability to select and use the better of two tools or ways of doing something—these are the factors of cultural evolution. Darwin could tell us the consequences of variations, but he could not tell us how these variations were produced. We know the motive force as well as the means of cultural evolution. The culturologist knows more about cultural evolution than the biologist, even today, knows about biological evolution.

A word about man's motives with regard to cultural development. We do not say that man deliberately set about to improve his culture. It may well have been, as Morgan suggested, decades before Lowie emphasized the same point, that animals were first domesticated through whim or caprice rather than for practical, utilitarian reasons. Perhaps agriculture came about through accident. Hero's steam engine was a plaything. Gunpowder was first used to make pretty fireworks. The compass began as a toy. More than this, we know that peoples often resolutely oppose technological advances with a passionate devotion to the past and to the gods of their fathers. But all of this does not alter the fact that domesticated animals and cultivated plants have been used to make life more secure. Whatever may have been the intentions and motives (if any) of the inventors or discoverers of the bow and arrow, the wheel, the furnace and forge, the steam engine, the microscope, etc., the fact remains that these things have been seized upon by mankind and employed to make life more secure, comfortable, pleasant, and permanent. So we may disregard the psychological circumstances under which new cultural devices were brought into being. What is significant to the cultural evolutionist is that inventions and discoveries have been made, new tools invented, better ways of doing things found, and that these improved tools and techniques are kept and used until they are in turn replaced.

So much for the laws, or generalizations derived from our basic formula. Let us turn now to concrete facts and see how the history of culture is illuminated and made intelligible by these laws.

In the beginning of culture history, man had only the energy of his own body under his control and at his disposal for culture-living and culture-building. And for a very long period of time this was almost the only source of energy available to him. Wind, water, and fire were but rarely used as forms of energy. Thus we see that, in the first stage of cultural development, the only source of energy under man's control and at his disposal for culture-building was, except for the insignificant and limited use of wind, water and fire, his own body.

The amount of energy that could be derived from this source was very small. The amount of energy at the disposal of a community of 50, 100, or 300 persons would be 50, 100, or 300 times the energy of the average member of the community, which, when infants, the sick, the old and feeble are considered, would be considerably less than one "man-power" per capita. Since one "man-power" is about one-tenth of one horse-power, we see that the amount of energy per capita in the earliest stage of cultural development was very small indeed—perhaps 1/20th horse-power per person.

Since the amount of energy available for culture building in this stage was finite and limited, the extent to which culture could develop was limited. As we have seen, when the energy factor is a constant, cultural progress is made possible only by improvements in the means with which the energy is expended, namely, the technology. Thus, in the human-energy stage of cultural development progress is achieved only by inventing new tools—the bow and arrow, harpoon, needle, etc., or by improving old ones—new techniques of chipping flint implements, for example. But when man has achieved maximum efficiency in the expenditure of energy, and when he has reached the limits of his finite bodily energy resources, then his culture can develop no further. Unless he can harness additional quantities of energy—by tapping new sources—cultural development will come to an end. Man would have remained on the level of savagery indefinitely if he had not learned to augment the amount of energy under his control and at his disposal for culture-building by harnessing new sources of energy. This was first accomplished by the domestication of animals and by the cultivation of plants.

Man added greatly to the amount of energy under his control and at his disposal for culture-building when he domesticated animals and brought plants under cultivation. To be sure, man nourished himself with meat and grain and clothed himself with hides and fibers long before animal husbandry and agriculture came into being. But there is a vast difference between merely exploiting the resources of nature and of harnessing the forces of nature. In a wild food economy, a person, under given environmental conditions, expends a certain amount of energy (we will assume it is an average person so that the question of skill may be ignored) and in return he will secure, on the average, so much meat, fish, or plant food. But the food which he secures is itself a form and a magnitude of energy. Thus the hunter or wild plant-food gatherer exchanges one magnitude of energy for another: m units of labor for n calories of food. The ratio between the magnitude of energy obtained in the form of food and the magnitude expended in hunting and gathering may vary. The amount obtained may be greater than, less than (in which case the hunter-gatherer would eventually perish), or equal to, the amount expended. But although the ratio may vary from one situation to another, it is in any particular instance fixed: that is, the magnitude of energy-value of the game taken or plant-food gathered remains constant between the time that it is obtained and the time of its consumption. (At least it does not increase, it may in some instances decrease through natural deterioration.)

In a wild food economy, an animal or a plant is of value to man only after it has ceased to be an animal or a plant, i.e., a living organism. The hunter kills his game, the gatherer digs his roots and bulbs, plucks the fruit and seeds. It is different with the herdsman and the farmer. These persons make plants and animals work for them.

Living plants and animals are biochemical mechanisms which, of themselves, accumulate and store up energy derived originally from the sun. Under agriculture and animal husbandry these accumulations can be appropriated and utilized by man periodically in the form of milk, wool, eggs, fruits, nuts, seeds, sap, and so on. In the case of animals, energy generated by them may be utilized by man in the form of work, more or less continuously throughout their lifetime. Thus, when man domesticated animals and brought plants under cultivation, he harnessed powerful forces of nature, brought them under his control, and made them work for him just as he has harnessed rivers and made them run mills and dynamos, just as he has harnessed the tremendous reservoirs of solar energy that are coal and oil. Thus the difference between a wild plant and animal economy and a domestic economy is that in the former the return for an expenditure of human energy, no matter how large, is fixed, limited, whereas in agriculture and animal husbandry the initial return for the expenditure of human labor, augments itself indefinitely. And so it has come about that with the development and perfection of the arts of animal husbandry and agriculture—selective breeding, protection from their competitors in the Darwinian struggle for survival, feeding, fertilizer, irrigation, drainage, etc.—a given quantity of human labor produces much more than it could before these forces were harnessed. It is true, of course, that a given amount of human labor will produce more food in a wild economy under exceptionally favorable circumstances,—such, e.g., as in the Northwest Coast of America where salmon could be taken in vast numbers with little labor, or in the Great Plains of North America where, after the introduction of the horse and in favorable circumstances, a large quantity of bison meat could be procured with but little labor,—than could be produced by a feeble development of agriculture in unfavorable circumstances. But history and archeology prove that, by and large, the ability of man to procure the first necessity of life, food, was tremendously increased by the domestication of animals and by the cultivation of plants. Cultural progress was extremely rapid after the origin of agriculture. The great civilizations of China, India. Mesopotamia, Egypt, Mexico, and Peru sprang up quickly after the agricultural arts had attained to some degree of development and maturity. This was due, as we have already observed, to the fact that, by means of agriculture man was able to harness, control, and put to work for himself powerful forces of nature. With greatly augmented energy resources man was able to expand and develop his way of life, i.e., his culture.

In the development of culture agriculture is a much more important and powerful factor than animal husbandry. This is because man's control over the forces of nature is more immediate and more complete in agriculture than in animal husbandry. In a pastoral economy man exerts control over the animals only, he merely harnesses solar energy in animal form. But the animals themselves are dependent upon wild plants. Thus pastoral man is still dependent to a great extent upon the forces and caprices of nature. But in agriculture, his control is more intimate, direct, and, above all, greater. Plants receive and store up energy directly from the sun. Man's control over plants is direct and immediate. Further independence of nature is achieved by means of irrigation, drainage, and fertilizer. To be sure, man is always dependent upon nature to a greater or less extent; his control is never complete. But his dependence is less, his control greater, in agriculture than in animal husbandry. The extent to which man may harness natural forces in animal husbandry is limited. No matter how much animals are improved by selective breeding, no matter how carefully they are tended—defended from beasts of prey, protected from the elements—so long as they are dependent upon wild plant food, there is a limit, imposed by nature, to the extent to which man can receive profitable returns from his efforts expended on his herds. When this limit has been reached no further progress can be made. It is not until man controls also the growth of the plants upon which his animals feed that progress in animal husbandry can advance to higher levels. In agriculture, on the other hand, while there may be a limit to the increase of yield per unit of human labor, this limit has not yet been reached, and, indeed it is not yet even in sight. Thus there appears to be a limit to the return from the expenditure of a given amount of human labor in animal husbandry. But in agriculture this technological limit, if one be assumed to exist, lies so far ahead of us that we cannot see it or imagine where it might lie.

Added to all of the above, is the familiar fact that a nomadic life, which is customary in a pastoral economy, is not conducive to the development of advanced cultures. The sedentary life that goes with agriculture is much more conducive to the development of the arts and crafts, to the accumulation of wealth and surpluses, to urban life.

Agriculture increased tremendously the amount of energy per capita available for culture-building, and, as a consequence of the maturation of the agricultural arts, a tremendous growth of culture was experienced. Cultural progress was very slow during Eolithic and Paleolithic times. But after a relatively brief period in the Neolithic age, during which the agricultural arts were being developed, there was a tremendous acceleration of culture growth and, the great cultures of China, India, Mesopotamia, Egypt, Mexico, and Peru, came rapidly into being.

The sequence of events was somewhat as follows: agriculture transformed a roaming population into a sedentary one. It greatly increased the food supply, which in turn increased the population. As human labor became more productive in agriculture, an increasing portion of society became divorced from the task of food-getting, and was devoted to other occupations. Thus society becomes organized into occupational groups: masons, metal workers, jade carvers, weavers, scribes, priests. This has the effect of accelerating progress in the arts, crafts, and sciences (astronomy, mathematics, etc.), since they are now in the hands of specialists, rather than jacks-of-all-trades. With an increase in manufacturing, added to division of society into occupational groups, comes production for exchange and sale (instead of primarily for use as in tribal society), mediums of exchange, money, merchants, banks, mortgages, debtors, slaves. An accumulation of wealth and competition for favored regions provoke wars of conquest, and produce professional military and ruling classes, slavery and serfdom. Thus agriculture wrought a profound change in the life-and-culture of man as it had existed in the human-energy stage of development.

But the advance of culture was not continuous and without limit. Civilization had, in the main, reached the limit of its development on the basis of a merely agricultural and animal husbandry technology long before the next great cultural advance was initiated by the industrial revolution. As a matter of fact, marked cultural recessions took place in Mesopotamia, Egypt, Greece, Rome, perhaps in India, possibly in China. This is not to say that no cultural progress whatsoever was made; we are well aware of many steps forward from time to time in various places. But so far as general type of culture is concerned, there is no fundamental difference between the culture of Greece during the time of Archimedes and that of Western Europe at the beginning of the eighteenth century.

After the agricultural arts had become relatively mature, some six, eight or ten thousand years before the beginning of the Christian era, there was little cultural advance until the nineteenth century A.D. Agricultural methods in Europe and the United States in 1850 differed very little from those of Egypt of 2000 B.C. The Egyptians did not have an iron plow, but otherwise there was little difference in mode of production. Even today in many places in the United States and in Europe we can find agricultural practices which, the use of iron excepted, are essentially like those of dynastic Egypt. Production in other fields was essentially the same in western Europe at the beginning of the eighteenth (we might almost say nineteenth) century as in ancient Rome, Greece, or Egypt. Man, as freeman, serf, or slave, and beasts of burden and draft animals, supplemented to a meager extent by wind and water power, were the sources of energy. The Europeans had gunpowder whereas the ancients did not. But gunpowder cannot be said to be a culture-builder. There was no essential difference in type of social—political and economic— institutions. Banks, merchants, the political state, great land-owners, guilds of workmen, and so on were found in ancient Mesopotamia, Greece, and Rome.

Thus we may conclude that culture had developed about as far as it could upon the basis of an agricultural-animal husbandry economy, and that there were recessions from peaks attained in Mesopotamia, Egypt, Greece and Rome long before the beginning of the eighteenth century A.D. We may conclude further, that civilization would never have advanced substantially beyond the levels already reached in the great cultures of antiquity if a way had not been found to harness a greater magnitude of energy per capita per unit of time, by tapping a new source of energy: fuel.

The invention of the steam engine, and of all subsequent engines which derive power from fuels, inaugurated a new era in culture history. When man learned to harness energy in the form of fuel he opened the door of a vast treasure house of energy. Fuels and engines tremendously increased the amount of energy under man's control and at his disposal for culture-building. The extent to which energy has been thus harnessed in the modern world is indicated by the eminent physicist, Robert A. Millikan (1939:211) as follows:

In this country [the U.S.A.] there is now expended about 13.5 horsepower hours per day per capita—the equivalent of 100 human slaves for each of us; in England the figure is 6.7, in Germany 6.0, in France 4.5; in Japan 1.8, in Russia 0.9, in China, 0.5.

Let us return now, for a moment, to our basic principle—culture develops as (1) the amount of energy harnessed and put to work per capita per unit of time increases, and (2) as the efficiency of the means with which this energy is expended increases—and consider the evolution of culture from a slightly different angle. In the course of human history various sources of energy are tapped and harnessed by man and put to work at culture-living and culture-building. The original source of energy was, as we have seen, the human organism. Subsequently, energy has been harnessed in other forms—agriculture, animal husbandry, fire, wind, water, fuel. Energy is energy, and from the point of view of technology it makes no difference whether the energy with which a bushel of wheat is ground comes from a free man, a slave, an ox, the flowing stream or a pile of coal. But it makes a big difference to human beings where the energy comes from, and an important index of cultural development is derived from this fact.

To refer once more to our basic equation: On the one hand we have energy expended; on the other, human need-serving goods and services are produced. Culture advances as these two factors increase, hand in hand. But the energy component is resolvable into two factors: the human energy, and the non-human energy, factors. Of these, the human energy factor is a constant; the non-human energy factor, a variable. The increase in quantity of need-serving goods goes hand in hand with an increase in the amount of non-human energy expended. But, since the human energy factor remains constant, an increase in amount of goods and services produced means more goods and services per unit of human labor. Hence, we obtain the law: *Other things being equal, culture evolves as the productivity of human labor increases.*

In Savagery (wild food economy) the productivity of human labor is low; only a small amount of human need-serving goods and services are produced per unit of human energy. In Barbarism (agriculture, animal husbandry), this productivity is greatly increased. And in Civilization (fuels, engines) it is still further increased.

We must now consider another factor in the process of cultural development, and an important one it is, viz., the *social system within which energy is harnessed and put to work.*

We may distinguish two kinds of determinants in social organization, two kinds of social groupings. On the one hand we have social groupings which serve those needs of man which can be fed by drawing upon resources within man's own organism: clubs for companionship, classes or castes in so far as they feed the desire for distinction, will serve as examples. On the other hand, social organization is concerned with man's adjustment to the external world; social organization *is* the way in which human beings organize themselves for the three great processes of adjustment and survival—food getting, defense from enemies, protection from the elements. Thus, we may distinguish two factors in any social system, those elements which are *ends in themselves,* which we may call E; and elements which are *means to ends* (food, defense, etc.) which we may term M.

In any social system M is more important than E, because E is dependent upon M. There can be no men's clubs or classes of distinction unless food is provided and enemies guarded against. In the development of culture, moreover, we may regard E as a constant: a men's club is a men's club whether among savage or civilized peoples. Being a constant, we may ignore factor E in our consideration of cultural evolution and deal only with the factor M.

M is a variable factor in the process of cultural evolution. It is, moreover, a dependent variable, dependent upon the technological way in which energy is harnessed and put to work. It is obvious, of course, that it is the technological activities of hunting people that determine, in general, their form of social organization (in so far as that social organization is correlated with hunting rather than with defense against enemies). We of the United States have a certain type of social system (in part) because we have factories, railroads, automobiles, etc.; we do not possess these things *as a consequence* of a certain kind of social system. Technological systems engender social systems rather than the reverse. Disregarding the factor E, social organization is to be regarded as the way in which human beings organize themselves to wield their respective technologies. Thus we obtain another important law of culture: *The social organization (E excluded) of a people is dependent upon and determined by the mechanical means with which food is secured, shelter provided, and defense maintained.* In the process of cultural development, *social evolution is a consequence of technological evolution.*

But this is not the whole story. While it is true that social systems are engendered by, and dependent upon, their respective underlying technologies, it is also true that social systems condition the operation of the technological systems upon which they rest; the relationship is one of mutual, though not necessarily equal, interaction and influence. A social system may foster the effective operation of its underlying technology or it may tend to restrain and thwart it. In short, in any given situation the social system may play a progressive role or it may play a reactionary role.

We have noted that after the agricultural arts had attained a certain degree of development, the great civilizations of China, India, Egypt, the Near East, Central America and Peru came rapidly into being as a consequence of the greatly augmented energy resources of the peoples of these regions. But these great civilizations did not continue to advance indefinitely. On the contrary they even receded from maximum levels in a number of instances. Why did they not continue progressively to advance? According to our law culture will advance, other things being equal, as long as the amount of energy harnessed and put to work per capita per unit of time increases. The answer to our question, Why did not these great cultures continue to advance? is, therefore, that the amount of energy per capita per unit of time, *ceased to increase,* and, furthermore, the efficiency of the means with which this energy was expended *was not advanced beyond a certain limit.* In short, there was no fundamental improvement in the agricultural arts from say 2000 B.C. to 1800 A.D.

The next question is, Why did not the agricultural arts advance and improve during this time? We know that the agricultural arts are still capable of tremendous improvement, and the urge of man for plenty, security and efficiency was as great then as now. Why, then, did agriculture fail to progress beyond a certain point in the great civilizations of antiquity? The answer is, The social system, within which these arts functioned, curbed further expansion, thwarted progress.

All great civilizations resting upon intensive agriculture are divided into classes: a ruling class and the masses who are ruled. The masses produced the means of life. But the distribution of these goods is in accordance with rules which are administered by the ruling class. By one method of control or another—by levies, taxes, rents, or some other means—the ruling class takes a portion of the wealth produced by the masses from them, and consumes it according to their liking or as the exigencies of the time dictate.

In this sort of situation cultural advancement may cease at a certain point for lack of incentive. No incentive to progress came from the ruling class in the ancient civilizations of which we are speaking. What they appropriated from their subjects they consumed or wasted. To obtain more wealth the ruling class merely inceased taxes, rents, or other levies upon the producers of wealth. This was easier, quicker, and surer than increasing the efficiency of production and thereby augmenting the total product. On the other hand, there was no incentive to progress among the masses—if they produced more by increasing efficiency it would only mean more for the tax-gatherers of the ruling class. The culture history of China during the past few centuries, or indeed, since the Han dynasty, well illustrates situations of this sort.

We come then to the following conclusion: *A social system may so condition the operation of a technological system as to impose a limit upon the extent to which it can expand and develop. When this occurs, cultural evolution ceases.* Neither evolution nor progress in culture is inevitable (neither Morgan nor Tylor ever said, or even intimated, that they are). When cultural advance has thus been arrested, it can be renewed only by tapping some new source of energy and by harnessing it in sufficient magnitude to burst asunder the social system which binds it. Thus freed, the new technology will form a new social system, one congenial to its growth, and culture will again advance until, perhaps, the social system once more checks it.

It seems quite clear that mankind would never have advanced materially beyond the maximum levels attained by culture between 2000 B.C. and 1700 A.D. had it not tapped a new source of energy (fuel) and harnessed it in substantial magnitudes. The speed with which man could travel, the range of his projectiles, and many other things, could not have advanced beyond a certain point had he not learned to harness more energy in new forms. And so it was with culture as a whole.

The steam engine ushered in a new era. With it, and various kinds of internal combustion engines, the energy resources of vast deposits of coal and oil were tapped and harnessed in progressively increasing magnitudes. Hydroelectric plants contributed a substantial amount from rivers. Populations grew, production expanded, wealth increased. The limits of growth of the new technology have not yet been reached; indeed, it is probably not an exaggeration to say that they have not yet even been foreseen, so vast are the possibilities and so close are we still to the beginning of this new era. But already the new technology has come into conflict with the old social system. The new technology is being curbed and thwarted. The progressive tendencies of the new technology are being held back by a social system that was adapted to the pre-fuel technology. This fact has become commonplace today.

In our present society, goods are produced for sale at a profit. To sell one must have a market. Our market is a world market, but it is, nevertheless, finite in magnitude. When the limit of the market has been reached production ceases to expand: no market, no sale; no sale, no profit; no profit, no production. Drastic curtailment of production, wholesale destruction of surpluses follow. Factories, mills, and mines close; millions of men are divorced from industrial production and thrown upon relief. Population growth recedes. National incomes cease to expand. Stagnation sets in.

When, in the course of cultural development, the expanding technology comes into conflict with the social system, one of two things will happen: either the social system will give way, or technological advance will be arrested. If the latter occurs, cultural evolution will, of course, cease. The outcome of situations such as this is not preordained. The triumph of technology and the continued evolution and progress of culture are not assured merely because we wish it or because it would be

Leslie A. White

better thus. In culture as in mechanics, the greater force prevails. A force is applied to a boulder. If the force be great enough, the rock is moved. If the rock be large enough to withstand the force it will remain stationary. So in the case of technology-institutions conflicts: if the force of the growing technology be great enough the restraining institutions will give way; if this force is not strong enough to overcome institutional opposition, it must submit to it.

There was undoubtedly much institutional resistance to the expanding agricultural technology in late neolithic times. Such staunch institutions as the tribe and clan which had served man well for thousands of years did not give way to the political state without a fight; the "liberty, equality and fraternity" of primitive society were not surrendered for the class-divided, serf and lord, slave and master, society of feudalism without a struggle. But the ancient and time-honored institutions of tribal society could not accommodate the greatly augmented forces of the agricultural technology. Neither could they successfully oppose these new forces. Consequently, tribal institutions gave way and a new social system came into being.

Similarly in our day, our institutions have shown themselves incapable of accommodating the vast technological forces of the Power Age. What the outcome of the present conflict between modern fuel technology and the social system of an earlier era will be, time alone will tell. It seems likely, however, that the old social system is now in the process of destruction. The tremendous forces of the Power Age are not to be denied. The great wars of the twentieth century derive their chief significance from this fact: they are the means by which an old social order is to be scrapped, and a new one to be brought into being. The first World War wiped out the old ruling families of the Hapsburgs, Romanoffs, and Hohenzollerns, hulking relics of Feudalism, and brought Communist and Fascist systems into being. We do not venture to predict the social changes which the present war will bring about. But we may confidently expect them to be as profound and as far-reaching as those effected by World War I.

Thus, in the history of cultural evolution, we have witnessed one complete cultural revolution, and the first stage of a second. The technological transition from a wild food economy to a relatively mature agricultural and animal husbandry economy was followed by an equally profound institutional change: from tribal society to civil society. Thus the first fundamental and all-inclusive cultural change, or revolution, took place. At the present time we are entering upon the second stage of the second great cultural revolution of human history. The Industrial Revolution was but the first stage, the technological stage, of this great cultural revolution. The Industrial Revolution has run its course, and we are now entering upon the second stage, one of profound institutional change, of social revolution. Barring collapse and chaos, which is of course possible, a new social order will emerge. It appears likely that the human race will occupy the earth for some million years to come. It seems probable, also, that man, after having won his way up through savagery and barbarism, is not likely to stop, when at last he finds himself upon the very threshold of civilization.

The key to the future, in any event, lies in the energy situation. If we can continue to harness as much energy per capita per year in the future as we are doing now, there is little doubt but that our old social system will give way to a new one, a new era of civilization. Should, however, the amount of energy that we are able to harness diminish materially, then culture would cease to advance or even recede. A return to a cultural level comparable to that of China during the Ming dynasty is neither inconceivable nor impossible. It all depends upon how man harnesses the forces of nature and the extent to which this is done.

At the present time "the petroleum in sight is only a twelve year supply, . . . and new discoveries [of oil] are not keeping pace with use" (Furnas 1941:425). Coal is more abundant. Even so, many of the best deposits in the United States—which has over half of the world's known coal reserves—will some day be depleted. "Eventually, no matter how much we conserve, this sponging off past ages for fossil energy must cease . . . What then?" (Furnas 1941:426). The answer is, of course, that culture will decline unless man is able to maintain the amount of energy harnessed per capita per year by tapping new sources.

Wind, water, waves, tides, solar boilers, photochemical reactions, atomic energy, etc., are sources which might be tapped or further exploited. One of the most intriguing possibilities is that of harnessing atomic energy. When the nucleus of an atom of uranium (U 235) is split it "releases 200,000,000 electron volts, the largest conversion of mass into energy that has yet been produced by terrestrial means." Weight for weight, uranium (as a source of energy produced by nuclear fission) is 5,000,000 times as effective as coal. If harnessing sub-atomic energy could be made a practical success, our energy resources would be multiplied a thousand fold. As Dr. R. M. Langer (1940), research associate in physics at California Institute of Technology, has put it;

The face of the earth will be changed. . . . Privilege and class distinctions . . . will become relics because things that make up the good life will be so abundant and inexpensive. War will become obsolete because of the disappearance of those economic stresses that immemorially have caused it. . . . The kind of civilization we might expect . . . is so different in kind from anything we know that even guesses about it are futile.

To be able to harness sub-atomic energy would, without doubt, create a civilization surpassing sober imagination of today. But not everyone is as confident as Dr. Langer that this advance is imminent. Some experts have their doubts, some think it a possibility. Time alone will tell.

But there is always the sun, from which man has derived all of his energy, directly or indirectly, in the past. And it may be that it will become, directly, our chief source of power in the future. Energy in enormous amounts reaches the earth daily from the sun. "The average intensity of solar energy in this latitude amounts to about 0.1 of a horse power per square foot" (Furnas 1941:426). "Enough energy falls on about 200 square miles of an arid region like the Mojave Desert to supply the [present needs of the] United States" (Furnas 1941:427). But the problem is, of course, to harness it effectively and efficiently. The difficulties do not seem insuperable. It will doubtless be done, and probably before a serious diminution of power from dwindling resources of oil and coal overtakes us. From a power standpoint the outlook for the future is not too dark for optimism.

We turn now to an interesting and important fact, one highly significant to the history of anthropology: The thesis set forth in the preceding pages is substantially the same as that advanced by Lewis H. Morgan and E. B. Tylor many decades ago. We have expounded it in somewhat different form and words; our presentation is, perhaps, more systematic and explicit. At one point we have made a significant change in their theoretical scheme: we begin the third great stage of cultural evolution with engines rather than with writing. But essentially our thesis is that of the Evolutionist school as typified by Morgan and Tylor. . . .

In the foregoing we have, we believe, a sound and illuminating theory of cultural evolution. We have hold of principles, fundamental principles, which are operative in all cultures at all times and places. The motive force of cultural evolution is laid bare, the mechanisms of development made clear. The nature of the relationship between social institutions on the one hand and technological instruments on the other is indicated. Understanding that the function of culture is to serve the needs of man, we find that we have an objective criterion for evaluating culture in terms of the extent to which, and the efficiency with which, human needs are satisfied by cultural means. We can measure the amounts of energy expended; we can calculate the efficiency of the expenditure of energy in terms of measurable quantities of goods and services produced. And, finally, as we see, these measurements can be expressed in mathematical terms.

The theory set forth in the preceding pages was, as we have made clear, held by the foremost thinkers of the Evolutionist school of the nineteenth century, both in England and in America. Today they seem to us as sound as they did to Tylor and Morgan, and, if anything, more obvious. It seems almost incredible that anthropologists of the twentieth century could have turned their backs upon and repudiated such a simple, sound, and illuminating generalization, one that makes the vast range of tens of thousands of years of culture history intelligible. But they have done just this. The anti-evolutionists, led in America by Franz Boas, have rejected the theory of evolution in cultural anthropology— and have given us instead a philosophy of "planless hodge-podge-ism."

It is not surprising, therefore, to find at the present time the most impressive recognition of the significance of technological progress in cultural evolution in the writings of a distinguished physicist, the Nobel prize winner, Robert A. Millikan (1939:211):

> The changes that have occurred within the past hundred years not only in the external conditions under which the average man, at least in this western world, passes life on earth, but in his superstitions . . . his fundamental beliefs, in his philosophy, in his conception of religion, in his whole world outlook, are probably greater than those that occurred during the preceding four thousand years all put together. Life seems to remain static for thousands of years and then to shoot forward with amazing speed. The last century has been one of those periods of extraordinary change, the most amazing in human history. If, then, you ask me to put into one sentence the cause of that recent rapid and enormous change I should reply: "It is found in the discovery and utilization of the means by which heat energy can be made to do man's work for him."

Tucked away in the pages of Volume II of a manual on European archeology, too, we find a similar expression from a distinguished American scholar, George G. MacCurdy (1933:134–135):

> The *degree of civilization* of any epoch, people, or group of peoples *is measured by ability to utilize energy for human advancement or needs.* Energy is of two kinds, internal and external or free. Internal energy is that of the human body or machine, and its basis is food. External energy is that outside the human body and its basis is fuel. Man has been able to tap the great storehouse of external energy. Through his internal energy and that acquired from external sources, he has been able to overcome the opposing energy of his natural environment. *The difference between these two opposing forces is the gauge of civilization* (emphasis ours).

Thus, this view is not wholly absent in anthropological theory in America today although extremely rare and lightly regarded. The time will come, we may confidently expect, when the theory of evolution will again prevail in the science of culture as it has in the biological and the physical sciences. It is a significant fact that in cultural anthropology alone among the sciences is a philosophy of anti-evolutionism respectable—a fact we would do well to ponder.

Ronald Cohen

16. Evolutionary Epistemology and Human Values[1]

Introduction

Within anthropology, and to a lesser extent among its sister social science disciplines, there is widespread acceptance of evolution as an overall perspective. There seems, however, to be no consensus about the appropriateness of such an approach or about the meanings of its constituent concepts and units or their relations to one another when the perspective is applied as social theory. Some see evolution as a process that involves trends in definable and predictable directions (Spencer 1900 [1876], Carneiro 1973); others see predictability as either impossible (Popper 1972 [1957]) or quite out of keeping with evolutionary theory (Monod 1972). Within the notion of directionality, some would have us judge the direction normatively, as progressive or retrogressive (Waddington 1960), giving to human history a moral quality in which evolution operates to help or hinder the development of a "better society." Others see the concepts of biological evolution as inapplicable to sociocultural phenomena because there is no easily extended genetic basis for the changes observed (cf. Sahlins 1976). Some see the major utility of evolutionary theory to be at the macrolevel (Gellner 1975, Goody 1976); others wish to concentrate on micro- events and processes (Mead 1964). Still others are concerned with the relationship between biological theory and cultural behavior (Chagnon and Irons 1979). Reviewing this problem, Dunnell and Wenke (1979:3) conclude that the difficulties involved in transferring evolutionary theory from natural science to sociocultural change are so great that the notion of evolution in social anthropology is confined to a prescientific, Spencerian mode of inquiry. In other words, although evolution is a much-respected paradigm, there are disagreements about its concepts, its propositions, and their applicability to sociocultural materials.

I intend to examine the logic of evolutionary theory and its applicability to social and cultural phenomena. I shall argue that the theory is

255

indeed applicable to comparative social science at both micro- and macro- levels, that it overcomes the positivistic fact/value dichotomy, and that it implies a much more intimate relation than is commonly recognized between fundamental and applied social science.

Evolution as Theory

The basic ideas of evolution refer to the means by which definable entities change from one form into another. The process is irreversible. It is possible for later forms to show great resemblance to earlier ones, for they retain clearly identifiable features from prior forms. For them to converge towards ancestral ones in every respect, however, would require far too many coincidental and simultaneous changes to be statistically feasible (Monod 1972); convergence is never complete.

To understand this process, one must begin by defining the evolving phenomenon as an entity occupying a space-time continuum. Once this is done, the next step is *taxonomy*—subdivision of the entity into a series of subentities, all of which are taxa or "kinds of" the generic phenomenon (trees, types or species of trees; rock, types of rocks; societies, types of societies, etc.). To be evolutionary, taxa are assumed to be developmentally related. Thus, evolutionary theory includes a set of *explanatory relations* by which taxa can be shown to change into one another in a developmental sequence, and it includes a set of *processes* by which these changes take place. Developmental relations among taxa may be observed to be repetitive, i.e., to have occurred similarly in differing locations such that taxa *a, b, c, . . . n* appear to follow one another with more than chance regularity. The repetition is not necessarily universal, but it is clearly not random. Thus evolution also involves *directionality.* I shall quickly go over these components.

Taxonomy

In the course of evolution, change is not constant in rate. Like all other evolving entities, human sociocultural systems manifest periods in which change rates are low. When local environmental forces—social, cultural, and physical—remain relatively constant, there is a tendency towards stabilization. This allows us to assume that many societal forms are sufficiently stable to provide an empirical basis for the identification of socialevolutionary forms and subforms. A taxonomy of societal forms, therefore, has real-world referents and is an important starting point for evolutionary study. Because such stabilization occurs in time, entities that evolve can be shown to exhibit periodicity.

Human societal forms are, however, the products of living persons—

aspects of individuals and their collective activities. As Irons (1979:35) points out, evolutionary theory suggests that culture and social forms evolve through the aggregation of individual interactions. Not only do culture and society determine individual differences, but also the reverse is true (Irons 1979:33–34). On the other hand, social forms are not simply persons writ large. Organizational complexity results from interactions which persist beyond individual life-spans. As we shall see, social forms are to some extent independent of individual actors and to some extent dependent on them. Factors affecting interactions result in the change and persistence of social forms. Because this is so, we can think of social forms as evolving phenomena with their own reproductive processes, their own mechanisms of change and stability, while at the same time accepting that living persons interacting as persons and groups *energize* evolving social systems. In this sense, a social form may be viewed as an entity dependent upon interpersonal and intergroup relations that persists and evolves over generations. My model here is Waddington's (1960) definition of biological taxa as classifiable constellations of transmittable potentialities. This means that problems of individual vs. group selection are just as applicable at the sociocultural level as they are at the biogenetic one.[2]

Taxonomy involves obtaining operationally reliable qualities that sort the evolving phenomenon into a series of stabilized types. In effect, this means theorizing that the most important taxa can best be differentiated through the use of a particular determinant as a criterion. The overall pattern of development is, however, quite well known and documented, at least in terms of the different forms available for study. Thus all criteria must in some way generate a taxonomy of known forms.

On the other hand, within the widely accepted macrodevelopmental sequences there is a good deal of variation, even among workers whose research is closely related. For example, Claessen and Skalník (1978) classify early states into three subvarieties—"inchoate," "typical," and "transitional"—based on a rather complex set of indices. In my own work (Cohen 1978a, b, 1981) on the same topic I use only one criterion, presence or absence of institutions for obviating fission. This allows me to separate very early centralized groups into chieftaincies (centralized polities subject to fission) and states (centralized polities that have evolved means for avoiding fission). Claessen and Skalník's criteria direct research towards the study of changes in markers or indicators (kinship, religion, mode of production, etc.) and the effects of such changes on centralized governmental institutions. My own criterion points research towards factors that select for fission-avoidance and the effects of this capability on the evolution of governmental structures and operations. Theoretical effects vary as well. The Marxist theory that class formation and antagonism precede and cause state development is affected by the two schemas in different ways. The Claessen and Skalník schema includes in its earliest forms "inchoate" states, i.e., centralized polities without classes (in the Marxist sense); thus classes do not precede statehood or cause it. In my work, states are generally correlated with class formation, but previous class conflict may be present or absent and when present operates in ways not predicted by the theory. Claessen and Skalník's classification produces a clear disconfirmation of the Marxist hypothesis, while my own fails to support but does not negate it. Taxonomy makes a difference in the way ideas are addressed. Clearly, there must be ways of classifying early states that would support the Marxist theory of origins (cf. Krader 1975).

Taxonomy is, therefore, not a simple set of inelastic inductive or deductive procedures. There is as yet no agreement as to what constitutes a complete set of human social forms; these vary from researcher to researcher and across theoretical traditions. Nevertheless, taxonomy is a major determinant of the entitivity—the "thing"-ness—of the evolving phenomenon and of the search for causes and the outcome of tests of current theories.

What is needed is a means of choosing among taxonomies, of determining which criteria will do the best job. I will return to this question in a moment.

Developmental Relations

Evolutionary taxonomy is based on the assumption that its taxa are, or can be shown to be, developmentally related, and in general the claim is supported by empirical observations. Some links are, however, nonexistent or missing. For example, we may create a taxonomy of descent systems which includes patri- and matri- systems, but the literature contains few, if any, cases in which a patri-dominant descent system becomes matrilineal. Thus it is more accurate to say that the number of specific instances of the development of one type into another is sufficiently large that we tend to accept it as fact. Research may uncover other instances; human history may even produce new possibilities, such as postindustrial hunter/gatherers or a new form of stateless, anarchic communal life. In evolution, all bets are on. Nevertheless, the main point stands: evolutionary forms as parts of an overall taxonomy are, theoretically at least, developmentally related.

Taxonomies vary in scale. Some take in all varieties of human societies (e.g., pre- and postcapitalist systems), others describe the subsocieties of a particular form (e.g., types of bands); developmental relations occur at both micro- and macro- levels. This is variously referred to as general and specific evolution (Sahlins and Service 1960) or as succession and branching (Dobzhansky 1962). For the sake of consistency and parsimony across disciplines I prefer the latter.

Succession refers to a set of intercorrelated permanent changes producing a significantly different order of internal complexity for all taxa classified at that level. Succession levels aggregate entities that are (*a*) structurally similar to one another in definable terms and (*b*) definably more complex or less complex than those of other succession levels. In other words, part-to-whole relations may vary in their particulars, but basic features such as the number and kinds of internal relations, subdivisions, and levels of activity—for example, authority chains—are comparable within levels and different across them. Thus I classify sedentary villages, pastoral nomads with no continuing supralocal authority, and other polities of this kind as "localized autonomies." They differ from one another in ecology, culture, social organization, and other particulars, but they are similar in level of political complexity and qualitatively different from band polities, at the simpler level, and chieftaincies, at the more complex one.

The processes that constitute succession have been of central importance in ecological studies for over half a century (see Clements 1965 [1916]). More recently, succession has been defined (for plant populations) by Odum (1969:262) as an orderly process of community development that is reasonably directional and predictable, resulting in the mutual modification of the community and its environment in which the environment sets the pattern of development, the rate of change, and the limits to which it can evolve. The outcome of the process is "a stabilized ecosystem," a condition in which the evolving community has achieved maximum protection against environmental perturbations for its level of efficiency and organization.

There is some confusion in the literature as to how inclusive a succession level should be, i.e., how comparable forms should be within it. Some writers widen the scale of generality as far as it can go to discuss social evolution in global and species terms. This is, in my view, analogous to the use of such inclusive terms as "vertebrate"/"invertebrate" in biology. For example, classic Marxist taxonomy divides all humanity into five basic levels—primitive communal, slave, feudal, capitalist, and communist—and assumes these levels to be the pathway through which the entire species *as a unit* evolves. (More recently, a number of Marxist writers [see, e.g., Dunn and Dunn 1974:5–9; Godelier 1978:768] have suggested giving up or changing these levels and the criteria used to

define them.) Except for obvious relations of population size and location to resources and technology, this macro- level of succession offers
little insight into actual sequences of development. All polities, for example, are now parts of nation-states. Thus the nation-state has succeeded all other levels of evolution for the species as a whole; put another way, as a species we are at the nation-state level of evolution.
Humankind as a whole did not, however, pass through all the steps in
the sequence. In many places very simple polities were destroyed or
incorporated. Humanity-wide schemas provide some overall perspective, but developmental relations among taxa are the results of underlying processes and real events, while succession levels are *abstract generalizations* that summarize large-scale trends.

For social evolution, succession applies to repetitive sequences of
developments in which similar "stages" or levels are passed through by a
number of societies in a particular world region. Steward (1949), like the
19th-century evolutionists before him, was looking for a universally
applicable succession sequence, and as a result the generalities he discovered omitted the all-important feature of locality. In plant ecology,
the special character, rate, and quality of each set of succession levels is
highly dependent upon the local environment. This is also true of human social evolution. Over a decade ago, Schlegel and I (Cohen and
Schlegel 1968) disregarded research findings indicating that *continental
location* explained much of the difference among systems of servility and
stratification around the world. We reasoned that this was a result of
"diffusion" effects and therefore of little or no theoretical significance.
Biased by the methodological canons of "Galton's problem," we overlooked what may have been our most important finding. This occurred
to me recently when I read the seminal work of Goody (1976), who
demonstrates historically and statistically that the mode of production
associated with continental land-mass is also associated with vast differences in the evolution of family and descent systems between Africa
south of the Sahara and Eurasia.

In summary, succession levels are highly abstracted sets of form-
features, arranged into antecedent-consequent relations, that are comparable across many localities and regions. These relations are not causal—Steward used the wrong term—but they do provide a framework
within which specific studies of causal relations can be carried out. They
are also in no way assumed to be inevitable. Their classifiable cooccur-
rence results from comparable progressions of sociocultural evolution,
no more and no less.

It is also possible to classify forms within any particular succession
level. Such forms are referred to as branches. Branches differ from one

another significantly in the internal structuring of their parts. As with matri- and patri- descent, it is a moot point whether all branches are capable of changing into one another within any one level, but it is important to note that actual changes in the real world occur among branches, *not* among succession levels. Continental or smaller regional developments often show a skewing to one set of branches, leaving others either not represented or rare. Some branches, e.g., polyandrous marriage or double descent systems, are infrequent and/or localized for complex reasons not always well understood, while others, e.g., patrilocal extended-family organizations or local village councils, are widespread and frequent within many separate lines of development.

Processes of Change

Processes of evolutionary change are discussed for cultural traditions by Plog (1974), who speaks of variety generation and selection as ways of analyzing change. Campbell (1975) and Durham (1979) do much the same kind of thing at the psychological and the behavioral levels.[3] On the other hand, Dunnell and Wenke (1979:22) argue that the causal explanations of evolutionary theory have yet to be applied successfully to sociocultural phenomena because (1) there is an unwillingness to deal with genetic effects on behavior and (2) the theory cannot yet cope with human consciousness and its cumulative effects, which make social evolution Lamarckian rather than, or as well as, Darwinian. The difficulties they pose are serious but not insurmountable. In offering my own rendition of the position taken by those who see evolutionary theory as a perspective for understanding human social change and development, I shall attempt to deal with some of the criticism that Dunnell and Wenke quite rightly apply to this view.

In evolutionary theory, three sets of mechanisms generate change: (1) random variation, (2) selection of successful variants, and (3) retention and reproduction of the changes selected.

Random variation. Nothing in evolutionary epistemology requires that variation be causally related to biochemically based genetic structures resulting from sexual reproduction. At the behavioral level, organizations (human and nonhuman), or at least varieties of organizational adaptations, persist beyond the individual careers of the actors. This makes recruitment a necessary part of organizational activity, and recruitment cannot be totally replicative. Participation in organized activity creates random variation in social process because new recruits are never the exact replicas of those they replace. Furthermore, situations demanding organizational response are never completely the same through time. Interrelations among members who vary and specific responses by each actor vary enough to provide grounds for accidental innovation in the way ordinary (i.e., repetitive) or extraordinary tasks are carried out.

Variation in biology is also dependent upon biased-sample effects or drift. This occurs when a significantly unrepresentative set of individuals is separated from the parent population. Migration, colonization, and disaster often produce such effects on sociocultural patterns. No one familiar with 20th-century England would ever say that colonial whites in Africa were a representative sample of the English population. Many of them hankered after a society no longer viable in England itself. Yet they were the bearers and transmitters of European culture and society in Africa, and this sampling bias in relation to the parent population deeply affected African history.

This approach suggests yet another source of variation, gene flow. New components are introduced into a population from outside when differentially evolving populations of the same species come into contact. The concept of contact and the borrowing or interchange of traits is obviously applicable to sociocultural systems. Cultural diffusion is the behavioral analogue of gene flow. Each has its own set of determinants, but the structure of change and the effects are similar.

Thus social evolution occurs for the very same reasons as its biological counterpart. At the level of culture, society, and behavior, there is a constant stream of chance variations generated by the very nature of social life. This is the seedbed of social evolution. How it proceeds depends on mechanisms of selection and retention that produce continuity and change in the evolving entity.

Selection. Biologists describe selection as *normalizing, balancing,* or *directional.* Even a brief glance indicates that all of these fitness mechanisms apply as well to sociocultural systems.

Normalizing selection occurs when new traits or variants are strongly disfavored, so that there is selection pressure against their increase in the population. This favors stability. Normal mutations are simply not adaptive; i.e., they do not contribute to any increased reproductive capacity for breeding populations. In sociocultural terms, normalizing selection occurs wherever forces or institutions in a society are used to combat or suppress change or variation from community norms. In small egalitarian and locally autonomous polities there are many ways of suppressing variations and innovations; gossip, witchcraft and sorcery accusations, obligatory sharing and redistribution, and strict adherence to local values are only a few. In factory work groups, norms of productivity develop, and individual workers are pressured to maintain them by other workers, the union, management, friends, and kin and also by socialization that instills into most participants an acceptance of the legitimacy of the system. In modern states, dissident political groups may be suppressed by police action. Although the causes are quite different, the effects are identical to those that biologists describe for normalizing selection in the genetic makeup of a population.

Balanced selection occurs when new traits are accepted into a population and are adaptive within certain limits of gene frequency. Below these limits the traits would disappear, making the selection a normalizing one; above these limits they would be harmful to reproductive success, i.e., maladaptive. At the sociocultural level, some tolerance of variation exists and is even institutionalized. In some societies, the variation allowable in adult roles is less than that normally predictable in human groups. It is highly unlikely that all adult men of Sparta were ideal Spartans; some variation must have been tolerated. Among the Plains Indians, a similar very brave and strong role for adult men was prescribed, and it is significant that this same culture evolved the concept of berdache, or man-woman, i.e., a man who rejected the adult male role and was tolerated because of his womanly skills. Conversely, women in several West African societies who wish to head their own households and not become subordinate to husbands may take on the role of household head and marry other women in a public ceremony. In these examples, the role normally assigned to a sex is rejected, and an institution has evolved to give a minority the opportunity to live contrary to the usual expectations. As societies become complex, not only are deviation and opposition institutionalized (e.g., in the king's jester, who verbalizes opposition to the throne), but dissent and variability are more tolerated. Although it varies with the sociopolitical environment, some form of dissent is tolerated in all modern states—again, within upper and lower limits depending upon local conditions and history. It is clear that in both the biological and the social realm, there must be some means for the maintenance of variance in the population. How much variation—how much dissent, role reversal, or rejection—is optimal is impossible to say at present. Like total suppression of variation, complete acceptance of all personal points of view and behavior is maladaptive. Complex society requires organization, coordination, and some minimal predictability, therefore discipline and a consensual recognition of authority.[4]

Directional selection occurs when there is pressure to increase or decrease components resulting in a significant change in the genotype of the population. This is the traditional Darwinian statement, in effect the heart of evolutionary theory. Whether it occurs through processes of individual or group selection or both is still unclear in both biology and sociocultural evolution (Irons 1979). Today we know that it occurs through selection factors internal and external to the evolving entity— i.e., "environment" is too general a term (Donald Sade, personal communication). The basic mechanism, change resulting from reproductive success, is clear. The same paradigm applies to social evolution. In my own research on the origins of the state in precolonial Nigeria, I found that small autonomous villages compacted and swelled in numbers behind large earthworks built for defensive purposes (Cohen 1976, 1978*b*, 1981). Once this occurred, the most common form of pre-state dispute settlement, through community fission, became much more difficult. Members of these larger communities gave up farms near their own households, lived closer to one another, experienced more disputes, and increased their reliance on leadership for dispute settlement. This produced strong pressure on the leaders to specialize, and they ultimately differentiated into a titled nobility under a monarch and his royal court. (The situation is in fact more complex, since some villagers chose to run away, others to join the raiders, and the emerging kingdom developed a nascent set of center-periphery relations with the surrounding villages.) The evolution of a village polity into a kingdom is here conceived in terms of inherent capacities for variation and a series of selective factors, internal as well as external to the society, operating to change the political system from non-state to state.

Such things happen all the time. Systems of interrelationships produce variations which are favored by factors external and internal to the system. For example, the end of European imperialism has brought more freedom to Third World nations. Previously, exports from these nations were based on local cost, held down by low standards of living and the interests of industrialized states. Self-interest and a conscious desire to raise living standards in the Third World have led to destabilization of colonial "normalization" processes. We now hear of a New Economic Order in which world trade is to be "indexed," i.e., changed so that prices for exports from poorer nations approximate their "true" market value and are tied to prices of goods those nations must buy from the developed world. Thus world trade is evolving from a system dominated by the richer nations to one in which the poorer nations have more power and derive greater benefits. Within the entity "world trade," variability in pricing is always possible; greater autonomy and self-interest on the part of poorer trading partners has therefore acted as a selective factor to produce pressure towards a different system.[5]

In summary, whether we are dealing with biological or sociocultural entities, tension (referred to as conflicts or dialectics in social analysis) between components of the evolving entity and the system of relations (internal and external to the entity) can create normalizing, balanced, or directional selection. These interactions determine whether the entity will remain stable, tolerate wide variation, or change in form.

Retention and reproduction. Given variation and selection, the evolving entity must be assumed to contain means by which successful variants can be retained in the population beyond the life-spans of individual participants. In biological evolution, retention is accomplished through biochemical processes of genetic structuring which are part of reproductive activity. In effect, genetic codes are unconscious biochemical instructions given by parents to their progeny in the living material making up the stuff out of which the progeny develop into new individuals in a breeding population. I have phrased this last sentence in such a way as to show the analogy between biochemically based processes of reproduction and sociocultural ones. In both biochemically based genes and learning-based socialization, the primary agents are parents or teaching agents who pass on coded behavior patterns to children, and in both cases much of this transmission is unconscious. Thus human parents give their normal children a (biologically based) capacity for speech and language. At the same time they pass on extremely complex rules for the ordering of words into meaningful sentences, again (for the most part) unconsciously. Like biochemical intergenerational transmission, much learned behavior that allows for the retention of social patterns is also unconscious. To a quintessentially important degree, however, human intergenerational transmission, along with other emergent modes of transmission, is *conscious*. And at this point, humans can be said to have evolved their own unique modes of retention and reproduction.

As Waddington (1960: 26–29) first noted, the transmission and retention of human constellations of potentialities involve the capacity (*a*) to learn the beliefs, values, and traditions of the particular social groups into which a person is recruited during a lifetime; (*b*) to accept the authority of those persons and rules that constrain, guide, and instruct members of groups; and (*c*) to process and compare information cognitively in terms of means, ends, and values, so that the learner is not just a trained automaton, but a critical individual who can, when necessary, assess present modes of behavior and either reject, accept, or innovate means and/or ends to obtain greater personal or collective satisfaction.[6] Much of this is a commonsense (albeit analytic and systematic) rephrasing of anthropological thinking about socialization. Language, social practices, roles, traditions, beliefs, etc., are passed on to new members by teaching agents—as often as not parents. The learning situation is the sociocultural means of reproduction.

For this process to work, especially with very young members, there must be a capacity for respect on the part of the learners for the teacher-socializer or for rules that govern and constrain behavior. Respect comes from several sources. First, there is the capacity of the teacher-socializer (or the group) to coerce compliance by force, by shame, by pressures of all sorts. The learner has no choice; he/she must learn the ways of the society into which he/she is to be socialized. Respect also stems from the *sapiens* quality par excellence—moralizing. Moralizing provides the teacher with directions which both teacher and learner accept; there is a "right" and a "wrong" way of carrying out an activity, and the teacher attempts to pass on the *proper* information and skills. Recent research (Klein n.d.) suggests that pre-*sapiens* cultures relied much more on genetic programming than on behavioral learning and that this accounts for their lack of variation. The large-brained *sapiens*, on the other hand, was able to vary cultural adaptations because of his greater intellectual capacity and to compensate for the reduction of genetic programming with moralizing prescriptions and proscriptions. In a very real sense, human evolution turns the "is" into the "ought." Where genetic evolution must experiment in hit-or-miss fashion, social evolution stabilizes and innovates species activity *consciously.* Incest *avoidance* is older than human culture, but incest *prohibition* is our way of stabilizing this cross-species behavioral regularity. By creating and by transmitting conscious prescriptions and proscriptions, we have shifted the locus and accelerated the rate of evolution. Our moralizing capability is the truly human mode of adaptation. No other species transmits so much across generations by labelling behavior as "right" and "wrong."

The human capacity to pass information on through learning adds enormous potential to the biochemical transmission upon which retention and reproduction are based and out of which they emerged. Socioculturally based transmission across generations (and to new role recruits in general) is not only unconscious, as before, but conscious as well. The emergence of learning-based cognitive and evaluative capabilities as primary mechanisms of reproduction and retention shifted a large part of human adaptation to the behavioral realm and to its collective continuity in human cultures.

Directionality

Directionality in evolution, especially social evolution, is both difficult to understand and paradoxical. From one point of view, it is a valid generalization, from another a logical impossibility, and from still another the gateway to moral philosophy and public policy.

As I have said, selection can be, among other things, directional. Imbalances within societal components and their relation to selective factors produce directional changes. In that sense, and after the fact, we can say that directional changes have occurred which produced branching away from an original form. As Wilson (1975) notes, evolution is a tracking of the environment. What he does not say is that the "environment" is also evolving, and so are the factors determining its change and/or stability, ad infinitum. And to know the outcome of all this beforehand is impossible—there is an infinite set of unknowns. Some selectors are therefore assumed to be constants, *which they are not*, and error and unpredictability are thereby introduced into our theories.

A number of writers (e.g., Waddington 1960, Carneiro 1973) deduce directionality in evolution from a comparison of successions across many species. The general tendency among succession series for developmentally related species is modification towards more efficient adaptation of reproductive communities.[7] We can apply this notion to human social evolution as well, but I see two problems with it. First, species and successions are viewed as communities in an ecosystem, within which they proliferate and/or diminish in relation to other communities. This means that succession series *may or may not* achieve more efficient adaptation, depending upon the total set of ecosystem processes including internal features of the community, competing communities, and the resources of the ecosystem required for a succession series to occur. And this means that there can be no predictability for any particular succession set. If and when succession developments occur, they do tend, at least for a while, to be in the generally predicted direction. It is this *partial* set of observations that underlies the notion of directionality. The second difficulty is thus methodological. Directionality is, in effect, an artifact of evolutionary analysis. Arranging data in developmental series makes evolution look directional because the data sets have been chosen to show a full evolutionary sequence, but what of all the instances in which this full sequence did not occur, in which development was cut off, or in which there was a return to a previous level? How often, where evolution has moved a community, or a set of them, towards greater efficiency or reproductive success, has there been a subsequent decline or even extinction? Adaptation through successions is not a never-ending spiral upwards. Given all these unknowns, and given knowledge of earlier forms, can we ever predict later ones?

In strictly logical terms, then, evolutionary change is directional only after the fact and predictable only within serious constraints. Within limits, social evolution does go from less to more complexity, from less to more heterogeneity, from less to more efficiency, but there are also significant numbers of human societal developments that have achieved very long-term homeostasis or devolved to resemble simpler levels of organization or become extinct. If we had come from Mars to Earth 20,000 years ago, knowing what we do now about social evolution, could we have predicted which regions of the world would produce full ranges of civilizational growth? Why the Near East, Middle America, Southeast Asia, but not southwestern Australia? The latter area is well watered; could it possibly have supported denser populations and stimulated complex societal development? Why the Lake Chad basin but not the Great Lakes of North America? Once social evolution occurs, it is possible to say a great deal about directional developments, but before it happens there is a long list of imponderables. Social evolution is limited and nonrandom, but whether it will occur at all and the particular branchings it will involve are not predictable.

Humanity as a species seems headed through a known, and possibly a knowable, set of succession levels. Has not the modern state now taken over all previous forms of society? Are there not clear attempts to create a basis for world order, for international organization? Possibly. But again, it seems clear that while we can plot out and explain where we have been the future is unclear. Humankind could change in a dozen different directions, including extinction, and it is impossible to say which. Directionality is always limited by past, present, and future unknowns. Whether we like it or not, they are considerable and significant. This is our fate.

Notes

1. Previous versions of this paper have been presented at the annual meeting of the American Anthropological Association, Los Angeles, 1978, and the Northwestern University Political Science Conference on Values in Social Science, Evanston, 1979. I wish to thank William Irons, John Paden, Roy D'Andrade, Bruce Trigger, James Caparaso, and Oswald Werner for their comments and criticism of previous drafts.

2. Irons (1979) has centered his recent research on this issue.

3. I wrote this section (in 1978) before reading Durham's (1979:72–74) argument. I encourage the reader to consult his useful paper and compare his views with mine.

4. By "recognition" I mean that the powers used by authorities are not successfully opposed by those within the authority structure (Cohen 1973).

5. I say "pressure" rather than "a trend" because it is unclear to me whether the ideological plea for a New Economic Order is based on real or only imagined forces (cf. Aron 1977:154–61).

6. I have paraphrased the original, especially the last idea.

7. Granovetter (1979) shows how many writers on social evolution have assumed, often on shaky grounds, that some notion of advance or progress is part and parcel of the evolution concept.

Donald L. Hardesty

17. Introduction:
Ecological Anthropology

Cultural Ecology

Ecology as a science blossomed in the twentieth century but has been mostly restricted to the study of plants and animals other than man. However, the ecological vantage point in anthropology was expressed as early as the 1930s by Julian H. Steward. Perhaps the most important contribution of his "method of cultural ecology" was the recognition that environment and culture are not separate spheres but are involved in "dialectic interplay . . . or what is called *feedback* or *reciprocal* casuality" (Kaplan and Manners, 1972, p. 79). Two ideas essential to the ecological viewpoint are inherent in the concept of reciprocal causality: the idea that neither environment nor culture is a "given" but that each is defined in terms of the other, and the idea that environment plays an *active,* not just a limiting or selective, role in human affairs. At the same time it must be kept in mind that the relative influence of environment and culture in a feedback relationship is not equal (Kaplan and Manners, 1972, p. 79). According to this view, sometimes culture plays a more active role and sometimes environment has the upper hand. Steward believed that some sectors of culture are more prone to a strong environmental relationship than other sectors and that ecological analysis could be used to explain cross-cultural similarities *only* in this "culture core." The culture core consisted of the *economic* sector of society, those features that are "most closely related to subsistence activities and economic arrangements" (Steward, 1955, p. 37). The "method" of cultural ecology then involved the analysis of

1. The interrelationship between environment and exploitative or productive technology.
2. The interrelationship between "behavior" patterns and exploitative technology.

3. The extent to which those "behavior" patterns affect other sectors of culture (Steward, 1955, pp. 40–41).

Steward's culture core did not include many aspects of social structure and almost no ritual behavior. Neither of these were considered to be significantly related to environment. Furthermore, Steward excluded from cultural ecology the study of biology, stating that "culture, rather than genetic potential for adaptation, accommodation, and survival, explains the nature of human societies" (1955, p. 32).

Cultural ecology retained the possibilist's interest in the study of *specific* cultural features. Steward's goal was "to explain the origin of particular cultural features and patterns which characterize different areas" (1955, p. 36). His method required that *detailed* studies of local groups in their environment be conducted as a prerequisite to making ecological generalizations (Vayda and Rappaport, 1968, p. 489). There can be no question that this focus is responsible for the present florescence of ecological studies in anthropology.

Andrew Vayda and Roy Rappaport (1968, pp. 483–87), while recognizing the importance of Steward's contribution, have criticized his approach as being inadequate. Steward gives as his primary objective the explanation of *origins* of certain cultural traits. However, his approach is to show first how a cultural feature and an environmental feature *covary*, that is, how they are functionally interrelated, and second, to show that the same relationship *recurs* in historically distinct areas. Vayda and Rappaport argue that this approach does not necessarily mean that the environmental feature *caused* the cultural feature for the following reasons:

1. Sampling procedures are not adequate to eliminate the possibility of spurious correlations.
2. Even if the correlations are statistically significant, correlations do not necessarily mean a cause and effect relationship.
3. Even if significant correlations and causality were shown, it does not necessarily mean that the relationship is inevitable, as Steward believed.

The second weakness of Steward's cultural ecology was to treat the culture core as if it included *only* technology. Several studies, as we shall see, have shown that ritual and ideology also interact with the environment. Vayda and Rappaport point out additionally that Steward's selection of environmental features for study does not include other organisms (e.g., disease microorganisms) nor does it include other human groups, perhaps the greatest weakness of all. (However, more recent applications of cultural ecology have taken "social environment" into consideration, and fruitfully so.) Finally, his approach does not include the study of interaction between culture and biology, neither genetic nor physiological. Yet numerous studies have shown that culture and biology go hand in hand in several areas, such as nutrition, and that one cannot be understood without the other.

Population Ecology

The study of the environmental relations of *particular* human groups, introduced by Steward's cultural ecology, marked the beginning of population ecology in anthropology. The *ecological population* is a local group of organisms, belonging to the same species, with a distinctive life style; that is, the members of the group get food in the same,distinctive way, have essentially the same tolerances for things in the environment, are fed upon by the same predators, and so forth. Population ecology is the study of those processes that affect the *distribution* and *abundance* of ecological populations. External processes affect a population's relationships with food, water, weather, and other organisms, among other things. By contrast internal processes include such things as behavioral, physiological, and genetic responses to population density. The study of populations has several distinct advantages for human ecology. In the first place the population is a more or less "bounded" unit, subject to quantitative description and analysis. Populations can be counted, their size and distribution measured, and so forth. In the second place the ecological population is the traditional unit of study in nonhuman ecology. Therefore, human populations

are commensurate with the other units with which they interact to form food webs, biotic communities, and ecosystems. Their capture of energy from, and exchanges of materials with these other units can be measured and then described in quantitative terms. No such advantage of commensurability obtains if cultures are made the units, for cultures, unlike human populations, are not fed upon by predators, limited by food supplies, or debilitated by disease. (Vayda and Rappaport, 1968, p. 494)

In other words the concept of the ecological population gives a quantifiable common denominator suitable for the study of human and nonhuman ecology alike.

The suggestion by Vayda and Rappaport that the population be made the *focal point* of human ecological studies should not be taken to mean that anthropologists have not until now been interested in population ecology. Julian Steward's cultural ecological studies in the 1930s on the

Great Basin and Southwestern Indians are explicitly aimed at understanding the relationship between human populations and their environment. Steward particularly studied the effect of environment upon
the *distribution* of human populations. Thus in his classic study of the
aboriginal Great Basin, he focused upon "interrelated physical features
of the landscape" as determinants of population distribution, including
water, altitude, temperature, geographical barriers, and the annual variation in the occurrence of eatable foods (1938). The intellectual descendants of Steward have continued his interest in the distribution of populations through *settlement pattern* studies. A settlement pattern is the
disposition of a population's settlements vis-à-vis the natural landscape
and the "social" environment. The determinants of a settlement pattern
are numerous but include such things as physical barriers, technology
and subsistence, political organization, kinship, warfare, and ideology
and symbolism (Trigger, 1968). Complex interaction among these variables is responsible for the actual distribution of a population. Settlement
pattern studies have particularly been stressed in archaeology, receiving
an important impetus from Gordon Willey's (1953) study of the Viru
Valley in coastal Peru. Since the publication of that study in 1953, interest
in the interrelationship between the distribution of a population and its
physical and social environment has been continued. Most recently, that
interrelationship has been formalized into an explicit "systems" approach, such as the "settlement-subsistence system" of Stuart Streuver
(1968b).

Steward also was interested in the interrelationships between environment and the *abundance* of human populations. However, his orientation in this regard was possibilistic. Thus, in the Great Basin, he saw
population density as "correlated with the fertility of the natural environment" (1938, p. 48). The possibilistic view of population abundance
was also expressed by A. L. Kroeber in his classic work *Cultural and
Natural Areas of Native North America*, published in 1939. Kroeber drew
upon earlier population estimates of North American tribes and his own
estimates to support a general correlation between "natural" areas and
population density. He concluded that "other things being equal, we
(can) infer a denser population from a richer ecology, or, among agriculturalists, from a larger area of more fertile soil" (1939, p. 180).

In 1953 Joseph Birdsell published a landmark study of the relationship
between *mean annual rainfall* and population abundance in aboriginal
Australia. Rather than define environment in terms of "fertility" or
"ecological richness," Birdsell chose a single variable, mean annual rainfall, to represent the relevant environment. Birdsell's reasoning was that
mean annual rainfall determines plant growth and that plant growth sets

limits on the food available to humans, either directly through plant foods or indirectly through animal foods. Consequently, variation in mean annual rainfall (allowing for "unearned" water from, for example, rivers with drainage basins outside the area under study) should be correlated with population density, and Birdsell's study supported such a correlation. Note that the study is possibilistic in orientation, since increased mean annual rainfall *allows*, but does not cause, higher population densities. The concept of *carrying capacity* has been used in similar studies (e.g., Zubrow, 1975). Carrying capacity is the theoretical limit to which a population can grow and still be supported permanently by the environment. As a population approaches this limit, it places "pressure" on the environment to provide the resources needed for subsistence. Population pressure, in turn, sets into motion demographic forces to limit further growth, forces that include *cultural* means of reducing birth rates (abortion, contraception) and increasing death rate (warfare).

The carrying capacity of an environment depends, of course, upon the subsistence methods available to a population and can be changed by technological innovations making possible more efficient exploitation or production. The late archaeologist V. Gordon Childe, in fact, saw population growth as being *dependent* upon subsistence (e.g., 1951). Thus the abundance of foragers is severely restricted by a low carrying capacity, but the adoption of farming raises the carrying capacity and makes possible a "population explosion." Childe coined the name "neolithic revolution" to stress the relationship between farming and population growth, among other things.

In recent years the "possibilistic" view of population growth has been questioned by a number of persons. Many anthropologists now accept a *causal* model of population growth, and a popular, if controversial, position is that taken by the economist Ester Boserup. Boserup (1965) argues that population growth causes a higher carrying capacity by forcing people to use land more intensively and to adopt technological innovations that make more intensive land use possible. For example, a shift from an extensive method of farming, such as slash-and-burn, to a more intensive method based upon fertilization and irrigation is brought about by population pressure, and that shift increases the carrying capacity of the land. (Observe that carrying capacity is not conceptualized as a constant but varies according to technology and environment.) Others have taken a less deterministic stance and see population growth and subsistence as *interdependent*. That is, population pressure stimulates technological innovations that, in turn, not only make more intensive land use possible but also increase the carrying capacity and stimulate a new population explosion. This kind of mutual causality is essential to ecological thinking, as we have noted.

The study of human population ecology is plagued by the same problem of definition that has handicapped so many other endeavors. The boundaries of local groups are not always clear, often blending into neighboring groups and rendering arbitrary the definition of the population. Perhaps more important is that local human groups are not always economically independent and, therefore, do not constitute a distinctive life style. For example, local groups of advanced farmers may produce a few specialized crops and depend upon trade with other groups to obtain whatever else is needed. The "ecological population" in this case is not the local group but *all* of the groups participating in the trading network. A similar problem is encountered with the concept of the genetic or "Mendelian" population. The genetic population is defined by a mating system, that is, a group within which most mating takes place. However, local groups of humans are not always synonomous with a mating system. Marriages may be arranged with persons in neighboring groups or groups farther away. In these cases the effective genetic population is the *network* of local or more distant groups, a network that is sometimes called a "commune" or "connubium." The problem of definition is obviously critical to any kind of quantitative or comparative study and will be discussed throughout this book.

Systems Ecology

The publication of Clifford Geertz; *Agricultural Involution* (1963) was another milestone in ecological anthropology. His approach is rooted in cultural ecology, indeed that is what he calls it, but his perspective is based upon the concept of the *system* . A system is a "set of objects together with relationships between the objects and between their attributes" (Hall and Fagan, 1956, p. 18). Instead of focusing upon "reciprocal causality" between two objects or processes, the system focuses upon a *complex* network of mutual causality. The methods of systems analysis are used, first, to define the boundaries and environment of a system and, second, to model its complexity in such a way that system behavior can be studied and predicted.

Geertz believes that the concept of the *ecosystem* (we shall use *ecological system* to avoid the biological bias associated with the name ecosystem) is the logical conclusion to the idea of constant interplay between culture, biology, and environment. Theoretically, the ecological system is a dynamic set of relationships between living and nonliving things through which energy flows and materials cycle and because of which other problems of survival are worked out. In practice the ecological system is identified by a group of plants and animals, along with their nonliving environment, that make up a "food web" and generally affect each other's chances of survival.

The ecological system in which humans participate can be studied, according to Geertz, in the same general way as those in which humans do not. This method of study

is of a sort which trains attention on the pervasive properties of systems qua *systems (system structure, system equilibrium, system change) rather than on the point-to-point relationship between paired variables of the "culture" and "nature" variety [italics added]. The guiding question shifts from: "Do habitat conditions . . . cause culture or do they merely limit it?" to such incisive queries as: "Given an ecosystem defined through the parallel discrimination of cultural core and relevant environments, how is it organized?" "What are the mechanisms which regulate its functioning?" "What degree and type of stability does it have?" "What is its characteristic line of development and decline?" "How does it compare in these matters with other such systems?" And so on. . . . (1963, p. 10)*

Although Geertz presents an elegant argument for the use of systems theory, he does not take advantage of the conceptual and analytical tools that are associated with the theory. In effect, he uses it only as a point of view. Some later studies, however, have done so, particularly those of Richard Lee (1969, 1972a, 1972b) and Roy Rappaport (1968). Rappaport's study, for example, is concerned with energy relationships between the Tsembaga Maring (New Guinea) farmers and the ecological system in which they participate. Carefully quantified data on caloric and protein consumption, physiological stress, energy expended in subsistence activities, carrying capacity, limiting factors, and demography were collected. Among other things, he was able to show that the ritual killing of domestic pigs by the Tsembaga Maring

helps to maintain an undegraded environment, limits fighting to frequencies that do not endanger the existence of regional populations, adjusts man-land ratios, facilitates trade, distributes local surpluses of pig in the form of pork throughout the regional population, and assures people of high-quality protein when they most need it. (1968, p. 224)

Rappaport's work demonstrates dramatically the advantages of using the concepts and tools of systems theory.

That such "holistic" studies in ecological anthropology are still in their infancy, however, is suggested by the criticism that Rappaport's work has drawn (J. Anderson, 1973, pp. 199–200):

1. The geographical scale of the ecological system used to study the Tsembaga Maring is too small to understand many relevant ecological processes (e.g., material cycles and other limiting factors),

2. His data on human nutrition are taken from a sample that is too small and representative of only a short time period, and their interpretation is too simplistic,
3. The analysis of quantitative data is not sufficiently sophisticated (only descriptive mathematics were used), and his use of system theory is incomplete,
4. He does not extend the study of energy flow to include exchanges among human groups.

The systems approach to ecological anthropology has also been criticized for emphasizing the processes of self-regulation and neglecting "disruptive" processes that upset systems and cause evolutionary change (e.g., E. Anderson, 1973; Diener, 1974). That is, the ecological systems in which humans participate are viewed as delicately balanced "machines" kept in equilibrium by mechanisms that counteract deviations. In large part this view has come from ecologists studying "natural" systems; however, the recent literature strongly suggests that nature is not in a state of balance but subject to "traumas and shocks imposed by climatic changes and other geophysical processes" (Holling and Goldberg, 1971). The ecologist Crawford Holling (1973) points out that the "self-regulation" of ecological systems really includes two types of processes: equilibrium and resilience. Equilibrium processes act to keep a system from *fluctuating* too much and may not be that important in nature. By contrast, resilience processes act to prevent the system from self-destructing, to make sure that it *persists* through time. These are the important processes and under some circumstances may actually give an advantage to systems that fluctuate rather than to those that are stable. For example, if energy flows in "spurts" through a system, a species or population that is able to grow rapidly and then to "crash" to a much smaller size without becoming extinct has a selective advantage. Vayda and McCay (1975) suggest that studies of the ecological systems in which humans participate should shift from equilibrium to resilience processes. It should also be pointed out that some anthropologists using a system approach have studied instability and evolutionary change, most notably the archaeologist Kent Flannery (e.g., 1972b). Nevertheless, the early stage of development of systems ecology in anthropology is apparent.

Ethnoecology

All of the approaches to ecological anthropology that have been discussed to this point are "objective;" that is, they study man-environmental relationships from the *observer's* point of view. Another approach that has gained popularity in recent years attempts to study ecological relationships from the *participant's* point of view. Usually called ethnoscience, ethnographic semantics, or cognitive ethnography, it uses the concepts of structural linguistics to get at what Rappaport (1963) calls the "cognized" environment, the environment that is actually perceived by a human group (J. Anderson, 1973, p. 188). Informants are used to construct "folk classifications" of nature with the assumption that the classifications are clues to the way that people have coped with environmental problems. Rather than being a first step toward understanding the processes of human ecology, however, folk classifications are all too often an end in themselves.

Summary

The study of the relationship between humans and their environment has been of interest to scholars for a long time. In anthropology environment has been used to explain cultural origins and diversity in at least three ways: environmental determinism, environmental possibilism, and ecology. In recent years the ecological approach has replaced the other two and today is one of the most popular kinds of anthropological explanation. Nevertheless, ecological anthropology should not be viewed as the "anthropology of the future." Problems in anthropology are varied and, as in any other science, require a variety of explanations. Nor is it likely that an ecological approach will provide the best answers to *all* problems with which it can potentially deal. Human behavior is simply too complex to be understood by a single set of principles. At the same time ecological anthropology has been shown to provide a powerful explanation for some questions, questions that will be discussed throughout this book.

Allen Johnson

18. Reductionism in Cultural Ecology: The Amazon Case[1]

In the effort to understand the influence of ecology on the cultures of native lowland South Americans, a number of related disputes have centered on the degree to which population pressure on resources and the resulting competition between local populations can explain major features of social life, such as community size, permanence of settlement, and patterns of political alliance and warfare. Although there has been a certain polarization between those who favor ecological explanations of Amazon cultures and those who oppose them, the underlying issue has been made more subtle and difficult to disentangle by the willingness of all parties to acknowledge that *some* resource scarcity exists and is responded to by community members. Therefore, at the outset we must state the central issue as follows: Is the scarcity of resources *sufficiently great* to explain significant features of native Amazon cultures?

Prior to the 1950s, this issue received little explicit attention among Amazon specialists, although it had been addressed by students of native North America (Lowie 1920:356; Wissler 1926; Kroeber 1939; Newcomb 1950). Lowie's (1949) comparative discussion of social and political organization of South American Indians did not even mention the issue. Métraux (1949:385) did suggest that competition over resources was a factor in some conflict but saw warfare as rooted mainly in "the system of values connected with warfare. Warfare was the principal means of acquiring prestige and high status." This view, with its emphasis on the explanatory power of "values" and a corresponding reluctance to ask where values come from (what causes them), is representative of what I shall refer to in this paper as a "structural" position.

Steward (1949) took an "ecological" position. He argued that the small size of Amazon communities reflected poor agricultural land and other environmental or technological shortcomings (pp. 677, 699) and that nucleated villages were a response to defense needs in the presence of warfare (pp. 704–5), but he did not suggest that warfare itself resulted from competition over resources.

Meggers (1954) strengthened Steward's argument by marshalling the emerging evidence on the poverty and fragility of tropical soils. It seems unlikely on the face of it that the native peoples of Amazonia, living at population *densities* of less than one person per square mile, surrounded by an enormous rain forest, could be experiencing any significant population *pressure* on resources. Yet here is a good case for the need to keep the abstract theoretical concept "population pressure" distinct from the concrete, operational concept "population density": Meggers in effect argued that soils were so poor and vulnerable that serious local population pressure could be felt even under low density unless people lived in small, frequently moving communities.

Meggers's argument focused on land for horticultural food production. By implication this refers in the Amazon to food energy (calories), since gardens emphasize starchy staples, while other nutrients tend to be obtained from forests and rivers. This was a single-factor hypothesis that was soon thrown into doubt by Carneiro's (1960) discovery of a tropical-forest community that had many times as much land as it needed to remain permanently in one location. Carneiro's data made such a convincing case that Chagnon and Hames (1979:911) recently concluded: "Since Carneiro's insightful empirical test of the soil poverty hypothesis, very few anthropologists hazard explanations of native Amazonian cultural forms and cultural limitations by invoking a soil-depletion or soil-poverty argument." I shall present evidence suggesting that rejection of Meggers's hypothesis has been too complete and that we may reasonably identify soil poverty as one factor of many that have shaped native Amazonian cultures.

Carneiro's empirical rejection of Meggers's view, in combination with a growing criticism of energy-based models in ecology (e.g., Brookfield's [1972:46] charge of a "calorific obsession"), influenced cultural ecologists in turning their attention to protein scarcity. Gross (1975) compiled data suggesting that protein intake levels in the Amazon were generally low, barely equal to recommended intake levels. He saw this as evidence that higher population densities would result in significant protein deficiency in Amazon diets.

It is relevant for my argument that these emphases—first on food energy, then on protein—were not arbitrary. They represented natural choices for researchers working in the framework of ecological theory, since food needs are primary in the theory, and calories alone or in combination with protein are often used by nutritionists as measures of overall dietary adequacy for comparative purposes (see, for example,

Slesser 1976, United Nations World Food Conference 1975). Hence, the turn to protein was the theoretically reasonable next step after the calorie-deficiency hypothesis had been tested and found wanting.

Shortly thereafter, however, data of much higher quality than those available to Gross began to appear showing that native. Amazon communities typically obtain more than twice as much protein as recommended for minimum health maintenance (Berlin and Markell 1977:78; Ross 1978:4; Chagnon and Hames 1979:912; Beckerman 1979; Johnson and Behrens 1982). As in the case of land shortage, therefore, protein shortage as a variable explaining culture process has seemed less than adequate.

Over time a polarization has developed between ecologists and structuralists over this issue. The main structuralist criticism has been that ecologists are reductionists. I will return below to a consideration of whether and to what degree "reductionism" is to be considered a criticism, and not simply a description, of ecological (and structural) explanations in the Amazon case. An example of the polarization around this issue is Ross's (1978) attempt to reduce the structural feature of food taboos in Amazon cultures to an ecological explanation, viz., that animals whose flesh is taboo are precisely those most in danger of extinction by overhunting. In addition to presenting evidence in support of his case, Ross criticizes structuralists for taking native belief systems as givens, rather than viewing them as "metaphysical systems" whose reason for existence is the selective advantage they confer in adaptation to the material environment. He charges structuralists with a "rhetorical use of obscurity" in elaborating their analyses without regard for the adaptive functions of belief systems.

Ross's attack has drawn much structuralist counterfire, exemplified by the following (Lizot 1979:151, emphasis added):

[Ross's argument] has its basis in a whole school of thought which claims that social and religious facts can be *reduced* to a bundle of external constraints to which man is subject. Structuralism and symbolism, we are told, are mere idealistic dreams: social life, beliefs, food taboos, and warfare are only an expression of the material conditions and the physical environment. . . .

Proponents of both viewpoints take the polemical stance that they are reasonable scientists viewing with alarm the extremism of the opposition. The majority of cultural anthropologists would rather avoid this degree of polarization and make opportunistic use of both perspectives. As Linares (1978:23) observes: "the sooner we abandon these academic polarizations . . . the sooner we will begin to understand such phenomena as hunting taboos in their full and subtle complexity . . . [as reflections of] both resource availability *and* necessary ways of ordering the social-spatial world."

I have given this brief and oversimplified history of a complex issue in order to place my own data and arguments in context. This is a most complex issue, with few people falling clearly on one side or the other. It is of great significance to specialists in native Amazon cultures and will by no means be resolved by the few new facts I introduce here. What I wish to do, rather, is examine the issue of reductionism as it has surfaced in the Amazon case and reinforce a view which I believe many colleagues share—that we need more "bridging" between structural and ecological positions in order to begin to answer the question, "Granting that more and more of us want [nonreductionistic cross-disciplinary work], how do we get it, and how do we get it right?" (Burton-Bradley and Pataki-Schweizer 1977:464).

Resource Scarcity and Structural Ecology in an Amazon Community

My examples will be drawn from the Machiguenga, slash-and-burn horticulturalists of the tropical rain forest of the Peruvian Amazon. The Machiguenga expend just over half (55%) of their directly productive work effort in gardening, from which they obtain the vast majority of their calories; the remainder of productive work is evenly divided between fishing and hunting-and-gathering, from which most of their protein and dietary diversity are obtained (for a discussion of data sources and research methods, see Johnson and Behrens 1982). Although they number about 10,000 and, in conjunction with the closely related and even more numerous Campa, constitute one of the most vital of traditional Amazon Indian groups, their settlements seldom exceed 35 persons, living in independent households or small clusters of such households isolated from one another by large expanses of unbroken rain forest. From the air, signs of human impact are nearly impossible to discern in the indescribable immensity of the forest carpet. Although the wave of destruction of the rain forest by human activity is rapidly approaching (see Richards 1973; Holden 1980:378), the Machiguenga are hardly aware of this and do not consider the Forest (in the large sense) destructible. Population density in the watershed of the Kompiroshiato River, where this research was done, is about 0.8 persons per square mile.

The impression of an abundance of resources relative to population pressure is strengthened by nutritional evidence. With a comparatively modest work effort (Johnson 1978a), the Machiguenga manage to produce not only more than twice as much food energy and protein as they need according to published recommendations, but an abundance of all major nutritional requirements: 210% of the National Academy of Sciences' recommended daily allowance of calories, 248% of the protein, 128% of the calcium, 196% of the phosphorus, 251% of the iron, 88% of the Vitamin A, 230% of the thiamine, 120% of the riboflavin, 183% of the niacin, and 1,208% of the Vitamin C (Johnson and Behrens 1982).[2]

Thus the Machiguenga (in addition to the cases cited above) support the general conclusion that aboriginal groups of Amazonia are well nourished (Berlin and Markell 1977:69). This finding provides still further evidence seemingly contrary to the idea that resource scarcity exists for such groups.

This conclusion may appear correct in an ecological frame of reference, but it does not reflect the Machiguenga perception. They regard "good" agricultural land as scarce and give this scarcity as one explanation for their frequent resettlement (usually within five years of the previous resettlement). Structurally, the Machiguenga divide *kipatsi* 'earth' into four major types: *shimentyapatsari* 'gravel soil,' *potsitapatsari* 'black soil,' *kiraapatsari* 'red soil,' and *imvanekipatsari* 'sandy soil' (table 18–1). Of these, gravel soil and sandy soil are highly preferred as "soft soils" (*metsopatsari*) over the other two "hard soils" (*kusopatsari*). At the time of the initial research in 1972, all the available sandy soil had been under cultivation for three to four years, and only one area of uncultivated gravel soil remained (it had come under cultivation at the time of a revisit in 1975). There was some black soil still available and a great abundance of red soil. The soft soils are preferred because they are much easier and more enjoyable to work with and drain well in this humid climate. We can translate these structural data into ecological terms by analysis of the soils. Both soft soils are unusually high in sand and gravel by comparison with silt and clay, while the reverse is true of the hard soils.

Table 18–1

Machiguenga Soil Types and Soil Analysis

Soil Type	Fertility Rank	"Hard"/ "Soft"	N	% Organic Matter	% Nitrogen	% Sand and Gravel	% Silt	% Clay
shimentya 'gravel'	1	soft	6	8.2	0.40	58	24	18
potsita 'black'	2	hard	5	5.4	0.27	34	42	24
kiraa 'red'	3	hard	9	5.1	0.24	28	44	28
imvaneki 'sand' ..	...	soft	2	1.8	0.08	72	20	8

Gravel, black, and red soils are similar in occurring on hillsides. The
Machiguenga consider them of declining fertility in that order, as measured by their ability to support maize cultivation (*oshivokonake* 'it
grows,' *otimanakera okitsoki* 'there are kernels'). All informants are enthu-
siastic about growing maize in gravel soil, and all agree, though without
enthusiasm, that black soil will permit maize to grow; they are divided,
however, about whether maize will even produce edible seed on red soil.
Again, the Machiguenga view can be interpreted in terms of the scientific data: soil fertility, as measured by the percentages of both organic
matter and nitrogen in the soil, decreases consistently in the same order
as the Machiguenga preferences.

It seems that the Machiguenga manage to find land scarcity in the
midst of abundance, or, rather, by attending to details of their environment that an outside observer might overlook, discriminate structurally
among qualities of land that affect their labor inputs and productivity.
These discriminations in turn influence their behavior: they plan their
clearing of new gardens at least two years in advance and, in the absence
of a system of land tenure, lay public (political) claim to the use of
particular plots in advance to avoid disputes when the time comes to
clear a new garden. Furthermore, when such preferred lands are difficult or impossible to obtain within a comfortable walking distance (about
one-half hour from home), they seriously consider moving their households to new locations. It would be out of touch with reality as the
Machiguenga perceive it to suggest that land scarcity was anything less
than a highly significant element of their cultural response to the environment.

Although the Machiguenga produce two and a half times their dietary
recommendation of protein, a similar and stronger case can be made for
the perceived scarcity of protein. We may begin by noting that the
Machiguenga spend fully 45% of their productive labor inputs in collecting protein-rich wild foods. Although it takes only 80 kcal. of labor to
produce 1 kg of garden food, as compared with 740 kcal. to produce 1 kg
of riverine foods and 1,150 kcal. to produce 1 g of forest foods (that is,
wild foods are roughly 10 to 15 times as energy-expensive to produce as
garden foods), the cost of protein is roughly comparable in both cases
because of the scarcity of protein in garden foods. A linear-programming
model predicts that by reorienting their garden labor around a different
mix of traditional crops, they *could* produce a nutritionally adequate diet
without needing to include either riverine or forest foods (Johnson and
Behrens 1982). But the Machiguenga have a strong preference for animal
proteins over vegetable proteins (which may have a physiological basis
[see Harris 1979a, Spath 1981]), and they work very hard to obtain them.
Fish and game elicit exclamations of pleasure when they are brought into

the house and are never wasted (which is not true of garden foods); wild food-getting activities are also pleasurable in themselves (see Johnson 1980:31).

As a specific example of how protein scarcity is reflected in behavior, we may look at the varieties of fishing distinguished by the Machiguenga (table 18–2). The four varieties (poisoning with barbasco, hook and line, net, and hand fishing; bow and arrow fishing is extremely rare) differ in productivity. With the exception of hand fishing, the Machiguenga match their time inputs to the productivity of the technique. Although from a strict maximization or optimization viewpoint it would seem rational for them to invest all their labor in the most productive alternative (poison), two reasons may be given for preferring a matching strategy.[3] First, there is always sufficient risk in all forms of fishing to make diversification desirable: I have observed cases in which the normally productive poison fishing produced almost no yield after large labor investments, and I have seen a hook-and-line fisherman bring in three large fish in two days even though he had caught nothing in the previous two weeks. Second, these strategies are not all directly competitive with one another. Poisoning and hook-and-line fishing are done when the river is low and clear, generally in the dry season: poison fishing takes place during the main part of the day, while the much less productive hook-and-line fishing is done in early mornings and later afternoons. By contrast, net and hand fishing are done when the river is muddy and turbulent, when the fish cannot hear or see the approaching fishers. The reason hand fishing is unexpectedly popular is that it is the only fishing that requires no special equipment or skills. Whenever it rains, and the river rises and becomes muddy, everyone, including small children, goes to the river to search for small fish and other river creatures. Only some of the adults will have nets, which are very costly to manufacture, but the others use what would otherwise be idle time to try their luck with small fish that they often eat on the spot as they catch them.

Table 18–2

Fishing Yields and Time Allocation

Fishing Strategy	Efficiency (Grams Fish/ Kcal. Work)	% Fishing Time Allocated
nonkamotera 'poison'	2.5	43
nontsagatera 'hook and line'	0.8	16
nonkitsatera/noshiriatera 'net'	0.6	11
nonpamuatera 'hand'	0.2	30

Despite an objective "sufficiency" or even abundance of food, we find that a perceived scarcity exists that influences individual behavior. Since my purpose is to establish the plausibility of the idea that, in the native's perception, there is environmental scarcity in many domains of native Amazon life, however, I will give an example from outside the realm of food production. Table 18–3 presents a Machiguenga typology for firewood. This is a general, high-order typology; a more detailed examination reveals a much finer set of discriminations than the "fast/slow" and "log/kindling" distinctions presented here. The most preferred firewoods are fast-burning kindling and slow-burning logs (but these latter must burn slow and hot, without smoke). Since much of the available firewood actually lies on the other diagonal (slow kindling and fast logs), there is a scarcity of the preferred firewoods.

Table 18–3

Machiguenga Firewood: Basic Use Typology

	tsitsi ("firewood")	
	omarapoani "big stick" (log)	*otiomiapoani* "little stick" (kindling)
otsonkanaka shintsi "finishes fast"	"fast-burning logs"	"fast-burning kindling"
okusotanaketyo "long lasting"	"long-lasting logs"	"long-lasting kindling"

Firewood is a good example for my purposes because less than 1% of the total Machiguenga energy expenditure is invested in obtaining firewood. Yet the Machiguenga pay careful attention to the kinds of firewood because even this labor must not be wasted and because the wrong choice of firewoods can cause great inconvenience in food preparation. During 1972 people complained frequently that there was "no firewood." This seemed unlikely to us, because there was nothing but potential firewood in the forest as far as the eye could see. Yet when we tried to obtain our own firewood we learned that the best woods had already been consumed from the rubbish lying around in gardens during the four or five years of previous residence in this area. Firewood had either to be cut from living plants or else brought in at great pains from distant gardens. Observations made in newly settled areas showed that firewood was being obtained in about half the time spent by the members of our sample.

Taken together, the preceding examples establish that environmental scarcity exists for the Machiguenga, calling for behavioral choices some of which are encoded in structural elements like soil and firewood typologies. These choices in turn have an impact on the size of social groups and the permanence of settlement. Under conditions of greater local population density, which are being encouraged by the Peruvian government's "native communities" policy, these pressures are being intensified. M. Baksh (personal communication, 1980), working in a Machiguenga community of over 300 that was established only in 1976, reports that the local fish and game have been all but depleted, requiring long trips to find productive hunting and fishing grounds; furthermore, firewood and materials used in building and manufacture have become extremely scarce within two to three hours' hard walk of the community. By 1980 these pressures had resulted in much political strife and efforts to split the village.

It is not so much the pressure on any single resource, therefore, as the accumulating effect of many scarcities in all areas of the economy, compared with the levels of abundance to which the people are accustomed and believe they are entitled as part of their quality of life, that brings about population movements and social realignments.

Discussion

Although structuralists (and others) have often criticized cultural ecologists working in Amazonia for reductionism, they have not fully specified what they find wrong with reductionism or what mode of explanation or understanding of culture process they think is better. It is true that ecological research has been reductionistic and that some ecologists may be fairly criticized for being extremely so, but the structuralist critics have also been reductionistic without apparently being aware of it and without acknowledging that some degree of reductionism is a necessary part of all scientific work.

"Reductionism" refers primarily to the effort to explain phenomena at one level of analysis entirely by reference to theoretical principles operating at another level. Usually, but not necessarily, the explanatory principles are thought to apply at a more "fundamental" level than the phenomena being explained. For example, "biostructuralism" attempts to explain phenomena labelled "cultural" solely by reference to underlying biological processes, particularly using theoretical models of neurophysiology and information processing (Rubinstein and Laughlin 1977). If any residue remains at the cultural level that cannot be explained biostructurally, the reduction is incomplete and to that degree unsuccessful.

A paradox of reductionism is that there is no rule saying where to stop. Hence we may aspire to reduce culture to the biostructural level, the biostructural to the biochemical, the biochemical to the physical chemical, the physical chemical to the physical, and so on in infinite regress until the smallest particles and their fundamental laws are found from which all higher orders of nature can be predicted (Bohm 1957:61–67). Skeptics of this "ultimate reductionism" point out that it has never been achieved and may be nothing more than a chimera, since the basic "elements" being sought do not exist immutably, but are determined in fundamental respects by their environments (i.e., the "wholes" in which they occur [Whitehead 1925, Bohm, 1957, Emerson 1960]).

The alternative to reductionism is usually some form of holism (Phillips 1976), asserting that the whole must be understood as such, not reduced to a part of itself. The structural critics of Amazon cultural ecology argue that features of Amazon cultures are too complex and too interrelated with myriad other variables to be explained ecologically (Chagnon 1968). This is, in essence, the structural-functional principle that culture must be described or explained in its own terms and not in terms of biology, economics, psychology, or any other approach that comprises only a part of the cultural whole.

It is not often explicitly noted that holism presents a paradox equal to that of reductionism in that there is also the possibility of "infinte egress," toward higher-order "wholes." Why stop with just one culture at one point in time? It is possible to interpret cultural features as a pattern believed to apply to a whole region of related cultures and their postulated historical antecedents (e.g., Lévi-Strauss 1978:25–43). Although the analysis quickly becomes "mystical" and outside the bounds of "normal science," the search for larger wholes need not end until the ultimate Whole has been reached. In the words of the Zen master Suzuki (1960:11–12), who calls his approach to reality "the Zen way, the antescientific or metascientific or even antiscientific way":

The Zen approach is to enter right into the object itself and see it, as it were, from the inside. To know the flower is to become the flower, to be the flower, to bloom as the flower, and to enjoy the sunlight as well as the rainfall. When this is done, the flower speaks to me and I know all its secrets, all its joys, all its sufferings; that is, all its life vibrating within itself. Not only that: along with my "knowledge" of the flower I know all the secrets of the universe.

In short, one man's reductionism is another's holism, depending on where each stands in the chain of inclusiveness from basic-particle elementism to universal oneness. For example, Harris (1979a) is self-consciously reductionistic in explaining Yanomamö warfare in terms of protein scarcity. Chagnon (1968), on the other hand, is self-consciously eclectic, emphasizing the many considerations, both ecological and structural, that influence Yanomamö warfare. It is within this context that Chagnon criticizes Harris for reductionism. However, Chagnon (1979) also entertains the possibility that features of Yanomamö population dynamics must be understood biostructurally and in that context comes within the scope of Harris's own criticism of biostructuralism for biological reductionism (Harris 1979b: 119–40).

It must be clear that reductionism is a natural and proper part of doing science and that we all are "guilty" of it at various times and to varying degrees. Since anyone who seeks knowledge in less comprehensive ways than the mystical all-knowingness described by Suzuki is reductionistic, it is not enough to dismiss the work of cultural ecologists as reductionistic; it is also necessary to show how that reductionism is somehow inferior to the reductionism of the critics. For example, in "Structuralism and Ecology" Lévi-Strauss (1972:7) seeks to discover how "human history and natural ecology become articulated so as to make up a meaningful whole," but it becomes apparent that what interests him is not a balance between ecological and structural theories, but a structural analysis of certain elements in Bella Bella mythology that occur in the natural environment (clams, owls, porcupines, etc.). Indeed, Lévi-Strauss is so uninterested in the ecological facts about these animals that he makes some obvious errors (Harris 1976); he has "reduced" ecology to something so peripheral that it hardly catches his attention.

This is an example of "inter-level reductionism" (Wimsatt 1976), in which the phenomena appropriate to one level of analysis (the ecological relations between the Bella Bella and the animal species in their natural environment) are understood exclusively in terms of another (structural analysis of the ways in which these animals are used in mythology). Lévi-Strauss's structural analyses are rich and provocative, but his use of ecology is correspondingly impoverished. He has made a firm *prescientific* commitment to center his work around structuralist themes, including the view of culture as an integrated system of meaning and as a source of evidence concerning the existence of "structures in the mind." He shows virtually no appreciation of the central themes of the ecological orientation, which focuses upon the existence of basic biological needs and environmental constraints in an interplay that influences a broad range of cultural phenomena.

In the case of population density and settlement in Amazonia, it is not necessary to postulate a single biological factor in order to develop a consistently ecological explanation. I cannot make sense of the Machiguenga case materials provided earlier with fewer than three levels of analysis. Viewed in narrowly ecological terms, we have data showing that the Machiguenga's population density is "low," that they produce more food than they need to meet recommended nutritional levels, that they obtain fuel (firewood) with less than 1% of their total energy output, and so on.

What these ecological facts mean is not always clear, however. For example, Carneiro (1978:19), upon learning that the Achuarä Jivaro obtain 58 g of protein per person per day from hunting, says they have "more than adequate protein." Diener et al. (1980) also assume that when people have more protein in their diet than the laboratory-established minimum they must have "plenty" of protein. But the phrasing of the problem has become unintentionally ethnocentric: Some of us are arguing that, for example, 55 g of protein a day is inadequate on scientific grounds, whereas others say that it is adequate, again on scientific grounds. We need also to "ask" the people themselves (i.e., try to understand their motives as they see them). Perhaps they want more meat because of wants we have not yet taken into account in our theories, such as the taste of meat, its fat content, diversity of nutrients, etc. Since the ultimate theoretical issue concerns motivation (willingness to move settlement or fight a battle), external and impersonal measures of biological need are not enough in themselves to support or to deny the protein hypothesis.

On the structural level, we learn that native Amazonians are profoundly cognizant of their environment and of their own interactions with it. They distinguish types of soil, modes of fishing, kinds of firewood, and so forth in ways that reflect important ecological realities like labor cost and quality of resources. This knowledge is, for the individual, often "prior" to real experience in the environment and helps shape that experience (see Bennett 1976). It is not necessary to insist either that all structural features are ecologically determined or that all ecological behavior is culturally encoded to acknowledge that there is a significant correspondence between the two.

Finally, we need an "economic" perspective on decision making to breathe life into our scheme. Both ecological and structural perspectives sometimes tend to imply that their subjects are mechanical followers of preordained strategies who either blindly pursue adaptive routes or blindly enact cultural rules. This is not to say that habitual, unreflective behavior never occurs, only that very often the people are aware of what they are doing and must balance complex options in order to meet the whole range of their wants and needs effectively.

Improved understanding comes from working back and forth between levels or orientations in a manner that Radnitsky (1973:194) calls "tacking." I suspect that most anthropologists working in Amazonia do tack in attempting to "make sense" of the diversity of cultures to be found there (e.g., Turner 1979). Perhaps it is in order to publish clear and unequivocal statements that they sometimes do not. Lévi-Strauss, in the works cited above, hardly ventures a step from the structural position, except occasionally to add a biostructural assumption about innate mental properties. Ross, in criticizing structural approaches to food taboos, similarly remains rooted in the ecological position. Tacking involves moving away from these "pure" points of view into the open spaces where multiple perspectives apply.

The open spaces do present problems of their own. A kind of eclectic ennui can set in in which either nothing seems important or everything seems so at once. In Redfield's (1953:157) wise observation, "we do not want ethnologists so balanced that they have no humanity. We want a balanced profession, a varied lot of anthropologists." I would place my present argument off-center in the direction of the ecological standpoint. Structural and economic perspectives are relevant to my approach to the extent that they help me understand Machiguenga cultural ecology, but it is natural and inevitable that other observers will migrate toward one of the other two corners according to their predilections or the demands of the problem before them.

Summary

Population density, village size, intravillage factionalism, and intervillage alliances in Amazonia are all determined or substantially influenced by the aggregate of decisions taken by individuals, households, and kinship groups concerning whether to remain where they are or move elsewhere. I assume that this is done in an effort to defend or improve upon an existing quality of life. One learns by participating in everyday conversations that individuals are continuously evaluating, alone and in groups, the extent to which available land, fish, firewood, and many other features of the environment are acceptable. This evaluation is done in terms of categories and understandings that exist, culturally or structurally, prior to any particular decision but are capable of change to reflect significant changes in circumstances. These structural categories and understandings refer to objective, ecologically relevant, and measurable attributes of the world, such as the energy cost of labor, the nutritional value of the diet, the yields of alternative procurement strategies, and the constituents of the soil.

On the whole, such decisions are taken not suddenly, but after thought and discussion, and only after a certain inertia is overcome or, in the case of group action, a consensus has been reached. The individual participant in the decision, the structural framework, and the ecological imperatives are all present simultaneously and influence one another through interaction effects. Structurally, one prefers "soft" soils; this influences the decision about which lands to clear for gardening; this in turn influences the availability of soft soils in the future and hence the decision to stay or move. If conditions were to change (say, population density to increase), it might conceivably turn out that "hard" soils retained nutrients and sustained crop production for longer periods without fallow, allowing greater population on the same land; if this led people to prefer "hard" soils, it would be a hypothetical case in which environmental change, itself brought about by the impact of decisions made under a prior structural set of assumptions, led to a new structural set. In all of this, the researcher may choose to emphasize one—the decision process, the structural framework, or the ecological imperatives—over the others. But reductionistic elimination of one or two of the three, which might be justified in the name of "theoretical purity," seems more likely to lead to unrealistic analyses and sterile debates than to the kind of realistic complexity and intuitive reasonableness conducive to improved research and more comprehensive understanding.

Notes

1. This paper was originally presented in a lecture to the School of Social Sciences, University of California, Irvine, on April 3, 1980. I gratefully acknowledge comments from that audience and extensive and thoughtful criticisms of an earlier draft by David Boyd, Robert Carneiro, Raymond Hames, and Kenneth Kensinger.

2. Estimates refer to an "average household." Thus to say that production of protein is 248% of the recommended daily allowance means that the average household produces food with a protein value 2.48 times the recommended level of protein intake for a family of average composition. Only Vitamin A is produced in less than recommended levels, and the shortfall is small considering that recommended levels are set high and clinical evidence of health problems with such a small deficit is weak (see discussion in Johnson and Behrens 1982). Major crops include manioc, maize, and cocoyam (*Xanthosoma*); wild foods are obtained in small quantities but great diveristy.

3. A matching strategy is known to economists as the "gambler's fallacy," since one should invest in the most profitable alternative, not in several less productive ones. Yet the behavior of people and some animals often follows a matching strategy, probably because security as well as profit is a goal.

Herbert Applebaum

VII

Cultural Materialism and Marxism

Introduction

Materialism is based on the concept that the world consists of material objects which interact and intersect with one another in various states of rest and motion. Materialists view the human being as a material, concrete reality, along with the products of the human mind and human behavior, consisting of physical objects such as tools and goods and the products of the mind, such as technology, science, knowledge, values, laws, religion, and culture. Anthropologists who are materialists insist that culture has no existence apart from human beings. They also include mental, and well as material, products under the materialist orientation.

Materialism as an approach to the study of human behavior has a long history, going back to Descartes, and before that, to Democritus and Lucretius in the ancient world. It was always part of anthropology, with its emphasis on cultural traits and artifacts. It is a part of archaeology, which is based, in large measure, on material artifacts unearthed as evidence of human cultures. The main attraction of materialism today is the way it fits in with scientific theory and method, based, as it is, on empirical data to support and verify hypotheses in the social sciences.

Cultural materialism is associated with the name of Marvin Harris, who coined the term (1968; 1979b). It is based on the concept that the material conditions of society determine the consciousness of human beings, rather than the other way around. Harris uses the Marxist idea of base and superstructure. He calls the base "infrastructure," a common term in other social sciences, i.e. geography. Harris modifies the Marxist scheme by including in the base (infrastructure) human reproduction, along with the economic mode of production. He also has an intermediary category, *structure*, between the base and superstructure, which is not in the Marxist scheme. The reader should check Chapter 19 for the social categories which Harris includes in his three-part division of society.

Harris considers all *three* categories—base, structure and superstructure—to be etic phenomena; that is, they are discoverable by social scientists investigating them as scientists. One category, superstructure—broadly, the ideological and mental phenomena—contains both etic and emic phenomena. Emic phenomena are mental components in the minds of persons residing in a culture or society, who view themselves and the world from their own, specific perspective, based on the values, knowledge, and attitudes fostered within the culture. Language is a category, apart from all the others, which Harris views as serving an instrumental role by coordinating base, structural, and superstructural activities. Thus, it infuses and belongs to all three groups, since all human social behavior implies the use of language.

Harris regards the etic approach (from the viewpoint of the social scientist) as the priority research strategy for developing explanations of human social phenomena. He does not deny that mental, superstructural, *emic*, explanations have a degree of autonomy apart from etic explanations. But he gives first priority to etic analysis. And he also gives first priority to an investigation of the base or infrastructure, since he, like the Marxists, believes that it will yield the basic regularities in the interface between culture and nature. In Harris' view, the strategic advantage of etic, infrastructural analysis lies in its amenability to quantification and measurement, always a plus in scientific endeavors.

Harris states that cultural materialism, or any other general theory such as Marxism or structuralism, is a body of concepts and a theoretical orientation which is not in itself testable or subject to empirical verification. General theories instead, serve as guides for the construction of plausible and testable hypotheses, which are subject to proofs through the assemblage of data (1982:143). Harris avers that cultural materialism as a general theory may be conducive to the developing of hypotheses; however, it cannot be predicted in advance what its success rate will be. This will depend on those using it as a theory, on how well they marshal empirical evidence and how expertly they develop their canons of proof.

Harris' cultural materialism is based on Marx, but it is differentiated from Marxism through its insistence on the priority of a research strategy which declares: first study base (infrastructure), then structure, then superstructure. Marxism insists that all social life is interrelated and considers any concentration on base, without relating it to the superstructure, a "vulgar" or "mechanical" materialism. Marxism stresses human consciousness (class consciousness, in many instances). It imparts an important historical role to classes of people, who can recognize and change social conditions whenever conditions become unbearable and no longer solve human needs. Cultural materialism tends to concentrate on objective phenomena, while Marxism stresses the interconnectedness of objective and subjective phenomena. At times, cultural materialism hypothesizes that people's behavior is controlled by protein requirements, energy levels, or other naturalistic factors. Marxism considers such an approach overly mechanistic and determinist and insists on the necessity to incorporate all levels of social reality in an explanatory analysis.

The methodology of cultural materialism relies on the scientific method and its rules for gathering of data, verifying hypotheses, and developing logical analysis and parsimonious proofs. Cultural materialism accepts the notion that empirical reality exists independently of human consciousness. Harris insists that, given a sufficient number of cases, generalizations can be developed regarding human society. And further, that cultural materialism can explain and isolate the reasons for similarities and differences between societies by concentrating on the study of material infrastructures (base) of societies.

In a short article in the American Anthropologist (1982:138–142, reproduced in this section as Chapter 20), Paul Magnarella posits some questions about cultural materialism's methods and results. Magnarella's points and Harris' reply (1982:142–145) help further to clarify cultural materialism theory. Magnarella claims that cultural materialists have not operationalized their theories so as to make them testable; and Harris replies that cultural materialism, as a corpus of theory, is not itself testable but that it can provide the guide for developing hypotheses that are. Magnarella challenges cultural materialists to deal with emic behavior as a test of their theory, and Harris replies that the ultimate test for the efficacy of cultural materialist theory is to relate infrastructural conditions to emic behavior, on the premise that superstructural innovations will be short-lived if they are out of touch with infrastructural social foundations. While Magnarella states that in dealing with hunting and gathering societies, Harris is rather narrow and only explains what is already known, a reading of Harris' explanation belies this accusation (1979b:79–85). In his analysis, he presents theories and data about subsistence strategies, technological and environmental influences, kinship relations, reciprocity relationships, food sharing based on band size, attitudes toward women, marriage patterns, and the division of labor. His approach is neither narrow nor reductionist.

To be fair to Harris, one must take his effort in a total context. While his writing is often polemical, which has irritated some and been enjoyed by others (myself, for instance), his views of scientific theory and the anthropological endeavor is sound and reasonable. His major works (1968; 1979b) are written in clear prose and contain many stimulating propositions. He argues that the value of a research strategy does not lie in its abstract theories but in the "cogency of its substantive theories (1979b:77). Like others (Marxists, structuralists), Harris seeks to penetrate beneath the surface of phenomena to reveal unsuspected relationships. He doesn't purport to have definitive answers, but only *probable* ones, the only kind that are possible in dealing with human behavior.

Some critics of cultural materialism, particular Marxists, see it, with its concentration on infrastructure, as belittling the importance of ideology and political activities as forces for change. Harris does not deny the role of political activism in changing social systems. He sees ideology as an accelerating or decelerating process to changes in the infrastructure. He insists that when conditions within the infrastructure are not ripe, no amount of political activism can bring about change. He cites the United States in the 1960s as an example. In spite of the plethora of manifestos by the counter-cultural movement, no lasting effects were produced. This was because the capitalist infrastructure of the United States was stable and functioning effectively, so that the general population was not ripe for, nor did it desire, a fundamental shift in its sociocultural conditions.

Replying to critics, who claim that cultural materialism underestimates the importance of ideology and politics, Harris writes (1979b:157–58):

Like dialectical materialism, cultural materialism accepts and affirms the interdependence of science and politics. It also vigorously rejects the myth of value-free science. It insists that there is a determined relationship between dominant research strategies and political-economic structures and infrastructures . . . cultural materialist strategy inevitably contributes to a radical critique of the status quo.

Harris is critical of cultural idealists, as he calls them, such as cognitive and symbolic anthropologists or Lévi-Strauss structuralists. He believes that their research strategies will never deal with "the guts of contemporary life" (1979b:285). As Harris puts it, no amount of knowledge of competent natives, nor information about rules and codes of behavior, can account for such phenomena as poverty, unemployment, ethnic and class conflict, exploitation, taxation, pollution, political repression, crime, urban blight, war, the military-industrial complex, and a host of other modern social phenomena.

Harris is also critical of dialectical materialists. He sees them as relying on their dialectical analysis as a means for predicting the future. This creates an inevitability and an idealistic certainty in the way they view social phenomena. This leads, in Harris' view, toward either ignoring empirical data, distorting it to suit the Marxist view, or an unnecessary denouncing of an empirical program for the gathering of data (1979b:149–151).

In summary, no matter how one views cultural materialism, it has generated discussion, debate, and even excitement in the field of anthropology. It is a theoretical orientation that vigorously asserts the need to found anthropology on a sound empirical and scientific basis. It offers a general theory, a grand theory, if you will, which is rare in a field that continues to fissure and specialize. Its originator, Marvin Harris, is steeped in a knowledge of anthropological literature and continues to offer the field new and challenging works in anthropological theory.

Marxist anthropology is based on applying the concepts and methods of Marx and Engels to society. Since anthropologists have traditionally concentrated on preindustrial societies, Marxist anthropologists have, in the main, bent their efforts toward the relevance of Marxist principles to these societies and cultures. This is difficult since Marx concentrated on capitalist society, and the clues to what he thought of primitive cultures are sparse. Mostly they are contained in what are now called *Ethnological Notebooks of Karl Marx* (Krader 1972) and in Engels' work, *The Origin of the Family, Private Property and the State* (1940). This work of Engels is based on the researches of Lewis H. Morgan.

The application of Marxism to anthropology is in the approach which sees the mode and relations of production as the primary social force determining the structure and development of any society or culture. The specific content of the mode of production and its accompanying social relations are researched by Marxist scholars using the same ethnographic methods as other anthropologists. Methods include moving back and forth between the abstract and the concrete. The Marxist anthropologist starts with a conception of society in which the base of the society, its subsistence or production mode and relations, are determining, *in the final analysis*, the course and development of a society, along with its superstructure, the ideology and values of the society.

Marxists are often accused of "economic determinism" in their approach to understanding society. They would reply that they do not believe in a direct, mechanistic relationship between economics and politics or economics and ideology. They call such an approach "vulgar Marxism." Engels is often quoted on this matter (1963:204):

According to the materialist concept of history the determining element in history is *ultimately* the production and reproduction in real life. More than this neither Marx nor I have ever asserted. If therefore somebody twists this into the statement that the economic element is the *only* determining one, he transforms it into a meaningless, abstract and absurd phrase.

Marxists insist on the human factor as a necessary part of social analysis. They see human actors bringing about change in a society.

Marx believed in the idea that human beings have control over their own destiny but not complete control. They must take into consideration their cultural traditions and historical past. He expressed it this way:

People make their own history, but they do not make it just as they please; they do not make it under circumstances chosen by themselves, but under circumstances directly encountered, given and transmitted from the past.

(Marx 1968:97)

The dynamics of change, in the Marxist view, involves the intervention of human beings to create new institutional relationships to cope with changing social conditions and bring them in line with the material base of a society. The Marxist view reinforced for anthropologists the necessity of adding a dynamic perspective to a static one in the study of societies. There was a growing concern among anthropologists for explanations which related behavior, ideology, and values of the impoverished to the oppressive social, economic, educational and political restraints imposed on them by dominant social groups (Lewis 1961; Foster 1965; Valentine 1968). Just as Marxists believed that they should not only study society but should become politically involved, many Marxist anthropologists were calling for the same thing (Diamond 1964; Gjessing 1968; Gough 1968; Ribiero 1970).

While Marx concentrated on the analysis of capitalist society, he was interested in the process through which primitive, classless societies evolved into class and state societies. His concepts of the nature of pre-class and pre-state cultures were derived from his study of the works of Lewis H. Morgan (1964); John Budd Phear (1880); Henry S. Maine (1914) and John Lubbock (1870). His studies were recorded in two of his notebooks. These two notebooks have been compiled and published as *The Ethnological Notebooks of Karl Marx*, edited by Lawrence Krader (1972).

Krader points out that Marx's well-known scheme on the evolutionary transformation of societies—Primitive Communism to Ancient Slave Class Society to Feudalism to Capitalism to Socialism to Communism—is based on a Middle East/European perspective. Marx realized that there was, in addition, an Asiatic mode of production which did not fit into his scheme. This Asiatic mode of production, with its particular social relations, is an important one for Marxist anthropologists. It refers to the type of small-scale, village societies that anthropologists have traditionally studied.

The small-scale societies studied by anthropologists often coexist within larger state systems. They are often allowed to function autonomously, provided that they pay their taxes and give fealty to the state system. If these village societies were the sequel to Asiastic primitive societies, then they did not conform to the Marxist scheme of the evolution from primitive society to capitalist society. Stanley Diamond (1979:7–10) reports that this question provoked a split between Soviet anthropologists and western Marxist anthropologists at a world conference. Soviet anthropologists tend to view peasants as retarding revolutionary change, whereas Chinese anthropologists take the opposite view, and western Marxist anthropologists are willing to examine the empirical data without taking any doctrinaire stand. It is important to realize that the term "Marxist anthropologist" represents a range of viewpoints—Soviet, West European, United States, Chinese, Latin-American, African.

Another issue of interest to Marxist anthropologists stemming from the ethnological views of Marx and Engels is research on the motive force which changed primitive society into class society. The Marxist dialectic of social transformation is based upon internal contradictions within societies between material forces and social relations. These contradictions reflect class differences and conflicts. The problem is that there are no such divisions in primitive societies. Furthermore, Engels stated that it was the kinship organization, not the mode of production, that was the key force in primitive society (Dunn 1979:173–174). This, too, has caused a split between doctrinaire Marxist anthropologists and others who believe the views of Marx and Engels should be "corrected" when the empirical data warrants it.

Stanley Diamond has identified two types of Marxist anthropologists—"ideological" and "critical" (1979:1–4). The ideological Marxists are those for whom Marxism is part of an ideology used to support a ruling bureaucracy. Under this rubric, it constitutes an official doctrine as much as it does an instrument for social research. This view can be found in the Soviet Union, Eastern Europe, China, and Cuba. The critical Marxists consider the works of Marx and Engels as a cutting edge for the analysis of human societies. They recognize that social conditions since the time of Marx have changed enormously, along with the state of knowledge and empirical research. They use Marxism as a method and general theory and are not reluctant to revise, critique, modify, or question Marx and Engels when their studies warrant it. Critical Marxists are found in the noncommunist world, though there are some, no doubt, in the communist world, as well. Since 1960, there has arisen a profusion of interest in Marxism among academics, including anthropologists.

Since both cultural materialists and Marxist anthropologists use the ideas of Marx as the basis for their theoretical corpus, it might be well to point out some differences between the two perspectives.

Marxists accuse cultural materialism and cultural ecology of being too mechanical and deterministic. Concentrating on technological and environmental factors, cultural ecology and cultural materialism often proceed with their analysis as if individuals play no part in the sociocultural process. Marxists insist on the unity between base and superstructure. Cultural materialism gives priority to the base and sees studies on the superstructure as a last resort when studies of the base yield no satisfactory explanation.

Another disagreement between Marxist anthropology and cultural materialism revolves around the method of dialectics. Harris (1979b:141–164) sees the dialectical method as directing Marxists away from seeking empirical evidence. By relying on inevitable outcomes of social developments, Harris charges that this leads to ignoring or distorting facts which do not conform to doctrinaire theory. However, Harris makes no distinction between ideological and critical Marxist anthropologists. It is evident from Diamond's discussion of Marxist anthropology that critical Marxist anthropologists are not explicitly bound to a political ideology. One area where cultural materialism and Marxist anthropology do converge is on the question of a value-free science. Marxist anthropologists and cultural materialists reject the notion that anthropology or any social science can be totally value free and not take into consideration that all observers have a particular perspective and a value system, implied or otherwise. Harris says that he does not believe in a value-free social science, but he does believe in an objective one, which faces the world as it is and not as one would like it to be.

In summary, Marxist anthropology and cultural materialism share an orientation which see the base, or infrastructure, of a society as the foundation for social development and social consciousness. The two orientations share the view that anthropologists should seek underlying relationships rather than surface ones based mainly on the way people in a society view their own behavior. The two viewpoints differ with regard to the role of ideology and dialectics as a part of the strategy for social analysis.

Marvin Harris

19. Theoretical Principles of Cultural Materialism: The Struggle for a Science of Culture

Universal Pattern in Cultural Materialist Strategy

The universal structure of sociocultural systems posited by cultural materialism rests on the biological and psychological constants of human nature, and on the distinction between thought and behavior and emics and etics. To begin with, each society must cope with the problems of production—behaviorally satisfying minimal requirements for subsistence; hence there must be an *etic behavioral mode of production*. Second, each society must behaviorally cope with the problem of reproduction—avoiding destructive increases or decreases in population size; hence there must be an *etic behavioral mode of reproduction*. Third, each society must cope with the necessity of maintaining secure and orderly behavioral relationships among its constituent groups and with other societies. In conformity with mundane and practical considerations, cultural materialists see the threat of disorder arising primarily from the economic processes which allocate labor and the material products of labor to individuals and groups. Hence, depending on whether the focus of organization is on domestic groups or the internal and external relationships of the whole society, one may infer the universal existence of *etic behavioral domestic economies* and *etic behavioral political economies*. Finally, given the prominence of human speech acts and the importance of symbolic processes for the human psyche, one can infer the universal recurrence of productive behavior that leads to etic, recreational, sportive, and aesthetic products and services. *Behavioral superstructure* is a convenient label for this universally recurrent etic sector.

In sum, the major etic behavioral categories together with some examples of sociocultural phenomena that fall within each domain are:

301

Mode of Production

The technology and the practices employed for expanding or limiting basic subsistence production, especially the production of food and other forms of energy, given the restrictions and opportunities provided by a specific technology interacting with a specific habitat.

Technology of subsistence
Techno-environmental relationships
Ecosystems
Work patterns

Mode of Reproduction

The technology and the practices employed for expanding, limiting, and maintaining population size.

Demography
Mating patterns
Fertility, natality, mortality
Nurturance of infants
Medical control of demographic patterns
Contraception, abortion, infanticide

Domestic Economy

The organization of reproduction and basic production, exchange, and consumption within camps, houses, apartments, or other domestic settings.

Family structure
Domestic division of labor
Domestic socialization, enculturation, education
Age and sex roles
Domestic discipline, hierarchies, sanctions

Political Economy

The organization of reproduction, production, exchange, and consumption within and between bands, villages, chiefdoms, states, and empires.

Political organization, factions, clubs, associations, corporations
Division of labor, taxation, tribute
Political socialization, enculturation, education
Class, caste, urban, rural hierarchies
Discipline, police/military control
War

Behavioral Superstructure

Art, music, dance, literature, advertising
Rituals
Sports, games, hobbies
Science

I can simplify the above by lumping the modes of production and reproduction together under the rubric *infrastructure;* and by lumping domestic and political economy under the rubric *structure.* This yields a tripar-
tite scheme:

Infrastructure
Structure
Superstructure

However, these rubrics embrace only the etic behavioral components of
sociocultural systems. What about the mental components? Running
roughly parallel to the etic behavioral components are a set of mental
components whose conventional designations are as follows:

Etic Behavioral Components	*Mental and Emic Components*
Infrastructure	Ethnobotany, ethnozoology, subsistence lore, magic, religion, taboos

Etic Behavioral Components	*Mental and Emic Components*
Structure	Kinship, political ideology, ethnic and national ideologies, magic, religion, taboos

Etic superstructure   Symbols, myths, aesthetic
standards and philosophies,
epistemologies, ideologies,
magic, religion, taboos

Rather than distinguish the mental and emic components according to the strength of their relationship to specific etic behavioral components, I shall lump them together and designate them in their entirety as the *mental and emic superstructure*, meaning the conscious and unconscious cognitive goals, categories, rules, plans, values, philosophies, and beliefs about behavior elicited from the participants or inferred by the observer. Four major universal components of sociocultural systems are now before us: the etic behavioral infrastructure, structure, and superstructure, and the mental and emic superstructure.

Language Again

One conspicuous omission from the above scheme is the category "language." It should be clear from the discussion of speech acts that studies of etic components usually involve the identification of speech acts and other communication events. For example, the description of domestic hierarchies by means of requests and compliances to requests shows that such hierarchies involve communication components that can be studied by means of etic operations. Since communication acts, especially speech acts, usually occur in human scenes of even moderate duration, all major etic rubrics are to some degree built up out of the observation of communication events.

Communication, including speech, serves a vital instrumental role in coordinating infrastructural, structural, and superstructural activities; hence it cannot be regarded as belonging exclusively to any one of these divisions. Moreover, communication in the form of speech acts is also the very stuff out of which much of the mental and emic superstructure is built. Hence language per se cannot be viewed as an exclusively infrastructural, structural, or superstructural component, nor as an exclusively behavioral or mental phenomenon.

Another important reason for not including language as a separate component in the universal pattern is that cultural materialism makes no claims concerning the functional relationship between infrastructure and the *major* phonemic and grammatical features of particular families of languages. Cultural materialism does not hold, for example, that particular modes of production and reproduction cause people to speak Indo-European rather than Uto-Aztecan languages. (But cultural idealists have proposed the now discredited theory that Indo-European grammatical categories led to the Industrial Revolution—see Whorf, 1956.)

We are now finally in a position to state the theoretical principles of cultural materialism.

The Major Principles of Cultural Materialism

The kernel of the principles that guide the development of interrelated sets of theories in the strategy of cultural materialism was anticipated by Marx (1970 [1859]:21) in the following words: "The mode of production in material life determines the general character of the social, political, and spiritual processes of life. It is not the consciousness of men that determines their existence, but on the contrary, their social existence determines their consciousness." As stated, this principle was a great advance in human knowledge, surely equivalent in its time to the formulation of the principle of natural selection by Alfred Wallace and Charles Darwin. However, in the context of modern anthropological research, the epistemological ambiguities inherent in the phrase "the mode of production," the neglect of "the mode of reproduction," and the failure to distinguish emics from etics and behavioral from mental impose the need for reformulation.

The cultural materialist version of Marx's great principle is as follows: The etic behavioral modes of production and reproduction probabilistically determine the etic behavioral domestic and political economy, which in turn probabilistically determine the behavioral and mental emic superstructures. For brevity's sake, this principle can be referred to as the principle of infrastructural determinism.

The strategic significance of the principle of infrastructural determinism is that it provides a set of priorities for the formulation and testing of theories and hypotheses about the causes of sociocultural phenomena. Cultural materialists give highest priority to the effort to formulate and test theories in which infrastructural variables are the primary causal factors. Failure to identify such factors in the infrastructure warrants the formulation of theories in which structural variables are tested for causal primacy. Cultural materialists give still less priority to exploring the possibility that the solution to sociocultural puzzles lies primarily within the behavioral superstructure; and finally, theories that bestow causal primacy upon the mental and emic superstructure are to be formulated and tested only as an ultimate recourse when no testable etic behavioral theories can be formulated or when all that have been formulated have been decisively discredited. In other words, cultural materialism asserts the strategic priority of etic and behavioral conditions and processes over emic and mental conditions and processes, and of infrastructural over structural and superstructural conditions and processes; but it does not deny the possibility that emic, mental, superstructural, and structural components may achieve a degree of autonomy from the etic behavioral infrastructure. Rather, it merely postpones and delays that possibility in order to guarantee the fullest exploration of the determining influences exerted by the etic behavioral infrastructure.

Paul J. Magnarella

20. Cultural Materialism and the Problem of Probabilities

The time is ripe . . . to replace the inchoate and unconscious paradigms under whose auspices most anthropologists conduct their research with explicit descriptions of basic objectives, rules, and assumptions. That is why I have written this book. [Harris 1979:26]

Marvin Harris's *Cultural Materialism: The Struggle for a Science of Culture* (1979) will very likely rank as one of the most important anthropology works of the past quarter century. In it Harris calls for the full explication of existing sociocultural research strategies and for the operationalization of their key variables. He also offers a systematic presentation of the theoretical principles of his brand of cultural materialism (C.M.), and challenges all rivals to test their explanatory powers against it. Harris even provides a round of action by taking on sociobiology, dialectical materialism, structuralism, structural marxism, psychological and cognitive idealism, "eclecticism," and "obscurantism."

Rater than enter the skirmish by offering an alternative to C.M., this paper critically examines certain aspects of C.M. as a research strategy. It looks particularly at some of the incongruencies between Harris's stated logic and his logic in use, and offers suggestions for addressing some of the difficulties noted. It is written in a positive spirit, in accordance with Harris's claim that C.M. is an imperfect strategy open to correction and improvement. I begin by briefly summarizing C.M.'s theoretical principles.

The Theoretical Principles of Cultural Materialism

Harris presents C.M. primarily as a scientific research strategy, which he defines as "an explicit set of guidelines pertaining to the epistemological status of the variables to be studied, the kinds of lawful relationships or principles that such variables probably exhibit, and the growing corpus of interrelated theories to which the strategy has thus far given rise" (ibid.: 26).

Harris states that the kernel principle of C.M. was established by Karl Marx when Marx postulated that "the mode of production in material life determines the general character of the social, political, and spiritual processes of life. It is not the consciousness of men that determines their existence, but on the contrary, their social existence determines their consciousness" (quoted in Harris 1979:55). C.M. improves on Marx's original strategy, says Harris, by omitting the Hegelian dialectic mechanisms of system change, and by adding reproductive pressure and ecological variables to the conjunction of material conditions.

Harris says that the universal structure of sociocultural systems rests on the following biopsychological constants:

1. People need to eat and will generally choose diets that offer more rather than fewer calories and proteins and other nutrients.
2. People cannot be totally inactive, but when confronted with a given task, they prefer to carry it out by expanding less rather than more energy.
3. People are highly sexed and generally find reinforcing pleasure from sexual intercourse—more often from heterosexual intercourse.
4. People need love and affection in order to feel secure and happy, and other things being equal, they will act to increase the love and affection which others give them (ibid.: 63).

He justifies this brief list on the basis of its generality, which "is guaranteed by the existence of similar bio-psychological predispositions among most members of the primate order" (ibid.), and on the basis of the adequacy of the theories it helps generate. In addition to the above bio-psychological constants, Harris explains that the universal structure of sociocultural systems rests on the distinction between thought and behavior and emics and etics.

According to C.M., the four major universal components of sociocultural systems and examples of some of their subcomponents are as follows (ibid.: 52-54):

Infrastructure

Mode of production: The technology and practices employed for producing food and other forms of energy, including technology of subsistence, techno-environmental relationships, ecosystems, work patterns, etc.

Mode of reproduction: The technology and practices employed to regulate population size, including demography, mating patterns, fertility, natality, mortality, nurturance of infants, medical control of demographic patterns, contraception, abortion, infanticide, etc.

Structure

Domestic Economy: The organization of reproduction and basic production, exchange and consumption within domestic settings, including family structure, domestic division of labor, domestic enculturation, age and sex roles, domestic discipline, hierarchies, sanctions, etc.

Political Economy: The organization of reproduction, production, exchange, and consumption within and between bands, villages, chiefdoms, states, and empires. It includes political organization, division of labor, taxation, tribute, political enculturation, class, caste, urban and rural hierarchies, discipline, police/military control, war, etc.

Behavioral Superstructure

"Given the prominence of human speech acts and the importance of symbolic processes for the human psyche, one can infer the universal recurrence of productive behavior that leads to etic, recreational, sportive, and aesthetic products . . . [ibid.:52] [including art, music, dance, literature, advertising, rituals), games, science, etc.]

Mental and Emic Superstructure

[According to Harris, these components run] "roughly parallel to the [above] etic behavioral components. . . . Rather than distinguish the mental and emic components according to the strength of their relationship to specific etic behavioral components, I shall lump them together and designate them in their entirety as the *mental and emic superstructure,* meaning the conscious and unconscious cognitive goals, categories, rules, plans, values, philosophies, and beliefs about behavior elicited from the participants or inferred by the observer." [ibid.: 53-54]

These include such phenomena as ethnobotany, religion, kinship, political ideology, myths, philosophies, epistemologies, taboos, and so forth.

The basic principle guiding C.M. strategy is the principle of infrastructural determinism, which holds that "the etic behavioral modes of production and reproduction probabilistically determine the etic behavioral domestic and political economy, which in turn probabilistically determine the behavioral and mental emic superstructures" (ibid.: 55-56). Hence, the principle of infrastructural determinism provides a set of priorities for the formulation and testing of theories about the causes of sociocultural phenomena.

According to Harris, "theories that bestow causal primacy upon the mental and emic superstructure are to be formulated and tested only as an ultimate recourse when no testable etic behavioral theories can be formulated or when all that have been formulated have been decisively discredited" (ibid.: 56). To my knowledge, cultural materialists have never reached this point, partly because their enterprise is comparatively new, partly because their faith in or commitment to their enterprise may prevent them from doing so. Cases where cultural materialists do resort to the emic superstructure for causal explanations would tell us a great deal more about their theories and stated logic then we now know.

The Problem of Probabilities

In his explication of C.M. as a scientific research strategy, Harris appeals to two different kinds of probabilities, both of which create difficulties. The first kind of probability helps structure the principle of infrastructural determinism, which maintains that "the etic behavioral modes of production and reproduction probabilistically determine the etic behavioral domestic and political economy, which in turn probabilistically determine the behavioral and mental emic superstructure (ibid.: 55-56).

On the surface, this may seem simple enough. If we are optimistic about our probabilities, assuming that each link in the infrastructural-structural-etic superstructural-emic superstructural chain has a causal probability of .8, then the ultimate probability would be $(.8)^3$ or .51. However, an actual situation would involve many more links, because infrastructure is not a single-factor prime mover, but rather "a vast conjunction of demographic, technological, economic, and environmental variables" (ibid.: 74). Each of the four universal components of sociocultural systems is loaded with a vast conjunction of subcomponents.

Unfortunately, C.M. as presented thus far lacks operational instructions for identifying the causally decisive connections between or among the large number of subcomponents comprising infrastructure with the large number comprising structure, and so on. The task of making the connections at this point requires more imagination and art than science.

In addition, it is important to point out that the type of probability being called upon here is of a nonfrequency nature. It is not based on empirically derived frequencies, but rather on an unexplicated logic of decision making in the face of the unknown and on psychological factors, one of which may be faith in the research strategy involved. The more strongly one believes in the causal connection of two or more phenomena (such as the veiling of Muslim women and veiling's biopsychological rewards for men [ibid.: 61]), the higher will be the probability assigned to the inferred causal link. The process is more procedural than validating. Hence, we should not expect adherents to rival research strategies to agree often on the magnitude of the causal probabilities connecting sociocultural phenomena.

Most behavioral and mental phenomena are associated with a wide array of infrastructural phenomena. Hence, a cultural materialist has no problem locating associations and calling them causal links. There is a problem in scientifically determining (in a fashion open to independent replication) which associations are crucial. To avoid a situation of "infrastructural eclectics," cultural materialists must devise explicit methodologies for discovering the critical causal links among the vast conjunction of variables and for assessing the causal probabilities of those links. Lacking an explicit basis for quantification, such posited probabilities are not open to rigorous scientific testing and cannot be falsified.[1]

According to Harris, C.M. also depends on frequency probability as a justification for its competitive edge over rival strategies.

Cultural materialism does not deal with unique specifications but with probabilistic causes . . . probabilistic causality exists whenever there is the expectation that theories can never be verified in 100% of all tests. Probabilistic theories are not falsified by negative instances as long as positive instances occur with greater-than-random frequencies. [ibid.: 244]

Harris has also written that "we would today seek to qualify any deterministic statement in probabilistic terms, *given a sufficient number of cases and in the long run*" (1968:244).

In order to translate this stated logic into an appropriate logic-in-use, Harris must define "the long run" in a nontautological, quantitative manner and must define what constitutes comparable sets of cases for purposes of theory testing. Thus far, he has not been clear on either point. Below, I take up the "comparable cases" issue only.

In his book, *Cows, Pigs, Wars and Witches* (1974), Harris offers an ecological or infrastructural deterministic theory to explain the Jewish and Muslim prohibitions on eating pork. It would seem that the other prohibited animals in these two religious systems should constitute an appropriate set of cases to test his theory. However, Harris avoids applying this theory to them. Shortly after mentioning them, he writes that "this is an appropriate moment to deny the claim that all religiously sanctioned food practices have ecological explanations. Taboos also have social functions, such as helping people think of themselves as a distinctive community" (ibid.: 45). If, of the dozens of prohibited animals in Judaism and Islam, Harris's theory can adequately deal with only one, then it lacks the generality which he claims. In this respect, Mary Doug-las's (1966) structural theory is more nomothetic than Harris's because it applies to all the prohibited animals of the book of Leviticus.

Harris's treatments of India's sacred cow and of Aztec cannibalism provide similar examples. The first, Harris treats as a unique member of a cultural complex, which includes other animals regarded as sacred by Hindus; the second Harris refuses to admit to membership of any set of cases. He writes:

> The Aztec are a unique case, and they therefore demand a unique explanation. Sahlins, however, tries to lump the Aztec complex with instances of small-scale pre-state ritual cannibalism in Oceania and elsewhere. He distorts the problem from one of explaining Aztec cannibalism in particular to one of the explaining cannibalism in general. [1979: 335]

Harris's treatment of the Aztec case appears to contradict his own state-ment that "at the heart of the cultural materialist theoretical corpus is a set of theories dealing with . . . the nomothetic process giving rise to a *type* of institution under a set of recurrent conditions" (ibid.: 78). Harris also maintains that C.M. is not concerned with "the unique concatena-tion of historical events leading to the first appearance of a particular thought or practice in a particular geographical spot . . ." (ibid.).

Rather than being nomothetic and explicitly objective, probabilities relating to single, nonrepetitive events are idiographic and subjective. "Such probabilities are measures of the strength of a person's belief concerning the occurrence or nonoccurrence of events, and they are arrived at by mental processes which are generally difficult to recon-struct or evaluate" (Freund 1967:100-101).

The relative frequency concept of probability relies on experience; it is empirical and self-corrective (e.g., an actuarial table). However, since it can only be assigned to a class or series or events, it does not explain any one particular event. Cultural materialists need to be more careful about the specification of such classes and series. For each theoretical problem solution, they should clearly stipulate the criteria by which cases will be admitted to a set considered appropriate for purposes of theory testing on a broad scale. Ideally, the resultant set will be large enough to permit the employment of appropriate statistic techniques for measuring prob-ability. Failing to do this, cultural materialists render their theories un-testable by the very scientific procedures they advocate.

A related problem involves Harris's frequent employment of known frequency distributions as support for "predictions" made on the basis of C.M. principles. For instance, in his attempt to offer a nomothetic C.M. explanation of the origins of hunter-gatherer political organization, Harris writes that historically hunter-gatherers have relied on dispersed wild flora and fauna over whose reproduction they have no control. This necessitated low densities of population. "Hence," Harris claims, "political organization into bands is a predictable theoretical consequence of the infrastructure of paleolithic peoples and of many surviving groups of recent and modern-day hunter-gatherers" (ibid.: 80).

This, of course, is not a prediction supported by post hoc frequencies, but a plausible explanation of what is already known, i.e., that a variety of people who for various reasons have been labeled "hunter-gatherers" tend to have a variety of political organizations that for various reasons have been labeled "bands." Harris's use of known frequencies in this way has aroused some extreme negative criticism. For example, Friedman writes "it is absolutely impossible for Harris's framework to do anything other than restate in a deceptive form that which we already know as a fact. Once again, explanation dissolves into redescription, but the original distribution remains forever unexplained" (1974:465).

I disagree with the first part of Friedman's statement. A central part of the problem is that any nomothetic prediction is impossible if there can be no expectation of a sufficient number of new cases against which to test the prediction. This is the situation with respect to hunter-gatherers and some other types of societies based on traditional technologies. Because a sufficiently large number of such societies have already been studied and have had their sociocultural components categorized in the Human Relations Area File, the distributions of various "traits," such as band organization, are already known. Explanations of the origins or causes of these traits can at best be plausible, not predictive. Predictions of previously unknown distributions where a sufficient number of test cases exist or will exist are, of course, possible and should be the focus of those wishing to demonstrate the nomothetic and predictive powers of C.M.

Harris has laid down a proper challenge for anthropology—the reexamination of research assumptions and their explication. All research strategies, including C.M., can benefit from such critical analysis and disclosure. Without such explications, we will need a special "emics" of C.M., just as we already need a special emics of French Structuralism and of other heavily intuitive research strategies.

Notes

Acknowledgments. I wish to thank Leslie Sue Lieberman for reading and commenting on an earlier version of this paper. She is in no way responsible for the ideas expressed.

1. This criticism parallels the one made by Harris of dialectical materialism ("The Hegelian Monkey"). Harris (1979:145) writes:

The central weakness of dialectical epistemology is the lack of operational instructions for identifying causally decisive "negations." If every event has a negation, then every component in the event also has a negation . . . Which negation is the crucial "contradiction"? . . . Since there are no instructions for identifying the properties or components that are the crucial negations, dialectical relationships can never be falsified.

Maurice Godelier

21. The Scope and Boundaries of Anthropology: Perspectives in Marxist Anthropology

The Scope and Boundaries of Anthropology

Quite bluntly, there exists no principle or theoretical axiom which would give to anthropology an exclusive content, which would provide it with a restricted sphere of research devoted solely to the analysis of specific and exclusive realities.[1] Or rather, there does exist a principle as to the scope of anthropology, but it is primarily negative, based on practical grounds and not on any theoretical necessity. In practice, anthropology was founded when Europe discovered the non-Western world, along with the development of the different forms of Western colonial domination throughout the world, from the first forms of capitalist genesis to twentieth century world imperialism.[2] Little by little, a field of studies was evolved, peopled by all those non-Western societies which the West discovered during its period of world expansion and which historians abandoned to anthropologists when they found they could not substantiate their studies with written sources—which could also have dated buildings and material elements of a historic past—and when these historians saw it was necessary to use direct observation and verbal enquiries.

At the same time, and for the same reasons, entire sections of Western history, ancient and modern, were abandoned to ethnology or rural sociology—fields often confused with each other. Anthropology was handed the study of all aspects of regional or rural life which appeared to be survivals of precapitalist and preindustrialist modes of production and social organisation or which had very old ethnic and cultural characteristics—the Serbian zadruga, the family organisation of the Southern Slavs, Basque and Albanian customs, etc.; realities and facts which appeared rarely in written documents and had therefore been cast aside by historians; these facts required further on-the-spot enquiry, followed by the collection of practices found mostly in folklore and oral traditions and customary laws.[3] Furthermore, there was the evolutionist idea, current in the 19th century, whereby it was held that European customs were survivals, relics of former stages of evolution, which could still be found flourishing and preserved among non-Western peoples; in this way two fields abandoned by historians were taken over by anthropologists. Only they could provide the missing links by studying European customs and their exotic practices (or the other way round if necessary). Thus, they achieved their theoretical task—considered as a duty—of reconstructing a complete and faithful picture of the first stages of mankind, at least from those of its representatives who had left no written record.[4]

But if anthropology grew up from the convergence of two bodies of material ignored or discarded by historians, this does not mean that history itself, as a scientific discipline, was founded on any strict theoretical principles: in fact there is the same absence of any strict basis for the development of history's sphere of enquiry. On the one hand, for a long time it remained totally oriented toward western realities, if only for practical reasons. On the other hand, historians—since most aspects of popular or village life hardly appeared in written documents—had little choice but to view western reality through the testimonies of those people who, in the West as elsewhere, have always used and controlled writing processes, namely the cultured dominant classes and the various state administrations.[5] There is therefore no idea of inferiority or superiority as far as the relations between anthropology and history are concerned; nor is one more or less scientifically objective. All attempts to get them apart from each other or to forget the history of their development or their respective content, can only turn them into fetishist domains, into theoretical fetishes from which scientific enquiry is debarred.

This reminder of how history and anthropology were founded and developed is necessary for understanding two basic points: firstly, the enormous diversity of the modes of production and societies studied by anthropologists, a diversity which includes the last remaining bands of Bushmen hunters-gatherers of the Kalahari desert, farming tribes of New Guinea's high plateaux, agricultural tribes and opium producers, many of them mercenaries in the South-East Asian wars, the castes and sub-castes of India, African kingdoms and traditional Indonesian States, today integrated into modern nations, pre-Columbian empires which have disappeared and which modern ethno-history and archaeology are attempting to interpret, peasant communities of Mexico and Turkey, Macedonia and Wales. This is the vast extent of the realities studied in anthropology. They seem to be societies with little in common, results of the historical development of different economic and social systems; they have adapted at different speeds by processes of change which have gradually eliminated almost all archaic modes of production in favour of other systems, both more dynamic and more encroaching, of which the capitalist one is the most recent and most devastating example. We must not forget that, since the beginning of the Neolithic Age (9000 BC), the economies and societies of hunter-gatherers have been gradually eliminated and driven back into ecological niches which are unsuitable for farming and herding; today they are near to complete extinction.[6] We should also remember that intensive farming methods now compete with the older extensive forms, a fact made necessary by increases in population and the need to produce goods for the market, etc.

Secondly, due to the logic and circumstances of its development, history has become the science and knowledge of civilisation (identified with the West and with some few exceptional cases such as China), and anthropology as the knowledge of barbarians, savages or backward, rural European populations at an inferior stage of civilisation. At the same time, the relationship between anthropology and history became a preferred means of expression; it was also a justification of ideological prejudices held in Western society by the dominant classes and about those societies which gradually fell under their control and exploitation. These included Western, rural populations which today have become an urban, industrial proletariat, or were forced to abandon their former way of life and adopt economic and social forms of organisation which allow them to produce, under the most favourable conditions, for a market where they confront organised competition following the criteria of capitalist economic 'rationality'.

For this reason we can now see why anthropology, among the social sciences, has always been one of the great sources—on the theoretical side—for the production and accumulation of ideological fetishes, ambiguities and—on the practical side—for acute embarrassment. Fetishisation and ambiguity are, moreover, complementary products of an inherent contradiction in the anthropologist's profession; he must dedicate himself to the study and reconstruction of their societies' way of life which his own society is changing or destroying, and he cannot avoid either facilitating or contesting these changes, accepting or denouncing this destruction. This contradiction shows how the anthropologist, paradoxically, is more intimately and more dramatically linked to the contradictions in history's development—that is of living history—than the historian himself who studies the history of things past, a past where the outcome, already known in advance, is less disturbing since we are already beyond it. The anthropologist, on the contrary is inevitably involved and must take part in history; he must justify or criticise changes in those societies he studies and through them justify or criticise his own society which, for the main part, has imposed these changes. For the most part the anthropologist justifies these changes as progress, with some reservations, or denounces them as irremediably decadent. These two attitudes, in fact, presuppose the same ideological postulate; the assumption of the existence of a 'veritable' human essence which is being lost for ever (shades of Rousseau) or which will triumph finally and for ever (an attitude adopted by the philosophers of the enlightenment or English Victorians). Now, no such thing as the 'veritable' essence of man exists, which can be placed in any past, future or present time and which would accord with everyone's ideological involvement or with every epoch; this means the devaluation of societies and periods in human history where one or other of these two choices has not been given a special manifestation, an exceptional moment of the existence of this 'real' essence of man. And since there is no 'real human nature', the anthropologist cannot be given the sublime and privileged task of disclosing this secret. An Amazonian Indian, victim of genocide and the white man's 'peace', is no nearer to the true essence of man than a worker at Renault's or a Vietnamese peasant fighting imperialism. It is not through any normative ideology about the essence of man that we must analyse reasons for a given historical situation and the exploitation of human groups, or that we should suggest a means of ending them or abandoning them to fate. For this, one needs to have not an ideology but rather a true 'science' of history and its needs, which are neither 'natural' nor 'eternal'. History has placed as its starting point, 'man', as the evolution of matter has made him: a new nature not ready-made or prefabricated within Nature.

In order to grow and expand, the 'science' of history—since this is a developing science—demands, among other things, a new understanding and articulation between anthropology and history; a combination which cannot be effected without radical criticism of their ideological content and without a new progression, a hitherto unknown enrichment of their scientific content. We have already had an inkling how Marxism can furnish the means for such a radical criticism, we must now show more precisely how it may also provide a means for a new development of scientific matter in anthropology and history. In our view, the central problem in a science of history is to explain the circumstances behind the appearance of different social structures, articulated in a determined and specific manner with the circumstances of reproduction, for change and for the disappearance of these structures and their articulation. At the same time this is the problem of analysing the specific causality of overlying structures, of their particular role and different meanings in the processes of the appearance, reproduction and disappearance of the various articulated entities, called social relations, which are the content of History and, indeed, Man.

In order to resolve these problems, a method is required which allows an analysis of structures and the discovery of reciprocal laws of compatibility or incompatibility and their concrete, historic effectiveness. Such a method seems to have been elaborated and applied for the first time by Marx in his efforts to analyse the modes of capitalist production and bourgeois society. Marx's answer to the problem of the differential causality of various instances of social life—in other words 'the mode of production of material life conditions, in the last analysis, the process of social, political and intellectual life in general'—seems to us to be the essential hypothesis to be taken up and systematically explored in order to renew the scientific content of history and anthropology.

For a Marxist such a method and general hypothesis act as a *unique* problematic theory as much for the study of so-called 'primitive' societies as for other types of society, ancient or modern; is it not wise for Marxism to use anthropology in its relation to history or vice versa, and do not oppositions of this kind have their place? There is only one science now[7] and this covers both the *comparative* theory of *social* relations and the explanation of *concrete societies* during the irreversible course of history. This science combines history and anthropology, political economy, sociology and psychology and will replace what historians call universal history and what anthropologists try to aim at in their studies of general anthropology.[8]

With this kind of analysis we hope to explain and clear up a fundamental paradox in Marxist anthropology—a complex practice which systematically tries to develop and broaden the analysis of the modes of production in societies left to anthropologists so that they might develop their theories of kinship, politics and religion. This paradox results from the practices whereby Marxists appear as specialists in economic anthropology who, at the same time as they are radically contesting the possibility and rationality of such a narrow specialisation, are also striving to produce conditions for a general renewal of the different fields of anthropological science, reanalysed and reconstructed in their reciprocal interconnections with the structures of the different modes of production—a theory which has to be constructed. This complex theoretical situation determines the critical relationships which the Marxist approach has with anthropology along with two other trends which attempt to create conditions for a general renewal of this scientific discipline, i.e., the neofunctionalism of 'cultural ecology' and the structuralist approach of Claude Lévi-Strauss. Both use a materialistic approach. The first studies societies afresh, considering them as parts of larger wholes, different ecosystems of nature. Like Marxism it pays particular attention to the material bases of society's functioning. The second, again like Marxism, rejects the methods of positivist empiricism and endeavours to take into account the social realities in terms of structure. This dual confrontation permits us to elaborate further the concept of structural causality in economics.

In the meantime let us take a last look at the content and limits of the traditional scope of anthropology—a scope derived from two fragments of human history, those of non-western societies, usually non-literate and colonised by Europe, and rural Europeans with a backward mode of production and precapitalist and preindustrial types of social organisation. This is why the anthropologist is considered a specialist of primitive and peasant societies although there are radical differences. Let us look at the remarkable 'Memorandum' as to the use of the term 'primitive' in anthropology drawn up by Lois Mednick in 1960 and commented on subsequently by Francis Hsu in 1964 in *Current Anthropology.*[9] Two sets of characteristic features, negative and positive, are designated by the term primitive. The negative traits include the absence of positive traits found in Western societies (*non-literate, uncivilised, arrested in development, moneyless, non-industrialised, non-urban, lacking economic specialisation*), or the presence of these traits to a lesser degree (*less civilised, low level of technical achievement, traditional, simple tools, small scale*). In both cases, 'primitive' societies are understood to be 'inferior'. Their positive features, on the other hand, are considered to be those absent from civilised societies (*societies in which social relations are based primarily on kinship, with all-pervasive religion, in which cooperation for common goals is frequent,* etc.). The absence of these traits in modern Western and capitalist societies, far from being interpreted as a sign of inferiority, is more often considered, in prevailing Western ideology, as a further proof of their superiority. However, we are now faced not with ideological phantasms, but with realities. This presents a problem since the anthropologist must now explain what he understands by the dominant role of kinship and the reasons for the appearance or disappearance of this dominance. Anthropologists like Marshall Sahlins, Morton Fried, Eric Wolf, have made great efforts to define primitive and peasant societies, avoiding the usual ideological implications of these terms. For them, primitive societies are those lacking exploiting classes, and organised in social forms, such as bands or tribes. On the other hand, so-called 'peasant' societies are class societies within which the peasantry constitutes an exploited class, dominated economically, politically and culturally by a class which no longer participates directly in production.

In primitive society producers control the means of production, including their own labor, and exchange their own labor and its products for the culturally defined equivalent goods and services of others . . . Peasants, however, are rural cultivators whose surpluses are transferred to a dominant group of rulers that uses the surpluses both to underwrite its own standard of living and to distribute the remainder to groups in society that do not farm but must be fed for their specific goods and services in turn.[10]

Peasants then, do not form a 'society', nor even a 'subsociety', a subculture (in Redfield's terminology), but a 'dominated class', and the nature and role of this class differs according to specific relations of production which make them dependent on the ruling class. One has, therefore, to characterise these relations of production each time and that is exactly what Eric Wolf has tried to do when, following on from Maine, Max Weber and Polanyi, he distinguishes the feudal domain, the prebendal domain (i.e., the domain conceded by a centralised State, as in China or in Persia at the time of the Sassanides, to functionaries who levy a revenue in the name of services rendered to the State) and the 'mercantile' domain which is based upon the private ownership of land for buying or selling on the market. The distinctions are far from corresponding to what Marx called the 'feudal mode of production', the 'Asiatic mode of production' and the 'mode of production founded on private property, independent landowning and the means of production'. Eric Wolf adds the 'administrative domain',[11] of the twentieth century, such as Russian kolkhozes or sovkhozes and Chinese communes or the *ejidos* established after the Mexican revolution, which resemble the 'prebendal domain', but are not organised as institutions to levy ground rent. They constitute forms, directly maintained by the State, of the organisation of agricultural processes. We can easily see that Eric Wolf has taken as his own Marx's analysis of the various precapitalist and capitalist forms of large-scale and small-scale land tenure, but the Marxist concept of 'modes of production', has disappeared along with the theoretical attempt to discover and reconstruct the structures of the mode of production within which the peasantry is an exploited class. This applies even more to George Dalton[12] and especially Daniel Thorner,[13] both of whom have tried to define a concept of 'peasant economy', but succeeded only in assembling a few common determining factors of all societies, where production is based on agriculture and where there is opposition between town and country and submission to an 'organised political power'. Such 'common' factors do not constitute any real undestanding; they are at best, as Marx emphasised, apropos general categories in political economy, abstractions which are not brought up again in the discussion.[14] We must also stress the danger— avoided by Marshall Sahlins, but not Eric Wolf—of presenting producers in classless societies as all equal controllers of the means of production. In 1877, Engels warned against those who hoped to find in earlier communities the exact image of social equality: 'In the oldest primitive communities equality of rights existed at most for members of the community; women, slaves and strangers were excluded from this equality as a matter of course.[15]

The whole of modern ethnology has confirmed this view, providing much information on economic and political inequalities to be found in classless societies—between older and younger siblings, men and women, 'big-men' and commoners,[16] founder lineages and stranger lineages, etc. Faced with the enormity of anthropology's theoretical task, due to the accumulation of valuable information on the multiple forms of social relations, one feels obliged to construct a theory of this multiplicity and to provide the reasons for differential evolution. At the same time, we have the huge problem of the circumstances and gradual changeover from classless societies to class societies, the question of the origins of rank, caste, class, the different types of State. It is also clear that any solution of such problems demands a radical redefinition of methods and concepts in anthropology, and above all, a rigorous elaboration of notions of causality and structural correspondences and—in the Marxist perspective we have defined—the elaboration of the concept of causality in economics, of social norms as engendered by the functioning of a mode of production.

Notes

1. This point is specifically illustrated in a recent anthropological manual published in the United States, *An Introduction to Cultural and Social Anthropology*, The Macmillan Company, New York, 1971, 456 pages, in which the author, Peter B. Hammond, having defined anthropology in vague and general terms as 'the study of man', and having divided, as is usual in American methods, physical, archaeological anthropology from social and cultural anthropology, dedicates his well-written book to the customary study of hunting, agricultural, pastoral, etc., societies, without any analysis of Western societies.

2. Cf. John Howland Rowes's very useful article 'Ethnography and Ethnology in the Sixteenth Century', *The Kroeber Anthropological Papers*, No. 30, 1964,

pp. 1–19, and his address, in April 1963, to the same society, 'The Renaissance Foundations of Anthropology'. Only in 1590 did José de Acosta invent the term 'moral history' to designate what was to be called 'ethnography', i.e., 'the description of customs, rites, ceremonies, laws, government and wars' of Indian peoples. Before him, in 1520, Johann Boem had published a general work comparing the customs of Europe, Asia and Africa, *Omnium gentium mores, leges et ritus ex multis, clarissimis rerum scriptoribus . . . super collectos*. See also a posthumous and incomplete work of J. S. Slotkin, *Readings in Early Anthropology*, Methuen, 1965, and James H. Gunnerson's address 'A Survey of Ethnohistoric sources' to the Kroeber Anthropological Society in 1958.

3.   A. Van Gennep's work illustrates these efforts.

4.   As did the two founders of anthropology, in their own way: E. B. Tylor in 1865 with his *Researches into the Early History of Mankind and the Development of Civilization*, London; and L. Morgan, in 1877, with *Ancient Society*, op. cit.

5.   Cf. Chapter I of Georges Lefebvre's course of lectures at the Sorbonne in 1945–6, re-edited in 1971 by Flammarion under the title *La Naissance de l'historiographie moderne*.

6.   Cf. De Vore and Lee, *Man the Hunter*, Aldine, Prentice-Hall, 1968.

7.   For this new orientation, see the works of J. Le Goff, E. Le Roy-Ladurie, J.-P. Vernant, P. Vidal-Naquet, M. Détienne, N. Wachtel, C. Parain, etc.

8.   M. Godelier, *Rationalité et irrationalité en économie*, op. cit., pp. 230–1.

9.   Sol Tax, 'Primitive Peoples', and Lois Mednick, 'Memorandum on the use of Primitive', *Current Anthropology*, September-November 1960, pp. 441–5; Francis L. Hsu, 'Rethinking the Concept "Primitive"', *Current Anthropology*, Vol. 5, No. 3, June 1964, pp. 169–78.

10. E. Wolf, *Peasants*, Prentice-Hall, 1966, pp. 3, 4.

11. Ibid., pp. 57, 58.

12. George Dalton, 'Peasantries in Anthropology and History', *Current Anthropology*, 1971, and *Traditional Tribal and Peasant Economies: an Introductory Survey of Economic Anthropology*, A. McCaleb Module in Anthropology, Addison-Wesley Publishing House, 1971.

13. Daniel Thorner, 'L'Economie paysanne, concept pour l'histoire économique', *Annales*, May-June, 1964, pp. 417–32.

14. K. Marx, *Introduction to a criticism of Political Economy, in Contribution to a criticism of political economy*, op. cit., p. 153.

15. F. Engels, *Anti-Dühring*, op. cit. p. 117.

16. M. Sahlins, 'Poor Man, Rich Man, Big-Man, Chief: Political Types in Melanesia and Polynesia', *Comparative Studies in Society and History*, vol. v, No. 3, April, 1963, pp. 285–303.

Gerald Berthoud

22. Genetic Epistemology, Marxism, and Anthropology

All science would be superfluous if the *outward appearance* and the *essence* of things directly coincided (Marx 1967 3:817. Italics added).

For a scientific mind, any knowledge is an answer to a question . . . Nothing is *given*. Everything is *constructed* (Bachelard 1967:14. Author's translation, italics added).

The total structuralism sticks to the system of *observable relations* or interactions, . . . whereas the characteristic of a methodical structuralism is to search for the explanation of this system in an *underlying structure* (Piaget 1968:83. Author's translation, italics added).

So far, anthropologists have not been really attracted by an epistemological evaluation of their own field. Such a reflexive and critical attitude toward their own intellectual production is frequently equated with a pure philosophical speculation devoid of any scientific relevance. If science is reduced, as is often the case among anthropologists, to the solid grounds of "facts," any epistemological quest is outside the realm of anthropology. But if epistemology, as it is practiced by Piaget and others, enlightens experimentally the process of scientific knowledge, anthropologists can no longer ignore the instrumentality of this multidisciplinary undertaking which is genetic epistemology.[1]

The main result of genetic epistemology is a condemnation of "apriorism" and empiricism,[2] as two reductive modes of knowledge which, respectively, tend to minimize the part of the object or the subject (see Piaget 1970:5).

The main blunder of any cognitive reductionism is to use an atomistic or associationistic approach, dealing at an elemental level. To insist, as do a great many anthropologists, on the unilateral importance of "facts," and simultaneously to stigmatize any theoretical endeavor as being simple speculation or jargon, is a dangerous tendency toward mediocrity. These very scholars, who quite easily accuse other anthropologists who

have theoretical concern, of "jargonization," are themselves unconsciously victims of this bias by way of an indiscriminate use of concepts
(note, for example, the intersocietal use of "capital," in which its material
and formal meaning are totally confused). In a way, we are flooded with
data which very often are of limited use, precisely because they have
been collected with a principle of classic ethnography in mind: "data
first, theory after." This is an excellent application of an atomistic view.
   Many anthropologists are blinded by the unilateral primacy of facts,
so that they quite naturally neglect to *conceptualize* their ethnographies.
They easily dichotomize between those who are looking for "substance"
(i.e. data) and those who are interested in so-called speculation (i.e.
theory in my own terms). To insist rigidly that "theory must be based on
substance" is to reject the relational preponderance between an object
and a subject in the process of knowledge. To argue that anthropologists
are "more and more involved in theoretical discussions with plays on
words, ideological and intellectual discriminations, precisely because
they do not have any data to work"[3] is to be ignorant of the Piagetian
opposition between "objectivity" and "realism":

There are two ways of being a realist. Or rather, objectivity and realism must be
distinguished. Objectivity consists in knowing so well the thousand intrusions
which derive from it—illusions of the senses, language, points of view, values.
etc.—that, to be allowed to judge, one starts to get free from the obstacles of
oneself. Realism, on the contrary, consists in ignoring the existence of oneself,
and, consequently, in taking one's proper view for immediately objective, and
for absolute (Piaget, in Battro 1966:122. Author's translation).

   The cognitive process in anthropology, as in any similar field, must be
conceptualized as a dialectic, i.e. as a relationship in constant transformations between two active elements, or a subject and an object. It is
therefore easy to see that in this case the emphasis is no longer placed on
the elements themselves but on the relation.[4]
   In short, subject and object are not dissociable. If we reject an atomistic or associationistic way of thinking, the process of knowledge must be
viewed as a specific *mode of production* of the concrete, or, as I am inclined
to call it, a "cognitive dialectic." There is an ever-renewed effort to reach
the *construct*. On the contrary, empiricism, whatever its form and its
degree may be, can be viewed as a *mode of perception* by which we remain
at the level of the *given*. Empiricism is thus an unsuccessful way of
reaching scientific knowledge. By reducing or neglecting the active role
of the "epistemic" subject (e.g. the anthropologist) in any process of
knowledge, the result is an explicative impotence—by remaining at a
pure descriptive level, and holding to an ideological view of the "lived"

level of social phenomena. Empiricism is thus alien to any conceptual construction trying to reach the underlying structural causes explaining any kind of social situation.

This can easily be illustrated by a classical example borrowed from celestial mechanics, which discriminates between apparent and actual or true movement. For the perception of any subject the sun rises and sets. This observation does not go beyond the superficial level of appearance or immediacy. At the explicative level, such a perceptive given is invalidate. Similarly, in the production of knowledge, in fields centered on man, we meet the same kind of paradox.

Anthropologists, like any scientists, cannot escape the epistemological problem of knowledge. From all the preceding statements, it follows that a clear discrimination must be established between *ideology* and *science*. For Piaget, "to know is to *produce* in thought, in a way to reconstitute the mode of production of phenomena" (Battro 1966:35. Author's translation). Such a conception of the cognitive process is exemplified in the works of Marx and in those of his serious followers.

What is at issue here is not the particular knowledge of Marx on a specific object traditionally included in anthropology. The main potentialities of Marxism lie on a methodological basis, whatever the real concrete object of study may be. To accept Marxism as a recipe would be to bury oneself in an ideological pitfall. Any actual scholar, trying to use Marxist problematics, is aware that he has to work according to Marx's method and not to follow him slavishly.

Critical Remarks on the Production of Anthropological Knowledge

From now on I want to stress the relevance of my previous arguments[5] for an evaluation of various anthropological results, as possible explanations[6] of ethnographic material. Although the construction of an actual dialectical anthropology is still in a quite early stage, the joint teaching of genetic epistemology and Marxism allows me not only to appeal to humanistic and ethical views (i.e. non-explicative) about anthropology, but also to formulate radical criticisms, which claim a scientific status, however limited.

According to my present level of knowledge, I will isolate four modalities of empiricism, or *modes of perception*. These four ideological conceptions of knowledge correspond to four forms of reduction based on (1) things, (2) individuals, (3) social groups, and (4) a sociocentric model of reference, implicit or not.

What could be labeled reductionism, in its four occurrences, is equated in my view with rejection of a relational complexity, and its replace-

ment by elements which belong to a directly visible and thence ideological level, quite typical of any empiricism. We do not then *produce*
knowledge, but rather *perceive* ideas and notions. All four of these elements are modalities of a global phenomenal reductionism.

Each of these empiricist reductionisms will be discussed separately,
although it should be understood that one may find a combination of at
least two forms within the intellectual production of a single scholar.

Reifying Reductionism

This ideological approach in the process of anthropological knowledge is adequately represented by what is loosely termed the "substantivist" tendency in economic anthropology.

Following Polanyi, the substantivists emphasize exchange at the expense of production to explain any economic system (Bohannan
1963:231). This restrictive view is particularly obvious in the widely used
ideological notions (here purely descriptive, hence superficial) of
"spheres of exchange," "multicentric economy," and the like (Bohannan
and Bohannan 1968; Bohannan and Dalton 1965; etc.).

The shift from exchange to production brings the question "what is
production?" To oppose a mode of production to a mode of exchange is
far from being a mere reversal of the economic order, in which production is simply taking the place of exchange. It is not the process of
immediate or effective production which is opposed to the "exchange
tendency," but the whole process of production obviously comprising
the three other moments: distribution, exchange, and consumption.
This total repetitive performance is in fact a process of *reproduction*, not
only of things, but also of specific social relations. This process of reproduction is, in its complex totality, a mode of material production (i.e. the
economic level), in which the dominant moment is always the social
relations of production opposing two sets of economic agents in a hierarchical position, according to modalities defined by the specific social
totality (i.e. lineage, feudal, capitalist structures, etc.).

To posit the primacy of exchange tends to view this particular moment
of the total economic process as a set of reified relations among products,
and to forget that these relations are external manifestations (i.e. mere
observation) of specific social relations already defined in production.
Anthropologists, unable to go beyond a deceptive clarity of a perceptive
given, do not realize that "the scientific truth is always paradoxical to the
judgments of daily experience which perceives only the misleading appearance of things" (Marx 1965:508. Author's translation).

Notions like "spheres of exchange," "multicentric economy," "prestige goods," and so on are not erroneous, but they are *percepts*, which

here means terms devoid of any cognitive power, and thus unfit to explain "real-concrete" facts. Indeed such categories, designed primarily to deal with exchange, become highly embarrassing if we accept the postulate that an analysis of exchange itself passes through the explicative mediation of the process of social production. In the pseudotheory of "multicentricity," the material appearance of things is the essential factor to discriminate "spheres of exchange." As long as this approach is applied to a single society, in which a material differentiation of goods is operative to distinguish various spheres, the deficiency of the theory is not manifest. It becomes obvious when a cross-societal analysis is attempted with such a tool (see Berthoud 1969–1970).

To equate economy strictly with a flow of things is a very serious anthropological blunder.[7] Such a reified image prevents one from seeing that economic relations are a specific kind of social relations in which human beings and things are structurally determined.

Unquestionably, terms like "spheres of exchange" and others are simple ethnographic observations. When the ethnographer has seen, or has been told that the exchange of anything for anything is not possible, the task for him is to find out why goods and services are so categorized. To define an economy as "multicentric" tells us nothing about the actual mechanisms of the system, but favors the mere *result* of exchange at the expense of the process (already determined in production). What should be the starting point of a theoretical work is offered as an end product. No knowledge is produced; only an arrangement of perceptive givens is described. We remain in the realm of things: appearance, or determined indices, and essence, or determinant factors, are thus confused at the expense of the latter. From any ethnographic observation we must construct *concepts*, which will explain the presence or absence of a so-called multicentric economy. The objective is thus to reach the specific underlying causes of any mode of exchange.

To view certain total economic processes in terms of "multicentric economy" leads to a consideration of reciprocal and hierarchical relations only among things, and to the neglect of similar relations among economic agents (e.g. youths, elders, women) who produce, exchange, and consume these things. Indeed, as Marx has cogently demonstrated for capital (1965:212), "prestige goods," whether as a discrete material domain or not, are not in essence things but the external expression of a specific distribution peculiar to lineage modes of production, in which juniors and elders, as distinctive sets, and not as individual subjects, are in opposition in the social relations of production.

An arbitrary selection of ethnographic data results from such a theoretical distortion. For instance, the monograph *Tiv economy* does not escape this deficiency. A fair description of the production (technical and social relations), and of the appropriation of so-called prestige goods is lacking. Instead, market places, considered as "peripheral" and "important beyond their economic importance" (Bohannan and Bohannan), fill four chapters of this book, maybe because "market places are among the most obvious and easily observed of Tiv institutions" (1968:146–147).

So far I have brought my criticisms to bear on the internal complexity of what is loosely termed "segmentary" society, or, more ideologically, "stateless" society, with no reference to any change. Indeed, the substantivists, by emphasizing the most immediate level of any ethnographic observation, as their reifying reductionism proves it, are unable to explain various modalities of articulation of modes of production.

Today, the main problem faced by anthropologists, especially when involved in the study of marginal areas by reference to the main centers of capitalistic development, is to conceptualize various forms of articulation of an internationally dominant capitalist mode of production with a certain number of pre- and noncapitalist modes of production.

In this respect, the substantivists, practicing in their own way a well-founded approach to classic anthropology (i.e. typical or representative of established principles in this discipline), evacuate this complexity of the second degree, which is the articulation of modes of production, and the transition from one to the other, by using a comparative-static view. Dalton, one of the main proponents of the substantive view in economic anthropology, reaches an extreme relativistic position when he postulates that two *unrelated* particular theories are needed to explain the so-called primitives and industrial capitalism. Economic anthropology on one side would produce the necessary tool for knowledge of the first, whereas economics would do the same for the second (Dalton 1969). Such a particularistic position is even more obvious when Dalton argues that "conventional economics is relevant to the commercialized sectors of peasant economic *organization* and useful in quantifying economic *performance*" (1969:65), thus implying that economic anthropology is relevant in the "subsistence" sectors. Such a division of labor between economic anthropology and economics would be total denial of the existence of the articulation, and hence a unilateral view unable to explain the complexity of the situation.

"Intersubjectivistic" Reductionism

This form of empiricism presents several modalities of existence in anthropology. Although my critical remarks seem to me to be valid for the technique of network analysis, or the psychologistic[8] approach, "culture and personality," I will concentrate on the economic anthropological tendency known as "formalist."

Any approach whose objective is knowledge of a *social* reality should be particularly cautious about any preferential treatment of individuals, in the various analytical steps. The obvious danger is to leave society as such out of consideration. An idealistic explanation,[9] stipulating that what is in the minds of the people is an essential causative factor, is illusory because it confuses effect with cause. An actual dialectical conception of knowledge implies the acceptance of a logical order of priority, in which the structural determinants or constraints take precedence over individual variations in the form of choices of subjective motivation. To record an individual strategy is not to explain it—unless the structural constraints are taken into account—as being the causative factors in the last instance. Although individuals present behavioral variations, they are determined by their positions in the power structures (economic, political, and ideological), and their actions can be understood only within an analysis of *social relations* which should not be confused with interpersonal or intersubjective relations (Marx 1970:122; or Piaget, in Battro 1966:168).

Such a theoretical position is opposed to a fashionable conception in anthropology which favors, in a psychologistic manner, specific individuals as units of inquiry, and considers them primarily as autonomous centers of decisions. The individual as such is not a free element, even if ideologically he sees his competitive behavior as a pure manifestation of his own ability. In other words, society tends to be an aggregate of subjects *consciously* maximizing and making choices.

Thus, a widespread inclination in economic anthropology tends to accept the explanatory universality of a marginalistic-oriented economic theory, centered on the individuals (see Goldschmidt 1972). There are two ways of viewing economy, at the individual level and at the societal or structural level. However, in an anthropological perspective, social structure should come first.

The society is not a sum of individuals or even a sum of intersubjective relations, as opposed to the superficial view of perception. A unilateral insistence upon the explanatory value of interindividual transactions[10] illustrates the individualistic bias[11] found in "formalist" economic anthropology.

Both the classical economists and the marginalists favor the abstraction of the "autonomous individual," by accepting the invariance of human nature throughout time and space. This view was reinforced when the capitalist mode of production became more and more dominant in its liberal form of free trade, and does not seem to have been seriously questioned in the succeeding era of monopoly capital and the increasing intervention of the state.

Consequently, a projection in economic anthropology of the marginalists' positions, regarding their definitional level of economy, raises serious problems. Such an emphasis on individual behavior, and not on the social whole, impairs any methodological and theoretical transference, particularly if we accept the holistic tendency of anthropology, or at least its intentional refusal to neglect the societal context of any studied element. I must insist here that, contrary to a formalist view (see, for example, Schneider 1970:1–3), a societal approach does not mean at all a communalistic view marked by an absence of dissent and conflict. Indeed, a dialectical analysis is a way of isolating conceptually relevant contradictions within any social whole.

Other considerations, such as the possible universal validity of master concepts (e.g. capital, profit, wage labor, etc.), question the adoption of a marginalist practice by economic anthropologists, if they are really interested in a cross-societal or comparative approach.

If the substantivists are unable theoretically to account for the specific articulations of various modes of production with capitalism, the formalists are not more successful. However, with them we are moving within a homogeneous field in which everything acquires a capitalist nature (with variations in degree). An extreme, even caricatured, view of such a position is exemplified by Pospisil's "discovery" of "primitive capitalism" among the Kapauku of New Guinea (1963).

This human naturalization is a sociocentric view which seriously impedes any progress in the development of a genuine anthropological discipline, based on a search for similarities, but also differences, among past and present existing social forms.

Any particular concept, like capital for instance, denotes *socially* and *historically* determined ties among agents, of specific social relations. It does not denote a thing, relations among things, or pure intersubjective ties, according to a point of view peculiar to the ideological discourse of the subjects. The concept, capital, must not be reified by being defined materially, and thus confused with any means of production. Marx, quite cogently, stigmatizes this so-called universal validity of capital:

The means and objects of labor . . . play their part in any labor process, at all times and in any case. If then I give them the name of capital . . . I shall have demonstrated that the existence of capital is, for human production, an eternal law of nature and that a Kirghiz who, with a knife stolen from Russians, cuts rushes to make his boat is as much a capitalist as Mr. Rothschild. I could as well demonstrate that Greeks and Romans celebrated the Lord's Supper, because they drank wine and ate bread, and that Turks sprinkle themselves daily with

Catholic holy water, because they wash themselves every day (Marx 1968:425. Author's translation).

Pseudostructural Reductionism

This third version of empiricism is found in the classic structural-functional approach of British social anthropology, emphasizing group-ings[12] as part of an empirical social structure. This widespread approach shows how anthropology fails to distinguish conceptually between two hierarchical levels of any process of knowledge. Indeed, a structure, to have the explanatory power of directly observable, or *given* sociocultural phenomena, must be *constructed*. An actual cognitive process rejects any form of skin-deep structuralism. Such an ideological approach (i.e. remaining at the "lived" level) is radically opposed to any kind of conceptual structuralism (i.e. produced and not simply perceived). Social structure, in the empiricist conception of structuralism, is equated to clearly visible structures. In other words, there seem to exist immediately perceivable centers revealing as such the structural order (i.e. economic, juridico-political, and ideological); whereas for a conceptual structuralism, any real-concrete element, individual, or group, is the locus of multiple and complex structural determinations. A concrete social relation may very well depend on the three structural domains, according to a combination in dominance. Fundamentally, this methodological structuralism, in the words of Piaget (1968:83), contradicts what Fortes claims to be scientific: "a good theoretical model—that is, one which tells us . . . how the social system works—must correspond to the pragmatic model" (1969:82). With such a high degree of concordance between the constructed "model" of the anthropologist and the "lived model" of the subjects, ideology as a social domain is blurred, with the exception of directly visible sectors such as the religious one.

In contradistinction to an idealistic approach, emphasizing the effective role of consciousness as a causative factor of sociocultural phenomena, it is interesting to find again a consensual view, betweeen Marx and Piaget, on the explicative relevance of a certain kind of materialism. Thus, in a review of *Capital* in a Russian journal (1872) and quoted by Marx with approval, we can read:

Marx treats the social movement as a process of natural history, governed by laws not only independent of human will, consciousness and intelligence, but rather, on the contrary, determining that will, consciousness, and intelligence. . . . If in the history of civilisation the conscious elements plays a part so subordinate, then it is self-evident that a critical inquiry whose subject matter is civilisation, can, less than anything else, have for its basis any form of, or any result of, consciousness. That is to say, that not the idea, but the material phenomen alone can serve as its starting point (quoted in Marx 1967:18).

For Piaget:

The merit of K. Marx is . . . to have distinguished in the social phenomena an effective infrastructure and a superstructure oscillating between symbolism and adequate taking of conscience, in the same direction . . . in which psychology is obliged to distinguish between actual behavior and conscience The social superstructure is then dependent on infrastructure as the conscience may be a self-apology, a symbolic transposition or an inadequate reflection of behavior, or as it succeeds in extending this one in the form of interiorized actions and operations developing real action; so the social superstructure will oscillate between ideology and science (1967:76–77. Author's translation).

When ideology is not viewed as the specific domain of any social reality, which must be isolated by analytical work and articulated with other sectors, one reaches a theoretical dead end, by creating categories lacking any internal homogeneity. The categories become an analytical jumble, in which economic, juridical, political, and ideological dimensions are confused. The following assertion seems to me to be a very good illustration of such a mixture: "The realm of custom, belief, and social organization, which we descriptively identify by the overall rubric of kinship, is both *analytically* distinguishable and *empirically* specifiable as a relatively discrete domain of social structure" (Fortes 1969:250. Emphasis added).

On the contrary, for a methodological structuralism, the ideological discourse on the subjects (representations, ideas, value judgments) gives only a distorted knowledge of their own social structure. This ideological discourse constitutes the superficial level of the structure and only a theoretical work allows one to reach the deep and hidden level of social relations.

Another essential shortcoming of the structural-functional approach is its refusal to consider a diachronic perspective (see Fortes 1969:308–309). This negligence precludes an explanation of structural transformations, dissolutions, transitions, and other forms of change in African societies and others in precolonial times, under the impact of the colonial (political dominance) and postcolonial (economic dominance) periods. A classic structural-functional approach is in fact static and consensual by overemphasizing the jural domain (normative aspect of social relations).

To go beyond the idealistic view of so many ethnographies, which describe various ethnic groups as if they have never known any exogenous intervention or, at best, as if they had been quite marginally affected, we strongly need a theory of the passage from one social form to another, or more broadly, a theory of the articulation of modes of production (including the corresponding superstructural domains).

The genetic-structural approach of Piaget—for whom genesis and structure are not antinomic but two elements of the same methodological whole and of Marxism with important concepts such as mode of production, reproduction, etc.—could help anthropologists to build a theory of diachrony. To refuse to construct the dialectical anthropology, articulating genesis and structure and insisting on processes, is to relegate this discipline to a purely gratuitous intellectual exercise, passionately looking for archaic and exotic customs. The result is that it is useless in reference to relevant problems of the present time: imperialism, neocolonialism, "underdevelopment," poverty, minorities, etc.

"Continuistic" Reductionism

My adopted conception of knowledge is based on a fundamental principle of discontinuity. Suffice it to mention here the concept of mode of production with all its concomitants, which establishes a periodication of specific historical processes, ideologically perceived as continuous developments.

On the contrary, a "continuistic" approach has been flourishing in anthropology for some time. The idea of an absolute continuum—differing in degree only—has been, and still is, widely used for all kinds of typologies (see, for example, Frankenburg 1966:130). The following pairs of opposition are widespread examples of the theoretical level reached by anthropology in the intrasocietal and intersocietal comparisons: traditional-modern, rural-urban, primitive-civilized, simple-complex, marketless-market, stateless-state, classless-class.

With such a comparative-static view, the theoretical problem of the passage is excluded and replaced by an empiricist vision, in which only gradual changes occur. Moreover with the refusal to admit conceptually (as opposed to descriptively) the passage by leaps from one social mode to another, one element of the dichotomy is simply defined, implicitly (but sometimes explicitly), in relation to the other one. A rural situation, a "simple" society, a "primitive" people, or a traditional organization are referred to their counterparts at the other end of the continuum, and appear very often as no more than their rigorous negatives.

Such results pertain to sociocentrism, and thus, in the last analysis, to the egocentrism[13] of the anthropologist, who is unable to get rid of a model of reference, which is, in effect, his own actual experience.

Within a dialectical anthropological approach, the pairs "rural-urban," "simple-complex" are poor abstractions of the real-concrete. They are pure *givens*, whereas they should be *constructs* resulting from an effective cognitive production. Indeed, these terms are external and thus quite superficial expressions of specific modes of production, which are at various stages of their history, and which could be scientifically known only by a theoretical work, and not by intuitive abstractions.

"Continuistic" perspectives are a recurrent theme in economic and political anthropology. They are examples of a widely used practice of defining so-called segmentary societies and even more differentiated ones in negative terms.

A quick look at the literature of anthropology shows a profusion of terms and categories simply denoting the absence of something that is specific to our own social system. Capitalistic institutions are accepted as standards established for the evaluation of any society. If we push such reasoning to its very end, we could define any "segmentary" society without recourse to painstaking theoretical work. Taking as models our familiar institutions—market, state, court, and church—we could then specify a "segmentary" society, in a strict sense, as a nonentity:[14] a marketless, stateless, courtless, and churchless society. The first two terms, at least, belong integrally to the conceptual equipment of anthropologists.

Negative terms tell us what a social system is not, but not what it is intrinsically. To explain an empirical reality with negations is to elevate them to constituent elements of an actual theoretical discourse. There is no question that in our present state of knowledge, certain negative and privative terms are useful, although they should always be considered as ideological devices.

Ultimately it is imperative to explain any social system in positive terms, which does not mean by use of a particularistic approach, such as the recourse to the ideology of the folk view. What we need is a general problematic that places all social forms on an equal basis, rather than favoring one to the extent of using it as an explicit or implicit pattern for the others. Such problematics, on a highly abstract theoretical level, is a prerequisite for the formulation of particular theories, producing the knowledge of specific real-concrete situations.

Conclusion

This paper has been centered on a discussion of scientific production versus ideological perception. A critical anthropology, based on a theoretical radicalism, appears to be an absolute necessity for a diagnosis of any social situation, and for any practical intervention, if spontaneity in knowledge and action is to be avoided.

My four recorded modalities of ideological reductionism, although quite sketchy, reveal that many contemporary anthropologists, unlike Marx, have not yet realized their Copernican revolution and are entangled in a Ptolemaic system—by mistaking a subjective perception for a scientific explanation.

Unquestionably, the mode of anthropological knowledge proposed here is only in embryo for various reasons. Suffice it to mention the strong traditional submission in social anthropology to a certain idealistic strategy through Durkheimian thought, and the disproportionate emphasis by Marxists upon analyses of the mode of capitalist production, at the expense of its articulation with other modes of production, and of a knowledge of these modes as such.

Anthropologists should seriously consider, with adequate epistemological criteria to appraise their own scientific production, if, for instance, they want to take up the challenge of such a sentential statement:

As a mass, the intellectuals . . . have not really recognized, or have refused to recognize, the unprecedented scope of Marx's scientific discovery, which they have condemned and despised, and which they distort when they do discuss it. *With a few exceptions*, they are still "dabbling" in political economy, sociology, ethnology, anthropology, social psychology, etc., etc. . . , even today, *100 years after Capital*, just as some Aristotelian physicists were "dabbling" in physics, *50 years after* Galileo. Their "theories" are ideological anachronisms, rejuvenated with a large dose of intellectual subtleties and ultra-modern mathematical techniques (Althusser 1970:6–7).

Undoubtedly, those anthropologists deeply rooted in the security of empiricism, and advocating, with an unshakable belief, the unilateral importance of fact, see nothing but pure jargon in any attempt to conceptualize these facts within a theoretical discourse. The mystifying power of empiricism is so strong that it can only be successfully eliminated through scientific knowledge concerning the role of the social scientist in the cognitive process. An appeal to genetic epistemology, viewed as a multidisciplinary field and not as a philosophical quest, is essential to avoid the insidious attraction of ideology. Empiricists claim that we should stick close to the "lived," or actual experience, whereas genetic epistemology and scientific Marxism teach us to depart from it, if we want to reach the intelligibility of any real-concrete phenomena.

Notes

1. Genetic epistemology, as developed by Piaget, has an unquestionable scientific status: "he [Piaget] tackled questions so far exclusively philosophical with a resolutely empirical manner and constituted epistemology as a science separated from philosophy but linked with all the human sciences" (quoted in Piaget 1970:6–7. Author's translation).

2. Here empiricism corresponds to the French term *empiriste* and not *empirique*. It is viewed as "a disregarding of scientific methods and relying solely on experience," or "the theory that sensory experience is the only source of knowledge" (*Webster's New World dictionary*).

3. Remarks heard at the symposium "New directions in formal economic anthropology: operationalizing the method," held at the meeting of the American Anthropological Association in New York City (November, 1971).

4. "It is in the logic of constructivism, of the relational method and of any dialectic synthesizing in an effective way structures and geneses, to result sooner or later in an unseparable interaction between the contributions of the subject and those of the object in the mechanism, not only of knowledge in general but of all the particular varieties of scientific knowledge" (Piaget 1967:1243. Author's translation).

5. Readers who would like to study thoroughly the process of cognitive production, presented here in a quite epitomized version, could delve into the works of Piaget (1967, 1968, 1970, 1972).

6. The search for causation, the attempt to reach an explicative level, is not an obvious anthropological objective today. The position of Kroeber (around 1925) on that matter, as it is reported by J. Steward, cannot be considered as obsolete: "I asked Kroeber when I would learn about explanations, upon which he said in some horror, 'What do you mean? I deal with cultural phenomena, not explanations'." (Personal letter to M. Harris, 1969).

7. "The economist abstracts from the untidy complexities of social life a neat world of commodities. It is the behavior of commodities, not the behavior of men which is the prime focus of interest in economic studies. The economist's world is a world of prices, quantities, interest rates, production, consumption, income, etc." (Boulding 1956:82).

8. "Psychologistic" is opposed to psychological. Such an opposition is parallel to that of "empiricist—empirical." According to Piaget, "the individualistic touch of numerous sociologies" is predominantly generated by "an insufficient psychology" (1965:29).

9. At the other extreme, a fatalistic explanation, or a pure mechanistic materialism, which is a deeply rooted belief in oversimplistic principles wrongly attributed to Marx, is also to be condemned. Marx and his serious followers (i.e. those who keep a critical point of view) have never accepted viewer history, on the one hand, without alternative, and individuals, on the other, as simple cogs in a machine.

10. A large consensus among economic anthropologists illustrates this preferential attitude toward transactions. Firth, for instance, asserts: "The significance of the economy is seen to lie in the *transactions* of which it is composed and therefore in the quality of *relationships* which these transactions create, express, sustain, and modify. . . . The emphasis of interest is still upon the transaction rather than upon the production" (1967:4).

11.   Piaget points out the universal existence in science of a "reductionistic tendency, striving to bring down the superior to the inferior or the complex to the simple," and one of the examples he gives is the reduction of "society to combinations of elementary individual characters" (1967:1228).

12.   See Harris' statement: "Domestic groupings and political groupings constitute the most important categories of social structure" (1971:145).

13.   Analogous with the Piagetian concept of egocentrism, sociocentrism may be viewed as "the confusion of ego and the other," or an "inability to differentiate between other and ego" (Piaget, in Battro 1966:57).

14.   The following quotation is a rigorous illustration of a definition as a nonentity: "The Tiv have a *subsistence* economy whose chief charactristics are households that are capable of self-sufficiency, *lack* of external trade, *lack* of general-purpose money, *lack* of a market for the factors of production [i.e. land and labor], market places that are used for 'economic' exchange of certain goods but not others and have '*non*-economic' uses, and a *lack* of a general profit incentive, coupled with egalitarianism and *lack* of a concept of ownership in the Western sense" (Schneider 1969:931. Emphasis added).

Herbert Applebaum

VIII

Economic Anthropology and the Anthropology of Work

Introduction

Economic anthropology has, as its general aim, the study and analysis of different economic systems in various cultures and societies. Economic anthropology uses comparative analysis in order to develop a general theory of economic functions, growth, and development. It derives its data from the work of ethnographers who record data which describes how people produce, distribute, and consume the economic goods and services required for their survival and cultural needs.

Economic anthropology specifically studies subsistence patterns, divisions of labor, trading relationships, systems of land ownership, work and food taboos, concepts of reciprocity and exchange, systems of taxation, tribute and gifts, redistribution systems, and the general relationship of economic institutions to other social institutions in various cultures and societies. The study of economics is as old as anthropology itself, since there can be no understanding of a society without an examination of its economic system. For a discussion of the nature of economic systems, see Chapter 24 by George Dalton.

One of the first anthropologists to deal with economics was Bronislaw Malinowski (1935). He demonstrated that horticulture among the Trobriand Islanders was not only an economic system but that it related to every aspect of Trobriand society. It was part of its value and prestige system and intertwined with its kinship organization. Malinowski analyzed the *kula* ring, created by the Trobriand Islanders and other island chains over a vast area of the western Pacific. It was a trading system which involved the exchange of prestige goods, subsistence items and tools (1922). In particular, the kula ring highlighted the importance of reciprocity as a

339

concept that related to prestige and survival among primitive societies. Economic anthropology later developed as a distinct specialization within anthropology. Some of the significant studies in economic anthropology were Raymond Firth's description of the Maori economy (1929) and that of the Tikopia (1939); A. I. Richard's work on land, labor, and diet among the Bemba of Northern Rhodesia (1939); Karl Polanyi's influential theoretical work on trade and market systems (1957); and Melville Herskovits who summed up the state of the subfield in his book, *Economic Anthropology* (1952). There were many others, too numerous to mention.

In 1981, the Society for Economic Anthropology was formed in the United States. Almost from its inception, economic anthropology produced a debate, sometimes quite furious, between those identified as "formalists" and those identified as "substantivists."

The formalists define economic theory as the classic formula that it is concerned with the allocation of scarce resources to meet unlimited needs. In this overall view, formalists believe that economic actors make rational decisions to maximize the allocation of resources and time to meet their demands. Maximizing, rationalizing behavior is viewed by formalists as a universal tendency that can be applied to every type of society.

Substantivists believe that peasant and primitive economies are so fundamentally different from industrial ones that the same concepts cannot be applied to both. Substantivists believe that the cultural substance of a society is a crucial determinant of the organizational rules for producing and distributing goods and services. Substantivists see a qualitative difference between an industrial society which distributes its goods through commodities and money and a small-scale society where producers consume their own produce and exchange through barter and gifts. Substantivists believe that concepts such as "capital" have no meaning in primitive societies.

Peasant societies, as units of analysis, occupy an important middle position. They are often part of national or world market systems in having to sell their products for cash. At the same time they use a nonindustrial type of technology and often rely upon growing their own subsistence goods for their survival.

The substantivist-formalist debate was over the view that social considerations predominated in economic exchanges in primitive economies (substantivist) or that humans everywhere were alike in their pursuit of self-interest by maximizing and manipulating economic relationships and goods. Karl Polanyi argued that exchange in primitive economies was embedded in the reciprocities of kinship. In the economies of centralized, nonindustrial economies—archaic states, tribal chieftainships, headmen village societies—services and goods were collected by the centralized authority and then redistributed to the population in the form of community functions, maintenance of the temple, storage of goods for bad times, organizations of feasts, and so on. Polanyi called these economies redistributive. He considered market economies to be unique to the industrial transformation of Europe during the eighteenth and nineteenth centuries. A market economy was an integrated system unifying local markets into a national and international network. It was a system relying upon the universal use of money, credit, and financial institutions, the use of capital for the employment of machines and labor with the aim of making profit as the reason for production. The heart of the substantivist approach on which Polanyi wished to rest his case was the empirical investigation of institutionalized connections between humans and their environment by which a steady flow of goods for satisfying wants would be assured.

As Voget (1975:649) explains, the formalists wished to reduce all humans to an economic archetype, the maximizing everyman. They saw this behavior as a universal of human nature. In this sense they were in line with similar trends in Lévi-Strauss structuralism and cognitive anthropology, trends in anthropology which also sought to use universal aspects of human nature as the basis for their theoretical orientation. The view of humans as maximizers also converged with a growing view in anthropology, namely, that human beings were positive actors in the social and cultural process. We saw previously how this was a growing trend among cultural ecologists. This view was also congruent with game theory (Von Neumann and Morgenstern 1944) which fostered the idea that human beings universally operated in situations regulated by rules, that these situations offered a choice of goals and strategies, and that the situations contained solutions that were rational. Schneider (a formalist), in criticizing Dalton (a substantivist), said that the two sides should stop arguing, that both approaches could exist side by side. Schneider declared that the substantivist approach was historical and the formalist was scientific.

In the two chapters on economic anthropology, there is one by a formalist (Salisbury) and one by a substantivist (Dalton).

The unusually rapid social changes taking place after the second World War could not help but have an effect on economic anthropologists and their choice of problems to research. Peasant communities, with their unique position between traditional and modern societies, came to occupy a special place in studies by economic anthropologists. The study of traditional and modernizing economies provided insights into the structures and functions of economies in the process of change.

Primitive and peasant economies undergoing social transformation offered opportunities to test the role and importance of different societal institutions for change and stability. Economic and technical aid was given by industrialized nations, both directly and through the United Nations, thus implying that economic factors were crucial to developing nations in their intent to modernize. Technology was thought to be more important than value systems as a catalyst for change.

In the 1950s and 1960s, many anthropologists were convinced that economic forces, in combination with class and nationalist aspirations, were about to transform traditional, static cultures. Theories of cultural integration and structural-functionalism were deemed inadequate to meet new conditions. There was also a strong desire on the part of anthropologists to offer more than just objective science to the struggle against economic backwardness and poverty in the former colonial nations where many of them were doing their field work (Valentine 1968; Frank 1970). The new analysis by economic anthropologists (Nash 1966; Ribeiro 1968; Wolf 1959; Geertz 1966; Worsley 1970) stressed a small-scale economy's involvement in the larger regional, national, and international system of economic arrangements. Though many wished to take control of their own lives and livelihood, they were faced with former systems of social and political control over the means of production, the land, and the financial institutions. No matter how much the individual peasant or craftsman wished to maximize his resources, he was faced with institutional arrangements blocking his access to the chance to maximize. It was clear that political arrangements, value systems, prestige systems, and kinship organization were all interrelated to the economic realities of these changing societies. These other social institutions would have to be taken into account in any analysis, as well as any program for change.

The perspective on change in these emergent societies did not always confirm the determinism of the economic variable. Both economic and noneconomic factors were relevant to the process of change, and their relative importance and sequence varied according to the particular society or culture. In some cases, it was necessary first to win over human minds and ideas before social change could proceed and new economic arrangements introduced. According to Foster (1967:314–320), changes in the social order involving political and religious orientations preceded by nearly a generation any serious input of economic factors, before changes were effected in Tzintzuntzan, Mexico.

Focus on exchange by anthropologists accentuated differences between the kin-obligated, reciprocity-minded systems of preindustrial economies and the impersonal, profit-oriented economies of industrial society. This distinction received support from Karl Polanyi, who stressed differences between the reciprocal (primitive societies), redistributive (centralized, empire societies and chieftainships), and market (industrial) types of exchange systems. The position that primitive economics and industrial economics were worlds apart prevailed until the post–World War II period.

Economic anthropology received its greatest impetus during the post–World War II period, when many participated in aid programs associated with the goal of transforming former colonial nations into modern states through economic and sociopolitical change. In the course of their work in these programs, economic anthropologists became convinced that economic incentives and motivations, as such, were more important than had previously been recognized. The theory that, despite kinship obligations, people in preindustrial societies operated in ways similar to economic actors in industrial cultures led to the spirited formalist-substantivist debate. The formalists felt that they recognized even among preindustrial people the impulse for economic maximization and proceeded to challenge those who maintained that primitive economics was embedded in the kinship system. The debate reached its climax during the sixties, with neither side able to claim a clear victory. However, the debate did broaden the perspective regarding kin-based societies. It was realized that there was greater variability within primitive economics than previously believed.

Participation in aid programs also convinced many economic anthropologists that political and ideological factors, along with economic ones, were of great significance in the struggle for change among formerly underprivileged cultures. Evidence on postwar economic developments suggested that ideological changes frequently preceded political ones, which, in turn, provided the social context for the introduction of economic and technological innovations. Traditional sociopolitical and economic institutions were not swept away easily, and various forms of mixed modern-traditional social organizations continued to function in these new nations. It gave support to those who believed that the groundwork for social change must first take place in the minds of people and stressed the importance of shared values, meanings, and expectations as part of the evolution of social process.

The *anthropology of work*, as a formal subdiscipline within the broad field of anthropology, is a very recent phenomenon. The Society for the Anthropology of Work was formed in 1981. Previously, the study of work by anthropologists was called "industrial ethnology," and before that, in the 1930s, "industrial anthropology." There is also a group within the anthropological enterprise which identifies itself as "business anthropologists." And finally, the Society for Applied Anthropology, as part of its orientation of applying anthropological research to the solution of social problems, touches upon the subject of work.

Work is a pervasive activity which influences and affects all individuals and social phenomena. Work is a part of the human condition and is a main determinant in the way societies are organized and function. It affects kinship and family structure, moral and religious teachings, the legal system, and property and human rights. Work is a crucial factor in a person's self-esteem and the way people are viewed by others. Control over other people's work has been a motivator of wars, revolutions, political upheavals, strikes, and social conflict. Work has also been a focal point for human cooperation, from the simple reciprocity of exchanging a helping hand to the cooperative effort of achievement of grand projects which involve science, engineering, art, and physical labor. Through work, human beings express their physical capacities, manual dexterity, and mental faculties.

The study of work today takes place within an ideological framework which sees work as a "social problem." Increasingly, there is talk of the social malaise of work and the lack of work satisfaction (Terkel 1971; Blauner 1966). In the past, the study of work was undertaken by industrial engineers and psychologists concerned with management goals to create a work force that would accept, unquestioningly, corporate objectives. However, despite all the years of scientific management, human relations in industry programs, and job redesign methods, worker dissatisfaction and alienation persists. The fall in productivity, the rise in absenteeism, and the growing use of drugs and alcohol in the workplace are all signs that something has gone wrong with work in modern society. Corporations and governments are continually sponsoring new studies about work and the workplace as it relates to various problems. All this signals that work, taken for granted as a norm in society, needs greater attention and study.

What has changed from the past? One change is that people work less and have more leisure. From this, some draw the conclusion that work is not as improtant as it was in the past and that one goal should be to reduce work to a bare minimum. David Macarov (1980) states that we are now on the verge of a "leisure society." In this society, people would measure self-esteem, not by their work, but by the nature of their leisure. Work would be an interruption of leisure, rather than the other way around. Everyone could be as creative as they wished during their leisure hours, since society would be productive enough to satisfy the material needs of its inhabitants with a minimum of work. Given the billions of work-years needed to feed and clothe the world, to provide health and social services, to build roads, bridges, waste treatment plants, and to clean up our air and water, the promise of a leisure society with work in a subordinate position seems utopian and far in the future.

Macarov's ideal seems attractive. But aside from the practical consideration that nature does not give up her bounty without humans performing work, there are social scientists and philosophers who believe that work is a fundamental condition of human existence (Heilbroner 1970; Thompson 1978; Udy 1970; Harris 1975; Arendt 1959; Heidegger 1971). Indeed, as work has been a creative force in the past, it can be likewise in the present and future. It is not necessary to have a split between work and leisure. Studies have shown that those who lack satisfaction in work often lack the imagination and resources to have satisfaction in their leisure (Kasl 1974).

Another change making work a "problem" is the loss in industrial cultures of aspects of work associated with small-scale societies. What are some of these aspects? With the mechanization of work, there is a reduction in creative and manual dexterity in work. Work performed in nonmarket societies, though arduous, calls upon a person's total faculties. The !Kung San hunter is a totally involved individual in the enterprise of gaining his livelihood. He must cooperate with others; he must prepare and care for his tools; he shares his catch with his community and gains prestige and status through his act of giving. The same is true for the herder, the farmer, the blacksmith, the potter, the fisherman, the gardener, the weaver, and the shoemaker in small-scale society. They control their work and its product. In industrial cultures, control over work is relinquished by the overwhelming majority of people. There is now a search to bring more autonomy in the workplace, to give workers greater control over the work process, and to motivate workers to become more involved with their work.

The social environment of the workplace, which ties workers to machines or computers, has left office and factory workers with a sense of isolation. Bureaucratization has made work so impersonal that social relations on the job are superficial and without affect. Work in the past and in nonmarket cultures features comradeship and community. Social scientists, including anthropologists, are now studying ways to rekindle such features in the workplace. The study of crafts and apprenticeship programs (Gamst 1986) by anthropologists, with a view of how to apply the experiences of preindustrial contexts to industrial situations, is one example of the effort to recapture aspects of work lost through modernization.

Another attribute of work relinquished with the transition from nonmarket to market society is the informal nature of work in the past. In its place, there is a hierarchical system which creates levels of authority and supervision. The personalized, face-to-face character of work, with direct exchange of services and cooperative effort, fosters satisfaction and solidarity in the workplace. Replaced by an impersonal hierarchy, people lose interest in the goals of the work because the work is not of their own making nor under their control. When human beings are not motivated, they do not work well.

These three factors, and no doubt others, have contributed to a sense of insecurity about work and the need to provide people who work with more control over the social, organizational, and environmental conditions in their workplaces. There is a sense of malaise about work and a desire for change. Anthropologists conducting research on work can contribute to making work and workplaces sources of self-esteem, more satisfying, and a means for mental and manual creativity.

Anthropologists bring to the study of work the same methods used in other ethnographic research, participant observation and, sometimes, full participant and observer (Applebaum 1981; Gamst 1980; Pilcher 1972). Sociologists use the same methods (Roy 1952; Burawoy 1974).

The study of work in nonindustrial societies was touched upon, but was not a focus, in many earlier ethnographic accounts (Applebaum 1984; Herskovits 1952). The significant characteristic of work in nonmarket cultures is the embeddedness of work in the total fabric of such societies. Unlike industrial cultures, where work is a separate sphere from the family, religion, and politics, in nonindustrial cultures work is an integral part of the rearing of children, magical and religious rites, the prestige status of chiefs, and the obligations of kinship groups. It is also an integral part of the value systems of these small-scale cultures, just as it is in industrial ones. Work and family, for a hunter or gatherer, are part of a continuum of roles and status. In industrial cultures, a person can have one life and status at home and a separate one at work. One can be totally subordinate at work and totally dominant in the home. This separation of life into sharply delineated spheres is not present in small-scale societies.

Anthropologists stress the importance of capturing the "native" or "folk" concepts of the world around them. The folk concept of work in industrial society sees work as associated with "paid work" and the notion of "occupations." Work is viewed in opposition to leisure. Work is something one is forced to do; leisure is something one does in "free time." The folk concept of work is changing as the occupational structure of industrial society changes. The folk concept of work is also changing in response to the increase in leisure and to the increase in the percentage of the population that has income without working for wages (social security, welfare, pensions). There is also the "hidden economy," where people work outside the market. This, too, is modifying the folk concept of work. There is, in addition, an increasing awareness that the value of work in the home, which is unpaid, should be counted as part of the national product of a society. This kind of work is also becoming part of the folk concept of work.

In an informal study of Norwegian folk concepts of work, Cato Wadel (1979:370) suggests the following folk concepts of work:

1. Work involves the use of physical energy.
2. Work is routine and repetitive.
3. Work takes place in a special place, outside the home.
4. Work takes place at certain times—"working hours."
5. Work is necessary—to earn the means for survival.
6. Work is done mostly for other people—employers.
7. Work is oriented toward a product or service.
8. Work implies a limitation of choice. At work one does as one is told.

An addition to Wadel's folk concept of work outlined above is the norm or moral aspect of the work "ethic." People in industrial and other types of cultures believe it is "right" or "a good thing" to work. One's standing in the community is, to a large extent, based on one's work—the type of work one does and manner in which work is performed. Trobriand Islanders display their yams in a special house as a public demonstration of their gardening skills. Master plumbers are given state certification as a demonstration of their knowledge of their craft. Dentists, doctors, and lawyers must fulfill certain educational requirements and pass certification tests before they can practice their occupational profession. The work ethic still retains a strong philosophical hold on the values of people in all cultures. It is for this very reason that so much alarm has been expressed over the expressed lack of satisfaction with work as reflected in surveys and interviews in industrial societies (Terkel 1971; Herzberg 1957; Blauner 1966).

Informal work is a domain largely unexplored and ripe for anthropological analysis. It involves the informal work experiences within society. Frederick C. Gamst discusses this type of work (1981: 59–61) by pointing out that,

under the customery in-depth and long-term research of ethnology, our folk-formal distinctions should dissolve between: time of gainful work and of other similar activity, monetarily paid work and unpaid work-like activity, workplace and nonworkplace.

Volitional work, which is uncompensated but widespread, is essential to societal well-being and preservation. Within the categories of volitional work, Gamst includes do-it-yourself work, community service work, expressive work (art, music, literature), and political work.

Summarizing, the anthropology of work involves a cross-cultural comparison in order to isolate the universal aspects of work. This can lead to identification of significant units of study, with the goal of developing an anthropological theory about work. The anthropology of work has also concentrated on researching the folk concept of work, so as to provide a survey and sequence of the evolution and transformation in the way work is perceived in various types of societies. For an example of the search for universals, the reader can find Applebaum's chapter in this section. for an example of the folk concept of work, Cato Wadel's research is a good illustration (1979).

Richard F. Salisbury

23. Economic Anthropology

In 1965, a review of economic anthropology, authored by Manning Nash, appeared in the *Biennial Review of Anthropology*. Since then there have been articles by Dalton (1967) and Firth (1967) and a book by LeClair & Schneider (1968) summarizing earlier materials. LeClaire & Schneider also repesented the arguments in the major 1967 controversy between substantivists and formalists. A concluding assessment by the present author (1968) saw the controversy as fruitless. Substantive analyses of production and distribution were clearly needed to permit formal analysis of choices made in the allocation of resources. Neither approach alone could predict behavior in new situations. Classifying economies in substantivist terms yielded a static (or comparatively static) analysis portraying economies either as in equilibrium or as between two equilibrium states. Assuming that all decisions aim at maximizing production (as formalists were accused of doing), or are "rational," ignores the vast literature on societies pursuing multiple cultural goals. The two approaches need to be fused—we need total models of economic systems in which decision making, particularly by the peasant or the worker, is seen as producing the observed behavior and its derived model. Barth (1967) formulated an essentially similar view of social change as requiring both systemic studies and studies of personal decisions which generated the systems.

Since 1967, unfortunately, the debate has continued, but materials presented in strictly dialectic terms of substantivist-formalist have yielded little of value. A spate of articles, for example, on the characteristics of "primitive money" have not added to the analyses widely current by the mid-1950s. They have illustrated their writers' lack of knowledge of the existing literature. Melitz (1970) has also shown how the idea that specialized forms of exchange items are found only in "primitive" societies is based on a naive analysis of what happens in "modern" societies.

The present review ignores these post-mortem spasms of the substantivist-formalist debate and considers three fields of economic anthropology where "live" work has been published since 1967: marketing, production, and entrepreneurial organization. The concern is with an issue implicit in Barth's formulation and explicit in my own—how far the decision processes at the local level "generate" the system, and how far they reflect a "system" determined otherwise. As of 1972 the most salient theoretical controversy lies between environmental determinists and those who see anthropology as showing human culture and knowledge as influencing behavior. The final section reviews relations between economic anthropology and cultural ecology.

Marketing

Studies of peasant marketing of foodstuffs and export commodities had by 1967 developed models of total systems and of individual decision making by marketers. The model was of a multilevel network of markets and traders through which individually produced goods were bulked and transported, while bulk imports of manufactures were distributed into progressively smaller units. Individual decision analysis had focused on the fixing of prices, how long-term relationships between sellers and buyers entered into price decisions, and the degree of rationality of sellers in calculating their returns.

Two systemic models have dominated the last 5 years—(*a*) the ecological analysis of how regional complementarity determines market systems, and (*b*) the central place and location theory model, derived ultimately from von Thünen's work of the early nineteenth century, where relative positions of towns and their hinterlands are seen as determinant.

Harding (1967) makes an ecological analysis of long-distance canoe trading in the Vitiaz Strait area of New Guinea, which long antedated pacification and political unification of the area, and which has only modified itself with modern changes in crops and the availability of manufactured goods. Ecological complementarity is highly significant, as between island communities, coastal communities, and inland communities, and between communities with seasonal shortages occurring at different periods of the year. Trading permits more local specialization in such areas, which are not forced to diversify production inefficiently in order to avoid the risks of periodic scarcity. Yet the specialization between independent communities appeared almost to have gone to extremes—coastal villages possessed no large canoes for long-distance voyaging, while pigs and dogs were seen as almost exclusively products of particular regions. Several islands with relatively large populations and very little land depended almost entirely on middleman profits, coupled with the manufacture of pots or carving (often from materials obtained in trade).

Societal differentiation has thus proceeded far beyond the level indicated by ecological variation. In explaining how such specialization originally began, how the existing differentiation is maintained, and how it is spread to new communities, Harding (1967) considers the relationship between trading and "big-man" feast giving. He shows how specific trading voyages are motivated by the desire of individuals to accumulate goods required for gaining prestige within their own village by giving feasts. It is their activity which establishes the network of trade friendships, and it is their innovativeness which introduces new commodities into the system. They amplify the system, but at a rate regulated by their limited arena for prestige competition. The system needed ecological diversity to emerge, but its present form is conditioned by the decisions of the traders.

Other studies of non-monetary trade show how social and cultural factors constrain decisions within the potential provided by ecological diversity. Salisbury (1969), for example, shows how New Britain women's attitude to trade has affected their response to the advent of expatriate buyers. Traditional trade using shell money as a medium of exchange was based on a system of nominally "fixed equivalent" prices. Exchanges were viewed as "delayed barter" with no profit involved, although varying size of units did make for limited price variation. This attitude did cushion against immense price variations for highly seasonal products when long-term supplies were balanced. Relatively few local producers have entered the market to supply expatriates with vegetables, since this is risky and no ideology has been developed to eliminate risk. By contrast an open, price-fixing market has developed to supply the steady demand for nonseasonal foodstuffs by native peri-urban villages.

The central place and location theory model of geographers has only recently been adopted by anthropologists. Studies by Hill & Smith (1972) for Africa, Smith (1972) for Latin America, and Brookfield (1969) for the Pacific provide good introductions to the field. General consideration of the costs of transportation, for example, suggest that on a flat plain they will be at a minimum if second-order centers for trading rural products against manufacturers are symmetrically grouped around major centers, and that the location of third-order centers are symmetrically located with respect to the other centers. Mapping shows that if modifications are made for situations that do not correspond to the ideal "flat plain," most systems of marketing centers fit this spatial model reasonably well.

Can one then conclude that transportation costs are the deciding factor in determining the location of centers and where market women sell their goods? Smith (1972) points out how the costs of land, the problems of maintaining highly productive but not full-time occupations, and difficulties of maintaining cultural identity, in fact, account for the distribution of Guatemalan Indian rural marketing centers. Hodder & Hassall (1971) reanalyze the location of Roman administrative centers in England, which were located, not in relation to the distribution of the indigenous population, but arbitrarily on a hexagonal grid to facilitate regional administration. It was only subsequently that many of them developed into market centers. Brookfield (1969), while starting from a spatial model, explicitly looks for cultural factors that might explain deviations from such a model. He finds "fixed unit" selling general in the Pacific. There is also a general nonemergence of the predicted zones of close-in market gardening and distant pastoralism. Instead, areas distant from markets specialize in export crops. The limited purchasing of indigenous foodstuffs by expatriates in administrative towns, as in New Britain, would explain the former, and visiting of towns by islanders only to obtain cash would explain the latter. Whether or not towns play the role indicated by the spatial model is clearly affected by cultural factors.

Gladwin & Gladwin (1971) explicitly study the criteria used by market women in Ghana to decide where to sell fish. It is common knowledge (at least among the 27 successful traders interviewed) that there is a threshold size of catch below which it is unprofitable to transport fish to inland markets, as the spatial model would predict. But they also share knowledge of how to estimate profits when the state of demand is unknown (and risky) but the supply is known. They can estimate profits for about 12 conditions of supply and risk, and it is these estimates which determine where they go. It would be a Herculean task to determine what the risks are objectively, even for a social scientist. Folk categories, in fact, determine behavior, and it is relatively simple to produce a *descriptive* model predicting actual behavior from a knowledge of folk categories.

The fact that folk models of relatively simple nature have analogs in complex formal mathematical terms has been recognized in other areas. Norvell & Thompson (1968) show that Jamaican higglers talking in terms of catering to preferred customers, specializing in particular commodities, and expecting partners to share unexpected losses are making the calculations that would be appropriate in a formal mathematical model derived from the assumption that there exists only a limited number of "places" in any market, and sellers must aim to preserve their "place." Plattner (1969) uses multiple regression analyses and production functions to show what factors affect the profits of itinerant peddlers in Southern Mexico. It turns out that amount of capital, number of mules used, and the route traveled do affect profits, but quite as important is what traders explicitly say is significant—"knowing one's customers." Plattner shows that an indirect measure of knowledge—the mark-up a trader can get away with—correlates most highly with profits.

Production

Before 1967 the charge was often made that anthropologists ignored production and concentrated on exchange. While this has never been true regarding food production, a group including Sahlins and headed by Godelier and Meillassoux, based in Paris, has deliberately attempted to develop a general neo-Marxian model of "primitive production." They try to correct errors due to Marx' nineteenth century view of primitive society, while confirming that in subsistence economies "what counts is that there should be enough to satisfy the needs."

Sahlins (1971) follows Chayanov's 1927 analysis of peasant production in Czarist Russia, asserting that in domestic production a worker works as hard as is needed to supply his dependents rather than to maximize returns. Sahlins calls this "intensity of production" and sees how far it follows Chayanov's rule in societies with available data— Gwembe Tonga, Tiv, Kapauku, Moala, and Maring. The first approximately follows the rule, but the last three show many deviant households which produce far more than they need for their dependents. In Moala the chiefly lineages produce a surplus, in Kapauku the "big men" do, while in Maring the scatter is extreme. The societies that reveal most scatter are those producing most above the bare-subsistence level, accumulating the surplus as capital in the form of animals to be "converted ultimately into social and political benefits." The strongest incentive there for intensive production would appear to be the desire for prestige or political power.

Sahlins seems to consider Chayanov's rule still valid, if one ignores overproducers. His data show, however, that in two of the five societies the correlation between intensity and the ratio of dependents is opposite to that predicted by Chayanov, and in no case is the correlation significant—it is "inappropriate as a predictive relationship" (1971: p. 45). Nonetheless, even if the results are unclear, they point to a new way to study production incentives in non-monetary societies.

Godelier's (1971) most available work for anglophones analyzes the determinants of exchange rates for locally produced salt in a part of New Guinea only recently brought into a monetary economy. He tests the Marxian hypothesis that rates would parallel labor costs, and finds this untrue. The Baruya group, who monopolize salt production, obtain a twofold advantage in exchanges. To explain why they do not charge more, why allies may use salt-producing facilities without payment, and why "big men" give salt to widows and orphans, Godelier says that "in trade between groups what counts is reciprocal satisfaction of their needs rather than an even balance in their labor output" (1971: p. 69). They are not motivated by profit.

Again the conclusion is naive. One break in the Baruya monopoly brought bitter rage and a cut in the rate of one third; the cost of travel clearly forces distant groups to accept even worse rates; the high valuation of leisure by the Baruya (who work only one-third of the time) indicates production restriction; "big men" build political support by calculated generosity. The observed level of production and pricing seems nicely adjusted to labor costs, transport costs, monopoly advantages, and political power. Baruya appear typically human, using very familiar techniques of economic decision making.

Polly Hill (1970) has continued to advocate studies of non-Western but monetary production. Her case studies of enterprises in Ghana, which use minimal amounts of cash and operate predominantly on kin relationships, show how each factor of production—land, capital in various forms, and organization—may be provided by different parties. Returns are allocated independently to each factor (or party), using traditional forms. Thus, for example, Accra is supplied with milk from cows owned by Ga-speakers, herded by Fulani, in kraals owned by other Ga. Expansion has followed economic opportunity without requiring employer-employee relationships. Ewe fishermen form "companies" for seasonal seine fishing, but divide the catch to reward the factors. After the workers are fed and the net repaired, the balance is divided into fixed "shares" for the workers, the net owner, the bos'n, and the entrepreneur who recruited and "staked" the company. It would appear that such co-adventurer systems of "shares" in fishing are worldwide. The Ewe companies are distinctively formal, even excluding the wives of crew men who must "buy" fish to market it, and distinctively they separate the role of net-owner and crew member. Nonfishermen among the Ewe accumulate wealth by building up numbers of nets owned. As her title shows, Polly Hill focuses on the variant ways in which capital accumulations are built up in non-monetary forms.

Fishing has been the subject of studies in Norway, Newfoundland, and Great Britain, stimulated in part by Barth's (1966) work on crew organization. Anderson & Wade (1972) collect several of these to show how technological change has had variable effects on "traditional" production organizations. Nineteenth century inshore fishing from small out-ports used simple gear and small boats, adapted to family production units. The same unit accumulated, controlled, and maintained capital, recruited and trained labor, and handed down knowledge. Fission in crews and steady expansion in numbers of boats were part of the family growth cycle. Engines, deep-water seines, and electronic fish-finding equipment require organizational changes. Crews are larger, the costly capital items cannot be maintained by crew members alone, skippers need greater knowledge to be effective, and the risk of loss from faulty or poorly informed decisions is greater. The diversity of needed skills places a premium on stable crews, yet the previous organization for ensuring stability no longer works.

Very different patterns emerge in each locality in reaction to local ecology, local culture, local government measures, and the structure of international trade. Skipper-crew relations vary with the uncertainty of catches; divisions into "shares" and relations between owners and skippers vary with technology; family and affinal patterns vary with the types of information flow and mobility of crews. The overall economy of world fishing may be sharply constrained by the marine food chain and by factory-ship technology, but within this global constraint, a multitude of variables of local origin condition what is actually produced.

Entrepreneurship

The local social condition that has most commonly been seen in the past as distinguishing "modern" societies from "traditional" ones has been the relative prevalence of "entrepreneurship." A number of articles dealing with "entrepreneurship" as a psychological trait have appeared during the past 5 years. Also, there has been an increasing amount of literature indicating that "enterprise" is by no means uncommon in "traditional" societies, even if it takes forms other than the creation of private businesses oriented to monetary profit making.

The studies of Hill (1970) and Salisbury (1969) have already been mentioned. Other examples include: Forman's (1970) study of raft fishermen in Brazil; studies of village manufacturers in Mexico by Acheson (1972), M. Belshaw (1967), and Cook (1970); the report by Owens (1971) on engineering firms near Calcutta; Marris & Somerset (1971) on Tanzanian businessmen; Pitt's (1970) study of tradition and progress in Samoa; Finney's (1968) and Strathern's (1972) work on entrepreneurs in New Guinea.

Two major themes emerge. The first, from the work of Finney, Salisbury, and Pitt, and from the earlier work of Cyril Belshaw and Geertz, is the way in which entrepreneurs can be motivated, not by goals of personal profit but by desires to advance the status of a larger grouping.

Where this is the case, the operation of their enterprise takes a distinctive form. The larger grouping combines to contribute capital for the enterprise, whether this is in the form of land, or labor to make buildings or improvements to land, or directly as cash. Local labor is used where possible, and generation of employment is seen as an aim of the enterprise. Returns may be made to the grouping in the form of intangible services, while accounting may aim either at increasing the capital assets of the group or at making no profits but providing services at low cost.

The second theme, stemming from Benedict's (1968) seminal article, is that these small-scale enterprises are analyzable in much the same terms as "family firms" have been in the economic literature. Implicit in this approach is the idea that they present an intermediary "stage" between individual enterprise and the emergence of large "universalistic" firms (either state or corporately owned). The previously mentioned studies of Ewe and North Atlantic fishermen clearly fit in this field, and indicate the problems that such firms face in acquiring capital stocks, in keeping up wide-ranging relationships with outsiders, and in mobilizing labor when special skills are required.

Owens (1971) in particular considers the limits on the expansion of such firms by studying the households of engineering entrepreneurs near Calcutta. Entrepreneurs live in larger, more joint-family households than do non-entrepreneurs. Capital stocks can be kept together if the owning "co-parsenary" group lives together (is "commmensal"), and a major skill of entrepreneurs is averting domestic splits which would lower stocks below critical levels. However, this is significant only when the firm is expanding and joint living can reduce consumption expenditures to permit capital accumulation. Joint-family households, and by implication family firms, become less useful when the firm has exceeded a critical size. At this point joint living is raising the level of too many nonproductive family members, while reducing too greatly the level of the entrepreneur. At that point he usually builds his own single-family house.

Entrepreneurship, in short, is an ability that is extremely widely dispersed and is by no means restricted to monetary societies or to joint stock corporations. The innovative organizer of production or distribution must adapt his enterprise to his existing social milieu as much as to existing nonsocial resources, and what one empirically finds is a wide range of organization forms. Barth's (1963, 1967) specification of two social niches to which entrepreneurs can adapt their enterprises—the brokerage niche when two cultural groups are in interaction, and the conversion niche, when a society formally has discrete spheres of exchange—does not exhaust the adaptations made by entrepreneurs.

Ecology and Economics

Two themes—the environmental constraints on human behavior to which humans adapt, and the way in which human decisions are made voluntarily in awareness of many of the constraints but also arbitrarily— have run through the listing of studies in earlier sections. In the past 5 years these themes have tended to become phrased as polar positions in a debate between "cultural ecologists" and "formalist" anthropologists. The intensification of work on the resources available to nonindustrial societies has added much to our understanding of the relationship at particular points in time of cultural behavior to available resources. Extremists have phrased this either in a variant of Radcliffe-Brownian functionalism, as though *every* element of behavior contributed to the maintenance of the society in its existing form, or as *adaptation* to the surrounding natural resources which are taken as given. It is a short step from such a stance to one of environmental determinism.

In the opposite direction the great increase in mathematical analysis and model building that has characterized recent formalist economic anthropology has led to a tendency to argue that models built on the basis of decisions taken at the individual level "explain" the operation of the system as a whole. This concentration on individual decision making has been reinforced even more by the development of techniques for eliciting statements from the decision makers themselves about how they make decisions. Models so based seem psychologically real, at the same time that they appear to fulfil Barth's (1967) demand for being "generative."

The possibility for sterile debate is clearly present, if polarization proceeds further. What may be ignored is the degree of complementarity between the analyses. For the social scientist, as for people who live in a particular environment, "natural" resources do exist and do provide a basis for human action; these resources need closer study. But they provide only part of the total resources available. Other humans, and their potentialities for being organized in different ways, provide yet another resource base, while knowledge, technology, and human cognition provide other resources. Davis (1972) has shown, for example, that over £ 140 million of consumer expenditure in the United Kingdom is generated by the gift economy.

However, it is impossible to segregate the role of "resources" and the role of individual decisions in determining the level of an economy *at one point in time*. All one can do is to say that all elements are interrelated. Where, over time, a group of humans has remained in the same environment but has changed in terms of knowledge and/or organization, and has also changed its level of production, one can begin to analyze the effects of environment and decisions. So, too, when different groups of humans inhabit the same environment but utilize it differently, one can analyze what factors are determinant and what are permissive.

Among the New Guinea Tolai, Salisbury (1969) has documented how four major technological innovations have been adopted over the hundred years since first European contact. The initial adoption of each innovation occurred because individuals were able to evaluate the likely gains from it in terms of their existing knowledge and experience. Though each innovation was in fact not used most efficiently at its initial introduction, a political ferment at the time of introduction permitted this inefficiency to pass unnoticed, and enabled modifications in social organization to occur later and permit the new technology to operate efficiently. Existing economic concepts and the structure of local opportunity costs are crucial determinants of whether change will occur, as is the existence of political ferment. Many alternative levels of production are possible with the same availability of natural resources, but which level in fact occurs is determined by local decisions about technology and sociopolitical organization. Especially is this true when a local political unit can maintain its autonomy in decision making and can prevent itself becoming entirely dependent on decisions made by larger political units which are unaware of the local structure of opportunity costs.

John Bennett (1969) analyzes the ways in which four distinct cultural groups—Hutterites, Indians, farmers, and ranchers—utilize the same available resources on the Saskatchewan prairies. Each uses a different *adaptive strategy,* or pattern of resource use, chosen by evaluating the costs of alternative uses so as to meet goals set in cultural and human terms. Over time, however, a selective process occurs whereby a strategy that can be viewed as adaptive to the resources available at one time actually changes the total resources. Hutterite communal living, for example, that was initially valued as a means of preserving a way of life, creates large family units which can smooth out the riskiness of prairies farming, while by giving children less schooling it lowers the opportunity costs of labor. They flourish far from towns, while small farmers have developed close relationships with town centers and depend on collective political action to avoid risks, and so have tended to gather around towns. What has thus happened is an *adaptive process* (1969: p. 14) in which new specializations of society and microenvironments occur at the initiation of cultural factors.

In short, provided one is aware of the need for analyzing the other side of the equation, it does not matter whether one starts by studying human strategies and organizations or by looking at resources. The economic anthropologist who focuses on how humans cognize their resources, organize for their use, and plan for the long term can profitably and equitably share the field with the cultural ecologist. The more sophisticated he becomes in developing a decision model of behavior, the more likely his work is to mesh with the work of a cultural ecologist.

George Dalton

24. Theoretical Issues in Economic Anthropology

A good theoretical framework for economic anthropology should be clear about the similarities and differences between our own economy and primitive and peasant economies, about the relevance of conventional economics to economic anthropology, and it should contain an explicit statement of the matters to be analyzed, economic anthropology, for example:

Table 24–1

1. Socio-Economic Structure: Primitive Economics,   before modernization   Peasant Economics   before modernization
2. Economic Performance: Primitive Economies,   before modernization   Peasant Economies,   before modernization
3. Socio-economic Organization and Economic Performance in Primitive and Peasant Economies Compared to Industrial Capitalism.
4. Processes and Problems of Socio-Economic Change, Growth, and Development in Primitive and Peasant Communities.

I shall discuss some of the conceptual categories I think most useful in economic anthropology, indicate the questions they help answer, and the leading ideas they are associated with (see Tables 24–2 and 24–3). In doing so I hope to make several points: to show how much at the beginnings of theoretical analysis we are in economic anthropology; to show what a wide variety of structures, processes and problems are dealt with in the subject; and to suggest lines of analysis and conceptual categories that seem promising.

Table 24–2

Economies of Record and Social Science Sub-fields

| | Economies of Record | | | | |
| | Small-scale | | National | | |
	Primitive and Peasant, Change and Development	Utopian [a]	19th-Century Capitalism	Welfare State and Fascism	Communist
Economic Anthropology	Economic Anthropology Applied Anthropology	European and American History	Economic History	Comparative Economic Systems	Soviet Economy [b]
Pre-industrial Economic and Social History (e.g., Europe and Asia)	Economic Development		History of Economic Thought	Economic History	Comparative Economic Systems
	Economic History		Classical and Neoclassical Economic Theory	Modern Economic Theory	
			Industrial Sociology	Industrial Sociology	Industrial Sociology

[a] The important connections between the structure of traditional, primitive economies and utopian communities (Noyes 1870; Nordhoff 1961; Bestor 1950; Bishop 1950) have never been systematically analyzed. Both kinds are small-scale economies whose internal organization is of nonmarket sorts; where production processes—especially land tenure, work organization, and produce allocation—express social relationships. It is this feature which makes writers like Nyerere (1964) and Senghor (1964) assert that traditional African communities had a "socialist" ethos.

[b] Soviet economy has developed as a separate field of specialization within economics; see Nove (1962).

Economic Anthropology as Part of Comparative Economy

The economies of direct interest to anthropologists are the large set of subsistence and peasant communities in Africa, Asia, Latin America, Oceania, and the Middle East. The focus of analytical interest is either their traditional structure and performance before serious Western incursion (Malinowski 1922; 1935), or matters relating to socioeconomic change and development (Epstein 1962; Firth 1966). In either case there is an important literature outside of anthropology. The fields within economics which provide complementary information are pre-industrial economic history (Postan 1966; Takizawa 1927), comparative economic systems (Grossman 1967; Myrdal 1960; Carr 1951), and the institutional literature of economic development (Lewis 1955; Myrdal 1957; Hagen 1962; Adelman and Morris 1967).

Economic anthropology is best done within a framework of comparative economic systems which draws on all economies of record. The analysis of pre-industrial, developed, and developing economies is now scattered in various branches of economics, history, sociology, and anthropology, all of which contribute information of use to the broad range of topics considered in economic anthropology (see Table 24–2).

What Is an Economic "System"?

One of the many semantic difficulties in economic anthropology is that the word "economy" (like the words "society" and "culture") has no size dimension attached to it. We can speak of the economy of a hunting band comprising a few dozen persons or the economy of Communist China comprising several hundred million.

Whatever the size of the economy it will have several features in common, three of which are of special interest.

(1) Whether the human group is called band, tribe, village, or nation, and whether its economy is called primitive, peasant, capitalist, or communist, it consists of people with recognized social and cultural affinities—kinship, religion, language, neighborhood—expressed in some sort of shared community or social life. This means that two kinds of goods and specialist services[1] must be provided for use within the community (however defined): food and other material requisites of *physical* existence, and goods and services for religion, defense, settlement of dispute, rites of passage, and other aspects of *social* and community life. The acquisition or production of material items and specialist services necessary for physical and social existence are never left to chance because neither individuals nor communities can survive without them. It is for this reason that it is useful to regard all communities or societies as

having economic systems. The world "system" refers to structured arrangements and rules which assure that material goods and specialist services are provided in repetitive fashion. One task of economic anthropology is to spell out these rules and systematic arrangements for that set of societies of interest to anthropologists.

(2) A second similarity among economies is that they all make use of some form(s) of natural resources (land, waterways, minerals), human co-operation (division of labor), and technology (tools, and knowledge of production or acquisition processes). Each of these features is structured: the use of tools, natural resources, and division of labor require social rules—specified rights and obligations. The rules for the acquisition, use, and transfer of rights to land, we call "land tenure"; the rules specifying human co-operation in production processes, we call "division of labor" or "work organization"; if tools and technical knowledge are important in any economy there will be rules for their acquisition, use, and transfer.

Two general points emerge: when the rules specifying rights of acquisition or usage of any of these components of an economy are expressions of kinship or political relationships, the economic component is inextricably related to the social, and we have a *socio-economic* practice, institution, or process. Aboriginal land tenure in parts of Africa are obvious examples, where land is acquired through kinship right or tribal affiliation (Bohannan 1954; Schapera and Goodwin 1937:157). Secondly, what we call economic organization is the set of rules in force through which natural resources, human co-operation, and technology are brought together to provide material items and specialist services in sustained and repetitive fashion.

(3) A third similarity is the incorporation of superficially similar devices and practices in economies differently organized. Economies as different as the U.S., the U.S.S.R., and the Tiv make use of market places, foreign trade, monetary objects, and devices for measuring and record-keeping.

In summary, all societies of record—those studied by anthropologists, historians, and economists—have structured arrangements to provide the material means of individual and community life. It is these structured rules that we call an economic system. Economic anthropology delineates these social rules of economy by describing activities and folkviews, and analyzing transactional processes and relationships in the small-scale, pre-industrial communities of the underdeveloped world, and makes comparisons between primitive, peasant, and industrialized developed economies. So too with comparing the components and sectors of economy: the allocation of land and labor, the organization of work, the disposition of produce, and the organization and usage of forms of money, markets, and external trade. There are very important differences among economies, however, differences in structure and in performance, and much valuable analysis lies in contrasting them.

Table 24 – 3

Analytical Categories and Relevant Questions
in Economic Anthropology

I. TRADITIONAL ECONOMIES

    A. *Types*
        1. Primitive, without centralized polity (Tiv).
        2. Primitive, with centralized polity: chiefdoms, kingdoms, empires (Nupe, Bantu, Inca).
        3. Peasant (Malay fishermen, Latin American peasantries).

    B. *Analytical Distinctions*
        1. Organization
           a. Size of economy; technology; natural resource endowment.
           b. Transactional modes (reciprocity, redistribution, market-exchange; dominant-integrative modes distinguished from petty modes).
           c. Production processes: (1) allocation of resources (land acquisition, use, and transfer; labor acquisition and use; the acquisition, use and transfer of tools and equipment); (2) work organization; (3) disposition of produce; (4) specialist services and their remuneration.
           d. Organization and role(s) of external trade (reciprocal gift trade; politically administered trade; market trade).
           e. Organization and role(s) of internal markets and market places (marketless economies, petty market places, small-scale market-integrated economies; resource markets and produce markets).
           f. Organization of money and money uses (general-purpose and special-purpose monies; commercial and non-commercial uses of money; relation of money uses to transactional modes).
           g. Operational devices: record-keeping, accounting, and measurement devices (quipu strings, pebble counts); devices of culture contact (silent trade, border markets, ports of trade).
           h. Prestige economy contrasted with subsistence economy (transactional spheres and conversions; bridewealth; ceremonial transfers; valuables and treasures as special-purpose monies).
           i. The relation of economic to social organization (the place of economy in society): social control of resource allocation, work organization, and produce disposition; social guarantee of livelihood through resource allocation and the provision of emergency subsistence.
        2. Performance
           a. Number of goods and specialist services produced or acquired.
           b. Level of output; fluctuations in output; frequency of dearth or famine (emergency devices in dearth or famine: use of trade partners for

emergency gifts; use of less-preferred foods; emergency conversions, e.g., sale of treasures and people for food).
c. Distribution of real income: equal or unequal? Why?
d. Distribution of subsistence goods contrasted with distribution of prestige goods (spheres of exchange; conversion between spheres).

C. *Special Problems Relating to Peasant Economies*
1. The nature of market organization and dependence contrasted with national, developed market economies; why "penny capitalism" is an appropriate description of peasant economy.
2. Peasant economy and culture before and after the Industrial Revolution.
3. The mixture of traditional and market economy; of traditional and modern technology; of traditional social organization and culture and elements of modern culture.
4. Peasant economy and society in contrast to primitive economy and society, and in contrast to industrial capitalist economy and society.

II. SOCIO-ECONOMIC CHANGE, GROWTH, AND DEVELOPMENT: SEQUENTIAL PROCESS ANALYSIS
A. *Contexts of change and development: colonialism-culture contact, independence-explicit national and village level modernization*

B. *Types of change*
1. Degenerative: cultural disruption and absence of substitute forms of organization.
2. Cash income growth without development: primitive economies becoming peasant; adoption of cash-earning activities with little or no disruption of ordinary life and without concomitant technological and other innovations which diversifies and sustains income growth.
3. Development: sustained income growth for the local community through integration-economic, political, cultural—into the larger socio-economic unit of which it is a part, without loss of ethnic identity or group malaise.

Traditional, Primitive Economies: Structure and Performance[2]

The questions about primitive economies of most interest to anthropologists relate to their organization (structure), and to comparisons of their organization with that of other types of economy (peasant, industrial capitalist). With regard to their performance, one can indicate the relatively narrow range of goods and specialist services produced or acquired. The level of output and fluctuations in output can be measured in terms of quantities produced (Deane 1953: Reynders 1963). Input measures can be devised (Salisbury 1962), indicating amounts of equipment used in production processes and work-days employed, and so arrive at some estimates of productivity. Dietary standards can be scrutinized (Richards 1939). Some impressions of the equality or inequality in real-income distribution can be conveyed. Given the absence of Western money and pricing and the relatively few resources used and goods produced, these measures of performance can only be rough indicators stated in terms of the resource and product units themselves.

The Scale of Primitive Economies

It is this smallness of scale, so hard for a modern European to grasp imaginatively, which is the fundamental characteristic of primitive life . . . (Wilson 1941:10).

There are some useful distinctions to be made among traditional economies. Much of the literature of primitive economies describes those without centralized polities—"tribes without rulers"—Malinowski's Trobriands being the most minutely described case in the literature. In saying that most primitive economies without centralized polity are small, one means several things: that the economy of the Tiv, the Nuer, or the Trobriand Islanders is small relative to modern, nationally-integrated economies of Europe and America; that most (but not all) resource, goods, and service transactions take place within a small geographical area and within a community of persons numbered in the hundreds or thousands. It is true that external trade is common and, as with the Kula, sometimes is carried out over long distances. Typically, however, it is intermittent, petty in amount, or confined to very few goods. It is rare (except in peasant economies) for foreign trade transactions to be frequent, quantitatively important, or essential to livelihood.

There are two other ways in which primitive economies are small-scale. Frequently one or two staple items (yams in the Trobriands, cattle among the Nuer) comprise an unusually large proportion of total produce. It is common for these important staples to be produced within the small framework of village, tribe, or lineage. Lastly, a relatively small number of goods and services is produced or acquired—dozens of items and specialist services rather than hundreds of thousands as in developed, industrial economies.

There are mutually reinforcing connections between the size and other aspects of the structure and performance of an economy. Two widely shared characteristics of the small economies anthropologists study are a simple technology (compared to the industrialized economies of the West), and geographical or cultural isolation (again, compared to those of Europe and North America). The absence of sophisticated machines and applied science, and of the extreme labor specialization characteristic of national economies numbering their participants in the millions, means a relatively low level of productivity. Two direct consequences for primitive economies of their simple technology and small size is that their peoples are sharply constrained in production activities by physical resource endowment (ecology), and that their peoples depend greatly on human co-operation for ordinary production[3] processes as well as emergencies such as famine and personal misfortune. Low-level technology combined with small size and relative isolation results in ingrained mutual dependence among people sharing many relationships: those with whom one is economically involved are the same as those with whom one is involved through neighborhood, religion, kinship and polity. The primitive economy in that sense is "embedded" in other community relationships and is not composed of associations separate from these (Dalton 1962; 1964).

Association is a group specifically organized for the purpose of an interest or group of interests which its members have in common. . . . Community is a circle of people who live together, who belong together, so that they share not this or that particular interest, but a whole set of interests wide enough and comprehensive enough to include their lives (MacIver 1933:9, 10, 12, quoted in Nadel 1942:xi).

Some points may here be underscored: (1) "Primitive" or "subsistence" economies require for the analysis of their *organization* conceptual categories which are socio-economic because material and service transactions are frequently expressions of kinship, religious, or political relationships. (2) Two general features of primitive or subsistence economies are the pervasive social control of production and distribution, and the assurance of subsistence livelihood to persons through the social determination of labor and land allocation and the social right to receive emergency material aid in time of need.

These points have frequently been made before: to Tönnies, primitive economies are *Gemeinschaft* rather than *Gesellschaft*; to Maine, they are characterized by status rather than contract; to Weber and MacIver, they are communities rather than associations; to Karl Polanyi (1944: Chap. 4; 1957), the economy is "embedded" in the society; to Raymond Firth (1951:142), the formula is "From each according to his status obligations in the social system, to each according to his rights in that system."

Primitive economies are so organized that the allocation of labor and land, the organization of work within production processes (farming, herding, construction of buildings and equipment), and the disposition of produced goods and specialist services are expressions of underlying kinship obligation, tribal affiliation, and religious and moral duty. Unlike the economist who can analyze important features of industrial capitalism (such as price and income determination) without considering social relationships, the economic anthropologist concerned with the *organization* of primitive economies finds there is no separate economic system that can be analyzed independently of social organization. The ways in which tools and implements are acquired, used, and disposed of is another point of contrast between primitive, peasant, and industrial capitalist economies. Typically in primitive economies tools are either made by the user himself, acquired for a fee from a specialist craftsman, or, as is sometimes the case with dwellings, storehouses, and canoes, acquired from a construction group specifically organized for the task. The construction group providing ordinary labor as well as the services of craftsmen specialists is remunerated either by food provided by the host (Thurnwald's *Bittarbeit* and barn-raising in the American West), or with food and luxury tidbits (tobacco, betel), or with these as well as payments in valuables or special-purpose money to the craftsmen-specialists (Dalton 1965*a*). Western cash is not paid. The making of tools, canoes, and dwellings is an occasional event rather than a continuous activity, and the construction workers do not derive the bulk of their livelihood from providing such services. The tools, canoes, and buildings when put to use do not yield their owners a cash income. Typically, the implements are used until they are physically worn out, when they are either repaired or discarded. Unlike some peasant economies (Firth 1946), primitive economies have no second-hand markets for tools and buildings.

Polyanyi's analytical distinctions between reciprocity, redistribution, and (market) exchange and their application to specific cases have been written up in detail (Polanyi 1944: Chap. 4; 1947, 1957, 1966; Dalton 1961; 1962, 1965*c*). Unfortunately, they have been misconstrued as applying only to transactions of produce (Smelser 1958; Burling 1962; Nash 1966). These socio-economic categories apply to inanimate resource and labor allocation and to work organization as well as to produce disposition— to production as well as to distribution of goods and craft services (LeClair 1962). It is misleading to regard "systems of exchange" as something apart from production processes because exchange transactions enter into *each* of the three component processes of production (Dalton 1962: 1964).

Consider any production process: automobile manufacturing in the U.S., yam growing in the Trobriands, collective farming in the U.S.S.R., Malay peasant fishing, or cattle raising among the Nuer. All these production lines require the allocation of land, labor, and other resource ingredients to the production process; the organization of work tasks within the production process; and the disposition of the items produced. Among the Tiv, acquiring farm land (in accordance with one's lineage affiliation) is as much a "reciprocal" transaction as yam-giving (in accordance with one's *urigubu* obligation) is in the Trobriands.

Primitive States: Internal Redistribution and External Administered Trade

As in other branches of anthropology, the typical unit of analytical interest in economic anthropology is a relatively small group, the tribe, the lineage segment, the village community. There is a small, internal economy to be analyzed whether our focus of interest is a primitive economy without centralized polity (such as the Tiv), a primitive economy within a centralized polity, such as the local farming communities in Nupe (Nadal 1942), or a peasant economy, such as the Malay fishermen (Firth 1946). To be sure, persons or groups within each of these small economies may carry out transactions with outsiders—external trade, tax and tribute payments to outside political authorities—but it is meaningful to distinguish between internal (local community) transactions and those external to the local group, however defined.

Primitive economics which are part of centralized political authority—what Polanyi called archaic societies and Evans-Pritchard and Fortes (1940) called primitive states—have socio-economic transactions in addition to those found within the local community and between local communities (see Figure 24–1). These are of two principal sorts, transactions between the political center and its local constituencies, and external trade transactions between the political center and foreigners (Arnold 1957a, 1957b; Polanyi 1963, 1966). The local constituents pay tribute to the political center—ordinary subsistence goods, luxuries reserved for elite usage, labor for construction projects and military service—and usually receive from the center military protection, juridical services, and emergency subsistence in time of local famine or disaster.

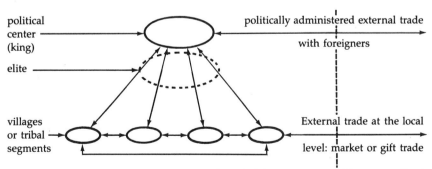

Fig. 24–1 Socio-economic transactions is the primitive economy within a centralized political authority system.

Where there is a centralized political authority, there is a redistributive sector which has no counterpart in primitive economies without a centralized polity (i.e., that are not chiefdoms, kingdoms, or empires). Indeed, where there is an intermediary elite between the king (his royal household economy and his domain), and the villages or tribal segments which express their political subordination through tax and tribute payments and other upward transactions, there are socio-economic sectors that some writers call feudal (Nadel 1942; Maquet 1961), although others question the usefulness of so labeling them (Goody 1963; Beattie 1964).

Peasant Economy

Writers on peasantry (Redfield 1956; Wolf 1966) emphasize the special nature of peasant personality and culture as that which distinguishes peasant from primitive: the semi-isolation from urban culture with which it shares religion and (in Europe) language; that peasants and peasant communities are the rank and file, so to speak, of larger political groupings, so that in Latin America, Europe, and India there are political authorities externally located who exercise some formal political jurisdiction over the peasant villages.

It is important to note that if we confine ourselves to cultural aspects such as religion, language, and political subordination, we can point up what is common to an enormous number of peasantries, and, at the same time justify the use of the special category, peasant culture, by showing it is different in these ways from primitive culture. Trobriand Island culture has none of the characteristics so far enumerated for peasants.

To go further, however, requires some special distinctions because of the long periods of historical time over which groups called peasant by social analysts have existed intact, and because there are other criteria used to differentiate peasant from primitive and modern.

One line of demarcation is the Industrial Revolution. Before the Industrial Revolution occurred in their regions, all peasantries used primitive technology, differing in no important way from the technologies used by those groups (Tiv, Lele, Nuer) anthropologists identify as being primitive. Let us call peasant communities as they existed before the Industrial Revolution in their regions, "traditional" peasantries. Then we can point out immediately that traditional peasantries, although differing from primitive societies in those cultural ways specified earlier, were like primitive communities in their use of simple (machineless) technology, their small units of production (principally but not exclusively agricultural) and the relatively few items produced within a peasant community. In traditional peasantries as in primitive communities, there is the same reliance upon one or two staple foodstuffs which comprise a large proportion of total output, and the same unusually large reliance upon natural resource endowment because of the simple technology used and the absence of complicated fabrication processes. With regard to the size of production units, technology, dependence on physical resource endowment, and the narrow range of items produced, traditional peasant communities resemble the primitive much more closely than they do with regard to culture. Moreover, material performance is roughly the same as in primitive communities, and for the same reasons. The ethnographic record does not indicate that traditional peasantries were typically less poor materially than primitive societies.[4]

What anthropologists mean by peasant culture is clear; what they mean by peasant economy is sometimes not clear.

By a peasant economy one means a system of small-scale producers, with a simple technology and equipment often relying primarily for their subsistence on what they themselves produce. The primary means of livelihood of the peasant is cultivation of the soil (Firth 1951:87).

But this is a perfect description of the Lele (Douglas 1965), The Tiv (Bohannan 1968), and the Trobriand Islanders in Malinowski's time—all have primitive economies. If we are to make analytical sense of the large literature of economic anthropology we need some finer distinctions.

It is as useful to distinguish between peasant and primitive economy as it is to distinguish between peasant and primitive culture. The *economic* organization of a peasant community has two sets of distinguishing characteristics: (1) most people depend for the bulk of their livelihood on production for market sale or selling in markets; purchase and sale transactions with cash are frequent and quantitatively important; and, frequently, resource markets are present: significant quantities of labor, land, tools, and equipment are available for purchase, rent, or hire at money price. It is the relative importance of markets for resources and products and of cash transactions that is the principal difference between peasant and primitive *economies*. It is this feature which gives peasant economies their crude resemblance to the least productive of our own farming sectors and which justifies Tax's appropriate phrase, "penny capitalism." But in all other ways relating to productive activities, peasant economies—especially traditional peasantries—more closely resemble the primitive than they do the modern: small-scale, simple technology, a narrow range of output, a few staples comprising the bulk of output, unusual reliance on physical resource endowment because of the absence of applied science and the technology of extensive fabrication; low levels of output—poverty and material insecurity.

(2) What strikes the economist is that although the rudiments of capitalist (i.e., market) economy are present and important in peasant

communities, they are *incomplete* and *underdeveloped* compared to market organization in a modern national economy. By incomplete is meant that within a given peasant community, some markets may be absent or petty—land may be frequently purchased or rented but labor is not, (Chayanov 1966) or vice versa; and that subsistence production may still be quantitatively important in some households. By underdeveloped is meant the absence of facilitative institutions and social capital of advanced capitalist countries: on the one hand, banks, insurance companies, and stock markets; on the other, electricity, paved roads, and educational facilities beyond the elementary school. In peasant comunities the extent of economic, cultural, and technological integration with the province and nation is markedly less than is the case with hinterland communities in developed nations.

In summary, peasant society, like primitive society (and also feudalism, *jajmani* in village India, and slavery) is a socio-economic category (Firth 1964a:17). If we include peasantries of all times and places within our analysis, then it is fair to say that peasant culture is more homogeneous and distinctive than is peasant economy (Fallers 1961). The spectrum of peasantries is wide, and contains varying mixtures of primitive and modern institutions. At one end are those in medieval Europe—the Russian mir, the feudal village (Bennett 1962) and some of present-day Latin America, which are peasant cultures (in religion, language, political subordination) with primitive economies (because of the absence of market dependence and cash transactions). There are also cases of peasant economy with a primitive culture, as in the early transition period of African groups enlarging their cash-earning production while retaining their tribal organization and culture (Fallers 1961; Gulliver 1965; Dalton 1964).[5]

Community Change and Development

The most promising area for fruitful interchange and collaboration between economics and anthropology is the field of economic development. Most development economists, however, are interested in processes and problems of *national* economic growth and development that have little in common with anthropologists' interests in local community social and economic change. But a growing number of economists are working on matters requiring anthropological insight: creating an industrial labor force, transforming subsistence agriculture (Yudelman 1964), devising policies for investment in educational facilities. Others are devising techniques of measurement and analysis to show the connections between socio-political organization and economic development (Adelman and Morris 1965, 1967). And yet other economists are making use of anthropology, sociology, and psychology to analyze—what is for economists—an unusual range of processes and problems entailed in economic growth and development (Hagen 1962; Myrdal 1957).

Matters relating to what I shall call socio-economic change, growth and development at the local community level conventionally appear in anthropology under the headings of evolution, diffusion of innovations, social change, culture change, culture contact, acculturation, and applied anthropology. There are two points about this literature of socio-economic change that I should like to emphasize.

The subject is extraordinarily diverse and complicated. It includes a wide range of complex processes: urbanization, industrialization, commercialization, national integration (cf. Southall 1961, UNESCO 1963). Moreover, these processes take place over much longer periods of time than anthropologists customarily remain in the field, and their analysis requires consideration of the policies of central government which impinge on the small group (village or tribal segment) that traditionally has been the focus of interest in anthropology.

The case studies of socio-economic change reach back to the early days of European colonization of Africa (Schapera 1934; Hunter 1961), Latin America (Chevalier 1963), and Asia (Boeke 1942), when neither political independence was a fact nor economic development of indigenous peoples an explicit intention. The recent case studies are of socio-economic change taking place in villages which are now parts of independent nation-states whose central governments are initiating nationwide development and modernization. The literature includes cases of piecemeal change, where a new cash crop or a new school or a new religion is introduced in an otherwise traditional community development, such as the famous case of Vicos (Holmberg et al. 1965).

Given the complexity of the processes, the large number and diversity of case studies on record, and the changed political and economic national conditions under which local community development now proceeds, it is not surprising that relatively few theoretical insights and conceptual categories with which to analyze socio-economic change have been contrived. Some notable contributions are Myrdal (1957), Hagen (1962), Smelser (1963), and Adelman and Morris (1967).

Socio-economic change as an anthropological subject is unusual in another way, as well. Many of us who work on problems of development and modernization hope not only to come to understand these processes, but also to use such knowledge to reduce the social costs of economic improvement. Therefore, this extension of the traditional concerns of economic anthropology into processes of socio-economic change and development has policy implications to an extent that is unusual in anthropology (Erasmus 1961; Goodenough 1963; Arensberg and Niehoff 1964).

What is also true is that each of us—the anthropologist, the economist, the sociologist—comes to a novel situation such as change and development in an African village community with two kinds of professional knowledge, the theory of one's subject, and an intimate knowledge of some portion(s) of the real world. The economist (typically) comes with price, income, growth, and development theory, plus his knowledge of the structure and performance of his own and perhaps several other economies. If he is a specialist in economic history or Soviet economy (Gershenkron 1963), he brings with him knowledge of the sequential processes through which England, Japan, Russia, or the U.S. developed. When he comes to examine local development in an African community, he is struck by similarities to and differences from what he is already familiar with.

First, with the exception of agricultural economics, there is no counterpart in conventional economic analysis to the study of local community change and development. European and American villages and townships—the local community counterparts of the Tiv lineage segment or an Indian village—are never the focus of analytical concern. Economics is about national economies and the component activities of business firms and households thoroughly integrated with their national economy through purchase and sale transactions. Immediately we can feed back into our new concerns knowledge that we know is important from our old ones. Empirically, *how do small groups—the tribe, the village— become part of a regional or national economy?*

Similarly, local community change or development seems never to be a "natural" process of immanent expansion of the village or tribe, but rather the local community's response to incursion from outside itself. Whether it is the Conquistadores' invasion of Peru 400 years ago, or Cornell University's invasion of Vicos 15 years ago, or European colonial incursion into Africa, or the slave-raider, missionary, or merchant who comes, the process of community change starts with impingement from without. Therefore, a second question we can ask of the empirical case studies is, *what is the nature of the initial incursion which starts the processes of socio-economic change, and to what extent does the character of the initial incursion shape the sequential changes that follows?*[6]

Most of the ethnographic case studies fall into one of three broad categories that I shall designate (*a*) degenerative change; (*b*) cash income growth without development; and (*c*) socio-economic development. The three categories—which are really ideal types—are not stages of progression. Moreover, they are clearly overlapping. Some of the empirical literature fits neatly into these categories, some does not. My point is to make sharp analytical distinctions, and to do so I must oversimplify.

Degenerative Change

Much of the early literature of culture contact consists of European and American incursions which produced decimation, misery, and community degeneration among indigenous groups (Rivers 1922; Jaspan 1953).

Native [Fiji] society [in the 1880's] was severely disrupted by war, by catastrophic epidemics of European diseases, by the introduction of alcohol, by the devastations of generations of warfare, and by the depredations of labor recruiters (Worsley 1957:19).

By degenerative change I mean severe disruption of the traditional life of a community over several generations with accompanying indicators of novel sorts and frequencies of personal social malaise. I do not postulate frictionless bliss in the traditional society; but whatever conflicts and malaise were generated by traditional society—warfare, vendetta, sorcery—were coped with by traditional institutions (Malinowski 1959), without prolonged disruption of ordinary life. Where degenerative change occurs, it is, obviously, because the situation is such that traditional institutions designed to deal with traditional sorts of stress and conflict are unable to deal with the novel change because it embodies forces which are at the same time without precedent, irreversible, and overwhelming to traditional organization.

The extreme cases are marked by military conquest and displacement of traditional political authority by conquerers who neither understand nor respect the culture of the society they now control. The indigenous people are unable to resist imposed changes, are prohibited from pursuing rituals or activities which are meaningful and integrative within traditional society, and are made to pursue new activities (e.g., forced labor in mines and plantations) which are not integrative—do not fulfill social obligation and so reinforce social relationships—in traditional society (Steiner 1957).

For the sting of change lies not in change itself but in change which is devoid of social meaning (Frankel 1955:27).

Degenerative situations and the psychological processes of individual and group reaction to them have caught the attention of many writers, perhaps because the consequences are so dramatic. Having lost the primary ties of meaningful culture, social relationships, and activities (Fromm 1941), and having been forced into meaningless activities and degrading helplessness, individuals and groups react to the bewildering changes with fantasy, aggression, withdrawal, and escape (Hagen 1962: Chap. 17; Smelser 1963). And so we have the ethnography of cultural disintegration, from the Pawnee Ghost Dance to Melanesian Cargo Cults[7] and Navaho alcoholism.

If one examines these cases of degenerative change from the viewpoint of community development, several features stand out:

(i) *The nature of the initial incursion.* In cases of severe degenerative change, the initial incursion causes cultural decimation: military conquest, political subjugation, and severe disruption of usual activities. A by-product of the incursion may be material worsening, or, indeed, slight material improvement. But these economic consequences are really beside the point because the force of change is perceived and felt to be deprivation of valued activities and the community's subjugation to militarily superior foreigners with hostile intentions and contempt for indigenous ways. The foreigners may come with the intent to deprive the people of gold or land, but typically it is not the deprivation of gold or land which causes the deep disruption.

Not economic exploitation, as often assumed, but the disintegration of the cultural environment of the victim is then the cause of degradation. The economic process may, naturally, supply the vehicle of the destruction, and almost invariably economic inferiority will make the weaker yield, but the immediate cause of his undoing is not for that reason economic; *it lies in the lethal injury to the institutions in which his social existence is embodied.* The result is loss of self-respect and standards, whether the unit is a people or a class, whether the process springs from so-called "culture conflict" or from a change in the position of a class within the confines of a society (Polanyi 1944:157. Italics added).

The nature of the initial incursion seems invariably important, not only to the generation experiencing the initial impact but also—in its shaping the sequences of socio-economic change—to successive generations (Hagen 1962). The group's cultural memory of what they regard as early injustice is long (Schapera 1928), and sometimes is nurtured several generations later (Colson 1949).

(ii) *The absence of new economic, technological, and cultural achievement.* The incursion prevents the society from functioning in customary ways without providing substitute ways which are meaningful to the people in terms of traditional culture (Steiner 1957, Frankel 1955). It is disintegrative to traditional organization without providing new forms of organization which re-integrate the society along new lines (Smelser 1963).

These are useful ways to state the problem, but much detailed analysis of socio-economic change needs to be done: What are the sequential processes of distintegration and subsequent re-integration? Which specific features of traditional society are most vulnerable? How long do these processes take? Under what conditions has re-integration taken place? We are here concerned with historical processes to be analyzed in sociological terms. The problems require explicit concern with long stretches of calendar time and with sequential process analysis of old and new economy, technology, polity, social organization, and culture

Degenerative change does not mean that some people believe themselves to be worse off materially or culturally under the new conditions. Some people are made worse off by any kind of social change. Rather, it means that the old society ceases to function in important ways, most people perceive the changes as worsenings, and in no important area of social or private life is there widespread absorption of new culture (e.g., literacy), new technology and economy (e.g., new farming methods and enlarged production for sale), of the sorts which create social reintegration. Neither is degenerative change necessarily a permanent state of affairs. Worsley (1957b) argues that Melanesian cargo cults, despite their traumatic symptoms of malaise, misunderstanding of European economy, and distorted religiosity, contain the beginnings of wider political organization of an anti-colonial sort which may possibly evolve into more orthodox and productive political activity (see also Hagen 1962).

Growth Without Development

Most of the case studies of community change reported in the literature differ from the one described above in two principal ways. First, the incursion was not severely disruptive of traditional society. The Trobriands (during Malinowski's residence), the Tiv (at the time of Bohannan's fieldwork), and many other groups carried on their traditional activities largely intact for generations after the foreign presence was felt. Second, the peoples became engaged in new cash-earning activities (principally growing cash crops and selling wage-labor), and this was the *only* innovation of importance widely adopted. Subsistence economies became peasant economies as cash earnings and dependence for livelihood on market sale of crops or wage-labor grew, while traditional culture and society remained largely intact (except for those changes induced by the enlarged commercial production or cash-earning).

Here we have the two salient features experienced by a large number of primitive societies: untraumatic incursion which allows ordinary activities, ceremony, and social relationships to continue on much as before; and enlarged cash-earning activities without the concomitant adoption of improved technology, literacy, or any of the other important accoutrements of "modernization" (Gulliver 1965).

I call this situation "cash income growth without development." The community's cash income grows somewhat because of its enlarged sales of crops or labor, but those structural changes in economy, technology, and culture necessary for sustained income growth and the integration over time of the local community with the nation, are not forthcoming. During the period when cash income grows while old culture, values, and folk-views remain initially unchanged (because literacy, new vocational skills, new lines of production, new technology, are not adopted), some characteristic responses are generated:

(1) The use of new cash income for old status prerogatives (bridewealth, potlatch).

(2) New conflict situations (land tenure litigation).

(3) The undermining of traditional arrangements providing material security through social relationships (cash-earning and individualism).

Typically, cash income is earned by individual or household activities rather than lineage or large cooperative group activities (such as canoe building and reciprocal land clearing). Writers on peasant economy (Chayanov 1966; Yang 1945: Chap. 7) stress the economic importance of the *family household* as a production unit for good reasons. The growth of dependence on market sale of labor or crops for livelihood means the lessened dependence on political heads, extended kin, age-mates, friends, and neighbors—in a word, lessened dependence on local social relationships—to acquire labor or land to use in production processes.

The new form of income, Western cash, is utterly different from anything known in traditional marketless economies. It is indefinitely storable, and so provides material security for its individual owner. It can be used to purchase a variety of goods and discharge a variety of obligations which no money-stuff or treasure item does in primitive economy. Not only a potentially enormous range of European imports—gin, tobacco, canned foods, steel tools, crucifixes, transistor radios—school fees, and colonial taxes, but also traditional subsistence goods (foodstuffs), traditional prestige sphere services, obligations, and labor, all become purchasable or payable with cash. This is what is meant by Western cash being a "general purpose" money (Dalton 1965*a*). The process of acquisition as well as the transactional use or disposition of Western cash in formerly primitive economies break down the traditional separation between spheres of subsistence and prestige goods and services (Firth 1958: Chap. 3; Bohannan 1959).

The use of new cash income for old status prerogatives, new conflict situations, and the undermining of traditional arrangements providing material security are related consequences of earning cash income *within an otherwise traditional setting*. For example, that bridewealth has come to be paid in cash rather than, as formerly, in high prestige items such as cows, indicates the great importance placed on cash (and what it will buy and pay for). The *social* consequences of such displacement are several. Consider the contrasting situations before and after cash has displaced traditional valuables as bridewealth. Indigenously, bridewealth in cows could be got by a young man wanting to marry only by soliciting the required cows from kin, friends, elders, chiefs, i.e., by drawing on social relationships and thus creating obligations to repay them (reciprocate) in some form (e.g., labor service, clientship, etc.). After cash becomes acceptable as bridewealth, young men can raise their own cash and pay their own bridewealth, thus weakening their dependence on traditional superiors.

Indigenously, where bridewealth required the payment of prestige goods, the items (such as cows) could be disposed of by the bridewealth recipients in very few ways. Cows (like kula bracelets) could only be exchanged or paid within the prestige sphere which was narrowly circumscribed. But cash received as bridewealth has no such limitations. It can be used for traditional prestige or subsistence goods, or any of the array of new goods. Bohannan (1959) has pointed out the moral ambivalence which results in the changed situation where bridewealth receipts in cash can be spent on goods in a lower prestige sphere.

Socio-Economic Development

Economists can answer the question, "What constitutes successful development?" with little difficulty. Their unit of analysis is the nation-state, and their base of reference is the already developed nations of North America and Europe. The indicators of successful development from the viewpoint of economics are impersonal, having little to do with folk-views, attitudes, social relationships, or culture. Development is characterized in terms of the country's yearly percentage rate of growth in gross national product, the size of per capita income and its distribution, and the use of advanced technology in major production lines.

If anthropologists are asked, "What constitutes successful development?" the answer is more difficult. The anthropologists' unit of analysis is the tribal or village community, not the nation-state[8]; anthropologists are not only concerned with economy and technology, but also with folkviews, attitudes, social relationships, and the rest of culture. And they do not use the already developed nations of Europe and North America as a base of reference for successful development. Moreover, anthropologists are analytically concerned with the wider social process of which economic development is a part, and sensitive to social and cultural costs of economic change.

There is no such thing as a small-scale community's development independent of the larger units of economy and society external to the tribe or village. The several kinds of change that constitute modernization all entail integration with external groupings, i.e., increased dependence upon external groups with whom new economic and cultural transactions take place.

Sustained income growth for the local community requires enlarged production for sale to regional, national, or international markets, and a return flow of consumption goods, producer's goods, and social services (health and education) purchased with the ever-increasing cash income. The community becomes economically integrated (and dependent upon) the regional, national, or international economy through a continual enlargement and diversification of purchase and sale transactions. These can be enlarged and made to grow only with the use of improved technology (tools and technical knowledge) acquired or purchased initially from outside the local community. Moreover, the experience of a significant growth in income seems frequently to be a necessary pump-priming condition if traditional groups are to become willing to take the risk of producing new kinds of crops and goods, or old ones with new, expensive, and unfamiliar techniques of production. Primitive and peasant unwillingness to change production is frequently a sensible expression of their poverty and material insecurity. They cannot afford unsuccessful experiments. The old techniques are not very productive, but they keep the people alive. One of the important lessons of the unusual (and unusually quick) development progress in Vicos (Holmberg *et al.* 1965), was that the *Cornell group* assumed the financial risk of planting improved varieties of potatoes. The demonstration effect of the sharp increase in the value product of the new potatoes convinced the people of Vicos to follow suit. A legitimate role for any central government wanting to accelerate local community development is for it to bear some portion of the financial risk of economic and technological innovation.

The local community's integration politically is yet another aspect of community development. But when central government acts only as a tax gatherer, the local community is likely to perceive any governmentally initiated project to expand community output as a device to increase taxes, and therefore to be resisted. Here too there must be demonstration effects: that government can provide the local community with important economic and social services and confine itself to taxing only a portion of enlarged income forthcoming.

Lastly, there is cultural integration with the larger society: learning new language, new vocational skills, literacy, private and public health practices, and acquiring a participant awareness of alternatives, events, and institutions of the larger world.[9]

What perhaps deserves emphasis is that successful development from the economist's viewpoint is compatible with successful development from the anthropologist's viewpoint. Anthropologists are concerned with minimizing the social costs of community transformation, and with preserving the community's ethnic identity in the new society of income growth, machines, and literacy. But we know from examining the subcultures in already developed nations, such as Japan, England, the U.S.S.R., and especially the U.S. (with its unusual ethnic diversity), that the retention of identity in both new and old institutional forms is compatible with modern activities. The point surely is to work with those powerful levers of new achievement which the people themselves perceive as desirable and which induce other positive changes—higher income through new economic and technological performance, and wider alternatives through education. If such developmental achievements are in fact incorporated, those features of traditional culture and social organization incompatible with the new are sloughed off without the personal and community malaise that characterize degenerative change and growth without development.

Social policy has . . . to assure that the individual in losing both the benefits and the burdens of the old society acquire no weightier burdens and at least as many benefits as he had in his previous station (Okigbo 1956).

Conclusion

Karl Polanyi's analytical concepts, insights, and generalizations relate to the socio-economic organization of primitive and archaic economies in which market organization is absent or confined to petty transactions. Here, the components of economy—labor and resource allocation, work organization, product disposition—are expressions of kinship, polity, religion, etc. His analysis is not general in three senses. (1) He did not analyze peasant economies, where market organization, market dependence for livelihood, and the use of Western money are important. (2) He was not concerned with the quantifiable performance of primitive economies, but only with their organization. (3) His analysis of socio-economic change and development was confined principally to Europe (Polanyi 1944: Chaps. 3, 6, 7, 8, 13). Much of the criticism of his work (and mine) is due to a misunderstanding of the range of economies we are referring to. Several anthropologists who have done fieldwork in peasant economies (Firth 1946), or in primitive economies at the beginnings of commercialization and use of Western money (Salisbury 1962, Pospisil 1963), look for a universal theory. They complain that Polanyi's categories and generalizations (designed for primitive, static economies), do not fit their peasant and changing economies, and so criticism of Polanyi's work ensues.

If, as with Polly Hill, the agricultural economist who specializes in Ghanaian cocoa farming (1963, 1966), the investigator is interested exclusively in peasant economy, cash crops, and economic growth, and particularly with measurable performance rather than socio-economic organization, then he is being rather short tempered when he criticizes those of us who are interested in economies different from those of Ghanaian cocoa farming, and with aspects of economy and society other than measurable performance.

If, as with Firth and Salisbury, anthropologists are interested in comparative economic performance—how much is produced, how much equipment and labor are used, how income is divided—questions economists put to our own economy, then (in vastly simplified fashion) some of the measurement concepts of conventional economics are usefully applicable, and they fail to understand Polanyi's criticism of conventional economics as inappropriate for analyzing the *structure* of primitive economies.

Some, like Pospisil (1963) and Burling (1962), perceive an economy not as a set of rules of social organization but as economic behavior of individuals and their subjective motivations; when they detect greed and self-aggrandizement they equate these with capitalism and assert that economic "behavior" in primitive societies is the same as in market societies and that Polanyi's conceptual categories are wrong and "romantic" (Cook 1966).

Finally, some anthropologists obliterate all distinctions between descriptive statements, analytical statements, and statements about folkviews, by describing and analyzing the economy, and stating folkviews about it exclusively in market terminology (supply, demand, price, maximizing, capital), and thus quite understandably convince themselves that conventional economics provides all the concepts necessary for economic anthropology (Pospisil 1963).

What must be recognized is that economic anthropology deals with two different sorts of economies, primitive and peasant, under two different sets of conditions, static and dynamic, and with two very different aspects of economy, organization and material performance. Polanyi's theoretical categories are addressed principally, but not exclusively, to the organization of primitive and archaic economies under static conditions. That he did not analyze peasant economies and small-scale economies undergoing change, growth, and development does not vitiate his important contributions to the analysis of nonmarket economies and the transformations of 18th and 19th-century capitalism.[10]

Notes

1.   The concept of "services" causes difficulty in economic anthropology (as do the concepts of "capital" and "market") because the term is used to cover a wide range of items or activities in our own economy, only a few of which are found in primitive economies. In our own economy, the term "services" is used to describe ordinary labor, mechanized utilities (telephone and electricity services), the services performed by craftsmen and professional specialists, e.g., dentistry, TV repairs, musicians; and also the functions performed by political and religious office-holders. In our own economy, all but the latter services are organized for purchase and sale. In relation to primitive and peasant economies, I prefer to use the term "specialist services" to refer to those provided by craftsmen, such as blacksmiths, woodcarvers, and dancers, and those provided by persons performing political, religious, and ritual roles.

2.   The literature of primitive (subsistence) economies—traditional economies most different from our own—is richest for Africa and Oceania, for small-scale communities rather than kingdoms and empires, and for agriculturalists rather than hunters, gatherers, herders, etc. Malinowski's work (1921; 1922; 1926; 1935; also, Uberoi 1962) is the single best source. On the economies of kingdoms and other politically centralized societies, see Nadel (1942), Maquet (1961), Arnold (1957), and Polanyi (1966).

3.   The extraordinary dependence on immediate physical environment for livelihood made it seem reasonable for an older generation of anthropologists to use classifications such as gathering, hunting, fishing, pastoral, and agricultural "economies." These categories do not classify according to *economic organization*, but rather according to principal source of subsistence, physical environment, and technology. Note that if we used these categories for developed economies, the U.S. and the U.S.S.R. would appear in the same category, both being manufacturing and agricultural "economies."

4.   For many traditional peasant economies (village communities), it is undoubtedly true that real income is no higher than in most primitive economies. But, aside from difficulties of measuring real output, there are complicating

features of peasant society which make it difficult to say whether many peasantries had consistently higher levels of output than is typical in primitive communities. Peasant communities, for example, seem invariably to be subordinate units of larger political (and religious) groupings, which means that significant portions of peasant produce and labor are paid "upward" as taxes, tributes, rents, and tithes. The elite recipients of such taxes and tributes channelled portions of them into the creation of churches, palaces, pyramids, armies, etc., some of the services of which were received back by the local peasant communities. Again, the slow growth of improvement in agricultural and marketing techniques in some European peasant communities for several hundred years before the Industrial Revolution may have given some European peasant communities of, say, the 18th century higher incomes than is typical of other peasant and most primitive economies.

5. In this paper I can only call attention to how little work has been done on the economic aspects of peasantry (in the anthropological literature) and suggest that similar cultural features accompany dissimilar economic arrangements in the broad spectrum of peasant societies. There is a great deal more to be said about peasant economy. I am preparing an essay which classifies peasant societies into three sorts. Type I consists of peasant communities which have dependent (non-market) land tenure (such as those under European Feudalism) in which land is acquired by clients from patrons as part of a long-run social and political relationship. Clients reciprocate with obligatory payments of material goods or labor services (farm labor, military labor, road repair, etc.), as well as with more diffuse social and political "payments"—loyalty, respect, homage, ceremonial services. Type II consists of peasant communities of a post-French Revolution sort, in which land tenure is strictly a matter of market purchase (or rental at money price) with no social or political obligations attached to land acquisition or usage. Types I and II refer to communities of long settlement. Type III is a hybrid sort, referring to communities of persons resettled within relatively recent historical times, frequently, as the aftermath of slavery in the Caribbean and the Spanish conquest of Latin America. Kroeber and Redfield, understandably, seized upon cultural attributes to differentiate "peasant" from "primitive" cultures. What remains to be done is socio-economic analysis of peasant groups from an anthropological perspective which takes account of the rich historical literature of European peasantries (e.g., Chayanov 1966) as well as the more recent ethnographies.

6. A third general point of significance I believe to be the time rate of change which is experienced (Polanyi 1944; Chap. 3). This is not, however, independent of the other features of the transformation process.

7. Cargo cults are complicated movements of expressing several aspects of fission and fusion. Here, I simply want to emphasize that among other things, they are symptoms of malaise that indicate deep misunderstanding of the processes of modernization through which Western goods are acquired.

8. Clifford Geertz's work is a notable exception.

9.   Gunnar Myrdal's point about the mutually reinforcing nature of developmental activities is indispensable for understanding the processes of sequential change, whether they be degenerative, cash income growth, or the structural changes entailed in successful development. (Myrdal 1957: Chaps. 1–3).

10.   Much that Polanyi said in *The Great Transformation* (1944) about the social and cultural consequences of the British Industrial Revolution is relevant to current socio-economic change in underdeveloped areas.

Herbert Applebaum

25. The Universal Aspects of Work

I have surveyed work in nonmarket and market societies in two volumes, with a global survey of work organizations in all types of societies. Now I propose to sum up the analysis by outlining basic patterns of work found in all or almost all work systems. What is the value of these universals? Hopefully, they will point to the significant variables in any work organization. They can provide a cognitive map for anthropologists and other social scientists researching the subject of work. These patterns can be useful bearing points as one pilots through the intricacies of the social matrix of work found in even the simplest society. Universals of work organization are not the same as a theory about the nature of work. They are guideposts rather than concepts, empirical regularities rather than laws, and suggestions for what is significant about the nature of work rather than dogmatic assertions that these, and only these, universals are the important variables to look for in the research on work.

What are the universal patterns found in work and work organizations in societies and cultures throughout the world?

All human work involves the mastery of knowledge and its transmission to the next generation

All forms of life appropriate the natural products of their environment for their own use. But to seize upon the materials of nature ready made is not work. Work is an activity that alters these materials from their natural states in order to improve their usefulness. Human beings share with other species, such as the beaver, spider, bee, and termite, the work of acting upon nature in a manner which changes its forms to make them suitable for special needs. What is important about human work, and what differentiates it from the work of other animals, is the purposive nature of human labor. Human work is conscious, while the work of most other species is instinctive. Thus, human work involves not only the physical act of labor but the accumulation of knowledge which can be passed on from generation to generation. Leslie White said:

Culture without continuity of experience, is, of course, impossible. But what sort of continuity of experience is prerequisite to culture? It is not the continuity which comes from the communication of experience by imitation, for we find this among apes. Clearly, it is continuity on the subjective side rather than on the objective, or overt, that is essential. . . . it is the symbol, particularly in word form, which provides this element of continuity in the tool-experience of man. And finally, it is this factor of continuity in man's tool-experience that has made accumulation and progress, in short, a material culture possible. (1949:48)

Work is so basic to the development of culture that the requirements for survival are the same for both. Clearly, man's ability to work constitutes one of the great domains of human activity which in one way or another shapes the lives of human beings and, like cultural inheritance, passes on from generation to generation.

All work has a communal dimension

This notion flows from the notion in the section above. No work can proceed in complete isolation, if only because techniques, skills, and knowledge must be passed from generation to generation for humans to know how to work. But the communal nature of human work extends further. Work in every society is related to social obligations—whether to one's immediate family, to one's kinship group, or to the community as a whole. No person or family can survive without the cooperation of others. In modern, industrial states, our interdependence is evident from the fact that almost none of us directly produces the items we require for survival. In nonmarket societies, work is a matter of obligation to others, and one who does not fulfill his or her obligation is considered a disturbing element in the community. Raymond Firth describes the communal nature of work as it appears in all types of societies:

In such societies (primitive, traditional, non-market), work is not just an economic service, it is a social service. . . . The basis of recruitment is not directly the offer of material reward, it is the social relationship between the person who wants labour and the person who has it to give. . . . In the long run, one can really only withdraw from work by leaving the community.

Let us now turn to consider the organization of work in a peasant society. . . . This is intermediate between the very simple society just discussed and our own complex industrial society. . . . The society (peasant) is still one where economic ties are largely personalized. . . . People usually work together for reasons other than just money. . . . In other words, work and the use of wealth are to them governed by social, community sanctions, and not by sheer economic individualism.

Let us compare this with an industrial society. As one tours through a modern factory, nothing seems to be more alien than the primitive or peasant working community. Yet despite . . . contrasts I think our analysis so far has some relevance to modern industrial conditions. A factory is not simply a place where goods are produced and wages are paid. It, too, is a little social world. Much as they may rely on their families and on other associations outside for companionship, amusement and other human interests, the workers all depend on the factory to some extent for some of these things. No one is insensible to the opinions of his workmates. (1972:10–13)

The communal aspect of work derives from the value system which determines what and how work is to be performed; it stems from the need to rely upon others in the performance of work or in the need to exchange the products of work; and it comes from the social obligations that come into play as soon as one undertakes to contribute to the sustenance and survival of the group. In essence, the social environment in any work situation is just as crucial as the physical environment; and part of the social environment is the ideology of work, an ideology which rests on the cultural values of the society. Since work has a cultural dimension, it must also have a communal dimension.

All work is involved with the allocation of time and is affected by attitudes toward time

The scarcity of goods in the face of the wants of a given society at a given period of history is a universal fact of human experience. No economic system exists in which enough goods are produced in enough variety to satisfy all the wants of all members of the society. This is true whether the group is small or large or whether the technology of the society is simple or complex. It is true whether the society is in a stage of dynamic transition, stable equilibrium, or stagnation and depression. For these reasons all societies and cultures are faced with the need to allocate the amount of working time of its members in order to produce the tools, implements, and subsistence requirements for survival. This notion involves the conscious exercise of choice as to which activities one will engage in during a daily, weekly, or yearly cycle of work. Such allocation and choosing takes place in every society, in spite of cultural differences, regarding tools, technology, or the kinds of goods and services desired.

In addition to the allocation of time, all cultures and societies are affected by their attitudes toward time. Each culture has a view of time which stems from its traditions and customs and which is appropriate for its social structure. The view of time will determine whether work is task-oriented or time-oriented, whether compensation for work is based on the amount of time one works or whether it is based on exchange and reciprocity. The view of time can be based on dividing and subdividing each unit of time and compressing one's activities into rigid norms of the work day; or time can be viewed in relation to concrete events and cycles of days and nights and the seasons of the year. Every society has a way of reckoning time which affects the manner in which work activities are planned and regulated.

All work requires a set of rules or norms

Work and work environments, like subcultures, have a set of rules and norms. First, there are the techniques and procedures for using tools and materials. Second, in every work environment there is an appropriate form of dress that is peculiar to the workplace. Third, there is a particular language associated with the performance of work. Finally, there are rules of behavior in the workplace.

Lee (1980:Chap. 8) describes how the !Kung San hunters follow certain procedures with regard to the animals they track, their preparation for the hunt, and their interrelations with one another. Gamst (1980a:Chap. 4) relates how railroad workers are constrained by rules which are codified and printed and have to be mastered by every worker in railroading. Malinowski (1965:52–68) talks about the rules of magic used by the Trobriand garden magician to regulate gardening procedures—a combination of magical and practical rules that pay homage to the needs of the gods, as well as to the needs of the soil. Whether the rules are written and codified, as in the case of railroaders, or are part of unwritten custom, as in the case of the !Kung San and the Trobriand Islanders, every work organization is governed by procedures and rules passed on from generation to generation. These rules and norms embody the collective experience of contemporaries and ancestors.

Work in all societies assumes some form of reciprocity and exchange

Techniques of production represent only one part of the organization of work in any society. Human work that produces or gathers what is necessary for subsistence and survival must be linked with some method of distributing what has been produced. Systems of exchange take on many forms, depending on the level of technology, the complexity of the social structure, and the value system of the society.

Given the fact that no human society exists in which there is not at least the division of labor along sex lines, it follows that even within the most self-sufficient household there is some kind of exchange of services. There can be no division of labor without a consequent system of reciprocity and exchange. The universality of reciprocity and exchange emphasizes human interdependence in work and culture.

In nonmarket societies the form of exchange is the gift, and the offer of labor is part of one's kinship obligations (Mauss 1967). In transitional peasant societies, exchange can take several forms from barter to selling in a marketplace or patron/client relations based on mutual obligations and duties. In industrialized cultures where virtually all goods are produced for market exchange, people are interconnected through the money nexus which moves goods and services throughout the society. In industrial society, there are exchanges of work on a voluntary basis and exchanges of gifts during holidays, birthdays, and anniversaries, mostly confined to kinship and friendship circles.

Reciprocity and exchange are not only associated with work but also with the total fabric of any human culture. An indication of the fundamental nature of work is that many of the universal attributes of culture, in general, are also associated with the nature of work.

The performance of work involves incentives and motivations

Performing work in any type of society involves incentives—concern with why people work and what they expect to receive in the way of gain or prestige for their efforts. In nonmarket societies, incentives are bound up with social forces and kinship obligations, whereas in industrial societies, economic gain is the main, but by no means the only, motivation and incentive for work. In all societies, prestige is a motivating force for work. In industrial societies, where the work ethic was part of the rise of industrialism and the factory system, having a job in itself carries prestige, and unemployment results in social stigma (Wadel 1973).

In all societies, incentives to work are embodied in a total set of values:

Work is at one time an economic, political and religious act and it is experienced as such. (Godelier 1972:266)

The social aspect of work also plays a part. Many people seek the sociability of the workplace to avoid the loneliness of staying at home (Neff 1977:171–172). In other cases people are motivated by the prestige of engaging in a particular kind of work and working well. Incentives to work operate in all societies because, wherever we find work organizations, we discover that people tend to work hard, or little, when they are forced to, as well as when they are not. Motivations and incentives for work are often hidden and elusive, but they have a significant impact on how hard or how well people work.

All work requires some form of organization

Work in all societies has some form of organization. In preindustrial, nonmarket societies, the organization is based on a division of labor by sex and age group. Within each category and within each task, there is some form of organization. Among the !Kung San of southwest Africa, there is one type of organization for stalking a giraffe and another for the trapping of animals. Among the Cheyennes of North America, there was an elaborate ceremony and organization for the buffalo hunt, while for quilling work the organization was based on a guild system and confined to women.

Work organization is a function of both the work itself and the cultural traditions of the society. In nonmarket societies, it is quite easy to establish correlations between work tasks and work organization. This is because everyone is a jack-of-all-trades, and work is associated with all the institutions of the society. Some have argued that, in industrial cultures, technology plays a crucial role in the nature of work organizations. William Form (1976) studied auto workers in four countries and found a remarkable coincidence of work organization in all countries, despite the diversity of background and history. Professor Inkeles commented:

Like conditions of work, especially a similar technological milieu and the characteristic accompanying socio-economic ambience, seem, on many dimensions, to elicit like response under the tutelage and pressure of the standard patterns of organization found in industrial operations. (1981:5)

Work in all societies needs organization to separate the various tasks and coordinate them. As work projects become more complex, so does the work organization. At some point, the planning of work becomes separated from the execution of work. At that juncture, people are trained as organizers and planners of work while others are trained to perform work. This happened in the development and growth of civilizations when specialists in the planning of work organized the monumental projects that still stand as testimony to their organizational skill.

All work groups require leadership

Wherever people work in groups, they require leadership. Leadership in work is a necessity, if only from the viewpoint that work technology must be passed on to the younger generation. Leadership in a preindustrial, nonmarket society may come from a shaman or magician who is not only in charge of religious and ceremonial rites but also directs the practical work. Leadership may also come from a headman or chief who not only assembles people and materials but also directs the work (Hogbin 1964).

As societies become more complex, leadership in work becomes hierarchically organized. The undertaking of a large construction project or the organization of a factory requires a division of tasks and a degree of coordination that necessitates supervision and planning. This need separates leadership from participation in work. In the past, as societies developed, there arose a number of specialists/leaders—priests, merchants, entrepreneurs, managers, engineers, and overseers. In modern, industrial societies, it is only in those industries where hand methods still predominate that people can undertake work without leadership from others. In addition to the leadership required for the functioning of work tasks, leadership also involves imparting values, teaching skills, and providing models of behavior considered appropriate for particular work cultures.

Work groups require controls and spurs to effort

All work groups require some form of control. Control is a product of leadership and organization. It flows from the division of labor and the assignment of tasks, as well as the management of these tasks by leaders. It also stems from the recognition that each person has a place in the work group—his or her role in relation to others. Control can be imposed from above, as indeed it is in all repressive work systems like slavery, serfdom, or peonage. In industrial society, it is imposed by the threat of dismissal. In nonmarket, preindustrial societies, it is imposed through the demands of kinship obligations and threats of loss of social standing in the society. In some nonmarket societies, control over those who work is enforced by the danger of accusations of sorcery or the possibility of banishment.

The most effective kind of control over work groups is one in which the members of the group accept the aims of the work organization. Among modern, industrial societies, the Japanese have had great success in imparting this kind of attitude among people in their work organizations. Where people are self-motivated to work well for the benefit of the group, controls are no longer viewed as such but become spurs to effort in which everyone shares. Work songs and chants are forms of self-imposed spurs people use to help them work rhythmically and in unison with others.

The element of prestige is present in all work

In every type of society, prestige has been associated with work. The Trobriand gardener displays his yams in a storehouse to be viewed by the entire community (Malinowski 1922); the woodcarver among the Kwakiutls is admired for his totem poles and receives commissions to work for others (Boas 1921); the Malay fisherman can display his fishing pole in the bow of his boat, if he has a large catch of bonito fish (Firth 1966); even a street sweeper in India, whose occupation is considered dirty and fit only for outcastes, enjoys prestige in being able to command high wages and exclusive control over the work (Searle-Chatterjee 1979). Work that is well done receives the admiration of peers in every society and sometimes finds expression in folklore—sagas of railroaders (John Henry); tales of seamen (Billy Budd); stories of hunters and trappers (Tom Horn); myths of forest men (Paul Bunyan). The term craftsmanship stems from the notion of prestige gained from the quality of workmanship, and every society accords recognition to high quality workers.

All cultures and societies have a work ethic, whether explicitly expounded, as in western society with its Protestant ethic, or based upon the obligations of persons toward their kinship group and community, as in nonmarket societies. In industrial society, work is a basis for determining a person's standing in the community. The kind of work one does is used to determine the value people place upon each other and upon themselves. Having a job is associated with such positive values as independence, autonomy, and citizenship. The unemployed face many varieties of derogation, even if they are not at fault for their situation (Wadel 1973). Even the wealthy and powerful derive prestige from being engaged in some kind of productive work. In societies dominated by males, work associated with males is accorded more prestige than that associated with females. In modern, industrial societies, with its stress on education, mental work has more prestige than manual work.

The question of work and prestige viewed universally is a complex question because it is a function of the total value system prevailing in various societies. There have been entire societies in which all work was perceived as servile—to be performed by slaves or pariahs—and only people entirely freed from work received any prestige (Arendt 1958). In still other societies, certain kinds of work were prestigeful (pastoralism, ranching), while others were considered contemptible (agriculture) (Goldschmidt 1971).

In modern, industrial society, being a worker as it relates to society's values is not simple. There are counter-culture groups among whom being a worker is tantamount to being a "square" or a "sucker," and "making it" through illegal means is considered prestigeful. For many others, performing work that is heavy or dirty is a burden to be endured, and those performing it do not expect to gain much prestige. At the same time, even in the least skilled occupations it is possible to gain the respect of others by doing good work. In general, the amount of prestige to be gained from work depends on a varied set of factors, including the amount of training necessary for the work and the evaluation placed by society on the social importance of the work being done (Neff 1977:161–176).

Work in all societies has both material and nonmaterial rewards

Social scientists in the United States and in other nations have reported that all work involves both material and nonmaterial rewards (Herzberg et al 1957; Touraine 1971; Vroom 1964). Herskovits (1948:Chap. 23) describes how people in nonmarket societies decorate their tools and implements even though the decoration has no practical function. Malinowski (1922) reports how Trobriand Islanders not only pride themselves on creating gardens that are highly productive but they also take great pains to line up their rows of yams and their fences so they look even when sighted. In construction work, I have seen steamfitters lay out and install piping in a boiler room so that they all line up in parallel planes vertically and horizontally. The question is why do people spend the extra effort in their work to add something that is beyond what is needed for the utilitarian aspects of work? And the answer is that there is something present in all work beyond the material reward sought after.

Though prestige is part of the nonmaterial rewards, there is something beyond prestige which relates to the fact that work reflects one's unique capabilities as a person. There is a need for creativity in the sphere of work which brings into existence an additional unit of something which is not known to others and which is ultimately one's own contribution. Ken Kusterer puts the idea this way:

Working knowledge, like other cultural forms, is a mode of adaptation on the part of workers to their work environment . . . the learning of working knowledge is a mode of adapting to the work place which increases the worker's ability to be effective in that environment, to manipulate it, or even to transform it. (1978:163)

Among the nonmaterial elements in work ideally sought after, three are prominent: first, the ideal of autonomy; second, the ideal of a workplace community where one may find meaningful friendships; and third, the chance for collaborative participation in a work enterprise that produces something with which one can be proud to be associated.

Work involves human interaction with nature

Human beings are not the only creatures who perform work. Caterpillars weave cacoons, beavers build dams, and apes use crude instruments to secure food. But human beings are the only creatures who do not merge into the materials of their undertakings. Human beings are the only creatures who can establish an objectivity with nature because they can separate themselves from nature through the objects they produce. These products have an existence apart from those who created them. Human beings build shelters which are separate from nature and which continue to exist apart from those who created the house. Eventually, the shelter will decay, but others can be erected in its place. Humans, like all other creatures, are dependent upon nature for food and the materials with which to perform work, but they do not merge with nature. Instead, they wrest from the natural environment what they have planned and willed, based on their knowledge of the laws of nature. This is the essence of human interaction with nature, and it occurs through work.

Agriculture is an example of human interaction with the natural environment. Where it is practiced, humans do not rely upon what nature has given but, through knowledge and skill, wrest from nature what they will. The tilling of the soil must follow the biological and natural cycles of the seasons, but, through working the soil year in and year out, such work will eventually transform a wilderness into cultivated land. At that point, the environment is man-made and subject to human control. Work on the soil not only secures a means of subsistence but eventually prepares the earth for the building of cities. Nature is never truly owned by human beings. The natural environment has a permanence and existence of its own, but it is subject to man's intervention.

Humans not only interact with nature but also destroy living processes in nature. To build houses, trees have to be killed. Iron, stone, and marble are torn out of the earth through mining and excavation work. Humans experience a sense of joy and strength when they pit their will and endurance against the natural environment. Hannah Arendt expresses it in this manner:

Most descriptions of the joys of labor in so far as they are not late reflections of the biblical contented bliss of life and death and do not simply mistake the pride of having done a job with the joy of accomplishing it, are related to the elation felt by the violent exertion of a strength with which man measures himself against the overwhelming forces of the elements and which through the cunning invention of tools he knows how to multiply far beyond its natural measure. (1958:123)

All work involves the expenditure of energy

"Work is the application of human energy to things; which applica-tion converts, maintains, or adds value to the worker, the thing worked on and the system in which the work is performed" (Wallman 1979:4). The expenditure of energy relates both to individuals, who use energy to work, and to work organizations, which use technological energy. Prein-dustrial societies use human energy as the main source of power. In these systems, the input of food energy obtained from plants and ani-mals is a crucial element in the output of human energy. In industrial systems, fuels, electricity, wind, and water, are the predominant forms of energy used to power tools and machines.

Marvin Harris cites energy as a crucial relationship between humans and their environment:

The most important aspect of any ecosystem is the pattern of energy flow characteristic of its organic and inorganic components. (1975:233)

Harris also cites energy as a crucial element in the relations between human beings:

Power in human affairs, as in nature, consists of the ability to control energy. Control over energy is mediated by the tools, machines and techniques for applying that energy to individual or collective enterprises. To control energy in this sense is to possess the means for making, moving, shaping and destroying minerals, vegetables, animals and people. (1975:397)

Leslie White based his theory of the evolution of culture on the con-cept of energy:

Other factors remaining constant, culture evolves as the amount of energy har-nessed per capita per year is increased, or as the efficiency of the means of putting energy to work is increased. (1959:363–369)

The utilization of energy is a broader issue than its relationship to work. Yet, in the discussion of energy as it relates to the growth of society, there is the explicit and implicit idea that it is crucial because it enhances the ability to work. Thus, the role of energy relates both to the anthropology of work and to the wider range of ideas involving the growth and decline, development and stagnation of entire societies, cultures, and civilizations.

Work is associated with the notion of value

Since no society is so isolated that it does not engage in some form of trade, exchange, or barter, and since every society has some form of internal reciprocal exchange between and among kinship groups, every society must have some notion of the value of the things it makes. The notion of value may be approached etically, from the point of view of the scientific observer, or it can be viewed emically, from the viewpoint of those wanting goods and services and who have their subjective ideas of what something is worth to them. In an industrialized society, the notion of value is expressed in monetary terms. Most goods and services are exchanged in the market, and the value of work embodied in those goods and services is measured quantitatively. In societies without money, the value of goods can only be expressed in terms of other goods. In societies without money, there are also prestige values associated with the giving and exchanging of gifts between trading partners or kinship groups or in marriage arrangements where two families exchange goods and gifts.

Firth has discussed the notion of value and work from an anthropological perspective (Wallman 1979:177–206). He describes how Marx, following the ideas of Adam Smith, saw commodities as being composed of two elements, exchange value and use value. Exchange value is determined by the amount of labor incorporated in the product, and use value is the utility that the object has for the purchaser. In trying to apply this notion to nonindustrial cutures, Firth found it did not fit situations where money was not used to exchange goods. He found that the value of a prestige good, such as turmeric (a crimson pigment) in Tikopia, was dependent upon a number of factors—scarcity of labor, alternative uses of labor, uncertainty, and a set of power considerations involving the mobilization of labor. Value, in Firth's view, is the result of a complex set of variables, of which the amount of labor in a product was only one. Firth states that normative elements, based on the cultural significance of certain objects in a particular society, are important in establishing value in work.

Sandra Wallman (1979:7–10) argues that the extent to which a person values one kind of work above another depends not only on the values of the society but on other options, other constraints, other obligations. In her view, value changes with historical and social context and with personal circumstances, depending on the role of the actor, what part of the work is focused upon, what kind of criteria is used, and when the work is done. Herskovits (1965:237) agreed with Wallman and Firth that "the phenomenon of value . . . can only be understood as . . . part of the wider phenomenon of culture." Whatever the viewpoint, we find inescapably that wherever there is work there is value. Even in a society such as the !Kung San, which is relatively isolated and self-sufficient, there is an evaluation of the worth of different parts of the animals they kill. There is also value given to the different contributions made by various hunters. Every society has a set of norms and values which inevitably affects the way work performed in the society is "evaluated." All work, no matter where it is performed, will become impregnated with the values of the society.

All work is carried on within a specific location, area, place or boundary

All work occurs within a particular space—hunters have territories, pastoralists have routes, auto workers work in factories, seaman sail on ships, and longshoremen work on docks. The physical environment of a workplace sets the kind of social environment one experiences at work. Work settings can either separate people from one another or bring them together. They will have significant effects on the communal ties within the workplace (Mills 1977:3–32).

Place becomes significant in the way certain work is viewed. The most common example is housework, which is characteristically undervalued in industrial societies. Bernard (1982:80–87) argues that housework has low status because it takes place in an environment where there is no competition, no wages paid for the work, where the work is isolating, and where there is no organization or hierarchy. Work in the household of American Pawnee Indians, on the other hand, carried as much prestige as that performed by the hunter, warrior, or medicine man (Weltfish 1979:233–235). The reason for this was that the Pawnee Roundhouse was a subsistence workshop where food was prepared and all manner of craft goods were made. Some types of work require mobility of workplace—herding, trucking, and seamanship. Work which requires shifting workplaces sometimes produces work styles and cultures associated with independence and aggressiveness. Other workplaces, like banks and libraries, foster quietness and decorum.

Places and boundaries for performing work are necessary aspects of exercising control in the workplace. All enterprises engaged in work seek to control entry and egress into and out of the work environment.

This is required for a number of reasons: 1. there are materials and tools to be safeguarded; 2. outsiders must not be allowed to interfere with the work process; 3. in the case of hunters, pastoralists, and agriculturalists, jurisdiction must be established over the land or territory to prevent outside encroachment and competition for the resources within the territory.

The nature of the workplace and the physical arrangements are crucial considerations in establishing consensus and communication at work. Anthropologists can make significant contributions to the understanding of social cohesion in the workplace. In the societies they have studied, people group themselves for the performance of work, based on a set of common feelings and mutual exchange. A knowledge of these arrangements and these principles may provide clues to enhance work and increase the personal fulfillment of humans at their work.

Herbert Applebaum

IX

Structuralism and Cognitive Anthropology

Introduction

Ino Rossi describes Lévi-Strauss' "epistemological attitude" as one which is based on the hypothesis that there is an underlying, hidden dimension to social phenomena, called social structure, which can be understood only through the use of some model. The underlying structure is "unconscious," by which Lévi-Strauss means that it is not within the heads of the actors of a society. The unconscious is used by Lévi-Strauss in the Kantian sense, namely that there are mechanisms within the human mind which permit it to close on relational connections. The structuralism of Lévi-Strauss contradicts the notions of empiricism, that objective reality can be understood and explained through objective observations. The Lévi-Straussian view sees the mental perceptions of humans as a mediating factor standing between the human being and the objective world.

The Lévi-Straussian view of the natural world is that it does not exist *for human beings* as a reality beyond the human conception of it. He does not say that it has no existence independently of human beings. He insists upon a dialectical relationship between human beings and their natural environment. In this way, he hopes to avoid the shortcomings of both the mechanistic and idealistic conception of reality. In his view, the human mind mediates between everyday life and the superstructure which human beings erect into institutions. Events are turned into signs and human beings communicate through symbols, thus imposing a

401

mental construct onto objective reality outside of themselves but related to themselves. In this connection, Lévi-Strauss said,

men communicate by means of symbols and signs . . . all cultural domains are pregnant with meaning and the anthropologist must work with meaning (1966b:115).

The structuralism applied to Lévi-Strauss is quite different from that of Radcliffe-Brown. Radcliffe-Brown was using structure within the context of society, as a set of institutions and organizational forms which preserved and maintained the stability of a society. Lévi-Strauss uses structure as a set of universal characteristics, innate structures of a psychobiological nature common to all human beings. Other scholars have sought universal structures of human nature, though from a different standpoint. Freud believed there were universal, psychological mechanisms and motives. Marx sought universals in the economic production of the necessities of life. Piaget researched child behavior with the idea of identifying universal patterns underlying cultural surface behavior.

Basic to the unity of human beings, according to Lévi-Strauss is a mental demand for order, a universal impulse toward classification (Garbarino 1983:85). While "primitive" classification may not coincide with our categories, it nevertheless imposes some sort of order on reality. Naming is one way of classifying experience and perceptions and communicating them. Information is stored and transmitted through such systematization. People sharing in one such system of classification are participants in the same culture. But even those who do not share that particular culture still participate in a common human foundation through the universal infrastructures posited by Lévi-Strauss, and that foundation makes possible communication across cultural borders.

While Freud was named by Lévi-Strauss as one of his major influences, he differed with Freud in his concept of the unconscious. Freud stressed the psychic content of unconscious mental activity. He saw it as a set of impulses striving for discharge. It included sensations, emotions, feelings, and conceptions connected with averted impulses. For Lévi-Strauss, the unconscious was not based on content but on form. It does not contain emotional feelings or psychic energy. Rather, its function is to impose structural laws upon psychic content, which originates elsewhere. Psychic content becomes significant when it is transformed into language, which is structured by the unconscious. Lévi-Strauss' concept of the unconscious led to some of his most important views:

1. The priority of a structural or synchronic view of society rather than a diachronic, things-in-change view.

2. The priority of collective and universal structures over individual ones.
3. Concern with a theory of the mind rather than the content of psychological research.

Though he stresses form over content, Lévi-Strauss does recognize the importance of concrete phenomena in scientific investigation. He sees concrete phenomena as needed for verification of underlying structures. He sees the mind in tune with the inherent structures in the objective world of nature. Thus, he has the grandiose notion that structuralism would finally unite human beings with the natural world. He believes basic thinking occurs as a set of contrasts, and these contrasts exist in the objective world—day, night; black, white; life, death; spirit, body. The dualism also appears in myths and in kinship organization. Thus, Lévi-Strauss' structuralism is an eclectic effort to integrate ideas from linguistics, biology, anthropology, philosophy (Kant), and other social sciences and to combine them into an integrating effort which views the human mind as imposing an order and comprehension upon the world by being in tune with its natural order and function.

The structuralism of Lévi-Strauss had its origins in linguistic analysis, particularly that of Ferdinand de Saussure. Saussure developed a synchronic analysis of language, as contrasted with an historical approach. Saussure differentiated between *la langue* (language) and *la parole* (spoken words), in which the former was the idea studied by specialists, while the latter was speech spoken by people communicating with one another. Saussure, like others, saw language as a way of ordering one's world.

What attracted Lévi-Strauss to Saussure and, later, Jakobson (1965) was their concepts of the universality of language and its binary character. Lévi-Strauss was attracted to linguistics and its universality, believing that it provided tools by which anthropologists could go beyond mechanical models toward more statistical ones. He distinguished between mechanical models, which are based on empirical data, and statistical models, where the population is too large for a mechanical model and a sampling for a statistical model is used. He saw human phenomena as somewhere between the two.

Regarding the binary nature of language, Lévi-Strauss expanded on this idea and used a duality and a dialectic to present various theories on myth, kinship, food, and other cultural phenomena. In the *Elementary Structures of Kinship* (1969a), he bases his concept of exchange on the reciprocity and duality of the fact that men exchange women, and not vice versa. In the *Raw and The Cooked* (1969b), he posits that a large body of mythology, in one way or another, is based on the fundamental opposition of nature versus culture. He presents a number of conceptions as to how myths are transformed, one into another: through a weakening of polar opposites, inversion of explicit ethnological content, mutation of the hero, correlative inversion, mutation of attitudes, and relation of hero's function to hero's mutation. He differentiates between elementary transformations and global transformations. His insights seem to have thrown light on universal laws of metaphor, and thus Lévi-Strauss has attracted the attention of literature scholars. In sum, Lévi-Strauss bases his binary dialectics on his belief that preoccupation with the contrast of nature and culture is a universal concern of mankind.

Structuralism is meaningful if one believes that the human realm cannot be treated as a series of events similar to those in the physical world. A natural scientist can talk about the physical world without taking into account lay impressions. But in the human realm, events having meaning, and include, in addition to scientific explanations or description, interpretations which people, at large, give to events. The difference between the scientist's view and the layman's view is analogous to the difference between Saussure's language (*la langue*) and actual speech (*la parole*). The difference between *la langue* and *la parole* is important to structuralism. It is the difference between institution and event, between underlying systems and instances of behavior. The system of underlying systems involves abstracting and conceptualizing in order to see how forms are related to one another. The study of concrete behavior focuses on reasons for actions to take place and the probabilities that actions will occur in particular circumstances. Lévi-Strauss expresses his debt to linguistics as follows (1967b:31):

First, structural linguistics shifts from the study of 'conscious' linguistic phenomena to the study of their 'unconscious' infrastructure; second, it does not treat 'terms' as independent entities, taking instead as its basis of analysis the 'relations' between terms; third, it introduces the concept of 'system'; . . . finally, linguistics aims at discovering 'general laws,' either by induction or . . . by logical deduction, which would give them absolute character.

The structuralist view is a systems view. A whole set of relations between elements must be studied to discover the relational patterns. Structure is not an observable fact. It is not derived through the accumulation of empirical data. It is discovered because the human brain has the capacity to devise meaning patterns. Structures are not simply theoretical constructs devised by the observer. They exist in the mind of the observer as the "source" of the relations observed. They are part of the observer's psyche. For Lévi-Strauss, structures emanating from the human mind existed before social systems and are not derivative. And they are the same unconscious mechanisms for all people. Lévi-Strauss stated (1967b:21–22):

> If as we believe to be the case, the unconscious activity of the mind consists in imposing form upon content, and if these forms are fundamentally the same for all minds—ancient or modern, primitive or civilized (as the study of the symbolic function, as expressed in language, so strikingly indicates)—it is necessary and sufficient to grasp the unconscious structure underlying each institution and each custom in order to obtain a principle of interpretation valid for other institutions and other customs, provided, of course, that the analysis is carried far enough.

Structuralism studies human phenomena in societies as incarnated mental activities which are made concrete by their appearance at a certain time and place. In Lévi-Strauss' view, man's relationship to the world is mediated by the instrument used to conceptualize the relationship. In this sense, the structure of the brain is the first constraint imposed on human beings. The brain follows its genetically inherited program in the fashion of a computer, through the binary code. Society is a machine for the exchange of communication; social phenomena are messages; the structure of language is a code used to convert messages. As a computer is based on the binary code, so is the human brain which functions through oppositional distinctions. The clue to the functioning of the brain is the way language is mastered, through the Saussurian method of distinctions.

Lévi-Strauss ranged over many subjects, but certain common threads run through his ideas and methods:

1. the concern with underlying structures beneath appearances,
2. the binary nature of phenomena and thought,
3. the principle of exchange in social relations, and
4. the search for universals.

Like Sartre, Lévi-Strauss is one of the rare modern thinkers who has created an overarching theoretical system. He has attracted much attention, not only in anthropology but in the humanities and in the study of literature and poetics. For a comparison of his grand system with that of Sartre, the reader can consult Rosen (1974). For a full explanation of Lévi-Strauss' ideas and those of his critics, the reader should look at the complete volume of Ino Rossi, from which Chapter 27 was taken.

Cognitive anthropology developed in the 1950s, when a group of anthropologists, including Ward Goodenough, H. C. Conklin, and Paul Kay, sought to study cultures from the viewpoint of the people living within the cultures studied. This was not a new idea. Boas had said that cultures should be studied from the native point of view. And Malinowski stressed the same thing. What was new with this approach was the attempt to eliminate the ethnographer's categories entirely.

The term cognitive anthropology, while increasingly used to encompass the various cognitive approaches in anthropology, has not been entirely standardized to include all of them. In the past, cognitive studies have been identified as ethnoscience, ethnosemantics, componential analysis, new ethnography, ethnolinguistics, psycholinguistics, new structuralism, and French structuralism. They are all founded on the notion that there is a pan-human way of knowing, based on deep structures within the human mind. The attempt to understand native categories is what is implied by cognitive anthropology. It is an effort to get at the organizing principles that underlie behavior within each society. It does not study what people actually do. Rather, it studies the rules for behavior. It does not predict how people will actually behave. It searches for what behavior is appropriate for particular situations or contexts within a particular culture.

Recognition of cognitive anthropology, called ethnoscience in the past, can be traced to Ward Goodenough, particularly his article, "Componential Analysis" (1956). While ethnoscience is basically a methodology, its theoretical underpinning is that real culture exists only in the minds of the culture bearers (Garbarino 1983:82). Each person in a particular culture has his or her own mental template or map of the culture. Goodenough defines this as what the individual must know to operate successfully within his society.

Those using the method of ethnoscience were seeking ways of eliciting information without imposing their own preconceived ideas on them. To avoid using his own classifications, the ethnoscientist used linguistic procedures based on the native language to get the informant's own categories. If correct procedures were followed, a taxonomy or model of all components germane to the native's concept of a subject and free of the anthropologist's categories, could be developed. Most of the early inquiries by ethnoscientists dealt with rather restricted domains like color categories, folk medicine, and plant classifications. It was an exhaustive and time-consuming technique, and just to recover the total perceptions of a single individual involved enormous amounts of a researcher's time.

In the past, researchers using various types of cognitive anthropology concentrated on perfecting their methods of eliciting information. They won some important grounds for insight and analysis of kinship, color, cuisine, botany, and disease. However, sometimes the techniques were deemed more important than the phenomena studied. The relationships between the data being sought and the larger workings of the societies were often not worked out, so that the data, while interesting in and of itself, did not lead to explanations of how the people in the cultures viewed their world.

In the past, cognitive anthropologists have been hazy about their goals. At present, they are more explicit. Through comparative study, they seek insights about the cognitive processes which they believe are universal. This is a modern version of Adolph Bastian's "psychic unity" of mankind wherein, regardless of which society, people shared certain basic biopsychological mental processes. The ideas of Noam Chomsky (1966) have influenced cognitive anthropologists. Chomsky and other linguists proceed on the hypothesis that the ability to create and use language is uniquely human and genetically transmitted through neurophysiological structures in the brain. Linguistics and cognitive anthropologists both seek to understand the nature of these innate structures and thereby gain an understanding of both language and culture.

In recent years, as this new field came to be called cognitive anthropology, the focus shifted. Rather than stressing eliciting techniques to get at native classifications, researchers now seek to discover the ways the mind functions to draw inferences and supply keys to action. Decision theory was developed in which attempts are made to ascertain the informational base upon which certain actors in a market make decisions about economic activities (Richardson 1982:421–436). Cognitive anthropology delved into the logical processes and abstract thinking patterns of people in various cultures (Colby, Fernandez, and Kronenfeld 1981:422–450). Attempts were made not only to study the content of cognition but also the mental processes by which ideas, symbols, and norms are interrelated. Clifford Geertz (1973) described a cock fight in Bali, using that event to explain and identify the norms of Balinese society. The Balinese were all involved in the preparations, features, and personal relationships associated with the holding of the cock fight.

One problem with using native informants to discover the rules of a society is that the rules will vary with the informant. This was illustrated in the Margaret Mead-Derek Freeman controversy. Freeman's conclusions regarding the nature of Samoan culture was at variance with Mead's. But so were his informants. Mead questioned young girls, while Freeman relied on old men. Margaret Mead herself was quite young when she did her study, *Coming of Age in Samoa*. There was no way an older man like Freeman could have been privy to honest and private views regarding sex habits of the young girls. Freeman relied on older men, leaders of the Samoan society, and, predictably, received a different impression of the essence of Samoan society. Probably both were right, and probably both were reflecting a different segment of Samoan society. For a discussion of this controversy, see Chapter 30 by Nancy Scheper-Hughes.

Cognitive anthropologists have begun to focus on text analysis and the cognitive process associated with writing (Colby, Fernandez, and Kronenberg 1981). The ability to fix ideas on paper, where they can be perused, studied, analyzed, and taken apart enables human beings to develop and enlarge their capacities for abstract and logical thought. When communication is restricted to verbal messages only, they tend to be event specific. They are subject to error or misunderstanding. And there can be omitted messages or just plain lying. A written text can be checked for misinformation. The study of texts and the interpretation of texts is part of a discipline called hermeneutics and will be dealt with in the section on Symbolic Anthropology (Part 11).

In the study of a society, the anthropologist is faced with the task of making sense out of the seeming chaos in the multiplicity of behavior and ideas facing him as he or she looks at another culture. There are two ways of bringing order out of chaos—impose order based on the categories of the anthropologist, or discover the order or classifications used by people within the culture. The cognitive anthropoligist relies on the second method. Often, the cognitive anthropologist will take the native categories, discovered through field research and interviews, and arrange them in some logical order. This logical order often takes the form of taxonomies, paradigms, and trees (Tyler 1969). A *taxonomy* is a logical order in which classes of phenomena are hierarchically arranged by a process of *inclusion*. For example, sofas, tables, chairs each constitute a class but are contained within a larger grouping called "furniture." A *paradigm* is a logical arrangement in which *features* of a class are arranged to show their *multiple* dimensions and their *intersecting* dimensions. For example, a horse is a kind of animal. This is part of a taxonomy. But an *adult* horse which is also (intersecting) a *female* is a "mare." This is a paradigm. It arranges features of a class. In addition to taxonomies and paradigms, features can be arranged in a logical diagram called a *tree*. Features in a tree are ordered by sequential contrast of only one feature at a time. Trees are arranged on successive *choices* between two *alternatives*. Trees are used in botony to illustrate contrastive features. Unlike a taxonomy, items at a lower level are not included in the higher one. Unlike a paradigm, features in a tree do not intersect. For example, in a tree, a flower can be spurred or not spurred. If it is not spurred, it has no petals. If it has no petals, it can be a ranunculus or an involucre. If it is an involucre, it can be an anemone or a clematis—and so on. One can see the value of a tree for setting out decision alternatives. In their research, cognitive anthropologists used these logics, relying on the communication and linguistic repertories of native speakers.

Cognitive anthropology, with its emphasis on the rules of behavior rather than behavior itself, can be called a formal approach to culture. Just as the grammar of a language provides the rules of a language, but cannot predict what actually will be spoken or written, so cognitive anthropology seeks to discover the rules of a culture, but does not claim it can predict behavior in the culture under study. It hopes to outline what is expected or appropriate behavior in particular situations. Cognitive anthropology does not aim at a description of events to discover process or change. It is mainly concerned with underlying ideas and the logical connections of ideas about the world. Some cognitive anthropologists (Tyler 1969; Colby, Fernandez, and Kronenberg 1981) believe that, at present, it is not possible to develop a general theory of culture. They hope through a series of cognitive studies to develop multiple theories of particular cultures, which one day may provide the basis for a comparative study leading to a general theory of culture.

There is a continuing debate among anthropologists as to whether anthropology is a formal or an empirical science. Many anthropologists believe that social analysis should be based on empirical data, involving material and mental phenomena which are observable and orderable into a system of generalizations which are testable on a probabilistic basis (Harris 1979b). Most cultural anthropologists realize that the social science cannot hope to achieve the levels of exactness and predictability possible in the natural sciences. But given the limitations of studying human behavior, many social scientists still regard the scientific method as the basis for their field. Cognitive anthropologists operate on the assumption that their data are mental phenomena to be dissected by formal operations comparable to the rules of logic. Each culture under study has a set of principles which order the relevant events, material life, and ideas. For the cognitive anthropologist, these logical principles should be the object of investigation by those seeking an understanding of a particular culture. To them, the logical rules are the culture. For them, cultural anthropology is a formal science. Comparative analysis of these logical rules, in the view of cognitive anthropology, can lead to a general theory of culture, which will be the formal features of cultures rather than substantive variables.

In conclusion, cognitive anthropology represents a relatively new development in cultural anthropology. It involves studying the organizing principles underlying behavior, rather than behavior itself. It assumes that every culture contains its own unique system for perceiving things, events, and behavior. The object of anthropological study, for them, is not the material phenomena but the ways they are categorized. Cognitive anthropology is a mentalist approach to the study of society. To the cognitive anthropologist, cultures are not material things, they are ideas. Cultures are not behavior, they are rules for behavior. Cultures are not institutions, they are organizing principles for institutions. And finally, cognitive anthropologists seek generalizations and regularities by relying on the generalizations and regularities perceived by the people living in the culture under investigation.

Claude Lévi-Strauss

26. Social Structure: Structural Anthropology

Definition and Problems of Method

Passing now to the task of defining "social structure," there is a point which should be cleared up immediately. The term "social structure" has nothing to do with empirical reality but with models which are built up after it. This should help one to clarify the difference between two concepts which are so close to each other that they have often been confused, namely, those of *social structure* and of *social relations*. It will be enough to state at this time that social relations consist of the raw materials out of which the models making up the social structure are built, while social structure can, by no means, be reduced to the ensemble of the social relations to be described in a given society. Therefore, social structure cannot claim a field of its own among others in the social studies. It is rather a method to be applied to any kind of social studies, similar to the structural analysis current in other disciplines.

The question then becomes that of ascertaining what kind of model deserves the name "structure." This is not an anthropological question, but one which belongs to the methodology of science in general. Keeping this in mind, we can say that a structure consists of a model meeting with several requirements.

First, the structure exhibits the characteristics of a system. It is made up of several elements, none of which can undergo a change without effecting changes in all the other elements.

Second, for any given model there should be a possibility of ordering a series of transformations resulting in a group of models of the same type.

Third, the above properties make it possible to predict how the model will react if one or more of its elements are submitted to certain modifications.

Finally, the model should be constituted so as to make immediately intelligible all the observed facts.

These being the requirements for any model with structural value, several consequences follow. These, however, do not pertain to the definition of structure, but have to do with the chief properties exhibited and problems raised by structural analysis when contemplated in the social and other fields.

Order of Orders. Thus anthropology considers the whole social fabric as a network of different types of orders. The kinship system provides a way to order individuals according to certain rules; social organization is another way of ordering individuals and groups; social stratifications, whether economic or political, provide us with a third type; and all these orders can themselves be orderd by showing the kind of relationships which exist among them, how they interact with one another in both the synchronic and the diachronic levels. Meyer Fortes has successfully tried to construct models valid not only for one type of order (kinship, social organization, economic relations, etc.) but where numerous models for all types of orders are themselves ordered inside a total model.

When dealing with these orders, however, anthropologists are confronted with a basic problem which was taken up at the beginning of this paper, that is, to what extent does the manner according to which a society conceives its orders and their ordering correspond to the real situation? It has been shown that this problem can be solved in different ways, depending on the data at hand.

All the models considered so far, however, are "lived-in" orders: they correspond to mechanisms which can be studied from the outside as a part of objective reality. But no systematic studies of these orders can be undertaken without acknowledging the fact that social groups, to achieve their reciprocal ordering, need to call upon orders of different types, corresponding to a field external to objective reality and which we call the "supernatural." These "thought-of" orders cannot be checked against the experience to which they refer, since they are one and the same as this experience. Therefore, we are in the position of studying them only in their relationships with the other types of "lived-in" orders. The "thought-of" orders are those of myth and religion. The question may be raised whether, in our own society, political ideology does not belong to the same category.

After Durkheim, Radcliffe-Brown has contributed greatly to the demonstration that religion is a part of the social structure. The anthropologist's task is to discover correlations between different types of religions and different types of social organization. Radcliffe-Brown failed to achieve significant results, however, for two reasons. In the first place, he tried to link ritual and beliefs directly to sentiments; besides, he was more concerned with giving universal formulation to the kind of correlation prevailing between religion and social structure than in showing the variability of one in relation to the other. It is perhaps as a result of this that the study of religion has fallen into the background, to the extent that the word "religion" does not even appear in the program of this symposium. The field of myth, ritual, and religion seems nevertheless to be one of the more fruitful for the study of social structure; though relatively little has been done in this respect, the results which have been obtained recently are among the most rewarding in our field.

Great strides have been made toward the study of religious systems as coordinated wholes. Documentary material, such as P. Radin's *The Road of Life and Death*[1] and R. M. Berndt's *Kunapipi*,[2] should help in undertaking, with respect to several religious cults, the kind of ordering of data so masterfully achieved by Gladys Reichard for the Navaho.[3] This should be complemented by small-scale comparative studies on the permanent and non-permanent elements in religious thought as exemplified by Lowie.

With the help of such well-organized material it becomes possible, as Nadel puts it, to prepare "small-scale models of a comparative analysis . . . of an analysis of 'concomitant variations' . . . such as any inquiry concerned with the explanation of social facts must employ."[4] The results thus achieved may be small; they are, however, some of the most convincing and rigorous in the entire field of social organization. Nadel himself had demonstrated a correlation between shamanism and some aspects of psychological development;[5] using Indo-European comparative material borrowed from Iceland, Ireland, and the Caucasus, Dumézil has interpreted an enigmatic mythological figure in relation to specific features of social organization;[6] Wittfogel and Goldfrank have shown how significant variations in mythological themes can be related to the socioeconomic background.[7] Monica Hunter has established beyond doubt that the structure of magical beliefs may vary in correlation with the structure of the society itself.[8] These results, together with some others (on which space prevents our commenting), give hope that we may be close to understanding not only what kind of function religious beliefs fulfill in social life (this has been known more or less clearly since Lucretius' time) but how they fulfill this function.

A few words may be added as a conclusion. This chapter was started by working out the notion of "model," and the same notion has reappeared at its end. Social anthropology, in its incipient stage, could only seek, as model for its first models, among those of the simplest kinds provided by more advanced sciences, and it was natural enough to seek them in the field of classical mechanics. However, in doing so, anthropology has been working under some sort of illusion, since, as Von Neumann puts it, "an almost exact theory of a gas, containing about 10^{25} freely moving particles, is incomparably easier than that of the solar system, made up of 9 major bodies."[9] But when it tries to construct its models, anthropology finds itself in a situation which is neither the one nor the other: The objects with which we deal—social roles and human beings—are considerably more numerous than those dealt with in Newtonian mechanics, and at the same time, far less numerous than would be required to allow a satisfactory use of the laws of statistics and probability. Thus we find ourselves in an intermediate zone: too complicated for one treatment and not complicated enough for the other.

The tremendous change brought about by the theory of communication consists precisely in the discovery of methods to deal with objects—signs—which can be subjected to a rigorous study despite the fact that they are altogether much more numerous than those of classical mechanics and much less than those of thermodynamics. Language consists of morphemes, a few thousand in number; significant regularities in phoneme frequencies can be obtained by limited counts. The threshold for the use of statistical laws becomes lower, and that for operating with mechanical models higher, than was the case when operating on other grounds. And, at the same time, the size-order of the phenomena has become significantly closer to that of anthropological data.

Therefore, the present conditions of social-structure studies can be summarized as follows: Phenomena are found to be of the same kind as those which, in strategics and communication theory, were made the subject of a rigorous approach. Anthropological facts are on a scale which is sufficiently close to that of these other phenomena as not to preclude their similar treatment. Surprisingly enough, it is at the very moment when anthropology finds itself closer than ever to the long-awaited goal of becoming a true science that the ground seems to fail where it was expected to be the firmest: The facts themselves are lacking, either not numerous enough or not collected under conditions insuring their comparability.

Though it is not our fault, we have been behaving like amateur botanists, haphazardly picking up heterogeneous specimens, which were further distorted and mutilated by preservation in our herbarium. And we are, all of a sudden, confronted with the need of ordering complete series, ascertaining original shades, and measuring minute parts which have either shrunk or been lost. When we come to realize not only what should be done but also what we should be in a position to do, and when we make at the same time an inventory of our material, we cannot help feeling in a disheartened mood. It looks almost as if cosmic physics were asked to work with Babylonian observations. The celestial bodies are still there, but unfortunately the native cultures from which we used to gather our data are rapidly disappearing and that which they are being replaced by can only furnish data of a very different type. To adjust our techniques of observation to a theoretical framework which is far more advanced is a paradoxical situation, quite opposite to that which has prevailed in the history of sciences. Nevertheless, such is the challenge to modern anthropology.

Notes

1. A. L. Kroeber, *Anthropology* (New York: 1948), p. 325. Compare with the statement by the same author: ". . . the term 'social structure' which is tending to replace 'social organization' without appearing to add either content or emphasis of meaning." A. L. Kroeber, "Structure, Function and Pattern in Biology and Anthropology," *Scientific Monthly,* LVI (1943), p. 105.

2. The same idea appears to underlie E. R. Leach's remarkable study, "Jinghpaw Kinship Terminology," *Journal of the Royal Anthropological Institute,* LXXV (1945).

3. Compare Von Neumann: "Such models [as games] are theoretical constructs with a precise, exhaustive and not too complicated definition; and they must be similar to reality in those respects which are essential to the investigation at hand. To recapitulate in detail: The definition must be precise and exhaustive in order to make a mathematical treatment possible. The construct must not be unduly complicated so that the mathematical treatment can be brought beyond the mere formalism to the point where it yields complete numerical results. Similarity to reality is needed to make the operation significant. And this similarity must usually be restricted to a few traits deemed 'essential' *pro tempore*—since otherwise the above requirements would conflict with each other." J. Von Neumann and O. Morgenstern, *Theory of Games and Economic Behavior* (Princeton: 1944).

4. K. Goldstein, *Der Aufbau des Organismus.* French translation (Paris: 1951), pp. 18–25. [English translation, New York: 1939.]

5. F. Boas (ed.), *Handbook of American Indian Languages,* Bureau of American Ethnology Bulletin 40 (1908), 1911, Part I.

6. See "Introduction: History and Anthropology," Chapter I of the *Lévi-Strauss* volume.

7. For examples and detailed discussion, see C. Lévi-Strauss, *Les Structures élémentaires de la parenté* (Paris: 1949), p. 558 ff.

8. R. Firth, *Elements of Social Organization* (London: 1951), pp. 28–31.

9. On this point, see Chapters VII and VIII of the *Lévi-Strauss* volume.

Ino Rossi

27. Intellectual Antecedents of Lévi-Strauss' Notion of Unconscious[1]

Lévi-Strauss' epistemological attitude is based on the hypothesized existence of an unconscious meaning of cultural phenomena and on the
methodological concepts of structure and model. Since his early writings, Lévi-Strauss has explicitly rejected immediate and spontaneous
evidence as a criterion of truth. As a consequence, he has questioned the
adequacy of the empiricist method insofar as it claims to reach reality
only through sensory perceptions and has rejected the phenomenological and existentialist methods insofar as they maintain that reality can be
reached through our conscious experience without offering any guarantee against the illusions of subjectivity (1965:61–62).

Lévi-Strauss compares his own approach to the geological method
and claims that his major sources of inspiration are Freud, Marx, and
Saussure. These masters have shown him that true reality rather than
being obvious evades our efforts of detection (*ibid.*). Consequently, the
operation of understanding consists of reducing apparent reality to its
hidden dimension through a process of decoding (1966c:33). What is,
then, the relation between rational and sensory knowledge? Marx and
Rousseau have shown that knowledge in physics and social sciences is
not based on sense perception, but on the construction of a model
(1965:61) through which we can interpret empirical reality and discover
its unconscious infrastructure.

Lévi-Strauss' notion of unconscious cannot be reduced to an arbitrary
epistemological idiosyncrasy, since he claims that this notion is present
in some social thinkers opposed to the empiricist mode of analysis.
There has been a good deal of literature on the issue of the intellectual
antecedents of Lévi-Strauss, but there is not always agreement on how
important is the influence of particular thinkers on his works. Some of
the intellectual influences have been denied by Lévi-Strauss in various

416

private correspondences, while others have been admitted by him with some qualifications (1969b:11).

Lévi-Strauss does not belong to one specific anthropological tradition or to a homogeneous group of traditions. Rather, he borrows some elements, and not necessarily the most important ones, from certain theoretical perspectives in psychology (Gestalt, Freud), sociology and anthropology (Rousseau, Durkheim, Mauss, Marx), linguistics (Saussure, Troubetzkoy, Jakobson), philosophy (Kant, Rousseau), cybernetics (Wiener, von Neumann, Shannon), etc. The elements which Lévi-Strauss borrows from these thinkers do not make up a heterogeneous eclecticism, but are organized in a consistent epistemological and methodological perspective. However, the highly personal way in which Lévi-Strauss has selected, systematized, and applied these elements has made it difficult for many social scientists to understand and even label his approach to sociocultural phenomena.

In this paper I limit my attention to those intellectual antecedents of Lévi-Strauss which are important to clarify the postulate of the unconscious dimension of cultural phenomena. In explaining the reason for not choosing the individual and its consciousness as the central perspective of his approach, Lévi-Strauss has very recently mentioned the same masters he mentioned in 1955 (1965:59–63). What structuralism wants to accomplish after Rousseau, Marx, Durkheim, Saussure, and Freud is to unveil to consciousness an "object other" and more important than consciousness itself (1971:563), that is, its unconscious infrastructure or the mechanisms and conditions of its functioning. Since I am discussing the influence of the intellectual antecedents of Lévi-Strauss' works from the point of view of their most fundamental epistemological notion, I will follow a systematic rather than a historical method of exposition.[2]

The Symbolic Meaning of Sociocultural Phenomena Is Made Possible by Their Unconscious Infrastructure

Lévi-Strauss has repeatedly refused to consider structuralism as a philosophy and has denied having or even being interested in one. However, he has participated comfortably in philosophical round-table discussions (see Lévi-Strauss, 1963a) and doesn't dislike interviews with professional philosophers. In these circumstances Lévi-Strauss explicitly recognizes his philosophical training as an important component of his anthropological method. In one of these interviews Lévi-Strauss states the following: "Philosophically I find myself more and more Kantian, not so much because of the particular content of Kant's doctrine, but rather for the specific way of posing the problem of knowledge. First of all, because anthropology appears to me as a philosophy of knowledge, a philosophy of concept; I think that anthropology can make progress only if it is situated at the level of the concept" (1963b:38). Elsewhere, Lévi-Strauss quotes Mauss' assertion that "the mental and the social [component of social reality] are undistinguishable" (1966b:22) and explains that the raw material of social phenomena consists in the common aspects of mental structures and institutional schemata (1969a:95).

Lévi-Strauss' position is characterized by the peculiar conception of the symbolic component of culture. Lévi-Strauss, trained in philosophy at the Sorbonne, finds congenial the task of purifying and continuing some elements of Durkheimian thought, which was under the influence of Kant (1945:518). In Lévi-Strauss' view, both Durkheim and Mauss insisted on the psychic nature of social phenomena, and Durkheim did not limit himself to stress "the mental side of social processes" but went so far as to conclude that they belong to the realm of ideals (*ibid.*:508–509).

Among the various deficiencies or contradictions of Durkheim's thinking Lévi-Strauss mentions his conceptualization of social phenomena. In Lévi-Strauss' opinion, Durkheim was at his best when he stated that intellectual activity, far from being the reflection of social organization, is presupposed by the latter, and therefore was at his worst when he proposed the opposite view of the primacy of the social over the intellectual component of culture. Lévi-Strauss praises Bergson for having clearly perceived that the concepts of class and opposition are the immediate data of "understanding," which are used in the formation of social order; in Lévi-Strauss' view, this conception constitutes "the foundations of a genuine sociological logic" (1967:96–97).

In *The Savage Mind*, Lévi-Strauss has somewhat elaborated his idea of "socio-logic" as the basis of sociology (1966:76). He asserts that "the universe is an object of thought" (*ibid.*:3), and against the Naturalist school he maintains that natural conditions, rather than being passively accepted, are defined, given meaning, and developed in specific directions. Man reduces natural reality to concepts which are organized into an unpredetermined system, and this is the reason why facts are "not of a natural but a logical order" (*ibid.*:95). Lévi-Strauss clarifies the Durkheimian thesis of the social origin of logical thought by stating that between social structures and the conceptual system there is a dialectical relationship rather than a causal relationship. The relationship between man and universe is the common substratum of the social and intellectual system, a substratum from which each one of these systems translates specific historical and spacial modalities (*ibid.*:214). One can see here elements of a dialectical view capable of avoiding the shortcomings of a causal and/or idealistic conception of culture.

Lévi-Strauss explains that the human mind mediates between infra-structure or praxis (man's activity) and superstructure or practices (cultural institutions) by elaborating a conceptual system which is a synthesizing operation between ideas and facts; through this mediation facts are turned into signs (*ibid.*:131).[3] It follows that since "men communicate by means of symbols and signs," all cultural domains are "pregnant with meaning," and the anthropologist must work with meaning (1966a:115).

Because social phenomena are made possible by the fundamental mediation of the conceptual schemata and are pregnant with meaning, their only suitable explanation must be dialectical. In an early theoretical essay Lévi-Strauss peculiarly defines dialectic explanation in opposition to mechanical explanation, that is, as an explanation which consists in "rethinking [social phenomena] in their logical order." Durkheim advocates this type of sociological explanation since social phenomena are "objectivated systems of ideas." At the same time, Durkheim also advocates the "methodical experiment" to study social facts as if they were "things." How can we apply both the dialectical and the experimental methods? Lévi-Strauss solves this Durkheimian antinomy by saying that the objectivated systems of ideas are unconscious "or that unconscious psychical structures underlie them and make them possible"; "the unconscious teleology of mind" explains "how social phenomena may present the character of meaningful wholes and of structuralized ensembles." Because of this basic fact, social phenomena present the character of "things" and at the same time can be treated as ideas to be rethought in their logical order (1945:518, 528, 534). Since it is a question of unconscious logical order, the anthropologist must aim at discovering the mechanisms of an objectivated (unconscious) thought on an ethnographic basis (1963a:640; 1969b:10–11), that is, at finding out how the human mind works in the most different societies or "incarnated mental activities" (1963b:31).

One question immediately arises: Where should we search for the meaning that Lévi-Strauss defines as being the proper concern of social anthropology? Does the notion of unconscious structures and objectivated thought imply that the meaning of which social actors are aware has to be totally rejected as a spurious or deceptive meaning?

The Unconscious Meaning Is More Important Than the Conscious One

Lévi-Strauss recognizes that social facts "are lived by man, and that subjective consciousness is as much a form of their reality as their objective characteristics" (1966a:113). In his view, however, the conscious level of social processes is the proper object of history, while anthropology should be concerned with its "unconscious foundations" (1963:18).

I omit the discussion of the evidence and authorities that Lévi-Strauss cites to prove the existence of an unconscious meaning underlying the apparent and conscious one (on this point see Rossi, 1973), and I examine the arguments by which Lévi-Strauss claims to prove the greater importance of the unconscious meaning over the conscious one.

Lévi-Strauss refers to Boas when he assserts that "all types of social phenomena (language, beliefs, techniques and customs) have this in common, that their elaboration in the mind is at the level of unconscious thought" (1969a:108). Boas made the point that the classificatory concepts of primitives never rise into consciousness and, therefore, must originate in unconscious mental processes (Boas, 1911/1968:63). Linguistic and other cultural facts are grouped together under certain ideas and categories which are unconscious. Our experience gives evidence of the unconscious origin of certain clusters of activities, such as table manners, habits, and automatic repetition of actions. For example, the danger of cutting the lips is easily given as the reason for not bringing the table knife to the mouth; however, this explanation is only a "secondary rationalistic" explanation, since we know that the fork came into being later than the knife and that in certain areas people use sharply pointed forks no less dangerous than the knife, while in other areas people use dull knives. The conclusion is that we do not know the origin of this particular custom, which may have been created for entirely different reasons than those we give (*ibid.*:64–65). In Lévi-Strauss' perspective, one could say that in this sense the unconscious reason or origin of cultural phenomena is more genuine and important than the conscious explanation.

Freud and Marx are the other two masters who have convinced Lévi-Strauss of the fundamental importance of the unconscious. From Freud he has learned that "what is not conscious is more important than what is conscious" (1963a:648), "and that the true meaning is not the one we are aware of, but the one hidden behind it" (1963b:41). This belief has been reinforced by the Marxian creed that "men are always victims of their own as well as other people's frauds" (*ibid.*:41).

Lévi-Strauss' thinking can be further clarified if we consider its relationship with the French socioanthropological school. According to Lévi-Strauss, Mauss constantly referred to the unconscious as the common and specific character of social facts; "in magic as in religion as in linguistics, the unconscious ideas are the ones which act" (1966b:30). The "unconscious categories" for Mauss are not just one component of cultural phenomena, but rather their "determinants" (1966a:113).

Lévi-Strauss comments on Mauss' effort in connection with the work of the linguistic school of Prague. At the same time that Mauss wrote "The Gift," Troubetzkoy and Jakobson, with the help of a new operational technique, were capable of distinguishing more phenomenological data, which evade scientific analysis, from their simpler infrastructure to which they owe all of their reality. It was unfortunate that Mauss did not apply his new discovery in the anthropological analysis of the ethnographic material (1966b:35). Durkheim and Mauss in surveying the native categories of thought substituted the conscious representations of the natives for those of the anthropologist, but in Lévi-Strauss' opinion, this important step was still inadequate since conscious representations may be quite remote from unconscious reality (1963:282).

Echoing Boas' formulation, Lévi-Strauss asserts that the conscious representations of the natives are "rationalized interpretations" of the unconscious categories (1966a:113) or "a sort of 'dialectical average' among multiplicity of unconscious systems" (*ibid.*:117). Consequently, anthropological analysis can be scientific only if moved to the level of the simpler unconscious infrastructure.[4]

The Unconscious Activity of Mind Imposes Structures upon Physical and Psychic Content. The Aggregate of These Structures Constitutes the Unconscious (Lévi-Strauss, 1963:202–203)

The term "unconscious" needs clarification since it has been used to refer to social behavior which is "unresponsive, indiscriminating, conditional, subliminal, unattending, insightless, unremembering, unlearned, unrecognizing, ignored and unavailable to awareness" (Machotka, 1964, in Bowman, 1965:320). Besides, the philosopher von Hartmann saw in the unconscious the primordial foundation of reality, that is, "a mysterious and hidden power [which] guides to a definite end and goal all the phenomena of the objective real world [nature] as well as that of the subjective ideal [mind]" (Darnoi, 1967:50). The notion that unconscious behavior influences our conscious behavior is found even among poets, physicians, essayists, mystics, and in the philosophies of Schopenhauer and Schelling (Whyte, 1962).

Lévi-Strauss' notion of the unconscious is a product of his interpretation of certain elements he claims to borrow from such disparate sources as structural linguistics, Freud, Kant, and cybernetics.

The Unconscious and Structural Linguistics

Lévi-Strauss gives credit to Jakobson and Troubetzkoy for having proved the existence of unconscious linguistic structures (1963:33;

1966b:35), a contention that, as we shall see, has been questioned by more recent critics. The linguistic facts that Lévi-Strauss mentions are mainly related to the phonological level of language. Modern linguistics has discovered the reality of phonemes and distinctive features, and has shown that the same pairs of oppositions exist in different languages (1963:20). Lévi-Strauss explicitly states that the distinctive features have an objective existence from a psychological as well as physical point of view; in other words, they are not merely theoretical and methodological devices, as mathematical tools of analysis, but rather they provide a "picture of reality," as do the Mendelian genetic characteristics (1969a:109). In the last volume of *Mythologiques*, Lévi-Strauss contradicts Sartre by asserting that the oppositions described by linguists are also present in biological and physical reality; an objective dialectics is inherent within the physical world (1971:616).

In Lévi-Strauss' view, language is structured not only at the phonological level, but also at the grammatical and lexical level, and even the structure of discourse "is not altogether random" (1963:85; also 1960:33).

Let us examine the argument that he develops from what he accepts as established linguistic facts.

(*a*) Following the linguistic views of the Prague school, he conceptualizes phonological structures as systems of relations, and the phoneme as "a bundle of distinctive features" (1963:57). For this reason language can be analyzed into constituent elements which can be organized according to "certain structures of opposition and correlation" (*ibid.*:86).

(*b*) These relations are constitutive and determinants of language, since language owes all of its reality to its simple infrastructure, and the infrastructure consists of small and constant relations (1966b:35). For the first time modern phonemics has made possible a social science capable of formulating "necessary relations" (1963:33), and anthropology should emulate its vestiges by trying to establish, like the natural sciences, "certain abstract and measurable relations, which constitute the basic nature of the phenomena under study" (*ibid.*:59).

(*c*) Then Lévi-Strauss links this presumed linguistic evidence to the dynamism of the human mind: "Language . . . is human reason, which has its reasons and of which man knows nothing" (1966:252). The laws of language "rigorously determine man's way of communicating, and therefore, his way of thinking" (1963b:43). Linguistics reveals that the basic phenomena, which determine the most general forms of mental life, are to be found at the unconscious level (1966b:31). It appears that Lévi-Strauss makes two crucial assumptions in reaching such conclusions on the basis of the highly selective linguistic evidence he uses.

The first postulate is that the fundamental and objective phonemic realities, which consist of systems of relations, are "the product of unconscious thought processes" (1963:58). Obviously, Lévi-Strauss does not simply mean that we learn, more or less consciously, collective habits of behavior or linguistic patterns, as it is implied by Geza de Rohan-Csermack's interpretation of collective unconscious (1967:145). Instead, Lévi-Strauss says that linguistic phenomena, as well as all other social phenomena, are "the projection, on the level of conscious and socialized thought, of universal laws which regulate the unconscious activity of the mind" (1963:59). "'Collective consciousness' would in the final analysis be no more than the expression, on the level of individual thought and behavior, of certain time and space modalities of the universal laws which make up the unconscious activity of the mind" (ibid.:65).

The second basic assumption of Lévi-Strauss' reasoning is that the "'natural basis' of the phonemic system" is "the structure of the brain" (ibid.:92); since the brain is the basic mediator and constraining influence on human thought (1963b:33), it is easy to conclude that the unconscious laws of language rigorously determine man's mode of thinking.

Were we to accept these two assumptions as self-evident, from the character of linguistic structures we could conclude that the human mind has built-in internal constraints by which it structures psychic and physical content; since we are unaware of this set of constraints or structures, they can properly be called the "unconscious infrastructure" of our psychic activity.

Lévi-Strauss draws on psychology and philosophy to strengthen and clarify this notion further.

Notes

1. An earlier version of this paper was read at the symposium on "The Unconscious in Lévi-Strauss' Anthropology" organized by the author at the 1970 meeting of the American Anthropological Association, November 20, San Diego, California. A much longer version of this paper, containing an evaluative section of Lévi-Strauss' ideas, appears in the volume 75 (I) of the American Anthropologist (Rossi, 1973). I acknowledge the helpful suggestions that Peter Caws, Georges Mounin, David Sapir, Bob Scholte, Yvan Simonis have made on earlier versions of this paper.

2. I do not discuss the influence of Rousseau on Lévi-Strauss' works but his importance cannot be emphasized enough. See for instance Lévi-Strauss, 1962, 1965, 1966a, 1967, etc.

3. Barthes clearly explains why Lévi-Strauss' socio-logic has to be understood as a semiology or sociology of signs rather than as the traditional sociology of symbolism (Barthes, 1962:119–120). On the cybernetic conceptualization of social phenomena as messages see, among other passages, *The Savage Mind*, pp. 267–268. On the structuralist notion of meaning as opposed to the phenomenological notion see Lévi-Strauss, 1963a:637–644.

4. However, Simonis has called my attention to a recent text where Lévi-Strauss states, "After all, if customs of neighboring people reveal relations of symmetry, one does not have to look for a cause in a somewhat mysterious law of nature or mind. This geometric perfection presently sums up more or less conscious but innumerable efforts accumulated by history and all aimed at the same end" (1971a:177). Simonis rightly remarks that this passage "seems to indicate a certain prudence (or a certain evolution!) of the author [Lévi-Strauss] on his thesis of the unconscious and the human mind" (Simonis, 1972). For an excellent exposition on Lévi-Strauss' notion of unconscious see Simonis, 1968, Chapter 3.

Michael H. Agar

28. Whatever Happened to Cognitive Anthropology: A Partial Review

Cognitive anthropology is usually dated from Goodenough's (1957) notion of culture as shared knowledge. With a blend of ethnography,
linguistics, and cognitive psychology, a framework was developed that
centered on the relationships of lexemes and the categories that they
labeled, where categories were defined in terms of a conjunction of
necessary and sufficient features. This framework, together with the
emic/etic distinction and a general concern for explicit method, still
characterizes the field for many anthropologists.

The characterization is accurate, but partial and dated. I do not have
the space in this essay to recapitulate the history and various current
forms of cognitive anthropological research, although such discussions
are available (see, for example, D'Andrade 1980; Clement 1976). Let me
mention, just as one example, that the recently collected works of
Charles Frake (1980) show both the incompleteness of this characterization of early work in the field, while at the same time displaying some of
the recent thinking of one of its founders.

The current diversity creates a problem for this essay, which I developed in response to the invitation of the editor of *Human Organization* to
do a "state of the art" review of cognitive anthropology centered on
Edwin Hutchins's recent book, *Culture and Inference* (1980). The problem
is that the "state" consists of a variety of regions, each with its own
dialect. Further, some of the regions are heavily populated with noncog-
nitive anthropologists, not to mention nonanthropologists as well.

To further confuse the issue, any of the regions could be reviewed
with an eye toward application. Again, to offer just one example, Doro-
thy Clement and Joe Harding, drawing on approaches developed by
Volney Stefflre and Kimball Romney, have used one version of cognitive
anthropology in projects as diverse as mental health in Samoa, fertility
in Korea, and urban planning in California (Harding and Clement 1974;
Harding, Clement, and Lammers 1972; Clement 1980). In fact, Clement,

in her review essay on the uses of cognitive anthropology in educational research (1976), notes with amusement the responses of anthropological colleagues to an announced interest in "applied ethnographic semantics."

Clement and Harding's work, drawing on approaches that involve belief matrices and multidimensional scaling, is just one example of several "regions" that will not be covered here. In this essay, I propose to use Hutchins's book, together with a few additional examples, to characterize only one of the current trends in cognitive anthropology. It is a trend that blends in with the new interdisciplinary field of "cognitive science," a mixture of people from cognitive psychology, artificial intelligence, philosophy, neurophysiology, sociology, and anthropology. This new field has a journal and a name, but no clearly bounded identity. However, one of its characteristics is a shared concern with the representation and use of complex knowledge structures. It also overlaps with another growing field—discourse analysis—which like cognitive science has its new journals (*Discourse Process* and *Text*) and which also lacks clear boundaries. However, many of its members concern themselves with extensive stretches of naturally situated talk.

The samples of recent cognitive anthropological work discussed here address both of these concerns. At the same time, they maintain a primary focus on the problems of doing ethnography. This blending of three interests—cognitive science, discourse analysis, and ethnography—roughly outlines a new cognitive anthropological region, in the middle of which sits Hutchins's new book. Interestingly enough, this mixture is an updated version of the blend that initiated the field of cognitive anthropology in the late 1950s and early 1960s. So, with apologies to colleagues whose work is neglected—for lack of space rather than for lack of significance or interest—I hope to give a sense of the nature of this new territory.

Culture and Inference

Hutchins sets out to understand the discourse involved in public land litigation in the Trobriands. He weaves together two major sources for theoretical guidance in his effort. The first is that stream of cognitive anthropology that runs through Kay's (1966) theory of culture as underlying propositions and rules of inference (further elaborated in D'Andrade 1976), together with Frake's (1964) notion of cultural knowledge as more akin to semantic nets than bounded taxonomic and componential structures. The second is the work in artificial intelligence that forces the development of explicit knowledge structures to guide the inferences required for everyday understanding. The conclusion is that

. . . with a little care, the ethnographer's finest tool—his ability as a human being to learn another's culture—can be used to produce scientific knowledge. To do so, however, the ethnographer must make some attempt to discover and explicitly represent the knowledge structure on which understandings are based. [Hutchins 1980:13]

Hutchins first gives an elaborate introduction to the core folk knowledge involved in land tenure. He then develops a formal model of that knowledge, along with a notational scheme that allows him to express the inferences that tie chunks of knowledge with each other and with events in the world. Then he picks a sample case—intentionally, one with "a minimal cast of characters and a relatively uncomplicated history of events" (1980:62)—and applies the model to demonstrate its role in understanding discourse.

These chapters are tough going. A wealth of Trobriand knowledge is presented, often using Trobriand terms. In a way, this is a strong reporting strategy, since Hutchins's book forces one to comprehend a chunk of knowledge before subsequent portions of the discussion can be understood. It is also a problem in another way, since at least for me, the flow of new knowledge and new terminology was a bit overwhelming. Besides, no sooner does the reader finish the information on land tenure than he or she is taken through an equally intense development of a formal representation for that knowledge.

However, for present purposes the culture-specific content is less important than the general approach. Besides, the required work is worth the effort. By showing how detailed analyses of land tenure litigation require the development of key schemas, Hutchins makes a contribution to Trobriand studies. Again, I won't cover the details here, but among other things Hutchins shows how Lee's (1949) characterization of Trobriand thought is simply nonsense when applied to litigation discourse, and he is also able to show both the strengths and weaknesses of other accounts in the ethnographies of Malinowski (1965) and Weiner (1976).

At the end of the book, Hutchins places his approach in broader context, and it is this discussion that characterizes the version of cognitive anthropology of interest here:

1. Understanding the discourse depends on knowledge that is not explicit in the text. This knowledge is applied both "bottom-up"—knowledge is called on depending on features of the situation—as well as "top-down"—the situation

is understood from the broad knowledge schemas that are applied. Some of this knowledge deals with specific historical events, but other parts of it are general and shared.

2. The knowledge is "referentially transparent"; that is, it is not "seen" by its users, but rather is something in terms of which the "seeing" gets done. Put another way, the knowledge is not a system of propositions that informants articulate; rather, it is a "set of instructions for the construction of propositions" (Hutchins 1980:117).

3. The knowledge is a resource for a variety of cognitive tasks—understanding and explanation; problem solving; judgments of sense, truth, and likelihood; and decision making, among others.

4. The knowledge, in short, is not a framework that is mechanically applied to the world to make sense of it. Instead, it is a resource in terms of which things get done, given the historical contingencies and human purposes of the moment. In land litigation, one sees this most prominently displayed, since the actors have conflicting goals and interpretations of experience that must be publicly evaluated and resolved.

There is of course more in the book than what I have mentioned here. In discussing the "redundancy in related groups of schemata" (1980:127), for example, Hutchins points toward a way to handle the traditional anthropological notion of "themes." He also makes the strong claim that cultural differences are reflected in the representation of the world rather than in the processes employed in doing the thinking. As a final note, he concludes: "By setting the goal of describing a model that is sufficient to perform the task, the anthropologist can bring some formal rigor to otherwise impressionistic field methods" (1980:128).

In a moment, I will say more on these issues. However, for the present I hope that this brief characterization of Hutchins's book serves to give a sense of the general approach. Before discussing the changes in cognitive anthropology that are implied, I want to first sketch some examples of related work. I do so for two reasons. First, the examples to be discussed fit more closely into "U.S. applied" work. Second, they show that Hutchins's work is not an isolated case; rather, it is an example of a more pervasive change in one form of cognitive anthropology.

Three Examples

The first example consists of some ongoing research conducted by Charles Fillmore and Paul Kay on schoolchildren's comprehension of reading test items (Fillmore 1981). In the same spirit as Hutchins, Fillmore and Kay argue that understanding the passage that constitutes a reading test item requires inferences to be made. However, there are three different levels. The first has to do with those inferences required to understand a single sentence; the second, with the inferences drawn on to understand the interrelationships of sentences within a test; and the third, with inferences drawn from the general knowledge and experience of the reader to connect the passages sensibly with his or her world.

When one examines the questions designed to test comprehension, one finds that there is necessarily an assumption that there are "correct" inferential links from question to text. However, when "general knowledge" inferences are part of the assumed chain, all hell can break loose. If the adult test designer draws on inferences that are part of a world that the child reader does not share, the child must work to construct a plausible reasoning solution that connects questions with text as mediated by his or her experiences. A "wrong" answer may be diagnostic of an adult's distance from the current world of children rather than an indication of faulty comprehension by the test taker.

Fillmore and Kay use informal interviews with the children as ways to get at the adequacy of the constructed schemas. The schemas, at whatever levels, should indicate where problems in comprehension might occur, and in the informal interviews the children discuss the test, often showing difficulties in just those areas that the schemas would predict. Further, their discussions also show where the child may be using world knowledge based on his or her experience that generates a "correct" answer that is wrong from the point of view of the adult test designer. Some of the initial child/adult differences that have been described are fascinating, involving, for example, mention of technological objects whose reality for the adult contrast with the object's obsolescence and consequent lack of reality for the child.

Fillmore and Kay are working with constructed texts that play a critical role in evaluation of a child's reading ability. In contrast, Naomi Quinn (1981a,b) has been working on several ethnographic interviews with American couples about their marriages. Like Hutchins, she is after constructed schemas that allow the understanding of stretches of native discourse. Her work, like all the examples mentioned in this section, is ongoing. It involves different strategies, such as a search for the metaphors that people use to characterize the state of their relationships. I will focus on her use of "key words" to understand folk conceptions of marriage.

A key word is the linguistic anchor for the organization of a wealth of background understandings. One example of a key word that Quinn analyzes is the term "commitment." By examining its use in the many pages of transcribed discussion, she finds that the term is used in three ways, indicating "promise," "dedication," and "attachment." Drawing on the work of Fillmore and Langacker, she notes that the three different uses are "related as three different aspects of one interpersonal relationship" (1981a:12).

In other words, the three different senses of "commitment" link up when one understands that they represent different takes on the cultural institution of marriage. "Promise" highlights the speech that initiates it; "dedication" focuses on the intention entailed by it; and "attachment" brings out the emotional aspects of the relationship (1981a:12). In brief, the analysis of the key word in interview context brings out its rich analytical differences. At the same time, the differences point to the construction of a schema for "marriage" that shows them to result from an emphasis on one part of the schema at the expense of others.

Quinn discusses other issues as well, such as the permitted diversity within the constraints set by the schema. She also, like Hutchins, relates the schemas to social action, showing how they play a role as "goal-generating knowledge structures" (1981a:28). For present purposes, though, these additional issues are neglected as we turn to the third example.

Jerry Hobbs and I, like Quinn, have been working with an informal ethnographic interview, in this case an extensive life history of a career heroin addict (Agar and Hobbs 1981a,b; Hobbs and Agar 1981). We are also looking for some way to arrive at and specify that broader knowledge that provides the inferential wherewithal to understand stretches of discourse. Unlike the others, though, our approach is explicitly emergent and interpretive, in that we highlight the role of intuition in coming up with a "best guess" schema that is then enriched and developed through progressive iteration through the text.

Like Hutchins, we also use the text as a whole to guide the development of schemas. We do so by asking what contiguous segments have to do with each other (local coherence), what a segment has to do with the overall goals of the speaker (global coherence), and what a segment has in common with other segments scattered throughout the text (thematic coherence). Forming the inference structures that enable us to answer those questions is something, we believe (along with the others), at the heart of ethnographic description.

So far, in our ongoing work, these inference structures are varied. Some may involve conventions of junkie life, while others may involve the interacting goals of different actors. In other cases, there may be conflicts among conventions and/or goals, especially interesting when the "street" and the "straight" world are simultaneously relevant to the understanding of a portion of the text. Finally, other inferences involve methodological considerations, such as the effect of the interviewer on the interview, or the problems in the differences between "then" and "now" that recur in a life-historical account.

Hopefully these three examples show that Hutchins's work is not an isolated case. Rather, it is the most thoroughly developed ethnographic example of an emergent style of cognitive anthropology. There are other styles, as noted in the introduction, that have been neglected here. Further, there are some differences among the examples of work discussed here that have also been neglected. However, the purpose of this essay is to paint this perspective in broad strokes and to contrast it with the traditional image of "cognitive anthropology" sketched at the beginning of this essay.

So What's New

So far I have tried to give a sense of the general argument in Hutchins's book, together with a few selected examples to further illustrate it. Now it is time to return to the question of the introduction and show how it differs from the traditional image of cognitive anthropology.

1. The data taken for analysis are elaborate stretches of discourse rather than related sets of lexemes. In the work sampled here, the discourse takes a variety of forms: social interaction, informal ethnographic interviews, and constructed test items. With this change, the perspective moves to ethnographic center stage, since "discourse" covers much of the data that goes into ethnographic work.

2. The knowledge structures are schematic rather than taxonomic and/or componential. Schematic representation allows for a more holistic presentation of knowledge, one that admits a variety of kinds of knowledge, inference links, and levels. It requires only explicitness. Taxonomic representations, in contrast, are limited to subset/superset relations while componential structures deal with simple conjunction of features. The increased breadth of schematic representations allows for potentially explicit discussions of almost any sort of knowledge that might go into an ethnographic account.

3. The constructed schemas are not necessarily explicit in native talk, but rather are put together by the ethnographer to understand it. Notable by their absence are the concerns with explicit "discovery" or "elicitation" strategies that gave early cognitive anthropology what Frake calls a "bag of tricks" image (1977). Schemas come from a mix of a general sense of the group, intuition, and things the folks say and do. However, even though there is less concern with formal elicitation of schemas, they require an explicitness in both their representation and in their relation to the discourse data.

4. In most of the examples, there is a concern with the relation between knowledge structures and situated purpose of actors. Though not yet well worked
out, this concern should help correct the earlier cognitive anthropological bias
towards representing a static world of conventions while neglecting the intentions of actors who move through it.

5. In discussions of "themes" in Quinn and Agar and Hobbs, and in the notion
of "schema redundancy" in Hutchins, theoretical pointers are set up to medi-
ate between the local detailed analysis of transcripts and the more global
statements about a group to which ethnographers aspire. Again, this is not
well worked out, but it moves toward a resolution of earlier problems with an
overly narrow focus on a specific domain.

In short, the examples discussed in this brief review article preserve
the classic premise of cognitive anthropology: the focus on language as
the prime inroad to understanding group life. However, by shifting to
discourse and schemas, by decreasing concern with mechanical elicitation strategies, and by beginning to worry about the relation of knowledge structures to actor's intentions and broader cultural themes, this
more recent version adds breadth and depth, retaining the old strengths
while enabling it to confront other issues of ethnographic concern.

Lest all of this sound too cheery, many problems remain. However,
my purpose here has been to accentuate the positive changes in one
branch of cognitive anthropology as reflected in the examples. At the
same time, there are problems with the ontological claims for the schemas, the limits on coverage that still remain, the unmonitored decision
by which some intuitions are formally represented while others remain
as background, and so on. Important as these and other issues are, there
is simply not enough space to deal with them here.

Nevertheless, I hope that this essay shows some of the directions in
which one part of cognitive anthropology is moving. Now, what does
this have to do with "applied anthropology"? On a general level, there is
a concern among ethnographers doing applied work over the problems
in articulately characterizing ethnography—its epistemological basis,
theory, and method. (See the recent issue of *Practicing Anthropology*
[1980] which has this concern as its theme.) Though I obviously have a
personal interest in the evaluation, it seems to me that the work represented in the examples I discussed in this article is a strong contribution
to this discussion in the area of theory and method.

More specifically, most of the examples are, in fact, applied. By "applied" ethnography, I mean any ethnography that in part connects its
account of group life with a current social issue such that the ethnography, implicitly or explicitly, constrains the possible actions that would be

appropriate to address that issue. This definition is problematic, but adequate for now. Hutchins's ethnography is not applied, though one can easily imagine circumstances under which it could be. Besides, in his research with computer based instruction systems, he is using the perspective in clearly applied ways. The other three examples—on reading tests, marriage, and heroin addiction—all connect directly with current issues of concern in our society.

But then a division of anthropology into "pure" and "applied" has never made much sense to me anyway. True, application requires an increased sophistication about and sensitivity to the various worlds of the audiences that one addresses, but that is an added skill, not one that replaces a concern with key issues in theory and method among professional colleagues. As I hope I have shown here, some recent work in cognitive anthropology represents at the same time a broadening of the original perspective and a contribution to some key ethnographic issues. The contributions, I think, will be of interest to any ethnographer, whatever his or her research context.

Laboratory of Comparative
Human Cognition

29. Cognition as a Residual
Category in Anthropology

Cognition Anthropology

In the mid-1950s, a small group of young anthropologists concerned with how to do better ethnographies borrowed some techniques from structural linguistics which seemed so impressively scientific at the time. They started a movement known variously as ethnographic semantics, cognitive anthropology, ethnoscience, and even the New Ethnography. Its basic concern for adequate description, well stated by Conklin (1964) and Frake (1964), for example, was obscured in the controversy surrounding its methods and its rhetoric.

Perhaps the first principle of cognitive anthropology was the quite sensible notion that people must somehow communicate about whatever is most important to them. Accordingly, a record of what it is that they talk about and name can offer an interesting gloss on what it is that they know. To paraphrase Frake's most cognitive sounding programmatic paper (1962), such a record will not capture all of a cognitive system, but it will certainly represent an important part of it, namely, the part that people use in getting each other organized to attend to certain issues in everyday life. This definition of contrast and inclusion across native terms became the measure of native concern and knowledge. (Conklin 1964, Frake 1962, Goodenough 1956).

The approach produced some quick victories, particularly in the area of kinship terminology (Lounsbury 1964), and also in the description of the use of native knowledge in the organization of subsistence (Conklin 1965) and social interactional systems (Frake 1964, Goodenough 1965). The important thing to note about most of the advances is that they were embedded in long-term ethnographic research. The new ethnography offered some new data gathering and data presentation techniques, but

434

it was successful to the extent that it was embedded in traditional ethnography by participant observation.

In the excitement of new advances, methods and claims began to outrun their original purposes, and the specifics of the taxonomic representation of people's knowledge began to replace a concern for the people and the uses they might make of their knowledge. Although Frake (1961) was clear to warn that *use* had to be the primary starting point of analysis and behavior the ultimate criterion for success in any analysis, we have had to wait until recent years to get a systematic body of accounts of the situational variability in the meaning of terms [e.g. Casson (1975), Rosaldo (1972)]. Between its ethnographic beginning and most recent developments, cognitive anthropology earned its name as an attempt to understand the thought patterns of peoples in different cultures. There are three strands to this effort for us to review for their statements about cognition.

Testing for Psychological Reality

Once ethnographic accounts of various cultural domains began to record conflicting taxonomies or domains too fuzzy to put within the confines of a taxonomic chart, one immediate response was to probe deeper into native naming behavior to uncover a more real (in the sense of "psychologically real") representation of native knowledge. Although the effort was unfailingly ethnographic in the sense that analysts were still interested in the best ways to represent the specifics of the knowledge system of a particular people, the techniques used in these accounts of psychological reality (triads tests, for example) were quite divorced from participation in the everyday life of the people under analysis. This is an intriguing development in that it marks a move to more careful constraining of task environments and shows that some anthropologists shared the psychologists' belief that to make statements about the psychological relevance of any description, the task the subject works on must be well defined (if only in terms of constraints arranged by the analyst).

With the advent of multidimensional scaling, the dimensions of native classificatory systems came to be represented by a delineation across a large data field of "what-goes-with-what" (Romney, Shepard and Nerlove 1972). A basic assumption of this approach (particulars of the statistical aggregating assumptions aside) is that objects are located in relation to each other conceptually on the basis of the conjunction of a limited number of their common attributes or features. These features are discovered in the "dimensions" which emerge from the data-analytic technique.

While these techniques may be a useful way economically to display regular relations in a body of data, we agree with D'Andrade (1976) that "The multidimensional techniques gave us one representation about what people believe, but not a representation of how people go about believing" (p. 155). D'Andrade's "implicational analysis" adds to the richness of the descriptions of the relations between concepts that have heretofore been studied by multidimensional scaling techniques. In a discussion of this work, D'Andrade tells us that ". . . thinking consists of more than classification. Thinking involves inferences, and an effective structure for making inferences requires at least the use of relations" (p. 179). This statement is undoubtedly true, but it should not be construed as a claim on D'Andrade's part that he is discovering "how people think" in a cognitive psychologist's sense owing to his use of a new data analysis technique. Rather, he is continuing his search for ways to make explicit the operations by which analysts come to make statements about the concepts and relations that constitute belief systems.

Principles of Folk Classification

A second literature within anthropology which has been given to cognitive claims has focused on the semantics of folk classifications of objects (particularly living ones) in the natural world and their colors. This literature differs from the literature actively engaged in testing the psychological reality of taxonomies by concerning itself with the principles of classification across persons, domains and even cultures rather than with the particulars of a taxonomy as it is elaborated by a particular people for particular purposes. This tradition strays far from the ethnographic base from which it emerged in order to make broader claims about the human mind and its evolution, a diversion which causes considerable problems in the interpretation of the taxonomic data it has to work with, as they are not constrained by their normal contexts of occurrence in a natural community (Conklin 1973, Saglins 1976).

The major event in this literature is Berlin & Kay's (1969) book on *Basic Color Terms*, which displayed an apparently universal organization of options in the arrangement of color terms in the world's languages and suggested an evolutionary progression in the organization of color terms across cultures of differing complexity. In moving to other domains of classification, similar results have been accumulating; folk taxonomies of different domains appear to be organized according to similar structural principles (Berlin, Breedlove and Raven 1973, Brown 1976, Rosaldo 1972). Although this work has produced some rhetoric about the structure of the human mind (for example, because there is evidence that taxonomies of things appear to have a ceiling of five hierarchic levels), few practitioners of the research try to claim that such folk taxonomies (or alternative representations) actually represent how the world is perceived and known by particular persons (e.g. Hunn 1976). Most investigators appear content to live with the less powerful claim that the folk taxonomies represent only the categories available to people if and when they do some thinking about the domains in question.

In view of their data-gathering techniques, students of folk classification are well advised to avoid psychological claims. Formal interviews on the similarities and differences in named objects or colors, and dictionary forays with the same ends in mind, cannot give strong data on how people are processing the information in question. In the terms of this paper, the task is ill defined from the points of view of either analysts or natives. When the distinctions the people make fall into a pattern, something interesting must be going on, but it is hard to know about it in any detail.

One of the most interesting statements about the current status and the future course of this effort has been offered recently by Rosch (1975, 1978). Although her work has often been interpreted as defining a competence model for the kinds of conceptual structuring systems people have in their heads, Rosch has recently stated that: "the issues in categorization with which we are primarily concerned have to do with explaining the categories found in a culture and coded by the language of that culture" (1978, p. 2). She specifically rejects the idea that her research is designed to specify how the categories are processed. Before more detailed psychological statements can be made, the objects specified in the classifications would have to be detailed in terms of their use "in the events of everyday life" (p. 25). In line with this objective, Rosch has initiated a study of people's classification of events and objects in events. If it is the case that "events stand at the interface between an analysis of social structure and culture and analysis of individual psychology" (p. 27), then her future work will be of special interest to anthropologists.

Models of Native Decision Making

A third development in the literature growing out of ethnographic semantics has focused on decison making in everyday life. In assuming that members of a society do not simply have knowledge about cultural principles, but act in accord with them, decision theorists appear to be making a number of claims about psychological processes, but the exact status of cognitive psychological claims is often difficult to pin down, a situation which is mirrored in studies of social decision making by psychologists (Simon 1976).

In Goodenough's (1956) classic discussion of Trukese residence rules, psychological claims are almost incidental. His concern was to show that the ethnographer must develop a theory of the choices available to the members of the particular culture. He suggests that the categories of residence and criteria of choice can be validated by using them to predict where actual married couples would choose to live or to predict where hypothetical couples would live and seeing if these predictions "would agree with those which members of society would also make for such hypothetical marriages" (p. 29).

Similar to Goodenough's discussion of residence choices are Keesing's model of fosterage (1970) and Fjellman's (1976) and Ebihara's (1977) accounts of residence decisions. While each of these authors infers that individuals have the cultural knowledge needed to make decisions, how the decisions are made is not necessarily attributed to individual actors and no claims are made concerning psychological process.

In contrast to the work of Goodenough, Geoghegan's studies on the use of address terms (1973) and residential decision making (1978) among the Eastern Samal of the Philippines contain explicit psychological claims. In the residence study he promises "a formal model of the cognitive process underlying a native actor's decisions about residence" (p. 1). Geoghegan derives his model of residence rules from interviews of one principal informant, "and the resultant model is intended to represent a portion of the cognitive organization of only this one informant." The model is claimed to have generality for both the individual informant and "native actor competence in general." The test of this claim is to use residence and status information for members of the population as input; their actual residence mode is then predicted within a small margin of error.

C. Gladwin (1975) modeled Mfantse fish sellers' decisions of whether to take their fish to market, and if so, where. She developed a model on the basis of interviews with fish sellers and output data from a large number of actual trips to market. The model which consists of a series of steps that Gladwin assumed "a fish seller mentally goes through" (p. 99), accounts for 90% of the variance in market trip data. The model assumes that individual fish sellers calculate the probability of a particular market being good given its condition the day before. Although the Mfantse do not talk about such calculations, the model assumes that over many years of observing market conditions the fish sellers have as part of their knowledge something equivalent to a contingency table for making this calculation. Validation for this model does not come directly from informants' verbal reports but from the success of the model for predicting the data on when the traders went to market.

In a study of fish sellers from a village neighboring the one studied by Gladwin, Quinn (1978) has argued strongly in favor of the importance of verbal reports. Based on interview data alone, she addressed Gladwin's assumption that fish sellers make probability estimates. Quinn suggests a model of fish sellers' decisions which offers a "cognitively plausible" alternative to the assumption "that individual decision makers can and do construct probability distributions against which to assess the riskiness of uncertain decisions" (p. 3). Quinn does not test her alternative model against actual outcome as did Gladwin, although she acknowledges the usefulness of such a test. Her argument is intended to demonstrate how verbal reports can be used in the initial modeling of economic choices. Quinn's argument that sellers do not construct probability distributions is based on her failure to find any mention of such a procedure by any of the individual sellers. Whether it better predicts economic behavior is left unclear because Quinn shifts the criterion, defending the new model on the grounds that it is more consistent with accounts of how decisions are made.

In order to evaluate the psychological claims in any of these studies of decision making, we must examine the suitability of interview data for making statements about cognitive processes. Verbal reports can say a great deal about the kinds of things it is possible to know about in a culture, and cognitive anthropologists have gone to great lengths to show how this can be done carefully (Agar 1975), but considerable data have been reported recently about the limits of treating what people say in interviews as literal data about thought processes. D'Andrade (1974) has reported that interview data about remembered events are particularly unreliable because they are strongly skewed in the direction of semantic relations between the descriptive terms used. Nisbett & Wilson (1977) have shown that subjects asked to report on their own decision making consistently answer on the basis of their own a priori theories about how certain stimuli and plausible responses go together rather than on the basis of veridical introspective recall. Bilmes has argued and demonstrated on the basis of some Thai data (1975) that misinformation and ambiguity are essential elements in the social organization of verbal interaction.

An important example of the dangers of drawing cognitive conclusions from interview data and decontextualized cognitive tests is available in the growing literature on navigational knowledge in Micronesia. For two decades now, T. Gladwin has been producing excellent descriptions of canoe voyages by Micronesians crossing hundreds of miles of open sea. He has also been using their navigational system to reach conclusions about their thinking. In the 1950s, before he began to study navigation, his conclusion was that Micronesians could not think abstractly (Gladwin and Sarason 1953). In the 1960s, after his initial research on navigation, the conclusion changed to allow Micronesians abstract thought but an inability to plan (Gladwin 1964). Finally, in *East is a Big Bird* (Gladwin 1967), in many ways an excellent book, the last chapter discusses the thinking of the Micronesian, arguing now that navigators can think abstractly and clearly. They must organize elaborate plans for their voyages, but they do no more conceptual problem solving than they have to do; they don't think "heuristically." After extensive interviews, and a few small voyages, Gladwin concluded that navigation on Pulawat was a closed rote system of knowledge about sailing under local conditions. This fact, in conjunction with the results of some tests in which the navigators performed at the level of preadolescent minors, was the basis for Gladwin's claim that the navigators were nonheuristic thinkers who were given to solving intellectual problems only when there was no other choice.

Fortunately, Gladwin's analysis was followed by the work of Lewis, who increased the range of observation by going with the navigators for long trips to strange places under their guidance. In his exciting book, *We the Navigators* (1972), Lewis shows that the Micronesian navigational system is not as closed as Gladwin reports. Taken far off course, the navigators were consistently able to reconstruct their location and the way home by an intensive study of the stars and waves about them in ways that Gladwin would characterize as reflecting heuristic thinking. Recently these skills were further displayed by a Micronesian navigating a canoe thousands of miles across Polynesia from Hawaii to Tahiti (Lewis 1977). This entire enterprise shows how the typical range of verbal reports, from open interviews to constrained psychological experiments, proves inadequate if it is not embedded in data gained from a more systematic analysis of the actual doing of the task in question.

Conclusion

In light of the many difficulties facing the ethnographer who seeks to make inferences about the cognitive processes of the people he studies, it is tempting to counsel retreat; the rumor that psychologists have been learning something recently that ethnographers need to know is false. Insofar as this conclusion depends upon the hope that psychologists have techniques which can determine "what goes on inside people's heads," such a retreat is more than warranted by the evidence.

However, in our opinion, the relevant contribution from psychology should not be sought in presumed privileged access to people's thought processes because it is not to be found there; rather the virtue of cognitive psychology is to be found in its procedures for limiting uncontrolled speculation about thinking. These procedures (the specification of task environment, behavior, and their relations) can yield plausible warranted statements about the activities that organize the behavior we observe as long as the constraints on behavior are well described, by either experimental manipulation or intensive behavioral analysis. But with few exceptions, the theoretical statements which are cognitive processes for the psychologist are so limited in score and predictive value that unless there is a special ethnographic interest in the task in question, the anthropologist is unlikely to wish to follow the psychologist in the quest for process specification.

In our view, the very extremes to which the psychologist is pushed are resources for the anthropologist. We believe that the ethnographer's question, "What is going on here?" is not different in kind from the psychologist's question, "What thought processes are involved in this task?" Rather, it differs in the level of context which is being questioned. In each of the substantive areas that we reviewed, crucial disagreement among anthropologists has turned exactly on this point—disagreement about what it is that people are doing in the task under study. In the modes of thought discussion, disagreement about task takes the form of arguments between "intellectualist, neo-Tylorians," and those who claim that the native task is not to explain the world in causal terms, but to exert social control; literacy is seen as a technology which fundamentally changes the structure of the information provided by the environment for thinking. In cognitive ethnography, the focus on native questions as a key to locating native tasks is a close analog to the psychologist's desire for task specification. Unfortunately, as Frake (1977:3), p. 3) has pointed out,

. . . The notion that answers are there, that the job is to find the questions, while often cited, did not seem really to take hold. Frames began to be called eliciting frames, to be thought of not as contexts for behavior but as prods to behavior. The ethnographer rather than the informant (became) the questioner.

With the aim of substantiating cognitive claims, some anthropologists have increased the constraints on their tasks, but have fallen short of the criteria applied by psychology. In such cases, neither psychological nor ethnographic inferences benefit; the result is indeterminacy.

In our view, each of the lines of work reviewed here makes important contributions to our understanding of human thought. Most often, however, it is not thought-as-process but the content of thought which is the topic of inquiry. Although there is no room to discuss the matter here, we would claim that all but the most exacting of psychological cognitive research fits (albeit imperfectly) the same characterization (1951).

In concluding we can do no better than cite Nadel's (1951) wise comment

. . . unless the relations between social and psychological enquiry are precisely stated, certain dangers, all-too-evident in the anthropological and psychological literature, will never be banished. Psychologists will overstate their claims and produce, by valid psychological methods, spurious sociological explanations; or the student of society, while officially disregarding psychology, will smuggle it in by the backdoor; or he may assign to psychology merely the residue of his enquiry—all the facts with which his own methods seem incapable of dealing (p. 289).

And so it goes.

Nancy Scheper-Hughes

30. The Margaret Mead Controversy: Culture, Biology and Anthropological Inquiry

It is indeed an event when a little known anthropologist publishes a book some 40 years in the making that promises to debunk the foremost proponent of cultural relativism, the late Margaret Mead, in the name of biology and sociobiology. The media of course have a heyday whenever social scientists disagree, and so the press was quick to turn Derek Freeman's book, *Margaret Mead and Samoa: The Making and Unmaking of an Anthropological Myth* (Cambridge. MA: Harvard University Press, 1983) into what we used to call a happening in the late 1960s. Due to a well-oiled publicity campaign by Harvard University Press, cover stories in *Time, Life,* and the *New York Times* preceded the general release of the book, and many anthropologists were asked to "respond" publicly to the Freeman thesis before even having had the opportunity to read it.

In broad strokes the controversy is as follows. In 1925, Margaret Mead, then a young woman of 23, set sail for American Samoa in order to "field test" Stanley Hall's adolescent stress hypothesis—that is, the idea that the characteristic rebelliousness, turmoil, and mood swings of adolescence were part of an innate, biological script, a fixed stage in the human maturational process. Hall, like many of the developmental psychologists of his day, believed that the stages of human development were biologically determined and had little reference to social or cultural conditioning. Freud, of course, had also posited invariant developmental stages and accompanying conflicts, such as the Oedipus Complex of the phallic stage. One psychologist, during the 1920s, even suggested that *all* human infants had to pass through a stage of wet diapers in order to achieve normal psychosexual development, a theory guaranteed to make anthropologists snicker at the absurdity of assuming a universal human nature amidst the richness of variety and diversity in human behavior. Not to mention the fact that for most of human history, of course, our species survived quite well without diapers.

So psychological anthropology emerged in the 1920s and 1930s as a little field with a big bite—for it took upon itself the task of testing among unacculturated non-western peoples the deterministic theories of Piaget, Freud, Hall and many others. Margaret Mead, one of the founders of Psychological Anthropology, soon became famous for developing a deceptively simple methodological approach called the "negative instance" or the "anthropological veto"—that is, the attempt to find a single negative case that could disprove a general tenet or axiom—such as the universality and *biological* basis of adolescent stress.

After nine months of fieldwork in Samoa, Mead returned to report in her first and most popular book, *Coming of Age in Samoa*, that among her young female informants adolescence was a very privileged and favored period in the life cycle—a time of casual pre-marital sex, few responsibilities, easy relations with parents and other kin, and consequently a period of harmony rather than disequilibrium and strife. Here, then, Mead had found her first single negative instance to disprove (to falsify in Popperian terms) the psycho-biological theory of adolescent stress, and to conclude that it was culture and not biology that was largely responsible for the "storm and stress" of Amerian youth. In the last two chapters of *Coming of Age* Mead suggests that there are lessons here for American parents, teachers, and physicians. If *our* adolescents could be given more freedom to explore and experiment, if American institutions like the nuclear family and public schools were less rigid, authoritarian and coercive, and if American parents were less puritanical and guilt-ridden about sexuality, then we could reduce the tensions, conflicts and rebelliousness of our youth. The book and its thesis had an almost immediate impact on social scientists and on the American public. It has been said that with the publication of *Coming of Age* Mead actually began the sexual revolution in America. It became a bible for reform-minded and progressive parents, educators, pediatricians, and guidance counsellors throughout America, and it greatly influenced the man who, in later years, was to become the pediatrician of Mead's only child, Cathy: Dr. Benjamin Spock. Social scientists praised the book as well, and welcomed the radically new idea that isolated and so-called "primitive" communities might be used as laboratories for the testing of sweeping hypotheses about human nature generated within the limited, in-bred, intellectual hot houses of academia.

The book had important political ramifications as well. It introduced cultural relativism and cultural determinism at a time when racist thinking was rampant in American society—among scholars and intellectuals as well as in the general population. In the early decades of the 20th century Darwinian ideas about natural selection were inappropriately applied to social behavior including class and race relations. "Survival of the fittest" became the rallying cry behind the eugenics movement, a racist immigration policy, and miscegenation laws throughout the South. Biology and genetics (but poorly understood in this period) were invoked to explain human differences and the apparent "inferiority" of some types of people: immigrants (especially from Ireland, Italy and Eastern Europe); women; blacks; the "underserving" poor; as well as, of course, the "inferiority" of all the darker-skinned "pagans and savages" living in impossibly remote areas of the world, like Samoa. As Mead writes in a preface to the 3rd edition of *Coming of Age:*

The idea that our every thought and movement was a product *not of race, not of instinct,* but derived from the society within which an individual was reared, was new and unfamiliar. (1961:iii)

But the book caught on, and gradually so too did the idea of *culture* as a non-biological script—as a coherent system of ideas, beliefs, and values that is transmitted to children both verbally and non-verbally in everything from the way in which an infant is held, nursed and disciplined, to the way in which the growing child is taught the formal rules of society. After Mead, culture was increasingly invoked by nonanthropologists to explain human differences. The book also caught on because of a general mood of optimism within the country and because the theory of cultural relativism contained within itself the very *American* notion that one can tinker with and change one's society, one's social, economic, and political destiny. It "fit" the American ideal of the *self-made* man or woman.

And so, with Mead's help, by the late 1920s the pendulum swung away from the social Darwinist and biological justifications of the status quo. Anthropologists along with other social scientists were coming to reject the view that western civilization, the white race, and the male sex represented the pinnacle of the human evolutionary process. Along with racism, however, many also rejected the relevance of the biological sciences for illuminating *anything* about social behavior and social organization. It was in this way that biology became split off from the social sciences with consequences that are still felt today in, for example, the continuing hostilities between physical and cultural anthropologists.

But Mead is dead and times have changed, including the political mood of the nation. The pessimistic spirit of the 1980s has encouraged the proliferation of social theories that deny the possibilities for change and for the development of new human potentials, and which argue instead for the biological rootedness and determinants of sex roles, temperament, intelligence, and achievement. In the vastly popular and popularized sociobiology of E. O. Wilson and his followers, for example, we have the attempt to explain virtually all of human social institutions as responses to a few biological imperatives.

The new innatist mood can be felt in many quarters of American life as well as within scientific inquiry. I believe it is at the basis of some popular movements with which I share some empathy. I see it, for example, in the holistic health movement with its rejection of medical technology and its search for natural foods and herbal cures. The home birth and hospice movements are, as well, part of the quest, the desire to return to our essential, "natural" and *biological* selves. Birth without drugs and without medical interventions and breastfeeding are encouraged in order to facilitate that almost mystical "bonding" between mother and infant, interpreted as a *natural* social script, rooted in woman's evolutionary biology. There is a growing tendency within the American media to question the wisdom of the radical changes in American sex roles and family life: the two career family; child care centers; househusbands; single parent families; lesbian parents, and so forth. There is a fear that we have moved too far and too fast from our supposed genetic inheritance, and a feeling that we must somehow strive to get back in touch and in rhythm with that biology.

The time is ripe and it is no accident that the refutation of Mead's first (and most strongly culturally relativist) book by Derek Freeman had to wait for more than half a century, and appeared at an historical moment when the mood of the country was receptive. In *Margaret Mead and Samoa* Freeman attempts to overturn not only Mead's idyllic picture of Samoan adolescent life, but also the theory of cultural relativism from which the description sprang.

Based on several field trips to Western (i.e., British) Samoa[1] between 1940 and 1967, Freeman amassed a significant amount of contradictory evidence to charge the young Mead with naivete, methodological incompetence, and self-delusion. Where Mead's Samoans were described as peaceful, loving, sexually relaxed and free of major psychological conflict, the Samoans that Freeman describes are aggressive, brittle, touchy, impulsive, sexually hung up, status hungry and violent. Freeman gives relentless examples of Samoans ". . . knocking each other on heads, breaking each other's jaws, battering babies, committing suicide, wishing their mothers were dead, and punishing sex offenders" (Nader 1983). In short, Freeman presents us with a description that is just exactly the opposite of what Mead had written, so that we are left with almost a caricature of Benedict's (1934) Appollonian versus Dionysian culture types.

In one interview with the press Freeman made the extraordinary claim for his work that: "this is the first time in anthropology, or in the human sciences generally, that such an established scientist has been proven so wrong" (*TIME* 2/14/83:68). In his 300 page refutation, *Margaret Mead and Samoa*, he suggests that Mead's ethnographic blindness came from her dedication to her mentor, Franz Boas of Coumbia University, and to his supposedly anti-biological and culturally determinist school of thought. The young Mead, depicted here as a dependent and some-what frivolous woman, "needed," Freeman suggests, for complex per-sonal/psychological reasons (i.e., pleasing her fatherly mentor), as well as for theoretical and political reasons (i.e., building a case against bio-logical reductionism, racism, and eugenic philosophies), to see Samoan adolescents as remarkably free of biological constraints and as gentle children of culture, rather than as aggressive and violent children of nature. Meads' blindness, no matter how well intentioned, represents for Freeman an unpardonable abrogation of scientific objectivity and neutrality. In short, he charges Mead with setting out to prove a point of view to which she was so committed that it actually obscured her ability to describe accurately what she observed. "Mead," he writes, "dis-missed biology, or nature, as being of no significance whatsoever" (p. 78). Later, he refers to her "avowed absolute cultural determinism with its assumption of human nature as *tabula rasa*" (p. 295). Nowhere does he substantiate these claims with relevant quotations from Mead's own writings and copious self-reflections.[2]

While Freeman does not accuse Mead of intentional deceit, he does accuse her of selecting, assembling and presenting facts in such a way as to downplay the *biological* and to exaggerate the *cultural* influences on Samoan behavior in general and on the behavior of adolescents in par-ticular. In a moment we will look at the case Freeman builds for the biological basis of Samoan temperament and behavior.

Where does this lead us with respect to the status of anthropology as a social and behavioral science? Who was right, who was wrong? And what accounts for the discrepancies? What kinds of scientific claims can anthropology make for itself? Perhaps the most painful part of this controversy has been the erosion of the "public trust" in the social sciences to which many educated Americans have traditionally looked for guidance with respect to how to raise their families. The following portions of a letter to the *New York Times* on February 17, 1983 from a concerned citizen of Far Rockaway, N.Y.C., poignantly captures this disillusionment and sense of betrayal:

. . Margaret Mead's work became a bible to a generation of people. It gave scientific credibility for the permissiveness which we *now* feel is responsible for our current social disintegration. That the scientific underpinnings of the present permissiveness, lawlessness, and disorganization may have been arrived at by some faulty or careless research or even by conscious distortion is really too much to bear.

So, here we are left once again with the mandate and the challenge to explain to the American public what anthropology is all about.

The general scholarly reaction to date seeems to be that Derek Freeman is more correct with respect to Samoan aggression, but that Mead was more correct with respect to Samoan sexuality (*see*, for example: Nader 1983; Marcus 1983; Clifford 1983). But it seems to me that both were wrong in approaching the ethnographic field as if it were a battleground for the simple true/false proof of hypotheses generated outside that culture.

In fact, there is quite abundant evidence in the writings of contemporary Samoan experts such as Bradd Shore (1981, 1982), that Samoan culture is a dual system containing many paradoxes, contradictions, and "mysteries," as Shore calls them, that are culturally structured but never actually resolved. The really interesting point is that a complex culture like Samoa can contain *both* behavioral poles (the Dionysian-aggressive and the Appollonian-harmonious) operating at the same time, so that in certain contexts Samoans are exceedingly nasty and in other contexts they are decorous, controlled and polite to a fault. There *is*, as Freeman suggests, a strong virginity cult in Samoa, but (as Mead was able to capture in *her* ethnography), most youth manage to escape it, and have a jolly good time for themselves without tremendous guilt. In a recent publication Bradd Shore juxtaposes the public Samoan ideology to private attitudes and behavior. He writes:

Premarital sex is part of growing up for many Samoan boys and girls. . . . Privately, at least, many Samoan youth see sex as an important part of youthful adventure. (1981:197).

The most common term for sexual intercourse used by Samoan adolescents is the Samoan word for "play." Shore also suggests that there exists in Samoa a temporal "double-standard"—a formal daytime morality and an informal, relaxed and relatively free-wheeling "nighttime" morality. What marred the early Mead work as well as Freeman's much later refutation is the old culturalist idea that everything in a society must adhere to a single configuration or a pattern: that is, either the Samoans are peaceful *or* violent, sexy *or* repressed—rather than an examination of the many contradictions that exist in almost every society. The point is that Mead had given up configurationalist thinking by about 1938; Derek

Freeman still clings to the paradigm in 1983. Thus he defends the existence of a single Samoan *ethos*, a term used extremely cautiously, if at all,
by contemporary anthropologists.

Our more sophisticated understanding of Samoan culture today suggests that Mead was responsive to and wrote about one dimension of
Samoan culture—she captured a Samoan truth, as James Clifford called
it (1983:476), but not *the* Samoan truth. Derek Freeman, it appears, had
access to another Samoan truth—again, not *the* truth. And this difference can be explained in turn by the differences between Mead and
Freeman and their respective informants. Mead was a young woman
who interviewed Samoan girls exhilarated by the first blush of sexual
experience. Freeman began studying the Samoans as a mature, later as
an old, man. His Samoan informants were high ranking chiefs. Freeman
could never have asked Samoan girls of 13 and 14 the kinds of questions
that Mead had asked without being run off the island as a "dirty old
man!" Samoan pre-marital sex is relaxed among adolescent boys and
girls—but it is decidedly not cross-generational. Due to the great status
differences between old and young, intimate questions posed to young
girls would be highly deviant and suggestive coming from a middle-aged
American male. Freeman's informants on Samoan sexuality were, like
himself, mature men who were the chiefly guardians of the "public"
morality. Freeman had access to what Erving Goffman called the "front
stage" performance: the "official" social script on sexual behavior. Mead,
however, had access to the "back stage" performance—the views and
behaviors of adolescent girls. And these low-status, relatively "unimportant" girls shared with Mead a number of "cultural secrets," that is, the
kinds of knowledge anthropologists gain from submerged, marginal,
and non-dominant groups in society, individuals with a less vested interest in preserving the official image of the society. In any highly stratified
or ranked society such as Samoa, it obviously makes a huge difference
whether your informants are males or females, old or young, high or low
ranking persons. The Indian caste system, to give another example,
means something entirely different to a Brahmin than to an untouch-
able. And if you begin working with one group, that alone may automatically exclude your having access or trust with the other group. It is
easier to talk about getting a whole or a "balanced" ethnographic "truth"
than it is to actually get it.

If there is one thing we have learned from the past two decades of
feminist revisions of the classic ethnographies, it is the extent to which
these early studies suffered from a pervasive and largely unconscious
male bias—that is, ethnographers interviewed *male* informants about
male domains such as politics, warfare, and economics. Based on the

widespread assumption that women, by and large, make poor ethnographic informants, it is still common practice to question male informants about their own lives as well as about the lives and activities of women (*see* Scheper-Hughes 1983b). It was entirely possible for whole ethnographies to be written without *any* female informants, whereas the reverse has never been the case. Edwin Ardener (1975:4) implies that Evans-Pritchard treated Nuer women in roughly the same way he treated Nuer cattle—that is, as omnipresent and important, but equally as mute with respect to their ability to tell us anything significant about Nuer culture and social relations. Once women, and more important, "feminized" anthropologists began to enter the field in greater numbers and began to seriously interview women (and children) about their lives, we began to get a very different picture of those same societies. Margaret Mead was, of course, the groundbreaker in this new line of inquiry. Jane Goodale's (1971) restudy of the Tiwi and Annette Weiner's (1976) restudy of the Trobriand Islanders demonstrate the difference between male and female renditions of the same culture. Freeman's "restudy," however is based on the implausible method of interviewing middle-aged men as a means of "correcting" Mead's interviews of adolescent girls! The error is to think of "culture" as a single integrated reality somewhere "out there" waiting to be accurately described.

We know now that when we are talking about Samoan culture or Irish culture we are talking about an interpretation that is the result of a complex series of interactions between the anthropologist and his or her informants. Cultural understanding is essentially produced, not merely recovered. Ethnography is a very special kind of intellectual autobiography, a deeply personal record through which a whole view of the human condition, an entire sensibility, is elaborated. We no longer try to approach the world (as the natural scientists would) as a fixed array of objects, but rather as a reality that cannot be fully separated from our perceptions of it. It shifts over time and in response to our gaze. It interacts with us. And the knowledge that it yields must always be interpreted by us, by the particular kind of complex social, cultural and psychological self that we bring with us into the field. This "self" cannot be denied. It structures the questions we ask and filters what we see and hear as well as what we do not think to ask or fail to see and hear.

Hence there can be no "falsification" of a 1925 ethnography by a 1940 or a 1965 "restudy" because the particular ethnographic moment in the stream of time that Mead captured is long since gone. The cast of characters has changed. The colonial world has thankfully vanished. There are, today, no "timeless" primitive or traditional peoples—we are all equally contemporary and are all faced with the same fears and challenges of the

20th century in a world united by global markets and divided by global hostilities.

As Elizabeth Colson (1983) so eloquently pointed out in her Distinguished Faculty Research Lecture given on the Berkeley campus last spring, in which she reflected on the past 35 years of her research on the Tonga speaking people of central Africa, cultures are not static and people are not content to play out (for the benefit of the ethnographer!) the same routines day in and day out. She notes that through many decades of anthropological restudy and longitudinal research we have finally learned to date our observations carefully and to drop, once and for all, the use of that "odd tense," the ethnographic present. We have also learned that what *can* be learned is always changing, and we have had to accept the fact that communities can change even more rapidly than the anthropologists who try to study them.

Mead made no claim in *Coming of Age in Samoa* of documenting an eternal truth. And she resisted all requests from Americans and Samoans alike to revise and "update" the book. She maintained that this would be impossible. Were she to study Samoa today she would have to write a very different kind of book based on a very different cultural and historical reality. Her science, too, had changed. In the 1973 edition of *Coming of Age* she writes in the new Preface:

It seems more than ever necessary to stress, shout as loud as I can, this is about Samoa and the United States of 1926–1928. When you read it, remember this. . . . Remember it is your grandparents and great-grandparents I am writing about when they were young and carefree in Samoa or plagued by our expectations from adolescents in the United States. . . . It must remain, exactly as it was written, and true to what I saw in Samoa and what I was able to convey of what I saw; true to the state of our knowledge of human behavior as it was in the mid-twenties; true to our hopes and fears for the future of the world. (1973:ii).

Had the mature Mead returned to Samoa (as she had to Manus, New Guinea), she would have found not only a vastly changed and modernized society with adolescents wearing Walkmen and watching Superman III videotapes, but she would have found the new generation of youth reluctant to talk with a middle-aged, motherly woman. And what's more, *she* might have found *them* less interesting than older men and women, including the high status chiefs. The older Mead, staff in hand, was herself a tribal elder and she understood and could enjoy the feel of power.

The mature Mead had given up the "hypothesis testing" scientific model that had formed her early work. She came to reject the metaphor of field situations as "laboratories" where scientific experiments would be conducted, and she came to recognize (as Freeman apparently does not) that human communities are *not* laboratories and we cannot hold conditions constant for the purposes of scientific replicability. Mead begins her chapter on fieldwork in Spindler's edited volume on *The Making of Psychological Anthropology* with the following statement:

Scientific anthropology differs from the experimental sciences in that it is almost never possible to set up a satisfactory experiment in the field (1978:89).

Moreover, she thought it unfair to the people studied to use them in order to prove theoretical points that meant little to them in the first place. Rather, the mature Mead became increasingly preoccupied with the contemporary situation of rapidly acculturating "primitive" peoples and with the destruction of traditional cultures. She became engaged in an applied ethnography in which she accepted ". . . the task to cherish and protect the lives of all human kind and the life of the world itself" (Spindler 1978:88). She became impatient with petty or internecine disciplinary squabbles, and with the preoccupation with "scientific" methodologies. "Time is running out," she cautioned.

National states are closing their doors to anthropologists, the jungle is being bulldozed and roads are being built through the Kalahari Desert and the Ituri Forest. However much an anthropologist may be interested in exploring or demonstrating some point which has arisen in the course of conventional experimental work in psychology, he or she will in the end, I believe, do better to accept conditions as they come, learn to use every possibility within a given field context, make do and mend with givens, rather than spending months looking for perfect sites, different sized populations or predetermined contrasts (1978:90).

Mead saw the anthropologist as a cultural broker, as a mediator between the collision of cultures and the clash of interpretations. A most compelling image comes from the Odyssey television series documentary on Mead. It showed the older Mead sitting under a tree with a rag-tag bunch of tribal New Guinea revolutionaries discussing Manus politics in pidgin. Mead had a vision of the anthropologist as a "keeper of the records" for preliterate peoples, prodding the old to remember and the young to cherish ways of life the likes of which will never be seen again. And as the rooms of Mead archives at the Museum of Natural History in New York City, filled with hundreds of thousands of tapes, photographs, children's drawings, diaries, journals and endless boxes of field notes, testify, she had a passionate dedication to getting it down right.

Mead was, in a sense, the mother of my generation. She and Benjamin Spock influenced the way we were reared and dared our parents to experiment with such "radical" notions as tolerance, open communication, and "permissiveness." Need I mention that she was a role model to hundreds of women who followed her into the field and into their rightful places within the discipline. She was with us through the civil rights movement, the anti-war movement, and she was a leader in the "second wave" of American feminism, having never left the first wave. Within anthropology she was a moral center as well as an intellectual and personal dynamo, and we have missed her large, although sometimes obtrusive, presence in our midst. I cannot help but recall the awkward way in which her death was announced in the midst of the 1978 American Anthropological Association Meetings. She *would* manage to die when all several thousand of us were gathered together to receive the news! It occurred to me then in the rather silent and frozen void of the moment that it was no wonder we were mute. It was to Margaret we had always turned to handle the significant ritual events of the day; *she* would not have floundered. She would have known exactly what to do, and she could have celebrated the passing so much better herself. We were then, as we are now, a bit adrift without her.

But in the South Seas, on the island of Peri, where Mead was known both as a somewhat brash young woman *and* as a mature, thoughtful and sympathetic elder, the announcement of her death was greeted by no awkward silence. Rather, a communal mourning chant for the death of a high chief filled the long, peaceful night. And no higher tribute can be paid to the eternal student of human culture and to one who spent, as Emilie de Brigard phrased it (1983:494), "the first half of her life trying to save the world's tribal cultures, and the second half trying to save the world from itself."

Notes

1. The island of Upolu, where Freeman conducted his research, is 200 miles away from the island of Ta'u where Mead did her study. During the period covering both their original studies Upolu was under British colonial rule and Ta'u was under American control. Both Mead and Freeman can be accused of making the common ethnographic error of generalizing to the rest of Samoa from the small community each knew best.

2. Even a cursory reading of Mead's early writings reveals the unfairness and inaccuracy of Freeman's description and labeling of Mead's intellectual tradition. Like Franz Boas (who also comes under attack in this book) Mead was a cultural *relativist*, not a cultural *determinist*. She was fascinated with cultural

variations which were assumed to take place, as George Mardus put it, "within the context of general biological tendencies in human behavior" (1983:3). In Mead's *Sex and Temperament in Three Primitive Societies* (1935) this theoretical orientation is quite explicit. She argues in her concluding chapter that temperament varies independent of sex, and is influenced by a host of individual, genetic, and constitutional tendencies, as well as by early childhood conditioning. She rejects the *tabula rasa* metaphor as incorrect and misleading. In reflecting on her own theoretical assumptions Mead wrote: "During the two year period between my field work in Samoa and the Manus field work, I continued to work with the broad assumption that human potentialities were universal, but which ones would be expressed and the form they would take depended upon culture" (1978:99). Freeman's depiction of Mead's supposed theoretical assumptions is a gross distortion of the facts, just as his description of the relationship between Mead and Boas is obscured by his own male bias. Mead's foremost mentor and guiding influence was Ruth Benedict and not Professor Boas.

3. See, for example, Thomas and Chess 1977; Caudill and Frost 1973; Kilbride and Kilbride 1975; and Super and Harkness 1982.

Herbert Applebaum

X

Sociobiology

Introduction

Sociobiology seeks to explain human social behavior through the use of evolutionary theory. In Darwinian and Neo-Darwinian concepts, the social behavior of various animal species evolves as the result of differential reproductive success among individuals. Reproduction is part of the code within genes. Thus, the evolution of patterns of animal social life is the outcome of the preservation and reproduction of the organization of DNA in the chromosomes of animal sex cells.

Sociobiology utilizes various aspects of evolutionary theory, such as adaptation, selection, fitness, and reproductive success, to relate human genetics to human behavior. Evolution is a lengthy process, involving hundreds of thousands and millions of years, particularly in the more complex animals. Change occurs on a random basis through mutations and recombinations of genes effected by sexual reproduction. Adaptation and selection is based on individuals who are better able to fit into their environment and better able to reproduce their kind and increase their contribution to the population. Sociobiology uses expressions such as "concerned with," "is better off doing," or "wants to." This implies that organisms are selected for behaving "as though" they are aware of how to maximize their fitness. It is a shorthand way of saying that they were more successful for having behaved differently, but it requires neither an assumption as to what is going on inside the head of organisms nor that they are aware. Adaptation and selection mechanisms refer to individuals doing what is appropriate, and it is neither required nor expected that they know why. Adaptation and selection operate over many successive generations of individuals, who are unaware of the structure of their DNA or their own fitness.

455

Even among the simplest organisms, behavior is not exclusively determined by genetic instruction. Observations of most organisms indicate that behavior results from a combination of genetic instructions and environment. Each organism, including humans, has a behavioral *genotype*—the hereditary instructions in the genes. There is also a behavioral *phenotype*—the genetically orchestrated products of an individual's experience in a particular environment.

Sociobiologists do not claim that genetics alone determines human behavior. Alexander states, "I hypothesize that the vast bulk of cultural variations among people alive today will eventually be shown to have virtually nothing to do with their genetic differences" (1979:6). And E. O. Wilson (1977:133) has remarked: "The evidence is strong that almost but probably not quite all differences among cultures are based on learning and socialization rather than on genes." While stressing culture and learning, rather than genetics, as explaining social behavior, sociobiologists point out that human beings are still a biologically evolved species. As such they share some evolutionary and genetic mechanisms with other, nonhuman animal species. Sociobiologists admit that they cannot say at this time to what extent these mechanisms influence human behavior. Sociobiology is a young field. It was not until 1975, with the publication of E. O. Wilson's book, *Sociobiology: The New Synthesis*, that sociobiology gained the attention it now receives. The theories it utilizes, evolution and genetics, are much older.

Most of the studies relied upon by sociobiologists to date involve animals and nonhuman organisms. E. O. Wilson's early career was devoted to the study of ants (1971). His second major work (1975), which contained his theories about animal social behavior, has a chapter that argues that the essentially biological principles associated with animal behavior apply to human social behavior. This inflamed many social scientists (Harris and Wilson 1978; Montagu 1980; Handwerker and Crosbie 1982). Even though he said that as little as ten percent of human behavior was genetically induced, Wilson (1975) tended to stress the continuities between human and nonhuman species and to down play the discontinuities, the biggest of which is language.

Humans are genetically programmed to have the capacity for communicating through abstract, symbolic language. It is through langauge, oral and written, that human beings transmit learned behavior to succeeding generations and to contemporaries. Wilson stressed the evolutionary function of organisms to reproduce their kind. However, humans produce more than just themselves. Humans produce wealth, tools, technology, arts, literature, and cultural artifacts. Wealth produced by human beings confers power and control to those who possess it. It gives selective advantage to some individuals over others, based on this cultural and social reality. Adaptation among human beings is culturally mediated, and biological programming has never been separated from cultural learning in human studies.

Sociobiologists argue against the nature/nurture dichotomy or instinct/culture duality. They believe all behavior involves both, in that human behavior is neither one-hundred percent environmentally nor one-hundred percent biologically determined. They agree that human behavior is overwhelmingly culturally influenced. But they insist that biology cannot be ignored. Sociobiology, as a young discipline, has not accumulated enough data, nor performed enough studies, to test many of its hypotheses. In a survey of sociobiology in the *Annual Review of Anthropology*, B. J. Williams concludes that most of the sociobiological models have yet to be applied effectively in field research (1981:189).

One of the propositions of sociobiologists is that altruism among human and nonhuman organisms is genetically based and evolved through natural selection. Traditionally, natural selection was thought to foster physical and behavioral traits which increase an individual's chance of reproducing its kind. Altruistic behavior, sacrificing oneself to save other members of the group, would seem to be incompatible with natural selection. Wilson maintains that such behavior is consistent with natural selection. The sacrifice is made in order to save closely related individuals who share the traits and genes of the sacrificed individual. Wilson argues that it is the preservation of the gene which is decisive, not the individual. W. D. Hamilton (1964) uses the term "inclusive fitness," to describe sacrifice for the benefit of the group. It has also been called "kin selection." Sahlins (1976a), argues that altruism among humans is learned, not genetically programmed. He maintains that, even if kin selection operated in human evolution in the past, it does not imply that it is operating at the present time. It has been replaced by cultural mechanisms.

In behavioral studies, a particular trait can have multiple origins—genetic, learned or a combination of the two. Barash comments (1977:301) that the environment is neutral; it does not "know" if the behavior is genetically or culturally controlled. If the behavior fits the environment, it is adaptive and survives. In human cultures, it makes little difference if the innovative individual is reproductively successful, since he can pass on his knowledge and information to his current generation through language and need not have to pass it on to his offspring for it to survive. Learned behavior does not depend on genetics for survival, but on culture. Cultural change can take place independently of natural selection. Human variation within six to nine thousand years belies the influence of genetics, which takes tens and hundreds of thousands of years to have effect. The enormous variation in human society only over the last three hundred years is testimony to the cultural predominance in explaining variation among human beings.

Sociobiologists theorize that sex relations between males and females is based on differential investment in the fertilized egg (Blute 1984). According to this view, males and females have evolved different reproductive strategies. Females employ a "quality" strategy by producing a small number of large gametes (eggs), while males employ a "quantity" strategy by producing a large number of small gametes (sperm). By providing an egg, plentifully supplied with cytoplasm, a female makes a much greater investment in each offspring than the male, whose sperm carries little more than a set of genes. Both, however, benefit from the cytoplasm provided by the female. In mammals, the female adds internal fertilization, gestation, the placenta, and lactation, thus sharply accentuating their disproportionately high investment in each offspring. The sociobiological thesis is that the sex that invests more in each offspring becomes a resource for which members of the other sex will compete. The low-investing sex (male) competes strenuously for mates and matings, with variable chances for reproductive success. The high-investing sex (female), with more risk in each act of reproduction, is more discriminating in its choice of mates and has a high rate of matings and reproductive success.

Based on the above, sociobiologists predict that, since females have the greater investment in offspring, they have a greater investment in nurturing, and, thus, women in most societies have the primary offspring-care role. Sociobiologists (Barash 1977) also assert that, since the female has a greater investment in offspring, males are more intolerant of female infidelity than females are of male infidelity. Without condoning it, sociobiologists have attempted to provide a hypothesis to explain the double standard between males and females. Sociobiologists believe that certain patterns, like male-female relations, have had their basis laid in the distant past, when humans were hunters and gatherers, and that these have carried over into modern society. The problem is that the arguments for the establishment of these behavior patterns cannot be tested, since they are based on hypothetical situations in human prehistory which are uncheckable.

Sociobiology stresses the notion that reproductive success is the basic mechanism for natural selection and surviving behavioral patterns. They also stress that such an orientation requires no human will or volition. This is where cultural anthropology differs in its orientation, which is based on the notion that human beings, unlike other species, have volition and act consciously to achieve certain ends, even if there are often unintended consequences from their actions. Sociobiology tends to treat human beings in terms of gross populations, rather than people living in particular societies. By doing so, the theory of sociobiology tends to factor out the determinants of human behavior based on type of society, culture, community, or group. Concentrating on populations, rather than types of societies, sociobiologists tend to search for universals rather than variations in human behavior.

In analyzing sociobiological theory, it can be noted that, with its evolutionary perspective and its concentrations on populations rather than societies, the theory largely deals with general traits—aggression, competition, altruism, reproductive success, kin selection, and so on. Sociobiologists are constrained from exploring the specific content of social behavior, since these are given specific expression by particular societies and cultures. To the extent that sociobiology deals mainly with general behavioral patterns, they will have difficulty in addressing the major questions of explaining differences in human behavior which is found in various types of societies and cultures.

If sociobiologists could solve the question as to how social groups adapt to their environment by evolution (Wilson 1978:15–16), it would be of great interest to cultural anthropologists. Different environments presumably impose a variety of problems for human beings and permit a variety of solutions. The sociobiological problem is to account for the differences in behavior, say, between a hunting and gathering society and an industrial one, based on genetic endowment. But since sociobiologists would admit that there is no appreciable difference in a present day hunting and gathering society's genetic endowment and that of an industrial society, differences between the two societies cannot be explained by genetic inheritance.

Sociobiologists must then turn to the prehistoric period, two or three million years ago, when the genetic factor was presumably operable in human adaptation. Evidence for behavior during the prehistoric period is scarce. Thus, sociobiologists must investigate modern day hunters and gatherers, whose way of life is hypothesized to be similar to the hunters and gatherers of prehistoric times. Use of such evidence would be valid, if we knew what prehistoric social life was like. Then, through comparative analysis, some measure of the degree of influence of genetics on behavior might be possible. This was a problem for nineteenth century evolutionary anthropologists, just as it is for sociobiologists today. Natural selection may have been a factor in human behavior two million years ago, but this is no longer true. People may carry genetic dispositions evolved in response to life in prehistoric times, but these dispositions are either no longer serviceable or have been overwhelmed by cultural factors. Sociobiologists concede (Barash 1977) that genetic evolution proceeds slowly by minute increments over many generations, while cultural evolution creates vast changes in a single lifetime. In order to sustain their theories, sociobiologists will have to devise some form of social experiment or research strategy in which they can compare populations after controlling for the cultural factors. Only in this way can they isolate the genetic determinants which they postulate are factors influencing human behavior patterns.

In summary, sociobiology is a discipline which uses evolutionary theory to argue that human behavior is influenced, to some important extent, by the genetic inheritance of the human organism. The basic mechanism for this influence on human behavior is natural selection and reproductive success, just as it is in other species. Cultural anthropologists have taken issue with sociobiologists, arguing that human beings must be considered within the context of societies, where culture and shared learning is the dominant determinant of social behavior. Cultural anthropology, being, in part, an empirical social science, bases its theories on data accumulated through observations and interactions with people in living cultures and societies. Sociobiology has been "frankly speculative" (Barash 1977:54, 61) about the mechanisms of natural selection during the millions of years in prehistory when human beings were evolving into hunting and gathering cultures. To date, sociobiology has provided models and hypotheses. It has started to provide some studies of substance (Turke 1984:663–668), addressing the problem of relating some human behavioral patterns to evolution and genetics. Sociobiologists contend that, while their field is still young, their theoretical foundation, evolutionary theory, is quite sound (Turke 1984). Sociobiologists ask that cultural anthropologists not close the book on them but give them time to develop and demonstrate the validity of their hypotheses.

Edward O. Wilson

31. "Hope"
From: "On Human Nature"

The first dilemma has been created by the seemingly fatal deterioration of the myths of traditional religion and its secular equivalents, principal among which are ideologies based on a Marxian interpretation of history. The price of these failures has been a loss of moral consensus, a greater sense of helplessness about the human condition and a shrinking of concern back toward the self and the immediate future. The intellectual solution of the first dilemma can be achieved by a deeper and more courageous examination of human nature that combines the findings of biology with those of the social sciences. The mind will be more precisely explained as an epiphenomenon of the neuronal machinery of the brain. That machinery is in turn the product of genetic evolution by natural selection acting on human populations for hundreds of thousands of years in their ancient environments. By a judicious extension of the methods and ideas of neurobiology, ethology, and sociobiology a proper foundation can be laid for the social sciences, and the discontinuity still separating the natural sciences on the one side and the social sciences and humanities on the other might be erased.

If this solution to the first dilemma proves even partially correct, it will lead directly to the second dilemma: the conscious choices that must be made among our innate mental propensities. The elements of human nature are the learning rules, emotional reinforcers, and hormonal feedback loops that guide the development of social behavior into certain channels as opposed to others. Human nature is not just the array of outcomes attained in existing societies. It is also the potential array that might be achieved through conscious design by future societies. By looking over the realized social systems of hundreds of animal species and deriving the principles by which these systems have evolved, we can be certain that all human choices represent only a tiny subset of those theoretically possible. Human nature is, moreover, a hodgepodge of special genetic adaptations to an environment largely vanished, the

461

world of the Ice-Age hunter-gatherer. Modern life, as rich and rapidly changing as it appears to those caught in it, is nevertheless only a mosaic of cultural hypertrophies of the archaic behavioral adaptations. And at the center of the second dilemma is found a circularity: we are forced to choose among the elements of human nature by reference to value systems which these same elements created in an evolutionary age now long vanished.

Fortunately, this circularity of the human predicament is not so tight that it cannot be broken through an exercise of will. The principal task of human biology is to identify and to measure the constraints that influence the decisions of ethical philosophers and everyone else, and to infer their significance through neurophysiological and phylogenetic reconstructions of the mind. This enterprise is a necessary complement to the continued study of cultural evolution. It will alter the foundation of the social sciences but in no way diminish their richness and importance. In the process it will fashion a biology of ethics, which will make possible the selection of a more deeply understood and enduring code of moral values.

In the beginning the new ethicists will want to ponder the cardinal value of the survival of human genes in the form of a common pool over generations. Few persons realize the true consequences of the dissolving action of sexual reproduction and the corresponding unimportance of "lines" of descent. The DNA of an individual is made up of about equal contributions of all the ancestors in any given generation, and it will be divided about equally among all descendants at any future moment. All of us have more than two hundred ancestors who were living in 1700— each of whom contributed far less than one chromosome to the living descendant—and, depending on the amount of outbreeding that took place, up to millions in 1066. Henry Adams put it nicely for those of Norman-English descent when he noted that if "we could go back and live again in all our two hundred and fifty million arithmetical ancestors of the eleventh century, we should find ourselves doing many surprising things, but among the rest we should certainly be ploughing most of the fields of the Contentin and Calvados; going to mass in every parish church in Normandy; rendering military service to every lord, spiritual or temporal, in all this region; and helping to build the Abbey Church at Mont-Saint-Michel." Go back another few thousands of years—only a tick in the evolutionary clock—and the gene pool from which one modern Briton has emerged spreads over Europe, to North Africa, the Middle East, and beyond. The individual is an evanescent combination of genes drawn from this pool, one whose hereditary material will soon be dissolved back into it. Because natural selection has acted on the behavior of individuals who benefit themselves and their immediate relatives, human nature bends us to the imperatives of selfishness and tribalism. But a more detached view of the long-range course of evolution should allow us to see beyond the blind decision-making process of natural selection and to envision the history and future of our own genes against the background of the entire human species. A word already in use intuitively defines this view: nobility. Had dinosaurs grasped the concept they might have survived. They might have been us.

I believe that a correct application of evolutionary theory also favors diversity in the gene pool as a cardinal value. If variation in mental and athletic ability is influenced to a moderate degree by heredity, as the evidence suggests, we should expect individuals of truly extraordinary capacity to emerge unexpectedly in otherwise undistinguished families, and then fail to transmit these qualities to their children. The biologist George C. Williams has written of such productions in plants and animals as Sisyphean genotypes; his reasoning is based on the following argument from elementary genetics. Almost all capacities are prescribed by combinations of genes at many sites on the chromosomes. Truly exceptional individuals, weak or strong, are, by definition, to be found at the extremes of statistical curves, and the hereditary substrate of their traits come together in rare combinations that arise from random processes in the formation of new sex cells and the fusion of sex cells to create new organisms. Since each individual produced by the sexual process contains a unique set of genes, very exceptional combinations of genes are unlikely to appear twice even within the same family. So if genius is to any extent hereditary, it winks on and off through the gene pool in a way that would be difficult to measure or predict. Like Sisyphus rolling his boulder up and over to the top of the hill only to have it tumble down again, the human gene pool creates hereditary genius in many ways in many places only to have it come apart the next generation. The genes of the Sisyphean combinations are probably spread throughout populations. For this reason alone, we are justified in considering the preservation of the entire gene pool as a contingent primary value until such time as an almost unimaginably greater knowledge of human heredity provides us with the option of a democratically contrived eugenics.

Universal human rights might properly be regarded as a third primary value. The idea is not general; it is largely the invention of recent European-American civilization. I suggest that we will want to give it primary status not because it is a divine ordinance (kings used to rule by divine right) or through obedience to an abstract principle of unknown extraneous origin, but because we are mammals. Our societies are based on the mammalian plan: the individual strives for personal reproductive success foremost and that of his immediate kin secondarily; further grudging cooperation represents a compromise struck in order to enjoy the benefits of group membership. A rational ant—let us imagine for a moment that ants and other social insects had succeeded in evolving high intelligence—would find such an arrangement biologically unsound and the very concept of individual freedom intrinsically evil. We will accede to universal rights because power is too fluid in advanced technological societies to circumvent this mammalian imperative; the long-term consequences of inequity will always be visibly dangerous to its temporary beneficiaries. I suggest that this is the true reason for the universal rights movement and that an understanding of its raw biological causation will be more compelling in the end than any rationalization contrived by culture to reinforce and euphemize it.

The search for values will then go beyond the utilitarian calculus of genetic fitness. Although natural selection has been the prime mover, it works through a cascade of decisions based on secondary values that have historically served as the enabling mechanisms for survival and reproductive success. These values are defined to a large extent by our most intense emotions: enthusiasm and a sharpening of the senses from exploration; exaltation from discovery; triumph in battle and competitive sports; the restful satisfaction from an altruistic act well and truly placed; the stirring of ethnic and national pride; the strength from family ties; and the secure biophilic pleasure from the nearness of animals and growing plants.

There is a neurophysiology of such responses to be deciphered, and their evolutionary history awaits reconstruction. A kind of principle of the conservation of energy operates among them, such that the emphasis of any one over others still retains the potential summing power of all. Poets have noted it well, as in the calm phrasing of Mary Barnard's Sappho:

Some say a cavalry corps,
some infantry, some, again,
will maintain that the swift oars

of our fleet are the finest
sight on dark earth; but I say
that whatever one loves, is.

Although the means to measure these energies are lacking, I suspect psychologists would agree that they can be rechanneled substantially without losing strength, that the mind fights to retain a certain level of order and emotional reward. Recent evidence suggests that dreams are produced when giant fibers in the brainstem fire upward through the brain during sleep, stirring the cerebral cortex to activity. In the absence of ordinary sensory information from the outside, the cortex responds by calling up images from the memory banks and fabricating plausible stories. In an analogous manner the mind will always create morality, religion, and mythology and empower them with emotional force. When blind ideologies and religious beliefs are stripped away, others are quickly manufactured as replacements. If the cerebral cortex is rigidly trained in the techniques of critical analysis and packed with tested information, it will reorder all that into some form of morality, religion, and mythology. If the mind is instructed that its pararational activity cannot be combined with the rational, it will divide itself into two compartments so that both activities can continue to flourish side by side.

This mythopoeic drive can be harnessed to learning and the rational serach for human progress if we finally concede that scientific materialism is itself a mythology defined in the noble sense. So let me give again the reasons why I consider the scientific ethos superior to religion: its repeated triumphs in explaining and controlling the physical world; its self-correcting nature open to all competent to devise and conduct the tests; its readiness to examine all subjects sacred and profane; and now the possibility of explaining traditional religion by the mechanistic models of evolutionary biology. The last achievement will be crucial. If religion, including the dogmatic secular ideologies, can be systematically analyzed and explained as a product of the brain's evolution, its power as an external source of morality will be gone forever and the solution of the second dilemma will have become a practical necessity.

The core of scientific materialism is the evolutionary epic. Let me repeat its minimum claims: that the laws of the physical sciences are consistent with those of the biological and social sciences and can be linked in chains of causal explanation; that life and mind have a physical basis; that the world as we know it has evolved from earlier worlds obedient to the same laws; and that the visible universe today is everywhere subject to these materialist explanations. The epic can be indefinitely strengthened up and down the line, but its most sweeping assertions cannot be proved with finality.

What I am suggesting, in the end, is that the evolutionary epic is probably the best myth we will ever have. It can be adjusted until it comes as close to truth as the human mind is constructed to judge the truth. And if that is the case, the mythopoeic requirements of the mind must somehow be met by scientific materialism so as to reinvest our superb energies. There are ways of managing such a shift honestly and without dogma. One is to cultivate more intensely the relationship between the sciences and humanities. The great British biologist J. B. S. Haldane said of science and literature, "I am absolutely convinced that science is vastly more stimulating to the imagination than are the classics, but the products of the stimulus do not normally see the light because scientific men as a class are devoid of any perception of literary form." Indeed the origin of the universe in the big bang of fifteen billion years ago, as deduced by astronomers and physicists, is far more awesome than the first chapter of Genesis or the Ninevite epic of Gilgamesh. When the scientists project physical processes backward to that moment with the aid of mathematical models they are talking about everything—literally everything—and when they move forward in time to pulsars, supernovas, and the collision of black holes they probe distances and mysteries beyond the imaginings of earlier generations. Recall how God lashed Job with concepts meant to overwhelm the human mind:

Who is this whose ignorant words
cloud my design in darkness?
Brace yourself and stand up like a man;
I will ask questions, and you shall answer . . .
Have you descended to the springs of the sea
or walked in the unfathomable deep?
Have the gates of death been revealed to you?
Have you ever seen the door-keepers of the place of darkness?
Have you comprehended the vast expanse of the world?
Come, tell me all this, if you know.

And yes, we *do* know and we have told. Jehovah's challenges have been met and scientists have pressed on to uncover and to solve even greater puzzles. The physical basis of life is known; we understand approximately how and when it started on earth. New species have been created in the laboratory and evolution has been traced at the molecular level. Genes can be spliced from one kind of organism into another. Molecular biologists have most of the knowledge needed to create elementary forms of life. Our machines, settled on Mars, have transmitted panoramic views and the results of chemical soil analysis. Could the Old Testament writers have conceived of such activity? And still the process of great scientific discovery gathers momentum.

Yet, astonishingly, the high culture of Western civilization exists largely apart from the natural sciences. In the United States intellectuals are virtually defined as those who work in the prevailing mode of the social sciences and humanities. Their reflections are devoid of the idioms of chemistry and biology, as though humankind were still in some sense a numinous spectator of physical reality. In the pages of *The New York Review of Books, Commentary, The New Republic, Daedalus, National Review, Saturday Review,* and other literary journals articles dominate that read as if most of basic science had halted during the nineteenth century. Their content consists largely of historical anecdotes, diachronic collating of outdated, verbalized theories of human behavior, and judgments of current events according to personal ideology—all enlivened by the pleasant but frustrating techniques of effervescence. Modern science is still regarded as a problem-solving activity and a set of technical marvels, the importance of which is to be valuated in an ethos extraneous to science. It is true that many "humanistic" scientists step outside scientific materialism to participate in the culture, sometimes as expert witnesses and sometimes as aspiring authors, but they almost never close the gap between the two worlds of discourse. With rare exceptions they are the tame scientists, the token emissaries of what must be viewed by their hosts as a barbaric culture still ungraced by a written language. They are degraded by the label they accept too readily: popularizers. Very few of the great writers, the ones who can trouble and move the deeper reaches of the mind, ever address real science on its own terms. Do they know the nature of the challenge?

The desired shift in attention could come more easily now that the human mind is subject to the network of causal explanation. Every epic needs a hero: the mind will do. Even astronomers, accustomed to thinking about ten billion galaxies and distances just short of infinity, must agree that the human brain is the most complex device that we know and the crossroads of investigation by every major natural science. The social scientists and humanistic scholars, not omitting theologians, will eventually have to concede that scientific naturalism is destined to alter the foundations of their systematic inquiry by redefining the mental process itself.

I began this book with an exposition of the often dialectic nature of scientific advance. The discipline abuts the antidiscipline; the antidiscipline succeeds in reordering the phenomena of the discipline by reduction to its more fundamental laws; but the new synthesis created in the discipline profoundly alters the antidiscipline as the interaction widens. I suggested that biology, and especially neurobiology and sociobiology, will serve as the antidiscipline of the social sciences. I will now go further and suggest that the scientific materialism embodied in biology will, through a reexamination of the mind and the foundations of social behavior, serve as a kind of antidiscipline to the humanities. No Comtian revolution will take place, no sudden creation of a primitively scientific culture. The translation will be gradual. In order to address the central issues of the humanities, including ideology and religious belief, science itself must become more sophisticated and in part specially crafted to deal with the peculiar features of human biology.

I hope that as this syncretism proceeds, a true sense of wonder will reinvade the broader culture. We need to speak more explicitly of the things we do not know. The epic of which natural scientists write in technical fragments still has immense gaps and absorbing mysteries, not the least of which is the physical basis of the mind. Like blank spaces on the map of a partly explored world, their near borders can be fixed but their inner magnitude only roughly guessed. Scientists and humanistic scholars can do far better than they have at articulating the great goals toward which literate people move as on a voyage of discovery. Unknown and surprising things await. They are as accessible as in those days of primitive wonder when the early European explorers went forth and came upon new worlds and the first microscopists watched bacteria swim across drops of water. As knowledge grows science must increasingly become the stimulus to imagination.

Such a view will undoubtedly be opposed as elitist by some who regard economic and social problems as everywhere overriding. There is an element of truth in that objection. Can anything really matter while people starve in the Sahel and India and rot in the prisons of Argentina and the Soviet Union? In response it can be asked, do we want to know, in depth and for all time, why we care? And when these problems are solved, what then? The stated purpose of governments everywhere is human fulfillment in some sense higher than animal survival. In almost all socialist revolutions the goals of highest priority, next to consecration of the revolution, are education, science, and technology—the combination that leads inexorably back to the first and second dilemmas.

This view will be rejected even more firmly by those whose emotional needs are satisfied by traditional organized religion. God and the church, they will claim, cannot be extinguished ex parte by a rival mythology based on science. They will be right. God remains a viable hypothesis as the prime mover, however undefinable and untestable that conception may be. The rituals of religion, especially the rites of passage and the sanctification of nationhood, are deeply entrenched and incorporate some of the most magnificent elements of existing cultures. They will certainly continue to be practiced long after their etiology has been disclosed. The anguish of death alone will be enough to keep them alive. It would be arrogant to suggest that a belief in a personal, moral God will disappear, just as it would be reckless to predict the forms that ritual will take as scientific materialism appropriates the mythopoeic energies to its own ends.

I also do not envision scientific generalization as a substitute for art or as anything more than a nourishing symbiont of art. The artist, including the creative writer, communicates his most personal experience and vision in a direct manner chosen to commit his audience emotionally to that perception. Science can hope to explain artists, and artistic genius, and even art, and it will increasingly use art to investigate human behavior, but it is not designed to transmit experience on a personal level or to reconstitute the full richness of the experience from the laws and principles which are its first concern by definition.

Above all, I am not suggesting that scientific naturalism be used as an alternative form of organized formal religion. My own reasoning follows in a direct line from the humanism of the Huxleys, Waddington, Monod, Pauli, Dobzhansky, Cattrell, and others who have risked looking this Gorgon in the face. Each has achieved less than his purpose, I believe, for one or the other of two reasons. He has either rejected religious belief as animism or else recommended that it be sequestered in some gentle preserve of the mind where it can live out its culture-spawned existence apart from the mainstream of intellectual endeavor. Humanists show a touching faith in the power of knowledge and the idea of evolutionary progress over the minds of men. I am suggesting a modification of scientific humanism through the recognition that the mental processes of religious belief—conscecration of personal and group identity, attention to charismatic leaders, mythopoeism, and others—represent programmed predispositions whose self-sufficient components were incorporated into the neural apparatus of the brain by thousands of generations of genetic evolution. As such they are powerful, ineradicable, and at the center of human social existence. They are also structured to a degree not previously appreciated by most philosophers. I suggest further that scientific materialism must accommodate them on two levels: as a scientific puzzle of great complexity and interest, and as a source of energies that can be shifted in new directions when scientific materialism itself is accepted as the more powerful mythology.

That transition will proceed at an accelerating rate. Man's destiny is to know, if only because societies with knowledge culturally dominate societies that lack it. Luddites and anti-intellectuals do not master the differential equations of thermodynamics or the biochemical cures of illness. They stay in thatched huts and die young. Cultures with unifying goals will learn more rapidly than those that lack them, and an autocatalytic growth of learning will follow because scientific materialism is the only mythology that can manufacture great goals from the sustained pursuit of pure knowledge.

I believe that a remarkable effect will be the increasingly precise specification of history. One of the great dreams of social theorists—Vico, Marx, Spencer, Spengler, Teggart, and Toynbee, among the most innovative—has been to devise laws of history that can foretell something of the future of mankind. Their schemes came to little because their understanding of human nature had no scientific basis; it was, to use a favored expression of scientific reporting, orders of magnitude too imprecise. The invisible hand remained invisible; the summed actions of thousands or millions of poorly understood individual human beings was not to be computed. Now there is reason to entertain the view that the culture of each society travels along one or the other of a set of evolutionary trajectories whose full array is constrained by the genetic rules of human nature. While broadly scattered from an anthropocentric point of view, this array still represents only a tiny subset of all the trajectories that would be possible in the absence of the genetic constraints.

As our knowledge of human nature grows, and we start to elect a system of values on a more objective basis, and our minds at last align with our hearts, the set of trajectories will narrow still more. We already know, to take two extreme and opposite examples, that the worlds of William Graham Sumner, the absolute Social Darwinist, and Mikhail Bakunin, the anarchist, are biologically impossible. As the social sciences mature into predictive disciplines, the permissible trajectories will not only diminish in number but our descendants will be able to sight farther along them.

Then mankind will face the third and perhaps final spiritual dilemma. Human genetics is now growing quickly along with all other branches of science. In time, much knowledge concerning the genetic foundation of social behavior will accumulate, and techniques may become available for altering gene complexes by molecular engineering and rapid selection through cloning. At the very least, slow evolutionary change will be feasible through conventional eugenics.The human species can change its own nature. What will it choose? Will it remain the same, teetering on a jerrybuilt foundation of partly obsolete Ice-Age adaptations? Or will it press on toward still higher intelligence and creativity, accompanied by a greater—or lesser—capacity for emotional response? New patterns of sociality could be installed in bits and pieces. It might be possible to imitate genetically the more nearly perfect nuclear family of the white-handed gibbon or the harmonious sisterhoods of the honeybees. But we are talking here about the very essence of humanity. Perhaps there is something already present in our nature that will prevent us from ever making such changes. In any case, and fortunately, this third dilemma belongs to later generations.

In the spirit of the enrichment of the evolutionary epic, modern writers often summon the classical mythic heroes to illustrate their view of the predicament of humankind: the existential Sisyphus, turning fate into the only means of expression open to him; hesitant Arjuna at war with his conscience on the Field of Righteousness; disastrous Pandora bestowing the ills of mortal existence on human beings; and uncomplaining Atlas, steward of the finite Earth. Prometheus has gone somewhat out of fashion in recent years as a concession to resource limitation and managerial prudence. But we should not lose faith in him. Come back with me for a moment to the original, Aeschylean Prometheus:

Chorus: Did you perhaps go further than you have told us?
Prometheus: I caused mortals to cease foreseeing doom.
Chorus: What cure did you provide them with against that sickness?
Prometheus: I placed in them blind hopes.

The true Promethean spirit of science means to liberate man by giving him knowledge and some measure of dominion over the physical environment. But at another level, and in a new age, it also constructs the mythology of scientific materialism, guided by the corrective devices of the scientific method, addressed with precise and deliberately affective appeal to the deepest needs of human nature, and kept strong by the blind hopes that the journey on which we are now embarked will be farther and better than the one just completed.

Napoleon A. Chagnon

32. Anthropology and the Nature of Things

Anthropologists familar with the history and tradition of the discipline might properly ask, at the end of this volume, what is so distinctive about considering human behavior in terms of evolutionary biology, viewing man and his behavior as a product of natural selection? After all, our craft began with the purpose of explaining both man's natural and cultural variations and has always held both social and biological questions as within its legitimate domain. Anthropology has always been, and will continue to be, what anthropologists do; and it is a prescient, if not presumptuous, soul who could hazard an accurate definition of what the future scope of the field will be.

One of my former teachers, Leslie A. White, was clearly aware of this. He whimsically advised his classes on the history of the discipline that "Anthropology is the study of anything that has to do with any primate at any point in time." On occasion White was dismayed by this prodigious scope, but he shared the vision of many of our academic forebears that anthropology by necessity incorporated and depended upon knowledge that other disciplines generated about the nature, history, and evolution of man. One of our distinguished intellectual ancestors, Edward B. Tylor, was more pointed and ebullient: he argued, with admirable confidence, that anthropology had a mission that entailed assembling all the knowledge about man and making it intelligible. In this enterprise, many of the other sciences, as Tylor expressly argued, served subordinate roles: "Various other sciences . . . must be regarded as subsidiary to anthropology, which yet hold their own independent places in the field of knowledge" (1910:109). Among these, Tylor explicitly included anatomy and physiology, psychology, philology, ethics, sociology, archaeology and geology. Tylor's boldly articulated vision presumably came unwelcomed to other scholars of his day, whose already mature disciplines were making notable advances in knowledge and shedding considerable light on the track of man. All the more, since anthropology was then a nascent discipline, just taking form and substance, yet rendering unto itself the supreme responsibility, if not privilege, of assuming the role of queen of the sciences.

All of this should remind us that anthropology has always concerned itself with the study of human behavior in a biological as well as a cultural sense, has always depended on the knowledge accumulated by other sciences to achieve this end, and has always represented itself as the most holistic of disciplines, destined to be supreme in a hierarchy of knowledge. Yet, one cannot help being amused by the fact that, despite Tylor's confident vision, there still exist as independent and vigorous disciplines all the "subsidiary" sciences he identified. Many of our colleagues seem to fear that evolutionary biology will aspire to the role that Tylor envisioned for anthropology. I am confident that their concerns are exaggerated. This is not because I share Tylor's view about the supremacy of anthropology but because, as the essays in this volume repeatedly show, man is at once a product of culture and nature and a comprehensive understanding of his behavior requires both a biology and an anthropology.

Claude Lévi-Strauss, who characteristically focuses his attention on enigmatic themes and who, for that reason, often determines major trends in anthropological inquiry, has always puzzled over a fundamental dichotomy characteristic of the intellectual concerns of most of the human species: the Nature/Culture opposition. The myths of peoples all over the globe reflect, elaborate upon, and attempt to reconcile the contradictions of an almost unacceptable Truth: that Man is at once part of Nature but yet, as distinct from other animals, independent of it because he has Culture—fire, tools, souls, language and immortality. Thus, in the *tristes tropiques* of Amazonas, Jaguar can successfully hunt and devour men unarmed and uncultured, but we deny this to him in our stories about him: in myth, he is a fool and invariably duped by Men. In a curious and amusing sense, the ideology of cultural anthropology is very much like the ambivalence of myth regarding Jaguar's nature: Yes, we say early in our textbooks, humans are primates and behave according to the laws of nature, but because humans can learn and have culture they are, in later sections of the textbook, almost immune to these laws and apart from nature. So prevalent is this attitude that Alexander (1979) concludes that two of the major obstacles to accepting general notions of evolution as applicable to humans are organized religion on the one hand, and cultural anthropology on the other!

This remarkable outgrowth of our philosophical tradition stems in part from a zealous and uncritical adherence to Durkheim's general admonition that the proper explanation of social facts had necessarily to be sociology in its narrowest form, a perspective that Leslie White himself elaborated in his compelling works on the science of culture. Their views, in their most exclusivist expressions, were challenged and modified by the cultural-ecological works of the 1960s and 1970s, when the "environment" was painfully admitted into the functional scheme of things. The deterministic dimension emerging in the harder side of social anthropology could hardly be incompatible with arguments that humans, like all other organisms, had to subsist to survive, and that their subsistence regimes reflected ecological realities which necessarily had to be considered in explanations of both human behavior and cultural adaptations (although the latter were the primary focus of attention).

But the conspicuous opposition of social anthropologists to biological models of human behavior is, in another sense, a consequence of the history of anthropology itself. Social and cultural anthropology set off on a specialized course nearly one hundred years ago while physical anthropology and human biology went a different way—and few of the respective practitioners had much awareness of what the others were doing. The fiction of a holistic anthropology was largely maintained through introductory textbooks and by the fact that all "good" departments had to include both physical and cultural anthropologists. Thus, much of the lack of understanding or even the suspicion, that characterizes the relationships between biologically oriented and culturally oriented anthropologists is built into the discipline itself, a product of increasing specialization and narrower and narrower focuses on smaller and smaller problems—coupled with stronger and stronger convictions about the symbolic nature of kinship, marriage, and even reproduction itself. Today it is commonplace for social and cultural anthropologists to scorn the very suggestion that kinship has biological attributes and functions, and that kinship behavior might make sense in terms of predictions from evolutionary biology. If in some quarters the significance of the "environment" has won a grudging acceptance, the possible significance of the "biogram" still incurs an apprehensive aversion.

Curiously, the reservations many of us in social anthropology have about the utility of biological models reflect in an uncanny way the theme that pervades the myths of tribesmen: Men are part of Culture and apart from Nature. Why is it so difficult, even repugnant, for humans to admit that they are as much a part of Nature as they are a part of Culture? We so willingly admit, both in scientific ideology and in myth, that humans and animals are one with each other and for many purposes interchangeable. We even permit them in fiction to beget each other, if not in enchanting stories of creation, then in evolutionary sequences. But in both instances we ultimately insist on a sharp break, a great divide, an insuperable gulf separating ourselves from the rest of the creatures. One is almost compelled to suggest that an idea so firmly entrenched in the minds of men has some adaptive function or meaning. Would admitting our "naturalness" reduce our capacity to effectively adapt to our surroundings? Does the optimistic conviction that Nature is subordinate to Culture confer any advantage in dealing with—struggling with—the external world, in the past or in the present?

Probably if the essays in this volume had been published ten years ago, they would have appeared in the context of physical anthropology without stirring much of a ripple among cultural anthropologists, but they may provoke more discussion now because the concerns of most of the authors can be simply expressed as an attempt to see beyond a Culture/Nature opposition, to reaffirm the kind of holistic view of human behavior that distinguished many of our academic ancestors. We can imagine nothing more exciting or scientifically profound than the possibility that much of human behavior conforms to predictions from evolutionary biology—and nothing more legitimate as a field of anthropological inquiry. But we also know that premature conclusions are not good science—they are not science at all. The recent impact of evolutionary biology on anthropological studies has come at a time when biological theory itself has gained new, powerful, and far-reaching insights into the nature of all behavior. The number of critical concepts or new ideas is small—inclusive fitness, nepotism, reciprocal altruism, kin selection, mating strategies, parental investment—but their implications for many kinds of characteristically human behavior are great. And behavior is the key word, particularly as it is relatable to strategies of reproduction and differences in reproductive success. The sexual asymmetries in reproductive physiology widespread in nature are likewise characteristic of our species, and in that simple truth a great many profound questions about human nature must necessarily lie. Anthropologists have been studying human kinship and marriage for over one hundred years, and yet we are hardly able to claim more than Morgan did in 1870: systems of consanguinity and affinity in the human family vary. But how does reproduction within them vary, individual by individual, sex by sex?

It should be obvious by now that definitive answers to the key questions will require new and highly detailed information. Lamentably, anthropology, in its traditional concerns, stands in the twilight of a rapidly disappearing era, for the kinds of societies in which new work can be done—or previous work extended—are vanishing, and many of those remaining societies are inaccessible for political reasons. While the now-limited ethnographic cosmos may hinder us, it does not preclude new studies altogether. Indeed, valuable work in this vein can be done in any society, for the variations of which we speak lie not only in the exotic hinterlands of remote places and anywhere therein, but everywhere. We believe that new studies of human behavior from the vantage of both evolutionary biology and traditional anthropology should be initiated on a broad scale with tests of natural selection hypotheses in mind, not only because such inquiries have always been within the traditional scope of our science, but also because they are scientifically important. We may enter blind alleys on some or make new discoveries on others, for such is the fate of those who take new paths and fresh ideas into unknown domains. Almost no explicitly sociobiological fieldwork in human societies has yet been accomplished. But, as the essays in this volume suggest, some existing data give us reason to believe that the return for such efforts will be great. To make this step, future field researchers must set aside the cliché of Nature-opposed-to-Culture, hold in abeyance some of the preconceptions and prejudices that mark our profession's recent parochial history, and responsibly reflect on the kinds of questions that aroused an earlier generation of students of man. It is entirely fitting to end this volume with an attempt to capture some of the caution and optimism that marked the measured words of Tylor:

None will deny that, as each man knows by the evidence of his own consciousness, definite and natural cause does, to a great extent, determine human action. Then, keeping aside from considerations of extra-natural interference and causeless spontaneity, let us take this admitted existence of natural cause and effect as our standing-ground, and travel on it so far as it will bear us [1958(1871):3.]

While Tylor had in mind the distinction between science and supernaturalism, which need not concern us here, his dismissal of causeless spontaneity surely applies to the question of the independence of man's behavior from his evolutionary and biological character. To deny any relationship or oppose any inquiry is to ignore the great aphorism of Lucretius: that nothing yet from nothing ever came.

Herbert Applebaum

XI

Symbolic and Humanistic Anthropology

Introduction

Edward Tylor, the nineteenth century pioneer in anthropology, wrote (1975:118):

> The power of using words as signs to express thoughts with which their sound does not directly connect them, in fact as arbitrary symbols, is the highest grade of the special human faculty in language, the presence of which binds together all races of mankind in substantial mental unity.

Symbols are objects, events, speech sounds, or written forms to which humans attribute meaning. The primary form of symbolizing by human beings is through language. But humans also communicate by using signs and symbols in art, dance, music, architecture, facial expressions, gestures, body postures, ornaments, clothing, ritual, religion, kinship, nationality, space arrangements, and material possessions, among many other things. Human beings can attribute meaning to any event, action, or object which can evoke thought, idea, and emotion. The perception of the use of symbols as a significant human feature has become an important object of study in anthropology and other disciplines. Susanne Langer (1951) sees it as a changing trend in modern human intellectual activity.

Leslie White (1940), in an article on humans as a symbolizing species, pointed to the importance of context in the meaning of symbols. Ernest Cassirer (1944:27–41) argues that without a complex of symbols, relational thought would not be possible. Humans have the capacity to isolate relations and consider them in their abstract meaning. Geometry is the classic example. Geometry, conceptually, deals with universal spatial relationships for which expression there is a symbolic language and a form of representation. Yet, this abstract system can be applied to building problems. Cassirer expresses the symbolic nature of human experience as follows (1976:20):

No longer in a merely physical universe, man lives in a symbolic universe. Language, myth, art, and religion are parts of this universe. They are the varied threads which weave the symbolic net, the tangled web of human experience. All human progress in thought and experience refines upon and strengthens this net.

As anthropologists began to develop a perspective of culture as a system of symbols, meanings, and values, various subdisciplines of anthropology with this orientation came into being. Two of these were semi.ic an^th-opology (the study of signs) and symbolic anthropology. While s ᐧtics will not be dealt with at length in this division, it is often group... .ogether with symbolic anthropology. Sign and symbol are often discussed together. Thus Charles S. Peirce, who laid the modern foundations for the discipline of semiotics, said, "the general answer to the question what is man? is that he is a symbol" (Singer 1980:485).

Symbols or signs can be viewed as concepts regarded by general consent as typifying something else by possession of analogous qualities or by association in thought or fact. Note the discussion in Victor Turner's article (chapter 33) about the symbol of the *mudyi* tree among the Ndembu people of Zambia. A symbol stimulates or conveys a message which stimulates thought or action. Peirce identified three types of signs: 1.) an *iconic* sign resembles its object in some respect (The cross is an iconic sign, evoking the idea and meaning of Christianity); 2.) an *indexical* sign is physically related to its object (A weathervane is an example, as is a flag flying at half mast to denote that an important public person has died); and 3.) symbols like language stand for its object because it is so interpreted by convention and usage. Some symbolic and sign system studies concentrate on the internal logic. Others, usually those not linguistically linked, stress the social action and social context of signs and symbols as they relate to the behavioral and value system of a culture or society.

Symbolic anthropology views human beings as the carriers and products, as subjects and objects, of a system of signs and symbols which serve as a means of communication to impart knowledge and messages. These provide the foundation for action and behavior, as well as ideas and values. The symbolic theory of culture is a model of human beings as a symbolizing species, as compared with a materialist theory of culture based on humans as primarily a producing species. Both models recognize the existence of both the material and mental aspects of human existence, but each views the other from its own perspective. The symbolic definition of culture is part of a trend which sees culture as the science of meanings. Symbolic anthropologists study the system of codes and messages received by human beings through their interaction with other human beings and with the natural world. Charles Peirce (Sebeok 1979:3) remarked that the entire universe is perfused with signs. Given this fact and the fact that all creatures communicate with some form of sign and symbol, symbolic anthropology is engaged in research which is universal in scope.

Most of the knowledge, thoughts, feelings, and perceptions of human beings is wrapped in language, a symbol system. Words convey meanings or name and classify objects and thoughts. As such, they are conceptual perceptions of the world, couched in symbols. Word symbols, languages, are appropriate to a society at a particular time and place. The word *planet* meant something different in the first century than it does in the twentieth. Language and its development provides the foundation for the symbolic view of culture. Linguistics, the study of language, has given the symbolic anthropologist the techniques with which to unravel the codes which represent the complex of motives, experiences, and knowledge which shape and express beliefs and actions. Thus, linguistics is the historical forerunner for symbolic anthropology.

Language is not the only form that symbolic expression takes. Symbols can take the form of public events, parades, funerals, tournaments, holidays and even the way leaders stand on a podium (see Dubinskas, Chapter 35). Many times a symbol will merge with a sign, as when pictures of public leaders are displayed. Symbolizing as a mental activity can draw upon any type of object or gesture.

The philosophical ideas of Immanuel Kant provide an important base to the orientation of symbolic and semiotic anthropologists, as does the structuralism of Lévi-Strauss. Kant argued that there were basic structures of thinking, which were independent of the content of thought. Kant developed a general theory of symbolic forms and their relation to thought which was influential in psychology and the social sciences. Weber, Durkheim, Mauss, Peirce, Saussure, and others were concerned with problems defined by Kant. Kant claimed that humans had no direct insight into the real world. He believed that it was only certain *pure* intellectual concepts, such as those of possibility, existence, necessity, substance, cause, time, and place, that enable humans to have the descriptive tools to gain knowledge about the external world. As Kant put it, in knowing, it is not the mind that conforms to things, but things that conform to the mind (Encyclopedia Britannica, 1985, Vol. 22:493–494).

Having said that communication is more than language, it must also be said that human knowledge is wrapped in language, a symbol system. Words convey knowledge or knowing, and knowing is couched in words. Words, which become signs when written, are appropriate to particular societies at particular times and places. Symbolic systems represent knowledge developed by a community of persons with a historic tradition and a particular system of communication. Symbolic analysis can proceed on an individual or a societal level. Though for purposes of analysis, we may abstract the individual from the community, or the present from the past or future, reality is a fabric of complex relationships, a totality that is continually taking shape, both in its objective reality and in the way we see it. The outside world and the subjective view of it are intertwined. Subject and object become one in the cognitive and symbolic view. Events, objects, and experiences are embedded in a set of meanings, enmeshed in a system of cultural symbols. Reality exists out there, but not as pure experience or as pure events. In the symbolic perspective, culture is the meaningful aspect of concrete or objective reality and the coming-to-be, the appropriation to consciousness, of objective reality.

Victor Turner (1975) groups the symbolic anthropologists into two groups: 1.) the abstract systems group which includes linguists, structuralists, and cognitive anthropologists (This group concentrates on formal analysis and is less concerned with content than with methods and logics), and 2.) the symbols and social dynamics group, which includes semiotic and symbolic anthropologists, sociolinguists, folklorists, and literary critics (This group tries to meld the formal analysis with content, and perception and meaning with social action).

Victor Turner states that the countermovement to the abstract systems of the formalists, especially in linguistics, was undertaken by symbolic anthropologists who concentrated on performance (acting) rather than competence (knowing). Referring to semiotics, Turner points out (1975:152) that signs are deliberate constructs for precise communicative purposes and, as such, play an important role in social action, particularly in technical, political, and economic action. In technology, there is the cad/cam computer system to drive machines. In politics, there are posters and pictures of leaders used to foster national support for leaders and their programs. In economics, there are indexes which signal the growth or decline of the economy and can stimulate or put a brake on actions in the market place.

Wherever symbol systems are guides to action, they operate within a social context. This gives a symbol or a sign its specific meaning, since a symbol or a sign can have one meaning in one social context and another in a different context. The word *father* has one meaning within a kinship structure and a different one within the context of the Catholic religious structure. Society is the result of the intersecting actions and behaviors of persons occupying different boundaries and social contexts, often simultaneously. Context can be place, organization, tribe, kinship group, institution, age, sex or occupational group, or any other social dimension which defines, regulates, and sets the limits of roles and behavior. Signs and symbols are cues which set humans in motion. In the symbolic view, the combinations of signs, symbols, and context give meaning and interpretation to human actions and behavior.

The increase in symbolic studies in anthropology is part of a general reevaluation of concepts in the social sciences. Faith in the scientific method and science assigned a high priority to physical phenomena over mental phenomena and to material processes which are independent of human will. With the development of cognitive and symbolic studies, the mental processes of both the observer and those observed have been added to the methodology for understanding and investigating human behavior.

With the development of language studies and the realization that language is related to human biological competency, an aspect of mental behavior appeared which could be subjected to formal analysis. The discovery of logical symbolic and sign systems, with internal consistency and with universal application, excited social scientists who saw new possibilities for precise, scientific analysis of mental structures, akin to studies in the physical sciences. In the earlier stages of these studies there was a concentration on methods. Later, symbolic studies focused on the internal logics of sign and symbol systems. In recent years, the thrust of semiotic and symbolic studies have leaned toward relating symbols and signs to social action and social context, an orientation which Schneider describes as the search for symbol systems that are codes for conduct on various levels (Schneider 1969:116–25). While the symbolic code may limit the range of possible meanings and provide materials and means for creating new meanings, behavior in a social process is not simply a mechanical use of codes in which actors are social dummies. Different groups and different individuals mobilize with different symbols for action. Dolgin, Demnitzer, and Schneider (1977:31–32) explain that sets and subsets of symbols are instruments for the human creativity capacity to use in different contexts, and symbols should not be reified into some mystical influence which automatically galvanizes people into thinking and acting in pre-set ways.

Clifford Geertz is another anthropologist who emphasized that anthropology should shift from the search for explanation to the search for meaning and who saw the importance of symbols in anthropological research. Geertz stressed the significance of social context as a crucial element in comprehending what symbols signify. He argued for turning away from an investigation of signs and symbols in abstraction, "toward an investigation of signs and symbols in their natural habitat—the common world in which men look, name, listen and make" (1983:119).

To summarize, *symbolic anthropology* is based on the notion that members of a society share a system of symbols and meanings called culture. The system represents the reality in which people live. Symbolic anthropologists stress system, whether it is loosely or tightly integrated, since members of a society must articulate and share to some degree. People must have some notion of what other people in their community believe, some expectation of what their response to others will be and others to them, so as to be able to interact and communicate. If communication is the sine qua non of human society, symboling (Leslie White's term), signing and conveying meaning on thoughts and actions, is what defines a culture. Symbolic anthropology is dedicated to studying and researching the process by which people give *meaning* to their world and their actions in it.

Humanistic or interpretive anthropology seeks to redirect cultural anthropology from a strategy of finding causal explanations for human behavior to one that seeks interpretations and meaning in human action. It is a strategy which sees the humanities rather than science as the model for anthropology. It seeks analogies based on theatre, play, drama, and literature rather than those based on crafts, mechanics, and organic structures.

Humanistic anthropology is mentalist in its orientation, seeing culture as a system of ideas, values, and meanings. It differs from other mentalist approaches which seek causes for human behavior. Interpretive or humanistic anthropology eschews the search for causal explanation in favor of a hermeneutic approach which seeks meanings through interpretations of behaviors or texts.

Interpretative anthropology, rather than seeking general propositions through the comparative study of many cases, takes an idiographic approach, that is, the study of the single case which can yield insights and meanings. In the study of the individual case, a particular society, for example, interpretive anthropology does not look at how people behave as much as the meanings which persons living in the society give to their actions and behavior. These meanings are conveyed through the use of symbols which stand for values, codes, and rules. This viewpoint does not deny the material world but believes that the material and social world of humans can be best understood by listening to the way persons living in the society explain and understand their institutions and customs. The job of the anthropologist is to interpret the interpretations of the "natives."

Clifford Geertz is the theoretical leader, if not the founder, of the approach to anthropology called "interpretive." He asserts that anthropology cannot aspire to be a science in the way that the physical sciences are, with laws and generalizations based on empirical and verifiable data. Geertz believes that anthropology must be based on concrete reality, but, from this reality, one derives meanings rather than predictions based on empirical data. Geertz argues against the use of models in social investigation. They are too abstract and strip social analysis of its living qualities. For Geertz, anthropology should base itself on the humanistic disciplines, utilizing description, poetics, literature, myths, symbols, and features of human beings which differentiate them from other species.

Geertz is not the first to develop the idea that the human sciences are different from the natural sciences. Nineteenth century German philosophers, like Rickert and Dilthey (Wilk 1984:276) believed the study of human phenomena should be historical and idiographic, as contrasted with the study of natural phenomena which is abstract and generalizing. Idiographic studies are particular and unique. They are based on the case study and, as such, can capture the totality of life within a society in its complexity and variation. Gaining a broader perspective is accomplished by accumulating many cases, abstracting the essential elements from them for comparison, and then summing them up into a generalization. Ruth Benedict (1934) stressed the idiographic study, as did her mentor, Franz Boas. Benedict believed there was a discontinuity, in kind, between two whole cultures which was often overlooked in the process of cross-cultural comparison and generalization.

German philosophers who saw a difference between the human and natural sciences, viewed human beings as part of the natural world but also differentiated humans from all other creatures (Polkinghorne 1983:20–32). They believed that, since human beings had the mental capacity for language and learned knowledge, this essential difference required methods, techniques, and orientations different from the study of other natural phenomena. Geertz and humanistic anthropologists share this view.

Miles Richardson (1984:275) makes the case for interpretive anthropology as a science of "humanity." He poses the question, Should anthropologists look to the physical sciences for predictive models, or to the humanities for interpretive insights? Richardson believes interpretive anthropology combines the concept of culture as symbol with the con-

cept of culture as social interaction. Interpretive and humanistic anthropology seeks to avoid reductionist analysis, in which human behavior is
reduced to singular, abstract dimensions based on the model of the
observer. Richardson states that the search for underlying causes for
human behavior often takes away the magic of real life. Geertz sees the
cultural context, not as a set of general propositions, but as webs of
significance which humans spin and in which they operate as they go
about their daily activities. In Geertz's view, to reduce the world to a
cause and effect perspective is to miss the human mode of being. This is
similar to Sartre's existentialist approach (1963) which, while acknowledging the materialist basis for existence, insists on the importance of
human everyday activities in any social analysis. Miles Richardson
stresses the importance of preserving the realism of life in anthropological analysis so as to make it become a truly human science.

Geertz's view of the importance of the single case is not a radical break
with the past. Boas, Malinowski, and Radcliffe-Brown used the study of
a single culture in depth to derive insights about the functioning of
human societies. Nor is Geertz's belief that meaning in a society should
be derived from the "native" point of view a radical departure from
anthropological tradition. The argument against ethnocentrism, and the
insistence on the integrity of all cultures, is part of the perspective that
tries to see other cultures from the "native" viewpoint. This was a strong
element in Boasian anthropology. Anthropologists also find the etic perspective important, that is, the observations of the outside observer
using his own theoretical orientation or model. This perspective is useful for comparative analysis and for an "objective" approach to search for
insights about a culture that may not be within the conscious purview of
those living within the society.

Geertz's orientation, to seek meanings based on the "native" view is
frankly relativistic. It is designed to make the anthropologist sensitive to
views other than his or her own. But, as Geertz emphasizes (1983:181), it
is one that does not accept nihilism, eclecticism, or an "anything goes"
attitude. Rather, what Geertz seeks, is a view that welds the processes of
self-knowledge, self-perception and self-understanding to those of oth-
er-knowledge, other-perception and other-understanding that identifies
and sorts out who the observer is and who the people are that he is
trying to understand. Geertz calls his latest books of essays, *Local Knowledge*. The title signifies his interest in the particular, the concrete, the
individual case, seeking knowledge by starting from the base of native
knowledge and combining it with that of the observer.

Geertz's perspective in anthropology can be called humanistic, as
well as interpretive, in the sense that he aims for expositions which
retain the individuality and complexity of human behavior usually

found in literature and art. He argues that a work of fiction, a play, a painting, or a poem captures and provides insights into the human condition often missed by abstract theorizing. He likens his type of anthropology to a "sort of cultural hermeneutics, a semantics of action" (1983:182). He wants anthropology to do what Frank O'Hara says of poetry, that it makes life's nebulous events tangible and restores their detail (1983:182). Most anthropologists would not argue against the view that there is room in anthropology for both abstract theorizing and concrete interpretation of the particular. It is when Geertz makes a claim for the superiority of his approach that grounds for disagreement arise. Shankman (1984:261–265) suggest that Geertz fails to offer the criteria upon which his and other theoretical positions can be compared. Geertz states that his orientation is *more human*. Shankman counters that the test of superiority should be based on whether it provides a *better understanding* of a particular phenomena.

There are two assumptions in Geertz's interpretive anthropology which could be subject to challenge. One is that a scientific approach is necessarily a dehumanizing one. The second is that people reveal the essence of their culture through symbolic forms. One could argue that scientific theory and data have been employed *against* the dehumanizing phenomena of fascism, sex discrimination, ethnocentrism, and superstition. One could also argue that people are unaware of the symbolic significance of their actions, ideas, and values. Therefore, a theory of culture benefits from the interpretive approach using the data of natives, as well as the scientific approach using the models and categories of social scientific observers.

Geertz states that his approach to anthropology is a hermeneutic one (1983:5). The hermeneutic approach to the human sciences was developed by a number of philosophers, including Wittgenstein, Gadamer, Heidegger, and Ricoeur, as well as Dilthey, Husserl, Merleau-Ponty, and Habermas (Kockelmans 1973:246). The hermeneutic view opposes the idea that the human sciences can be formal, functional, and quantitative. This view does not accept the notion that knowledge is derived from observing the world in such a manner that the observer is neutral or objective. Geertz has explicitly invoked the ideas of Ludwig Wittgenstein (1968) and Alfred Schutz (1973) in arguing against the idea that the observer can be neutral. Geertz's work has stressed that culture and social organization do not exist apart from individuals but rather in and through individuals' interpretations of events and objects around them. He has thereby asserted the idea that the social order is both subjective and objective, a matter of individual values and motivations, yet bound up in public symbols and communication.

It is interesting to compare Geertz's ideas with that of Heidegger

(1927). Truth, according to Heidegger, is sought through human engagement with the world. For Heidegger, hermeneutics, or interpretive understanding, is not a way of knowing the world; it is the way we are. It is the basic form of human existence. Interpretation is not a tool; it is the essence of being human. According to Heidegger, knowledge is not something we construct by using methods which distance us from what is to be known, thereby assuring objective knowledge untinged by personal bias or a personal perspective. Heidegger believes there is no way for the subject/observer to separate himself or herself from the object/observed. In this view, the search for knowledge is conditioned by culture, context, and history.

Gadamer (1975) insisted that consciousness is not historically neutral, as thought by Descartes. Rather, it is historically built up and is shaped by ways of seeing, by attitudes, and concepts embedded in our language and in our cultural norms and styles. Knowledge can never overcome the way of being human or appear outside the human condition based on historical conditions. Gadamer does not believe in the possibility of the social sciences carrying humans beyond their culturally shaped context to some standpoint from which they can see the things-in-themselves. Geertz's view of anthropology shares these perspectives of Heidegger and Gadamer. Geertz has written (1973:50):

Our ideas, our values, our acts, even our emotions, are like our nervous system itself, cultural products—manufactured, indeed, out of tendencies, capacities, and disposition with which we were born, but manufactured nevertheless.

Geertz cites Ricoeur's hermeneutics as having an influence on his interpretive approach. (See Taylor 1985 for a description of Ricoeur). Ricoeur recognizes that unconscious structures make up the content of human expression. He sought to develop a theory for understanding the intentions of the author of a text, as well as the author of an action. Ricoeur views the social science investigator as a reader of a text. Geertz also uses the notion of the "text analogy" as a procedure for interpreting cultures (1983:30–33).

Summarizing interpretive and humanistic anthropology, the problem of meaning is part of the problem of understanding in the social sciences. Positivism, a philosophic approach to understanding the world that dates from the nineteenth century, is an approach to knowledge based on sense perception and logic. The traditional anthropological view is that, if one is to understand the cultures of other people, one must take on the roles of others. Malinowski believed that only by actually doing what the native did could one understand what it meant to him. Geertz argues for a "native" point of view as one road to anthropological understanding (Dolgin, Kemnitzer, and Schneider 1977:480–492). He went beyond this to add an interpretive approach, allied to hermeneutics. In this approach, interpretations are assembled, one version of a text, speech, or action compared with another, one set of perceptions compared with another. The perceptions and knowledge of the observer are melded to those of the native. The medium for the comparison is a system of symbols which give meaning to individual and social life.

With the compilation of interpretations of texts, actions, symbols, social forms, and events, going from the particular to the general and back again, understanding and meaning slowly emerges. It is presented in the form of "thick description," it preserves the magic of life, it tacks back and forth from one viewpoint to another, from one level to another, and it leads to an understanding of the meaning of one's own, as well as other, cultures. This, briefly, is the interpretive and humanistic anthropology of Clifford Geertz. It takes the humanities as its model. It is a new trend in anthropology. It remains to be seen if it will be a lasting one. Whatever the outcome, interpretive anthropology is based, in part, on new trends in scientific methodologies in the human sciences. These methodologies and perspectives have modified the traditional, empirical epistemologies in favor of interpretive ones.

Victor W. Turner

33. Symbols in African Ritual[1]

No one who has lived for long in rural sub-Saharan Africa can fail to be struck by the importance of ritual in the lives of villagers and homesteaders and by the fact that rituals are composed of symbols.

A ritual is a stereotyped sequence of activities involving gestures, words, and objects, performed in a sequestered place, and designed to influence preternatural entities or forces on behalf of the actors' goals and interests. Rituals may be seasonal, hallowing a culturally defined moment of change in the climatic cycle or the inauguration of an activity such as planting, harvesting, or moving from winter to summer pasture; or they may be contingent, held in response to an individual or collective crisis. Contingent rituals may be further subdivided into life-crisis ceremonies, which are performed at birth, puberty, marriage, death, and so on, to demarcate the passage from one phase to another in the individual's life-cycle, and rituals of affliction, which are performed to placate or exorcise preternatural beings or forces believed to have afflicted villagers with illness, bad luck, gynecological troubles, severe physical injuries, and the like. Other classes of rituals include divinatory rituals; ceremonies performed by political authorities to ensure the health and fertility of human beings, animals, and crops in their territories; initiation into priesthoods devoted to certain deities, into religious associations, or into secret societies; and those accompanying the daily offering of food and libations to deities or ancestral spirits or both. Africa is rich indeed in ritual genres, and each involves many specific performances.

Each rural African society (which is often, though not always, coterminous with a linguistic community) possesses a finite number of distinguishable rituals that may include all or some of the types listed above. At varying intervals, from a year to several decades, all of a society's rituals will be performed, the most important (for example, the symbolic transference of political authority from one generation to another, as among the Nyakyusa (Wilson 1959) of Tanzania) being performed perhaps the least often. Since societies are processes responsive to change, not fixed structures, new rituals are devised or borrowed, and old ones decline and disappear. Nevertheless, forms survive through flux, and new ritual items, even new ritual configurations, tend more often to be variants of old themes than radical novelties. Thus it is possible for anthropologists to describe the main features of a ritual system, or rather ritual round (successive ritual performances), in those parts of rural Africa where change is occurring slowly.

The Semantic Structure of the Symbol

The ritual symbol is "the smallest unit of ritual which still retains the specific properties of ritual behavior . . . the ultimate unit of specific structure in a ritual context." This structure is a semantic one (that is, it deals with relationships between signs and symbols and the things to which they refer) and has the following attributes: (i) multiple meanings (significata)—actions or objects perceived by the senses in ritual contexts (that is, symbol vehicles) have many meanings: (ii) unification of apparently disparate significata—the essentially distinct significata are interconnected by analogy or by association in fact or thought; (iii) condensation—many ideas, relations between things, actions, interactions, and transactions are represented simultaneously by the symbol vehicle (the ritual use of such a vehicle abridges what would verbally be a lengthy statement or argument); (iv) polarization of significata—the referents assigned by custom to a major ritual symbol tend frequently to be grouped at opposed semantic poles. At one pole of meaning, empirical research has shown that the significata tend to refer to components of the moral and social orders—this might be termed the ideological (or normative) pole of symbolic meaning; at the other, the sensory (or orectic) pole, are concentrated references to phenomena and processes that may be expected to stimulate desires and feelings. Thus, I have shown that the mudyi tree, or milk-tree (*Diplorrhyncus mossambicensis*), which is the focal symbol of the girls' puberty ritual of the Ndembu people of northwestern Zambia, at its normative pole represents womanhood, motherhood, the mother-child bond, a novice undergoing initiation into mature womanhood, a specific matrilineage, the principle of matriliny, the process of learning "women's wisdom," the unity and perdurance of Ndembu society, and all of the values and virtues inherent in the various relationships—domestic, legal, and political—controlled by matrilineal descent. Each of these aspects of its normative meaning becomes paramount in a specific episode of the puberty ritual; together they form a condensed statement of the structural and communal importance of femaleness in Ndembu culture. At its sensory pole, the same symbol stands for breast milk (the tree exudes milky latex—indeed, the significata associated with the sensory pole often have a more or less direct connection with some sensorily perceptible attribute of the symbol), mother's breasts, and the bodily slenderness and mental pliancy of the novice (a young slender sapling of mudyi is used). The tree, situated a short distance from the novice's village, becomes the center of a sequence of ritual episodes rich in symbols (words, objects, and actions) that express important cultural themes.

Ritual Symbols and Cultural Themes

Opler has defined a theme as a part of a limited set of "dynamic affirmations" that "can be identified in every culture" (1945:198; 1968:215). In the "nature, expression, and relationship" of themes is to be found the "key to the character, structure, and direction of the specific culture" (ibid.). The term "theme" denotes "a postulate or position, declared or implied, and usually controlling behavior or stimulating activity, which is tacitly approved or openly promoted in a society" (ibid.). Every culture has multiple themes, and most themes have multiple expressions, some of which may be in one or more parts of the institutional culture. Ritual forms an important setting for the expression of themes, and ritual symbols transmit themes. Themes have multiple expressions, and ritual symbols, such as the mudyi tree (and thousands of others in the ethnographic literature of African ritual), have multiple significata (Turner 1974). The major difference between themes and symbols is that themes are postulates or ideas inferred by an observer from the data of a given culture, while ritual symbols are one class of such data. Ritual symbols are multivocal—that is, each symbol expresses not one theme but many themes simultaneously by the same perceptible object or activity (symbol vehicle). Symbols *have* significata, themes may *be* significata.

Themes, in their capacity as significata (including both conceptions and images), may be disparate or grouped, as we have seen, at opposed semantic poles. Thus the mudyi signifies aspects of female bodily imagery (milk, suckling, breasts, girlish slenderness) and conceptions about standards of womanhood and motherhood, as well as the normative ordering of these in relation to group membership, the inheritance of property, and succession to such political offices as chieftainship and village headmanship through matrilineal descent. There are rules of exclusion connected with the mudyi in this ritual context—all that is not concerned with the nurtural, procreative, and esthetic aspects of human femaleness and with their cultural control and structuring, is excluded from the semantic field of mudyi symbolism. This is a field of themes with varying degrees of concreteness, abstraction, and cognitive and orectic quality. The impulse that leads advanced cultures to the economical use of signs in mathematics finds its equivalent here in the use of a single symbol vehicle to represent simultaneously a variety of themes, most of which can be shown to be related, logically or pragmatically, but some of which depend for their association on a sensed likeness between variables rather than on cognitive criteria. One is dealing with a "mathematics" of sociocultural experience rather than with a mathematics of logical relationships.

Ritual symbols differ from other modes of thematic expression, particularly from those unformalized modes that arise in spontaneous behavior and allow for individual choice in expression (Opler 1945:200). Indeed, it might be argued that the more ritualized the expression, the wider the range of themes that may be signified by it. On the other hand, since a ritual symbol may represent disparate, even contradictory themes, the gain in economy may be offset by a loss in clarity of communication. This would be inevitable if such symbols existed in a vacuum, but they exist in cultural and operational contexts that to some extent overcome the loss in intelligibility and to some extent capitalize on it.

Dominant Symbols in Ritual Cycles

Rituals tend to be organized in a cycle of performances (annual, biennial, quinquennial, and so on); even in the case of contingent rituals, each is performed eventually. In each total assemblage, or system, there is a nucleus of dominant symbols, which are characterized by extreme multivocality (having many senses) and a central position in each ritual performance. Associated with this nucleus is a much larger number of enclitic (dependent) symbols. Some of these are univocal, while others, like prepositions in language, become mere relation or function signs that keep the ritual action going (for example, bowings, lustrations, sweepings, and objects indicative of joining or separation). Dominant symbols provide the fixed points of the total system and recur in many of its component rituals. For example, if 15 separate kinds of ritual can be empirically distinguished in a given ritual system, dominant symbol A may be found in 10 of them, B in 7, C in 5, and D in 12. The mudyi tree, for example, is found in boys' and girls' initiation ceremonies, in five rituals concerned with female reproductive disorders, in at least three rituals of the hunters' cults, and in various herbalistic practices of a magical cast. Other dominant symbols of Ndembu rituals, as I have shown elsewhere (Turner 1961; 1966; 1969a) recur almost as frequently in the ritual round. Each of these symbols then, has multiple referents, but on each occasion that is used—usually an episode within a ritual performance—only one or a related few of its referents are drawn to public attention. The process of "selectivity" consists in constructing around the dominant symbol a context of symbolic objects, activities, gestures, social relationships, between actors of ritual roles, and verbal behavior (prayers, formulas, chants, songs, recitation of sacred narratives, and so on) that both bracket and underline those of its referents deemed pertinent in the given situation. Thus, only a portion of a dominant symbol's full semantic wealth is deployed in a single kind of ritual or in one of its episodes. The semantic structure of a dominant symbol may be compared with a ratchet wheel, each of whose teeth represents a conception or theme. The ritual context is like a pawl, which engages the notches. The point of engagement represents a meaning that is important in the particular situation. The wheel is the symbol's total meaning, and the complete range is only exposed when the whole cycle of rituals has been performed. Dominant symbols represent sets of fundamental themes. The symbol appears in many rituals, and its meanings are emphasized separately in many episodes. Since the settings in which the themes are ritually presented vary, and since themes are linked in different combinations in each setting, members of the culture who have been exposed to the entire ritual cycle gradually learn, through repetition, variation, and contrast of symbols and themes, what the values, rules, behavioral styles, and cognitive postulates of their culture are. Even more important, they learn in what cultural domains and with what intensity in each domain the themes should apply.

Positional Role of Binary Opposition

The selection of a given theme from a symbol's theme assemblage is a function of positioning—that is, of the manner in which the object or activity assigned symbolic value is placed or arranged vis-à-vis similar objects or activities. One common mode of positioning is binary opposition, the relating of two symbol vehicles whose opposed perceptible qualities or quantities suggest, in terms of the associative rules of the culture, semantic opposition. Thus when a grass hut is made at the Ndembu girls' puberty ceremony for the seclusion of the novice for several months, the two principal laths of the wooden frame are made respectively from mudyi and mukula (blood tree) wood. Both species are dominant symbols. To the Ndembu, mukula represents the husband whom the girl will marry immediately after the puberty rites, and the mudyi stands for the bride, the novice herself. Yet when mukula is considered as a dominant symbol of the total ritual system, it is found to have a wide range (what has aptly been called a "fan") of significata (Turner 1967; 1968). Its primary and sensory meaning is blood—the Ndembu point to the dusky red gum secreted by the tree from cracks in its bark to justify their interpretation. But some bloods, they say, are masculine and some feminine. The former include blood shed by warriors, hunters, and circumcisers in the call of duty; the latter represents blood shown at menstruation and parturition. Another binary opposition within the semantic field of blood is between running blood and coagulating blood. The latter is good, the former is dangerous. Thus, prolonged menstruation means that a woman's blood is ebbing away uselessly; it should coagulate to form fetus and placenta. But since men are the dangerous sex, the blood they cause to flow in hunting and war may be good—that is, beneficial for their own group.

Mukula symbolism is adroitly manipulated in different rituals to express various aspects of the human condition as the Ndembu experience it. For example, in the *Nkula* ritual, performed to placate the spirit of a dead kinswoman afflicting the female patient with menstrual troubles causing barrenness, mukula and other red symbols are contextually connected with symbols characteristic of the male hunting cults to convey the message: the patient is behaving like a male shedder of blood, not like a female conserver of blood, as she should be. It is her "masculine protest" that the ritual is mainly directed at overcoming and domesticating into the service of her female role (Turner 1968:55–89). Mukula means many other things in other contexts, when used in religious ritual or in magical therapy. But the binary opposition of mudyi to mukula restricts the meaning of mudyi to young mature feminity and that of mukula restricts the meaning of mudyi to young mature masculinity, both of which are foundations of a hut, the prototypical domestic unit. The binding together of the laths taken from these trees is said to represent the sexual and the procreative union of the young couple. If these meanings form the sensory pole of the binary opposition as symbol, then the legitimated union by marriage represents the normative pole. In other words, even the binary opposition does not stand alone; it must be examined in the context of building the novice's seclusion hut and of the symbolic objects comprising the hut and its total meaning. There are, of course, many types of binary opposition. The members of pairs of symbols may be asymmetrical (A > B, A < B); they may be like or unlike but equal in value; they may be antithetical; one may be thought of as the product or offspring of the other; one may be active, the other passive; and so on. In this way, the Ndembu are induced to consider the nature and function of relationships as well as of the variables being related, for nonverbal symbol systems have the equivalents of grammar, syntax, accidence, and parts of speech.

Sometimes binary opposition may appear between complexes of symbol vehicles, each carrying a system of dominant and secondary symbols. Thus, in the circumcision rites of the Wiko, in Zambia (Gluckman 1949:165–67), one group of masked dancers may mime opposition to another group; each mask and headpiece is already a combination of multivocal symbols. Yet one team may represent protectiveness and the other, aggressiveness. It is, in fact, not uncommon to find complex symbol vehicles, such as statues or shrines, with simple meanings, while simple vehicles, such as marks drawn in white or red clay, may be highly multivocal in almost every ritual situation in which they are used. A simple vehicle, exhibiting some color, shape, texture, or contrast commonly found in one's experience (such as the whiteness of the mudyi or the redness of the mukula), can literally or metaphorically connect a great range of phenomena and ideas. By contrast, a complex vehicle is already committed, at the level of sensory perception, to a host of contrasts that narrow and specify its message. This is probably why the great religious symbol vehicles such as the cross, the lotus, the crescent moon, the ark, and so on are relatively simple, although their significata constitute whole theological systems and control liturgical and architectural structures of immense complexity. One might almost hypothesize that the more complex the ritual (many symbols, complex vehicles), the more particularistic, localized, and socially structured its message; the simpler the ritual (few symbols, simple vehicles), the more universalistic its message. Thus, ecumenical liturgiologists today are recommending that Christian ritual be essentially reduced to the blessing, distribution, and partaking of bread and wine, in order to provide most denominations with a common ground.

Actors Experience Symbols as Powers and as Meanings

The second characteristic of ritual condensation, which compensates in some measure for semantic obscurity, is its efficacy. Ritual is not just a concentration of referents, of messages about values and norms; nor is it simply a set of practical guidelines and a set of symbolic paradigms for everyday action, indicating how spouses should treat each other, how pastoralists should classify and regard cattle, how hunters should behave in different wild habitats, and so on. It is also a fusion of the powers believed to be inherent in the persons, objects, relationships, events, and histories represented by ritual symbols. It is a mobilization of energies as well as messages.[2] In this respect, the objects and activities in point are not merely things that stand for other things or something abstract, they participate in the powers and virtues they represent. I use "virtue" advisedly, for many objects termed symbols are also termed medicines. Thus, scrapings and leaves from such trees as the mudyi and the mukula are pounded together in meal mortars, mixed with water, and given to the afflicted to drink or to wash with. Here there is direct communication of the life-giving powers thought to inhere in certain objects under ritual conditions (a consecrated site, invocations or preternatural entities, and so on). When an object is used analogously, it functions unambiguously as a symbol. Thus, when the mudyi tree is used in puberty rites it clearly *represents* mother's milk; here the association is through sight, not taste. But when the mudyi is used as medicine in ritual, it is felt that certain qualities of motherhood and nurturing are being communicated physically. In the first case, the mudyi is used because it is "good to think" rather than "good to eat";[3] in the second, it is used because it has maternal power. The same objects are used both as powers and symbols, metonymically and metaphorically—it is the context that distinguishes them. The power aspect of a symbol derives from its being a part of a physical whole, the ideational aspect from an analogy between a symbol vehicle and its principal significata.

Each symbol expresses many themes, and each theme is expressed by many symbols. The cultural weave is made up of symbolic warp and thematic weft. This weaving of symbols and themes serves as a rich store of information, not only about the natural environment as perceived and evaluated by the ritual actors, but also about their ethical, esthetic, political, legal, and ludic (the domain of play, sport, and so forth in a culture) ideas, ideals, and rules. Each symbol is a store of information, both for actors and investigators, but in order to specify just which set of themes any particular ritual or ritual episode contains, one must determine the relations between the ritual's symbols and their vehicles, including verbal symbolic behavior. The advantages of communication by means of rituals in nonliterate societies are clearly great, for the individual symbols and the patterned relations between them have a mnemonic function. The symbolic vocabulary and grammar to some extent make up for the lack of written records.

The Semantic Dimensions

Symbols have three especially significant dimensions: the exegetic, the operational, and the positional. The exegetic dimension consists of the explanations given the investigator by actors in the ritual system. Actors of different age, sex, ritual role, status, grade of esoteric knowledge, and so forth provide data of varying richness, explicitness, and internal coherence. The investigator should infer from this information how members of a given society think about ritual. Not all African societies contain persons who are ready to make verbal statements about ritual, and the percentage of those prepared to offer interpretations varies from group to group and within groups. But, as much ethnographic work attests,[4] many African societies are well endowed with exegetes.

In the operational dimension, the investigator equates a symbol's meaning with its use—he observes what actors do with it and how they relate to one another in this process. He also records their gestures, expressions, and other nonverbal aspects of behavior and discovers what values they represent—grief, joy, anger, triumph, modesty, and so on. Anthropologists are now studying several genres of nonverbal language, from iconography (the study of symbols whose vehicles picture the conceptions they signify, rather than being arbitrary, conventional signs for them) to kinesics (the study of bodily movements, facial expressions, and so forth as ways of communication or adjuncts and intensifiers of speech). Several of these fall under the rubric of a symbol's operational meaning. Nonexegetical, ritualized speech, such as formalized prayers or invocations, would also fall into this category. Here verbal symbols approximate nonverbal symbols. The investigator is interested not only in the social organization and structure of those individuals who operate with symbols on this level, but also in what persons, categories, and groups are absent from the situation, for formal exclusion would reveal social values and attitudes.

In the positional dimension, the observer finds in the relations between one symbol and other symbols an important source of its meaning. I have shown how binary opposition may, in context, highlight one (or more) of a symbol's many referents by contrasting it with one (or more) of another symbol's referents. When used in a ritual context with three or more other symbols, a particular symbol reveals further facets of its total "meaning." Groups of symbols may be so arrayed as to state a message, in which some symbols function analogously to parts of speech and in which there may be conventional rules of connection. The message is not about specific actions and circumstances, but the given culture's basic structures of thought, ethics, esthetics, law, and modes of speculation about new experience.

In several African cultures, particularly in West Africa, a complex system of rituals is associated with myths.[5] These tell of the origins of the gods, the cosmos, human types and groups, and the key institutions of culture and society. Some ritual episodes reenact primordial events, drawing on their inherent power to achieve the contemporary goals of the members of the culture (for example, adjustment to puberty and the healing of the sick). Ritual systems are sometimes based on myths. There may coexist with myths and rituals standardized schemata of interpretation that may amount to theological doctrine. But in wide areas of East and Central Africa, there may be few myths connected with rituals and no religious system interrelating myths, rituals, and doctrine. In compensation, there may be much piecemeal exegesis of particular symbols.

Foundations of Meaning

Most African languages have terms for ritual symbol. The Nyakyusa, for example, speak of *ififwani* (likenesses); the Ndembu use *chijikijilu* (a landmark, or blaze), which derived from *kujikijila* (to blaze a trail or set up a landmark). The first connotes an association, a feeling of likeness between sign and signified, vehicle and concept; the second is a means of connecting known with unknown territory. (The Ndembu compare the ritual symbol to the trail a hunter blazes in order to find his way back from unexplored bush to his village.) Other languages possess similar terms. In societies that do not have myths, the meaning of a symbol is built up by analogy and association of three foundations—nominal, substantial, and artifactual—though in any given instance only one of these might be utilized. The nominal basis is the name of the symbol, an element in an acoustic system; the substantial basis is a symbol's sensori-ly perceptible physical or chemical properties as recognized by the cul-ture; and its artifactual basis is the technical changing of an object used in ritual by human purposive activity.

For example: At the start of a girl's puberty ritual among the Nya-kyusa of Tanzania (Wilson 1957), she is treated with a "medicine" called *undumila*. This medicine is also an elaborate symbol. Its nominal basis is the derivation of the term from *ukulumila*, meaning "to bite, to be pain-ful." The substantial basis is a natural property of the root after which the medicine is named—it is pungent-tasting. As an artifact, the medi-cine is a composite of several symbolic substances. The total symbol involves action as well as a set of objects. Wilson writes (1957:87) that the root "is pushed through the tip of a funnel or cup made of a leaf of the bark-cloth tree, and salt is poured into the cup. The girl takes the tip of the root in her mouth and pulls it inward with her teeth, thus causing the salt to trickle into her mouth." The root and leaf funnel, together with their ritual use, constitute an artifact. These three bases of signifi-cance are substantiated by the Nyakyusa Wilson talked to. One woman told her (1957:102): "The pungent root is the penis of the husband, the cup is her vagina, the salt, also pungent, is the semen of her husband."

Biting the root and eating the salt is copulation." Another woman confirmed this: "The *undumila* is put through the leaf of a bark-cloth tree, shaped into a cup, and it is a sign of man and woman, the penis in the vagina. It is similar to the plantains which we give her when we wash her. The plantains are a symbol of the husband. If we do not give her. . . the *undumila*, she constantly has periods and is barren." A third informant said: "It is the pain of periods that we symbolize in the sharpness of the *undumila* and salt." Thus *undumila* is at once a symbol of sexual intercourse, a prophylactic against pain in intercourse and against frequent or painful periods, and (according to other accounts) a ritual defense against those who are "heavy"—that is, those actively engaged in sexual intercourse, especially women who have just conceived. If a heavy person steps over the novice's footprints, the novice will not bear a child; but will menstruate continually. These explanations also demonstrate the multivocality and economy of reference of a single dominant symbol. The same symbol vehicles can represent different, even disparate, processes—marital intercourse and menstrual difficulty—although it may be argued that the Nyakyusa, at an unconscious level, regard a woman's "distaste" for intercourse as a cause of her barrenness or menorrhagia.

Symbols and Cosmologies

Similar examples abound in the ethnography of sub-Saharan Africa, but in the great West African cultures of the Fon, Ashanti, Yoruba, Dahomeyans, and Dogon, piecemeal exegesis gives way to explicit, complex cosmologies. Among the Dogon, for example (Calame-Griaule 1966; Dieterlen 1941 and 1963; Douglas 1968), a symbol becomes a fixed point of linkage between animal, vegetable, and mineral kingdoms, which are themselves regarded as parts of "un gigantesque organisme humaine." The doctrine of correspondences reigns—everything is a symbol of everything else, whether in ritual context or not. Thus the Dogon establish a correspondence between the different categories of mineral and the organs of the body. The various soils in the area are conceived of as the organs of "the interior of the stomach," rocks are regarded as the bones of the skeleton, and various hues of red clay are likened to the blood. Sometimes these correspondences are remarkably precise: one rock resting on another represents the chest; little white river pebbles stand for the toes of the feet. The same *parole du monde* principles hold true for the relationship between man and the vegetable kingdom. Man is not only the grain of the universe, but each distinct part of a single grain represents part of the human body. In fact, it is only science that has emanci-

pated man from the complex weave of correspondences, based on analogy, metaphor, and mystical participation, and that enables him to
regard all relations as problematical, not preordained, until they have
been experimentally tested or systematically compared.

The Dogon further conceive of a subtle and finely wrought interplay
between speech and the components of personality. The body constitutes
a magnet or focus for man's spiritual principles, which nevertheless are
capable of sustaining an independent existence. The Dogon contrast
visible and invisible ("spiritual") components of the human personality.
The body is made up of four elements: water (the blood and bodily
fluids), earth (the skeleton), air (breath), and fire (animal warmth). There
is a continuous interchange between these internal expressions of the
elements and their external aspects. The body has 22 parts: feet, shins,
thighs, lumbar region, stomach, chest, arms, neck, and head make up
nine parts (it would seem that Dogon reckon double parts, as they do
twins, as a unit); the fingers (each counting as a unit), make up ten parts;
and the male genitals make up three parts. Further numerical symbolism
is involved: there are believed to be eight symbolic grains—representing
the principal cereal crops of the region—lodged in the collarbones of
each Dogon. These grains represent the mystical bond between man and
his crops. The *body* of speech itself is, like the human body, composed of
four elements: water is saliva, without which speech is dry; air gives rise
to sound vibrations; earth gives speech its weight and signficance; and
fire gives speech its warmth. There is not only homology between personality and speech, but also a sort of functional interdependence, for
words are selected by the brain, stir up the liver, and rise as steam from
the lungs to the clavicles; which decide ultimately whether the speech is
to emerge from the mouth.

To the 22 parts of the personality must be added the 48 types of
speech, which are divided into two sets of 24. Each set is under the sign
of a supernatural being, one of the androgynous twins Nommo and
Yourougou. Here I must draw on Griaule's and Dieterlen's extensive
work on the Dogons' cosmogonic mythology (1963). The twins are the
creations of Amma. Yourougou rebelled against Amma and had sexual
relations with his mother—he was punished by being changed into a
pale fox. Nommo saved the world by an act of self-sacrifice, brought
humans, animals, and plants to the earth, and became the lord of
speech. Nommo's speech is human and can be heard; the fox's is silent, a
sign language made by his paw marks, and only diviners can interpret it.
These myths provide a classification and taxonomy of cosmos and society; explain many details of ritual, including the forms and color symbolism of elaborate masks; and, indeed, determine where and how houses

are constructed. Other West African cultures have equally elaborate cosmologies, which are manifested in ritual and divinatory symbolism. Their internal consistency and symmetry may be related to traditions of continuous residence and farming in a single habitat, combined with exposure to trans-Saharan cultural elements, including religious beliefs, for thousands of years—ancient Egyptian, Roman, Christian, Neo-Platonic, Gnostic, Islamic. The history of West Africa contrasts with that of Central Africa, where most societies descend from groups that migrated in a relatively short period of time across several distinct ecological habitats and that were then exposed to several centuries of slave raiding and slave trading. Groups were fragmented and then combined with the social detritus of other societies into new, temporary polities. There were conquest, assimilations, reconquests, the rise and fall of "kingdoms of the savannah," and temporary centralization followed by decentralization into localized clans. Swidden (slash-and-burn) agriculture kept people constantly on the move; hunting and pastoralism compounded the mobility. Because of these circumstances, there was less likelihood of complex, integrated religious and cosmological systems arising in Central Africa than in West Africa. Yet the needs and dangers of social and personal survival provided suitable conditions for the development of rituals as pragmatic instruments (from the standpoint of the actors) for coping with biological change, disease, and natural hazards of all kinds. Social action in response to material pressures was the systematic and systematizing factor. Order, cosmos, came from purpose, not from an elaborate and articulated cosmology. It is an order that accords well with human experience at preindustrial technological levels; even its discrepancies accurately reflect the "facts of life"—in contrast to consistent and harmonious cosmologies whose symbols and myths mask and cloak the basic contradictions between wishes and facts.

The Continuing Efficacy of African Ritual Symbols

Nevertheless, from the comparative viewpoint, there are remarkable similarities among symbols used in ritual throughout sub-Saharan Africa, in spite of differences in cosmological sophistication. The same ideas, analogies, and modes of association underlie symbol formation and manipulation from the Senegal River to the Cape of Good Hope. The same assumptions about powers prevail in kingdoms and nomadic bands. Whether these assemblages of similar symbols represent units of complex orders or the debris of formerly prevalent ones, the symbols remain extraordinarily viable and the themes they represent and embody tenaciously rooted. This may be because they arose in ecological and social experiences of a kind that still prevails in large areas of the continent. Since they are thus sustained and since there is a continuous flux and reflux of people between country and city, it is not surprising that much of the imagery found in the writings of modern African novelists and in the rhetoric of politicians is drawn from ritual symbolism—from which it derives its power to move and channel emotion.

Notes

1.   Reprinted by permission from *Science*, March 16, 1972, vol. 179, pp. 1100–05. Copyright © 1973 by the American Association for the advancement of Science.

2.   This problem of the sources of the effectiveness of symbols has been discussed by Lévi-Strauss (1963:186–205), Munn (1969a), and myself (Turner 1969).

3. ·   See Lévi-Strauss' formulation regarding "totemic" objects, countering the "common-sense" view of J. G. Frazer and other early twentieth-century anthropologists (Lévi-Strauss 1962a).

4.   For example, Beattie (1968), Beidelman (1961), Evans-Pritchard (1956), Griaule (1965), Morton-Williams, Bascom, and McClelland (1966), Richards (1956), and Wilson (1954).

5.   Examples of African cosmological systems may be found in D. Forde (1954). See also T. O. Beidelman on aspects of Swazi cosmology (1966).

David M. Schneider

34. Kinship, Nationality, and Religion in American Culture: Toward a Definition of Kinship[1]

Kinship has traditionally been defined in anthropology in terms of certain concrete elements, relations of blood and marriage, or in terms of some set functional prerequisites to which those concrete elements are crucial. Thus Morgan deals with kinship in terms of relations of consanguinity and affinity, Malinowski in terms of how sexual relations are regulated and how the family is formed, that unit being defined as primarily concerned with the problems of reproduction, socialization, and social placement. Levy, in line with Malinowski, defines kinship with reference to the facts of biological relatedness and/or sexual relations, and his view is not very different from that of Gellner in this respect (Gellner 1957, 1960; Levy 1965; Malinowski 1930).

In these views the facts of biological relatedness and sexual relations are treated as scientifically demonstrable facts of life and the question that is asked centers on how the particular society organizes its cultural forms with respect to these facts of life. These facts are treated as having determinate or causal value, imposing certain sharp, clear limits on whatever forms may be posed with respect to them. Thus a tribe of Australian aborigines, the Trobriand or Yap islanders may deny the causal link between coitus and conception in their cultural forms, but if their beliefs call a complete halt to coitus it can be shown that they could hardly survive long as a society.

Whatever the legitimacy or productivity of this way of dealing with kinship, it seemed to me that there was another view which might be worth pursuing. This view is implicit in much anthropological thinking, but was made most explicitly to me by Parsons (1951). In this view culture is defined as a system of symbols and meanings. That is, any given culture is seen to consist in a system of units and their interrelations, and these contain the fundamental definitions of the nature of the world, of what life is like, of man's place in it. Instead of asking how a society is organized so as to assure its continuity over time, one asks instead of what units it is built, how these units are defined and differentiated, how they articulate one with another. And one asks what meanings such a state of affairs has and how those meanings may be spelled out into patterns for action.

Studying American kinship from this point of view yielded some results which proved to be rather different from those deriving from the traditional functional or the traditional "consanguinity and affinity" or "facts of biological relatedness and/or sexual relations" views. For indeed, the fundamental question was how kinship was defined in American culture, not the question of how those externally devised definitions partitioned the material of American culture.

The purpose of this paper is to ask whether the results of the study of American kinship from this point of view are of any value in helping us to understand the nature of kinship and to define it most usefully for analytic purposes.

Perhaps the most important point to be made about American kinship is that there is a fundamental distinction between the distinctive features of kinship on the one hand and the kinsman as a person on the other (Schneider 1968a). The former embodies those aspects which distinguish kinship from any other domain of American culture—the domain of kinship as distinct from commerce, politics, friendship, etc. Those features which distinguish kinship from other domains are necessarily present in any of its parts as these are further differentiated. Thus although mother, father, brother, and sister are all different kinds of kinsmen, each is a kinsman as against the storekeeper, the mayor, or the policeman, and as kinsmen all share the distinctive features of kinship.

The distinctive features of the domain of kinship in American culture can be abstracted from a consideration of the classification of the different kinds of relatives. There are two kinds of relatives in American culture: those related "by blood" and those related "by marriage."

"Blood" or blood-relationship is the outcome of a single act of sexual intercourse which brings together sperm and egg and creates a child. Mother and father are thus related to the child by the fact that they create it and that the child is created out of material substance which each contributes. "Blood" is thus a state of shared physical substance. This shared physical substance is an "objective fact of nature," a natural phenomenon, a concrete or substantive part of nature. And this "objective fact of nature" cannot be terminated for it endures. A blood relationship is a relationship of identity, and those who share a blood relationship share a common identity. The phrase "the same flesh and blood" is a statement of this.

Where "blood" is a substance, a material thing whose constitution is whatever it is that is really in nature, and a natural entity which endures and cannot be terminated, "marriage" is just the opposite. It is not a material thing or a substance in the same sense as biogenetic heredity is. It is not a "natural thing" in the sense of a material object found free in nature. As a state of affairs it is of course natural, but it is not in itself a natural object. And it is terminable by death or divorce. Where blood is a natural material, marriage is not; where blood endures, marriage is terminable; and since there is no such "thing" as blood of which marriage consists, and since there is no such material which exists free in nature, persons related by marriage are not related "in nature."

If relatives "by marriage" are not related "in nature" how are they related? They are related by "a relationship," that is, by the fact that they follow a particular code for conduct, a particular pattern for behavior. It is in this sense that a stepmother is not a "real" mother, not the genetrix, but she is in a mother-child relationship to her husband's child.

The distinctive feature which defines the order of blood relatives is blood, a natural substance and blood relatives are thus "related by nature." This, I suggest, is but a special instance within the larger class of *the natural order* of things as defined by American culture. That is, the natural order is the way things are in nature, and one special class of things in the natural order consists in blood relatives.

Correspondingly, the feature which alone distinguishes relatives "by marriage" or "in law" is their relationship, the pattern for their behavior, the code for their conduct. This, I suggest, is a special instance within the larger class of *the order of law,* which is opposed to *the order of nature.* The order of law is imposed by man and consists in rules and regulations, customs and traditions. It is law in its special sense, where a foster parent who fails to care properly for a child can be brought to court, and it is law in its most general sense of law and order, custom, the rule of law, the government of action by morality and the restraint of human reason.

The domain of kinship, then, consists of two major parts, and each of these parts is but a special case of the two major orders of which the world is composed, the order of nature and the order of law. And it is this, of course, which makes sense of the fact that those who are relatives "by marriage" are also called "in-laws," for they are related through the order of law, not through the order of nature.

In fact of course the complete typology of kinds of relatives distinguished by American culture is built out of these two elements; *relationship as natural substance* and *relationship as code for conduct*. These two elements combine to make three major categories as follows:

RELATIVES	NATURE	LAW
(1) In Nature: The natural child, the illegitimate child, the natural mother, etc.	+	−
(2) In Law: Husband, wife, step-in-law, etc.	−	+
(3) By Blood: father, mother, brother,sister, uncle, aunt, etc.	+	+

Blood is a matter of birth, birth a matter of procreation, and procreation a matter of sexual intercourse. Sexual intercourse as an act of procreation creates the blood relationship of parent and child and makes genitor and genetrix out of husband and wife. And sexual intercourse is an act in which and through which love is expressed; indeed, it is often called "making love," and love is an explicit cultural symbol in American kinship.

There are two kinds of love in American kinship. One can be called *conjugal love*, the other *cognatic love*. Conjugal love is erotic, having the sexual act as its concrete embodiment. Cognatic love, on the contrary is not an act but a state of affairs and marks the blood relationship, the identity of natural substance which obtains between parent and child. Cognatic love has nothing erotic about it. The conjugal love of husband and wife is the opposite of the cognatic love of parent, child, and sibling. One is the union of opposites, the other the unity which identities have, the sharing of biogenetic substance.

It is the symbol of love which links conjugal and cognatic love together and relates them both to and through the symbol of sexual intercourse. Love in the sense of sexual intercourse is a natural act with natural consequences according to its cultural definition. And love in the sense of sexual intercourse at the same time stands for unity.

Finally, the contrast between home and work brings out aspects which complete the picture of the distinctive features of kinship in American culture. This can best be understood in terms of the contrast between love and money which stand for home and work. Indeed, what one does at home, it is said, one does for love, not for money, while what one does at work one does strictly for money, not for love. Money is material, it is power, it is impersonal and universalistic, unqualified by considerations of sentiment and morality. Relations of work and money are temporary, transient, contingent. Love on the other hand is highly personal and particularistic, and beset with considerations of sentiment and morality. Where love is spiritual, money is material. Where love is enduring and without qualification, money is transient and contingent. And finally, it is personal considerations which are paramount in love—who the person is, not how well he performs, while with work and money it does not matter who he is, but only how well he performs his task. Money is in this sense impersonal.

The facts of biological relatedness and sexual relations play a fundamental role in American kinship, for they are symbols, culturally formulated symbols in terms of which a system of social relationships is defined and differentiated. The beliefs about the facts of biological relatedness and sexual relations constitute a model in terms of which a series of conditions about the nature of kinship or about a domain of social relationships are stated. The statement of identity in terms of flesh and blood between mother and child, whatever significance the actual biological relations may have, is at the same time a symbolic statement of the kind of social relationship between them.

Once the symbolic significance of biological relatedness and sexual relations is perceived it becomes immediately apparent that an enormous number of other symbols might operate with almost equal effect for defining the domain of kinship and for providing for the internal differentiation of elements within that system.

And if it is indeed true that whatever it is that we are calling "kinship" might equally well be defined and differentiated in terms of any number of other symbols, we seem to have lost all hold on something we think of as "kinship in general," for if it could be anything how can it be something in particular?

But at this juncture there are some other important points to be made before we consider the question of definition. The problem that arises now is that of the boundary of the American kinship system. Where does kinship leave off and something else begin? Let us return to the problem with this question in mind.

The different symbols of American kinship seem to say one thing; they are all concerned with unity of some kind. The unity of those related by blood, of those joined in love, of the parent and child in the face of the child's growing up and going off to found a family of his own, of man and woman as husband and wife and so on. All of these different kinds of unity are expressed as the unity of substance or the unity required by a code for conduct.

Put somewhat differently, all of the symbols of American kinship seem to "say" one thing; they provide for relationships of diffuse, enduring solidarity. "Diffuse" because they are functionally diffuse rather than specific in Parsons' terms. That is, where the "job" is to get a specific thing "done" there is no such specific limitation on the aim or goal of any kinship relationship. Instead the goal is "solidarity," that is, the "good" or "well being" or "benefit" of ego with alter. Whatever it is that is "good for" the family, the spouse, the child, the relative, is the "right" thing to do. And "enduring" in the generalized sense symbolized by "blood"; there is no built-in termination point or termination date. Indeed, it "is" and cannot be terminated. But although a marital relationship can be terminated by death or divorce, it is, as the saying goes, "til death do us part"; it is supposed to endure and persevere and it is not to be regarded as transient or temporary or conditional.

The phrase "diffuse, enduring solidarity" is mine. The natives do not use it and although some of them understand it when I explain it to them, it falls like jargon on their ears. Which it should, of course, for that is just what it is.

Yet this generalization permits us to look at American culture and ask. Is this the only domain of diffuse, enduring solidarity? and see that the obvious answer is No! There are at least two others which obviously fit that description. One is called "nationality," the other "religion."

In American culture, one is "an American" either by birth or through a process which is called, appropriately enough, "naturalization." In precisely the same terms as kinship, there are the same two "kinds of citizens," those by birth and those by law. And indeed it would not be hard to show that the same three categories are derived from these two elements as three categories of kinsmen are derived from those elements. There is the person who is by birth an American but who has taken the citizenship of another country; there is the person who is American by naturalization but not by birth; and there is the person who by both birth and law is American.

What is the role of a national? To love his country, his father- or mother-land. Loyalty and support for his nation and all those who belong to it. Patriotism in the extreme of "My Country Right or Wrong" is one statement of it. But even where it does not take that particular form, loyalty to and love for one's country is the most generalized expression of diffuse, enduring solidarity.

I will not pursue this in any further detail. My point is not to demonstrate incontestably that kinship and nationality are structured in identical terms, but rather to make a plausible enough case for this so that we can consider its implications for the question of how to frame a useful definition of kinship.

One argument that might be presented against the view that kinship and nationality are structured in terms of the same set of symbols is that kinship contains things like family, uncle, in-laws, and so forth which do not have corresponding elements within the domain of nationality. States, counties, towns, and so forth do not seem at first glance like family, uncle, or in-laws, etc.

This argument brings us back to the opening statement in the description of American kinship; there is a fundamental difference between the distinctive features of kinship on the one hand and the relative as a person on the other.

As I have tried to show elsewhere (1968a:57–75), the structuring of the relative as a person is the outcome of the intersection of a series of different elements from different symbol systems of which kinship, age, sex, and class are but four among others, and only one of which is "kinship" in a "pure" sense. For example, not only is "father" a kinsman, but he is also male and the cultural definition of his maleness derives from the sex-identity symbol system; he is also older and those aspects of his definition as older derive from the age symbol system, and so forth.

What I am saying here is really quite simple but perhaps it appears to be somewhat radical. I am saying that what we have heretofore regarded as the single domain of kinship is really made up of two distinct domains. One is a "pure" domain of kinship *per se* which has as its defining element a single symbol, coitus (Schneider 1968a:30–54). The second is that domain which has traditionally been regarded as the domain of kinship, the system of person-based definitions. I believe that the importance of the difference between the "pure" domain of kinship and the "conglomerate" part has not been sufficiently appreciated.[2]

Now let us go back to the problem which is raised by comparing what seems at first glance to be the internal differentiation of the domains of kinship and nationality and finding them apparently quite disparate, the one being cast in apparently genealogical terms, the other in terms of states, cities, counties, and so on.

Once the distinction between the "pure" and the "conglomerate" domains of kinship is appreciated, the same distinction can be applied to nationality. It is not nationality as it applies to what makes a person a resident of a county for purposes of meeting the relief requirements that is at issue. It is instead the comparison of the domains of kinship and nationality as "pure" domains, each defined in terms of a single symbol or a single set of closely interlocked symbols. At this level these are internally undifferentiated domains, and it is in these terms that their identity is being postulated.

Let us turn now to religion and consider the situation there. As a convenience, and purely for the purposes of this paper, I assume that "religion" means the Judeo-Christian tradition. I know that this hardly exhausts the many different beliefs that are to be found in America, not the least of which I call "devout atheism." But once again my aim is not to try to exhaust the material to show indisputably that kinship, nationality, and religion are all the same thing, but rather to build that case for what it may suggest with regard to the problem of defining kinship.

There is a special problem, too, in that there is a historical continuity to the relationship between the Jewish and Christian traditions. At the same time both co-exist in America and their coexistence as well as their historical relations pose special problems.

In the tradition of Judaism nation, state, and kinship group are one, and certainly the identity between kinship and nationality in Judaism is very clear. To be a Jew one's mother must be Jewish even if one's father is not and to be converted to Judaism is not an easy thing. Thus, the modern state of Israel has encountered a number of problems which arise from this special view that anyone who is by birth a Jew is also necessarily by nationality a Jew and correspondingly a Jew by religious definition.[3]

With Christianity, as is well known, the criterion for membership shifted from birth to volition. That is, in the most general sense, one is a Christian by an act of faith and not an act of birth, and correspondingly conversion to the Faith becomes a very different matter and a real possibility since it takes only an act of will to effect.

But this view leaves out two very important facts. Being a Jew is not simply being born a Jew. There is a code for conduct which is linked to the fact of birth. What is true is that it is the act of birth which has the quality of the defining feature, and so the other element tends to be easily overlooked. And it is here that the parallel between kinship and religion in Judaism is quite clear, for in both there are those two features, relationship as substance and relationship as code for conduct; the substance element is bio-genetic, the code for conduct is one of diffuse, enduring solidarity.

Although the shift from Judaism to Christianity seems to drop the condition of substance as the defining feature and rest it entirely on the commitment to the code for conduct, this is not really so. Certainly there is a shift away from the particularistic, biogenetic, criterion of substance as the defining features. But the shift entails a realignment so that commitment to the code for conduct becomes paramount as the defining feature, and the substantive element is redefined from a material to a spiritual form. It is the triumph of the spirit over matter that is at issue here. Closely linked to this is the prominent place given to love as a symbol, to the spiritual aspects of love, and to the spiritual aspects of creation as against its rather more narrowly material or biogenetic aspects in Judaism.

The prevalence of the symbol of "love" in Christianity, the prevalence of the use of kinship terms in Christianity, the importance of such concepts as "faith" and "trust" and "belief" all testify, to me at least, that the domain of religion may well be structured in the same terms as kinship and nationality, and the historical fact that Judaism is indeed so clearly defined as one nation, one religion, and one family suggests to me that there may be something in what I say.

Let me add one more point. If Judaism is the clearest and simplest case where kinship, religion, and nationality are all a single domain, then the transformation of Christianity centers on the separation of a natural and a supernatural element, so that kinship becomes differentiated as being based on relationship as natural substance, religion as relationship as supernatural (spiritual) substance. In other words, kinship and religion are more highly differentiated in Christianity than in Judaism, and this differentiation depends on a different form of the distinction between supernatural and natural.[4]

There is certainly no doubt in my mind that I am far out of my depth in this discussion. I am no theologian and have little command of this material. If I were pressed to spell this out in detail I would have to resign from the discussion. On the other hand, once again, I am merely trying to make a plausible enough case for the guess that religion (in the Judeo-Christian tradition) is defined in the same terms as kinship so that this can be taken into consideration in trying to reach a useful definition of kinship.

But once again we are faced with the problem of the double-domain, for at one level it is certainly indisputable that people tend to join the church of their parents and they are in this sense born to a church as they are born to a family, and this is hardly an act of volition at this level. And if one takes even a passing look at the bureaucratic organization of some churches or synagogues many of the highest ideals are systematically transformed into petty schismatic differences. The internal differentiation of any particular religious organization or set of beliefs is one thing; the domain of religion I would suggest quite another. There is the "pure" domain of religion which I am comparing to that of kinship and nationality and there is the internally differentiated "conglomerate" domain which I am not.

Let me summarize the argument briefly. From a close study of American kinship it seems clear that this particular system depends first on a distinction between the "pure" domain of kinship, defined in terms of the symbol of coitus and differentiated into two major aspects, relationship as natural substance and relationship as code for conduct, and a "conglomerate" domain of kinship, differentiated into "the family" on one hand and an articulated system of person-defined statuses (genealogical?) on the other.

If we consider only the "pure" domain of kinship and treat this as a system of diffuse, enduring solidarity, it seems possible that what is called "nationality" and "religion" are defined and structured in identical terms, namely, in terms of the dual aspects of relationship as natural substance and relationship as code for conduct, and that most if not all of the major diacritical marks which are found in kinship are also found in nationality and religion.

If this is true—and I repeat that I offer it only as a very tentative hypothesis—then it might well be that at the level of the "pure" domain, religion, nationality, and kinship are all the same thing (culturally), and that their differences arise through the kinds of combinations and permutations they enter into with other "pure" domains, and at the level of the "conglomerate" domain.

Thus far I speak only of American culture not from having carefully surveyed its precise boundaries, but precisely because I don't know what those boundaries are. Hence the next step is to generalize the view of American kinship, religion, and nationality and ask how widely applicable this view may or may not be to other cultures. At the moment, and from but a small grasp of world ethnography, I would hazard the guess that this generalized view will obtain fairly widely, but this remains an empirical question which can be answered only by concrete studies.

Finally, if all this proves true, the question arises of the utility of any definition of "kinship" until we have more fully explored the ways in which culture as a system of symbols and meanings is formed and its different parts articulated.

Notes

1. Reprinted by permission of the publisher from *Forms of Symbolic Action*, V. Turner, ed. (New Orleans, La: American Ethnological Society. Tulane University, 1969), pp. 116–25.

2. I have spoken here of two domains, one a "pure" and one a "conglomerate" domain. Perhaps it would be better to treat these as two parts of a single domain rather than as two different domains. But this is not my problem here, and so I will proceed simply as if the two domain mode of expression is adequate to the exposition here and leave to another time the question of one domain of two parts or two domains intimately linked.

3. This may be a convenient point to note that I have omitted from this paper considerations of race and racism, which cannot be omitted from any comprehensive or systematic review of this problem. I can refer the reader to Louis Dumont's brilliant discussions of this subject for its bearing on the questions

before us and at the same time acknowledge the stimulus which his writings have provided for me, even when I have resisted his views. See his *Homo Hierarchicus* especially.

4. I think that I have absorbed this from Parsons somehow, but the closest form in which I have found the notion is in Parsons' article on Christianity (1968:427).

Frank A. Dubinskas

35. Leaders and Followers: Cultural Pattern and Political Symbolism in Yugoslavia[1]

Political leadership is often symbolized through processions, which share a common model for enacting a leader-to-followers relationship in rural Slavonia. The temporal/spatial precedence of leaders and their accompaniment by followers is a pervasive cultural pattern for enacting asymmetric or hierarchic relationships. This pattern is shared by religious processions, weddings, funerals, and secular parades of all sorts, and the everyday hospitality of hosts towards guests. It also informs the shape of verbal action and interchange in the structure of village-style "conversational" singing. Normal conversational usage casts all these activities in the same terms: vodit' ("to lead") and pratit' ("to follow"). Symbolizing the political leadership of Marshal Tito through this same model evokes a broad cultural nexus of historically-validated activities in village life. By enacting this processual symbol for hierarchy, participants create both the relationship and its meaning while they also enhance the legitimacy of the leader.

The leading role of Marshal Tito pervades Yugoslav political discourse, but it is most spectacularly enacted in public processions. A myriad of secular events include some symbolization of Tito's leadership: from state holidays and party rallies to harvest and calendrical festivities, sports tournaments, and folklore festivals. Parades most often open these events, and some symbols of Tito nearly always heads the procession.

Just such a parade opens the colorful annual festival of Slavonian village folklore groups in Djakovo in 1979. At the very front of a three-hour procession is a massive 6 x 6 foot portrait of Marshal Tito, bordered with white flowers, and borne by two teenagers in folk costume. Behind this "icon"[2] of Tito comes a phalanx of flags and banners—Yugoslav, republican, and Party—carried by select youth in folkloric finery. At many similar festivals, a gaggle of tiny tots is clustered near Tito, each dressed in a miniature replica of their village's fanciest traditional dress.

After Tito and the banners come the village folklore performers, singing as they walk along. The sequence of groups has an order: a hierarchy of prestige. The first groups in line are the "honored guests," those representing other republics and ethnic minorities, arranged roughly in decreasing order of the distance they travelled to attend. Then come Croatian groups from outside Slavonia, then groups from Slavonia and the Baranja, and finally those from the villages of Djakovo county—the "hosts" of the festival.

Many of these gaily-clad village performing groups are also internally ordered. A typical arrangement has little children at the head, followed by unmarried teenagers in brilliant embroidered costumes. A banner naming the ensemble and its village is often carried at the front by children or youths. Behind the younger performers, in slightly less elaborate garb, come married men, then married women, with the eldest last. A band of *tamburica* musicians brings up the rear, playing as the strolling performers sing or stop to dance in the road.

Tito's image leads the whole parade, and all others follow in his path. Behind Tito, the followers have their own subsidiary internal ordering; and they as well have been Party cadres at a political rally or athletes at a sports convocation. The trope of "following the path" of the leader pervades Yugoslav politics. From the mid-1970s, as Tito gradually withdrew from day-to-day state affairs, the emphasis has shifted subtly: From following Tito, the person, as leader, the image has changed to following the *path* of Tito's guiding ideas. This was nowhere more evident than in the time surrounding comrade Tito's death, when the air was filled constantly with one mournful song:

Druže Tito, mi ti se kunemo
da sa tvoga puta ne skrenemo.
Comrade Tito, we promise you
that from your path we will not turn.

Following in a leader's path is a pattern which belongs not only to a political context in Slavonia. It cross-cuts a wide variety of forms of social action where hierarchic relationships are symbolized. It orders religious processions as well as secular parades, it informs the action at weddings and funerals, it shapes verbal action in singing, and it patterns the interactions of guests and hosts in domestic hospitality.

In Clifford Geertz' (1973:87–125) terms, following a leader is a model *of* hierarchy: an image which displays asymmetry. At the same time, it is a blueprint *for* expressing difference—the Slavonian's familiar medium for playing out hierarchy. The ubiquity of this pattern is also suggested by Gregory Bateson's (1958) concept of *eidos*, that discernable consistency of shape which infuses disparate realms of cultural activity. What I suggest in this essay, on the other hand, is that a Slavonian *model* of and for hierarchy is a process. Movement and precedence are part and parcel of the symbol itself.

"Following a leader" is a Slavonian way of articulating status difference while acknowledging the joint social company of participants. The native expression for "following" or "accompaniment" is *pratnja*, the verb, *pratit'*. Its semantic implies both movement and precedence: followers proceed "behind" and "after" a leader. *Pratit'* also encapsulates several senses that "accompany" does in English: In spatial motion, it means to accompany someone in going someplace, for instance in a parade or procession, or when hosts accompany their guests to the door; in musical performance, a lead-singer begins, and all others *prate* or "accompany," singing in harmony . . . although just *how* harmonious they are depends a bit on how much plum brandy they have consumed! *Pratit'* also means "to pay attention to"; one can *pratit'* events in the news. Similarly, accompanying singers "pay attention to" the lead singer; and hosts "pay attention to" their guests.

Religious processions are one of the most conspicuous examples of *pratnja*.[3] Until the early 1950s, they filled the Slavonian village lanes on numerous saints' days and Holy Days, and they continue today, mostly within the confines of churchyards. Statues of saints or the Virgin, a monstrance with the Eucharist, or simply the crucifix was accompanied about the village to various ritual ends: blessing the fields, honoring the saints or God, and seeking grace or protection. The cross leads all sacred processions. The crucifix, Christ upon the cross, is at the same time God—apex of all status hierarchies and ultimate director of events—and also the "Saviour" *(spasitelj)*, deliverer of his followers and leader on the path of righteousness. The crucifix holds the position of honor—the front—and the villagers follow, by twos and threes, in its path.

Besides the primary division between the crucifix and the company of followers, religious processions are also internally ordered. Clustered closest behind the cross are little children, dearest in God's grace and most needful of his protection. Then, usually, come the males, younger to older as one goes back in the line, the priest—between the men and women—then younger girls to older women. This sequence is sometimes modified for specific ritual ends, adolescents commonly moving forward to carry statues, banners, or relics. A combination of purity and social status orders the column: Little children are purest and first, males are purer than females and also rank higher, youth are less corrupted than elders, married heads-of-household rank over grandparents, and priests, as liminal characters, tend to separate the sexes.

This common arrangement of sacred processions also recalls the order of secular ones like the folklore festival parade. In it, village performing groups often mirror the sequence of church processions. The whole parade, too, is modelled on this shared pattern: Tito, as the secular head of society, leads the way. "Following Tito's path" is as common a secular trope as following the Saviour's is for Catholics. Tito is also spoken of in political discourse and occasionally in common village conversation as our *spas* or "salvation" (but not spasitelj—"saviour"). In the folklore festival parade, to place little children nearest his portrait—his "icon"— is to invoke the same symbolic order, and thus the relation of protector, as the cross bears in leading religious processions. Also, adolescent youths bear religious paraphernalia near the head of a column, just as in the festival parade they follow behind Tito carrying emblems of the state. These two kinds of processions mutually inform each other's meaning by playing on a shared processual model for enacting hierarchy—of purity, honor, status, or whatever.

Besides these broadly public social events, there are numerous occasions for processions which focus on individual observances. Funerals, for instance, attract a representative of every village household (in theory at least) to accompany the corpse to the graveyard. The cross is followed by the coffin, then the chief or closest mourners. The rest of the villagers follow after, ordered roughly as in religious processions. Funerals are the only present occasion when a cross leads villagers through the streets; and at a Communist's funeral, a red star usually replaces the cross. Weddings, though, are the most extravagant occasions for parading about the village. The groom, his guests, and musicians file to the bride's home, where she and her guests join the company. Singing, talking, drinking, and smashing bottles in delight, this caravan of carousery proceeds to the village clerk's to record the marriage and to the church to consecrate it. The parade then returns to the groom's for a wedding party lasting through the night. Even in the wee hours, parading continues as hosts and musicians accompany their special guests home.

Turning from the festive to the mundane, a telling example of pratnja in domestic interactions is the everyday treatment of guests by hosts. It is, in secular microcosm, a model of more elaborate ritual events. A guest received into the home is treated with honor. The personal relationship may be friendly and familiar, but the cultural hierarchy of guests before hosts is revealed by the niceties of etiquette in the simple ritual of parting. A guest must initiate the move to leave. The host, and often the entire family, will rise *after* the guest and accompany him or her to the door. The guest must reach for the latch first and open it. (It would be a terrible *faux pas* to do as we might think cavalier and open the door for someone; that would be a "bum's rush" in Slavonia!) The guest steps first over the threshold and leads the little train of hosts out to the courtyard gate, which again the guest opens. It is impolite for a household having any visitor, no matter how ill-liked, not to send at least one family member to see them to the gate.

This act of everyday hospitality models on a small scale, the pattern of larger public events. The highest-status person, the main actor or "leader," has the first position in line. This might be Marshal Tito, a groom, bride, guest, or the crucifix. They lead the action temporally and spatially. Followers are included in a social company with the leader, and acknowledge this leadership by following in the same path.

This same pratnja pattern shapes the processes of singing in verbal action. Singing has long been a primary mode of domestic entertainment and recreation in Slavonia. Even now, with the widespread penetration of mechanically-reproduced music for *listening* (via radio, phonograph, and tape cassettes), *making* music by singing is still a common evening's pastime.

Two aspects of village singing will concern us: one is its topical flexibility and use in conversational interaction, and the other is its structure of a leading soloist and harmonizing group accompaniment. As to topics, songs do not usually wed a fixed text to a melody. Certain melodies are indeed commonly associated with two or three well-known verses; but once these verses are sung, anyone may add further couplets to the tune, as long as they fit the poetic meter of the verse. Couplets may either be made up on the spot or drawn from a virtually limitless pool of "known" texts.

These couplets are an opportunity to comment through song on all aspects of social relations and events, on selves or others, on politics or love. In the relaxed after-dinner ambience of a domestic party, singing is an alternative communication medium to talking. In the alternation of turn-taking in the conversation, amidst the drinking and talking, someone begins to sing, and the others join in. At the end of the couplet, talk resumes.

Some topics can be introduced at a party more easily through this "conversational" singing; politics and sex are noteworthy examples. As an informant explained: "Well, the songs are like a joke, they're sung in jest—you can't get angry at them . . . so you can say things in singing that you can't say [ordinary] talking." What I wish to draw attention to here is that singing, as a "marked" or special mode of conversation, is a device for initiating new topics into discourse, and, in the process, preempting a leading role in the flow of conversation.

In "normal" conversation, the order of turn-taking—who gets to speak next—is often an indicator of power, status, or prestige differences among a group of communicators. If you're on the high end of the totem pole, people are more likely to pay attention to you. If you're on the low end, it may be hard to get a word in edgewise. Singing, however, usually preempts a conversational turn for the person who starts to sing, no matter "who" he or she is. All ears turn to the singer, and conversation—in the form of sung accompaniment—reiterates the leader's words.

In musical terms, the *počimajlja* or "starter" of a song also preempts leadership. Only one person "begins" and sings the melody line *solo;* all others join in later in an *obbligato* harmony. Only after the "starter" reaches the last few syllables of the first line does the rest of the group join in singing. They are compelled by custom to follow or pratit' in a fixed style of accompaniment. The social asymmetry of musical leadership and pratnja, however, is largely ephemeral, since different singers continually take the lead to start new songs or add verses to current ones. Singing, like the rituals of hospitality, provides an arena in everyday life where the model for leadership and accompaniment is repeatedly practiced.

Looking back over these examples of pratnja, our original image of "following in Tito's path" has a rich field of associations. The pattern is reiterated in the minutiae of everyday life, from the sociability of singing to the interchange of daily hospitality. Diurnal repetition organizes expectations about the public enactment of status hierarchy. The grand spectacles of state ceremony, folklore festivals, religious processions, and rites-of-passage draw on that everyday groundwork of meaning, while they cross-fertilize each other. The symbolism of political leadership, seen in the wider context of symbolizing precedence, becomes another example of a pervasive cultural pattern. The legitimacy of a political leader is thus enhanced through this similitude and reinforced by the active participation of "followers."

The trope of "following a leader," though, may seem so "natural" to us that we lose sight of it as a particularly cultural construction. Our perspective is repaired by comparing it with "other sheep in other valleys": Zinacantecan ritual processions reverse the sequence of hierarchy, building to a climax at the end (Cancian 1965; Rosaldo 1972; Vogt 1972). In Balinese funerary rites, the apex of status hierarchy is at the exemplary center of the ritual train (Geertz 1980).

Slavonian leadership and accompaniment have their own distinctive cast. They convey not so much a static image of hierarchy, but rather a model for an active process. Just as rank and precedence are inherent in

Slavonian leading and following, so is motion. Our analytical model *of* and *for* social action is thus phrased in the same processual idiom of the action it symbolizes.

Notes

1. I would like to acknowledge the encouragement of my late teacher, mentor, and friend, Prof. Michelle Z. Rosaldo of Stanford, in developing this theme, and thank Prof. Shelly Errington for her detailed comments on the text. I also appreciate the critical commentaries of Mark Forry, Eugene A. Hammel, Anna Hargreaves, Gail Kligman, Olga Supek, and Sylvia Yanagisako.

Research for this paper was conducted during 21 months in Yugoslavia in 1978–80, 18 of these in Vinkovci county in souteastern Slavonia and was supported by Fulbright-Hays (DHEW) Doctoral Dissertation Research Award #G007802510 and an IREX Exchange Program Fellowship. I am also deeply indebted to my Yugoslav sponsors, the City Museum of Vinkovci and the Institute for Folklore Research in Zagreb, as well as to my many friends and consultants from Slavonian folklore groups.

2. I use the term *icon* with no intent of disrespect to Tito's memory. In English, *icon* captures some of the awe and respect paid to Marshal Tito, as it evokes, but need not "denote," religiosity. In Serbo-Croation, I would substitute the more neutral *simbol.*

3. Not all processions, even those with an internal ranking, are commonly called pratnja. It is the pattern of following the leader which implies, evokes, and enacts status difference. The term *pratit'* conveniently encompasses many of its occasions, but does not exhaust them.

Clifford Geertz

36. Interpretive Anthropology

Interpretive explanation—and it is a form of explanation, not just exalted glossography—trains its attention on what institutions, actions, images, utterances, events, customs, all the usual objects of social-scientific interest, mean to those whose institutions, actions, customs, and so on they are. As a result, it issues not in laws like Boyle's, or forces like Volta's, or mechanisms like Darwin's, but in constructions like Burckhardt's, Weber's, or Freud's: systematic unpackings of the conceptual world in which *condottiere*, Calvinists, or paranoids live.

The manner of these constructions itself varies: Burckhardt portrays, Weber models, Freud diagnoses. But they all represent attempts to formulate how this people or that, this period or that, this person or that makes sense to itself and, understanding that, what we understand about social order, historical change, or psychic functioning in general. Inquiry is directed toward cases or sets of cases, and toward the particular features that mark them off; but its aims are as far-reaching as those of mechanics or physiology: to distinguish the materials of human experience.

With such aims and such a manner of pursuing them come as well some novelties in analytical rhetoric, the tropes and imageries of explanation. Because theory, scientific or otherwise, moves mainly by analogy, a "seeing-as" comprehension of the less intelligible by the more (the earth is a magnet, the heart is a pump, light is a wave, the brain is a computer, and space is a balloon), when its course shifts, the conceits in which it expresses itself shift with it. In the earlier stages of the natural sciences, before the analogies became so heavily intramural—and in those (cybernetics, neurology) in which they still have not—it has been the world of the crafts and, later, of industry that have for the most part provided the well-understood realities (well-understood because, *certum quod factum*, as Vico said, man had made them) with which the ill-understood ones (ill-understood because he had not) could be brought into the circle of the known. Science owes more to the steam engine than the steam engine owes to science; without the dyer's art there would be no chemistry; metallurgy is mining theorized. In the social sciences, or at least in those that have abandoned a reductionist conception of what they are about, the analogies are coming more and more from the contrivances of cultural performance than from those of physical manipulation—from theater, painting, grammar, literature, law, play. What the lever did for physics, the chess move promises to do for sociology.

Promises are not always kept, of course, and when they are, they often turn out to have been threats; but the casting of social theory in terms more familiar to gamesters and aestheticians than to plumbers and engineers is clearly well under way. The recourse to the humanities for explanatory analogies in the social sciences is at once evidence of the destabilization of genres and of the rise of "the interpretive turn," and their most visible outcome is a revised style of discourse in social studies. The instruments of reasoning are changing and society is less and less represented as an elaborate machine or a quasi-organism and more as a serious game, a sidewalk drama, or a behavioral text.

All this fiddling around with the proprieties of composition, inquiry, and explanation represents, of course, a radical alteration in the sociological imagination, propelling it in directions both difficult and unfamiliar. And like all such changes in fashions of the mind, it is about as likely to lead to obscurity and illusion as it is to precision and truth. If the result is not to be elaborate chatter or the higher nonsense, a critical consciousness will have to be developed; and as so much more of the imagery, method, theory, and style is to be drawn from the humanities than previously, it will mostly have to come from humanists and their apologists rather than from natural scientists and theirs. That humanists, after years of regarding social scientists as technologists or interlopers, are ill-equipped to do this is something of an understatement.

Social scientists, having just freed themselves, and then only partially, from dreams of social physics—covering laws, unified science, operationalism, and all that—are hardly any better equipped. For them, the general muddling of vocational identities could not have come at a better time. If they are going to develop systems of analysis in which such conceptions as following a rule, constructing a representation, expressing an attitude, or forming an intention are going to play central roles—rather than such conceptions as isolating a cause, determining a variable, measuring a force, or defining a function—they are going to need all the help they can get from people who are more at home among such notions than they are. It is not interdisciplinary brotherhood that is needed, nor even less highbrow eclecticism. It is recognition on all sides that the lines grouping scholars together into intellectual communities, or (what is the same thing) sorting them out into different ones, are these days running at some highly eccentric angles.

The point at which the reflections of humanists on the practices of social scientists seems most urgent is with respect to the deployment in social analysis of models drawn from humanist domains—that "wary reasoning from analogy," as Locke called it, that "leads us often into the discovery of truths and useful productions, which would otherwise lie concealed." (Locke was talking about rubbing two sticks together to produce fire and the atomic-friction theory of heat, though business partnership and the social contract would have served him as well.) Keeping the reasoning wary, thus useful, thus true, is, as we say, the name of the game.

The game analogy is both increasingly popular in contemporary social theory and increasingly in need of critical examination. The impetus for seeing one or another sort of social behavior as one or another sort of game has come from a number of sources (not excluding, perhaps, the prominence of spectator sports in mass society). But the most important are Wittgenstein's conception of forms of life as language games, Huizinga's ludic view of culture, and the new strategies of von Neumann's and Morgenstern's *Theory of Games and Economic Behavior.* From Wittgenstein has come the notion of intentional action as "following a rule"; from Huizinga, of play as the paradigm form of collective life; from von Neumann and Morgenstern, of social behavior as a reciprocative maneuvering toward distributive payoffs. Taken together they conduce to a nervous and nervous-making style of interpretation in the social sciences that mixes a strong sense of the formal orderliness of things with an equally strong sense of the radical arbitrariness of the order: chessboard inevitability that could as well have been otherwise.

The writings of Erving Goffman—perhaps the most celebrated American sociologist right now, and certainly the most ingenious—rest, for example, almost entirely on the game analogy. (Goffman also employs the language of the stage quite extensively, but as his view of the theater is that it is an oddly mannered kind of interaction game—ping-pong in masks—his work is not, at base, really dramaturgical.) Goffman applies game imagery to just about everything he can lay his hands on, which, as he is no respecter of property rights, is a very great deal. The to-and-fro of lies, meta-lies, unbelievable truths, threats, tortures, bribes, and blackmail that comprises the world of espionage is construed as an "expression game"; a carnival of deceptions rather like life in general, because, in a phrase that could have come from Conrad or Le Carré, "agents [are] a little like us all and all of us [are] a little like agents." Etiquette, diplomacy, crime, finance, advertising, law, seduction, and the everyday "realm of bantering decorum" are seen as "information games"—mazy structures of players, teams, moves, positions, signals, information states, gambles, and outcomes, in which only the "gameworthy"—those willing and able "to dissemble about anything"—prosper.

What goes on in a psychiatric hospital, or any hospital or prison or even a boarding school in Goffman's work, is a "ritual game of having a self," where the staff holds most of the face cards and all of the trumps. A tête-à-tête, a jury deliberation, "a task jointly pursued by persons physically close to one another," a couple dancing, lovemaking, or boxing—indeed, all face-to-face encounters—are games in which, "as every psychotic and comic ought to know, any accurately improper move can poke through the thin sleeve of immediate reality." Social conflict, deviance, entrepreneurship, sex roles, religious rites, status ranking, and the simple need for human acceptance get the same treatment. Life is just a bowl of strategies.

Or, perhaps better, as Damon Runyon once remarked, it is three-to-two against. For the image of society that emerges from Goffman's work, and from that of the swarm of scholars who in one way or another follow or depend on him, is of an unbroken stream of gambits, ploys, artifices, bluffs, disguises, conspiracies, and outright impostures as individuals and coalitions of individuals struggle—sometimes cleverly, more often comically—to play enigmatical games whose structure is clear but whose point is not. Goffman's is a radically unromantic vision of things, acrid and bleakly knowing, and one that sits rather poorly with traditional humanistic pieties. But it is no less powerful for that. Nor, with its uncomplaining play-it-as-it-lays ethic, is it all that inhumane.

However that may be, not all gamelike conceptions of social life are quite so grim, and some are positively frolicsome. What connects them all is the view that human beings are less driven by forces than submissive to rules, that the rules are such as to suggest strategies, the strategies are such as to inspire actions, and the actions are such as to be self-rewarding—*pour le sport*. As literal games—baseball or poker or Parcheesi—create little universes of meaning, in which some things can be done and some cannot (you can't castle in dominoes), so too do the analogical ones of worship, government, or sexual courtship (you can't mutiny in a bank). Seeing society as a collection of games means seeing it as a grand plurality of accepted conventions and appropriate procedures—tight, airless worlds of move and countermove, life *en règle*. "I wonder," Prince Metternich is supposed to have said when an aide whispered into his ear at a royal ball that the czar of all the Russians was dead, "I wonder what his motive could have been."

The game analogy is not a view of things that is likely to commend itself to humanists, who like to think of people not as obeying the rules and angling for advantage but as acting freely and realizing their finer capacities. But that it seems to explain a great deal about a great many aspects of modern life, and in many ways to catch its tone, is hardly deniable. ("If you can't stand the Machiavellianism," as a recent *New Yorker* cartoon said, "get out of the cabal.") Thus if the game analogy is to be countered it cannot be by mere disdain, refusing to look through the telescope, or by passioned restatements of hallowed truths, quoting scripture against the sun. It is necessary to get down to the details of the matter, to examine the studies and to critique the interpretations— whether Goffman's of crime as character gambling, Harold Garfinkel's of sex change as identity play, Gregory Bateson's of schizophrenia as rule confusion, or my own of the complicated goings-on in a mideastern bazaar as an information contest. As social theory turns from propulsive metaphors (the language of pistons) toward ludic ones (the language of pastimes), the humanities are connected to its arguments not in the fashion of skeptical bystanders but, as the source of its imagery, chargeable accomplices.

Herbert Applebaum

XII

Concluding Remarks

Scientific inquiry in the human sciences today is not so much a method for getting at the "truth," as it is a recognition that knowledge claims are based on the orientations of observers and the context of the intellectual community and larger society in which they dwell. There is also the recognition that there is not one truth but many truths, based on orientation and context. Finally, there is the understanding that the nature of human reality can be reached only by conceptualizing it. Reality, human and otherwise, is not a thing-in-itself. We can only reach it with the mental apparatus we possess. That mental apparatus compels us to conceptualize the world through language, models, and focused observation.

We are presently in a period that could be labelled "postpositive." We no longer believe that knowledge claims have the same degree of certainty as we did in the past. Today, most social scientists recognize three major aspects of the search for knowledge:

1. The standard for what is acceptable as a knowledge claim has changed with the recognition that the criteria for near absolute knowledge is too stringent. Pure observation, untainted by theoretical assumptions, is unattainable. Deductive links between theoretical concepts are diluted by variation due to context and levels of analysis. What is now acceptable as knowledge is that which has stood the test of experience and experiment and that which provides a better explanation and solution to problems than competing theories.

2. A second aspect of human science which has received increased attention is the recognition that, as a human activity, the knower is central to the process of gaining knowledge. Knowledge is developed in a historical context and is a product of the conceptual and methodological tools at the command of the social investigator. Science is progressive, not in the sense that it is additive, but that later periods, by using literature and logic, can understand the

viewpoints of previous periods. Yet, solutions to problems in the present period cannot merely rely on previous understandings, but must be based on present day social realities.

3. A third modern trend in the human sciences has been the development of intellectual tools to supplement sense perception and data collection. Some of these new tools are systems logic, hermeneutics, field theory, linguistic analysis, mental cognition analysis, interactional analysis, and action theory. These modern tools are a response to the need for refinement of intellectual techniques, in the face of growing human diversity and increasing societal complexity.

In spite of these new trends, knowledge claims still require creative hypotheses, the testing and demonstration of hypotheses, and the communication of scientific findings to others. This book has presented a history of the main orientations leading to knowledge claims in anthropology. It has been representative, rather than exhaustive, since there is too much specialization in the field to be encompassed in one volume. Chapter 37 by I. C. Jarvie, which follows, caps this volume and summarizes the present state of theory in anthropology.

Being human ourselves, as well as researchers of human affairs, anthropologists have their particular interests and particular motives for choosing one or several points of view. The most scientific choice is the one that offers the best explanation for a particular case. The scientific choice depends on the problems and upon the level and context of inquiry. It is also legitimate for one to choose a particular line of inquiry because of one's particular bent of mind.

I encourage the reader to have respect for all points of view presented in this book. I encourage the reader to be open to argument and dispute. Knowledge and knowing is a polemical process, hammered out through the struggle of competing viewpoints and theories.

I. C. Jarvie

37. Epistle to the Anthropologists[1]

Lack of theoretical progress among other things, indicates a genuine intellectual crisis in anthropology. Previously, the author advocated a more consciously critical and falsificationist set of methodological rules as a remedy. Fabian has shown that this is not sufficient. He argues that there is an uncritical positivism built-in to anthropology, which leads to ontological, epistemological, and moral error. Metaphysics as well as method needs rectification. The paper urges doing this by rebuilding links to the broad philosophical concerns out of which anthropological theory grew.

This paper addresses itself to two problems: first, is there a crisis in anthropology; second, if there is, what caused it and what will resolve it. As a springboard for discussion, we look at the allegation of crisis and its diagnosis that has come from anthropologists of a phenomenological or "critical theory" persuasion. While agreeing with them that there is a crisis, the paper attributes it to theoretical stagnation, not to the influence of "positivism." A possible cure for theoretical stagnation is seen in critical reflection on the history of anthropology, and especially in coming to terms with the continuities (or lack of them) between its present concerns and those of the tradition of inquiry to which it belongs.

The Crisis

Crises in science are of great interest because they frequently presage an intellectual transformation of some kind (Agassi 1959). They are also treacherous, because some talk of crisis is spurious. There are those who take the view that there is a crisis when people say there is (Jarvie 1972:147–172). I am inclined to use "crisis" in a more objective manner, to refer to an insuperable intellectual difficulty—whether recognized as such or not. To take an example, was there a crisis or a sense of crisis immediately preceding the revolution in social anthropology initiated by Malinowski and Radcliffe-Brown in 1922? I see little evidence of a *sense* of crisis, but plenty that a crisis existed. The crisis was this: the ostensibly competing theories of evolution and diffusion had become so rubbery

527

that they could be reconciled with each other and with all facts. They were better described as metaphysical frameworks or research programs. Neither could specify facts that might refute them and hence would constitute a test, still less a crucial test that would decide between them. Theories which clash neither with other theories nor with the facts are said to have no explanatory power: even though no one denies evolution and diffusion go on, they do not serve to explain any society or social feature. The anthropologist in the field experiences this sharply: according to these theories, what should he look for and record?[2] Almost by accident, both Radcliffe-Brown and Malinowski found themselves plunged into lengthy and intense field experiences. If they were to present "their" people's lives in a coherent and intelligible manner it would virtually be necessary to reinvent anthropology. This they proceeded to do. The result was an immensely powerful new method which teated societies as integrated wholes peopled by recognizably human beings. This transformation and improvement of the practice of anthropology was all to the good; the new pseudo-theoretical dogma was bad. Its worst effect was that instead of continuing and extending the debate on traditional anthropological problems, the new anthropology dismissed them as misconceived or speculative (Jarvie 1964:7-28,170-176). Anthropology was claimed to be beginning anew, free from the errors of the past. This absurd radicalism merely succeeded in suppressing the past, not freeing us of it. If we junk the concerns of the past, where do we begin, what can anthropology now be about? This question was rudely shoved aside in the haste to get on with applying the new method. And the method was such a powerful novelty that it has powered the subject ever since. Now, however, that old question "What is anthropology about?" has re-emerged. Therein lie the fifty-year-old seeds of the present crisis. Anthropologists no longer know what their subject is about, they have lost the thread of those long-ago debates (Kupe 1973; Jarvie 1975a).

Outlining as I just have the intellectual origins of the present crisis—as it were its objective component—is to put things backward. Although the elements of this explanation of mine were developed ten years ago (Jarvie 1964), it was only five years ago that I began to see that a new social and psychological crisis in the subject was actually in the making. Fifty years after *The Andaman Islanders* and *Argonauts of the Western Pacific* flopped from the presses, what is the present situation in social anthropology? We have, I would say, all the signs, indeed a veritable syndrome, of intellectual crisis. There is, for example, the pursuit of intellectual fads, such as structuralism—whatever that is. There is reversion to the comfort of long-discredited theories, such as Marvin Harris's espousal of cultural materialism. There is the invocation of such gadgets as computers, linguistics, systems theory, communications theory, and animal ethology as the answers to all problems. Above all, perhaps, there are strenuous calls for radical reform of the subject, politically, ethically, theoretically, and methodologically. Anthropology, we have even been told, may have to be reinvented once more. So much, then, for the general syndrome of disorder.[3] Let us now look a little more closely at some of the things which are pointed to as causing the crisis. My list mixes the serious with the frivolous, but is none the worse for that: crises have their funny side.

First and above all there is the loss of recruits: the growth boom seems to be over in anthropology, student numbers are said to be levelling off or even falling. Even if this were true, the passing of a fashion for anthropology may be salutary.

Second, there is the loss of the great men: no one, it is said, now leads the subject. Malinowski and Radcliffe-Brown are long dead; their most brilliant pupil Evans-Pritchard had ceased to be a creative influence for some years before he joined them. Lévi-Strauss is looked to by some, but he has an off-putting habit of kicking away those who come to pay him homage that prevents effective leadership (Anonymous 1974). Besides, no Anglo-Saxon can seriously contemplate ceding the leadership to a Frenchman.

Third, as a result of the loss of recruits and loss of the great men, there is a social disorganization: *anomie;* charisma has been routinized into professorships; segmentary fission and fusion has been bureaucratized into departments; *rites de passages* have been secularized into university degrees; there is loss of the clear sense of what it is to be an anthropologist and hence of the direction to proceed.

Fourth, in addition to social disorganization, there is intellectual disorganization: instead of vigorous theoretical debate there are increasingly specialized and technical quibbles.[4] The reason is clear; expansion and specialization cause people to forget or neglect the broader debates on the basic issues.

Such disorganization leads to the fifth contributory cause to the crisis, and that is intellectual stagnation. There has been little movement, little new theory in anthropology since the fifties.[5] When I was an undergraduate at the London School of Economics in the fifties it was the anthropologists' proud boast that the subject was so dynamic and vigorous no one had the time, inclination, or opportunity to write a textbook. We learned the subject without benefit of textbooks. Nowadays there are many textbooks.[6] For this to be at all possible, the pace of the subject must have slowed down.

The dreary catalog of causes could go on, but I will halt at a sixth, in some ways the most serious, and also the best known. I refer to the loss of subject matter. Untouched simple societies are fewer and fewer, and newly decolonized governments are openly hostile and obstructionist toward anthropologists.

Six gloomy portents of a parlous state of affairs. If we add a seventh, to which I shall come later, namely the sweeping claim that the basic epistemological categories of anthropology are inadequate, it is no wonder some scholars develop an urge to throw it all up and begin again *ab initio*: to reinvent anthropology. It is my opinion that we must resist this urge, not so much because the problems and difficulties are not real, but more because the program of trying to start again from scratch is an impossible one: *ex nihilo nihil fit*. Instead, I suggest that we renew ourselves, refresh ourselves, by reexamining assumptions, by looking again at the history and metaphysics of anthropology, by trying to forge links to the past from which we have cut ourselves off, to recapture the identity of self and re-address ourselves to the central unsolved problems.

Philosophical Diagnoses

Two kinds of philosophical difficulties have been advanced as causes of the crisis in anthropology: one, that anthropology participates in the general methodological shortcomings of the empirical social sciences; the other an objection to empiricism itself. To begin with, I want briefly to consider the general methodological shortcomings of the social sciences. Methodological shortcomings in the social sciences are frequently alluded to. It was Poincaré who jibed that sociology was the subject with "the greatest number of methods and the least results" (n.d.: 19-20). Why are the social sciences preoccupied with their own method? One answer might be that when you have nothing to say, you talk about method. No one would claim there is a shortage of first-order problems in the social sciences; they are awash in problems. War, inflation, poverty, injustice, crime, neurosis, unemployment, racialism, underdevelopment, challenge us still—both socially and intellectually. To talk intelligently about a problem, however, one has to have something to say, a solution or theory to meet the problem, or a novel criticism of earlier solutions. In contrast to the problems and the methodologies, both of which abound in the social sciences, there are indeed pathetically few fully worked out theories on offer. Classical and neo-classical economics constitutes one such body of theory, a basis for debate at least. Marx, the great critic of classical economics, is also one of the few social scientists to have developed anything resembling a broad and linked theoretical system.[7] By contrast, his critic Max Weber left us only fragmentary insights in the form of a long drawn out critique of Marx. In social anthropology it could be said that the metaphysics of evolutionism, diffusionism, and functionalism were briefly specified as theories able to do explanatory work. They did not however solve any of the above problems. Moreover, all the examples we have given—classical economics, Marx's theory of society, evolutionism, diffusionism, and functionalism—have it in common that in all precise versions they are false,[8] known to be false, and have been known to be false for a long time; in all vague, imprecise, qualified, or otherwise hedged versions, they are irrefutably metaphysical.

Unlike many anthropologists, I regard theoretical breakdown as a fundamentally healthy event. If what we want is intellectual progress, better explanation, then the breakdown of existing theories is a prerequisite: we cannot supersede a theory until we know where it goes wrong. The more orthodox way to look on theoretical breakdown is that we must have used the wrong method, or not been conscientious enough in employing method to have landed up with false theories. The difference here is that I equate the discovery of error with progress: the more orthodox view is that error, mistake, going wrong, is a lurch that needs explanation. One often finds it suggested that there is a corect methodology that is like a path leading from our present state of error or shortcoming or lack, to a future state of possession of the truth or adequacy or wholeness.[9] Alas, to the best of my knowledge no such path exists; or, even if it does, there is no pathfinder to guide us along it. Method is not an algorithm. Method is the general set of rules governing rational or critical debate; it guides us in the appraisal of theories once we have them; it offers us no guidance as to how to get theories when we are without them. This is why theoretical crisis spawns methodological debate: to assess what has happened and its implications, whether a low-level theory, a global theory, or an entire type of theory has been undermined, etc. However critical our debates are, we may still go on making mistakes, or get nowhere at all, and there may be nothing for it but to go on arguing and thinking and hoping that ideas will come.

No doubt all this sounds hard, but life is hard. It is not as hard, however, as many social scientists like to maintain. There is the constantly reiterated complaint that social life is very complex, unpredictable, and afflicted with multiple causes, and that this accounts for whatever theoretical difficulties are current. Yet every methodological remedy proposed in its turn fails. Like cargo cultists, social scientists have yet to learn the basic lesson that spells are an inefficient way to get anything. A related complaint is that social scientists, being human, cannot escape human bias. The implication is that only Martians or perhaps viruses will ever produce a genuine social science, and in the meantime, social scientists should try to empathize the Martian or the viral viewpoint. The well-known answer to this complaint is that it is highly unlikely that the Martian or the virus would even notice man and his social life as a separate category of phenomena demanding a science to themselves; such beings would have no access to what is sometimes called the world of meanings which man inhabits. And this privileged access man has to himself. This grasp every human necessarily has of his social predicament actually simplifies the alleged complexity of social life.

Failure to appreciate this undoubtedly has to do with the issue of misunderstandings known as scientism. Scientism is the "slavish imitation of the method and language of science" (Hayek 1955:15). Originally exposed and criticized by Hayek in 1942, we nevertheless find it rearing its ugly head in anthropology as recently as Marvin Harris (1968).[10] The irony is that often enough what is so slavishly imitated are methods better known to philosophers than to scientists, e.g., observation, induction, operationalism, experimentalism. Much science obviously (e.g., astronomy, historical geology, and pencil and paper physics) does without experiment. All science is done without induction and operationalism, whatever scientists and philosophers may *say*. It would be doubly ironic if anthropologists of all people did not attend to what scientists do rather than what they say, and hence underestimate the influence of positivism or positivistic *talk* about science. The true methods of science are hard to get at.[11] That may explain why successive methodological revolutions are necessary, as each fails to deliver the goods to the waiting social scientists. Like the cargo cultists they study, anthropologists do not easily lose their credulousness toward manna from heaven.

Theoretical poverty cannot, however, be entirely explained by lack of method or misunderstood method. For such problems have not held back the natural sciences. Another possibility is that what little theoretical progress there is is simply not recognized as such by social scientists. Scientism, positivism, cultural materialism, refuse to recognize progress as such when it occurs unless it conforms to their mistaken ideas of what scientific theories should look like. Thus the sense of crisis brought on by the sense of getting nowhere may be simply a mistake. But I am not inclined to think so, at least as far as anthropology goes. It does seem as though anthropological theory has been stagnant for about twenty years. The question is, why? My answer: because anthropology constantly refuses to debate and acknowledge its philosophical, and espe-

cially metaphysical, ingredients. The fundamental philosophical problem of anthropology, as I have argued elsewhere, is how to reconcile
man's apparent diversity with his real unity (1964:8n, 1968). This problem is a metaphysical problem, and the theories proposed to solve it give
birth to concrete physical, biological, and sociological problems.[12] Scientism, and especially its positivistic variant, constantly tries to cleanse the
social sciences of metaphysics, on the mistaken premise that this will
make them more like the natural sciences. Yet without this metaphysical
problem of the unity of mankind and its surrounding debate there simply would be no anthropology.

Notes

1.   Earlier versions of this paper were read to anthropology seminars at
McMaster University (February 28, 1974), at York University (March 8, 1974), and
at the State University of New York at Buffalo (March 14, 1974).

2.   Boas's fieldwork was buried in 10,000 pages of unreadable prose, in which
there were contradictions, vacillations, and no coherent account of the social
organization (White 1966:6-7).

3.   This syndrome is not noted by that specialist in crises of science, Kuhn
(1962).

4.   The *American Anthropologist* is occasionally ludicrous in this respect, as one
can test by reading aloud a typical contents list (say, for October 1973, 75:1187) to
an audience of colleagues in neighboring fields.

5.   Bidney's survey (1953) is now more than twenty years old.

6.   Beattie (1964), Lienhardt (1964), Mair (1965), Harris (1971), Fried (1973), etc.

7.   Which is one reason why sociology takes as much of its subject matter what
amounts to commentary on Marx (cf. Jarvie 1972:124).

8.   What is true and what false (the sum is false) in Marx is discussed in Popper
(1962, Chs. 18-21). Classical and neo-classical economics consist of models based
on theoretical assumptions (perfect knowledge, free entry, infinite divisibility
and elasticity of supply and demand) which are *known* to be quite false. The
results are then compared to reality and adjustments made to the assumptions to
improve the approximation. The falsity of all current anthropological theories is
precisely the reason for the sense of crisis.

9.   Popper (1963:3-30) calls this the theory that truth is manifest, there for all
those with eyes to see it. On this theory, error equals blindness, distortion. It is
falling into error, rather than the achievement of truth that needs explanation.
Popper argues that the situation is the other way around.

10.   In his remarkable work, the author of that surrealist fantasy *The Nature of Cultural Things* (1964), comes forth with dogmatic pronouncements on complex philosophical questions such as what truly or genuinely constitutes science and scientific method, and proceeds to berate almost every figure in the long history of anthropology. Under the odd impression that Marx, White, Steward, and himself have found the secret of the universe ("cultural materialism"), he orchestrates the whole history of anthropology up to this climax (climacteric?). That there is a protracted and bitter debate about the nature of science; that the status of the social sciences has several quite odd features; that Hayek has warned about the dangers of aping science in garbled form; all this has apparently escaped Harris's selective reading. Of course it makes for exciting reading. History has a plot and the plot has a climax—the revolutionary take-over by cultural materialism. Unfortunately the plot is a travesty of the real dialogue going on in the history and encourages a cavalier hindsight attitude to the great minds of the past. Another inauthentic debunking and devaluing revolution. Malinowski at least had fieldwork to offer.

11.   May in a certain sense not exist. Popper's classic (1959) is in terms of proposed methodological rules (conventions) for science, not factual generalizations about science.

12.   Such a view of science has been developed by Agassi (1964), Popper (1963:97-119, 184-200), Watkins (1958) and Wisdom (1972).

Chapter Sources

Chapter 1.
Murphy, Robert F. 1976 A Quarter Century of American Anthropology, Introduction to Selected Papers from the *American Anthropologist*, 1946–1970. Washington, D.C.: American Anthropological Association, pp.1–19.

Chapter 2.
Tylor, Edward B. 1871 The Science of Culture. *Primitive Culture*. New York: Henry Holt and Co., pp. 1–9.

Chapter 3.
Morgan, Lewis H. 1878 Ethnical Periods. *Ancient Society*. New York: Henry Holt and Co., pp. 1–17.

Chapter 4.
Boas, Franz. 1940 The Limitations of the Comparative Method of Anthropology. *Race, Language and Culture*. New York: The Free Press, pp. 270–280.

Chapter 5.
Kroeber, Alfred L. 1948 The Nature of Culture. *Cultural Patterns and Processes*. New York: Harcourt, Brace and World, Inc., pp. 60–64.

Chapter 6.
Lowie, Robert H. 1929 The Determinants of Culture. *Culture and Ethnology*. New York: Peter Smith, pp. 66–97.

Chapter 7.
Benedict, Ruth Fulton. 1934 The Integration of Culture. *Patterns of Culture*. Boston: Houghton Mifflin, Co., pp. 45–56.

Chapter 8.
Malinowski, Bronislaw. 1939 The Group and the Individual in Functional Analysis. *American Journal of Sociology* 44:938–947.

Chapter 9.
Radcliffe-Brown, Alfred R. 1952 On Social Structure. *Structure and Function in Primitive Society*. New York: The Free Press, pp. 188–204.

Chapter 10.
Kardiner, Abram. 1981 The Technique of Psychodynamic Analysis. *The Psychological Frontiers of Society*. Westport, Conn.: Greenwood Press, pp. 23–34.

Chapter 11.
Mead, Margaret. 1939 Introduction: Coming of Age in Samoa. New York: William Morrow, pp. 1–13. Introduction: Growing up in New Guinea. New York: William Morrow, pp. 1–11.

Chapter 12.
Kluckhohn, Clyde. 1943 Covert Culture and Administrative Problems. *American Anthropologist* 43:413–419.

Chapter 13.
Whiting, John, and Beatrice Whiting. 1978 A Strategy for Psychocultural Research. *The Making of Psychological Anthropology,* edited by George and Louise Spindler. Berkeley: University of California Press, pp. 41–61.

Chapter 14.
Steward, Julian H. 1949 Cultural Causality and Law: A Trial Formulation of the Development of Early Civilizations. *American Anthropologist* Vol. 51, 1:56–82.

Chapter 15.
White, Leslie A. 1943 Energy and the Evolution of Culture. *American Anthropologist* Vol. 45, 3:335–350.

Chapter 16.
Cohen, Ronald. 1981 Evolutionary Epistemology and Human Values. *Current Anthropology* Vol. 22, 3 (June):201–206.

Chapter 17.
Hardesty, Donald L. 1977 Introduction, *Ecological Anthropology.* New York: John Wiley & Co., pp. 8–17.

Chapter 18.
Johnson, Allen. 1982 Reductionism in Cultural Ecology: The Amazon Case. *Current Anthropology* Vol. 23, 4 (August):413–418.

Chapter 19.
Harris, Marvin. 1979 "Theoretical Principles of Cultural Materialism." *Cultural Materialism: The Struggle for a Science of Culture.* New York: Random House, pp. 46–50.

Chapter 20.
Magnarella, Paul J. 1982 Cultural Materialism and the Problem of Probabilities. *American Anthropologist* Vol. 84, 1 (March):138–142.

Chapter 21.
Godelier, Maurice. 1977 *Perspectives in Marxist Anthropology,* New York: Cambridge University Press, pp. 25–32.

Chapter 22.
Berthoud, Gerald. 1979 Genetic Epistemology, Marxism, and Anthropology. *Toward a Marxist Anthropology,* edited by Stanley Diamond. New York: Mouton Publishers, pp. 124–138.

Chapter 23.
Salisbury, Richard F. 1973 Economic Anthropology. *Annual Review of Anthropology,* edited by Siegel, Beals and Tyler. Palo Alto, Calif.: Annual Reviews, Inc., pp. 85–93.

Chapter 24.
Dalton, George. 1969 Theoretical Issues in Economic Anthropology. *Current Anthropology* Vol. 10, 1 (February):63–80.

Chapter 25.
Applebaum, Herbert A. 1984 The Universal Aspects of Work. *Work in Market and Industrial Societies*, edited by Herbert Applebaum. Albany, N.Y.: State University of New York Press, pp. 18–32.

Chapter 26.
Lévi-Strauss, Claude. 1967 "Social Structure" *Structural Anthropology*. New York: Doubleday & Co., Inc., pp. 271–272; 305–309.

Chapter 27.
Rossi, Ino. 1974 Intellectual Antecedents of Lévi-Strauss' Notion of Unconscious. *The Unconscious in Culture: The Structuralism of Claude Lévi-Strauss in Perspective*, edited by Ino Rossi. New York: E. P. Dutton & Co., pp. 8–17.

Chapter 28.
Agar, Michael H. 1982 Whatever Happened to Cognitive Anthropology: A Partial Review. *Human Organization* Vol. 41, 1 (Spring):82–85.

Chapter 29.
Laboratory of Comparative Human Cognition. 1978 Cognition as a Residual Category in Anthropology. *Annual Review of Anthropology*, edited by Siegel, Beals and Tyler, Vol. 7. Annual Reviews, Inc.: Palo Alto, California, pp. 60–67.

Chapter 30.
Scheper-Hughes, Nancy. 1984 The Margaret Mead Controversy: Culture, Biology and Anthropological Inquiry. *Human Organization* Vol. 43, 1 (Spring):85–92.

Chapter 31.
Wilson, Edward O. 1978 *Hope. On Human Nature*. Cambridge, Mass.: Harvard University Press, pp. 195–209.

Chapter 32.
Chagnon, Napoleon A. 1979 Anthropology and the Nature of Things. *Evolutionary Biology and Human Social Behavior*, edited by N. A. Chagnon and W. Irons. North Scituate, Mass.: Duxbury Press, pp. 522–526.

Chapter 33.
Turner, Victor W. 1977 Symbols in African Ritual. *Symbolic Anthropology*, edited by Janet L. Dolgin, David S. Kemnitzer, and David M. Schneider. New York: Columbia University Press, pp. 183–194.

Chapter 34.
Schneider, David M. 1977 Kinship, Nationality, and Religion in American Culture: Toward a Definition of Kinship. *Symbolic Anthropology*, edited by Janet L. Dolgin, David S. Kemnitzer, and David M. Schneider. New York: Columbia University Press, pp. 63–71.

Chapter 35.
Dubinskas, Frank A. 1983 Leaders and Followers: Cultural Pattern and Political Symbolism in Yugoslavia. *Anthropological Quarterly* Vol. 56, 2:95–99.

Chapter 36.
Geertz, Clifford. 1983 Interpretive Anthropology. *Local Knowledge, Further Essays in Interpretive Anthropology.* New York: Basic Books, pp. 22–26.

Chapter 37.
Jarvie, I. C. 1975 Epistle to the Anthropologists. *American Anthropologist* Vol. 77, 2 (June):253–266.

Bibliography

Acheson, J. M.
1972 *Limited Good or Limited Goods: Response to Economic Opportunity in a Tarascan Pueblo. American Anthropologist,* Vol. 74: 1152–1169.

Adair, John, and Evon Vogt
1949 Navaho and Zuni Veterans: A Study of Contrasting Modes of Culture Change. *American Anthropologist* 51:547–61.

Adelman, Irma, and Cynthia Taft Morris
1965 Factor Analysis of the Interrelationship between Social and Political Variables and Per Capital Gross National Product. *The Quarterly Journal of Economics* 89:55–78.
1967 *Society, Politics and Economic Development.* Baltimore: Johns Hopkins.

Agar, Michael
1975 Selecting a Dealer. *American Ethnologist* 2:247–60.

Agar, M. H., and J. R. Hobbs
1981a Interpreting Discourse: Coherence and the Analysis of Ethnographic Interviews. *Discourse Processes* 5:1–32, 1982.
1981b Natural Plans: AI Planning in the Analysis of a Life History. *Ethos,* 11:33–48, 1983.

Agassi, J.
1959 Epistemology as an Aid to Science. *British Journal for the Philosophy of Science* 10:139–146.
1964 The Nature of Scientific Problems and Their Roots in Metaphysics. *The Critical Approach to Science and Philosophy,* Mario Bunge, ed. New York: Free Press.

Ainsworth, Mary
1967 *Infancy in Uganda: Infant Care and the Growth of Love.* Baltimore: Johns Hopkins Press.

Albright, William Foxwell
1946 *From the Stone Age to Christianity.* Baltimore: Johns Hopkins.

Alexander, Richard D.
1975 The Search for a General Theory of Behavior. *Behavioral Science* 20:77–100.
1979 Evolution and Culture. *Evolutionary Biology and Human Social Behavior,* N.A. Chagnon and W. Irons, eds. North Scituate: Duxbury Press, pp. 59–78.

Allen, L. et al.
1976   Sociobiology—Another Biological Determinism. *BioScience*   26:182–86.

Althusser, L.
1970   Philosophy as a Revolutionary Weapon. *New Left Review*   64:3–11.

Anderson, J. N.
1973   Ecological Anthropology and Anthropological Ecology. *Handbook of Social and Cultural Anthropology*, ed. by J. J. Honigmann. Chicago: Rand McNally, pp. 179–239.

Anderson, R., and C. Wadel, eds.
1972   North Atlantic Fishermen. *Newfoundland Society of Economics*. Paper No. 5. Newfoundland: Memorial University.

Andersson, J. G.
1934   *Children of the Yellow Earth*. London: Clarendon.

Anonymous
1974   Review of Tristes Tropiques, by C. Lévi-Strauss. *Times Literary Supplement*, Feb. 22:188.

Applebaum, Herbert
1981   *Royal Blue: The Culture of Construction Workers*. New York: Holt, Rinehart and Winston.
1984   *Work in Non-Market and Transitional Societies*. Albany, N.Y.: State University of New York Press.

Ardener, Edwin
1975   Belief and the Problem of Women. *Perceiving Women*, S. Ardender, ed. New York: John Wiley, pp. 1–16.

Arendt, Hannah
1959   *The Human Condition*. Chicago: University of Chicago Press.

Arensberg, Conrad
1961   The Community as Object and as Sample. *American Anthropologist* 63:241–64.
1968 (1937)   *The Irish Countrymen*. Garden City: Natural History Press.
1981   Cultural Holism Through Interactional Systems. *American Anthropologist* 83:562–81.

Arensberg, Conrad, and A. H. Niefhoff
1964   *Introducing Social Change*. Chicago: Aldine.

Armillas, Pedro
1948   A Sequence of Cultural Development in Mesoamerica. *A Reappraisal of Peruvian Archaeology*. Society of American Archaeology Memoir 4.

Arnold, Rosemary
1957a   A Port of Trade: Whydah on the Guinea Coast: *Trade and Market in the Early Empires*, K. Polanyi and C. Arensberg, and H. W. Pearson, eds. Glencoe: The Free Press.

1957b Separation of Trade and Market in the Early Empires. *Trade and Market in the Early Empires*, edited by K. Polanyi, C. Arensberg, and H. W. Pearson. Glencoe: The Free Press.

Aron, R.
1977 *In Defense of Decadent Europe*. Translated by Stephen Cox. South Bend, Indiana: Regenery Gateway.

Bachelard, G.
1967 *La formation de l'esprit scientifique*. Paris: Vrin.

Barash, David P.
1977 *Sociology and Behavior*. New York: Elsevier.

Barnard, C. I.
1938 *The Functions of the Executive*. Cambridge, Mass.: Harvard Univ. Press.

Barry, Herbert, III, Margaret K. Bacon, and Irvin I. Child
1967 Definitions, Rating and Bibliographic Sources for Child Training Practices of 110 Cultures. *Cross-Cultural Approaches: Readings in Comparative Research*, C. Ford, ed. New Haven: HRAF, pp. 293–331.

Barry, Herbert III, Irvin L. Child, and Margaret K. Bacon
1959 Relation of Child Training to Subsistence Economy. *American Anthropologist* 61:51–63.

Barth, Fredrik
1956 Ecologic Relationships of Ethnic Groups in Swat, North Pakistan. *American Anthropologist* 58:1079–1089.

1963 *The Role of the Entrepreneur in Social Change in North Norway*. Bergen: Norwegian University Press.

1966 Models of Social Organization. *Occasional Papers of the Royal Anthropological Institute*. London 23.

1967a Economic Spheres in Darfur. *Themes in Economic Anthropology*, edited by Raymond Firth. A.S.A. Monograph 6. London: Tavistock, pp. 149–74.

1967b On the Study of Social Change. *American Anthropologist* 69:661–69.

Bateson, Gregory
1958 (Orig. 1936) *Naven*. Stanford: Stanford University Press.

Battro, A. M.
1966 *Dictionnaire d'epistemologie genetique*. Dordrecht, Holland: Reidel.

Beals, Ralph
1951 Urbanism, Urbanization and Acculturation. *American Anthropologist* 53:1–10.

Beattie, John
1964a *Other Cultures*. London: Cohen and West.

1964b. Bunyoro: An African Feudality? *Journal of African History* 5:25–36.

1968 Aspects of Nyoro Symbolism. London: Oxford University Press. *Africa* 38:413–442.

Beckerman, Stephen
1979 The Abundance of Protein in Amazonia: A Reply to Gross. *American Anthropologist* 81:553–60.

Beidelman, T. O.
1961 Right and Left Among the Kaguru. *Africa* 31:250–257.
1966 Swazi Royal Ritual. *Africa* 36:373–405.

Belshaw, M.
1967 *A Village Economy: Land and People of Huecorio.* New York: Columbia University Press.

Benedict, B.
1968 Family Firms and Economic Development. *Southwestern Journal of Anthropology* 24:1–19.

Benedict, Ruth
1934 *Patterns of Culture.* Boston: Houghton Mifflin Co.

Bennett, J. W.
1969 *Northern Plainsmen.* Chicago: Aldine.
1976 Anticipation, Adaptation and the Concept of Culture in Anthropology. *Science* 192:847–53.

Bennett, Wendell C.
1946 The Andean Highlands: An Introduction. *Handbook of South American Indians,* J. H. Steward, ed. Bureau of American Ethnological Bulletin 143, 2:1–60.

Berlin, B., and P. Kay
1969 *Basic Color Terms: Their Universality and Evolution.* Berkeley: University of California Press.

Berlin, B., D. E. Breedlove, and P. H. Raven
1973 General Principles of Classification and Nomenclature in Folk Biology. *American Anthropologist* 75:214–42.

Berlin, E. A., and E. K. Markell
1977 An Assessment of the Nutritional and Health Status of an Aguarune Jivaro Community, Amazonas, Peru. *Ecology of Food and Nutrition* 6:69–81.

Berndt, R. M.
1951 *Kunapipi.* New York: Lippincourt.

Berreman, Gerald D.
1966 Anemic and Emetic Analyses in Social Anthropology. *American Anthropologist* 68:346–354.

Berthoud, G.
1969–1970 La validite des concepts de "multicentricite" et de "spheres d'echange" en anthropologie economique. *Archives Suisses d'Anthropologie Generale* 34:35–64.

Bestor, A. E., Jr.
1950   *Backwoods Utopias*. Philadelphia: University of Pennsylvania Press.

Bidney, David
1953a and 1968   *Theoretical Anthropology*. New York: Columbia University Press.
1953b   The Concept of Value in Modern Anthropology. *Anthropology Today, An Encyclopedic Inventory*, edited by A. L. Kroeber. Chicago: University of Chicago Press, pp. 682–699.

Biebuyck, Daniel, ed.
1963   *African Agrarian Systems*. London: Oxford University Press.

Bilmes, J.
1975   Misinformation and Ambiguity in Verbal Interaction. *International Journal of Sociological Language*   5:63–75.

Birdsell, J.
1953   Some Environmental and Cultural Factors Influencing the Structuring of Australian Aboriginal Populations. *American Naturalist*   87:171–207.

Bishop, C. W.
1942   Origin of the Far Eastern Civilizations. *War Background Studies No. 1*. Washington, D.C.: Smithsonian Institution.

Bishop, Claire
1950   *All Things Common*. New York: Harper.

Blauner, Robert
1966   Work Satisfaction and Industrial Trends in Modern Society. *Class, Status and Power*, R. Bendix and S. M. Lipset, eds. New York: The Free Press.

Blurton-Jones, N. G., ed.
1972   *Ethnological Studies of Child Behavior*. London: Cambridge University Press.

Blute, Marion
1984   The Sociobiology of Sex and Sexes Today. *Current Anthropology*   25:193–214.

Boas, Franz
1921   Ethnology of the Kwakiul based on data collected by George Hunt. *Bureau of American Ethnology Annual Report No. 35* (for 1913–14), Parts 1 and 2. Washington, D.C.
1960   The Aims of Anthropological Research. *The Golden Age of American Anthropology*, Margaret Mead and Ruth Bunzel, eds. New York: George Braziller, Inc., pp. 557–91.
1968 (orig. 1911)   *Introduction to Handbook of American Indian Languages*. Lincoln: University of Nebraska Press.

Boeke, J. H.
1942   *The Structure of Netherland Indian Economy*. New York: Institute of Pacific Relations.

Bohannan, Paul
1954　*Tiv Farm and Settlement.* London: His Majesty's Stationery Office.
1959　The Impact of Money on an African Subsistence Economy. *Journal of Economic History*　19:491–503.
1963　*Social Anthropology.* New York: Holt, Rinehart and Winston.
1968　*Tiv Economy.* Evanston: Northwestern Unversity Press.

Bohannan, Paul, and George Dalton
1965　Introduction. *Markets in Africa,* edited by P. Bohannan and G. Dalton. New York: Doubleday, pp. 1–32.

Bohn, D.
1957　*Causality and Change in Modern Physics.* New York: Harper.

Boserup, Ester
1965　*The Conditions of Agricultural Growth.* Chicago: Aldine.

Boulding, K. E.
1956　*The Image.* Ann Arbor: University of Michigan Press.

Bowlby, John
1969　*Attachment.* New York: Basic Books.
1973　*Separation.* New York: Basic Books.

Bowman, C. C.
1965　Review of the Unconscious in Social Relations, by O. Machotka. *American Sociological Review*　30(2):320.

Brace, C. Loring
1962　Refocusing on the Neanderthal Problem. *American Anthropologist* 64:729–741.

Brokensha, David W.
1966　*Social Change at Larteh, Ghana.* Oxford: Clarendon Press.

Brookfield, H. C.
1969　*Pacific Marketplaces.* Canberra: Australian National University.
1972　Intensification and Disintensification in Pacific Agriculture: A Theoretical Approach. *Pacific Viewpoint*　13:30–48.

Brown, C. H.
1976　General Principles of Human Anatomical Partonomy and Speculations on the Growth of Partonomic Nomenclature. *American Ethnologist*　3:400–24.

Burawoy, Michael
1974　*Manufacturing Consent, Changes in the Labor Process under Monopoly Capitalism.* Chicago: University of Chicago Press.

Burling, Robbins
1962　Maximization Theories and the Study of Economic Anthropology. *American Anthropologist*　64:802–21.
1964　Cognition and Componential Analysis: God's Truth or Hocus-Pocus. *American Anthropologist*　66:20–28.

Burton-Bradley, B. G., and K. J. Pataki-Schweizer
1977 Comment on: Bridging Levels of Systemic Organization, by R. A. Rubinstein and C. D. Laughlin, Jr. *Current Anthropology* 18:464.

Burton, R. R. V., and J. W. M. Whiting
1961 The Absent Father and Cross-Sex Identity. *Merrill-Palmer Quarterly of Behavior and Development* 7(2):85–95.

Calame-Griaule, Genevieve
1966 *Ethnologie et langage; Le Parole chez les Dogons.* Paris: Gallimard.

Campbell, Donald T.
1975 On the Conflicts Between Biological and Social Evolution and Between Psychology and Moral Tradition. *American Psychologist* 30:1103–1126.

Cancian, Frank
1965 *Economics and Prestige in a Maya Community.* Palo Alto: Stanford University Press.

Carlsmith, L.
1964 Effect of Early Father Absence on Scholastic Aptitude. *Harvard Educational Review* 34:3–21.

1973 Some Personality Characteristics of Boys Separated from their Fathers during World War II. *Ethos* 1(4):466–77.

Carneiro, R. L.
1960 Slash-and-Burn-Agriculture: A Closer Look at its Implications for Settlement Patterns. *Men and Culture,* edited by A. F. C. Wallace. Philadelphia: University of Pennsylvania Press.

1970 A Theory of the Origin of the State. *Science* 169:733–738.

1973a The Four Faces of Evolution. *Handbook of Social and Cultural Anthropology,* J. J. Honigmann, editor. Chicago: Rand McNally.

1973b Classical Evolution. *Main Currents in Cultural Anthropology,* Raoul and Frada Naroll, eds. New York: Appleton-Century-Crofts, pp. 57–123.

1978 Comment on: Food Taboos, Diet and Hunting Strategy, by E. B. Ross. *Current Anthropology* 19:1–36.

Carr, E. H.
1951 *The New Society.* London: Macmillan.

Cassirer, Ernst
1944 *An Essay on Man: An Introduction to a Philosophy of Human Culture.* New Haven: Yale University Press.

1976 A Clue to the Nature of Man: The Symbol. *Ideas of Culture,* F. C. Gamst and E. Norbeck, eds. New York: Holt, Rinehart and Winston.

Casson, R.
1975 The Semantics of Kin Term Usage. *American Ethnologist* 2:229–38.

Caudill, W., and L. Front
1973 A Comparison of Maternal Care and Infant Development and Behavior in Japanese-American and Japanese Families. *Youth, Socialization and Mental Health*, W. Lebra, ed. Honolulu: University Press of Hawaii.

Chagnon, N. A.
1968 Yanomamo Social Organization and Warfare. *War: The Anthropology of Armed Conflict*, M. Fried, M. Harris, and R. Murphy, eds. New York: Natural History Press.

1979 Is Reproductive Success Equal in Egalitarian Societies? *Evolutionay Biology and Human Social Behavior: An Anthropological Perspective*, N. A. Chagnon and W. Irons, eds. North Scituate, Mass.: Duxbury Press, pp. 347–401.

Chagnon, N. A., and R. Hames
1979 Protein Deficiency and Tribal Warfare in Amazonia: New Data. *Science* 203:901–13.

Chagnon, N. A., and W. Irons
1979 *Evolutionary Biology and Human Social Behavior: An Anthropological Perspective*. Belmont, Calif.: Wadsworth.

Chapple, Eliot D., and Conrad M. Arensberg
1940 Measuring Human Relations: An Introduction to the Study of the Interaction of Individuals. *Genetic Psychology Monograph* . Worchester, Mass.: Clark University.

Chayanov, A. V.
1966 (Orig. 1925, in Russian) *The Theory of Peasant Economy*. Homewood: Irwin.

Chevalier, Francois
1963 *Land and Society in Colonial Mexico*. Berkeley: University of California Press.

Chi, Ch'Ao-Ting
1936 *Key Economic Areas in Chinese History*. London: G. Allen and Unwin, Ltd.

Childe, V. Gordon
1934 *New Light on the Most Ancient East*. New York: Penguin.
1946 *What Happened in History*. New York: Pelican.
1951 *Social Evolution*. London: C. A. Watts.

Chomsky, Noam
1966 *Cartesian Linguistics*. New York: Harper and Row.

Claessen, H. J. M., and P. Skalnik, eds.
1978 *The Early State*. The Hague: Mouton.

Clement, D. C.
1976 Cognitive Anthropology and Applied Problems in Education. *Do Applied Anthropologists Apply Anthropology?* M. Angrosino, ed. Athens: University of Georgia Press.

1980 Samoan Folk Knowledge of Mental Disorders: A Partial Analysis with Some Comments on Cognitive Anthropology. Paper presented to a conference on Cultural Conceptions of Mental Health and Therapy. East-West Center, Honolulu.

Clements, F. E.
1965 (Orig. 1916) Plant Succession: An Analysis of the Development of Vegetation. *Readings in Ecology*, edited by J. E. Kormondy. Englewood Cliffs: Prentice-Hall, pp. 140–43.

Clifford, James
1983 The Other Side of Paradise. *Times Literary Supplement*. May 13, No. 4. 180:475–476.

Cohen, Ronald
1973 The Political System. *Handbook of Method in Cultural and Social Anthropology*, edited by R. Naroll and R. Cohen. New York: Columbia University Press.

1976 The Natural History of Hierarchy. *Power and Control: Social Structures and Their Transformation*, edited by T. Burns and W. Buckley. Beverley Hills: Sage Publications, pp. 185–214.

1978a State Origins: A Reappraisal. *The Early State*, edited by H. J. M. Claessen and P. Skalnik. The Hague: Mouton.

1978b State Foundations: A Controlled Comparison. *Origins of the State*, edited by R. Cohen and E. R. Service. Philadelphia: Institute for the Study of Human Issues.

1981 Evolution, Fission and the Early State. *The Study of the State*, edited by H. J. M. Claessen and P. Skalnik. The Hague: Mouton.

Cohen, Ronald and A. Schlegel
1968 The Tribe as a Socio-Political Unit: A Cross-Cultural Examination. *Essays on the Problem of the Tribe*, edited by J. Helm. Seattle: University of Washington Press, pp. 120–44.

Colby, Benjamin N., James W. Fernandez, and David B. Kronenfeld
1981 Toward a Convergence of Cognitive and Symbolic Anthropology. *American Ethnologist* 8:436–442.

Colson, Elizabeth
1949 Assimilation of an American Indian Group. *Human Problems in British Central Africa (Rhodes-Livingstone Journal)* 5:1–13.

1983 The Reordering of Experience: Anthropological Involvement with Time. Unpublished Faculty Research Lecture, April 20. Wheeler Auditorium, Berkeley Campus.

Conklin, Harold C.
1954 The Relation of Hanunoo Culture to the Plant World. Unpublished PhD. dissertation, Yale University.

1955 Hanunoo Color Categories. *Southwestern Journal of Anthropology* 11:339–344.

1964 Ethnogeneological Method. *Explorations in Cultural Anthropology,* edited by W. Goodenough. New York: McGraw Hill, pp. 25–56.

1972 Color Categorization. *American Anthropologist* 75:931–42.

Cook, S. F.

1947 The Interrelation of Population, Food Supply, and Building in Pre-Conquest Central Mexico. *American Antiquity* 13:45–52.

Cook, Scott

1966 The Obsolete "Anti-Market" Mentality: A Critique of the Substantive Approach to Economic Anthropology. *American Anthropologist* 68:323–45.

1970 Price and Output Variability in a Peasant-Artisan Stone Working Industry on Oaxaca. *American Anthropologist* 72:776–801.

Creel, H. G.

1937a *The Birth of China.* New York: Reynal and Mitchcock.

1937b *Studies in Early Chinese Culture.* Baltimore: Waverly Press.

Dalton, George

1960 A Note of Clarification on Economic Surplus. *American Anthropologist* 62:483–90.

1961 Economic Theory in Primitive Society. *American Anthropologist* 63:1–25.

1962 Traditional Production in Primitive African Economies. *The Quarterly Journal of Economics* 76:360–78.

1963 Economic Surplus, Once Again. *American Anthropologist* 65:389–94.

1964 The Development of Subsistence and Peasant Economies in Africa. *International Social Science Journal* 16:378–89.

1965a Primitive Money. *American Anthropologist* 67:44–65.

1965b Primitive, Archaic, and Modern Economies: Karl Polanyi's Contribution to Economic Anthropology and Comparative Economy. *Proceedings of the 1965 Annual Spring Symposium of the American Ethnological Society.* Seattle: University of Washington Press.

1965c History, Politics and Economic Development in Liberia. *Journal of Economic History* 25:569–91.

1967 *Tribal and Peasant Economies.* Garden City: N.Y.: Natural History Press.

1969 Theoretical Issues in Economic Anthropology. *Current Anthropology* 10:63–80.

D'Andrade, R. G.

1962 Father Absence and Cross-Sex Identifictation. PhD. dissertation. Harvard University.

1973 Father Absence, Identification and Identity. *Ethos* 1(4):440–55.

1974 Memory and the Assessment of Behavior. *Measurement in the Social Sciences,* edited by T. Blalock. Chicago: Aldine-Atherton, pp. 159–85.

1976 A Propositional Analysis of U.S. American Beliefs about Illness. *Meaning in Anthropology,* K. H. Basso and H. A. Selby, eds. Albuquerque: University of New Mexico Press.

1980 The Cultural Part of Cognition. Paper presented to the 2nd Annual Cognitive Science Conference. New Haven, Conn.

Daniels, R. E.
1970 By Rites a Man: A Study of the Societal and Individual Foundations of Tribal Identity among the Kipsigis of Kenya. PhD. dissertation. University of Chicago.

Darnoi, D. N. Kennedy
1967 *The Unconscious and Edward von Hartmann.* The Hague: Martinus Nijhoff.

Darwin, Charles
1965 *The Expression of the Emotions in Man and Animals.* Chicago: University of Chicago Press.

Davis, J.
1972 Gifts and the U.K. Economy. *Man* 7:408–29.

Deane, Phyllis
1953 *Colonial Social Accounting.* Cambridge: Cambridge University Press.

de Brigard, Emilie
1983 Review of: Margaret Mead: Taking Note. *American Anthropologist* 85:494–495.

Diamond, Stanley
1964 Anthropology and World Affairs as seen by U.S.A. Associates: A Revolutionary Discipline. *Current Anthropology* 5:432–441.

1979 *Toward a Marxist Anthropology: Problems and Perspectives.* The Hague: Mouton Publishers.

Diaz, May N.
1967 Opposition and Alliance in a Mexican Town. *Peasant Society,* Potter, Diaz and Foster, eds. Boston: Little, Brown, pp. 50–57.

Diener, Paul
1974 Ecology or Evolution?: The Hutterite Case. *American Ethnologist* 1:601–618.

Diener, Paul, Kurt Moore, and Robert Mutaw
1980 Meat, Markets and Mechanical Materialism: The Great Protein Fiasco in Anthropology. *Dialectical Anthropology* 5:171–92.

Dieterlen, Germaine
1941 *Ls Ames des Dogons.* Paris: Institut d'Ethnologie Travaux et Memories, XL.

Dieterlen, Germaine and Marcel Griaule
1963 *Le Renard Pale.* Paris: Institut d'Ethnologie Travaux et Memoires, LXXII.

Dobzhansky, T.
1962 *Mankind Evolving.* New Haven: Yale University Press.

Dolgin, Janet L., David S. Kemnitzer, and David M. Schneider
1977 *Symbolic Anthropology.* New York: Columbia University Press.

Douglas, Mary
1958 *Raffia Cloth Distribution in the Lele Economy. Africa* 28:109–22.
1965 The Lele: Resistance to Change. *Markets in Africa,* edited by P. J. Bohannan and G. Dalton. New York: Natural History Press.
1966 *Purity and Danger: An Analysis of the Concepts of Pollution and Taboo.* New York: Praeger.
1968 Dogon Culture—Profane and Arcane. *Africa* 38:16–24.

Draper, Patricia
1972 !Kung Childhood. PhD. dissertation. Harvard University.
1976 Social and Economic Constraints on !Kung Childhood. *Kalahari Hunter Gatherers,* R. B. Lee and I. DeVore, editors. Cambridge, Mass.: Harvard University Press.

Dumezil, G.
1948 *Loki,* Paris: Gallimard.

Dumont, Louis
1967 *Homo Hierarchicus.* Paris: Gallimard.

Dundes, Alan
1962 Earth-Diver: Creation of the Mythopoeic Male. *American Anthropologist* 64:1032–1051.

Dunn, Stephen P.
1979 The Position of the Primitive-Communal Social Order in the Soviet-Marxist Theory of History. *Toward Marxist Anthropology: Problems and Perspectives,* edited by Stanley Diamond. The Hague: Mouton Publishers.

Dunn, Stephen P., and E. Dunn
1975 The Intellectual Tradition of Soviet Ethnography. *Introduction to Soviet Ethnography,* edited by S. P. Dunn and E. Dunn. Berkeley: Highgate Social Science Research Station.

Dunnell, Robert C., and Robert J. Wenke
1979 An Evolutionary Model of the Development of Complex Society. Paper presented at the annual meeting of the American Association for the Advancement of Science. San Francisco, Calif.

Durham, L. H.
1979 Toward a Co-Evolutionary Theory of Human Biology and Culture. *Evolutionary Biology and Human Social Behavior,* edited by N. A. Chagnon and W. Irons. Belmont, Calif.: Wadsworth.

Durkheim, Emile
1938 (orig. 1895) *The Rules of Sociological Method.* S. Solvay and J. Mueller trans. G. E. G. Catlin, editor. Chicago: University of Chicago Press.
1947 (orig. 1912) *The Elementary Forms of the Religious Life: A Study in Religious Sociology.* J. W. Swain, trans. New York: The Free Press.
1949 (orig. 1893) *The Division of Labor in Society.* G. Simpson, trans. New York: The Free Press.
1951 (orig. 1887) *Suicide.* J. Spaulding and G. Simpson, trans. New York: The Free Press.
1960 (orig. 1892) *Montesquieu and Rousseau: Forerunners of Sociology.* R. Manheim, trans. Ann Arbor: University of Michigan Press.
1964 (orig. 1895) *The Rules of Sociological Method.* New York: The Free Press.

Ebihara, M.
1977 Residence Pattern in a Khmer Peasant Village. *Annals, New York Academy of Science* 243:51–68.

Eggan, Fred
1954 Social Anthropology and the Method of Controlled Comparison. *American Anthropologist* 56:743–63.

Eibl-Eibesfeldt, I.
1961 The Fighting Behavior of Animals. *Scientific American* 205:112–21.
1975 *Ethology, The Biology of Behavior.* New York: Holt, Rinehart and Winston.

Ekholm, Gordon P.
1946 Wheeled Toys in Mexico. *American Antiquity* 2:222–27.

Elliott-Smith, G.
1929 *Human History.* New York: Morrow.

Emerson, A. E.
1960 The Evolution of Adaptation in Population Systems. *Evolution After Darwin,* Vol. 1, edited by S. Tax. Chicago: University of Chicago Press.

Engels, Frederick
1940 and 1942 *Origin of the Family, Private Property and the State.* New York: International Publishers.
1959 *Karl Marx and Frederick Engels, Basic Writings on Politics and Philosophy,* edited by Lewis S. Feuer. Garden City, N.Y.: Doubleday & Co.
1963 Letter: F. Engels to J. Bloch. In Selsam, H., and H. Martel. *Reader in Marxist Philosophy.* New York: International Publishers.

Epstein, T. Scarlett
1962 *Economic Development and Social Change in South India.* Manchester: Manchester University Press.

Erasmus, Charles J.
1961 *Man Takes Control.* Minneapolis: University of Minneapolis Press.

Evans-Pritchard, E. E.
1956   *Nuer Religion.* Oxford: Clarendon Press.

Fallers, Lloyd A.
1961   Are African Cultivators to be called "Peasants?" *Current Anthropology* 2:108–110.

Fillmore, C. J.
1981   Ideal Readers and Real Readers. Paper presented to the 32nd Annual Georgetown University Round Table on Languages and Linguistics. Washington, D.C.

Finney, B.
1968   Big-fellow Man Belong Business in New Guinea. *Ethnology* 4:394–410.

Firth, Raymond
1929   *Primitive Economics of the New Zealand Maori.* London: George Routledge.

1939   *Primitive Polynesian Economy.* London: Routledge and Kegan Paul.

1946   *Malay Fishermen: Their Peasant Economy.* London: Routledge and Kegan Paul.

1951   *The Elements of Social Organization.* London: Watts.

1957 (Orig. 1939)   *We, the Tikopia: A Sociological Study of Kinship in Primitive Polynesia.* London: G. Allen.

1958   *Work and Wealth of Primitive Communities.* New York: Mentor Books.

1959   *Social Change in Tikopia.* London: George Allen and Unwin.

1964   Capital, Saving and Credit in Peasant Societies: A Viewpoint from Economic Anthropology. *Capital, Savings and Credit in Peasant Societies,* edited by R. Firth and B. Yamey. Chicago: Aldine.

1966a   *Malay Fishermen.* Hamden: Archer Books.

1966b   *Primitive Polynesian Economy,* Revised Edition. London: Routledge and Kegan Paul.

1967   *Themes in Economic Anthroplogy.* A.S.A. Monograph 6. London: Tavistock.

1972   Anthropological Background to Work. *The Social Dimensions of Work,* edited by Clifton D. Bryant. Englewood Cliffs, N.J.: Prentice-Hall.

Fjellman, S. M.
1976   Talking About Talking About Residence. *American Ethnologist* 3:671–82.

Flannery, Kent V.
1972   The Cultural Evolution of Civilizations. *Annual Review of Ecological Systems* 3:399–426.

Forde, Daryll, ed.
1954   *African Worlds.* London: Oxford University Press.

Form, William H.
1976 *Blue-Collar Stratification: Autoworkers in Four Countries.* Princeton: Princeton University Press.

Forman, S.
1970 *The Raft Fishermen: Tradition and Change in the Brazilian Peasant Economy.* Bloomington: Indiana University Press.

Fortes, Meyer
1953 The Structure of Unilineal Descent Groups. *American Anthropologist* 55:17–41.
1969 *Kinship and the Social Order: The Legacy of Lewis Henry Morgan.* Chicago: Aldine.

Fortes, M., and E. E. Evans-Pritchard
1940 *African Political Systems.* London: Oxford University Press.

Foster, George
1965 Peasant Society and the Image of Limited Good. *American Anthropologist* 67:293–315.
1967 *Tzintzuntzan: Mexican Peasants in a Changing World.* Boston: Little, Brown.

Frake, Charles O.
1962a Cultural Ecology and Ethnography. *American Anthropologist* 64:53–59.
1962b The Ethnographic Study of Cognitive Systems. *Anthropology and Human Behavior,* edited by T. Gladwin and W. C. Sturtevant. Washington, D.C.: Anthropological Society of Washington, pp. 72–85.
1964a Notes on Queries in Ethnography. *American Anthropologist* 66:132–45.
1964b A Structural Description of Subanum "Religious" Behavior. *Explorations in Cultural Anthropology,* edited by W. Goodenough. New York: McGraw-Hill, pp. 111–29.
1977 Plying Frames can be Dangerous: Some Reflections on Methodology in Cognitive Anthropology. *The Quarterly Newsletter of the Institute for Comparative Human Development* 1:1–7.
1980 *Language and Cultural Description.* Stanford: Stanford University Press

Frank, A. G.
1970 On Dalton's "Theoretical Issues in Economic Anthropology." *Current Anthropology* 11:67–71.

Frankel, S. H.
1955 *The Economic Impact on Under-Developed Societies.* Cambridge: Harvard University Press.

Frankenburg, R.
1966 British Community Studies: Problems of Synthesis. *The Social Anthropology of Complex Societies,* edited by M. Banton. A.S.A. Monographs 4. London: Tavistock, pp. 123–54.

Frazer, James G.
1915 (orig. 1890). *The Golden Bough*. London: Macmillan.

Freeman, Derek
1983 *Margaret Mead and Samoa: The Making and Unmaking of an Anthropological Myth*. Cambridge, Mass.: Harvard University Press.

Freud, Sigmund
1938 *Totem and Taboo, Basic Writings of Sigmund Freud*. Translated by A. A. Brill. New York: Modern Library.

Freud, John E.
1967 *Modern Elementary Statistics*. 3rd Ed. Englewood Cliffs: Prentice-Hall.

Fried, Morton H.
1957 The Classification of Corporate Unilineal Descent Groups. *Journal of the Royal Anthropological Institute* 87:1–29.
1967 *The Evolution of Political Society: An Essay in Political Anthropology*. New York: Random House.
1973 *Explorations in Anthropology*. New York: Thomas Y. Crowell.

Friedman, Jonathan
1974 Marxism, Structuralism, and Vulgar Materialism. *Man.* 9(3):444–469.

Fromm, Eric
1941 *Escape From Freedom*. New York: Rinehart.

Furnas, C. C.
1941 Future Sources of Power. *Science*. Nov. 7, 1941.

Gadamer, Hans-Georg
1975 *Truth and Method*. Trans. by Garren Burden and John Cumming. New York: Seabury Press.

Gamst, Frederick C.
1980 *The Hoghead: An Industrial Ethnology of the Locomotive Engineer*. New York: Holt, Rinehart and Winston.
1981 Considerations for an Anthropology of Work. *Anthropology of Work Newsletter* 2(1):2–7.
1986 Anthropological Perspectives on Apprenticeship. *Anthropology of Work Review*. 7:3–6.

Gamst, Frederick C., and Edward Norbeck
1976 *Ideas of Culture*. New York: Holt, Rinehart and Winston.

Garbarino, Merwyn S.
1983 *Sociocultural Theory in Anthropology, A Short History*. Prospect Heights, Ill.: Waveland Press.

Geertz, Clifford
1957 Ritual and Social Change: A Javanese Example. *American Anthropologist* 59:32–54.
1963 and 1966 *Agricultural Involution: The Processes of Ecological Change in Indonesia.* Berkeley: University of California Press.
1973 *The Interpretation of Cultures.* New York: Basic Books.
1980 *Negara: The Theatre State in Nineteenth Century Bali.* Princeton: Princeton University Press.
1983 *Local Knowledge: Further Essays in Interpretive Anthropology.* New York: Basic Books.

Gellner, Ernest
1957 Ideal Language and Kinship Structure. *Philosophy of Science* 24:235–242.
1960 The Concept of Kinship. *Philosophy of Science* 27:187–204.
1975 The Soviet and the Savage. *Current Anthropology* 16:595–617.

Geoghegan, W. H.
1973 *Natural Information Processing Rules: Formal Theory and Applications to Ethnography.* Monograph, Language Behavior Resources Laboratory No. 3. Berkeley: University of California.
1978 Decision Making and Residence on Tagtabon Island. *Journal of Anthropological Research.* 31:18–29.

Gershenkron, Alexander
1963 *Economic Backwardness in Historical Perspective.* Cambridge: The Bellknap Press of Harvard University Press.

Gjessing, G.
1968 The Social Responsibility of the Social Scientist. *Current Anthropology* 9:397–435.

Gladwin, C.
1975 A Model of the Supply of Smoked Fish from Cape Coast to Kumasi. *Formal Methods in Economic Anthropology,* edited by S. Plattner. Washington, D.C.: American Anthropological Association, p. 77–127.

Gladwin, Harold S.
1947 *Men Out of Asia.* New York: Wenner-Gren Foundation.

Gladwin, Harold S., and C. Gladwin
1971 Estimating Market Conditions and Profit Expectations of Fish-Sellers at Cape Coast. *Studies in Economic Anthropology,* G. Dalton, editor. Washington, D.C.: American Anthropological Association, pp. 123–43.

Gladwin, T.
1964 Culture and Logical Process. *Explorations in Cultural Anthropology,* edited by W. Goodenough. New York: McGraw-Hill. pp. 167–78.
1970 *East is a Big Bird: Navigation and Logic on Puluwat Atoll.* Cambridge, Mass.: Harvard University Press.

Gladwin, T., and S. Sarason
1953   Truk: Man in Paradise. *Viking Fund Publication in Anthropology No. 20.* New York: Wenner-Gren Foundation.

Gluckman, Max
1959   The Role of the Sexes in Wiko Circumcision Ceremonies. *Social Structure: Studies Presented to A. R. Radcliffe-Brown,* edited by M. Fortes. Oxford: Clarendon Press.
1968   The Utility of the Equilibrium Model in the Study of Social Change. *American Anthropologist* 70:219–37.

Godelier, Maurice
1971   Salt Currency and the Circulation of Commodities among the Baruya of New Guinea. *Studies in Economic Anthropology,* edited by George Dalton. Washington, D.C.: American Anthropological Association, pp. 52–73.
1972   *Rationality and Irrationality in Economics.* London: NLB
1978   Infrastructure, Society and History. *Current Anthropology* 19:763–71.

Goffman, Erving
1956   The Nature of Deference and Demeanor. *American Anthropologist* 58:473–512.

Goldenweiser, A. A.
1917   The Autonomy of the Social. *American Anthropologist* 19:447–49.

Goldschmidt, Walter
1971   Independence as an Element in Pastoral Social Systems. *Anthropological Quarterly* 44:132–141.
1972   The Operations of a Sebei Capitalist: A Contribution to Economic Anthropology. *Ethnology* 11:187–201.

Goodale, Jane
1971   *Tiwi Wives.* Seattle: Washington University Press.

Goodenough, Ward H.
1955   A Problem in Malayo-Polynesian Social Organization. *American Anthropologist* 57:71–83.
1956a   Componential Analysis and the Study of Meaning. *Language* 32:195–216.
1956b   Residence Rules. *Southwestern Journal of Anthropology* 12:22–37.
1957   Cultural Anthropology and Linguistics. *Report of the Seventh Annual Round Table Meeting on Linguistics and Language Study,* P. Garvin, editor. Georgetown University Monograph Series on Languages and Linguistics, No. 9. Washington, D.C.: Georgetown University.
1963   *Co-operation in Change.* New York: Russell Sage Foundation.
1965 (38)   Rethinking "status" and "role." *The Relevance of Models in Social Anthropology,* edited by M. Banton. London: Tavistock, pp. 1–24.

Goody, Jack
1963   Feudalism in Africa? *Journal of African History*   4:1–18.
1976   Production and Reproduction: A Comparative Study of the Domestic Domain. *Cambridge Studies in Social Anthropology 17*. Cambridge: Cambridge University Press.

Gough, K.
1968   New Proposals for Anthropologists. *Current Anthropology*   9:403–407.

Granovetter, M.
1979   The Idea of Advancement in Theories of Social Evolution and Development. *American Journal of Sociology*   85:489–515.

Griaule, Marcel
1965   *Conversations with Ogotemmeli*. London: Oxford University Press.

Gross, D.
1975   Protein Capture and Cultural Development in the Amazon Basin. *American Anthropologist*   77:526–49.

Grossman, Gregory
1967   *Economic Systems*. Englewood Cliffs, N.J.: Prentice-Hall.

Gulliver, P. H.
1965   The Arusha—Economic and Social Change. *Markets in Africa*, edited by P. J. Bohannan and G. Dalton. New York: Natural History Press.

Gunders, S. M., and J. W. M. Whiting
1968   Mother-Infant Separation and Physical Growth. *Ethnology*   7:196–206.

Hagen, Everett E.
1962   *On the Theory of Social Change: How Economic Growth Begins*. Homewood: Dorsey Press.

Hall, A. D., and R. E. Fagan
1956   Definition of System. *General Systems*   1:18–28.

Hallowell, A. Irving
1976   The Beginnings of Anthropology in America. *Selected Papers from the American Anthropologist, 1888-1920*, edited by A. Irving Hallowell. Washington, D.C.: American Anthropological Association, pp. 1–91.

Hamilton, William D.
1964   The Genetical Evolution of Social Behavior, Parts I and II. *Journal of Theoretical Biology*   7:1–52.
1975   Innate Social Aptitudes of Man: An Approach from Evolutionary Genetics. *Biosocial Anthropology*, edited by R. Fox. New York: J. Wiley.

Handwerker, P. W., and P. V. Crosbie
1982 Sex and Dominance. *American Anthropologist* 84:97–104.

Hardesty, Donald L.
1977 *Ecological Anthropology.* New York: John Wiley.

Harding, J. R., and D. C. Clement
1974 Features Affecting Acceptability of Fertility Regulating Methods in Korea. Paper presented at the meetings of the American Anthropological Association. Mexico City.

Harding, J. R., D. C. Clement, and K. Lammers
1972 *Perceptions of and Attitudes Toward Alternative Living Environments in Santa Clara County.* Berkeley: Policy Research and Planning Group.

Harding T. G.
1967 *Voyagers of the Vitiaz Strait.* Seattle: University of Washington Press.

Harkness, Sara
1980 The Cultural Context of Child Development. *Anthropological Perspectives on Child Development,* C. Super and S. Harkness, editors. New Directions for Child Development, 8:7–13.

Harris, Marvin
1964 *The Nature of Cultural Things.* New York: Random House.
1966 The Cultural Ecology of India's Sacred Cattle. *Current Anthropology* 7:51–59.
1968 *The Ries of Anthropological Theory.* New York: Crowell.
1971 *Culture, Man and Nature: An Introduction to General Anthropology.* New York: Crowell.
1974 *Cows, Pigs, Wars and Witches.* New York: Vintage.
1975 *Culture, People, Nature: An Introduction to General Anthropology.* New York: Crowell.
1976 Lévi-Strauss et la palourde. *L'Homme* 16:5–22.
1979a The Yanomamö and the Causes of War in Band and Village Societies. *Brazil: Anthropological Perspectives,* edited by Maxine L. Margolis and William E. Carter. New York: Columbia University Press.
1979b *Cultural Materialism.* New York: Random House.
1982 Reply to Paul J. Magnarella. *American Anthropologist* 84:142–45.

Harris, Marvin and E. O. Wilson
1978 Encounter: The Envelope and the Wig. *The Sciences* 18:9–15.

Hart, C. W. M.
1954 The Sons of Turimpi. *American Anthropologist* 56:242–61.

Hayek, F. A.
1955 The Counterrevolution of Science. Glencoe: The Free Press. Originally in *Economica* 1942 9:267–91; 1943 10:34–63; 1944 11:27–39.

Heidegger, Martin
1962 (orig. 1927) *Being and Time.* Trans. by John Macquarrie and Edward Robinson. New York: Harper and Row.
1971 *Poetry, Language, Thought.* New York: Harper and Row.

Heilbroner, Robert L.
1970 *The Economic Problem.* Englewood Cliffs, N.J.: Prentice-Hall.

Henry, Jules
1959 Culture, Personality and Evolution. *American Anthropologist* 61:221–26.

Herskovits, Melville
1948 *Man and His Works.* New York: Alfred A. Knopf.
1952 (1965, 2nd Edition) *Economic Anthropology.* New York: Knopf.

Herzberg, F.
1957 *Job Attitudes.* Pittsburgh: Psychological Service of Pittsburgh.

Herzog, J. D.
1968 Household Composition and Boys' School Performance in Barbados, West Indies. PhD. dissertation, Harvard University.
1973 Initiation and High School in the Development of a Kikuyu Youth's Self-Concept. *Ethos* 1(4):478–89.

Hill, Polly
1963 *Migrant Cocoa-Farmers of Southern Ghana.* Cambridge: Cambridge University Press.
1966 A Plea for Indigenous Economics.*Economic Development and Cultural Change* 15:10–20.
1970 *Studies in Rural Capitalism in West Africa.* Cambridge: Cambridge University Press.

Hill, P., and R. H. T. Smith
1972 Spatial and Temporal Synchronization of Periodic Markets: Evidence from Four Emirates in Northern Nigeria. *Economic Geography* 48:345–55.

Hobbs, J. H., and M. H. Agar
1981 Text Plans and World Plans. Proceedings of the International Joint Conference on Artificial Intelligence, Vancouver, B.C.

Hodder, I. and M. Hassal
1971 The Non-Random Spacing of Romano-British Walled Towns. *Man* 6:391–407.

Hogbin, H. I.
1964 *A Guadalcanal Society: The Kaoka Speakers.* New York: Holt, Rinehart and Winston.

Holden, C.
1980 Rain Forests Vanishing. *Science* 208:378.

Holling, C. S., and M. A. Goldberg
1971   Ecology and Planning. *Journal of the American Institute of Planners* 37:221–30.

Holmberg, Allan R.
1965   The Changing Values and Institutions of Vicos in the Context of National Development. *American Behavioral Scientist* 18:3–8.

Homans, George, and David M. Schneider
1955   *Marriage, Authority and Final Causes*. Glencoe: The Free Press.

Hull, Clark L.
1943   *Principles of Behavior.* New York: Appleton-Century-Crofts.

Hunn, E.
1976   Toward a Perceptual Model of Folk Biological Classification. *American Ethnologist* 3:508–24.

Hunter, Monica
1951   Witch Beliefs and Social Structure. *American Journal of Sociology* 56:307–13.
1961   *Reaction to Conquest.* 2nd edition. London: Oxford University Press.

Hutchins, E.
1980   *Culture and Inference.* Cambridge, Mass.: Harvard University Press.

Inkeles, Alex
1981   Book Review of Form's "Blue Collar Stratification." *Anthropology of Work Newsletter* 2(3):5.

Irons, William
1979   Natural Selection, Adaptation, and Human Social Behavior. *Evolutionary Biology and Human Social Behavior: An Anthropological Perspective*, edited by N. A. Chagnon and W. Irons. Belmont, Calif.: Wadsworth.

Jakobson, Roman O.
1965   *Preliminaries to Speech Analysis.* Cambridge, Mass.: M.I.T. Press.

Jarvie, I. C.
1964   *The Revolution in Anthropology.* New York: Humanities.
1972   *Concepts and Society.* Boston: Routledge and Kegan Paul.
1975   Review of Anthropologists and Anthropology, by Adam Kuper. *Philosophy of the Social Science* 4:302–305.

Jaspan, M. A.
1953   A Sociological Case Study: Communal Hostility to Imposed Social Change in South Africa. *Approaches to Community Development*, edited by Phillips Ruopp. The Hague: W. Van Hoeve.

Johnson, Allen
1978   In Search of the Affluent Society. *Human Nature*   1(9):51–59.
1980   The Limits of Formalism in Agricultural Decision Research. *Agricultural Decision Making*, edited by P. F. Barlet. New York: Academic.

Johnson A. and C. Behrens
1982   Nutritional Factors in Machiguenga Food Production Decisions: A Linear Programming Analysis. *Human Ecology*   10:167–190.

Kant, Immanuel
1985   Kant and Kantism. Encyclopaedia Britannica. Chicago: Encyclopaedia Britannica, Inc, pp. 491–499.

Kaplan, D. and R. Manners
1972   *Culture Theory.* Englewood Cliffs, N.J.: Prentice-Hall.

Kardiner, Abram
1981   *The Psychological Frontiers of Society.* Westport: Greenwood Press.

Kasl, Stanislav V.
1974   Work and Mental Health. *Work and the Quality of Life,* James O'Toole, editor. Cambridge, Mass.: M.I.T. Press.

Kay, P.
1966   Ethnography and Theory of Culture. *Bucknell Review*   19(2):106–13.

Keesing, Felix
1939   *The Menomini Indians of Wisconsin.* Philadelphia: Memoirs of the American Philosophical Society. Vol. 10.

Keesing R.
1970   Kwaio Fosterage. *American Anthropologist*   72:991–1019.

Keyfitz, Nathan
1959   The Interlocking of Social and Economic Factors in Asian Development. *The Canadian Journal of Economics and Political Science*   25:34–46.

Kidder, Alfred V.
1945   Excavations at Kaminaljuyu, Guatemala. *American Antiquity*   11:65–75.

Kidder, Alfred V., Jesse D. Jennings, and Edwin M. Shook
1946   Excavations at Kaminaljuyu. Publication No. 516. Washington, D.C.: Carnegie Institution of Washington.

Kilbridge, J. E., and P. L. Kilbride
1975   Sitting and Smiling Behavior of Baganda Infants: The Influence of Culturally Constituted Experience. *Journal of Cross-Cultural Psychology*   6:88–107.

Klein, R.
n.d.   Late Pleistocene Hunter-Gatherers. *Cambridge Encyclopaedia of Archaeology,* edited by A. Sherratt. Cambridge: Cambridge University Press.

Kluckhohn, Clyde
1941 Patterning as Exemplified in Navaho Culture. *Language, Culture and Personality*, edited by Leslie Spier. Menasha, Wisc.: Sapir Memorial Publication Fund, pp. 109–130.
1943 Covert Culture and Administrative Problems. *American Anthropologist*. 43:413–19.

Kockelmans, Joseph J.
1973 Theoretical Problems in Phenomenological Psychology. *Phenomenology and the Social Sciences*, edited by Maurice Natanson. Evanston, Ill.: Northwestern University Press, 2:225–280.

Konner, Melvin
1976 Maternal Care, Infant Behavior and Development Among the !Kung. *Kalahari Hunter-Gatherers*, R. B. Lee and I. DeVore, editors. Cambridge, Mass.: Harvard University Press, pp. 219–245.

Krader, Lawrence
1972 *The Ethnological Notebooks of Karl Marx*. Assen: Van Gorcum.
1975 *The Asiastic Mode of Production*. Assen: Van Gorcum.

Kroeber, Alfred L.
1909 Classificatory Systems of Relationship. *Journal of the Royal Anthropological Institute* 39:77–84.
1915 Eighteen Professions. *American Anthropologist* 17:283–88.
1939 *Cultural and Natural Areas of Native North America*. Berkeley: University of California Press.
1940 The Present Status of Americanist Problems. *The Maya and their Neighbors* New York: Harcourt Brace & Co., pp. 460–87.
1944 *Peruvian Archaeology in 1942*. Viking Fund Publications in Anthropology, Number 4.

Kuhn, Thomas
1962 *The Structure of Scientific Revolutions*. Chicago: University of Chicago Press.

Kuper, Adam
1973 Anthropologists and Anthropology. *The British School 1922–1972*. London: Allen Lane.

Kusterer, Ken
1978 *Know-How on the Job: The Important Working Knowledge of Unskilled Workers*. Boulder: Westview Press.

LeBarre, W.
1938 *The Peyote Cult*. New Haven: Yale Publications in Anthropology.

Landauer, T. K., and J. W. M. Whiting
1964 Infantile Stimulation and Adult Stature of Human Males. *American Anthropologist* 66:1007–1027.

Langer, R. M.
1940 Fast New World. *Collier's*, July 6, 1940.

Langer, Susanne K.
1951 *Philosophy in a New Key: A Study in the Symbolism of Reason, Rite and Art.* Cambridge, Mass.: Harvard University Press.

Larco Hoyle, Rafael
1946 A Culture Sequence for the North Coast of Peru. *Handbook of South American Indians*, J. H. Steward, editor. Bureau of American Ethnological Bulletin 143, 2:149–173.

Leach, Edmund
1954 *Political Systems of Highland Burma*. Boston: Beacon Press.

LeClair, Edward E.
1962 Economic Theory and Economic Anthropology. *American Anthropologist* 64:1179–1203.

LeClair, Edward E. and H. K. Schneider
1968 *Economic Anthropology*. New York: Holt, Rinehart and Winston.

Lee, D. D.
1949 Being and Value in a Primitive Culture. *Journal of Philosophy* 48:401–15.

Lee, Richard
1969 !Kung Bushman Subsistence: An Input-Output Analysis. *Contributions to Anthropology: Ecological Essays*, edited by D. Damas. Natural Museums of Canada. Bulletin 230. Ottawa, pp. 73–94. Also in *Environment and Cultural Behavior, Ecological Studies in Cultural Anthropology*. Garden City, N.Y.: Natural History Press, pp. 47–79.

1972a !Kung Spatial Organization: An Ecological and Historical Perspective. *Human Ecology* 1:125–147.

1972b Population Growth and Beginnings of Sedentary Life Among the !Kung Bushmen. *Population Growth: Anthropological Implications*, edited by B. Spooner. Cambridge, Mass.: M.I.T. Press, pp. 329–42.

1980 *The !Kung San*. New York: Cambridge University Press.

Lee, Richard, and Irven DeVore, eds.
1968 *Man the Hunter*. Chicago: Aldine.

Leinhardt, Godfrey
1964 *Social Anthropology*. New York: Oxford University Press.

Lesser, Alexander
1939 A Culture Sequence for the North Coast of Peru. *Handbook of South American Indians*, J. H. Steward, editor. Bureau of American Ethnology Bulletin 143, 2:149–173.

LeVine, R. A., and LeVine (Lloyd), B.
1966   Nyansongo: A Gusii Community in Kenya. *Six Cultures: Studies in Child Rearing*, Vol. 2, edited by John Whiting. New York: John Wiley.

Lévi-Strauss, Claude
1944   Reciprocity and Hierarchy. *American Anthropologist* 46:266–68.

1945   French Sociology. *Twentieth Century Sociology*, edited by G. Gurvitch and W. E. Moore. New York: Philosophical Library, pp. 503–537.

1949   *The Elementary Structures of Kinship*. Translated by J. Bell and J. von Sturmer, R. Neeham, editor. Boston: Beacon Press.

1951   Language and the Analysis of Social Laws. *American Anthropologist* 53:155–163.

1960   La Structure et la Forme. *Cahiers de l'Institut des Sciences Economiques Appliques* 99(7):3–36.

1961   *Tristes Tropiques*. New York: Criterion.

1962   *Le Totemisme Aujourd'hui*. Paris: Presses Universitaires de France.

1963a   *Structural Anthropology*. C. Jacobson and B. C. Shoepf, trans. New York: Basic Books.

1963b   Responses a qualques questions. *Esprit*   31(32):628–633.

1963c   Intervista a Claude Lévi-Strauss. *Aut Aut*   77:27–45.

1963d   *Totemism*. Boston: Beacon Press.

1965a   *Tristes Tropiques*. New York: Atheneum.

1965b   Riposta a un questionario sullo Strutturalismo. *Paragone* 16(187/2):125–27.

1966a   *The Savage Mind*. Chicago: University of Chicago Press.

1966b   The Scope of Anthropology. *Current Anthropology*   7(2):112–23.

1966c   Introduction a l'Oeuvre de Marcel Mauss. *Sociologie at Anthropologie*, by M. Mauss. Paris: Presses Universitaires de France, pp. ix–xi.

1966d   *Du Miel aux Cendres*. Paris: Plon.

1967a   *Totemism*. Boston: Beacon Press.

1967b   *Structural Anthropology*. Trans. by Claire Jacobson and Brooke Grundfest Schoepf. Garden City: Anchor Books.

1968   *The Savage Mind*. Chicago: University of Chicago Press.

1969a   *The Elementary Structures of Kinship*. Revised Edition. Translated J. H. Bell, edited by J. R. von Sturmer and Rodney Needham. Boston: Beacon Press.

1969b   *The Raw and the Cooked*. John Weightman, trans. New York: Harper and Row.

1971   *L'Homme Nu*. Paris: Plont

1972   *Structuralism and Ecology*. Gildersleeve Lecture, Barnard College, New York, N.Y. (Reprinted in *Readings in Anthropology 75/76*, edited by Andrew Weiss. Guilford, Conn.: Dushkin, 1976)

1978   *Myth and Meaning*. New York: Schocken.

Levy, Marion J., Jr.
1965 *Aspects of the Analysis of Family Structure*, A. J. Coale, editor. Princeton: Princeton University Press.

Levy, Robert
1983 The Attack on Mead. *Science* 220:829–832.

Lewis, D. (49)
1977 Mau Piailug's Navigation of Hokule'a from Hawaii to Tahiti. *Topics in Cultural Learning 5*. Honolulu: East-West Center.

Lewis, Oscar
1961 *The Children of Sanchez: Autobiography of a Mexican Family*. New York: Random House.

Lewis, W. Arthur
1955 *The Theory of Economic Growth*. London: Allen and Unwin.

Linares, O. F.
1978 Comment on: Food Taboos, Diet and Hunting Strategy, by E. B. Ross. *Current Anthropology* 19:23

Lizot, J.
1979 On Food Taboos and Amazon Cultural Ecology. *Current Anthropology* 20:150–51

Longabaugh, R. H. W.
1962 The Description of Mother-Child Interaction. PhD. dissertation. Harvard University.

1973 Mother Behavior as a Variable Moderating the Effect of Father Absence. *Ethos* 1(4):456–65.

Lorenz, Konrad Z.
1950 The Comparative Method in Studying Behaviour Patterns. *Symposia of the Society for Experimental Biology* 4:221–268.

1966 *On Aggression*. New York: Harcourt, Brace and World.

Lounsbury, F. G.
1956 A Semantic Analysis of the Pawnee Kinship Usage. *Language* 32:158–94.

1964 The Structural Analysis of Kinship Semantics. *Proceedings of the 19th International Congress of Linguistics*. The Hague: Mouton, pp. 1073–93.

Lowie, Robert H.
1925 *Primitive Society*. New York: Boni and Liverright.

1929a The Determinants of Culture. *Culture and Ethnology*. New York: Peter Smith, pp. 66–97.

1929b *Culture and Ethnology*. New York: Peter Smith.

1936 Cultural Anthropology: A Science. *American Journal of Sociology* 42:301–320.

1937   *The History of Ethnological Theory.* New York: Farrar and Rinehart.

1948   *Social Organization.* New York: Rinehart.

1949   Social and Political Organization of the Tropical Forest and Marginal Tribes. *Handbook of South American Indians,* Vol. 5, edited by J. H. Steward. Washington, D.C.: Smithsonian Institute, pp. 13–50.

Lubbock, Sir John
   1870   *The Origin of Civilization and the Primitive Condition of Man: Mental and Social Condition of Savages.* London: Longmans, Green.

Macarov, David
   1980   *Work and Welfare.* Beverly Hills: Sage Publications.

MacCurdy, George C.
   1933   *Human Origins.* New York: Lippincourt.

   1937   *Early Man.* New York: Lippincourt.

MacIver, R. M.
   1933   *Society, Its Structure and Changes.* New York: R. Long and R. R. Smith.

Magnarella, Paul J.
   1982   Cultural Materialism and the Problem of Probabilities. *American Anthropologist* 84:138–42.

Maine, Sir Henry Sumner
   1914   (Orig. 1875) *Lectures on the Early History of Institutions.* Port Washington: Kennikat.

Mair, Lucy
   1965   *An Introduction to Social Anthropology.* London: Oxford University Press.

Malinowski, Bronislaw
   1921   The Primitive Economics of the Trobriand Islanders. *Economic Journal* 31:1–15.

   1922   *Argonauts of the Western Pacific.* New York: Dutton.

   1930   Kinship. *Man* 30:19-29.

   1935   *Coral Gardens and Their Magic: A Study of the Method of Tilling the Soil and of Agricultural Rites in the Trobriand Islands.* (2 Volumes). London: G. Allen.

   1938   Method of Study of Culture Contact in Africa. *Memorandum XI of the International Institute of African Languages and Cultures.* Reprinted from *Africa,* Vols. VII (1934), VIII (1936), IX (1936). London: Oxford University Press.

   1939   The Group and the Individual in Functional Analysis. *American Journal of Sociology* 44:938–947.

1944 *A Scientific Theory of Culture.* Chapel Hill: North Carolina Press.

1959 (orig. 1926) *Crime and Custom in Savage Society.* Paterson: Littlefield, Adams.

1960 *A Scientific Theory of Culture and Other Essays.* New York: Oxford University Press.

1965 *Soil Tilling and Agricultural Rites in the Trobriand Islands.* Bloomington: Indiana University Press.

Maquet, Jacques
1961 *The Premise of Inequality in Ruanda.* London: Oxford University Press.

Marcus, George
1983 One Man's Mead. *New York Times Book Review.* March 28:3, 22, 24.

Marris, P., and A. Somerset
1971 *African Businessmen: A Study of Entrepreneurship and Development in Tanzania.* London: Routledge and Kegan Paul.

Marx, Karl
1965 *Oeuvres. Economie 1.* Paris: Gallimard.

1967 *Capital,* Volumes One and Three. New York: International Publishers.

1968 *Oeuvres. Economie 2.* Paris: Gallimard.

1970a Theses on Feuerbach. In the *German Ideology,* edited by C. J. Arthur. New York: International Publishers, pp. 121–23.

1970b (orig. 1859) *A Contribution to the Critique of Political Economy.* New York: International Publishers.

Marx, Karl, and Frederick Engels
1968 *Selected Works.* London: Lawrence and Wishart.

Mauss, Marcel
1954 *The Gift: Forms and Functions of Exchange in Archaic Societies.* Glencoe: The Free Press.

1967 *The Gift.* New York: W. W. Norton & Co.

McDowell, Nancy
1980 The Oceanic Ethnography of Margaret Mead. *American Anthropologist* 82:278–303

McGrew, William C.
1972 *An Ethnological Study of Children's Behavior.* New York: Academic Press.

Mead, Margaret
1938 The Mountain Arapesh, I: An Importing Culture. *Anthropological Papers of the American Museum of Natural History* 36:139–249. Also in New York: Natural History Press, 1970, pp. 1–206.

1950 *Sex and Temperament in Three Primitive Societies.* New York: New American Library.

1956   *New Lives For Old: Cultural Transformation—Manus.* New York: Morrow.

1963 (orig. 1935)   *Sex and Temperament in Three Primitive Societies.* New York: Morrow.

1964   *Continuities in Cultural Evolution.* New Haven: Yale University Press.

1973 (orig. 1928)   *Coming of Age in Samoa.* New York: Morrow.

1978   The Evocation of Psychologically Relevant Responses in Ethnological Field Work. *The Making of Psychological Anthropology,* George Spindler, editor. Berkeley: University of California Press.

Meggers, B. J.
1954   Environmental Limitation on the Development of Culture. *American Anthropologist*   54:801–824.

Meggitt, Mervyn J.
1965   *The Lineage System of the Mae-Enga of New Guinea.* Edinburgh: Oliver and Boyd.

Melitz, J.
1970   The Polanyi School of Anthropology on Money. *American Anthropologist*   72:1020–1040.

Metraux, A.
1949   Warfare, Cannibalism and Human Trophies. *Handbook of South American Indians,* Vol. 5, edited by J. H. Steward. Washington, D.C.: Smithsonian Institution, pp. 383–409.

Metzger, Duane, and Gerald Williams
1966   Some Procedures and Results in the Study of Native Categories: Tzeltal Firewood. *American Anthropologist*   68:389–407.

Miller, N., and J. Dollard
1941   *Social Learning and Imitation.* New Haven: Yale University Press.

Millikan, Robert A.
1939a   *Living Philosophies.* New York: Simon and Schuster.

1939b   *Cosmic Rays.* New York: Macmillan.

Mills, Herb
1977   The San Francisco Waterfront. *Urban Life and Culture*   6(1):Part 2.

Minturn, Leigh, and William W. Lambert
1964   *Mothers of Six Cultures: Antecedents of Child Rearing.* New York: John Wiley.

Monod, J.
1972   *Chance and Necessity.* New York: Vintage.

Montagu, Ashley
1962   The Concept of Race. *American Anthropologist*   64:919–928.

1980   *Sociobiology Examined.* Oxford: Oxford University Press.

Moore, Sally Falk
1964   Descent and Symbolic Filiation. *American Anthropologist*   66:1308–20.

Morgan, Lewis H.
1877   *Ancient Society.* New York: World Publishing

1910   *Ancient Society.* Chicago: University of Chicago Press.

1964   *Ancient Society,* Leslie White, editor. Cambridge, Mass.: Harvard University Press, Belknap Press.

Morley, Sylvanus G.
1946   *The Ancient Maya.* Stanford: Stanford University Press.

Morton-Williams, P., W. Bascom, and E. M. McClelland
1966   Two Studies of Ifa Divination. *Africa*   36.

Munn, Nancy
1969   The Effectiveness of Symbols in Murngin Rite and Myth. *Forms of Symbolic Action,* edited by R. R. Spencer. *Proceedings of the American Ethnological Society.* Seattle: University of Washington Press.

Munroe, R. L., and R. H. Munroe
1971   Male Pregnancy Symptoms and Cross-Sex Identity in Three Societies. *Journal of Social Psychology*   84:11–25.

1973   Psychological Interpretation of Male Initiation Rites: The Case of Male Pregnancy Symptoms. *Ethos* 1(4):490–98.

Munroe, R. L., R. H. Munroe, and J.W.M. Whiting
1973   The Couvade: A Psychological Analysis. *Ethos* 1(1):30–74.

Murdock, George P.
1949   *Social Structure.* New York: Macmillan.

1962-1966   Ethnographic Atlas. *Ethnology*   1–5.

Murdock, George P., and J.W.M. Whiting
1951   Cultural Determinants of Parental Attitudes: The Relationship between the Social Structure, Particularly the Family Structure and Parental Behavior. *Problems of Infancy and Childhood,* J. E. Senn, editor. *Transactions of the Fourth Conference.* New York: Josiah Macy, Jr., Foundation

Murphy, Robert F.
1967   Tuareg Kinship. *American Anthropologist*   69:163–71.

1976   A Quarter Century of American Anthropology. *Introduction to Selected Papers from the American Anthropologist, 1946–1970.* Washington, D.C.: American Anthropological Association, pp. 1–19.

Murphy, Robert F., and Leonard Kasdan
1959   The Structure of Parallel Cousin Marriage. *American Anthropologist* 61:17–29.

Murray, H. A.
1938   *Explorations in Personality.* New York: Oxford.

Myrdal, Gunnar
1957 *Rich Lands and Poor.* New York: Harper.
1960 *Beyond the Welfare State.* New Haven: Yale University Press.

Nadel, S. F.
1942 *A Black Byzantium: The Kingdom of Nupe in Nigeria.* London: Oxford University Press.
1951 *The Foundations of Social Anthropology.* London: Cohen and West.
1952 Witchcraft in Four African Societies: An Essay in Comparison. *American Anthropologist* 54:18–29.

Nader, Laura
1983 Book Review: Mead and Samoa. *Los Angeles Times,* April 10.

Nash, Manning
1966 *Primitive and Peasant Economic Systems.* San Francisco: Chandler.

Neff, Walter S.
1977 *Work and Human Behavior.* Chicago: Aldine.

Newcomb, W. W.
1950 A Re-Examination of the Causes of Plains Warfare. *American Anthropologist* 52:317–330.

Nisbett, R. E., and T. Wilson (56)
1977 Telling More Than We Know: Verbal Reports on Mental Processes. *Psychological Review* 84:231–59.

Nordhoff, Charles
1961 (orig. 1875) *The Communistic Societies of the United States.* New York: Hillary House.

Norvell, D. G., and M. Thompson
1968 Nigglering in Jamaica and the Mystique of Pure Competition. *Social Economic Studies* 17:407–16.

Nove, Alec
1962 *The Soviet Economy.* New York: Praeger.

Noyes, John Humphrey
1870 *American Socialisms.* Philadelphia: J. B. Lippincott.

Nyerere, Julius K.
1964 Ujamaa. *African Socialism,* edited by William H. Friedland and Carl G. Roseberg, Jr. Stanford: Stanford University Press.

Odum, E. P.
1969 The Strategy of Eco-System Development. *Science* 164:262–70.

Okigbo, Pius
1956   Social Consequences of Economic Development in West Africa. *Annals of the American Academy of Political Science*   125–33.

Opler, Morris E.
1945   Themes as Dynamic Forces in Culture. *American Journal of Sociology* 51:198-206.

1968   The Themal Approach in Cultural Anthropology and its Application to North Indian Data. *Southwestern Journal of Anthropology*, 24:215-228.

Orlove, Benjamin S.
1980   Ecological Anthropology. *Annual Review of Anthropology*, Siegel, Beals and Tyler, editors. Palo Alto: Annual Reviews, Inc.

Owens, R.
1971   Industrialization and the Indian Joint Family. *Ethnology*   10:223–50.

Parsons, Talcott
1951   *The Social System.* Glencoe: The Free Press.

1968   Christianity. *The Encyclopedia of the Social Sciences*   Vol. 2.

Pearson, Harry W.
1957   The Economy has no Surplus: Critique of a Theory of Development. *Trade and Market in the Early Empires,* edited by K. Polanyi, C. M. Arensberg and H. W. Pearson. Glencoe: The Free Press.

Perry, W. J.
1926   *Children of the Sun.* London: Methuen.

Phear, Sir John Budd
1880   *The Aryan Village in India and Ceylon.*

Phillips, D. C.
1976   *Holistic Thought in Social Science.* Stanford: Stanford University Press.

Phillips, Philip, and Gordon R. Willey
1953   Method and Theory in American Archaeology: An Operational Basis for Culture-Historical Integration. *American Anthropologist*   55:615–633.

Piaget, J.
1965   *Etudes Sociologiques.* Geneva: Droz.

1967   Les Courants de l'epistemologies scientifique contemporaine. *Logique et connaissance scientifique,* edited by J. Piaget. Paris: Gallimard, pp. 1225–1271.

1968   Le Structuralisme. *Que said-je?* 1311. Paris: Presses Universitaires de France.

1970   L'epistemologies genetique. *Que said-je?* 1399. Paris: Presses Universitaires de France.

1972   *Epistemologie des sciences de l'homme.* Paris: Gallimard.

Piddocke, S.
1965   The Potlatch System of the Southern Kwakiutl: A New Perspective. *Southwest Journal of Anthropology*   21:244–64.

Pilcher, William
1972   *The Portland Longshoreman.* New York: Holt, Rinehart and Winston.

Pitt, D.
1970   *Tradition and Economic Progress in Samoa.* London: Oxford University Press.

Plattner, S.
1969   Peddlers, Pigs and Profits. Itinerant Trading in Southeastern Mexico. PhD. dissertation. Stanford University.

Plog, Fred T.
1974   *The Study of Prehistoric Change.* New York: Academic Press.

Poincare, H.
n.d.   *Science and Method.* New York: Dover.

Polanyi, Karl
1944   *The Great Transformation.* New York: Rinehart.

1957   The Economy as Instituted Process. *Trade and Market in Early Empires,* edited by K. Polanyi, C. M. Arensberg and H. W. Pearson. Glencoe: The Free Press.

1963   Ports of Trade in Early Societies. *Journal of Economic History*   23:30–45.

1966   *Dahomey and the Slave Trade.* Seattle: University of Washington Press.

1968   The Semantics of Money Uses. *Primitive, Archaic and Modern Economies: Essays of Karl Polanyi,* edited by G. Dalton. New York: Doubleday, Anchor Books.

Polkinghorne, Donald
1983   *Methodology for the Human Sciences.* Albany, N.Y.: State University of New York Press.

Popper, Karl
1959   *The Logic of Scientific Discovery.* New York: Basic Books.

1962   *The Open Society and Its Enemies.* London: Routledge and Kegan Paul.

1963   *Conjectures and Refutations.* London: Routledge and Kegan Paul.

1969   *Conjectures and Refutations: The Growth of Scientific Knowledge.* New York: Harper and Row.

1972 (orig. 1957)   *The Poverty of Historicism.* London: Routledge and Kegan Paul.

Pospisil, L.
1963   *Kapauku Papuan Economy.* New Haven: Yale University Press.

Postan, M. M.
1966   The Agrarian Life of the Middle Ages. *Cambridge Economic History of Europe*, Vol. I, 2nd Edition. Cambridge: Cambridge University Press.

Practicing Anthropology
1980   *Special Issue on Applications of Ethnography*   Vol. 3, No. 1

Quinn, N.
1978   Do Mfantse Fish Sellers Estimate Probabilities in their Heads? *American Ethnologist*. Volume 5.

1981a   "Commitment" in American Marriage: Analysis of a Key Word. Paper presented at the American Anthropological Association annual meeting, Washington, D.C.

1981b   Theories of Marriage Implicit in Key Word and Metaphor. Paper presented at Symposium on the Anthropology of Women. University of Houston.

Radcliffe-Brown, Alfred R.
1935   Kinship Terminologies in California. *American Anthropologist*   27:30–35.

1952   On Social Structure. *Structure and Function in Primitive Society.* New York: The Free Press, pp. 188–204.

Radin, Paul
1945   *The Road of Life and Death*. New York: Pantheon Books, Inc.

Radnitsky, G.
1973   *Contemporary Schools of Metascience*. Chicago: Henry Regnery.

Rappaport, Roy A.
1963   Aspects of Man's Influence on Island Ecosystems: Alteration and Control. *Man's Place in the Island Ecosystem,* edited by F. R. Fosberg. Honolulu: Bishop Museum Press, pp. 155–74.

1967   *Pigs for the Ancestors*. New Haven: Yale University Press.

Redfield, Robert
1940 and 1941   *The Folk Culture of Yucatan*. Chicago: University of Chicago Press.

1947   The Folk Culture. *Journal of American Sociology*   52:293–308.

1953   *The Primitive World and its Transformation*. Ithaca: Cornell University Press.

1956   *Peasant Society and Culture*. Chicago: University of Chicago Press.

Redfield, Robert, Ralph Linton, and Melville Herskovits
1936 Memorandum on the Study of Acculturation. *American Anthropologist* 38:149–152.

Reichard, Gladys
1950 *Navaho Religion, A Study in Symbolism.* 2 Vols. New York: Pantheon.

Rensberger, Boyce
1983 Margaret Mead: The Nature-Nurture Debate. *Science* 83:4(3):28–37.

Reynders, H. J. J.
1963 The Geographical Income of the Bantu Areas in South Africa. *African Studies in Income and Wealth*, edited by L. H. Samuels. Chicago: Quadrangle Books.

Ribeiro, D.
1968 *The Civilization Process: Stages of Sociocultural Evolution.* Washington, D.C.: Smithsonian Institution.

1970 The Culture-Historical Configurations of the American Peoples. *Current Anthropology* 11:403–435.

Richards, A. I.
1939 *Land, Labour and Diet in Northern Rhodesia: An Economic Study of the Bemba Tribe.* London: Oxford University Press.

1956 *Chisungu.* London: Faber and Faber.

Richards, P. W.
1973 The Tropical Rain Forest. *Scientific American* 229:56–67.

Richardson, Miles
1982 Being-In-The-Market versus Being-In-The-Plaza: Material Culture and the Construction of Social Reality in Spanish America. *American Ethnologist* 9(2):421–36.

1984 Comment on Paul Shankman's Article, The Thick and the Thin: On The Interpretive Theoretical Program of Clifford Geertz. *Current Anthropology* 25:275.

Rivers, W.H.R.
1920 *Instinct and the Unconscious: A Contribution to a Biological Theory of the Psycho-Neuroses.* Cambridge: Cambridge University Press.

1922 *Essays on the Depopulation of Melanesia.* Cambridge: Cambridge University Press.

Romanucci-Ross, Lola
1983 Preface. *Anthropology of Medicine*, Romanucci-Ross, Moerman and Tancredi, editors. New York: Praeger, pp. vii–xiii.

Romney, A. K., R. N. Shepard, and S. B. Nerlove, eds.
1972 *Multidimensional Scaling.* Vol. 2. New York: Seminar.

Rosaldo, M. Z.
1972 Metaphors and Folk Classification. *Southwestern Journal of Anthropology* 27:83–99.

Rosaldo, Renato I.
1972 Metaphors of Hierarchy in a Mayan Ritual. *Reader in Comparative Religion: An Anthropological Approach*, A. W. Lessa and E. Z. Vogt, editors. New York: Harper and Row, pp. 359–369.

Rosch, E.
1975 Cognitive Representation of Semantic Categories. *Journal of Experimental Psychology* 104:192–233.

1978 Principles of Categorization. *Cognition and Categorization*, edited by B. Lloyd, E. Rosch. Hillsdale, N.J.: Erlbaum.

Rosen, Lawrence
1974 Language, History and the Logic of Inquiry in the Works of Lévi-Strauss and Sartre. *The Unconscious in Culture*, edited by Ino Rossi. New York: E. P. Dutton, pp. 389–423.

Ross, Eric B.
1978 Food Taboos, Diet and Hunting Strategy: The Adaptation to Animals in Amazon Cultural Ecology. *Current Anthropology* 19:1–36.

Rossi, Ino
1973 The Unconscious in Lévi-Strauss' Anthropology. *American Anthropologist* 75(1):20–48.

1974 *The Unconscious in Culture*, Ino Rossi, editor. New York: E.P. Dutton.

Roy, Donald
1952 Quota Restriction and Goldbricking in a Machine Shop. *American Journal of Sociology* 57:427–42.

Rubinstein, R. A., and C. D. Laughlin, Jr.
1977 Bridging Levels of Systemic Organization. *Current Anthropology* 18:459–81.

Sahlins, Marshall
1965 On The Ideology and Composition of Descent Groups. *Man* 65:104–07

1966 On the Delphic Writings of Claude Lévi-Strauss. *Scientific American* 214:131–36.

1971 The Intensity of Domestic Production in Primitive Societies. *Studies in Economic Anthropology*, edited by G. Dalton. Wash., D.C.: American Anthropological Association, pp. 30–51.

Bibliography

1976a   *The Use and Abuse of Biology: An Anthropological Critique of Sociobiology.* Ann Arbor: University of Michigan Press.

1976b   Colors and Cultures. *Semiotica*   16:1–22.

Sahlins, M., and E. R. Service
1960   *Evolution and Culture.* Ann Arbor: University of Michigan Press.

Salisbury, S. F.
1962   *From Stone to Steel.* London: Cambridge University Press.

1969a   Anthropology and Economics. *Economic Anthropology,* edited by E. E. LeClair and H. K. Schneider. New York: Holt, Rinehart and Winston, pp. 477–85.

1969b   *Vunamami: Economic Transformation in a Traditional Society.* Berkeley: University of California Press.

Sapir, Edward
1917   Do We Need a Superorganic? *American Anthropologist*   19:441–47.

1931   Fashion. *Encyclopedia of the Social Sciences*   VI:141. New York: MacMillan.

1933   Language. *Encyclopedia of the Social Sciences*   IX:157. New York: Macmillan.

1949   The Unconscious Patterning of Behavior in Society. *Selected Writings of Edward Sapir in Language, Culture and Personality,* edited by D. G. Mandelbaum. Berkeley: University of California Press, pp. 544–59.

Sartre, Jean-Paul
1963   *Search For A Method.* New York: Alfred A. Knopf.

Schapera, I.
1928   Economic Changes in South Africa Native Life. *Africa*   1:170–88.

1934   *Western Civilization and the Natives of South Africa.* London: Routledge.

Scheper-Hughes, Nancy
1979   *Saints, Scholars and Schizophrenics: Mental Illness in Rural Ireland.* Berkeley: University of California Press.

1983   Women, Work and Infant Mortality: A Case Study from Northeast Brazil. *The Proceedings of the Conference on Women, Work and the Impact of Industrialization and Global Economic Interdependence.* April 14–15. Berkeley, California: Center for the Study, Education and Advancement of Women, pp. 145–162.
(Forthcoming)   "Basic Strangeness": Maternal Detachment and Infant Survival in a Brazilian Shantytown—A Critique of Bonding Theory. *Studies in Comparative Human Development,* Vol. 1, C. Super and S. Harkness, editors. New York: Academic Press.

Schneider, David M.
1968 *American Kinship: A Cultural Account.* Englewood Cliffs, N.J.: Prentice-Hall.

1969 Kinship, Nationality and Religion in American Culture. *Forms of Symbolic Action,* edited by R. F. Spencer. Seattle: University of Washington Press, pp. 116–25.

1976 Notes Toward a Theory of Culture. *Meaning in Anthropology,* edited by Keith H. Basso and Henry A. Selby. Albuquerque: University of New Mexico Press.

Schneider, H. K.
1969 Review of Tiv Economic by P. and L. Bohannan. *American Anthropologist* 71:931–932.

1970 *The Wahi Wanyaturu: Economics in an African Society.* Chicago: Aldine.

Scholte, Bob
1966 Epistemic Paradigms: Some Problems in Cross-Cultural Research on Social Anthropological History and Theory. *American Anthropologist* 68:1192–1201.

Schutz, Alfred
1973 *Collected Papers,* edited by Maurice Natanson, 3 Vols. The Hague: Martinus Nijhoff.

Searle-Chatterjee, Mary
1979 The Polluted Identity of Work: A Study of Benares Sweepers. *Social Anthropology of Work,* edited by Sandra Wallman. New York: Academic.

Sebeok, Thomas A,
1979 *The Sign and Its Masters.* Austin: University of Texas Press.

Senghor, Leopold S.
1964 *On African Socialism.* New York: Praeger.

Service, Elman R.
1975 *Origins of the State and Civilization: The Process of Cultural Evolution.* New York: Norton.

1985 A Century of Controversy, Ethnological Issues from 1860 to 1960. New York: Academic Press.

Shankman, Paul
1984 The Thick and the Thin: On the Interpretive Theoretical Program of Clifford Geertz. *Current Anthropology* 25:261–79.

Shore, Bradd
1981 Sexuality and Gender in Samoa: Conceptions and Misconceptions. *Sexual Meanings,* edited by H. Whitehead and S. Ortner. Cambridge, England: Cambridge University Press.

1982 *Sala'ilua: A Samoan Mystery.* New York: Columbia University Press.

Simon, H. A.
1976 *Discussion: Cognition and Social Behavior,* edited by J. S. Carroll and J. W. Payne. Hillsdale, N.J.: Erlbaum, pp. 253–67.

Singer, Milton
1980 Signs of the Self: An Exploration in Semiotic Anthropology. *American Anthropologist* 82:485–507.

Slesser, M.
1976 Energy and Food. *Nutrition and Agricultural Development.* edited by N. Scrimshaw and M. Beshar. New York: Plenum

Smelser, Neil J.
1958 *Social Change in the Industrial Revolution.* London: Routledge and Kegan Paul.
1963 Mechanisms of Change and Adjustment to Change. *Industrialization and Society,* edited by B. F. Hoselitz and W. E. Moore. The Hague: UNESCO-Mouton.

Smith, C.
1972 Production in Western Guatemala: The Interaction of Markets, Distance and Geographical Givens. Presented at Conference of Mathematical Society of Economic Anthropology. St. Louis.

Southall, Aidan
1961 *Social Change in Modern Africa.* London: Oxford University Press.

Spath, Carl D.
1981 Getting to the Meat of the Problem: Some Comments on Protein as a Limiting Factor in Amazonia. *American Anthropologist* 83:377–79.

Spencer, Herbert
1897a *The Principles of Ethics.* New York: Appleton.
1897b *Social Statics.* New York: Appleton.
1900 (orig. 1876) *Principles of Sociology.* 5 Vols. New York: Appleton.
1912 *First Principles.* 6th Edition. New York: Appleton.

Spindler, George
1978 Introduction to Chapter Three. In *The Making of Psychological Anthropology,* edited by G. Spindler. Berkeley: University of California Press, pp. 87–89.

Steiner, Franz
1957 Towards a Classification of Labor. *Sociologus* 7:112–129.

Steward, Julian H.
1936 The Economic and Social Basis of Primitive Bands. *Essays in Honor of A. L. Kroeber.* Berkeley: University of California Press.
1937 Ecological Aspects of Southwestern Society. *Anthropos* 32:87–104.

1938   Basin-Plateau Aboriginal Sociopolitical Groups. *Bureau of American Ethnology Bulletin 120.* Wash., D.C.: Smithsonian Institution.

1940   Native Cultures of the Intermontane (Great Basin) Area. *Essays in Historical Anthropology of North America.* Wash., D.C.: Smithsonian Miscellaneous Collection   100:445–498.

1947   American Culture History in the Light of South America. *Southwestern Journal of Anthropology*   3:83–107.

1948   A Functional-Developmental Classification of the American High Cultures. *A Reappraisal of Peruvian Archaeology.* Society of American Archaeology Memoir No. 4. Wash. D.C.: U.S. Government Printing Office. Bound in *American Antiquity,* Vol. 13.

1946-1950   *Handbook of the South American Indians.* 6 Volumes. Washington, D.C.: Bureau of American Ethnology.

1949a   Cultural Causality and Law: A Trial Formulation of the Development of Early Civilizations. *American Anthropologist*   51:1–27.

1949b   South American Cultures: An Interpretive Summary. *Handbook of South American Indians,* edited by Julian H. Steward. Washington, D.C.: Smithsonian Institution   5:669–772.

1950   *Area Research: Theory and Practice.* New York: Social Science Research Council. No. 63.

1955a   *Theory of Culture Change.* Urbana: University of Illinois Press.

1955b   Lineage to Clan: Ecological Aspects of Southwestern Society. *Theory of Culture Change.* Urbana: University of Illinois Press, pp. 161–70.

1956   *The People of Puerto Rico.* Urbana: University of Illinois Press.

Steward, Julian H., and Frank M. Setzler
1938   Function and Configuration in Archaeology. *American Antiquity*   4:4–10.

Strathern, A.
1972   The Entrepreneurial Model of Social Change. *Ethnology*   11:368–79.

Streuver, Stuart
1968   Woodland Subsistence-Settlement Systems in the Lower Illinois Valley. *New Perspectives in Archaeology,* S. R. Binford and L. R. Binford, eds. Chicago: Aldine, pp. 285–312.

Strong, William Duncan
1936   Anthropological Theory and Archaeological Fact. *Essays in Honor of A. L. Kroeber.* Berkeley: University of California Press, pp. 359–370.

1943   *Cross Sections of New World Prehistory.* Wash., D.C.: Smithsonian Miscellaneous Collection   104, No. 2.

1947   Finding the Tomb of a Warrior-God. *National Geographic,* April, pp. 453–482.

Sumner, W. G.
    1906 *Folkways.* Boston: Ginn and Co.

Super, Charles, and Sara Harkness
    1982 The Development of Affect in Infancy and Early Childhood. *Cultural Perspectives on Child Development,* D. Wagner and H. Stevenson, editors. San Francisco: Freeman and Company.

Suzuki, D. T.
    1960 Lectures on Zen Buddhism. *Zen Buddhism and Psychoanalysis,* edited by E. Fromm, D. T. Suzuki and R. DeMartino. New York: Harper & Row.

Sweet, L. E.
    1965 Camel Raising of North Arabian Bedouin: A Mechanism of Ecological Adaptation. *American Anthropologist* 67:1132–1150.

Ta Chen
    1946 *Population in Modern China.* Chicago: University of Chicago Press.

Takizawa, Matsuyo
    1927 *The Penetration of Money Economy in Japan and its Effects Upon Social and Political Institutions.* New York: Columbia University Press.

Tancock, B.
    1961 A Study of Household Structure and Child Training in a Lower-Class Barbadian Group. EdD. dissertation. Harvard University.

Taylor, Mark Kline
    1985 Symbolic Dimensions in Cultural Anthropology. *Current Anthropology* 26:167–85.

Terkel, Studs
    1971 *Working.* New York: Pantheon Books.

Thomas, A., and S. Chess
    1977 *Temperament and Development.* New York: Brunner Mazel.

Thompson, E. P.
    1978 *The Poverty of Theory.* New York: Monthly Review Press.

Thompson, J. Eric
    1943 A Trial Survey of the Southern Maya Area. *American Antiquity* 9:106–134.

    1945 A Survey of the Northern Maya Area. *American Antiquity* 11:2–24.

Touraine, Alan
    1971 *The Post-Industrial Society.* New York: Random House.

Trigger, Bruce
    1968 The Determinants of Settlement Patterns. *Settlement Archaeology,* edited by K. C. Chang. Palo Alto, Calif.: National Press, pp. 53–78.

Trivers, Robert L.
1971 The Evolution of Reciprocal Altruism. *Quarterly Review of Biology* 46:35–57.

Turke, Paul W.
1984 On What's Not Wrong with a Darwinian Theory of Culture. *American Anthropologist* 86:663–668.

Turnbull, Colin
1983 Trouble in Paradise. *New Republic* March 28:32–34.

Turner, T. S.
1979 The Ge and Borro Societies as Dialectical Systems: A General Model. *Dialectical Societies*, edited by D. Maybury-Lewis. Cambridge, Mass.: Harvard University Press.

Turner, Victor
1961 *Ndembu Divination: Its Symbolism and Techniques*. Manchester: Manchester University Press.

1966 *Color Classification in Ndembu Ritual. Anthropological Approaches to the Study of Religion*, edited by M. Banton. Association of Social Anthropologists Monographs, 3. London: Tavistock.

1967 (Paper 1970) *The Forests of Symbols*. Ithaca: Cornell University Press.

1968 *The Drums of Affliction*. Oxford: Clarendon Press.

1969a *Forms of Symbolic Action*. New Orleans, La.: American Ethnological Society. Tulane University.

1969b Introduction to Forms of Symbolic Action. *Proceedings of the Annual Meeting of the America Ethnological Society*, edited by R. F. Spencer. Seattle: University of Washington Press.

1969c *The Ritual Process*. Chicago: Aldine.

1974 *Dramas, Fields, and Metaphors*. Ithaca: Cornell University Press.

1975 Symbolic Studies. *Annual Review of Anthropology*, edited by B. J. Siegel, A. R. Beals and S. A. Tyler. Palo Alto, Calif.: Annual Reviews, Inc., pp. 145–60.

Tyler, Stephen A.
1969 *Cognitive Anthropology*. New York: Holt, Rinehart and Winston.

Tylor, Edward B.
1865 *Researches into the Early History of Mankind and the Development of Civilization*. London: J. Murray.

1871 *Primitive Culture: Researchers into the Development of Mythology, Philosophy, Religion, Language, Art and Custom*. London: J. Murray.

1875 Anthropology. *Encyclopaedia Britannica*. 9th Edition. 2:107–123.

1910 Anthropology. *Encyclopaedia Britannica*. 11th Edition. 2:108–119.

1958 (orig. 1871, Primitive Culture). *The Origins of Culture, Part I*. New York: Harper and Row.

Uberoi, J. P. Singh
1962   *The Politics of the Kula*. Manchester: Manchester University Press.

Udy, Stanley H.
1970   *Work in Traditional and Modern Society*. Englewood Cliffs, N.J.: Prentice-Hall.

UNESCO
1963   *Social Aspects of Economic Development in Latin America*. New York: UNESCO.

United Nations World Food Conference
1975   Assessment of the World Food Situation, Present and Future: Extracts from the Papers of the United Nations World Food Conference. *Food and Nutrition*   1:8–40.

Vaillant, George C.
1944   *The Aztecs of Mexico*. New York: Penguin.

Valentine, Charles A.
1968   *Culture and Poverty: Critique and Counter-Proposals*. Chicago: University of Chicago Press.

Van den Berghe, Pierre L.
1974   Physiological Determination of Female and Male Roles: A Reply to Sharlotte Neely Williams. *American Anthropologist*   76:567–69.

Vayda, A. P., and B. MacKay
1975   New Directions in Ecology and Ecological Anthropology. *Annual Review of Anthropology*, edited by B. J. Siegel, Alan R. Beals and Stephen A. Tyler. Palo Alto, Calif.: Annual Reviews, Inc.   4:293–306.

Vayda, A. P., and R. Rappaport
1968   Ecology, Cultural and Non-Cultural. *Introduction to Cultural Anthropology*, edited by J. A. Clifton. Boston: Houghton Mifflin, pp. 476–98.

Voegelin, C. F., and Z. S. Harris
1947   The Scope of Linguistics. *American Anthropologist*   49:588–600.

Voget, Fred W.
1975   *A History of Ethnology*. New York: Holt, Rinehart and Winston.

Vogt, Evon Z.
1972   Structural and Conceptual Replication in Zinacantan Culture. *Reader in Comparative Religion: An Anthropological Approach*, A. W. Lessa and E. Z. Vogt, eds. New York: Harper and Row, pp. 231–237.

Von Neumann, J., and O. Morgenstern
1944 *Theory of Games and Economic Behavior.* Princeton: Princeton University Press.

Vroom, Victor H.
1964 *Work and Motivation.* New York: John Wiley.

Waddington, C. H.
1960 *The Ethical Animal.* London: George Allen and Unwin.

Wadel, Cato
1973 *Now, Whose Fault is That?* Newfoundland: Institute of Social and Economic Research.

1979 The Hidden Work of Everyday Life. *Social Anthropology of Work,* edited by Sandra Wallman. New York: Academic Press.

Wagley, Charles, and Marvin Harris
1955 A Typology of Latin American Culture. *American Anthropologist* 57:428–451.

Wallace, Anthony F. C., and John Atkins
1960 The Meaning of Kinship Terms. *American Anthropologist* 62:58–80.

Wallman, Sandra, editor
1979 *Social Anthropology of Work.* New York: Academic Press.

Watkins, J.W.N.
1958 Confirmable and Influential Metaphysics. *Mind* 67:344–365.

Weiner, Annette B.
1976 *Women of Value, Men of Renown.* Austin: University of Texas Press.

Weisner, T.
1973 Studying Rural-Urban Ties: A Matched Network Sample from Kenya. *Survey Research in Africa: It's Application and Limits,* W. M. O'Barr, D. H. Spain, M. Tissler, editors. Evanston, Ill.: Northwestern University Press.

Weltfish, Gene
1979 The Anthropology of Work. *Marxist Perspectives in Anthropology,* edited by Stanley Diamond. Chicago: Aldine.

Wenley, A. G., and John A. Pope
1944 *China.* Washington, D.C.: Smithsonian Institution War Background Studies No. 20.

White, Leslie
1940 The Symbol: the Origin and Basis of Human Behavior. *Philosophy of Science* 7:451–463.

1943   Energy and the Evolution of Culture. *American Anthropologist* 45:335–56.

1945a   Diffusion vs. Evolution: An Anti-Evolutionist Fallacy. *American Anthropologist*   47:339–356.

1945b   History, Evolutionism and Functionalism: Three Types of Interpretation of Culture. *Southwestern Journal of Anthropology*   1:221–248.

1947   Evolutionary Stages, Progress and the Evaluation of Cultures. *Southwestern Journal of Anthropology*   3:165–192.

1947b   The Expansion of the Scope of Science. *Journal of Washington Academic Science*   37:181–210.

1948   The Definition and Prohibition of Incest. *American Anthropologist* 50:416–435.

1949   *The Science of Culture.* New York: Grove Press.

1959a   The Concept of Culture. *American Anthropologist*   61:227–251.

1959b   *Evolution of Culture.* New York: McGraw-Hill.

1966   *The Social Organization of Ethnological Theory.* Houston: Rice University Studies. 52:1–66.

Whitehead, A. N.
1925   *Science and the Modern World.* New York: Free Press.

Whiting, Beatrice B.
1950   *Pauite Sorcery.* New York: Viking Fund.

1963   *Six Cultures: Studies of Child Rearing.* New York: John Wiley.

1965   Sex Identity Conflict and Physical Violence: A Comparative Study. *American Anthropologist*   67:123–40.

1969   *The Effect of Urbanization on the Behavior of Children.* Cambridge, Mass.: Harvard University, Graduate School of Education.

1973a   Folk Wisdom and Child Rearing. *Merrill-Palmer Quarterly of Behavior and Development*   20(1):1974

1973b   The Problem of the Packaged Variable. *Proceedings of the Biennial International Conference on Behavioral Development,* edited by K. Riegel. Ann Arbor: Michigan University Press.

1974   The Effect of Modernization on Socialization. Paper presented at Third Annual Meeting of the Society for Cross-Cultural Research. Boston, Mass.

Whiting, B. B., and Edwards, C.
1973   A Cross-Cultural Analysis of Sex Differences in the Behavior of Children Aged Three through Eleven. *Journal of Social Psychology* 91.

Whiting, Beatrice B., and John W. M. Whiting
1975   *Children of Six Cultures: A Psychological Analysis.* Cambridge, Mass.: Harvard University Press.

Whiting, John W. M.
1942   *On Becoming a Kwoma.* New Haven: Yale University Press.

1954   The Cross-Cultural Method. *Handbook of Social Psychology,* edited by G. Lindsay. Volume 2. Cambridge, Mass.: Addison-Wesley.

1959   Sorcery, Sin and the Superego: A Cross-Cultural Study of Some Mechanisms of Social Control. *Symposium on Motivation,* edited by M. R. Jones. Lincoln: University of Nebraska Press.

1964   Effects of Climate on Certain Cultural Practices. *Explorations in Cultural Anthropology: Essays in Honor of George Peter Murdock,* edited by Ward G. Goodenough. New York: McGraw-Hill.

1971   Causes and Consequences of the Amount of Body Contact Between Mother and Infant. Paper delivered at the 70th Annual Meeting of the American Anthropological Association in New York.

1973   A Model for Psychocultural Research. The 1973 Distinguished Lecture Address delivered at the Annual Meeting of the American Anthropological Association in New Orleans. Annual Report 1974.

Whiting, John W. M., and B. Ayres
1968   Inferences from the Shape of Dwellings. *Settlement Archaeology,* edited by K. C. Chang. Palo Alto: National Press Books.

Whiting, John W. M., Eleanor H. Chasdi, Helen F. Antonovsky, and Barbara C. Ayres
1966   The Learning of Values. *People of Rimrock: A Study of Values in Five Cultures.* Cambridge, Mass.: Harvard University Press.

Whiting, John W. M., and Irvin Child
1953   *Child Training and Personality: A Cross-Cultural Study.* New Haven: Yale University Press.

Whiting, John W. M., Irvin L. Child, and William W. Lambert
1966   Field Guide for a Study of Socialization. *Six Cultures: Studies in Child Rearing.* Vol. 1. New York: John Wiley.

Whiting, John W. M., F. Kluckhohn, and A. Anthony
1958   The Function of Male Initiation Ceremonies at Puberty. *Readings in Social Psychology,* Maccoby, Newcomb and Hartley, editors. New York: Henry Holt and Co.

Whiting, John W. M., and O. H. Mowrer
1943   Habit Progression and Regression: A Laboratory Study of Some Factors Relevant to Human Socialization. *Journal of Comparative Psychology* 36(3).

Whiting, John W. M., and Beatrice Whiting
1971   Task Assignment and Personality: A Consideration of the Effect of Herding on Boys. *Comparative Perspectives on Social Psychology,* W. E. Lambert and R. Weisbrod, editors. Boston: Little Brown, pp. 33–45.

Whorf, Benjamin
1956   *Language, Thought and Reality.* New York: John Wiley.

Whyte, L. L.
1962   *The Unconscious Before Freud.* London: Tavistock.

Wilk, Stan
1984   Comment on Paul Shankman's Article, The Thick and the Thin: On the Interpretive Theoretical Program of Clifford Geertz. *Current Anthropology* 25:276.

Willey, Gordon R.
1948   *New World Culture.* Byron Cummings Anniversary Volume. New Haven: Yale University Press.

1953   Prehistoric Settlement Patterns in the Viru Valley, Peru. *Bureau of American Ethnology Bulletin 155.* Washington, D.C.: Smithsonian Institution.

Williams, B. J.
1981   A Critical Review of Models in Sociobiology. *Annual Review of Anthropology,* edited by B. J. Siegel, A. R. Beals, and S. A. Tyler. Palo Alto, Calif.: Annual Reviews, Inc., 10:163–92.

Wilson, E. O.
1971   *The Insect Societies.* Cambridge, Mass.: Harvard University Press.

1975   *Sociobiology: The New Synthesis.* Cambridge, Mass.: Belknap Press.

1976   Academic Vigilantism and the Political Significance of Sociobiology. *BioScience* 26:183–190.

1977   Biology and the Social Sciences. *Daedalus* 106:127–140.

1978   *On Human Nature.* Cambridge, Mass.: Harvard University Press.

Wilson, Godfrey
1941   An Essay on the Economics of Detribalization in Northern Rhodesia. *The Rhodes-Livingston Papers.* No. 5. Livingstone, North Rhodesia: Rhodes-Livingstone Institute Journal.

Wilson, Monica
1954   Nyakusa Ritual and Symbolism. *American Anthropologist* 56:228–243.

1957   *Rituals of Kinship Among the Nyakusa.* London: Oxford University Press.

1959   *Communal Rituals of the Nyakusa.* London: Oxford University Press.

Wimsatt, W. C.
1976   Reductionism, Levels of Organization, and the Mind-Body Problem. *Consciousness and the Brain*, edited by G. Globus, G. Maxwell, and I. Savodnik. New York: Plenum.

Wisdom, J. O.
1972   Scientific Theory. Empirical Content, Embedded Ontology and Weltanschauung. *Philosophy and Phenomenological Research*   33:162–177.

Wissler, Clark
1926   *The Relation of Nature to Man in Aboriginal America*. Oxford: Oxford University Press.

Wittfogel, Karl A.
1935   The Foundations and Stages of Chinese Economic History. *Zeitschrift fur Sozialforschung*   4:26–60.

1938   Die Theorie de Orientalischen Gesselschaft. *Zeitschrift fur Sozialforschung*. 7:Nos. 1–2.

1939–1940   The Society of Prehistoric China. *Studies in Philosophy and Social Science*. Peking Institute of Social Research. 8:138–186.

Wittfogel, Karl A., and Feng Chia-Sheng
1946   General Introduction to History of Chinese Society, Liao. *American Philosophical Society Transactions*   36:1–35.

Wittfogel, Karl A., and E. S. Goldfrank
1943   Some Aspects of Pueblo Mythology and Society. *Journal of American Folklore*   Vol. 56.

Wittgenstein, Ludwig
1968   *Philosophical Investigations*. 3rd Edition. Translated by G.E.M. Anscombe. New York: Macmillan.

Wolf, Eric
1955   Types of Latin American Peasantry: A Preliminary Discussion. *American Anthropologist*   57:452–471.

1959   *Sons of the Shaking Earth*. Chicago: University of Chicago Press.

1966   *Peasants*. Englewood Cliffs, N.J.: Prentice-Hall.

Worseley, Peter M.
1956   The Kinship System of the Tallensi: A Reevaluation. *Journal of the Royal Anthropological Institute*   86:37–77.

1957a   *The Trumpet Shall Sound: A Study of 'Cargo' Cults in Melanesia*. London: MacGibbon & Kee.

1957b   *Millenarian Movements in Melanesia*. Livingstone, North Rhodesia: Rhodes-Livingstone Institute Journal, pp. 18–31.

1970   *The Third World*. Chicago: University of Chicago Press.

Wright, S.
1969   *Evolution and the Genetics of Populations.* Chicago: University of Chicago Press.

Yang, Martin C.
1945   The Family as a Primary Economic Group. *A Chinese Village.* New York: Columbia University Press.

Yudelman, Montague
1964   *Africans on the Land.* Cambridge, Mass.: Harvard University Press.

Zubrow, E. B. W.
1975   *Prehistoric Carrying Capacity: A Model.* Menlo Park, Calif.: Cummings.

Index

589

101; as social effect, discussed by
R. Cohen, 264.

Self-motivation and control in work,
described by H. Applebaum,
392-393.

Semantic structure of the symbol,
analyzed by V. Turner, 489-490.

Services, concept of, analyzed by
G. Dalton, Note 1, 383.

Setting, social, effect on parents and
children, 196-197.

Settlement pattern in ecological
anthropology, 273.

Sex behavior and differential
investment, 458; identity and
conflicts, 191.

Shankman, Paul, critique of
C. Geertz, 485.

Single configuration perspective,
Mead and Freeman, analyzed by
N. Scheper-Hughes, 448-449.

Singing, as public ritual and as
model for leadership, in
Slavonia, 517-518.

Size, labor, technology and
cooperation in primitive
economies, 366-367.

Skill, human, concept of by
L. White, 237-238.

Sleeping arrangements and child
rearing, discussed by the
Whitings, 191-192.

Small-scale and large scale
development, analyzed by
G. Dalton, 380-381; economies,
characteristics of, 366.

Social,
analysis requisites of primitive
economies, G. Dalton's view,
367; and biological evolution,
compared and contrasted, 202-
203; anthropology and Radcliffe-
Brown's method, 126; aspects of
work, 390-391; basis of primitive
economic systems, 367-368;
change, discussed by Radcliffe-

Brown, 132; environment,
M. Mead's view, 161-162;
experiments, M. Mead's view,
162-163; evolution, review of
theories, 255; facts in Emile
Durkheim's theory, 110;
organization and energy,
L. White's view, 246; personality
and social structure, Radcliffe-
Brown's view, 126; phenomena
and structure, Radcliffe-Brown's
view, 123; phenomena as viewed
by K. Marx and J. Piaget, 332-
333; problems, E. O. Wilson's
view, 468; relations and
economic goods, Marx's view,
328; relations and social
structure, Levi-Strauss' view,
411; role, as viewed by Radcliffe-
Brown, 124; sciences and
theoretical problems, 530-531;
scientists and systems of
analysis, 521-522; structure and
child rearing, 187-188; structure
in Radcliffe-Brown's theory, 122-
124, 127; structure in ancient
civilizations, J. Steward
analyzes, 229; structure and
communication theory, Levi-
Strauss' view, 414-415; survival
in Radcliffe-Brown's theory, 114;
systems, analyzed by L. White,
247; systems, as fetters on
development, L. White's view,
248-249; theories of the 1980's, as
commented on by N. Scheper-
Hughes, 445-456.

Socialization practices in six
societies, discussed by the
Whitings, 188-189.

Society,
any social structure, Radcliffe-
Brown's perspectives, 125; and
the individual, Malinowski's
perspective, 112-113; as an
organism, Radcliffe-Brown's
view, 114.

Societal development and
agriculture, L. White analyzes,